OFF THE RECO...
IS A "DOUBLE-PLATINUM...

D0970156

"Consistently titillating...Joe Smith forcefully pulls off the covers of superstars and others in the entertainment world, often showing them for what they really are." —**New York Daily News**

"Engaging and telling...paints a well-rounded portrait of popular music that is never less than entertaining." —**Variety**

"Smith has captured some amazing tales." —**Rolling Stone**

"Joe Smith has done what no historian, musician, pop critic or rock writer has been able to do: He's compiled a history of popular music, ranging from the big bands of the 30s to the chart-toppers of today...a paper jukebox that's chock-full of pop."
—**San Francisco Examiner-Chronicle**

"A gem of a book." —**The Trentonian**

"OFF THE RECORD is full of 'off the record' remarks about the history of the world's most famous popular musicians—in their own words, plain and simple. Pardon the pun, but it will definitely set most 'retro rock' fans' heads spinning!" —**Inside Books**

"Even readers who do not think of themselves as music lovers will find much to savor in the experiences recorded here....The sheer scope of the book is astounding. Nearly all the heavy hitters are here. Smith's introductory material, coupled with exemplary editing by Fink, columnist for the Los Angeles *Herald Examiner*, round out this double-platinum winner." —*****Publishers Weekly**

"Fun to read...these conversational pieces open entertaining, informative vistas on the popular music world during a period of great growth and immense change." —**Christian Science Monitor**

"A fascinating overview of rock history." —**Chattanooga Times**

"Delightful...candid...a must-have for rock fans who want to find out how the stars themselves feel about fortune and fame."
—**Celebrity Plus**

OFF THE RECORD

OFF THE RECORD

An Oral History of Popular Music

JOE SMITH

Edited by Mitchell Fink

WARNER BOOKS

A Warner Communications Company

Warner Books, Inc., 666 Fifth Avenue, New York, NY 10103

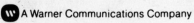A Warner Communications Company

Printed in the United States of America
First Trade Printing: November 1989
10   9   8   7   6   5   4   3   2   1

Book design by H. Roberts

Cover design by George Corsillo

Library of Congress Cataloging-in-Publication Data

Off the record : an oral history of popular music / [stories told to]
   Joe Smith ; edited by Mitchell Fink.
        p.   cm.
     1. Popular music—History and criticism.   2. Muscians—United
States—Interviews.   I. Smith, Joe.   II. Fink, Mitchell.
ML3477.034 1988
780′. 42′0922—dc19   88-24068
ISBN: 0-446-39090-9 (pbk.) (U.S.A. and Can.)   CIP
                                                                      MN

○ ○ ○

Dedicated to my wife and pal Donnie.
She knew what it took to complete this work
and hung in there all the way.

○ ○ ○

CONTENTS

Preface / xiii   Artie Shaw / 1   Tex Beneke / 3
Lionel Hampton / 4   Art Lund / 7   Sammy Cahn / 8
Woody Herman / 11   Charlie Barnet / 12   Ella Fitzgerald / 14
Lou Levy / 16   Billy May / 18   Sy Oliver / 19
Buddy Rich / 21   Milt Gabler / 23   Maxine Andrews / 25
Sammy Kaye / 27   Herb Jeffries / 28   Sammy Fain / 30
Ray Anthony / 32   Paul Weston / 34   Jo Stafford / 35
Jack Leonard / 36   Al Gallico / 38   Les Brown / 40
Peggy Lee / 41   Mitch Miller / 42   Margaret Whiting / 44
Frankie Laine / 46   Stan Getz / 48   Dave Brubeck / 49
Patti Page / 51   Henry Mancini / 53   Ed Ames / 55
Harry Belafonte / 56   Phyllis McGuire / 58   Bob Thiele / 60
Rosemary Clooney / 62   Ray Ellis / 64   Carmen McRae / 66
Les Baxter / 67   Johnnie Ray / 69   Ruth Brown / 71
Ahmet Ertegun / 73   Ray Charles / 75   Quincy Jones / 77
Jerry Wexler / 80   Les Paul / 83   Tony Bennett / 85
Barbra Streisand / 87   Joe Smith / 89   Bo Diddley / 93
Little Richard / 95   Jerry Lee Lewis / 97   Roy Orbison / 99
James Brown / 102   Dick Clark / 103   Hank Ballard / 105
Paul Robi / 107   Pat Boone / 109   Del Shannon / 111
Marshall Chess / 113   Phil Everly / 115   Dion / 118
Jerry Leiber / 120   Mike Stoller / 122   Ben E. King / 124
Barry Mann / 126   Gerry Goffin / 128   Duane Eddy / 129
Al Bennett / 131   Little Anthony / 133   Artie Ripp / 134
Jimmie Haskell / 137   Tom Jones / 139   Bob Marcucci / 140

viii / CONTENTS

Fabian / 142   Jeff Barry / 143   Ellie Greenwich / 145
George "Shadow" Morton / 147   B.B. King / 149
Harold Leventhal / 151   Pete Seeger / 154   Joan Baez / 156
John Stewart / 158   Mary Travers / 160   Peter Yarrow / 161
Bob Dylan / 163   Smokey Robinson / 165   Mary Wilson / 167
Lamont Dozier / 169   Levi Stubbs / 171   Eddie Kendricks / 172
Martha Reeves / 173   Mike Love / 174   Dean Torrence / 176
Bones Howe / 178   Burt Bacharach / 180   Jerry Ragavoy / 182
Herb Alpert / 183   Lester Sill / 185   Neil Diamond / 187
Bob Crewe / 190   Frankie Valli / 191   Bobby Vinton / 194
Chubby Checker / 195   Brooks Arthur / 197
Paul McCartney / 199   George Martin / 202   Dave Clark / 205
Mick Jagger / 206   Mickie Most / 209   Peter Noone / 211
Tony Stratton Smith / 212   Cliff Richard / 214
Peter Asher / 215   Roger Daltrey / 217   Donovan / 219
Mark Lindsay / 221   Michael Nesmith / 222   Johnny Rivers / 225
Lou Adler / 227   Country Joe McDonald / 229
Bill Graham / 231   Paul Kantner / 234   Al Schmidt / 235
Jann Wenner / 237   Joe Smith / 239   Jerry Garcia / 243
Mickey Hart / 245   Robbie Robertson / 246   John Fogerty / 248
Robby Krieger / 250   Paul Rothchild / 253   John Sebastian / 255
Clive Davis / 257   George Harrison / 260   Yoko Ono / 262
Booker T. Jones / 264   Isaac Hayes / 265   Al Green / 267
Al Kooper / 268   Van Morrison / 270   Alice Cooper / 273
Robert Hilburn / 275   Russ Regan / 277   Elton John / 279
Paul Simon / 281   Lou Rawls / 284   Jac Holzman / 286
Judy Collins / 288   Bill Medley / 290   Jimmy Webb / 292
Graham Nash / 294   Stephen Stills / 297   Joe Cocker / 298
Linda Ronstadt / 301   David Geffen / 303   Joni Mitchell / 305
James Taylor / 308   Carly Simon / 310   Jackson Browne / 312
Valerie Simpson / 314   Nick Ashford / 315   Ry Cooder / 317
Randy Newman / 319   Teddy Pendergrass / 321
Kenny Gamble / 323   Richard Carpenter / 324   Al Jarreau / 325
Kenny Rogers / 327   David Gates / 328   Herbie Hancock / 330
George Benson / 332   Walter Yetnikoff / 334   Bob Seger / 336

CONTENTS / ix

Robert Plant / 338   Chris Wright / 340   Ian Anderson / 342

Rod Stewart / 343   Joe Smith / 347   Don Henley / 351

Glenn Frey / 353   Irving Azoff / 355   David Bowie / 357

Roger Waters / 359   Richard Branson / 361   Robert Lamm / 363

Olivia Newton-John / 364   Justin Hayward / 366

Jon Anderson / 368   Chris Squire / 369   Gene Simmons / 370

Paul Stanley / 371   Dan Fogelberg / 373   Michael McDonald / 374

Lionel Richie / 376   Natalie Cole / 378   Richard Perry / 379

Peter Frampton / 382   Barry White / 383   Don McLean / 385

Boz Scaggs / 387   Leo Sayer / 388   Donna Summer / 390

Tommy Mottola / 392   Lindsey Buckingham / 393

Christine McVie / 395   Anita Pointer / 396

Michael Chapman / 398   Tom Petty / 401   Tina Turner / 403

Steven Tyler / 405   Joe Perry / 405   Pat Benatar / 406

Dee Snider / 407   Robert Palmer / 409

John Cougar Mellencamp / 411   Phil Ramone / 412

Billy Joel / 414   Phil Collins / 416   Sting / 418

George Michael / 420   Bono / 422   David Lee Roth / 424

Joe Smith / 427

OFF THE RECORD

PREFACE

Writing this book, or any book, was never in my game plan. You read books, you don't write them. When the opportunity arose to do one, however, it seemed that my 700 years in the music business—it only seemed that long when waiting for Jackson Browne or the Eagles to make an album—qualified me to get out and talk with a lot of people who made things happen in popular music.

As to how to do the book, it was the Studs Terkel approach that interested me the most. Reading Studs, I can't believe how hung up I got on his stories of people who otherwise would never have crossed my path—the steelworker, the retired army sergeant. But when they told their stories, they became very interesting people.

I thought, "What if I could get some of the major names in music all telling me stories about themselves?" Famous people who have all done terrific things in music. I wanted to stand alongside Woody Herman, not to get a comprehensive history on the man, but maybe he'd share some of his experiences with me. That's the kind of thinking that went into this book. Over 200 personalities who have affected our lives in some way. From Artie Shaw to a guy in the Platters. From Barbra Streisand to David Lee Roth. "Tell me a story?" I asked, and, over the course of the two-plus years it took to do this, most of them did.

There had to be a starting point, and the arrival of the swing era with the big bands felt like the logical place in that it was the first identifiable genre of pop music that caught fire. It was also where I entered music as a fan. I had been a big band groupie growing up in Boston, hanging around the theaters for five shows a day before working up the courage to sneak backstage to beg Count Basie's bass player for an autograph.

In beginning the interviewing process, I ran into disaster right away. I wanted to start with the 1938 Benny Goodman concert at Carnegie Hall, and who better to talk to but Benny Goodman? I finally had an appointment set up with Mr. Goodman, and he passed away. Certainly a greater inconvenience for Mr. Goodman than for me. It was not the most auspicious opening to the book, and it made me realize I'd better get a lot of the big band guys fast.

I've been lucky enough to have been in radio and in records, and I've seen and heard the music change, imperceptibly from year to year and dramatically over a decade or two. It was Patti Page and Mitch Miller when my career began and the gradations from Elvis Presley through Bob Dylan and the Beatles, through R&B and heavy metal, all combined to create the currency of my professional life. In other words, I figured I could cover the territory.

Acknowledging the help of personal managers, publicists, record company pals and others who surround the talent would take up too many pages and is therefore impractical. To work out the logistics with the artists themselves would have seriously affected my brain.

I want to first thank Mitchell Fink, who edited these talks into the form you'll read.

Andrea Boyce, Sandy Gibson, Paul Grein and Andi Stevens all pulled some of the load by researching, arranging, transcribing and caring.

Working with book editors was a brand-new experience. I lucked out when Warner Books assigned me to Nansey Neiman and Bob Miller. Bob said he loved Mel Brooks and the concept of this book. Nansey ran the show with firmness and patience. Like Larry Bird and Magic Johnson in basketball, Nansey and Bob know how the publishing game is played.

But the heart and soul of this effort are the conversations with these talented men and women whose work has touched the world for five decades, and will continue doing so for many years to come. Their willingness to share feelings, experiences and memories of their bad times as well as their good times is what sets this book apart from the many excellent writings on the business. I think you'll identify with many of them, and I hope you enjoy meeting all of them.

—*JOE SMITH*

Artie Shaw

○ ○ ○

Getting Artie Shaw to talk is not one of life's difficult challenges. A man of great intellect, he comments on anything and everything, especially the rationale for quitting a business when he was truly a superstar.

○ ○ ○

In 1938, I was the highest-paid bandleader in America, and yet I was beleaguered. The audience would not support me if I did what I wanted to do. I had to do what they wanted me to do. Music to order.

How do you do the same tune every night the same way? How many years can you play "Begin the Beguine" without getting a little vomity? I mean, it's a good tune if you are going to be associated with one tune, but I didn't want that. It was a song I played on the way to where I was going. I was trying to be an evolving musician, but the public isn't interested in that. Look at Mick Jagger. He's still doing "Jumpin' Jack Flash." And What's-his-name will have to do "Purple Rain" the rest of his life.

I got to a place where they said, "Stop, don't grow anymore." That's like telling a pregnant woman, "Stop, don't get more pregnant."

We used to do seven shows a day, seven days a week, months at a time. Do you know how boring it is to start a show with "S'Wonderful" and end it with "Concerto for Clarinet"? Whenever I changed a tune, the manager would come running back and say, "Damnit, don't do that. Those kids will be here all day." How could you live with that?

T. S. Eliot once made a very smart remark. He said, "No one who ever won the Nobel Prize ever wrote anything worth reading afterwards." You get monumentalized, you take yourself too seriously. The best music I made was when people left me alone. There would be a blizzard, and nobody was in the audience, and the managers would go home, and we would play for ourselves all night.

At the peak of that '38 band, I was making $60,000 a week, which is the equivalent of $600,000 today. It seemed insane. I began to ask myself, "How can I be getting $60,000 a week when the first clarinet in the philharmonic only gets $150 a week?" Maybe I'm one of the greatest clarinet players, maybe even the greatest that's ever come down the pike, but am I that much better than the first clarinet in the philharmonic? It began to dawn on me that it was lunacy.

Everything became totally irrational, and in order to live with that kind of schizophrenia, I had to become schizophrenic, and I wasn't going to become schizophrenic just to please an audience.

I would get restless. I'd want to quit. Then I would think about the life I was living and how I'd have to support myself if I did quit. So I'd go back into it. Quite obviously, the tail was wagging the dog.

I was enjoying myself, but that's when the demon "success" hit. Or the "bitch goddess," as Harry James used to say. Once I got the bitch goddess on my neck, it was no good anymore. The audience perceived me in a certain way, and it was in an insecure attempt to please the audience that I lost myself. Benny Goodman kept playing "Sing, Sing, Sing" until the day he died. I couldn't do that. I was through with playing. I never touched the instrument again.

Rubenstein once said, "If I don't practice one day, I know it. If I don't practice two days, my friends and family know it. If I don't practice three days, the whole world knows it." Well, I haven't practiced in thirty years.

There's a story about "Stardust" that bears repeating. Harry Myerson, an A & R man, called me one day said, "We want to do 'Stardust,' two sides with our biggest-selling artists—you and Tommy Dorsey. Two versions, same record. No A and B sides. How does that strike you?"

I said, "Fine," and we went into the studio to make the record of "Stardust." It worked on the first take. I said, "Fellas, let's go home because it ain't gonna get any better," and we left. About a week later, I called Harry. I said, "What happened?"

He said, "Well, Tommy came in and he wanted to hear what you did. The guys were sitting in the studio ready to go, and they put on your record, and Tommy says, 'I ain't getting on the back of that.' " So that was the end of that. My record came out, and Tommy lost out on the sale of about 16 million records.

It was difficult in those days for some of the black people in the band. Hot Lips Page could handle it. He was one of the only ones who could. Billie Holiday couldn't. It was murder for her. We played a gig, and afterwards she couldn't go eat with us. Lips could deal with it. He had a sunnier disposition, a more stable ego. Lips would say, "Don't fuck with my living, man." He was a spark plug. Roy Eldridge, on the other hand, couldn't handle it either. He'd go crazy.

When I hired these people, I told them, "It's going to be rough, but I wanted you in the band because I like the way you play."

We'd go into a town, and they couldn't stay in the same hotel. They'd have to go to a place called "nigger town." They'd have to find a cab and scuffle around. As a gag, we once got Billie into a hotel by painting a little red dot on her forehead between her eyes. Two guys carried her bags. She got the room, not as a black or a colored person, but as an Indian.

You know, it's funny. I ran into Reggie Jackson one time and we were talking about this whole syndrome of people paying you a lot of money. Somebody said to Reggie once, "You're nothing but a ball player."

And he said, "It has nothing to do with ball playing. I put asses in the seats." That's what I did. I put asses in the seats. And when you stop putting asses in the seats, it doesn't matter how well you play. No one is interested.

I was the biggest thing there was. I was going fine, but I didn't like the life. There were six of us who made that era—Dorsey, Goodman, me, Miller, Lunceford, and Basie. All of them are dead, and here I am. I must have done something right.

Tex Beneke

o o o

**If he'd recorded only "Chattanooga Choo Choo," Tex's voice would be
one of the world's most familiar. The Glenn Miller experience
constituted the glory time, and he's lived with it for forty years.**

o o o

Glenn Miller gave me a call and introduced himself. I didn't know who he
was, never heard of him. He said he was forming a band and asked if I was
interested in joining. I thought, "Hey, this may not be bad. I'll get to the
Apple. That's where things are happening. A band on every corner, in every
hotel."

So I asked him what he intended to pay. He said fifty dollars a week,
everybody gets the same. I thought for a second, and I don't know what
made me do it, but I told him I wanted fifty-two fifty, a little more than the
other guys.

Dead silence on the other end. You wouldn't want to print what he
called me, but he said, "All right, you so-and-so, I'll give it to you."

Glenn was a taskmaster. He used to stand up right in front of me while
I was playing, and we'd come to the end of the chorus and he'd say, "Take
another one, Texas. They're small." Sometimes I'd play as many as ten or
twelve choruses on something, or until I was about to drop.

He expected everybody to be dressed immaculately at all times. All the
jackets had to be buttoned, the handkerchiefs had to be just right in the
pockets. The shoes and socks had to match. There was no such thing as a
man crossing his legs on the bandstand, one leg over the other. You had to
sit there straight in your chair, legs together, with both feet flat on the floor.

We went into the Paramount for one of those long six- or eight-week
engagements, and Glenn told us, "You've got three days to memorize the
whole show. The music stands are coming out at the end of the third night.
We're going to sit up there and we're going to play the entire show, top to
bottom, without anybody having a note of music in front of him." It looked
fantastic. They audience ate it up. They thought, "Wow! How can they do
that?" After we did it, other bands started doing it, too. Glenn had a lot of
innovative ideas.

Records were everything to us, those thirty-five-cent Bluebirds. Glenn
watched the charts like crazy to see where he was standing in regard to record
sales. He was the first one, you know, to ever be given a gold record. It was
for "Chattanooga Choo Choo," which sold a million and two hundred and
some-odd thousand copies. That was a lot of records in those days.

It was also a very busy time. We were doing the theaters, anywhere
from four to six to eight shows a day at the Paramount. They were already
cutting out the feature movies and were just running short subjects in between
our shows.

At the same time, we were doing broadcasts from the Pennsylvania

Hotel. We had a fleet of cabs lined up, right outside the doors of the Paramount. We never had time to put the horns in the cases. We'd just grab the charts we needed for the broadcast and shove them down the bell of the horn, jump into the cab, do the broadcast from the Pennsylvania, and be back at the Paramount in time for another show.

Glenn would buy box lunches for the kids who would come to the Paramount and wouldn't leave. They'd stay all day for all the shows. The ushers would bring in the box lunches and pass them out. The kids would dance in the aisles. They worshiped Miller, and all the guys in the band. We all had our own little fan club. There was the Al Klink Fan Club, several Beneke fan clubs.

Benny Goodman and Jimmy Dorsey both came to the Café Rouge a couple of nights, and during the breaks they'd proposition some of the guys in a corner. Made Glenn madder than hell. I had a chance to go with several different bands, but I was happy with Glenn. I knew we had something going that was good, but a lot of people in the band wished it was a better swing band than it was. We would have liked it had Glenn given us more of a chance, like Charlie Barnet did with his band. Primarily, though, we were all happy to stay with what we knew was good.

It was a sad thing when Glenn told us we were going to disband. He first tried to enlist the whole band in the service, as a unit. We would have gone with him, but at that time no branch of the service would take an organized band. Shortly after we disbanded, they changed the rules and Clyde McCoy went in with his whole band.

When I heard the news of Glenn's disappearance, I was at Klink's house. I had come up to New York to do a radio show with the Modernaires. We were sitting there having dinner when it came over the air. We couldn't believe it. We thought, "OK, so his plane may have gone down someplace and he was captured, but he'll turn up." They're still looking for that airplane.

Lionel Hampton

o o o

A great musician and an effusive personality, Lionel's been showing his stuff for over fifty years. He lights it up when he recalls his days with Benny Goodman, Louis Armstrong, and other brilliant artists he's known and teamed with.

o o o

Louis Armstrong was an actor. I played drums with him when I was sixteen, and I watched his every move. It was like going to heaven.

Louis was a natural, right up until the day he died. I played one of his last jobs with him over in Europe, at the San Remo Song Festival in Italy. Louis was one of twelve American artists, and there were also twelve Italians. It was a four-day competition, us and the Italians.

We're ready to go into the finals. The Italians had loaned us a song called "Ciao." We're in this place that holds 9,000 people. You had to know someone to get a ticket.

Louis' sponsors had a roomful of Dom Perignon champagne. Everyone was ready to celebrate. Well, unbeknownst to us, Louis' manager sent down to Rome for the best Dixieland band to come up and assist us. That night, when the announcer introduced Louis, he came in playing "When the Saints Go Marching In" from the back of the auditorium, with the Dixieland band behind him. The people are going, "Bravo, bravo."

Louis comes up on the stage, and they give me the signal for the introduction to "Ciao." Louis says, "Ciao," and the newspaper guys run up on the stage, knock over Louis' easel, where he had the words, and it falls all over the floor. Louis' mind was running so quick he didn't remember he was in Italy. He said, "Ciao," the music hit the floor, and he said, "Spaghetti and meatballs." There was nothing else he could do. He just said, "Spaghetti and meatballs."

But the holy father had listened to the program, and he picked out two stars to be his guests—me and Louis. We went to Rome to see him at the Vatican. He treated us beautifully. He said if there's one thing we should see at the Vatican, it has to be the catacombs. Louis said, "What's that?"

And the people said, "It's way down in the basement, where they keep all the dead saints."

Louis looked at the holy father and said, "Hey, pops. I'm splitting because I'm a Baptist. I'm not going down to look at no dead things."

One time Louis saw some vibes sitting in the corner. He said, "What's that sitting in the corner?"

I said, "They call it a vibe harp."

He says, "Can you play it?"

I said, "Sure." I played a solo off one of Louis' records and he fell out. It was the first time jazz had ever been played on the vibes. Nobody had ever done it before.

I stayed with Louis for nine months. Then I got a little group of my own. We came to Los Angeles and got a little job in a place in San Pedro called the Paradise Night Club, right across the street from the Red Car depot. The Red Car depot was very important because the sailors would all come in from Long Beach. They'd get off the train, do the town, and come over to the Paradise to buy a twenty-five-cent pitcher of beer.

The place got real popular. We were packing the Paradise in with sailors, playing jazz. Lo and behold, I'm playing one night and I hear this clarinet playing next to me. Then I heard a piano, then drums. There was Benny Goodman playing clarinet, Teddy Wilson playing piano, and Gene Krupa playing drums. Well, we jammed for hours. People were standing out on the sidewalk, screaming, hollering.

That was the night I met Benny Goodman. John Hammond had told him to come down there. The next morning, Benny invited me to a recording session at RCA Victor. I came in and we recorded "Moonglow." I'll tell ya, after that jam session, the Paradise got so popular that they took the sawdust off the floor.

That was 1936. I joined the Benny Goodman quartet in New York City, at the Pennsylvania Hotel, in the Manhattan Room. Man, we made history.

Benny was my role model. A lot of things I do in the band business today are things I learned from him. I played some drums in Benny's band. When Gene Krupa left, several other drummers came in, but they could never play "Sing, Sing, Sing," so I played it.

I always tried to give youngsters a break. I found Dexter Gordon in Los Angeles. He was my doctor's son.

I went to Seattle one time and I saw a little kid who wanted to know if he could do arrangements for me. I said, "I'm going to Portland next. You wanna go there with me?"

He says, "I don't mind."

I said, "You better ask your parents." He was about eighteen years old. About the same time I get a notice that one of my trumpet players had to go report for the army. I said to the kid, "You want to play trumpet with me?"

He said, "Oh, yeah."

I said, "OK, get your things together." He came with his clothes in a cardboard box. I kid him about it now. That was Quincy Jones.

There were a lot of girls singers coming from my band. Like Dinah Washington. I discovered her in the ladies' washroom. She was working as a powder-room attendant. I had her come out to the Regal Theater in Chicago to do an audition. She came in and started singing. She was terrific. I asked her, "What's your name?

She said, "Ruth Jones."

I said, "I don't like that name. Can you change it?"

She said, "I don't care what you call me as long as you give me the job."

A guy standing next to us says, "Oh, well, there goes my chance. I wanted to get a job with the band, too."

I said, "You can do the next matinee." He did and it went over terrific, so I gave him a job with the band. His name was Joe Williams. I had Dinah Washington and Joe Williams, as a team. Imagine that.

Art Lund

o o o

He wound up on Broadway, but his time as band singer with Benny Goodman gives an insight into that great organization. While never on the A list, he had the pipes and a few hits along the way.

o o o

I was playing with Jimmy Joy in Chicago when Benny Goodman's brother, Fred, called me. He said, "There's a big band in town looking for a singer, but we don't want to let anybody know who it is because then he'll be mobbed." You have to understand, when I was going to school in Salt Lake City in the thirties, Benny's band was my favorite band.

Later, we were playing in Kansas City on a Saturday night when I got this long-distance call. "Hello," said the voice, "is this Art Lund?"

I said, "Yeah."

He said, "This is Benny Goodman." I couldn't talk. All the guys around me knew it was long-distance, and we all were sort of hoping that something like that would happen. Benny said, "I want you in the band. We're rehearsing Tuesday."

I told Jimmy I was leaving, and he got another guy to fill in for me. I went with Benny on November 11, 1941.

The first meeting was scary. I went to the New Yorker Hotel, and I was sitting in this chair right near the elevators. I must have had 17,000 cups of coffee. And then here comes Benny around the corner with his clarinet under his arm, and he walked by. He didn't see me. And I thought, "Shall I tell him? Shall I tell him?"

Then I heard the band strike up, and I went in. I'm going down the aisle, and Benny says, "Hey, Art Lund. Come on up and meet the guys." It was like meeting gods.

We had four broadcasts each night. If anybody goofed during those broadcasts, Benny would receive telegrams from other band leaders—Tommy Dorsey, Artie Shaw—saying, "What's the matter with that brass section of yours?" Or, "The singer had a dry spot there." They were picking on him. Benny would disappear, too, and listen to their broadcasts. I'm sure they were going back and forth, giving one another a bad time about their bands.

Benny would fire somebody if he smelled something on their breath. I saw it happen at the Pacific Theater in Passaic, New Jersey. We were playing seven shows, and one of the guys in the band went somewhere in between shows for a sandwich and a beer. When he came back to the theater, Benny happened to be standing by the stage door, and when the guy walked in and said, "Hi, Ben," Benny said, "Wait a minute. You've been drinking."

The guy said, "I had a beer with a sandwich."

Benny said, "I don't know how much you had, I can't tell that. But I'm not taking any chances on any mistakes up there. You're fired."

Benny was tough. I saw him woo a baritone man away from Gene

Krupa by promising the guy more money. The first night, the guy sat down in the baritone chair and played. Benny was walking up front, back and forth, and after the night was over, he gave the guy two weeks' pay and said, "I'm sorry kid. It won't work."

The guy said, "What am I gonna do? Krupa won't take me back."

And Benny said, "I'm sorry. It's not the sound I want," and that was it. The guy was out.

Sammy Cahn

○ ○ ○

Not a reluctant interviewee, Sammy was—and still is—an overwhelmingly prolific and eclectic lyric writer. When they select the best of them all, Mr. Cahn will be in the Final Four.

○ ○ ○

The only songwriter who was never demeaned was Irving Berlin. Berlin is one of the great phenomenons of American music. He is the only songwriter in the history of music who owns 100 percent of every song he ever wrote. Irving Berlin is also the only songwriter whose name appeared above the title of a film—Irving Berlin's *Blue Skies*, Irving Berlin's *Holiday Inn*, Irving Berlin's *There's No Business Like Show Business*.

I once met Cole Porter. It was one of the great thrills of my life. He said, "I've always wanted to meet you."

I said, "You've always wanted to meet me?"

He said, "Yes. I've always envied that you were born on the Lower East Side." From my area came many great writers.

I came before the Brill Building. The Tin Pan Alley I knew was the DeSilva Brown Henderson Building, on 49th Street at Seventh Avenue and Broadway. It was about a seven-story building that housed maybe a hundred publishers. With all the pianos going at the same time, it sounded like tin pans in an alley, which is how it got its name.

I look down at my fingers every once in a while and say, "God blessed me." I'm not talented, but I have talented fingers. Just put the piece of paper in the typewriter and I'll type a lyric.

I remember vividly seeing a fellow named Jackie Osterman at the Academy of Music on 14th Street. He was a comedian, and in the middle of his act he said, "I'd like to sing a song I've written," and he sang it. Walking home that night, I wrote a song, "Walking in the Street." That became a modus operandi for me. I could think of a whole song in my head, and I'd write it walking home.

I remember reading an article about the fellow who wrote only one song, "Yes, We Have No Bananas." I said to myself, "Am I one of those fellows who can only write one song?" I wrote about twenty songs that day just to show I could write more than one.

There would be no Woody Herman without Sammy Cahn. I was at the low part of my life. I gave up my apartment on 57th and Sixth and moved back to Brooklyn to my parents'. One day I get a call from the Woody Herman Orchestra. They were at Roseland in Brooklyn, could I please come and see them? I go out to Roseland, and they say, "Sammy, you gotta help us. If you don't help us, it's the end of the band."

I said, "Look, guys, I can't fight my own battles, I'm at the low point of my life. I can't take on your battle." But I went home and I called these lawyers, Michael Vallen and Chubby Goldfarb. I had them meet me at Roseland, and I sold them the Woody Herman band. That was the start of Woody's band.

Ten years later, Woody was king of Decca Records. I read in the papers that he's doing twenty-two sides before he goes into the hospital for an operation. I figure maybe he'll do a song of mine. I call up and Mike Vallen answers. I say, "Mike, I need a favor."

He says, "You need a favor? Come on."

So I go to where Woody is and I do two songs for him and he sends them back. I've never talked to him since. I'll tell you the difference between Woody Herman and Tommy Dorsey. I once went to Tommy and I said, "Tommy, I need this."

He took it out of my hand and handed it to someone, and he said, "Make this."

I said, "Don't you want to hear it?"

He said, "Quit while you're ahead."

My great lesson in life was: Do something for the joy of doing it and pray you won't be punished.

The first song I did with Jule Styne was "I've Heard that Song Before." He played the melody, and I said, "Play that again. I've heard that song before."

He said, "What are you, a tune detective?"

Julie and I were signed to do a film called "Pink Tights," starring Frank Sinatra and Marilyn Monroe. Just when the film is about to start Marilyn runs off to Japan with Joe DiMaggio. Picture's put on hold, I have nothing to do.

One afternoon, Sol Siegel walks into my office and says to us, "Can you fellows write me a song called 'Three Coins in the Fountain?'"

I said, "We can write you a song called 'Eh.'"

He said, "Just write me a song called 'Three Coins in the Fountain.'"

I said, "Can we see the picture?"

He said, "No, you can't see the picture. It's all over the lot."

"Can we at least read the script?"

"No, the script's in Italy."

"Can you give us a clue as to what the picture is about?"

"It's about three girls who go to Rome. They throw coins in a fountain and they also fall in love." And he leaves.

I go to the typewriter, I put a piece of paper in, and I type, "Each one seeking happiness," which is in the rhythm of "thrown by three hopeful lovers, which one will the fountain bless?" The title and three lines, and it's ready for music. I give the paper to Styne, he looks at it, and he starts to play. That's the entire process.

One day, it's the hottest day of the year. I don't make these stories up. I say to Julie, "Let's go down to the beach."

He says, "Why don't we stay here and write a winter song?"

I write, "Let it snow, let it snow, let it snow." I look around and I say, "The weather outside is frightful" on the hottest day of the year.

When the Dorsey band came to Los Angeles, I was at another low point of my life, living at the Castle Argyle, an apartment-hotel that a lot of band people used to stay in, just up the block from the Palladium. I lived there with Axel Stordahl. One night at the Palladium Frank Sinatra comes up to me and says, "I'm going to be the greatest singer in the whole world."

I looked at him and said, "You already are."

I often wake up in a cold sweat from dreaming I was born in today's world. I think, "What would I have done if Sinatra had written his own songs?" I don't think I could have dealt with that.

When Frank was doing *Anchors Aweigh*, they asked him who he wanted—Gershwin, Kern, Rodgers and Hammerstein? He said Sammy Cahn.

They said, "We don't mind hiring him. Who is he?"

Sinatra told them not to worry, but it started such a rhubarb that Lew Wasserman called me and said, "Sammy, if you don't tell Frank to stop asking for you, we're going to blow this picture."

I went to Frank and said, "Hey, Frank, yesterday nobody knew me. Today everybody hates me. Why don't you pass. I'll do the next one."

He said, "If you're not there Monday, I won't be there Monday."

Another of my partners, Jimmy Van Heusen, ran with Sinatra. I've often said that the real Sinatra is Van Heusen. People ask me, "Who is the most fascinating person you've ever met?"

I say, "Van Heusen."

They say, "What about Sinatra?"

I say, "Sinatra thinks he's Van Heusen."

People also ask me to pick the best song I ever wrote, and I pick "Call Me Irresponsible." Wrote it with Van Heusen. The song is the epitome of matching words with music. You put "undependable" here, "unreliable" there, which goes with "undeniably." That's the finesse of lyric writing. I've said to my children, "If someone asks you what your father did, say he was a lyric writer. If they ask you to prove it, hand them that lyric."

Woody Herman

∘ ∘ ∘

We talked on a sunny California afternoon on the patio of his Hollywood home. Woody was very much beloved, universally respected, and full of memories, and his spirit and love of the trade remained constant until his passing.

∘ ∘ ∘

I thought I was a pretty good coach. I knew how to handle guys, particularly musicians. I found that the less bothersome you were as a leader, the better the band you would have. I never looked at myself as being a guy who had to hold power in order to get guys to do things.

The Esquire Jazz Poll may have voted Duke Ellington the all-time number-one band, but we were the number-one new band in 1946. That was our peak period. We had everything going for us. You could get an audience. People were hungry to get their minds off the war and the conditions of the times. We were like a breath of fresh air to millions of people.

We put together Stan Getz, Zoot Sims, Herbie Steward, and a guy from Boston, Serge Chaloff, and called them the Four Brothers sax section. They were all budding, great musical minds. And they were nutty.

It was hip to get into drugs back then because it was corny to be an alcoholic. It was cool to be stoned out of your mind. Some guys won and some guys lost. Sonny Berman, a nineteen-year-old trumpet player, took an overdose and died in New York two weeks after the band broke up. It didn't seem to affect the band, which was usually at its peak on any night. But they looked so weird and acted so weird that it drove me up a wall. I didn't know how to cope with it.

We were in Washington playing a theater. After the show we went to a club that was crowded with people who had come over from a Truman political party. It was an after-hours place. They were ten-deep at the bar, and I couldn't get a drink. Serge Chaloff was so stoned, and he was causing me all this trouble.

He said, "Man, why are you so upset with me. I'm cool."

I said, "You're cool? I will knock you on your ass. You ain't cool."

Finally, I remember an old gimmick while we are standing there. I said to myself, "I gotta do it to him." So I'm talking, and he's going on, and all of a sudden I dig out my thing and I start pissing on him. I managed to keep it on him, out of everyone else's way. It takes a minute or two before he realizes what's happening, and he lets out a blood-curdling yell and races for a phone booth. I chased him, stuffing myself back in my pants and beating on the booth.

One of the bosses who owned the joint comes by and says, "I just love you and your guys. It's the greatest band in the world." They pulled me out and gave me another drink. It was quite an upsetting night for everyone.

We used black musicians on record dates because that was permissible.

Not in person, though. The prejudices were ridiculous. I was one of the first bands with a black and white mixture. Charlie Barnet and ourselves were the only predominantly white bands that could play the black theaters in Harlem and Baltimore and Washington. They ostracized all the rest, but we were OK because we were basically jazz bands.

But there were problems. I had a tour for Loews Theaters that was supposed to go for ten weeks. We had been out about two, three weeks when I get a letter from Loews, Inc., from some big man there saying, "I see you have a contract to play the Capitol Theater in Washington," on such-and-such date. "If you appear with the entire orchestra, all our contractual obligations are severed, or will be severed."

I took the bull by the horns and called the guys in. I showed them the letter. We had about five or six black guys. I told everyone what the problem was. I told them to do whatever they thought was right. I said, "You know where I am on this. I can easily go back to California." They all left, saying they'd be back in a week. We didn't play the Capitol, which was fine.

We kept the band together through 1949, but a major part of our audience didn't understand the bebop kind of music at all. They wanted more of that music from the '45, '46 band. I made a miscalculation, and it cost me a lot of money.

After that the bottom dropped out of the band business. There were a few bands hanging in there—Ellington, Basie, Harry James—the stubborn ones. Actually, the bands that were jazz oriented were the only ones that pulled through.

Charlie Barnet

o o o

Regarded as the playboy band leader, Charlie still looks the part in his Palm Springs home. But he played brilliantly, gave his band the room to grow, and loved every minute of his career.

o o o

I was strict about one thing—I didn't care about the guys drinking, just don't drink too much, don't make it a big drag on the other guys in the band. I did fire a couple of guys for drinking, but that was only because they fell off their chairs. I used to kid my band about it. I'd say, "We work four hours a night, from nine till one. Don't ask to work until one-thirty because everyone will be stone drunk by that last half hour."

I'm afraid, though, that I was guilty of the same thing. In my book, I said that all the trouble I ever got into in my life was from drinking.

New York's my hometown, like at the Cotton Club, although we didn't go up there too often because at the time there wasn't too much cash in hand and the Cotton Club was pretty expensive. It was especially hard to see the black bands. There was the Duke, Don Redman, and Fletcher Henderson. I heard a lot of Fletcher Henderson in those days. He used to play the Roseland Ballroom. He was a big favorite there. Fletcher even had tangos and waltzes in his repertoire. Can you imagine a band with Coleman Hawkins, Benny Carter, and Rex Stewart sitting there playing tangos and waltzes?

The problem with making records back then was that they expected us to make too many sides in not enough time. They never really cared about the quality of the record. It wasn't until a guy like John Hammond came along and started campaigning, although he did have a horrible experience with Fletcher Henderson. John wanted to do something for Fletcher so he rented a theater downtown in Greenwich Village to put on a show. He was going to have Fletcher play in the pit. Well, there wasn't a less disciplined band in the world than Fletcher Henderson's, possibly Duke Ellington's, definitely less disciplined than mine.

Well, Fletcher's band didn't show up. About three guys showed up for the opening show. John had to eat crow. It was horrible, but it wasn't done maliciously. They were just ungovernable. Fletcher himself was a fine gentleman, very well educated.

A lot of stealing of people went on in those days. For example, Glenn Miller stole Billy May from me. Simply, it was a matter of money. At the time I had to make the decision whether or not to match Glenn's offer, and I chose not to. Pretty soon word gets around, and then everybody in the band wants more and more and more, and then I wouldn't be able to operate. Billy swears I was trying to make money with the band. I wasn't. I was just trying to keep it going.

Contracts, too, in those days didn't mean much. I had Lena Horne under contract. I had Doc Severinsen under contract. I had Maynard Ferguson under contract. In the end, it didn't mean anything.

How "Cherokee" came about started with Count Basie playing it. The song was written by Ray Noble, and Basie's way was to play the song quite fast. We had a date coming up. I said to Billy May, "Let's make it our sixth number," our last one on the date. Billy wrote part of the arrangement in the car on the way to the studio.

I had a funny feeling about the song, but I'll tell you what Leonard Joy, the A & R man on the date, said when we finished it. He said, "Charlie, when's your birthday?"

I said, "October 26," not thinking.

Leonard said, "You can have that last one for your birthday." Because he didn't like it, we never bothered making a better cut of it. In fact, there's one place on the original record where the trombones slow down and then come back. Leonard thought so little of the cut that he didn't want to give us the time to make a better one.

But I had a feeling about it. When we played it, we got a reaction. I said, "I think this is going to happen, I think this is the one we've been looking for." And it was, no doubt about it. It doubled our price and made us known.

I guess I was a pretty good saxophone player, but being a band leader takes away the freedom of playing. I did not pursue the playing part as much as I perhaps should have, although I think I was respected right on through. I couldn't possibly compete with guys like Charlie Parker or Johnny Hodges in a melodic way, but I had the respect. I suppose I could have been a lot better, but I was more interested in having a good time. In a way, I regret it. On the other hand, think of all the fun I would have missed.

Ella Fitzgerald
∘ ∘ ∘

She's just Ella, a name known round the world. This kindly lady invented many of the techniques in pop and jazz singing, and she has always carried it off with dignity and style.

∘ ∘ ∘

Chick Webb had one of the greatest bands. Nobody gave him the credit for the band he had. When Chick died in 1939, everyone in the band tried to keep it together. I sang in that band, but I didn't do much leading. They finally ended up having one of the musicians direct the band, but all we were doing was trying to keep the band together. It was a way for me to work.

I did more dancing on the floor than I did singing. I used to love to do the Lindy hop. People called me a tomboy because on our day off I would go play ball. But I always wanted to be a dancer. I had gone on the "Amateur Hour" to dance, and my girlfriend and myself had made a bet that we would all be signed to work at the Apollo Theater, and I was the one that got the call to come down. I lived in Yonkers then. When I walked out on the stage, I was trying to do something good because they were going to call me "chicken" if I didn't show up. When I got out there, I saw all these people and I lost my nerve. The man said, "You're out there. Do something." So I started to sing a Connee Boswell song called "Judy, the Object of My Affection."

I never thought I was going to be a singer. What I really did was dance a lot. My cousins would say, "Let's go to the movies," and I'd end up dancing in the streets and people would give us money. At that time, they used to have block parties and I'd go and dance. When I got called to go audition at the Apollo, I was very surprised because there were two sisters who were the greatest dancers at that time, and they were closing the show. I was the first amateur. I tried to sing like Connee Boswell and I won first prize. A man had a radio show, and my mother had to sign for me because I was only fourteen and I wasn't old enough. From there, I went from amateur show to amateur show and I kept on winning.

I was promised a week at the Apollo, but that never came through. But I kept right on. The first time I lost a contest was at the Lafayette Theater in New York. I sang "Lost in the Fog," and the piano player couldn't get the chords right.

But I kept right on, and the man at the Apollo said, "If you win this time, I'll give you a week." Finally I did the week at the Apollo and then I went to the Harlem Opera House. They had number-one acts at the Harlem Opera House, acts like the Nicholas Brothers, and they put me on at the end of the show. They said, "We have a little girl here who sang at the Apollo." Then they all cheered at the end of my songs. I sang "Judy" and "Believe It, Beloved." Chick Webb was playing there and he finally gave in and said he'd listen to me. He was big time and that was a big job for me.

I did a show with a disc jockey somewhere, and on a song called "Simple Melody" I started doing a do-do-do-do-doodley-do, and this man said I was scat singing. I never considered it jazz or bop. I learned how to sing like that from Dizzy Gillespie. In New York there were plenty of after-hours clubs, and I hung out with the guys and learned that technique. I didn't pay much attention to what people were calling it. That's what's so funny.

I've worked with so many great people. For me, Louis Armstrong was a lesson in love. This was a man everybody loved, no matter what he did. He just had that "way" and that "want." There are just some people that you can come up to and say something to and you know something nice will be said back.

I messed up a lot on Louis' records because he always wore his socks rolled down, and I would look and see his socks down and I'd start laughing. Or he would say something funny while we were recording, and I would laugh. He made recording sessions a joy.

Count Basie was just like Louis. Everybody loved him so much. I could go to him with anything and he'd help me. I used to call him one of my lawyers. He would give me such beautiful advice. And he would phrase that advice into these little sayings. One saying of Count Basie's that I'll always remember pertains to when my husband and I broke up. Basie said, "It's like a toothache. It hurts now, but if you take that tooth out, you'll miss it but you'll feel better."

I also remember one my mother told me when I thought I was such a good dancer in Yonkers. She said, "Don't you ever, ever feel that you are bigger than anybody else, because some man could be lying in the gutter and he could get up the next day and be the one person to give you help. So always remember to speak to everybody."

In the fifties I started singing with a different kind of style. That came about because Norman Granz felt that there was something else to my voice besides just singing. Basin Street and Birdland had closed down, and I was wondering where I was going to work. All the bop/jazz clubs were gone. So we tried this new style, picking out songwriters and singing their songs. Cole Porter was the first. It was like beginning all over again. People who never heard me suddenly heard songs which surprised them because they didn't think I could sing them. People always figure you could only do one thing. It was like another education. Here I am with Cole Porter, and it became such a big hit that we tried it with Gershwin. Then we did a Harold Arlen songbook, then an Irving Berlin songbook. We just went from one songwriter to another, all the great ones, and it opened up another whole level of audience for me. People started saying, "You know, no matter what this lady sings, she's still singing a pretty tune."

Lou Levy

o o o

When music publishers talk about style, smarts, and success, Lou's name is in the Top 10. A legend in that world, he made it and spent it and could step in anytime and be a winner.

o o o

Sammy Cahn lived around the corner from me on the Lower East Side, and one day he came to me and said, "You're not tall, you're not good-looking, you can't sing. Would you please manage me and my partner, Sol Kaplan?"

Sammy's name was Sammy Cohen, so Cohen became Cahn, Sol Kaplan became Sol Chaplin, and Levy stayed Levy. And I managed them without a contract for twenty years.

Sammy Cahn paid for his first song to be published. When I met him, I said, "You paid to get your song published?"

And he said, "Will you manage us?" So I managed them. That's what got me into the music business, handling Cahn and Chaplin. I needed a name for a music company, and so we opened a company, looked on the inside of our clothes and it said Leeds Clothes. That's how my company became Leeds Music.

Besides managing Sammy and Sol, and being a publisher, I also managed the Andrews Sisters through their whole career. I managed and discovered Steve Lawrence. I managed and found a guy named Merv Griffin. He probably wouldn't admit it, but I brought Merv to my brother-in-law, Marty Melcher. But I was the one who found Merv in San Francisco.

The Andrews Sisters I handled for seventeen years. Through them I met Nelson Riddle. I was going into the service, and I went down to the Armed Forces Entertainment Group, and Nelson said to me, "You can do more as a civilian." Out of that came an idea that made me a lot of money.

I began photostatting every bandstand arrangement for the armed forces band, so they'd have an orchestration on Woody Herman, Harry James, Jimmie Lunceford, Benny Goodman, Gene Krupa, you name it. Out of that came the Leeds Manuscript Service, which was a big thing in its day.

Like everyone, the Andrews Sisters needed material. I taught them a song in Yiddish called "Bei Mir Bist du Shon." I had Sammy Cahn write the lyric to "Bei Mir Bist du Shon" faster than an audition. I asked him to do it, and he sent the lyric back over the telephone.

Songs also caused a lot of heartaches. I published one song, the dirtiest song I had ever heard, called "She Had to Go and Lose It at the Astor," written by a dancer, Don Raye. Don Raye wrote "I'll Remember April," "This Is My Country," "Boogie Woogie Bugle Boy" and "Cow Cow Boogie." I published all these songs. But it all came from "She Had to Go and Lose It at the Astor," which he had been doing in his vaudeville act.

I published Charlie Shavers' first songs. He gave me a hit song called "Undecided." That was the first hit I had, written by Charlie, a saxophone player who used to work with me in the Andrews Sisters' orchestra. Charlie said, "What'll we call it?"

I said, "Right now, it's called 'Undecided.'" Charlie Shavers was undecided about the title, which is why it was called "Undecided."

And then Sid Robin wrote the lyric, "First you say you do, and then you don't. You're undecided now." Charlie needed money so badly, I bought three songs from him for a hundred dollars, and "Undecided" was one of the songs. After the song hit—and this is the truth—I gave it back to Charlie. The song probably made three-quarters of a million dollars for his family.

I had a good sense for picking a song and then marrying it to an artist. I mean, Rosemary Clooney takes credit for a thing called "Come on-a My House." In truth, she had as much to do with it as Joe Smith. The real story is, Charlie Chaplin's son, Sid Chaplin, was doing a show in California that was written by William Saroyan. The show was called *The Son of a Bitch*, but they couldn't really call it that, so they tried *The SOB*, but the newspapers wouldn't stand for that either, so they settled on *The Son*.

The opening song in the show was "Come on-a My House," about a Greek fellow. I published the song, and the girl who actually deserves all the credit is a girl called Kay Armen, in New York. She recorded the song with three other songs on a custom date at CBS. Rosemary Clooney owes her entire career to Kay Armen. Kay made the record that Rosemary Clooney copied. And Kay was the only one in the whole thing who suffered. The song could have been her hit song. In the end, it's always the song more than the singer. If Kay Armen had the hit, she would have been as big as Rosemary Clooney.

Billy May

○ ○ ○

**Billy's career is full of starry associations. From Glenn Miller through
Frank Sinatra, he's put wondrous notes on paper while being
responsible for some of the most popular records ever.**

○ ○ ○

The difference between Glenn Miller and Charlie Barnet was like going
from a country club to work in a factory. With Miller's band, not only did
we all have to wear the same kind of socks, we had to make sure the socks
were up.

With Barnet, there were two uniforms—the blue suit that the guitar
player wore because he forgot, and the rest of us in brown suits.

With Miller, that would have been a disaster. In Barnet's band, he
made a big thing out of it. He would make the guy in the blue suit a soloist
and make a joke out of it. That was his attitude. Charlie was very relaxed.
We'd go down to do a record, and we'd have four charts and end up doing
six sides because we worked out so many things in our heads.

I joined Charlie in 1939 and was with him until the end of 1940. I
wrote "Cherokee" and "Pompton Turnpike" for him, and we were starting
to make some noise. Glenn needed trumpet players, but he hired me because
he wanted my writing.

I left for money, pure and simple. Miller offered me almost twice as
much as I was making with Charlie.

Miller had a songbook the size of a telephone book, about 120 tunes.
He was success oriented. He found a good thing and decided to make as
much money as he could. He had his own publishing company, and everything else he wanted he got.

I enjoyed the road. I learned a lot about human nature riding on a bus
and living intimately with guys in that kind of setting. There were idiosyn-
crasies and a lot of bullshit going on in the band. There were also a couple
of girl singers who were kind of loose with their morals, so it was fun.

By the early fifties, with my own band, the handwriting was on the
wall. I was playing all the same goddamn joints I had played with Barnet
and Miller ten years before. I could see that nothing was happening. We
were making money and doing business, but there were too many other
forms of entertainment to consider. Before, there was no television, no drive-
in movies. It was a much simpler time. The band was there and the broads
were there and the servicemen were there and the bars were open. It was
swinging, like the disco joints now.

So I moved on and went to work for Capitol Records when Sinatra was
finishing his deal with the record company. He was really getting picayunish
with Capitol. Nelson Riddle was leading a session with about thirty-five
musicians, and before they start playing it back, Frank says, "I don't know

how in the hell you can make records with that mike up there." Or something like that.

So finally, they get to, like, the twenty-eighth take, and Nelson stops the band, and Frank's looking around, and everyone's thinking, "Who's he gonna pick on next?"

And from the back Sweets Edison hollers, "Shit, daddy, you can't do it no better than that."

Everybody laughed, including Frank, and that was it. From then on, we'd say, "In the immortal words of Sweets Edison, 'Shit, daddy, you can't do it no better than that,'" and Frank would fall on the floor.

Sy Oliver

○ ○ ○

If you know anything about the swing era and big bands, you'll recognize that Sy was as great an arranger as ever lived. Talking with him in his New York apartment brought forth a litany of names, records, and stories.

○ ○ ○

The most exciting time for me was when I was with the Jimmie Lunceford Band. I was twenty-two. We came to New York and we opened at the Lafayette Theater. We were an overnight sensation. Literally.

Jimmie was very special. His was the first black band that crossed the line. White bands played for white people, and black bands played for black people. Lunceford's was the first band that played for both.

He was a man of great dignity. Very intellectual. You would never have even believed that he was in the music business. He wasn't like Ellington. Ellington was a charming man, an extrovert, a performer. Lunceford wasn't a performer.

We were on the road all the time. We worked darn near 352 days a year. Sometimes I wonder how we got from one date to the next. Some of them were very far apart. The big white bands, like Dorsey's, could come to New York and sit in the hotels and stay on the air doing remote broadcasts. The black bands couldn't do that. Black bands were like black baseball players. On the road we had to live in black neighborhoods. The accommodations were never good unless we were in the major cities—New York, Chicago, Los Angeles. In the boonies, it was never comfortable.

After six years with Jimmie I decided that this was not the way I wanted to spend my life. So I left the band to go back to school. And then Tommy

Dorsey offered me a job that I couldn't refuse. I joined the Dorsey band and stayed until I went into the army.

Dorsey would announce my name on the air. He'd say, "And that was a Sy Oliver arrangement." Nobody knew what an arranger was. I made the *Down Beat* poll three or four years in a row for the simple reason that I was the name people knew. In the meantime, there were hundreds of good arrangers. Every band that enjoyed any success at all owed it to whoever was doing the arrangements for them.

Then Jack Kapp, the man who founded Decca Records, called me and asked if I'd like to write for his artists. In those days, most record companies had two sections, white records and race records. It was like there were two musical worlds, the one below 110th Street and the one above 110th Street.

I told Jack Kapp I didn't know anything about race records. I said I didn't do that sort of thing. He said, "I don't want you to do that. I want you to write for all our artists."

That took me aback. I wasn't expecting him to say that. When I told him I wanted to use some black musicians, he hesitated. I guess it never occurred to him that there were no black musicians recording with either the Dorsey band or the Andrews Sisters. But he did say, "I don't care who you use. They all get paid the same. Just get the best person for the job." That's when I accepted the job.

Sometimes I'd get a call from Milt Gabler at the end of the day, just when I was getting ready to leave the office. He'd say, "Ella Fitzgerald's going to be in town tomorrow, and this is the only time we can do the dates. Can you have the arrangements ready by tomorrow morning at ten?"

I'd have to stay in the office all night and do four arrangements. I hadn't seen Ella, she didn't know what the songs were half the time, but I knew her keys and I knew how she sang, and that was all I needed to know.

I was a professional arranger who used to do whatever the situation called for. There are different types of musicians. There's the storybook musician, the guy who loves music and hangs around all night and jams as long as there's someone to play with. Then there's the professional musician, who is in the business to earn money, period. That's me.

Buddy Rich

o o o

**An amazing man, an incredibly gifted musician, Buddy may be the
greatest drummer of all time. Rock 'n' rollers as well as his swing
peers all agree that he set a standard. We talked a few months before
he died, and it was one of my most memorable conversations.**

o o o

I had what you might call an "attitude" in the old days. Unless a band
sounded like the way I wanted to play, I didn't sit in.

I can recall my first encounter with Tommy Dorsey. I had just left Artie
Shaw's band and I was sitting in at a place called Pick-A-Rib, a rib joint in
New York that was owned by Benny Goodman and his brother, Irving.
Incidentally, the best ribs ever on this planet.

OK, so I'm sitting in there one night and I get a call from my mother,
and she says Tommy Dorsey's manager had been trying to reach me, and
would I call the Palmer House in Chicago. So I call, and they ask me if I
would be interested in joining the Dorsey band. In those days, the Dorsey
band was strictly a dance band, more like a society band. No jazz in it,
except for the Clambake Seven, a seven-piece band Tommy used to pull
out of the big band to play a few tunes in Dixieland fashion.

I tell the manager I'm not interested in the job. He asks me to fly to
Chicago anyway to hear the band. He says they're in the process of making
some style changes. So I fly to Chicago and go to the Palmer House. After
listening to the first set, they ask me how I feel about joining the band. I
say I can't play their kind of music.

Then Tommy comes over and tells me Sy Oliver is going to be joining
the band and there's going to be a tremendous transition in the band's style.
He says they are going to try to be like the old Jimmie Lunceford band.
Tommy also tells me he has a group flying in called the Pied Pipers. And
also, that he's hired a singer by the name of Connie Haines.

The minute he mentions Sy Oliver's name, and Lunceford—I was a
big Lunceford fan—I think maybe I should stick around and listen. So Sy
Oliver flies in from New York, brings with him a couple of charts, I play
them and I'm delighted with the way they're written.

Now the band is cooking, and I figure this is a good place to be. Now
the Harry James band comes into Chicago, and there's a singer in the James
band by the name of Sinatra. Tommy goes over to hear him, and two weeks
later Frank joins the band. And that's where the band takes on the kind of
success it would enjoy for a lot of years.

Actually, I think Frank had intended to leave the James band all along.
But that was the way things happened in those days. If you offered a guy
twenty-five dollars more a week, he'd leave. I don't think that's proper. As
a band leader, I don't do that. But in those days, it was cutthroat and very
competitive. But that is how Frank Sinatra joined the Dorsey band.

I had the highest respect for Tommy's musicianship. He was the greatest trombone player, bar none, that ever lived. But I'm not talking about Tommy as a jazz player. He would have given anything to play jazz. But he was not a jazz player. He was strictly thirty-two bars of melody, and that he played better than anybody in the world, before or since.

Tommy had two personalities. He used to drink a lot. Me, I don't drink. Never did. I was always the straight guy in the band. When Tommy would have more than he should, he'd get reckless and we'd have our beefs. But he respected me as a player, and it was a mutual thing. That's probably why I stayed so long with Tommy.

Of course, Frank was another independent voice. Frank and I were roommates the first year he was in the band. In the beginning, we didn't battle each other too much. Within a couple of years, we were having personality conflicts, as any two young guys would who were trying to make a name for themselves. Everybody was trying to get the spotlight, everybody wanted to be successful.

With Frank it got to be hand-to-hand at times. At other times there was a lot of love. And there's still a lot of love. To me, the man is magic. There's nobody with a more vibrant, more demanding personality, than Frank, and I love him for that.

We were all a little nuts in the Dorsey band. Ziggy Elman, a great trumpet player. Joe Bushkin on piano, another nut. The Pied Pipers were all crazed, every one of them. Connie Haines was on the verge of becoming nuts.

With all the fights, there was a greater camaraderie in those days than there is today. When you finished working at night, you would either go uptown to Harlem and you'd play with all those guys from the Lunceford Band or you could go downtown to places like Nick's in the Village and meet all the Dixieland players.

When I started at the Hickory House in 1938, I had to wait three weeks for an audition. Every Sunday afternoon is jam-session day, and anybody who was anybody in the city would flock to the Hickory House.

The Hickory House is where I first met Gene Krupa and Benny Goodman and Bob Crosby and Roy Eldridge. The reason it took three weeks to get an audition, or even sit in with a band, was that so many other guys had first call.

Finally, they call me up. It's a Sunday afternoon. I finish playing—I'd never played in a band before—and Joe Marsala who was the band leader then, asks me if I want a job. I started working there two weeks later. Been working somewhere ever since.

I'll tell you, it was so romantic then. I remember coming out to L.A. in 1939 with Shaw's band and playing the Palomar. The old Palomar, before the Palladium was built. Opening night, Artie gets sick. For the first two weeks Tony Pastor leads the band. Even without Artie there the band was so good the place was packed every night.

It was a love thing that permeated places in those days. You could always feel it. Whatever you were doing, people just went, "Yeah," like, "Wow."

Today, kids feel like they have to light matches and scream whenever they're enjoying something. I don't understand the screaming. How can you listen? In the old days, people would save their yelling for the end of the chart. If you played a tune and they liked it, they'd let you know it. Today, you're out there playing and the people are making more noise than the music.

Milt Gabler

o o o

One of the behind-the-scenes manipulators, he put songs, singers, and musicians together for years of success. His early years with jazz have won him a permanent niche in that world.

o o o

My father owned the Commodore Music Shop, which was on 42nd Street in New York, diagonally across the street from the Commodore Hotel. It was a radio shop. I worked in the store. I would play music over the loud-speaker to attract customers. Everything started in the Commodore Music Shop. Writers and musicians would hang out there because I specialized in hot records. I started reissues in that store.

But it wasn't a big business, and when radio came in, it just about killed records. So we sold parts for people to build their own ham radios. In fact, we sold everything—cameras, golf clubs, tennis rackets, along with records.

My father said, "I don't know anything about music."

I said, "I got the radio on all day, so I know every song there ever was."

And my father said, "Get the telephone book and look up the record companies, and have them send salesmen down so we can begin stocking records."

Little by little, the store's record stock grew in size and I got rid of all the other stuff, including eventually radios, and we became just a record shop.

I had to finally begin making records when Columbia started putting out reissues at a cheaper price than what the Commodore Music Shop was selling them at. I realized it was no good unless you made your own masters.

Eddie Condon was my kind of guy, the free-style swing guys. I used to go down to the Village, and over to 52nd Street, and that was where all the free-style swing was happening. I got ahold of Eddie Condon and I said, "Eddie, I want to make a record." I had analyzed the records I was collecting—Chicago Rhythm Kings, "I Found a New Kind of Baby," "There'll

Be Some Changes Made." These things had a spirit, and it wasn't Dixieland. It was a four-four beat. So I wanted to make that kind of record, and it seemed that Eddie Condon was in the rhythm section on all those records.

Eddie's brother-in-law had brought him into the shop because I had all these jazz records. Eddie was like a promoter. He didn't like big band music. He just liked small-group stuff. So I said to him, "I want to make a record like the Chicago Rhythm Kings. I want Bud Freeman," my favorite tenor sax player. "I want Bobby Hackett on trumpet, George Wettling on drums, Artie Shapiro on bass, Jess Stacy on piano," and Condon, of course, on guitar.

But the problem was, Freeman was with the Tommy Dorsey band, George Wettling was with the Red Norvo band, and Jess Stacy was with Benny Goodman. I had to have three bands in town at the same time, and then book a studio. This particular time, Benny Goodman was in New York to do what turned out to be his famous Carnegie Hall concert. Which was on a Sunday, and I had a studio booked for Monday. Dorsey's band was in town, and so was Norvo's. So everything was set.

And then Condon calls me on Friday before the session and says, "Milt, Jess Stacy can't get off on Monday. Benny is recording before he leaves town."

I said, "Goddamnit, I gotta talk to Benny and get Jess off for Monday." So I walked over to where they were rehearsing for the Carnegie Hall concert, and I go through the back door, and Benny sees me and he says, "Hi, Milt. What are you doing here?"

I said, "Benny, I have a record date booked for Monday, and Jess called Eddie Condon and told him that he couldn't get off because you're recording on Monday."

Benny said, "That's right."

I said, "Benny, you have a record out every week and they're all starting to sound the same. You know? Formula arrangements? Why don't you take Monday off. Especially after the concert. Take a rest. Do some trio work with Teddy Wilson. Or use Teddy on your Monday date instead of Jess. I've been trying to do this date for six months. I'm dead if I have to cancel it."

Benny had been one of my customers when he lived in Jackson Heights. So he thought about it for a second and realized, maybe he should give the guys Monday off.

Speaking of Teddy Wilson, he had brought Billie Holiday into the shop. So I knew Billie around the time of "Billie's Blues" and "Summertime." Great gal.

The store was no longer on 42nd Street. I opened up on 52nd Street, to be right on Swing Alley. One night I was closing at about seven P.M., and Billie came in with a long face. She was very unhappy. She had just started to sing a song called "Strange Fruit," which was the first protest song, an antilynching song she'd been singing at the downtown Café Society.

She said to me, "Columbia won't record it because they're afraid of the content of the song." They were worried about the Southern record dealers, the adverse publicity. They also didn't think it was a pop hit. But it was a marvelous piece of music with a great message. Columbia didn't want to touch it, but I was all for it.

So I said, "Billie, ask them if they'll give you permission to do a record for me. I'm just a little record store, one of their good customers. What do they have to lose?"

The next day she came back with a smile on her face and said, "Milt, they'll let me do a record date with you." So we went into the studio with "Strange Fruit," "Fine and Mellow," "I Got a Right to Sing the Blues," and Jerome Kern's "Yesterdays." We went in with Frankie Newton's band, the band she'd been singing with at the Café Society. What happened, of course, was that "Strange Fruit" got publicity from the minute it came out, and "Fine and Mellow" turned out to be the big hit. Here I was, on my own Commodore label, named for the store, and I have Billie Holiday's two most important artistic and commercial releases.

Maxine Andrews

○ ○ ○

She and her sisters were truly stars at a time when female groups were not especially in fashion. They worked with anyone that mattered, and their records epitomized the escapist pop of World War II.

○ ○ ○

Whenever you see three girls, you automatically think of the Andrews Sisters. I get a big kick out of that. When Bette Midler came out with her version of "Boogie Woogie Bugle Boy," a lot of people said to me, "That wasn't very nice of her," but I was flattered. She did a wonderful job, and we are very indebted to Bette because she recreated interest in the Andrews Sisters.

From the beginning, we were the girls next door, the kid sisters. We were never glamorous, never great beauties, but we had a wonderful thing about us. When we went overseas during the war, the fellas would say, "Gee, you're just like my kid sister." Or, "It's so good being with you because you remind me of my family." That kind of feeling has stuck with the Andrews Sisters.

I was four when I did my first radio broadcast in Minneapolis. By the time I was six, I was entertaining at Veterans hospitals, for the mayor of Minneapolis, and at DAR luncheons.

LaVerne started the trio. Our great influence was the Boswell Sisters. They did a show on the radio with Bing Crosby that came on during the week at 4:00 P.M. Like everybody in those days, we'd put our chairs around the radio console and watch it and listen to the sounds coming out. LaVerne played great piano, all by ear, and she would remember the Boswell Sisters' intricate arrangements so we'd be better able to copy them. We got so good at copying the Boswell Sisters that we developed a southern accent. You couldn't sing their songs without having a southern accent.

The only kind of encouragement we got from our family was that they let us go. We were supposedly making $250 a week, but we never saw any of that money. We got a dollar a day between us. Our father, being Greek, did not think it was honorable to have female relatives in show business. He never said it to us directly, but it showed in his disapproval. He thought his daughters should go back to school and become private secretaries, which was the furthest thing from LaVerne's mind, from Patty's mind, and from my mind.

Actually, nobody wanted girls back then. What they wanted was a great girl singer, but a trio, no. Still, when we made our first record, we were so sure that everybody was going to get down on their knees and bow to Allah that it was quite a revelation when the record didn't sell. In fact, we went from a great high to thinking it was the end of our record career. We thought for sure that Mr. Jack Kapp, who the three of us idolized, was going to drop us because the last thing he needed was a girl trio that wasn't selling.

And then one day we got a call from Jack saying he had a hit song for us. I said to him, "What about the other side of the record?"

And he said, "I don't care. Pick anything you want."

It was just about the same time that Lou Levy walked in and said to us, "Have I got a song for you." He said there was no sheet music for the song, but that he'd sing for us.

Don't ever ask Lou Levy to sing because he can't. But he sang this melody, and somehow it grabbed us from the first note. The harmonies were easy and the melody was nothing to learn.

But the lyrics, there really weren't any. Lou said, "My mother used to sing me this melody when I was little." We were so naive. I think the corn husks were still coming out of my ear.

Well, what Lou did was, he taught us the lyrics phonetically because they were in Yiddish. So we got into the studio and first we do the arrangement of "Nice Work If You Can Get It." Then we do the second side.

Now what Jack used to do was have all the recording sessions piped into his office, which was two floors above the studio. In the middle of doing "Bei Mir Bist Du Schon," in Yiddish, Jack calls down to the studio and has the tape stopped. We were petrified.

He walked into the studio and looked at us and said, "Where did you get that song?" The three of us at the same time pointed right at Lou.

Sammy Kaye

o o o

**He accepted the role of schmaltzy band leader and created a business
out of the music. Many feel the band's commercial success outstripped
the talent, but Sammy managed to live with it and prosper.**

o o o

I was always a sweet band, not a jazz band. I wasn't a jazz guy, and as a
matter of fact, Guy Lombardo was my favorite band.

We were always disciplined, always spic 'n' span. When we played
theaters, between the next to last and the last show we always had a rehearsal,
whether we needed one or not. I would say, "Let's try number fifty-five.
Let's see if we can clean it up a little."

We also always traveled first-class. We would take Greyhound on the
theory that if one of the buses broke down, Greyhound would always send
another. And when we traveled by train, it was Pullman cars all the way.

We'd be out for one-nighters. MCA in Cleveland was booking us, and
New York never heard of us. I'd go into a place like the Sunnybrook Ballroom
with a $200 guarantee for the night and sixty percent, and we'd walk out of
there with $1,800 for the night.

When we sent the commission to MCA, and it got to New York, they
would say, "Sammy Kaye, $1,800? Who the hell is he, and where is he?"
They sent an office boy named Sonny Werblin to find me. After that, we
played the Paramount Theater for $3,500, which was terrific.

Well, enter Jim Peppe, my manager. He sees the contracts, and he says
to MCA, "Fellas, Sammy Kaye for $3,500? You're kidding, aren't you?"
The next thing you know, it's $6,500.

So I go in there for $6,500, following Tommy Dorsey, and I'm telling
you, they had to push me out there on the stage. I'm saying, "No way. I
can't. Oh, my God." When I look back, at least we weren't booed off the
stage. In fact, they accepted us.

The number-one break for me was "Swing and Sway." I'm playing at
a place in Cleveland called the Cabin Club, and with "Kaye" it's very easy
to rhyme. The announcer would come on and he would say, "Music in a
romantic way, played for you by Sammy Kaye." Or "Music in a rhythmic
way, played for you by Sammy Kaye."

Once in a while I'd throw in, "Now let's swing and sway with Sammy
Kaye."

One night some kids walked up to me and said, "Hi, swing and sway."

The minute I heard that, I said, "That's it." I dropped everything else.
From that moment on, it was, "Now let's swing and sway with Sammy
Kaye."

People used to say, "I'd like to lead a number with the band," and I
would just fluff them off. One time there was this kid with a very lovely girl,
and he said, "I'd sure like to lead the band."

"All right," I said, with an ulterior motive, "can I dance with your girl?"

So I danced with the girl, and I said, "Oh, how lovely you are. May I call you sometime?" She didn't answer me. She was too busy looking at her boyfriend leading the band. The next night I'm thinking, "If the people want to lead a band that badly, why not invite them to come up?"

I talked with my manager, and I said, "Give me a bottle of champagne, and we'll give it to the winner." Instantaneous hit. I mean, no matter where we went after that we had everybody—governors, senators, everybody wanted to lead a band.

Herb Jeffries

o o o

One of the very few band singers with Duke Ellington, Herb went on to a moderately successful solo career. His time with the band gives us a look into the workings of one of the world's great magical teams.

o o o

When I joined Earl Hines in Chicago, in 1936, the racial situation was terrible. When we played one-nighters throughout the South, in places like Jacksonville, Florida, I can remember vividly how blacks were roped off. They could come in and listen to the band, but they couldn't dance. Only white people could dance. The blacks would stand off in a corner behind a big rope and listen.

The bandleaders all fought it. I was in Moline, Illinois, with Duke Ellington's band that had just come back from Europe where it had played for the royal family. And of course the Prince of Wales had sat in, you know, and played drums. But in Moline, blacks couldn't go to the restaurants to eat. Still, when anyone came backstage, the musicians would be finishing a show and people would be standing in line for autographs.

I don't think anybody was thrilled about the conditions, but if you wanted to advance and develop you couldn't show anger. You had to accept it and resign yourself to it. Little by little, blacks started saying, "If I can't live in this hotel, I won't play this hotel."

After I left Hines, I went on the road with Blanche Calloway, Cab Calloway's sister. She had a very successful band. After that I made the first all-sepia cowboy picture. It was called *Harlem on the Prairie*, and it was so successful we made four more. I had the lead, like Gene Autry. The picture played the Apollo Theater, where Ellington was appearing. Later, I was in Detroit at the same time he was there, and I came in my cowboy regalia to hear his band. I was down in front, and he introduced me. He said, "I just finished playing the Apollo with your picture. Won't you come up and sing a song?" I wound up joining his band.

The camaraderie in his band was like a bunch of guys in college. You're talking about all-star musicians. My God, Duke's was the greatest all-star band there ever was. Ellington had a knack for developing talent and stars. He was a wonderful man. He shaped my way of life. He was impeccable in his dress and he was one of the most articulate speakers I'd ever heard. He was one of the most impressive people I have ever met, an all-around conglomerate. I believe he will go down in history as the Mozart or Beethoven of his time.

He was more like a father to me than a boss. He could scold you as easily as he could give you money. If he felt you needed clothes, he'd say, "Give him an advance for clothes."

I remember once sitting next to him, looking at him. He said, "What are you thinking?"

I said, "I'm just thinking about how great it must be to be standing up there where you are."

He said, "Yeah, yeah, it is. But there's no place for me to sit down." I never forgot that. It's great to be famous, but when you're famous you never get a chance to sit. You have to keep going for if you don't, your career starts to ebb. And it's the same with all performers.

I was the first male vocalist Duke had. He realized there were songs that needed to be broadcasted, and in order to do that, he had to have a singer. I was lucky to be selected.

I had a million-seller, "Flamingo," which Tony Martin covered about six months after I had the hit. He came down to see the show one night. I heard he was in the audience, and I peeked through the curtain and saw him sitting there. After the show, I'm driving up Wilshire Boulevard and who should pull up next to me at a light but Tony Martin. He yells out, "Hey, Jeffries, I caught the show. You were terrific."

I said, "Yeah, I saw you sitting in the audience."

We're rapping back and forth like that, and he says, "Incidentally, I recorded 'Flamingo.' "

I said, "I know. You copied my record."

He said, "How did you know that?"

I said, "Because you made the same mistake in the lyrics that I did."

He said, "Pull over, you son of a gun." And we pulled over on Wilshire Boulevard and I told him the story of how, when I went in to record that song, I didn't have any music with me. Once in the studio I got so excited that I couldn't think of two words in the song. So I made up words in their place. Tony recorded the song never knowing that some of the words I sang were made up.

Sammy Fain

○ ○ ○

**Provide a piano and three willing people, and Sammy will run down
highlights from one of the great songwriting careers. He remembers
every detail and delights in recounting stories of his creations.**

○ ○ ○

I came from a musical family. Even in public school I was writing songs—
words and music—and singing them. I remember this one time when George
Gershwin came up to visit us in the country with my uncle, who was
Gershwin's family doctor. I played a few of my songs for George, and he
said, "Gee, you have some great little tunes here."

The next time George visited us he brought with him a copy of "Rialto
Ripples." That was the first song he ever had published. The sheet music
was purple, I'll never forget that. I don't know what I ate yesterday, but I
remember that the color of "Rialto Ripples" was purple.

My first two big hits, "Let a Smile Be Your Umbrella" and "Wedding
Bells Are Breaking Up That Old Gang of Mine," were both published by
Waterson, Berlin and Snyder, big publishers at the time. Well, they wanted
to be really big so they expanded. It didn't work and they went bankrupt—
owing me $17,000, which is like $17 million today.

Now, mind you, this was Irving Berlin's company, even though he
himself was no longer with the firm by the time they declared.

So I got the credit for those songs, but not too much in royalties because
of the bankruptcy. I figured, if a publisher goes out of business owing a writer
money, the writer should at least get his songs back. I went to court with it.
I sort of became a test case. Well, I won it, and then the publishers won it
back, saying it was unfair because maybe they owed the printer, or something.
And that's the way it stands today. Publishers still win out.

Of course, publishers can also do wonders for you. I'll tell you a very
interesting story about one of my songs, "I'll Be Seeing You." Years ago, I
received this call from Max Dreyfuss in New York, and he said, "Sammy."

And I said, "Yeah, Mr. Dreyfuss."

And he said, "Call me Max." He had this thin little voice. He said,
"Richard Rodgers is crazy about 'I'll Be Seeing You.' He wants it for his
publishing company."

God, was I flattered. I was such a big fan of Dick's. In fact, he and I
got into ASCAP on the same day in 1926.

So I turned the song over to his company, and we did very well with
it.

On another occasion, I was walking along Broadway in New York and
I ran into someone from the Shubert office. He said, "Sammy, you're the
guy we gotta get."

I said, "For what?"

"For a show we're doing. We're in rehearsal, we got the sets, the costumes, we got the choreographer, and the thing doesn't work. Now, if you can get us four or five songs by the beginning of the week . . ."

I said, "By the beginning of the week? Are you kidding me?"

And he said, "No." So I got ahold of Charlie Tobias and we went away for three days and came back with five songs. The name of the show was *Hellzapoppin*. Terrific hit. Ran for years. Anyway, that's the way things happened in those days. Fast. A songwriter had to be ready for anything.

Another time, in New York, I got a call from Buddy Morris. He said, "Sammy, get on a plane."

I said, "For what?"

He said, "We gotta have a good song for *Footlight Parade*. Buz Berkeley needs it. He's important."

So I came. Brought along Irving Kahal. Wonderful lyricist who co-wrote "I'll Be Seeing You" with me. Died much too soon.

OK, so we got on the plane. Imagine, it took us twenty-three hours to fly from New York to Burbank. When we arrived in Burbank, Buddy was there to tell us that the song they needed had to be about a waterfall for this waterfall scene Berkeley wanted to shoot.

I had a little tune in my mind and I started humming it. Irving goes, "Gee, maybe," and he starts singing, " 'By a waterfall, I'm calling you.' "

Before we could get any further they're running to Berkeley with it, and he says, "That's it! That's it! I wanted something simple that the girls can swim to, and that's it."

Well, "By a Waterfall" went right in the picture. Berkeley loved it. He kept doing it and doing it. It seemed like it went on for 104 choruses.

But that wasn't the first picture song I did. The first one was "You Brought a New Kind of Love to Me," that Maurice Chevalier sang for *A New Kind of Love*. Sinatra has probably recorded that song three or four times, and Benny Goodman did a great record of it. I'm talking standard.

Billy Rose was a pretty good friend of mine, too. One time he said, "Sammy, you do such beautiful songs. You need to learn how to sing 'em so that performers who want to put 'em in their act can hear how they sound."

That turned out to be pretty good advice because it allowed me to get my foot in the door with some pretty heavyweight people like Eddie Cantor, Kate Smith, and Jimmy Durante.

E. Y. "Yip" Harburg, the great lyricist, got a hold of me once and said, "Sammy, I want to write a song called 'Goodnight, Mrs. Calabash, Wherever You Are.' "

I said, "That's Durante's sign-off."

Yip said, "I know, but I think it could be a great song."

So I took the title and I wrote up a tune, and Yip wrote the lyric that his wife, to this day, says has more heart than anything I've ever written.

Durante, now there was someone special. He would call me up at ten, eleven o'clock in the evening and say, "Hey, what are you doing?"

I'd say, "Jimmy, I'm taking it easy."

And he'd say, "Get dressed and come over. I gotta do this benefit for so-and-so. I want you to come with me. We'll both sing."

So I'd do this benefit with him. Jimmy liked certain of my songs, especially "I'll Be Seeing You." I'd start singing it, and he would never interrupt me, you know, like a lot of comics would break in if they thought they could get a laugh. But not Jimmy. He'd let me sing the entire song, and I would sing it with all my heart, and as soon as I finished and got a nice hand, he'd wait a few beats and then point to me and say to the audience, "He stole that from 'Inka Dinka Do.' "

Jimmy recorded "I'll Be Seeing You." He was fantastic doing it, as he was doing any kind of ballad. There was something about that type of voice doing that type of song. The first time I heard "September Song" was when Walter Huston sang it in *Knickerbocker Holiday*. Walter Huston wasn't a singer. But he could deliver a good song with style. Same with Jimmy. When he sang "September Song" and then took his hat off at the end, my God, you had to love him.

Ray Anthony

○ ○ ○

He looks back at a career with some regrets, but with the certainty that he was a great trumpet player who had trouble fitting in. Ray is a survivor and made records long after the band days had peaked.

○ ○ ○

I was seventeen, and I was touring in the New England area with Al Donahue's band, and we went to see Glenn Miller at the RKO in Boston. I was just flabbergasted. I mean, this machine! Sliding trombones, the hats flying, the organization—it was all so thrilling to me. Three months later, I was with the Glenn Miller band.

I was cocky and probably driving everybody else nuts. Here I was, a kid sitting on the top of the world, in a business I wanted to be in. Being in the band was not good enough. I wanted to be in the number-one chair.

I did dumb things. I was fired, rehired. But I was tremendous, and I'm not bragging. It amazed me I was so good. But to Miller I was "Junior," I was nothing. And so was everybody else. Which is why some of the younger guys disliked him so much.

Tex Beneke had a party recently for the Miller alumni, and somebody at the party told me that back then nobody liked me. I acknowledge that I must have been obnoxious. It's so hard to figure out what I was like then.

I don't care how much Miller was disliked, I admired him, and I still do. He did what he had to do. Musicians are like children. Dealing with musicians is like dealing with gypsies. You have to discipline them.

My life was disciplined. My dad was disciplined, Miller was disciplined, and the navy was disciplined. So when I got my own band, the sort of natural thing for me to do was discipline them.

Our band was always clean in the way it played. Everything was precise. I can remember seeing the Ellington band. One guy would come on the stand, five minutes later another guy would come up, and I'd say, "How can they run a band like that?" Halfway through the set the saxophone player might be sleeping. And the audience is watching all this. I could never handle such a lack of discipline.

When I went into the navy, my claim to fame was that I was in Glenn Miller's band. They wanted to hear that, and so we played mostly Miller-type arrangements. When the kids heard that sound, that was America to them, that was home. I thought, "Well, the thing to do is incorporate the sax part or the clarinet lead into our style and sound."

In other words, the trumpet was Harry James, the trombone was Tommy Dorsey. Put it all together and start something of your own. It's similar to Perry Como liking Russ Columbo and Bing Crosby, and then eventually becoming Perry Como. You imitate the best, and then, hopefully, you become something yourself.

In '54 we made a motion picture at 20th Century Fox, we replaced Perry Como for Chesterfield cigarettes on TV, we had a hit with "Dragnet," and at the end of the year we made "Daddy Longlegs." We grossed a million dollars that year.

In '55, I could have grossed $750,000 on just the momentum, but not me. I broke up the band because I wanted to stay in Los Angeles and study voice, acting, and further enhance my career as a performer, which was a mistake. I could have waited another year or so, but I'm impulsive that way.

"The Bunny Hop," which I wrote in '52 or '53, is still selling. I still get royalties on it. In fact, I did it recently at a dance. Musically, the piece is nothing, so I'd rather not play it. But then, people keep bugging me to play it. I guess it's so simple, a crowd thing, and everybody gets into it.

If kids don't know who Ray Anthony is, I ask them, "Do you know who Glenn Miller is?"

And they say, "Yeah, we know Glenn Miller, but we don't know Ray Anthony."

I say, "I wrote 'The Bunny Hop.' "

And they say, "You wrote that?" After all these years, "The Bunny Hop" is my claim to fame.

Paul Weston

o o o

"Respected" is the word most used when discussing this veteran arranger, conductor, and composer. Paul and his wife, Jo Stafford, represented the high style of pop music in the forties and fifties.

o o o

I was up to seventy-five dollars an arrangement, and my father had come down from Pittsfield, Massachusetts, and he said, "You gotta get out of this filthy show business. You went to Dartmouth. You need to get a decent job."

Well, when I sent my first check from Rudy Vallee up to Pittsfield, my father went into the bank with the check and he became a celebrity. People were running around the bank yelling, "Rudy Vallee! Rudy Vallee!" After that, I never heard another word from my old man.

Tommy Dorsey was great to write for. He very seldom changed anything. He never picked apart the arrangement. He was a bad guy to work for if you were sloppy and you didn't know what you were doing, but he didn't mind a guy making a mistake as long as he was trying hard. But if a guy played through a rest or left out a part, he could be "gone," just like that.

Tommy's was the most versatile of all the bands. Benny Goodman played swing, and Guy Lombardo and a lot of the other guys did the sweet stuff, but Tommy was always second in swing and in sweet stuff, which is just where he wanted to be.

We spent a lot of time back then with the music publishers. Jonie Taps was with Shapiro, Bernstein, and they published a lot of songs that Tommy hated, like "Heading for the Last Roundup." Whenever Jonie came into the Astor Hotel, he'd walk down the aisle to his table. No matter what Tommy was doing, even if he was in the middle of a trombone solo, he would stop and bark at Jonie because Tommy believed Jonie published dogs. People would be having dinner, and they would see this famous trombone player and bandleader stop what he was doing and go, "Arf, arf."

Later, I got a chance to be Dinah Shore's regular arranger, and so I went to Tommy and said, "I think I'd like to free-lance." At first, he got real bugged because he thought I was going with Glenn Miller.

Tommy said to people, "I bet we'll hear about him being with Glenn Miller." They were always raiding Tommy.

I arranged, and I started producing, too. I produced "Que Será Será." Doris Day cried and said she didn't like it—and didn't want to record it. Doris never knew how good she was.

Jo Stafford and I made 500 records together. A lot of jazz and black musicians loved Jo's singing. The day she made the record of "Daydream," somebody went over to Johnny Hodges and said, "Billy Strayhorn would have loved this."

When Jo met Louis Armstrong, he said to her, "I just want you to know, all us spades appreciate your work."

Jo Stafford

o o o

Completely identifiable and totally talented, Jo has won acclaim from her peers among musicians and vocalists. She walked calmly through the turmoil of the Dorsey-Sinatra-Rich wars and kept making hits long after.

o o o

Originally, the Pied Pipers were made up of seven boys and me. Alyce King of the King Sisters was going with Paul Weston, and Alyce's sister, Yvonne, was going with Axel Stordahl. Paul and Axel were arrangers with Tommy Dorsey's orchestra.

Alyce went to Paul one day and said, "You've got to hear this group that's just formed. They're really good." So we got together one afternoon and had a jam. Paul and Axel then told Tommy about the group, and he hired us, not as part of his orchestra, but as an act on his radio show.

We did Tommy's radio show for about seven weeks, and then we starved to death for the next seven months before returning to California.

Then, I'll never forget, it was a Friday. I had just picked up my last unemployment check, and when I got home there was a message for me to call an operator in Chicago. It was free, so I made the call. It was Tommy. He said he couldn't handle a group of eight, but if we were a quartet we could join his organization.

I said, "Funny you should ask. Some of the guys have dropped out, and we're already down to a quartet." That's how the Pied Pipers joined Tommy.

Two weeks later, Frank Sinatra joined the band. We'd just finished an engagement at the Palmer House in Chicago, and now we were on our way to another engagement in Minneapolis. We went up by train. It wasn't very far. We didn't have to rehearse because we knew our part of the presentation. But Frank was new and he had to rehearse.

The first time I ever saw him, or heard him, was that night when Tommy introduced him as the new vocalist, and he walked on to do his stint. About eight bars into the song I thought, "Boy, this is something else. This is new. No one has ever sounded like this before." And it was an entirely new sound. Most boy singers in those days sounded like Bing Crosby. Crosby was the big thing. But this kid didn't sound like Crosby. He didn't sound like anybody I'd ever heard before. And he was sensational.

The Pipers joined Tommy's orchestra in December of '39, and we stayed three years, until November of '42. We left because of a fight Tommy got into with one of the Pipers, Chuck Lowrey. We were at a train station, about to board our train. It was eight o'clock in the morning. It was during one of the periods when Tommy was drinking. He asked Chuck which train was ours, and Chuck gave him the wrong information. Not purposely. He'd just made a mistake. But "Little Tom," as we used to call him, had a bit of a hangover that morning, and he got very mad and started screaming and yelling. The four of us walked off the train in a huff and that was it.

Luckily for us, we had a big fan named Johnny Mercer. He liked our group and he liked me as a solo. He had told us, "If you ever leave Dorsey to go on your own, I'm starting this record company, and I would sure like to sign the Pipers, and Jo as a solo singer." So we went to see him, and he signed the Pipers and he signed me.

Paul Weston was at Capitol. He was Capitol's musical director at the time. He and Johnny both helped us pick material. One day in 1945, Paul and I looked at each other and said, "How long have we known each other?"

For years, Paul and I had been like passing ships through the night. It started off as a strictly platonic friendship. Later on, there were these two dumbbells, looking at each other one day and saying, "Hey there."

Jack Leonard

o o o

The answer to the trivia question "Who preceded Frank Sinatra as Tommy Dorsey's male singer?", Jack Leonard had a few hits—and has a few regrets.

o o o

I joined Tommy Dorsey in late '36 and stayed with him four and a half years. That's a record. Nobody stayed with Tommy that long. I used to get weary with Tommy's temperament. He would scream at the guys, but never at me. I guess I was doing what he wanted me to do. I was not like Sinatra. He rocked a lot of boats. I just went along and did my job.

Tommy made men out of boys. Some leaders just stood up with their baton and waved it like a stick, guys who knew beans about music. But Tommy knew what he wanted. He worked us hard. He was rough and very bombastic. A lot of guys disliked him because he could do some very cruel things. But I loved him.

Tommy was tough, even in front of an audience. People would be out there dancing, and Tommy would be giving one of the guys a hell of a time. He'd pick up his trombone and start giving the guy a lesson in front of all the customers. You know, showing him positions on the slide of the trombone.

It was a hard life. Days were upside-down. Dinner was at eight o'clock in the morning, breakfast at nine at night. We'd be on the road doing one-nighters, and we'd drive 400, 500 miles a night. It was murder. Tommy always insisted on getting to the next night's job right away. We'd do a job and be finished at, say, one o'clock in the morning. We'd pack up, get on the bus, and take off for the next town. We'd go to bed the next morning, sleep during the day, and then go to our job. There were times I'd say, "Hey, what day is this? What town are we in?"

I've made two big mistakes in my career. One was in 1941, when Glenn Miller asked me to join him. He said, "You can join us. We're rehearsing up at Yale."

And I said, "Yeah, but I'm at Fort Dix in New Jersey, and I'm leading a band up there."

The rest is history. Then came Pearl Harbor, and Glenn got Johnny Desmond, and I got sent overseas. Had I gone with Glenn it might have been different. Johnny Desmond made a name for himself with Glenn.

My other big mistake was quitting Tommy when I did. We were playing the Palmer House in Chicago. Tommy could be very vindictive. Anyway, we played the job, cleared the house, and Tommy said, "Hang around, guys, I'm calling a rehearsal."

So I'm sitting there, and Jimmy Blake, a trumpet player, went out and got a sandwich. Tommy spotted this, and he asks, "What the hell is happening here? Nobody eats on my bandstand when I'm rehearsing."

Jimmy says, "Tommy, we haven't had a break to get something to eat."

Tommy says, "Why, you sonofabitch."

The guy, who was a buddy of mine, thinks, "Well. I've had it."

I didn't say a word to Tommy. I just walked out and went to my hotel. Tommy's manager, Bobby Burns, calls and says, "Jack, what are you doing there?"

I said, "Well, I've had it. When he started screaming at Jimmy, I thought he was being grossly unfair. I took a hike," I said, "and I'm not going back."

After that, CBS wanted to sign me, and Tommy said, "If you ever sign Jack Leonard, my band will never do a remote on your station." Tommy did all kinds of horrible, vindictive things, but who knows what might have happened if I hadn't left?

Let me back up a minute. In 1938 we played the Canadian National Exhibition and I was lying on my bed in the Royal York Hotel in Toronto. My roommate in those days was Carmen Mastren, the guitar player. The telephone rings, and there's this girl on the line who I think is a fan, and she says, "Hi, is Carmen there? I have a song for him."

We had a lot of girls in those days, and I'm thinking, "Yeah, right, you have a song for Carmen."

Well, it turns out that she gives Carmen the song, and it's a knockout. It's called "I'll Never Smile Again." We said, "Wow, Tommy, you gotta hear this."

We finally nail Tommy, sit him down and play him the song, and he says, "Jack, as soon as we get off the road, this song is for you."

It was shortly after that, maybe two or three months, that we wind up in Chicago and I quit. Had I stayed, "I'll Never Smile Again" would have been mine, not Frank's. That was my big mistake. I left and he inherited the song.

Al Gallico

○ ○ ○

A publishing phenomenon who spanned forty years of frantic activity, Al worked the room well, allying himself with the men and women who made records.

○ ○ ○

I was an errand boy for a publisher on 43rd Street, and all I really wanted to be was a song plugger. One day I get an order to pick up two copies of one song. It was only two copies, and I was used to carrying a hundred, and I had never heard of the company, so I put the order in my pocket and I didn't go.

I get back to my office and my boss says, "Did you go to Leeds Music?"

I say, "No, I didn't."

He says, "Get your hat and coat, catch the Sixth Avenue bus, get the song, and get back here because the customer is in the shop."

I go up to Leeds Music and it's in an apartment house, Lou Levy's apartment. I ring the bell. He opens the door. I give him the order. He goes to the cupboard for the song. While he's filling the order, I'm looking around the room and I see all these young people. I say to myself, "Goddamnit, maybe this is the place."

He fills the order, and I say to him, "You got a job for me?"

He says, "Get lost."

I say, "Sonofabitch, this is the place." I go there every day, and every day he throws me out.

One day he says, "You want to make a quarter?"

I say, "I don't want the quarter, Lou. What do you want me to do?"

He says, "Take this package over to West 54th Street, by the river."

I deliver the package, then I come back and ring his bell. He says, "What the hell do you want?"

I plead for a job. He says, "How much do you make a week?"

I say, "Twelve dollars."

He says, "I'll give you eight."

I say, "I'll take it." He didn't pay me for a year and a half, but I didn't care. I was learning. By the time I was twenty-two, I was a manager and I was running a publishing company, unheard of in those days. Oh, yes— and by the way, the young people in Lou's apartment that day were the three ugly girls who became the Andrews Sisters.

I found the Ames Brothers and got them their record deal. I was running Shapiro-Bernstein at the time. One day Ed Ames calls and says, "Al, I think mambos are going to happen. Do you have a mambo?" I didn't. He says, "If you find a mambo, call me."

As God is my judge, five minutes later three writers come in—Al Hoffman, Dick Manning, and another guy—and they want me to listen to their song, "Papa Loves Mambo." I say, "I'll buy it."

They say, "Don't you want to hear it?"

I say, "I don't have to hear it. I love the title. I need a mambo." So I give them $500 in advance, draw up the contracts, and then I listen to the song.

Now I call back Ed Ames and I tell him I have the song. He says, "Great. We're meeting Hugo Winterhalter, noon tomorrow at RCA. Meet us there."

The next day I go to RCA. Al Hoffman sings the song live, and the Ames Brothers look at me as though I'm nuts. When I go to take my copy of the song away from Hugo Winterhalter, he winks at me. Two hours later, Hugo calls me and says, "Al, they're crazy. I think it's a hit. Even though I don't cut Perry Como, I'm going to tell him about the song." And that's what he did. He gave it to Como and Como recorded it.

In the fifties the publishers lost control. A & R guys lost their say, too. Artists started to write their own songs, and it marked the beginning of the end of the business as we had known it.

Les Brown

○ ○ ○

Les didn't cut a great swath through the big band annals, but as he says, he ran a tight entertaining group and has his name on many hits of the time—and he's still out there with his old-time buddy, Bob Hope.

○ ○ ○

I was a very big admirer of Benny Goodman. I went to Duke in the early thirties, during the depth of the Depression, and I fronted a band with clarinet. We were more or less a Goodman-style band.

Later on, we gradually got to play however the tune felt. To this day, we don't have an instant identification like, say, Billy May with his sliding saxophone, or Glenn Miller with his clarinet lead. But we did have a certain sound and a certain cleanliness that dilettantes could understand and recognize.

Frankly, my own opinion of the Glenn Miller clarinet lead is that it was so saccharine sweet it could give you diabetes. However, it certainly was commercially feasible and it made for instant recognition. The Glenn Miller band is no doubt the most popular band of all time, still going strong forty-some–odd years after Miller's death.

I preferred Benny Goodman's swing style. Tommy Dorsey's band was an all-around band, and that is more or less how I patterned our band. We did ballads pretty. Benny never did. Benny always kept the beat going. For a while we copied a lot of the Jimmie Lunceford stuff. In essence, we were a conglomeration of anything we thought was good.

In 1939, we needed a girl singer. We hadn't been very lucky with girl singers until that point. A song plugger told me that Bob Crosby was at the Strand Theater and he had a young kid from Cincinnati named Doris Day. Her real name was Doris Kappelhoff, and she'd given her notice. The song plugger said, "Why don't you go hear her."

After I heard her, I went backstage and we made a deal right away. I told her at the time, "I'm afraid we won't keep you long. The movies will be after you."

Actually, while we were at the Café Rouge, the hotel in Pennsylvania where we played twice a week for six weeks for five years in a row, they came in and set up screen tests for her. Twice she didn't even show up because she was scared. In '46 she left the band and finally did do a screen test. Then she made a movie, and the rest is history.

Doris' sound was very good and her pitch was perfect. I never heard her out of tune on any note, ever. Even when by mistake the arranger came in with something that was a little high for her, she still hit those notes. If anything, the only criticism I ever had of her was that she was a little too cute at first. She could have been a little more musical, but she got rid of that cuteness, and you'd have to put her down as one of the great singers of all time.

Doris could sing anything. It didn't make a difference what it was. I remember we had quite a hit on a thing called "My Dreams Are Getting Better All the Time," which she didn't want to do. She cried and everything. I talked her into doing it, and it became a hit. Later I kidded her. I'd say, "You didn't want to do 'My Dreams Are Getting Better All the Time,' and then when you get on your own, you start doing things like 'Que Será Será.' Where is your thinking?" I'd say, winking.

The bands were the big thing in the entertainment business, before the singers took over. We didn't know how long it was going to last. We got lucky. After it started going downhill, we joined Bob Hope. The other bands didn't have that advantage. We started in September of '47 with Bob's radio show, and we've been with him ever since.

Peggy Lee

○ ○ ○

An innovator among pop singers, Peggy's range as a song stylist has won her the absolute respect of great musicians as well as an international following that welcomes her every appearance.

○ ○ ○

I went from Chicago to Minneapolis, and then on the road to California, and then back to Chicago and I was singing at the Buttery. Benny Goodman was staying at the Ambassador Hotel and so was Lady Alice Duckworth, who later became Mrs. Goodman. She came in first and heard me sing. I think there was a lot of interest in me from various bandleaders, like Glenn Miller and Claude Thornhill. Jimmy Dorsey was also living at the Ambassador, but he didn't ask me to sing with him because he had Helen O'Connell. So we all became friends. But it was Alice Goodman who brought Benny in.

I was in awe of Benny, all the time. He was always very nice to me. He could be extremely difficult with the fellows, but with me it wasn't that way. Gordon MacRae tried out once, but Benny didn't accept him. Benny wasn't much for male vocalists.

I had no idea what traveling with a band would be like. I was glad I was healthy because I used to average approximately two hours sleep per night. I used to have long, long blonde hair and I tried to wash it and dry it with no hair dryer.

I believe my style of singing was a gift. I started singing professionally when I was fourteen. I sang any place I could. I was also a writer and a musician. It helped a lot that I listened to Count Basie, Maxine Sullivan, and especially Mel Powell, who is now a professor at Caltech.

I always picked my own songs, but usually I had to fight for most of them. I went to Glenn Wallichs, the founder of Capitol Records, with "Is That All There Is?," and I asked him if it was OK to do and he was embarrassed. He said, "Peggy, you don't have to ask me what to do. You've helped build this building. If you want to record it, go ahead." But up until Glenn I had nothing but nos.

Then, after I recorded it they didn't want to release it because they thought it was too long and far out. Plus, they had a million other reasons. Then they wanted me to do a TV show which I didn't particularly want to do. I agreed to do it on the condition that they release the record. And they did, and it became a hit across the board.

"Fever," by the way, was my arrangement. Jack Martin won the Grammy for it, but it was my arrangement. I remember Sammy Cahn was at my house and I showed him how I wanted to do it.

When rock 'n' roll came along, it scared me to death. I thought the sky had fallen. It took awhile to adjust and then I began to see where I could be a little more contemporary myself. I notice now that a lot of rock 'n' roll musicians are studying music more and getting more musical. It's not just a loud sound.

When I think of rock today I think of heavy metal. I don't even think of Paul McCartney as being in the rock field. He wrote a song for me called "Let's Love," which became a title cut for one of my albums.

Mitch Miller

o o o

There was a time in the early fifties when this man could not miss. His powerful personality got singers to record songs that didn't seem right, and constantly proved his judgment was near perfect. After a sing-along career on television and records, Mitch has returned to his classical training and is now doing concerts with symphony orchestras.

o o o

In the days of direct-to-disc, you went into the studio and people had to know their business. If you didn't get it on the take you were doing, you had to throw it all out and do it again. The whole point was to be ready when you did the take. Otherwise, it became an exercise in exhaustion. Nobody wanted to be the one who screwed up the record.

I will never forget one time with Sinatra. I played on the session. We'd just done a wonderful take in three minutes and seventeen seconds. Manny

Sachs says, "We can't use it because we can't go over three-twelve because then the record changer on the jukebox won't flip."

I piped up, "It's a great record. What's the difference?"

Sinatra said, "Yeah, what's the difference?" And he walked out. Manny Sachs banned me from the studio after that.

To me, the art of singing a pop song has always been to sing it very quietly. If anyone had to sing in a hall without a microphone, you couldn't hear them, even in the first row. In other words, the microphone and the amplifier made the popular song what it is—an intimate one-on-one experience through electronics. It's not like opera or classical singing. The whole idea is to take a very small thing and make it big.

In the recording studio, because of all the rugs and padding on the walls, everyone sounded like they were singing into a hunk of wall. I remember saying to Bob Fein, a wonderful engineer, "How could we put a halo around the voice?"

He said, "What do you mean?" I explained to him and he came right up with it—he put a loudspeaker in the toilet. He put a microphone in there, took the sound and sent it through a loudspeaker into the microphone, mixed it with the original sound, and that was the first echo chamber.

I got my opportunity to run Columbia Records when Manny Sachs left to go to RCA. Goddard Lieberson was looking for someone to take over the popular division. I was classmates with him at Eastman. He liked good jazz. He was a composer himself.

At the time, we had Sinatra and Dinah Shore, and that was it. The bands were now out. Harry James was playing, and we had Benny Goodman, but the mandate was to go and buy if necessary. I wouldn't buy because making a record is not like making a movie. You can't force anyone to make a record. I figured, if you buy somebody and pay out a lot of money, you have pressures that aren't necessary.

Be that as it may, in 1950 or '51, Columbia advanced Sinatra a big chunk of money to pay his back income taxes. The idea for us, of course, was to make this money back. I found two songs, "The Roving Kind" and "My Heart Cries for You," written anonymously by Percy Faith, who was trying to write a hit song with three chords, and when it turned out good, he was so embarrassed he didn't put his name on it.

Frank was going to see Ava in Spain, and on his way he stopped off in New York for one day. So I met him at the plane with the arrangements of both songs. The studio was set, the musicians, horns, orchestrations, everything. I wanted him to hear the songs, learn them during the day, and do them that night.

He landed at La Guardia at seven-thirty that morning. He was with Hank Sanicola and Benny Barton. They came up to the office to listen to the demos. After listening to them, they looked at each other, and Frank said he didn't want anything to do with them. Now I'm stuck. I've got men hired, and a chorus hired, and I don't know what to do.

And then I remembered hearing this young kid, Al Churnick, who had been sleeping on a desk at King Records. It was a desperation move, but it worked. Al Cernik became Al Grant, who became Guy Mitchell, and both records went to Number 1.

Those were not good times for Sinatra. He had lost his television show, lost his movie contract. Priests were telling the kids not to buy his records. And Columbia had given him this big advance, and now we don't want to resign him. So Capitol does, and now you have this incredible chain of events. First, he does the part of Maggio in *From Here to Eternity*. On top of that he makes a damn good record called "Young at Heart." He starts selling records again, Capitol's and the ones he did with us. Not only did we make back the money we advanced him, but he also made himself another quarter or half a million on the records he sold.

So now, some writers are going before Congress saying that BMI is taking over the business. Frank sends us a telegram saying I forced him to do BMI songs. The lawyers descend on us. In other words, Frank was trying to find a scapegoat for the dip in his career. He was the only reason for the dip in his career. He was the one who got sick and couldn't sing at the Copa. Blood was coming from his throat. He was punching photographers. The telegram he sent said that I only gave him bad songs, but the record is there and it speaks for itself.

Margaret Whiting

o o o

The breeding and background were impeccable, and the lady sang with great cool. Her choice of songs and the musical company she kept placed her among the best of female singers through the forties and fifties.

o o o

I was a Hollywood child. I knew everything about every picture being made. My girlfriend was Harry Warren's daughter, and we would go down to the Warner Brothers Theater in Hollywood, or Grauman's Chinese Theater, and then have a hot fudge sundae at C. C. Brown's, and then go into the theater and drool over whichever movie star happened to be on.

Growing up in Hollywood was wonderful, because, you know, if you were lucky, and your mothers and fathers did well, you had chauffeurs and you went to the best schools.

Everybody my father knew was either Maurice Chevalier or Jeanette MacDonald and her husband, Gene Raymond, or Shirley Temple or Harry Warren, Johnny Mercer, or Jerome Kern, who I called Uncle Jerry. All these people would come to the house, and they were either singing or writing their songs. But I thought this went on at everybody's house. I'd go to Paramount with my father, and Warner Brothers, and Fox. I watched pictures being made. I read *Variety* and the *Hollywood Reporter*. There wasn't anything I didn't know about the movies. I knew it all.

We had a two-story house at 732 South Beverly Glen, and I would look down at all the people from a balcony on the second floor. Chevalier was there, Benny Goodman, Fred Waring, Paul Whiteman, Bob Hope. My father's best friends were Buddy DeSilva, David Butler, and Leo McCarey, and they always brought the biggest stars to the house.

Johnny Mercer had been signed by Buddy Morris, and Buddy sent him out to Hollywood and said, "You're either going to write with Harry Warren or Richard Whiting."

And Johnny said, "I'd very much like to write with Whiting. I love the way he writes melodies. He's a true American songwriter," whatever that meant. One night at one of our parties they started writing, and my mother wanted me to sing for Johnny. I did, and he gave me this advice. He said, "Grow up." And then later on he said, "I know you're going to sing. You sing very well. But I want you to find a style that's your own. Who are your favorite singers?"

I said Judy Garland, Ethel Waters, Frances Langford, Mildred Bailey. Johnny said, "Fine. Listen to them. Copy them for a while, if you want. Find out what makes them different, and that way you'll find your own style."

I was seven years old when I met Johnny Mercer. I was twelve, in 1948, when my father passed away. He gave me the greatest piece of advice. He said, "You know, there's all kinds of music. Never be afraid to listen. You may not like opera, you may not like jazz or classical. But expose yourself to all of it, just as you should expose yourself to all of life. See everything, touch everything, be a part of everything."

So many parties, so many people. Judy Garland, Mel Torme, Nancy Walker, everyone from MGM, June Allyson, David Niven, Errol Flynn. Anybody and everybody. Our parties became famous, a hundred people a night. My mother would say, "My daughter is walking up and down Sunset and Vine with a sandwich sign saying, 'Come to the Whitings'.' "

On one particular night—this was after we had moved to Comstock and Loring, 336 Loring—Martha Raye was over, and Mel Torme was over. They used to come early, and we'd sit around and sing. We'd have piano players, Rob Blaine and Hugh Martin.

So Johnny Mercer calls and says, "Is there a gang there?"

I said, "There's about twenty of us."

He says, "We're coming over." He and Harold Arlen had just finished their score to the movie *Blues in the Night*. So they came over and sat down, and Torme was on the floor, and Judy and I were sitting together on the couch. Martha Raye was in the room, my mother, a few others. And Johnny and Harold started singing, "My momma done told me . . ."

Well, to hear those two men sing that song. They were a brilliant combination. They wrote so well together, and it probably had to do with their ethnic backgrounds. Johnny was a true son of the south, from Savannah. Harold was the son of a cantor from Buffalo. And yet, both of them understood the blues.

That night we made them do "Blues in the Night" seven times. It was the first time ever that Martha Raye had nothing to say. And Judy and I both ran to the piano to see who could learn it first. This is how I grew up.

Frankie Laine
o o o

His life could be a miniseries. The man wouldn't and couldn't quit even when all the signs said to get out. Sometimes bigger than life on record and in person, he was on anyone's Top 10 for many years.

o o o

I was a part of a group of dancers that danced at the Merry Garden Ballroom on Chicago's North Side. Every once in a while traveling orchestras came through, like on special holidays. That's where I first saw Paul Whiteman with Mildred Bailey. It was her version of "Rocking Chair" that gave me the inspiration to sing.

Every so often they'd get me up to sing with one of the orchestras that came through, just on a guest basis. I was fifteen, sixteen years old.

That's also where I first saw Cab Calloway. I flipped for him. His showmanship was great. In the meantime, I had seen Al Jolson three years earlier. I skipped school one day to see Jolson in *The Singing Fool*. I flipped over the way he did "Sonny Boy." I knew then that that was what I wanted to do. I wanted to do what he was doing.

Louis Armstrong came to town shortly after that, to a place called the Sunset Café, and boy, did he wrap up Chicago. I was crazy about the way he sang, too.

So, between Mildred Bailey, Cab Calloway, Jolson, and Louis Armstrong, those were my first jazz influences. I didn't know enough then to know that Jolson really wasn't a jazz singer. The way he sang was not jazz the way we know it today, or even knew it then. But I didn't know any better then.

I must not leave out Bessie Smith. I remember this old Victrola my parents had. Ma liked mostly opera. But I found this one record mixed in with all the operas, one by Bessie Smith. I didn't know what blues was at the time, but I fell in love with that record. Listened to it over and over again.

I did a long time as a marathon dancer, and when I wasn't dancing I was singing. In the mid-thirties, I was busy imitating Bing Crosby. People used to come up to me and say, "Gee, you sound more like him than he does."

As the years went by, I became influenced by more and more singers. Like Crosby. And Billie Holiday, who fractured me later on. I was so crazy about Crosby that I could do "East of the Sun" straight from the shoulder, right from the heart. And "Soon," and all those songs that he made famous, I could do them just like he did. I figured that somewhere down the line I might have a chance. But I had no idea all those years of struggling were still ahead of me.

In 1935 I came back to Chicago and I entered a contest at the Arcadia Ballroom. Anita O'Day was in the same contest. She was fourteen years old. I used to do a song then called "I Found a Dream," a gorgeous tune, and I would walk along beside her, and she was after me to find out "Why do you phrase so-and-so in such-and-such way? Why did you pick that song?" Then somebody found out that she was only fourteen years old, and they pulled her off the floor.

By the mid-forties I'm in with Al Jarvis, and he wants me to put a little group together. So I did—the Make-Believe Ballroom Four, with Frankie Laine and a girl on piano named Winnie Beatty. We started working around L.A. A guy named Billy Berg had just sold his swing club at Las Palmas and Hollywood Boulevard, and we went in there with his OK. We're working there maybe four nights when in walks this little saxophone player—we'd let guys jam with us—who is all of sixteen years old, I found out later. He gets out his horn and says, "Can I come up and play?"

I said, "Sure." Well, he broke everybody up. Tore the place up. We didn't hire him, but we let him come in every night and play. Four nights later, they pulled him off the stand for being too young. It was Stan Getz.

By '51 my recording contract with Mercury was about to end, and the company came to me with a couple of inducements. But in the meantime, CBS said they would put up $50,000 for a TV pilot. I had been doing "The Ed Sullivan Show," and I could see where TV was going. But I wanted to be fair with Mercury, so I went to Irv Green and said, "Irv, here's the way it looks. If I go to Columbia, they'll put up money for a TV pilot. If this were offered to you, what would you do?"

And Irv said, "I'd take it, Frank. Just make me a couple of albums before you leave." Which I did. And "Jezebel" was one of the songs I gave him.

People like to say, "Oh, I wouldn't change a thing." But if I had it to do over again, there is one thing I would change. I would make it happen maybe ten years sooner. Ten years is a good stretch of scuffling. But I scuffled for seventeen years before it happened, and seventeen is a bit much.

Stan Getz

○ ○ ○

No one ever played the saxophone better than Getz, and his music pops up with small groups, big bands, and great singers. Though he's lived in turmoil, his talent has been consistent and marvelous. Stan is and will remain a legend.

○ ○ ○

I'm glad that I started with a master like Jack Teagarden. You gotta walk before you can run, and you can imagine what it was like for a sixteen-year-old like me to be playing with Teagarden. He was a great trombone player, really great. I remember we played a theater in Fort Worth, and they used to run the movie first, and then the band came on. Well, there was this trailer for a Tommy Dorsey movie, and his theme song came on, "I'm Getting Sentimental Over You," and there was this huge speaker behind the screen—no stereo in those days—and we were getting ready to go on behind the speaker. Just before they pulled up the screen, Teagarden picked up his trombone, played along, and drowned out Dorsey playing his own theme song.

For me, it was like a nice orderly progression. From Teagarden, I went to Kenton, then Dorsey, then Goodman, then Woody Herman. I learned a lot from everyone. Goodman was such a perfectionist. I think he fired forty-five guys in one year just because he was looking for the right sound from every instrument, from the first trumpet player down to the fifth baritone.

Stan Kenton's band was more like a military band. Later on, he became better when he got guys like Shelly Manne and Kai Winding, and some better arrangements. When I was with Kenton, in '44, he still had that machine-gun sound, which for me wasn't all that good musically.

Woody Herman, though, from the first note you knew. It was great. Greatest white band ever, as far as I was concerned. Woody had a sense to let the guys go, put them all together and let them go. I mean, we were pretty feisty young guys. He'd call a tune, and we'd say, "Oh, let's not play that. Let's play something else."

I grew up fast, maybe too fast, playing with the musicians I played with. And what we did we did in spite of drugs, which were in our culture long before they reached the public.

I remember playing one time with Woody's band at this afternoon concert. Nine acts of vaudeville and a trained bear. The bear came on, and I mean, this bear had to be nine feet tall. And the band came out, and the two on each side of Sam Marowitz—the lead alto player who was very straight-laced, no drugs, no drinking—were Serge Chaloff, Zoot Simms, Al Cohn, and me, all stoned. The bear was doing this thing with the trainer, and at one point the bear came around and his arm went over the saxophone section. He could have killed the five of us, but only Sam Marowitz ducked. The rest of us were too stoned to even know that the bear was near us.

People used to claim that Woody's band was made up of a bunch of faggots because we were so stoned we didn't bother going after the women.

Much later, the kind of music that Miles Davis and I were playing came to be known as the backlash to bebop, which was so frenetic. And that backlash, or the "cool school," as it was known, is where the bossa nova came from. It was Antonio Carlos Jobim and Astrud Gilberto listening to the progenitors of the cool school, Miles and myself. Listening to the harmonies we played, the laconic approach. Jobim took the traditional street samba and combined it with our North American cool school and that's what came out—the bossa nova.

I was able to buy a mansion and put five kids through college, but I never got it into my head that I was a commercial musician. I was still a jazz musician, even when I was playing two bossa novas a night. I refused to go away from jazz. I probably could have milked the bossa nova for all that it was worth, but I didn't. The great thing about playing a bossa nova in concert was that it was a relief from jazz. It always felt good to have some of both.

But you know jazz musicians. Part of the thing that keeps them going is that thing about, "We don't just play the old shit, man, that's old shit. Let's have some new shit." They self-indulge themselves into a knot. They don't want to take something and play it because it's been already done. But I feel that music can be classic, too. Just nice music. Jazz music is supposed to be democratic music. Each man has a say in a jazz quartet. But they all must contribute to the whole. Egos have to be kept to a minimum. But you know jazz musicians. They're crying for attention. They always want something different.

Dave Brubeck

o o o

A leading exponent of the cool jazz feel in the fifties, Dave resents the perception that his music lacked soul. Our talk took place in northern California, where he continues performing and making that fine music, whatever the definition.

o o o

My mother was a classical pianist and my father was a cattleman, a rare combination to produce someone who would play jazz. My father was a champion rodeo roper, which means you have to be quick with your hands, have good coordination. He won shows. He was the town's top roper, and I was his son. He played harmonica, and he was always whistling, so I guess he was always interested in music. One of the first tunes I ever wrote was called "Dad Plays Harmonica," which was recently published in a piano book of my early piano pieces. The book is called "Reminiscences of the Cattle Country."

Early on people would say about me, "He has black blood in him." I was in college, working in places like the Cool Corner in Stockton, California. I was usually the only white person in the club. No one in college could understand why I'd be down there working every night.

One of my first jobs in school was intermission pianist for Cleo Brown. I had been influenced by Fats Waller and Art Tatum, but Cleo Brown was frightening. She was so good. And she's still alive. She recently played with me in one of the strangest concerts I've ever done. We were in Denver opening with a gospel choir, and we did "Gates of Justice," which is an Old Testament piece my wife and I wrote together. I invited Cleo to come up and sing. Understand, she's almost eighty, and I hadn't seen her since 1941. Well, she came up on stage and sang gospel music to a very mixed audience—whites, blacks, American Indians—and she bowled them over, sang as great as she ever sang in her life.

She once gave me a note to give Art Tatum. So I went to L.A. and handed Art this note from Cleo. What an influence she was. I may not sound like her, but all my early influences were people like her. And she was somebody I actually played with. She still amazes me, even at her age now.

I know because I was on the cover of *Time* magazine in 1954 that a lot of people think my career started with my *Time Out* album, but I can't stress enough how important those early years were, the period when the quartet first got going, when we played nothing but standards. In those years, almost every job I took I was lucky to break even. You'd work for scale and then have to give half the money back to the guy who owned the club. I'd get a check, then endorse it back to the owner. Maybe we'd wind up with twenty dollars a week, some ridiculous amount.

I'm trying to raise a family, so when I went on the road we'd drive all night instead of staying in a motel. Just drive from Los Angeles to New York without stopping.

I relate back to being white and playing in all the black places. There were many small black combos on the road in the fifties—the Modern Jazz Quartet, Nat Cole, Johnny Hodges after the Ellington band had split up, Dizzy, Miles. A lot of the clubs would have a rope down the middle with all the black people on one side and all the whites on the other. It didn't take long before everyone began ignoring the rope and having a good time. But I would not play a club unless it was integrated.

Like Eugene Wright, bless him, because he was black he'd have to put up with those situations where someone would try to deny him entrance to a hotel or a restaurant. They'd tell him, "You can't sleep here," and he just said he was going to have a good time and not hold anything against anybody. He never got angry, and there were a lot of bad situations, usually in the South.

But it even happened in the Midwest. We would be in Chicago, playing at the Blue Note, and blacks and whites couldn't stay at the same hotel in downtown Chicago. It wasn't a law, but you'd get the message from porters or elevator guys, the people who checked you in.

One night we couldn't get into a hotel, and Eugene and I were wondering where we were going to sleep, and Paul Desmond drove up in a Lincoln that somebody had let him ride in from the concert, and the guy whose car it was said to us, "What are you doing out here on the street?"

And we said, "We can't stay in the hotel."

And the guy said, "Do you mind if I go in and talk to them?"

I said, "Go ahead, but it won't do any good. I used every argument in the world."

So the guy goes in, then comes back out and says, "Go in and register."

I said, "What did you say to them?"

He said, "I told them that I'll foreclose on their little old hotel." The guy owned oil wells, a couple of jet planes. He told us, "If you need a plane in the morning, you got it."

Like Ellington, Louis Armstrong, and Beethoven, critics also bothered me. I've been on tour with guys who were so loaded they couldn't even go out and play, and yet they'd go out, destroy themselves, and then get a good review. They were people the critics knew. Unbelievable. In good papers.

My favorite was one night when we played Carnegie Hall. That night I had it planned for all of us to be playing this one piece in a different time signature. It came off perfectly, and the next day the critics said, "They couldn't even keep time together."

Patti Page
o o o

She came out of Oklahoma and ran a career that is still active. Along the way she produced several pop and novelty hits and later scored in the country field.

o o o

I was doing a show in Tulsa for the Page Milk Company. That's where I got my name. Jack Rael was a saxophone player and the road manager for Jimmy Joy's band, and they were doing a one-nighter in Tulsa.

They checked into the Bliss Hotel, and at that time they had those quarter-machine radios in all the hotels. Well, there was some time left on the machine, and my show—a fifteen-minute show with an organist—was on the air.

Jack heard me and he called the station. They said, "That's our own Patti Page."

I spoke to Jack and he asked if he could see me. We made an arrangement for dinner. When he saw me—five feet tall and baby fat—he knew I was not someone to front a band. He was looking for someone sexy, and so he tried to get out of it gracefully. He said, "If you ever want to take an air check off the show, you can send it to me."

I surprised him. I sent two songs.

He heard the songs and asked me if I'd come to Dallas to audition with the band. I went, I sang all the arrangements, and they asked if I'd join them in Chicago. I said yes, and I joined the band in December 1946.

Jack said he wanted to be my manager, so we signed a contract in early 1947. I worked with the band for only six weeks. I had thought it was going to be fun, and the guys would ask me out, but I found that Jack had gotten to all of them and said, "Hands off. Nobody asks her out. She's going to be a star." And I thought nobody liked me.

"Tennessee Waltz" was my biggest record. We had an office in the Brill Building. *Billboard* was a couple of floors above us. Jack was going into the office one morning when he ran into Jerry Wexler. Jerry was reviewing records for *Billboard* on Tuesday nights. He said, "Jack, I was just thinking of you. We reviewed a record last night in the rhythm and blues field called 'Tennessee Waltz,' by Erskine Hawkins. If Patti got it, I think it could be a pop hit."

We had been getting ready to go in and record a Christmas song because it was a rule in the record industry at that time that nothing comes out after November 15 except Christmas records.

So Jack decides we'll put "Tennessee Waltz" on the other side of our Christmas song, "Boogie Woogie Santa Claus." We don't want the disc jockeys to turn the record over. We just wanted them to play the Christmas song.

I was appearing at the Copa when the record came out. I opened for Joe E. Lewis. Nobody really knew me. I did five songs, and that was it. No encores. One night someone says, "Sing the waltz."

I thought, "What are they talking about?" I went upstairs to the dressing room after I finished, and I said, "Jack, somebody asked for the waltz. What are they talking about?"

He said, "I don't know."

The next morning, we called Harry Rosen, our record distributor in Philadelphia. He was like a friend in the business. Harry said, "Jack, hasn't anyone told you?"

And Jack says, "Told me what? What are you talking about?"

And Harry said, " 'Tennessee Waltz.' We've just ordered our second shipment of it."

Nobody had even heard the Christmas song.

Henry Mancini
o o o

This brilliant composer, conductor, and film scorer has stamped his signature on some of America's classiest music. Hank has racked up Grammys and Oscars and still spreads his touch over the concert stages of the world.

o o o

Sometimes I think I think orchestrally. I do think in terms of top lines, the melodic lines, because of my Italian heritage. But when I sit down to compose a film score, I'm always conscious of who will do what. A lot of fellows who don't orchestrate will make a piano guide, or a sketch, and then give it to an orchestrator. I can't do that. I have to have it all on the page.

I went to Juilliard wanting to learn about the orchestra. My dad took me to my audition in front of the school board. I went in with a Beethoven and Mozart prepared. After I played both pieces, they asked me, "Would you like to play something else?" So I took a flyer and I started in with what I call a bullshit arrangement of "Night and Day." When I say bullshit, I don't mean that really. I just mean it was off the top of my head.

Anyway, I put as many scales and flourishes in it as I could. It lasted four or five minutes, and it got me into the school. At the end of "Night and Day," they said, "That was very nice, Mr. Mancini." I had been winging it the whole time.

In the service, I had what amounted to a five-minute meeting that changed my life. It was with Glenn Miller and it took place at the Knights of Columbus Hotel in Atlantic City. I was in basic training in the air force, and Glenn's band was rehearsing in the ballroom of the hotel. I used to hang around hoping to see somebody.

Finally I got in and I became friends with Arnold Ross. He'd say, "You don't want to be a tail gunner, do you?"

I'd say, "Hell, no."

And he said, "Why don't you talk to Glenn," who was at the peak of his career.

Well, I went in there one time and Glenn was sitting behind his desk. He asked me what I do and I told him I'd been with Bob Allen in New

York, that I'd played with Johnny Long, and that I'd played second piano for Vincent Lopez but was fired because my part was better than his.

Glenn asked me if I wanted to be in another band, and I said yeah. Through his intervention, I wound up in the 528th Air Force band after my basic training. I probably wouldn't be sitting here talking about my career if it hadn't been for Glenn Miller's intervention when I was in the service.

There was no chance to get into the Miller band at that time because he already had piano players like Mel Powell and Jackie Russin. But what stuck with Glenn was that I was interested in arranging.

I eventually did get with Miller's band after the war, and that was because of Tex Beneke. I became Tex's pianist and arranger.

By the early fifties I was in Hollywood, a time when the studio orchestra was the staple and movie recording the backbone of the business. There were six or seven major studios, and each had a staff orchestra. Universal is where I ended up. I did an Abbott and Costello picture called *Lost in Alaska.* I also did things like *Creature from the Black Lagoon* and *It Came from Outer Space*. It was a learning experience. Nothing bothered me in those days.

In television, of course, there was "Peter Gunn," which was a studio breakthrough. The guts of the whole thing was the rhythm section—bass, guitar, drums and vibes, and the walking bass that opened the show. In a normal movie a walking bass would be lost. The sound of "Peter Gunn" was a totally contained sound, and it started a new approach to commercial recording.

Johnny Mercer wrote a lyric to a song of mine in "Peter Gunn" called "Joanna." He liked the song. Johnny was like that. If he heard a song on the radio he liked, he would call the DJ to find out the name. Then he would contact the composer. That's how "Midnight Sun" got done. He heard the instrumental on the radio.

Now I go in to do *Breakfast at Tiffany's*. There was a scene when Audrey Hepburn sings "Moon River" on the fire escape. The producers went to Blake Edwards and said, "This song is so New York. We'd like a New York songwriter in here," and Blake called me.

"Moon River" was one of the most difficult songs I've ever tried to write. I can't think of another song that gave me so much trouble. And in the end it was so simple. It all happened on the white keys. It was simple. It was Audrey.

Well, when Johnny got hold of "Moon River," it became a scene. It took two minutes to sing that song, and yet it was the glue that held that picture together. It told you everything you needed to know about Holly Golightly. Melodically it did, but mainly it was Johnny's words. I call it Audrey's "Over the Rainbow." It was a perfect example of what a song can do for a picture.

Front row, from left: **Count Basie, Lionel Hampton, Artie Shaw, Les Paul**

Back row, from left: **Illinois Jacquet, Tommy Dorsey, Ziggy Elman, Buddy Rich**

Ella Fitzgerald, 1986
(Photo by James Ruebsamen)

Art Lund
(Photo courtesy of George Simon)

Woody Herman, 1986
(Photo by James Ruebsamen)

Sammy Cahn, 1976

Lou Levy

Charlie Barnet, 1959

Tex Beneke, 1980

Milt Gabler

Sammy Fain, 1978

(AP Laserphoto)

Sammy Kaye

Billy May
(Michael Ochs Archives)

The Andrews Sisters: Maxine *(left)***, Patty, and LaVerne with Glenn Miller**
(Photo courtesy of Alan F. Timpson)

Herb Jeffries
(Michael Ochs Archives/Photo by Ray Whitten)

Ray Anthony with Jack Webb

Paul Weston

Jo Stafford, 1947

Jack Leonard, 1936

Les Brown

Al Gallico

Peggy Lee, 1982
(Photo by Rob Brown)

Mitch Miller, 1965

Margaret Whiting, 1948

Frankie Laine, 1950

Stan Getz, 1978
(Photo by Dean Musgrove)

Dave Brubeck, 1965

Patti Page
(Las Vegas News Bureau)

James Galway (left)
and Henry Mancini, 1985
(Photo by Leo Jarzomb)

Harry Belafonte, 1984
(Photo by Dean Musgrove)

Ed Ames, 1972

Rosemary Clooney, 1952
(Photo by Gerald K. Smith)

Bob Thiele

The McGuire Sisters *(left to right)*: **Chris, Phyllis, and Dottie, 1957**

Les Baxter, 1957

Carmen McRae

Johnnie Ray, 1952

Ray Ellis, 1959
(Photo by Popsie)

Ruth Brown, 1988
(Photo by James Ruebsamen)

Ahmet Ertegun

Ray Charles, 1980
(Photo by Henry Diltz)

Quincy Jones, 1978
(Photo by Ken Papaleo)

Jerry Wexler, 1986
(Photo by Sandy Gibson)

Barbra Streisand

Tony Bennett, 1983
(Photo by Mike Mullen)

Ed Ames

○ ○ ○

The Ames Brothers were part of the light pop music of their time. Ed was the trademark lead voice, and after the group split up, he continued his career with solo records and acting.

○ ○ ○

My mother and father were Russian Jews. They came from the Ukraine and they played in little balalaika orchestras around Boston. There were no professionals in the family. We were the first and only. To begin with, we were terribly poor, although I did go to Boston Public Latin School, as did my brother Joe. We prepared to go to college, but we always knew we couldn't afford to go to college.

There was this field where they played semipro baseball, Franklin Field. It was like an Andy Hardy movie. We'd be standing around on these huge granite boulders surrounding Franklin Field, and people would say, "Let's hear the singing brothers." At a ballgame. And we would do imitations of the Mills Brothers and the Ink Spots. And then this one kid got his uncle to come to a game by telling him, "These guys sing down on the field." The guy came. He was this sax player who played in this orchestra in a nightclub, and he got the nightclub owner to listen to us.

Lou Levy saw us in clubs. We were a bunch of raggedy kids, but Lou liked us. We sang, like everybody else at the time, at Leon and Eddie's on Sunday nights. Jerry Lewis performed there, Alan King, lots of people who later became very famous. But we were just a bunch of kids from Boston. I was the baby of the family.

Right about this time there was a musicians strike going on, and the record companies were really panicking. Lou Levy says, "I got an idea. I want you to sing for Milt Gabler." Milt was at Decca, and Lou says, "I know there's a strike, but I know you guys can sing without music. I've heard you sing without music. Maybe you can make records without music."

So we went up to see Milt. He was very sweet and kind, a wonderful man. And he signed us. But he didn't know what to do with us. We made some records, but I don't think they ever released them. We were still so young, all teenagers, and we probably weren't ready yet.

People in the business would ask us, "What is that low sound? You need some high voices, like some girls, on top. Tenors. Whatever. Get a sound like the big bands." It was the period after the big bands, and yet they wanted singers to sound like the big bands sounded.

We did one of the first Ed Sullivan shows. It was done down at Wanamaker's Department Store, where Ed did a lot of his early shows. It was sort of a makeshift studio, and the lights were so hot you had to keep your eyes closed until the last possible instant. The second you opened your eyes, you'd start tearing so much your socks would be soaked. I mean, every inch of you would be wet. It was so strange because as wet as everyone was, we all tried to be so charming.

The brothers didn't always get along. We would holler and yell at one another, and geez, I remember we were in a parking lot somewhere, and I don't know what caused it, but we were all hollering at one another, these four big guys with these big, booming basso voices. And the cops came. They laughed when they realized that we were having a silly row. But we had a lot of differences of opinion, usually about something artistic, probably something to do with the excessive traveling.

I'd come home from the road and my little baby girl would be waiting at the stoop, and she'd say, "He's home! He's home, Mommy!"

And my wife would say, "Who's home?"

And my little girl would answer, "One of the Ames Brothers."

Harry Belafonte

o o o

An incredible career involving politics, social causes, and his unique music has made Belafonte a true superstar. We talked in a recording studio while he readied his first album in almost a decade.

o o o

My earliest interests had to do with the theater. I studied at the New School for Social Research. The program I was in was called the New York Dramatic Workshop. My classmates were Marlon Brando, Walter Matthau, Tony Curtis, and Bea Arthur, among many others.

In the late forties I developed a relationship with this young kid from Brooklyn named Monte Kay. He had this incredible instinct for modern jazz. I, on the other hand, had no musical background whatsoever.

Well, besides performing in sketches with Walter Matthau and Tony Curtis, I wrote a song which was to be put in one of our plays. It was a writing assignment and it was meant for someone else to perform. At the audition they decided I should do it.

Monte saw the play. He said to me, "I heard you sing. Why don't you put together three or four songs and come down to the Royal Roost," a Broadway jazz club he was associated with.

I said, "You got it."

Monte put me together with a jazz piano player named Al Haig. The songs we rehearsed were "Pennies from Heaven," "Skylark," and the song I did in school, "Recognition." A friend of mine, a Jewish guy I roomed with, Alan Greene, had written a song called "Lean on Me," so these four songs, with only Al Haig playing, sounded beautiful.

Now comes the night for me to open at the Royal Roost. I walk on stage ready to do my thing, thinking it's going to be me and Al Haig, and there's the band from the main set—Charlie Parker on saxophone, Max Roach on drums, Miles Davis on trumpet, Tommy Potter on bass, and on piano the only white dude in the band, Al Haig. It blew me away. I was nervous and anxious because I wasn't in their league.

But people were kind to me, and that helped a lot. Billie Holiday got to be very friendly. Lester Young would always be sitting in the back of the club with his hat on and his horn on his lap. He'd see me and he'd say, "Hey, Bela, come sit here," and I would go over, and he would say, "How ya feeling?"

I'd say, "OK, Les."

And he would say, "Tell me about the world, man."

Monte then created the Roost label and became my manager. I married, had my first kid at twenty-two, and with the little money I had, we opened a restaurant down in Greenwich Village called the Sage, which exposed me to the Café Society Downtown and the Village Vanguard. The Café Society was presenting Lena Horne, Josh White, and Art Tatum. It was the Rolls-Royce of the club business.

Over at the Vanguard, Max Gordon had Burl Ives, Pete Seeger, Leadbelly. Because of the restaurant, I'd find myself going to these clubs. Well, when I saw people like Josh White, Pete Seeger, and Leadbelly, I was absolutely mesmerized. The songs these people were singing were different from Broadway, the Brill Building, Tin Pan Alley. I found a humanity in their songs. Fell in love with the stuff.

Meanwhile, the restaurant was getting harder and harder to sustain. The folk singers used to come in, and we carried more tabs on people. But they came in from all parts of America, black and white. They chatted, talked politics. It was a world that totally seduced me.

I began to see my place in that world. As an actor, I could be a guy from the badlands, or a chain-gang singer, or a soul singer, or I could sing Jewish folk songs. I could do anything I wanted. I could juggle emotions, becoming severe one minute and funny the next. I ain't no Leadbelly, and I certainly wasn't Seeger, but I decided I would mold the material and carve out a unique place as a conduit of all this rich music. I thought God had smiled down on me. I'd be able to sing these songs in every folk joint in America.

I remember sitting with Sonny Terry and Brownie McGhee, and somebody asked Sonny about a folk song, and Brownie answers, "All songs are folk songs. I never heard a horse sing."

Some years later, I'm playing in Vegas at the Riviera. The orchestra leader at the Riviera was Ray Sinatra, Frank's cousin. Ray and I were very close. Our families were close. Our kids grew up together in New York.

Ray says, "You're going to close in a couple of nights. We'll have a big dinner for you after the second show." I went to Ray's house expecting some drinks and something light. After all, after the second show it was two o'clock in the morning.

Well, everybody showed up. The whole strip was there, and Ray had nothing but heavy food—lasagne, cacciatore. I'm talking heavy. I look over in the corner of the room and there's Louis Armstrong rapping to somebody, and Louie's plate is vulgarly filled with a bit of everything. And he's devouring it with no conscience or concern.

I went over to him and I said, "Louie, how can you eat this heavily at this hour?"

He says, "A little Swiss Kriss, pops, is all it takes."

I ask, "What is Swiss Kriss?"

He says, "You mean you don't know what Swiss Kriss is?" And then he pulls out this little green packet with black lettering and a picture of a white girl in a one-piece bathing suit with long hair flowing in the wind, and the world, "Swiss Kriss keeps you normal, keeps you lovely, keeps you comfortable." It was a package of herbs, a laxative.

Louie says, "When I get through with this little packet of Swiss Kriss, and a glass of warm water, everything will be aces."

He goes to Europe, and in Italy reports start coming out that he's gravely ill. I write him a letter saying, "I hope you pull through."

Three or four days later, Louie walks out of the hospital. A month later, he reappears playing his horn and singing and bopping. That Christmas I get a Christmas card from him. The card is a profile shot of Louie on a white toilet. His pants are down, his black ass is sitting on the bowl, his fingers are dangling his trumpet, and he's staring into the camera with a Santa Claus hat on and a smile on his face. And the card says, "And a merry Swiss Kriss to you."

Phyllis McGuire

o o o

The McGuire Sisters looked great and sang well, and they took the country by storm. They still look great and are giving it another try, but the panache of the Godfrey connection is gone. It was a rare time, as Phyllis remembers.

o o o

I remember the first time we auditioned for "Arthur Godfrey's Talent Scouts." We went into CBS, and Larry Puck and Esther Stoll said, "Well, you girls are wonderful. Who is going to accompany you?"

We said, "We sing a cappella." I pulled out the pitch pipe, and we did our own arrangement of a Nat King Cole record, "Mona Lisa."

They said, "Arthur is away on vacation, but when he comes back, we want you on the first show."

The biggest town we had ever seen was Cincinnati, and here we are—Dorothy, Chris, and I—staying in New York at the Barbizon for women, walking around clutching each other, looking at the tall buildings.

But we went over to NBC and tried the same thing. We said we wanted to audition for RCA records, and we ended up in the studio with Manny Sachs and Ted Collins. We had on these lucky pink suits, had our hair pulled back, we were tall and thin and dressed alike. We were so green, but Manny and Ted thought we had guts. We sang for them and were signed instantly for the daytime Kate Smith show.

We were on the show for eight weeks, and then it was canceled. We were heartbroken. Kevin Johnson, who was the director, and Barry Wood said, "You girls are not going back to Ohio with tears in your eyes. You are going to meet a dear friend of ours."

We had no idea who they were talking about, but we walked into this small apartment and there sat Gordon Jenkins. He said, "Sing for me."

We started singing and the man fell in love with our sound. Four days later, we went back to Ohio with our contract. We carried it around for six months because we were so scared to death of any legal document.

That Christmas, the phone rings and it's Arthur Godfrey. My mother didn't believe it. She thought someone was playing a joke on her, so she hung up on him and he had to call back.

He said, "Mrs. McGuire, I am Arthur Godfrey, and you have three lovely daughters and I want to speak to one of them."

We did his "Talent Scouts" show on December 1st, 1952, and he asked us to join him regularly.

That was the beginning. We were on the show for seven years without a contract from CBS. They kept saying we had to sign a contract. We kept saying, "Later, later," scared to death of anything legal.

Then there were the scandals, Dorothy and Julius LaRosa, which got front-page news and was blown completely out of proportion.

Then I met Sam. I did not know who he was at first, and that is the truth. After I was already in love with the guy, the FBI came and said, "Do you know who you're consorting with?"

I said, "Yes. Sam Flynt."

They said, "No. Sam 'Momo' Giancana. He did this, and he did that, and he should be in jail and not out on the street with a nice girl like you." Sam and I sort of iced it for a while after that.

And then there was the time I dated Elvis Presley. It was right around the time he was getting over Ann-Margret. We were out in the desert in Vegas and he pulled out a gun. Elvis was quite a character.

I used to listen to Martin Block and his "Make-Believe Ballroom" on the radio, and I would say to myself, "Oh, God, do you think we will ever have a record played on his show?" When it happened, it was unbelievable.

The McGuire Sisters' first hit was "Goodnight, Sweetheart." We were in Detroit doing a thing for General Motors, and someone sent over a demo of the Moonglows doing the song, and we loved it.

Bob Thiele and Milt Gabler called saying we had to get back to New York because they wanted us to cover the DeJohn Sisters record of "No More." We hated that song. We said we were not going to do it because it sounded hiccuppy.

They said, "Do it. Their record is taking off."

We said, "The only way we will do this is if the other side is 'Sincerely.' "

So "Sincerely" was the B side, and the rest is history.

I remember one time when Johnny Mercer and Fred Astaire were at one of our sessions. We were doing "Picnic," which had already been an instrumental, when it was coupled with "Moonglow."

Anyway, Bob Thiele called and said, "You know, Steve Allen lives next door to us in New York, and Steve has written a great lyric to 'Picnic.' "

We said, "It's already a hit."

Bob said, "It's an instrumental hit with 'Moonglow.' If you do 'Picnic,' you'll have a hit on your own."

We adored Steve, so we went and did it and it was a biggy.

We remained very friendly with Arthur Godfrey to the very end. He was unbelievable and always very fair with us. The man was also always in terrible pain, and of course every now and then he was in a bad mood, and Arthur was, to a degree, a womanizer, but he did not mistreat anyone, and he was never cruel or sadistic.

Bob Thiele

o o o

A key man in American jazz, Thiele gave the shot to many players and put together some hellacious combinations on several labels. Married to Teresa Brewer, he still knows the jazz game as well as anyone.

o o o

The first record that I ever set out to make was four piano solo sides by Joe Sullivan. I booked the studio, I booked Joe, and then I didn't have enough money. Mind you, I was about sixteen years old. I couldn't pay for anything. So I never showed up, and we never made the records, and Joe never recorded, and that was the end of that.

But I had drive. I had to record people, anybody, or just be in the record business. I had to record unknown players, just find players that I felt were great and put them on records, and then put the records out.

I like to think of myself as maybe different from Milt Gabler, Mitch Miller, and those guys. Everybody made records based on what they thought would be big commercial hits. I honestly don't think I've ever made a record I didn't personally like. I love jazz. I recorded Coleman Hawkins, John Coltrane. I also recorded Lawrence Welk and the McGuire Sisters.

I remember being in Clovis, New Mexico, and we'd had some big hits with Buddy Holly and the Crickets, and there was some kid on the front porch somewhere. It was like a movie scene. We're all sitting on the porch, and there's this guy sitting on the steps playing guitar and singing "Sugar-time." I said, "Listen, don't play that for anyone else. When I get back, I'll give it to the McGuire Sisters."

I got back to New York, went into the brass at the company and said, "We're doing this song for the McGuire Sisters with Neil Hefti and a sixteen-piece band at Bell Sound on Eighth Avenue. Great place. You can isolate performers. There's some real technical advancement happening at Bell."

They said, "Oh, no, you can't do that. The union will scream at us. Can't do it."

I said, "Fuck it. I'm going to record it tomorrow morning at Bell Sound. They can fire me, but I'm going to make that record."

We went to Bell and started to record. Neil had a brilliant arrangement, very exciting, but I threw out the brass section. Then I threw out the sax-ophones, and all that was left was the rhythm section. Neil was getting pissed off. He said, "Bob, what are you doing to me?" But we made the record "Sugartime" with the rhythm section at Bell Sound, and it was a giant smash.

I also had Billy Williams' "Gonna Sit Right Down and Write Myself a Letter." We were sitting in the office one day talking about some old tunes, and I said to the arranger, "Why don't we dress up the arrangements a little," and all Billy would say was, "Oh, yeah."

I said, "Billy, at the end of 'Gonna Sit Right Down and Write Myself a Letter,' you might as well say, 'Oh, yeah.' "

When we first recorded Jackie Wilson, I said, "Let's record him with a big band." All R & B in those days was, like, nine guys, heavy rhythm section. And I took him in with a big band, and, like, the first five records were smashes. I must confess, though, it wasn't some genius thought on my part. I just did it that way because I wanted to hear him that way.

With Jackie, there was this fellow named Al Green who was the manager of a black group that Jackie sang with, the Dominoes. Al took me to the Apollo to hear the Dominoes. He wanted me to sign them, and I said, "Nah, I don't want to sign the Dominoes, but I'd love to sign that singer, Jackie Wilson."

Al said OK. He didn't care, you know, like, "Sign anybody." So we signed Jackie Wilson and I went to the Taft Hotel to pick up the contract.

I rang the room and Nat Tarnapol answered the door. Nat was a young kid, a go-fer, and he said, "Al Green died last night in the hotel room, but I have the contract signed." That's how I signed Jackie Wilson.

I also recorded Jack Kerouac. Steve Allen read Kerouac before I read him, and Steve made some sort of contact with Kerouac, and he agreed to record some poetry with Steve playing piano. And we decided to record it. I mean, it was as simple as that, really.

Later, I recorded Kerouac again. Kerouac really threw me. I asked him, "Do you want to use Steve Allen again?"

And he said, "No. I'd like to use my two favorite tenor sax players."

And I said, "Who are they?"

And he said, "Al Cohn and Zoot Sims."

And I said, "How are these guys going to play with you reading poetry? Two guys blowing against that?"

He said, "I want to do it." So we did it. It was a great LP. That was the last time I ever saw Kerouac. Zoot and Al left the date. When the session was over, they packed up their horns and they left. After they left, I found Kerouac in the studio crying against the wall.

He said, "My favorite saxophone players left me. They don't even want to listen to these playbacks." We went down to a bar on Eighth Avenue and he started to throw beer bottles at the taxi cabs on Eighth Avenue. I split, and that was the last time I ever saw him.

Rosemary Clooney
o o o

She sure could sing and still can. And she sure messed herself up. But Rosie has pulled it together and talks with relish about working with some of the greatest and about being a well person once again.

o o o

When that first hit came along, things changed overnight. I had been in Florida with Buddy Rich, working a theater in Miami. We flew back to New York and took a cab to go to 59th Street, and there was "Come on-a My House," blaring out of a horn that was attached to the outside of a record store.

I remember sticking my head out of the taxi window and saying, "My God, I think I've got a hit record." That was the beginning of 1951. It was like stepping onto a merry-go-round that was going fifty miles per hour. You could barely hold on. Actually, hold on was all you could do.

I remember being so tired. I didn't want to turn anything down. I didn't know how long the success was going to last. I had some prior experience, but boy, it was hard—hard to make the plane, hard to understand why everybody wants you, hard to rationalize why one week you're one person and the next week you're somebody else.

I worked all the time. I had five children in five years, from 1955 through 1960. During that time I did two television series. I was pregnant both times.

I simply didn't understand that "Come on-a My House" could be important, or that the feeling it had was as important as a death-defying love song that you're dying to sing. But the song has stayed with me all these years. No matter where I am, people tell me how they associate that song with a certain time in their lives.

Steve Martin had a funny thing with a lot of dancers, and he wanted me to come down and sing "Come on-a My House." This was just a few years ago. I did it, and it didn't sound bad. The kids who were dancing said, "What a wonderful record to dance to."

And I thought, "My God, thirty years."

I suppose Bing Crosby was the performer with whom I worked the most. I knew him from before I got married. It seemed I had admired Bing my entire life. As a fan, I wasn't in love with him the way I was in love with Frank Sinatra because Frank was always dangerous on stage and on records. Listening to him, there was always a sense of danger. But I felt very safe with Crosby.

There was also a kind of humor about Bing that I admired tremendously. He was wonderful company. He was always very nice to me, and he liked the fact that I understood all his subtle jokes. I was on his wavelength. We sang exactly in the same range. There was never a concession that had to be made musically because our ranges were so totally compatible. I could pick a key for him, and he could pick a key for me. If it was comfortable for me, it was fine for Bing.

We first sang together on radio. Then we did "White Christmas." Then I did his first television show. I worked with him from 1951 until he died in 1977. Bing's fiftieth anniversary show in March of 1976 was my first major performance in nearly ten years.

Before that, I sang in a lot of little saloons. I sang any place I could make money, really. But I couldn't travel very much because I was going to the shrink five times a week. I was in intensive therapy. That whole time I knew I wasn't singing well, so I took more drugs so I wouldn't have to be aware of it. Six months after my breakdown in 1968 I started singing better. I could sense after a long time that I was finally on my way back.

Ray Ellis

o o o

While you may not recognize his name, it appears on records by stars from Billie Holiday to Barbra Streisand as one of the quality arrangers and conductors. His memories of working with these people are fascinating.

o o o

It was 1950 and I was doing the "Paul Whiteman TV Teenage Club" on WFIL in Philadelphia. I was playing in the orchestra. I used to write a few things, but I wouldn't get paid for anything.

Paul Whiteman was a very nice man, the dean of American music, but unfortunately the man was a phony. He used to just wave his arm, and Glenn Osser was conducting on the side. Because it was television, and we were a big orchestra, nobody looked at Glenn on the side. You were in trouble if you looked at him. This was all live television, and believe me, it was scary. We'd finish a thing, and the mistress of ceremonies on the show would say, "Pops, what's the band going to do for its next number?"

And Whiteman would say, "You're Driving Me Crazy." We used to play the old Paul Whiteman corny arrangements, straw hats and everything. So he turns around, a big downbeat, and half of us are looking at him while the other half are following the guy on the side. After eight bars on live television the band fell apart.

After the show, Paul says he wants to see the band in the back. Now this is the dean of American music, and he says, "For Christ's sake, you guys don't know any better than to take a downbeat from me?" He couldn't have cared less. He made a joke out of the whole thing. God knows how he ever got through the *Rhapsody in Blue* concert with George Gershwin at Carnegie Hall. Everybody must have been watching Gershwin. That's probably how they did it, and that is definitely how we did it, by watching someone on the side.

After that whole thing folded, I started playing society parties, bar mitzvahs, and Jewish weddings. I was real depressed. I had a wife, two kids, and I'm saying to myself, "Is this all there is? I can't play Jewish weddings for the rest of my life. I know I have to do more than this."

At my first major record session, I was so naive about having written the arrangement that I did not know I was supposed to conduct the orchestra. I came walking in with the arrangement, and I panicked. The music is handed out, and Mitch Miller walks out and says, "What are you waiting for?" You gotta understand, I never gave a dog a downbeat. So this scared me completely, changed my personality. But I did get through it, and I vaguely remember it.

Anyway, I learned fast. All of a sudden I'm getting calls—"No, Not Much," "Moments to Remember," "Standing on the Corner." Within six months, I was the hottest arranger in New York City.

In 1955 Jerry Wexler calls me from Atlantic Records and asks if I can come around. He says, "I want to talk to you. Ever done any race records?"

I tell him, "Yeah, a little R & B."

He says, "We got this kid named Clyde McPhatter from the Drifters, and we want to break him out as a single. I figure with our R & B feel and your R & B feel, maybe we can come up with something."

So I go out and pick up some Top 10 rhythm & blues records, and I start listening to them. This was at the beginning of rock 'n' roll. "Cracker bands," as Lena Horne used to say.

But I had nineteen hits with Atlantic Records that year. "Treasure of Love," bunch of Drifters records, "Splish Splash" with Bobby Darin, "Since I Left You Baby," things with LaVern Baker.

Then I did some Tony Bennett, Johnny Mathis, Sarah Vaughan. Everything came down to who picked the songs. If it was Clyde McPhatter, I might have been sitting down with him, but Ahmet Ertegun picked the songs. If it was someone on Columbia, Mitch Miller picked the songs. Without the right song, forget it.

Johnny Mathis did not know a good song from a bad song. He just sang them all so beautifully. You could take the worst in the world and make it sound good with him. Incidentally, he recorded some of the worst songs in the world. But when Mitch had control over him, that was when he had big hits. Mitch made him do "It's Not for Me to Say," "Chances Are," "A Certain Smile," "Misty," "Maria." As soon as they lost control, as soon as Mathis insisted on going his own way, that was the end of that.

I did the arrangement for Sarah Vaughan's biggest hit, "Broken-Hearted Melody." At the time I was doing three, four sessions a week, and Clyde called me. He said, "Baby, you gotta do Sarah for me."

I said, "I can't, Clyde. I'd love to, but I'm doing a session tonight." So I talk him out of it.

It's now one o'clock in the morning, and I'm in my office at 1650 Broadway, and Clyde walks in with Sarah. He said, "One arrangement, please?" So, OK, I say I'll do it. But it's so late and I'm so punchy. I figure the key to probably be B-flat, but in my scribbling I write down E-flat. So I write the arrangement in the wrong key.

I get to the session, and Sarah's singing way up in the air. I say, "Jesus Christ, Sarah, what are you doing?" Then I realized what I had done, so I rewrote it quickly, and the thing was an absolute smash.

Carmen McRae

o o o

The lady is definite in her opinions and brilliant in her vocal styling. Carmen has had it good and not so good. When she turns on the instrument, you know it's her. A fine, fine singer.

o o o

I never thought I'd make it just singing because I always thought I wasn't good. But when I found I could make a living singing and playing the piano, I was the happiest broad in the world. I thought, "I'm getting my nuts off, doing what I want to do."

Maybe I should say, "Half of what I want to do," because I never wanted to play for myself. I never thought I played well. Which, over the years, has given me a great sense of appreciation for the people who've accompanied me. Like George Shearing, who comes to my mind because he was one of the greatest accompanists in the world.

I would visit him in clubs, and he would ask me to come up and sing, and I'd go up and sing with him. Maybe it's his blindness that made him that much more perceptive, but he sure was perceptive. I've had a lot of good piano players, players as good as George or better, but none who could accompany like him. You ad lib, he follows. I've had guys who have played with me forever, and they can't do it right.

George and I did this album together. We just chose the songs, chose the keys, and never rehearsed. We went in and did the whole album in three hours and forty minutes, something like that. Mostly first takes. And it turned out good, too. But I'm not the last judge anyway. The people who buy the records, they're the real last judge.

I had done a lot of things prior to my getting my first job singing and playing. I'd play piano one minute, and the next minute I'd be a secretary. But from 1948, when I went to Chicago, I haven't done anything else but be in this business one way or another.

I listened to the radio and played records all the time. I'd buy records and I'd try to learn by listening to them. Half the time I couldn't understand what the shit they were singing about. They would garble the words. Maybe that's what made me concentrate so heavily on my diction. Whatever the hell it did, it made me learn lyrics. When I got a lyric, I knew what the hell it was about.

And I also know that I've never played my audience cheap. By that I mean I've always prided myself on finding the best tunes I could find. Once I found them, I then tried to figure out the best way to do them. And it's paid off. Over the years, people have come up to me and said, "Boy, where did you find that tune?" Or, "My wife and I got married to that song." Or, "That song saved our marriage." When you hear that kind of stuff, it does something to you. I look for simple, straight-ahead lyrics. You don't need that double-shit meaning. If it has a double meaning, it better at least be clear. That's all you need—and a melody.

For me, the lyrics come first because you can always improvise on the melody. If the melody ain't too hip, you can always make it hip, if you're a jazz singer. That's how I try to approach it. I've been lucky. For forty years, my voice has held up. I just wish my body held up as well as my voice.

Les Baxter

o o o

An arranger and composer who made pretty music in the fifties, Baxter accompanied many of the best singers of the time, but he remains slightly bitter at what he perceives to be a lack of recognition. Judge for yourself.

o o o

I was considered a child prodigy, playing piano at the Detroit Conservatory at the age of five. As I grew up, I became a member of nothing. I've never joined organizations. This business is made up of cliques and people who like to hang together. I never did that. I was always a lone wolf. I felt my music was one of a kind. I felt I belonged in a special category.

I got into playing the tenor sax, and I played well enough to back Billie Holiday. I worked clubs with her, where they would let you sit in. Lester Young would be there, and I was allowed to sit next to him and play behind Billie. That was very special of them to let me do that.

Eventually, I got tired of playing the tenor sax, and I went with a small group that Mel Torme had just vacated to go into the army. So it was four of us, until Mel came out of the army, and the thinking was, "Which one of us is going to be dumped?" which logically would be me, and so I said, "No, five parts would be better than four." That's how Mel Torme and the Meltones were born. We used Duke Ellington's sax section for our voicing. It was five parts, open voicing, influenced by the six instruments in Duke Ellington's band.

I was also with a four-part vocal group on Bob Hope's radio show, singing the Pepsodent commercial. I did that for years. I was making a fortune singing on Bob's show, which was ridiculous. I compare it to the great ballets, which I love. When I traveled with Bob, I took down a big salary. Expense money filled my pockets, and most of our expenses were paid for. All this for doing a few seconds of commercial, once a week. We were flown to whatever city Bob was in, and we didn't even have to rehearse. We stood in the wings until the band played the intro, and we ran out and sang our commercial.

Well, one time in Phoenix I notice that the Ballet Russe de Monte Carlo is in town. I thought, "I have to see them, but how?"

I asked the cab driver if there was a good restaurant in town, and he said, "The Busy Bee is a great one, and there's also the American Boy Café."

I look out the window at the American Boy Café, and it says, "Booze for Ladies." And there, at American Boy Café, were all the principals of the Ballet Russe de Monte Carlo, eating blue-plate specials, making just a fraction with a lifetime of work what we were making singing commercials for less than fifteen seconds. That was my introduction to the unfairness of the music business.

My first album was a twelve-voice choir, one cello, one french horn, rhythm section, and theremin. No one had ever heard of a combination like that. It was a little weird. I didn't know what popular records were. I didn't know what I was doing.

I couldn't take a band on tour because I was never a band. Every album I did had different combinations. I wanted to be innovative. Perhaps I was the most innovative person in our business, I don't know. Nobody was going in with six drummers, a choir, and a flute. But I was. I was doing these little concert suites. I was a composer of concerts, writing little albums that could be played in music halls. I was doing African suites, tangos, Cuban rhythms. Nothing could have been further from pop music. "How Much Is That Doggie in the Window," "Tennesse Waltz," those were the hits of the day. I had no concept, and yet the stuff I was doing at Capitol—"April in Portgual," "Quiet Village," "Unchained Melody," "I Love Paris"—were all hits.

And it worked because I had the inclination to have men sing in a velvety low unison. That was a new thing, the low male unison.

The rhythm was also new, like the rhythm of "I Love Paris." There was no rock 'n' roll yet. It was like a stripper's beat. I don't know if I got it from Africa or Cuba, but it went, "Boom, ch, boom, boom, ch, boom, boom," which became rock 'n' roll. Before anyone heard of rock 'n' roll I had the rock 'n' roll drum beat.

Johnnie Ray

∘ ∘ ∘

He streaked across the pop sky with a voice and style like nothing ever heard before. It disappeared quickly, but it would be difficult to talk about the time without memories of Johnnie.

∘ ∘ ∘

The word "courage" seems to come up every time someone wants to know about how I managed to perform wearing a hearing aid. It's always been the big rock in my past. People think for some reason that I'm not a complete unit physically. For instance, I can't hear bass players. If I take the hearing aid out, I can't hear anything. I'm totally deaf. But with the hearing aid I still can't hear bass players, so I am constantly fighting to stay in tempo because time doesn't tick off in my head the way it does with a lot of jazz singers. I don't keep that perfect time in my head, and I've had to struggle with that for most of my years in show business. But it had nothing to do with courage. It never entered my mind.

There was a time when I did not wear my hearing aid on stage. Critics had been attacking me for wearing the hearing aid as a gimmick to get the audience's sympathy, and they used that against me in reviews. I thought that was a little below the belt. OK for feature writers to say maybe, but not in *Variety* and *Billboard*. That I didn't think was right.

But it did get me to take off the hearing aid for a couple of years. And I was still doing business without it. I remember it was in Buffalo one night that I decided to put the hearing aid back on. They were taking pictures of me for *Life* magazine, and I said, "For the picture, should I wear the hearing aid or take it off?"

They said, "Do whatever you want."

So I thought, "What the hell? I can't spend the rest of my life with people not knowing I wear a hearing aid." I really couldn't hear the band without it. Without it, I always had to maintain a sight line with the conductor.

It also never crossed my mind that I would lose my privacy after achieving some modest success. But something happened after "Cry." The night we recorded "Cry," I knew something was going on. When we played back the second take, I knew immediately I wasn't in tune. Technically, it was terrible. But nobody wanted to say anything to me. Like they figured I didn't know. They were all treating me with kid gloves. Nobody knew a flat note more than I did. But there was an electricity to that recording session that nobody could put their finger on.

Nobody was more shocked than I was when "Just Walking in the Rain" became so popular. I had closed at the Palladium in London, and I came home, and no one had done any promotion. Not a phone call to a DJ. I came back from England, got to my apartment, picked up *Variety* or *Billboard*, and "Walking in the Rain" was Number 4. The next week it went to Number 1. Other than the promotion from the Columbia Records guy, I didn't do anything. That's when I was grateful for the fact that I had never said no to anything Mitch Miller ever asked me. When we did "Walking in the Rain," I was trying to keep a straight face. We had four backup singers and a professional whistler. The whistler whistled and we kept messing around. Finally Mitch came out and said, "OK, let's get serious. This one could be a big one."

Performing was another story. I had been doing capacity business in Buffalo, Cleveland, Boston. Very successful. But I had not played New York. Nobody in New York had seen Johnnie Ray. I hadn't done any TV yet. So they booked me for a weekend at a place on Queens Boulevard, in Queens, on a show that had a couple of comedians. They put me on as, "Added attraction, Johnnie Ray," and all these people came out to see what is a Johnnie Ray. So many stories had been going around—that I was a black, that I was a woman. There was even a story that I had cancer. Ridiculous. But outside of a few eight-by-tens that had been sent in from Chicago, nobody knew what I looked like.

In April of '52 I opened at the Copa. Three shows a night, seven nights a week. For four weeks there was no way you could get near the Copa. As a bonus, they gave me a Cadillac convertible and a silver plaque given to me by the driver that read, "To Johnnie Ray, for breaking all the records at the Copacabana, 1952. We love you, the Copacabana." Unfortunately, the plaque was eventually stolen.

After a while, when all of a sudden I was no longer the hottest thing, I was forced to deal with it right off the bat. How do you become a former teenage idol? When Elvis hit, his popularity happened almost as rapidly as my own, and in those days I was accustomed to being met at the airport by a lot of people. Now I come back from England, from being on a particular tour, and somebody asked me the question, "What do you think of Elvis Presley?"

I said, "Who is Elvis Presley?" Big mistake. But I had been gone for two months and I didn't know what an Elvis Presley was. But the damage was done. The press got on it right away, saying it was sour grapes on my part. And that wasn't it at all.

A little later I came out to the Desert Inn, in Las Vegas, and Elvis was across the street. We played opposite each other, and I had my show down to a fast seventy minutes, the whole show. We had you in and out and back to the casino before you knew what was happening. So I was able to run across the street and find the maitre d' and ask him to point out Presley. The billing was Elvis Presley and the Freddy Martin Orchestra. Colonel Parker made a mistake by booking Elvis in there. The marquee said, "The Freddy Martin Orchestra with Elvis Presley," and no one remembers this because Elvis bombed. Parker took him out of there very quickly.

But in the meantime Elvis came over and we met and I finally realized what he did. By the time he had his second record out, my reaction was,

"This poor son of a bitch. I only hope he knows what he's going to go through. I only hope he's equipped to handle it."

Ruth Brown
o o o

I talked with Ruth at one of her engagements in the second life of her career. She was the R & B darling of the 1950s, and she just lit up when we talked about the hits and the great ride they provided.

o o o

After I finished high school, I began working in little clubs around Virginia. Mostly by word of mouth club owners would say, "I have a girl singer who is good," so that's how I'd go from club to club. I went from the B-Track in Norfolk to the Ballerina in Petersburg, which was owned by Mo Barney, who was friends with two brothers in Detroit, Hymie and Benny Gasman.

Hymie and Benny had a club called the Frolic Show Bar, and Mo told them he thought I was good enough to play that room. So they hired me, and I rode to Detroit by bus, and I was working there when Lucky Millinder and the Stan Kenton Band were at the old Paradise Theater in Detroit.

The Frolic Show Bar was the place everyone would come to hang out, and one night Lucky Millinder and Chico Alvarez and Billy Mitchell and Al Grey all came by and they heard me sing. They partied a long time, the drinks were flowing, and after a while Lucky said, "How would you like to sing with me?" I heard him, but I didn't believe him.

The next day I went to the Gotham Hotel where everybody was staying. They stood me up in the middle of the floor and I guess I sang ten songs for Lucky's pleasure. They'd go, "Do you know so-and-so?" and I'd sing it. Lucky said, "I think you are good. I want to hire you."

Hymie and Benny allowed me to be written out of my contract so I could tour with Lucky, which I did for three or four weeks without ever getting the chance to sing a note. I just rode around, running up hotel bills, food bills.

We got to Washington, D.C., to play a place called Turner's Arena, and this was supposed to be the first night that I was going to sing. Charts were done for me. One of the songs was a Dinah Washington song. Well, I sang my songs, and then after the show Billy Mitchell and Al Grey said, "Would you go to the snack bar and bring us some cold drinks?"

So I came back with this cardboard carton with all the sodas in it, and Lucky looked down and saw me with this tray, and he said, "I hired you as a singer, not as a waitress. On second thought, you don't sing very well anyway. I don't think it would make any sense for you to go any further with the band."

I was 220 miles from home. I didn't have the nerve to call home and ask for ticket money. Certainly not from my father because he didn't want me going in the first place. But I thought Lucky was kidding. I could not believe he was going to leave me, but when he insisted that he really was going to leave, I asked for the little money I had coming. He said I had nothing coming, that he'd been paying the hotel bills and feeding me. So I got nothing. They left me in Washington, and that was my first knowledge of the raw side of show business.

But I still wanted to sing. I got a job in Washington, at a little club called the Crystal Cavern, at 11th and U Street. One night the great Duke Ellington came into the nightclub with a man named Willis Conover, who was the Voice of America at the time, and after he listened to me sing, he went to the pay phone in the check room and called Ahmet Ertegun and Herb Abramson in New York and convinced them that it would be worthwhile for them to come down to hear this young singer at the Crystal Cavern. That's how I eventually got on the Atlantic label.

There was a closeness between Ahmet, Herb, and myself. I trusted their judgment. They came up with the right songs for me to sing. Ahmet and Herb said, "Trust us. You're gonna be great."

I had quite a few records, but I didn't believe I'd made it until the one and only time I worked with Nat King Cole at the Paramount. Ella Fitzgerald was going to be singing on the bill, but she was taken ill, so they sent me in her place. I couldn't believe they were sending Ruth Brown, an R & B singer, in to replace Ella.

I'll never forget the first thing I ever heard by Ella Fitzgerald. It was a song called "Have Mercy." The other side was called "Up a Tree," which I remember vividly. It went, "Am I your love or not, please make it clear. Why won't you tell me what I long to hear? Pity me, can't you see, I am up a tree."

So here I am on the same bill with Nat King Cole, and the Count Basie Orchestra, and it suddenly dawns on me, maybe I have made it.

When I got back home to Norfolk, Joe Louis came to our house and sat down at the table with my dad. For someone like the heavyweight champion of the world to come into our house was probably the greatest acknowledgment for a black family. Joe Louis coming to our house was so special that it no longer mattered to my dad what I did for a living.

Ahmet Ertegun

○ ○ ○

**The enigmatic and dynamite founder and boss of Atlantic Records,
Ahmet is as comfortable with the international set as he is in the
studio with a new rock group. He's a tremendous piece of pop music
history, with forays into jazz, R & B, and partying.**

○ ○ ○

Atlantic Records started because I got my dentist to lend me $10,000. He
mortgaged his house. I had a lot of rich friends, but nobody really thought
of a young kid with no experience who was still in college as a particularly
good investment. But my dentist, Dr. Sabet, was a crazy guy, a big gambler,
and so he gave me $10,000.

Then I went to Herb Abramson, who knew something about the record
business. I sure didn't know anything about the record business. Herb knew
how to get a record pressed, he knew an attorney who could write a contract,
and he knew where you could find cheap studio time. So we formed this
little partnership—Dr. Sabet, Herb, who put up $2,500, and me.

Jerry Wexler came in about five or six years after we started Atlantic.
Herb had to go do military service in Germany, and Jerry had become a
friend of ours, a terrific reviewer for *Billboard* magazine who had a great
love for the kind of music we made. With Jerry, things got better. He never
made records before, but he started off as my co-producer. Between Herb,
me, and Jerry, we signed people like Ruth Brown, the Clovers, the Cardinals,
Joe Turner, Ray Charles. I learned about making records from Ray Charles.
Atlantic's history is deeply tied in with Ray Charles' career.

Herb, myself, and Jerry, we were all fans of the music. So everybody
to us was a big star. We were in awe of all of them, and because we acted
that way around them, they felt maybe we were people who were not going
to exploit them. We were one of the few record companies at the time to
pay its royalties properly. That is how we kept so many of those people for
such a long time. They made a hit record, they got a decent royalty, and
they got paid on time.

The Joe Turner story is a great story. Joe grew up in Kansas City. He
never went to school very much, but he could sing over an entire brass
section without a microphone. Incredible voice. I knew him since 1941,
when he sang at a jazz concert in Washington. Herb Abramson had recorded
him for the National label, so we both knew him.

Well, Jimmy Rushing had left the Count Basie band because of illness,
and they hired Joe Turner to take his place. Herb and I went to the very
first show at the Apollo Theater, a Friday morning show after the first movie.
The audience was very cruel. They could be tough, and Joe hadn't had
much rehearsal time with the band. He didn't know the arrangements perfectly. He was coming in at the wrong place, they weren't finishing together,

and there was a lot of jeering and hooting in the audience. Joe was so embarrassed.

After the show, I went backstage but he had already left. So I went down to 126th Street, to a place called the Braddock Grill and Bar, and Joe was already sitting at the bar having a drink. Herb and I walked in, sat down, and consoled him. We told him he deserved to be a star on his own, with his own band, that he should make records on his own. I wrote the first song he recorded for Atlantic Records, "Chains of Love," which turned out to be the start of his second career. Of course, he eventually made a record which became the cornerstone of rock 'n' roll, "Shake, Rattle and Roll."

Wilson Pickett had a few big hits on Atlantic. I remember the time he was touring Great Britain, and we went there for some press conferences, and I gave a party for Wilson at the Scotch Club in London. There were a lot of press people there, and disc jockeys, and at one point we were having a drink, facing away from the bandstand where some people were jamming. I had my back to them, and suddenly I heard this blues guitar player. I said to myself, "This must be Pickett's guitarist." I turned to Wilson and I said, "Your guitar player sure sounds good."

Wilson said, "My guitar player is having a drink at the bar."

I turned around and saw this kid with an angelic face, a beautiful-looking young man playing like B. B. King. It was Eric Clapton. I said, "My God, he plays well."

Robert Stigwood was standing next to me, and he said, "You really think he's great?"

I said, "He's fabulous. We have to sign him up right away." So Stigwood got with him, and that is how Cream was formed. Cream was my first big British group. After that, I began concentrating on getting more British rock 'n' roll bands on the label. We got the Bee Gees, Led Zeppelin, Emerson, Lake and Palmer, Yes, and of course, the Rolling Stones.

Even though he is no longer on Atlantic, I have an ongoing, very strong personal relationship with Mick Jagger. It was '69 or '70, and I wasn't aware that the Rolling Stones contract with London Records was running out. I was in Los Angeles, and I was aware the Stones were in town because there was a traffic jam around the recording studio on Santa Monica and La Cienega where they were working.

One morning there's a knock on my bungalow door at the hotel where I'm staying, and it's a British roadie who tells me that Mick says it's OK if I want to come down to the studio where they are recording. I thank him very much, but I don't go because I have something else I have to do that night.

The next morning a knock on my door again, same roadie, he says, "Hey, listen, man, Mick wants you to come down," and the next evening I did. They gave me a tremendous reception, all the guys in the band. I leave the studio, and I go out with Bill Drake, who was a very powerful man in radio. He liked me because I drank with him. Well, that night we drank a couple of bottles of whiskey together. I tell him I've been to the studio where the Stones are recording, and Mick Jagger says he wants to talk to me, and I have a plan to meet him at the Whisky at midnight.

Drake says, "No kidding? Mick Jagger? Terrific." By this time I'm getting very tired from the jet lag the day before and all the drinking. Anyway, we go to the Whisky. I've called ahead for a table, and Bill had a couple of girls, the four of us are sitting at the table, and I have another drink.

Chuck Berry is onstage, and Mick arrives at twelve-thirty. I introduce him to Drake and the girls, and Mick sits down and starts telling me about their recording plans. He starts talking, and I doze off. I can remember this girl shaking me, going, "Wake up, wake up. It's Mick Jagger. He's telling you something important." Mick hates people who are into high pressure, but this was the opposite. Here he was telling me that the Rolling Stones have decided to sign with Atlantic, and I had fallen asleep.

Ray Charles

o o o

The man radiates enthusiasm, and love for what he does. And what he does and has done is to make some of the world's best music for many years. Ray is a one-man hall of fame who takes his genius title in stride.

o o o

I almost cried real tears when Artie Shaw stopped playing, and what a loss that was. I would not say this if I didn't mean it. Ever since I was a kid Artie Shaw was someone I loved. Everybody used to be excited about Benny Goodman. I'm not saying he wasn't great, but Artie Shaw had so much feeling in his notes. Every note you could feel in his heart.

Artie Shaw was one of the greatest musicians that ever lived. On any given night he was the best clarinet player in the world. When I went to school, I couldn't get into piano class because there were too many kids who were playing piano. So I took up the clarinet for a while, and mainly because that's what Artie Shaw played. And that is God's truth.

Now, I know it's none of my business, but it hurts me that Artie Shaw probably woke up one day and said, "Fuck it." And I know that feeling. He could do anything he wanted with his horn, but probably never the same way twice. And that can be frustrating. I don't sing "Georgia on My Mind" like the record. I don't sing "I Can't Stop Loving You" like the record. Or "Hit the Road, Jack." No way in the fuck that I can sing "Georgia" the same way twice. I'd have to study myself, and that's a chore. That's why I can't lip synch.

But Artie Shaw was an idol of mine, he certainly was. So was Art Tatum and Nat King Cole and Charles Brown. I love so many people, it just depends on the mood I'm in. I'm a great lover of people like Tampa Red and Blind Boy Phillips. I remember Big Joe Turner doing a thing with Art Tatum called "Wee Baby Blues," and I'm just a kid of eight sitting there going, "Oh, God."

Someone asked me once how I feel about being called a genius. Do I feel I have to live up to it? No, it ain't that kind of ball game. Whatever people say about me or call me, that's their business. I don't get hung up on it. It's the highest compliment, and I'm not trying to be cute, but I didn't create the fuss, so all I really have to do is continue what I'm doing for as long as God keeps breath in my body.

I ain't got nothing to do with all the little adjectives people put on me. I never said I was a genius. I never said I was a cornerstone, or a legend in my own time. I'm very thankful people recognize me for what I do, but I am not in the business of holding up some kind of picture someone has painted of me. If I did that, then I'd have to live up to it.

I try not to intimidate people, but I guess I do. I think most great artists who are extremely well-known tend to intimidate a little. If Aretha Franklin walked into the studio, or Barbra Streisand, or Frank Sinatra, they'd intimidate a whole lot of people. When a great conductor walks into a room full of musicians, you can almost hear a pin drop. I don't want to do that to people. As a matter of fact, when I am having a rehearsal and a new guy is coming in to try out for a job, I always let my conductor handle it. I don't want the guy getting bent out of shape because I'm there. I always stay out of the rehearsal room when they first come in. Once they've had a chance to play a little, then I walk in. I have seen guys fall apart because they felt intimidated.

I was lucky in the sense that I was with a real good company, Atlantic Records. The two guys there, Jerry Wexler and Ahmet Ertegun, were very smart. They saw something, and they did not interfere. It takes a smart person to know when not to interfere, even though you have the power to do it. It takes a smart person to say, "Hey, I think things would be better if I just kept my nose out of it." Atlantic did exactly that. They let me do the music and they did the marketing, which was smart.

When I would call Jerry or Ahmet and say, "Hey, man, I'm ready," they would say, "OK, come in whenever you want to record." They would send me songs, but they never ever told me I had to do them. They never once said, "Hey, man, we want you to do this song." That is why I wrote a lot of my own music in the early years. They would send me songs, and I didn't like them, so I had no choice. I knew I had to record, so I forced myself to sit down and write my own music.

My life has been like a ladder. I never had a bunch of things happen at once. It's always been a little bit at a time. Something good happens this year, then they hold back, then you get a little more next year.

I have had so many wonderful things happen to me over my lifetime that I don't know how the hell I could pick one particular year and say, "Yeah, that was the year." Maybe it was the year my version of "Georgia" became the state song of Georgia. That was a big thing for me, man. It really touched me. Here is a state that used to lynch people like me suddenly declaring my version of a song as its state song. That is touching.

Then there was the year the B'nai B'rith made me its Man of the Year. That was pretty incredible, too. Or the year I received a Life Achievement Award at the Kennedy Center. To receive one of those awards you usually have to be seventy-five or eighty or dead, and here I am, a young whipper-snapper, sitting with all these great people.

But you know, if I had to pick just one year, I would say 1954, the year I was first able to get a band of my own. I made no money that year, but I had my band, and they sent us on out on the road with Ruth Brown. I will never forget it. We drove almost 800 miles the first week, and had the time of our lives.

Today, I don't have any personal rivers to cross or any personal mountains to climb. For myself, I have won every kind of war you could possibly want to win in my profession. There is nothing in my profession that I have not won. You name it, I got it.

The thing that's really become important with me now is my involvement in ear research. I know you would think I'd be involved in eye research, but it is not so. It's ear research because I have so much respect for hearing. I don't know what would have happened to me if I hadn't been able to hear.

Quincy Jones

o o o

Possibly the most widespread talent in this entire book, Quincy tells how he plugged into jazz on two continents and carried through to make history with Michael Jackson and "We Are the World." Quincy is a best bet for any honor the industry might bestow at any time.

o o o

I came from the South Side of Chicago, meaning the ghetto. At four years old, we carried switchblades to protect ourselves. If you went from one black neighborhood to another, you got your butt kicked.

By the time I was ten, I was in Seattle, the only black kid in grade school, which was shocking. In Seattle, I started singing with a gospel quartet. From there, I went into school bands. I met Ray Charles when I was fourteen and he was sixteen. We played R & B every night. I didn't start with jazz, I started with R & B. We played the Seattle Country Club at seven o'clock at night, songs like "Roomful of Roses" and all that kind of shit, and then we'd go to the black clubs later on that night and play R & B.

We played for comedy acts, we played for strippers. That was the time during the war when they had nine military camps in the Seattle area, and the sailors and soldiers would stop there before they shipped out to Japan. So there was a lot of action there. East Coast pimps worked there. Ray's band, and my band, we had three jobs a night. We'd start off at the country club, then play the black clubs from ten to one A.M., and then go over to the Elks Club and play bebop.

I was with Lionel Hampton's band from '51 to '53. You're kind of isolated when you're in a band, and this was my first time out of high school. Drinking fountains for whites, drinking fountains for coloreds. Different restrooms, different places to sit at the bus stop.

Hamp's was a very popular band. We worked all year, six nights a week, seventeen dollars a night. We'd play New Orleans, and there'd be folding chairs facing each other, blacks on one side, whites on the other. Posters in Atlanta would say, "General admission—two fifty. White spectators—one fifty." We used to stay in people's homes because we couldn't afford hotels. Couldn't stay in the white hotels anyway. There was a group of dancers called the Brownskins, from the Cotton Club days. They would set up homes so the traveling musicians could spend a night, share a bathroom with a whole household, and have two meals. Sometimes we stayed in funeral parlors. But we always had a white bus driver. He was the one who would go in and get the food.

I went to New York in the early fifties, and that was something. Leonard Feather was an A & R man then. It was like a fairytale. Everybody was there —Charlie Parker, Art Tatum, Al Hibbler, Oscar Pettiford, Charles Mingus, Miles Davis. I freaked out that Miles had even heard about me. He heard this record, "Kingfish." It was the first solo I did with Hamp's band, and I was trying to play like Miles. Everybody was trying to play like Miles. They couldn't play like Dizzy Gillespie, so they tried to play like Miles.

Somehow Broadway then was a hundred times brighter than it is now. It was loaded with live theaters and jazz clubs. It was like Disneyland. And there I was, nineteen and going crazy. It was like the Golden Age—you could play with Hampton and still know what Bird was about, and Mingus, and Thelonious Monk, and Max Roach.

And then something happened, and it happened in Billy Eckstine's band. Billy Eckstine's band was like the spawning ground for a whole new turnaround in modern jazz. It was very revolutionary. It was like everyone all met in Billy's band—Dizzy, Bird, Sarah Vaughan, Miles. That was the band that turned everything around, where black musicians for the first time said, "We don't want to be just entertainers. We want to be artists. And we don't give a shit whether we dance. We just want to deal with our art."

That attitude brought on a lot of consequences. Number one, the audience was not ready for that kind of dance music. So there was a big risk in alienating the audience, which is why, I think, a lot of musicians turned to drugs, to escape the consequences.

Funny, but the Europeans understood the change in music better than the Americans. I did a State Department tour with Dizzy in '56, and we got more trouble from the U.S. Information Agency than we did from anybody else. When we went to North Africa, the USIA people there thought Dizzy was a baseball player—Dizzy Dean. They didn't have a clue. After the tour, we went to the White House. Nixon was vice president, and he asked Dizzy, "Was the tour fun?"

And Dizzy said, "It was the most fun I've had since I've been black." I never forgot that line.

To think, after all the people I've worked with, that I could still be around working with someone like Michael Jackson, it's like a dream. On paper, I should not be around. Let's face it, the music business is about eighteen-year-olds. I remember in 1959, when I was broke, and I was doing three weeks in Europe with Nat Cole, and Nat said, "Somehow it all works out. You can have a big spurt of five years, or else you can take your time, and just ease on for fifty years and get bigger all the time." That idea just knocked me out.

I would not have met Michael Jackson had I not agreed to do *The Wiz*. I didn't want to do *The Wiz*. Except for a couple of songs, I didn't like the music. But Sidney Lumet, who I've done six movies with, said, "You've got to do it," and so I did it.

I met Michael, and he said, "I'm looking for somebody to produce my record. Can you think of anybody?" He thought I was too busy, which I was.

I said, "Michael, don't bother me now. I've got Richard Pryor, Lena Horne, this one, that one. I have to get all this stuff together. Can we talk about this later on?"

But then I started to watch him on the set. He'd get in two hours early for makeup. He'd know everybody's lines, everybody's music. I thought he was a little bubble-gummer. But we connected during rehearsal. Something happened, and that's how we got started together. The next day I said, "OK, I'll do your album," and we did *Off the Wall*.

And then came *Thriller*, which was mind-boggling. It scared me. I thought, "Holy shit, what is going on?" I mean, everybody wants a big record, but this was outrageous. I was looking at sales reports, and we were doing 1.1 million albums a week. We had eleven weeks in a row of 1-million-plus albums. I couldn't believe it. Nobody could. The fever was so strong. Michaelmania was so powerful. I'd seen it with the Beatles, and I'd seen it with Presley. I worked with Tommy Dorsey, when Elvis came on Tommy's show in '55, so I've seen this phenomenon happen three times— Presley, the Beatles, and Michael.

The dark side to all this is that there is no other way to go but down.

But they will never take Michael out. He's going through his lumps, critically and otherwise, but he will continue to surface throughout. He has enormous talent, and he's a very nice person. He's not the weirdo people think he is.

Jerry Wexler

o o o

This executive, producer, and observer is a colorful reminder that the record business was begun by brilliant, gutsy men and women who, above all, loved the music first and made it a business later on.

o o o

Nobody really knew how to make a record when I started. You simply went into the studio, turned on the mike, and said, "Play." We didn't learn how to make records until probably sometime in 1976.

I used to hang out in Harlem long before I had any notion of being in the record business. Ahmet and Nesuhi Ertegun were these highly evolved European jazz fans who loved the mystique of the blues. Most of the other people around at the time didn't know squat about it. Leonard Chess and his brother, Phil, came to the United States with their father from Poland, who used to ride a junk wagon through Chicago, ringing a bell and offering cash for clothes.

The Chess boys started a saloon somewhere on the South Side of Chicago. They put a jukebox in. Then they had live talent. Leonard took me to one of his dives in 1955, and the new singer and star on the bill was Joe Williams, who had just started out.

See, there were three basic styles of making blues records then. Leonard Chess' was one. He would see Muddy Waters playing in some circular bar, and the next day he would take Muddy into the studio and tell him to play what he played last night. Leonard would document what he'd already heard.

Then there was the second style, the songwriter-arranger type of producer who would create the music, then arrange it. Like Johnny Otis and Arif Mardin.

We were the third type. I don't know what kind of name to give us, because I sort of feel like I came in on a pass.

Everything was a little crazy back then. The perfect example is Guitar Slim. He was a blues man who came out of the swamps of Louisiana. People used to follow him thinking he was a preacher.

We're doing our first session with him in Cosmo's little studio in New Orleans. Every time Slim comes to a certain point in the song, he hits a terrific chord and blows all the tubes out. Cosmo never has a spare tube because he can't afford it. He has a kid run down to Canal Street to a radio store. We have to wait until the kid comes back with another tube.

So we finally get going again trying to record a song called "Plenty Good Room in My House." Every time Slim gets to the bridge he makes the same mistake, and instead of going back to the last verse, he goes back to the top.

I say, "Slim, you need to go here, not to the top."

He looks at me and says, "My natural soul takes me back up there, not here."

Also, no matter what we did we couldn't get him to follow the lyrics. So we printed the lyrics on the back of a cardboard dance advertisement. Still, he keeps doing the same thing, going back up to the top instead of the last verse. We're trying to be resourceful, so we begin tearing the dance advertisement into strips. This way he can only see one verse at a time. We had up to eight people holding these strips, and it still wouldn't work.

Finally he gets through the song, but he leaves off the little coda at the end. I said, "Slim, you finally got through the whole song, but you left out the coda. You're supposed to sing the coda."

He says, "Motherfuck the motherfucking coda. I'm supposed to sing 'Plenty Good Room in My House.' "

The way it worked during the early days of Atlantic, we recorded four nights a week—only singles. We'd release three records at a time, every three weeks. To make the nut back in those days we needed to do 60,000 singles a month. We were lucky. All the records sold between 200,000 and 300,000, but hardly ever more than that. But it was enough to get us going.

We're at a meeting in Chicago and I get this bright idea that as long as our distributors are there, let's have a sales meeting. It won't cost us anything, just a cheap breakfast of sausage links and eggs. So we have this meeting. Amos Heilicher and Jim Schwartz are there, and Nesuhi is conducting the meeting with books and everything. He's going on and on about how we combined the Modern Jazz Quartet with Chris Connor, and Ahmet and I are dying. Heilicher and Schwartz are falling asleep, and Ahmet is cursing at Nesuhi in Turkish, "Why the fuck don't you shorten it? They are dying out there. They don't want to hear this shit."

And Nesuhi keeps going on, legitimizing us. Ours was a street-distributor mentality: We're in Chicago, "OK, who is going to pay off the R & B disc jockey so we can break a Joe Turner record?" We needed Nesuhi to guide us, putting up a patina of legitimacy.

We just never questioned anything anybody did. If there were piles of twenties and fifties laying around, Ahmet would say, "I think I need three inches of money." Nobody questioned anything. It was a fabulous relationship.

La Vern Baker was a wonderful singer and also very funny. Her aunt was a famous blues singer from Chicago. They used to call her the "Yas Yas Girl," which came from a song called "Ducks Yas Yas." It was a great jukebox race song. It went, "Mama bought a chicken, mistook it for a duck, stuck it on the table with the legs straight up. Yonder comes sister with a spoon and a glass, catch the gravy dripping from the yas yas yas."

Ray Charles was originally on a small label called Swing Time. He had a record called "Kissa Me, Baby," which Ahmet had fallen in love with. We knew this great agent in those days named Billy Shaw. He had his own agency. In those days, agents really used to create and nurture artists, sponsor them, finance them. They would bring them along, not just book them. Billy was the go-between with Ray. We bought his contract from Swing Time for $2,000. Who knew?

In the beginning, we recorded Ray like we recorded anybody. He didn't have a band, he hadn't been writing songs. We would give him songs, musicians. We would get Jessie Stone to do the arrangements. And then one day Ray called us from Atlanta and said, "Come down here. We'll record here. I got my own band."

It was a whole new genesis. He had his own songs, his own arrangements, a seven-piece band. I remember we recorded him once at a college radio station, in the news room. We had to stop every hour so they could do the news. But that's where Ray first did "I Got a Woman."

Music can be funny sometimes. The things you think are black can actually be rooted in country. Chuck Berry is a good example of that. "Maybellene" is really an update of an old country tune, "Ida Red." Listen to Chuck Berry sing. There's nothing black about his songs. He sounds like an American country person. That is part of the genius of his rhythm guitar playing, which had so much to do with rock 'n' roll. His songs aren't black, they're mid-American country. "School Days" and "Sweet Little Sixteen" have nothing to do with the idiosyncratic black experience. But his rhythm playing was extremely idiosyncratic.

Now turn it around to the white person who sounds black. Bobby Darin was our first white artist. He had been on Decca, nothing was happening, and he was discouraged. Ahmet said, "Let me take a shot with him."

Darin came in with this song, "Splish Splash," which was co-written by Bobby and Murray the K's mother. I hear this thing, "Splish splash, I was taking a bath," and I say, "Ahmet, are you crazy? This isn't a song, it's ridiculous."

Ahmet says, "No, it's a song."

So Bobby does a split date with Morgana King. They each do two songs. History may remember what Morgana King did on that date, but I certainly don't. Bobby did "Splish Splash," and we were off to the races. Nobody knew he was white. Thank God we didn't have video then.

Les Paul

∘ ∘ ∘

An amazing combination of a great musician and a commercial
success, he has an ability to totally recall every detail of his career.
Les is in the Rock 'n' Roll Hall of Fame, and his innovative recording
techniques make him one of pop music's all-time stars.

∘ ∘ ∘

The first guy to really floor me was Gene Autry. I was a thirteen-year-old
kid in Wisconsin, and he was appearing at the local auditorium. I went to
the show and I had a friend of mine go with me so he could hold a flashlight
so I'd be able to write down all the chords Gene Autry was playing on a
fingerboard I'd drawn. I put these little dots down on a fingerboard, the F
chord and so on, whatever he was playing.

Meanwhile, the flashlight is going on and off, on and off, and in the
middle of the show Gene says, "I have to stop the show, folks. Something
out there is bothering me, or intriguing me. Every time I hit this chord a
light goes on. I don't know what's going on. Would someone tell me what's
going on out there."

I stood up and said, "Mr. Autry, would you mind playing that chord
again? I'm trying to write down where you put your fingers."

So he calls me up to the stage, and I go up, this little skinny kid. He's
laughing. But he handed me his guitar and he said, "Play something." And
I did. And then he made some comment that brought the house down. But
he also showed me the chords, and after the show he took me to the back
room and he said, "When you're ready, you come down to Chicago and I
will take care of you."

Well, a western band then came through my hometown, and I would
work all night with them, go to school in the morning, and then sleep all
afternoon. I was a night worker anyway. I'd stay up all night and practice
with all these electronics. My brother thought I was real weird, but my
mother thought I was a genius. As far as my mother was concerned, I could
do no wrong. She always justified anything I did. If I tore the piano apart,
it was for a reason. She'd say, "Look at him. He wants to know why."

"How High the Moon," by Les Paul and Mary Ford, came out in 1950.
Mary had been described as the singer with a "plaintive, folksy, Wisconsin
dairy-maid voice." The name Ford came out of a phone book. Her real
name was Colleen Summer. We went on tour and opened at the Blue Note
in Chicago. Mary's dressed in a street dress, and I'm in my western outfit.
We looked like a relief band. The owner took one look at us and promptly
fired us. He said, "The girl with the housedress on, and you with the
moccasins. This whole thing has got to go." So we were given notice, and
they were going to bring in George Shearing to take our place. But all the
papers had been down on opening night to review us. *Down Beat*, *Variety*,
Billboard, the *Tribune*—they were all there. Two days later, the papers hit

the street and we're a hit. But I hadn't seen the reviews. I was out getting Mary a dress and me a tuxedo. So we put on our new clothes and we get to the club and on the marquee it says, "The world's greatest guitarist." The owner is waiting for us, and he says, "Forget the tuxedo, forget the dress. I just canceled Shearing. You can stay for six months if you want." Our whole world changed with those reviews. We were on our way.

By '52 we were very successful. Now we're playing in St. Paul, and there's a terrific snowstorm. Bad weather, but beautiful as far as I'm concerned. I probably should have been an Alaskan huskie. Anyway, we're in the room and I turn on the radio and I hear Anita O'Day singing a song called "Vaya con Dios." And she's singing the hell out of it. Mary is sewing her dress on the bed and I ask her what she thinks of it. She says, "I don't know what it is, but I like it."

I reach for the phone to call the disc jockey at the station so I can find out more about the record, and the disc jockey says, "You're really Les Paul? You can come down and have the record."

I call Hal Cooke at Capitol Records, and I say, "Hal, you gotta stop 'I'm a Fool to Care.' "

He says, "We already stamped out a half a million. We're on our way with it."

I say, "Stop it. I want to put out 'Vaya con Dios.' " Everyone at Capitol tells me I'm wasting my goddamn time, and I say, "Would you guys please do what I'm telling you?"

Finally they say, "OK, if you want to put it out, go ahead." So instead of saying, "Vaya con Dios, my darling, may God be with you, my love," which is the original lyric, I change it to, "Vaya con Dios, my darling, vaya con Dios, my love." No one knew what "Vaya con Dios" meant anyway, unless they read it on the label, where it said, "Go with God."

So we put the record out and the other side takes off—"Johnny Is the Boy for Me," not "Vaya con Dios." I tell my manager I want to go to seven cities to promote "Vaya." He says, "Are you crazy, trying to knock off your own hit?"

But I convinced him to let us go to these seven cities. So we went and one by one we convinced the disc jockeys to turn over the record. You can't believe how glad I am that they did. "Vaya con Dios" was the one that put us over the top.

It's very nice today how people give me credit for having the kind of impact I had on all the younger guitar players. When I was a kid, I would take a phonograph needle and the cartridge, put it in the guitar, and then turn it up. I had an electric guitar in 1929. When I joined the cowboy band, my guitar was already amplified. I simply never left the electric guitar. I just stuck with it and stuck with it. By 1940, '41, I was pleading with Gibson, which markets the electric guitar, to give me a solid-body electric guitar. They thought I was crazy, so I took a two-by-four and put two wings on the side of it so it would look like a guitar. Everybody laughed at me, but Leo Fender would sit in my back yard and look at it, and his mind was moving.

Gibson finally came out with one in 1952, and from '52 to '64 the Les Paul guitar became so big that it was probably the number-one instrument in the world. The president of Gibson came to me later and he said, "Les, did you ever in your wildest imagination think this was going to happen?"

And I said, "Sure."

Tony Bennett

o o o

A total class act, Tony won't compromise, feels rather strongly about rock 'n' roll and its impact on popular music, and continues to concertize around the world with homage to Porter, Gershwin, Kern, Arlen, and Mercer.

o o o

Bing Crosby was a pioneer. He created a psychological way of performing, and it had to do with how he learned to communicate on radio. He actually had people hypnotized for many years. No one could get past that. It must have been frustrating for the singers of the day. There was really no one else. No other singer got the exposure Bing got. He was like fifteen Beatles.

I never got to really know him, but he claimed I was the greatest singer he ever heard. I met him once with Bob Hope, but that was about it. Things did come back to me from musicians. For example, I did a Cole Porter suite one time with Arthur Fiedler and the Boston Pops. Arthur told me that Bing carried around a videotape of me doing that. Arthur said that Bing told him he liked the way I worked the mike. I learned it from him.

My first record was "Fascinating Rhythm," and my biggest influence was Bing. He was a pop singer who sang jazz. I am not a jazz singer either. Billie Holiday, now there was a jazz singer. Louis Armstrong, Ella Fitzgerald. But the rest don't really sing jazz, even though we're all trying to say something through music.

I just wanted to be a good, crafty singer. The thought of being in the Top 10 was more than I had ever dreamed. But it was a long battle. I took a lot of auditions, and I didn't look the way people thought a singer should look. Everybody told me to get a nose job. Today I look like the prototype of a nice Italian romantic singer, but in those days it was rough.

I was very self-conscious, very shy and nervous, because when you first start out you hope things will work out. But it's luck and a matter of learning your craft. It takes ten years to get really comfortable. I would think a lot of rock groups today must be scared stiff, just hoping it sustains.

Years ago, there was a circuit. You could go from town to town to break in. It was like George Burns said, "You were allowed to get lousy before you got good." And that's very true. You can't do it overnight. You may look good, you may have the energy and pizzazz, but to do a confident thirty, forty minutes onstage, you really have to know your craft. Took me ten years.

But I did manage to arrange every record I ever made. Musicians orchestrated the records, but I arranged the songs. I was influenced by Art Tatum because of how he dramatized simple, little songs. I got my style through Art Tatum's piano playing. I was told to imitate musicians rather than singers. If I had imitated singers—and in my day it probably would have been Dick Haymes, who I liked very much—I don't know where I would have been. But I took my teacher's advice and imitated musicians.

And in a way, all of them influenced me. Like Louis Armstrong. He invented jazz. A whole line of popular music that will be defined more as time goes by can be traced directly to him. He was the fountainhead that made everything happen. There isn't a note in popular music that Louis Armstrong did not do. He was what Caruso was to opera.

Basie was a very good philosopher with great charisma on stage. All he had to do was raise an eyebrow and the entire place would "ooh" and "aaah," and have fun with him. His secret was the economy of lines. He knew what to leave out. He knew what had to be in there, he knew what to take out, and he knew how to let the audience participate. He had a microphone on his piano. His guitarist, Freddie Green, never had a mike on his guitar, and yet he could be heard above the brass section if that's what Basie wanted.

I was the first white guy to sing with Basie. I had quite an adventure in the musical world. I sang with Woody Herman, Duke Ellington, Basie. You can't ask for anything more. Louis Bellson said it best. He called Duke the sky, and Basie the earth. You know how Shirley MacLaine talks about other lives and reincarnation? Duke talked that way all his life. He believed in this universal attitude, the infinity of the heavens.

Basie was down here on the ground, one of the guys. When the music business changed so drastically in the late sixties, and rock began happening in such a big way, I went to Count Basie and said, "It's a complete takeover. What should I do?"

Basie waited a beat, looked up at me with those big eyes of his and said, "Why change an apple?"

Barbra Streisand

o o o

**There are few individuals whose first name is all you need hear to
identify them. In this rare interview, Barbra gives us a perspective on
her feelings about music and stardom.**

o o o

I can remember being six or seven and singing with my friends on the stoop
in front of my apartment building in Brooklyn. I used to imitate Joni James
and other singers on the Hit Parade. And I used to like to sing in our hallway
because it had a great echo.

I always wanted to be an actress, that's why lyrics are so important to
me. I am drawn to songs that have a place to go, songs that have a beginning,
middle and end. They are like mini-theatrical pieces.

Whether an album sells or not is not of consequence. The reward for
me is in the process. If it sells . . . then that's a bonus.

Can I say something to new artists?

Don't be afraid of the establishment. There are always those who are
going to say, "No you can't, no you shouldn't . . ." Just like the line that
Stephen Sondheim wrote, "All they ever want is repetition, all they really
like is what they know."

You've got to do your own thing. Only the public can tell you if
something is commercial or not. Don't be maneuvered into doing something
that isn't you. Each person is unique.

I love to use the truth, and the truth sells. I wish more people would
realize that.

I never intellectualized my musical sound. I've always heard orchestrations in my head and other melodies when I sing. "Evergreen" began
with me learning some basic guitar chords and building a melody from that.
I get such a kick out of it when I hear other people sing it now because here
I was just fooling around with this instrument for a movie, and now other
people actually sing it at weddings! Winning the Oscar for "Best Song" was
more thrilling than getting it for "Best Actress." And writing the score for
Nuts was challenging. Since I don't read music I hummed the lines to an
orchestrator. I've written the music to six songs so far and the lyrics to one,
and I'd like the time to write more.

I don't know what to tell other singers when they ask me how I take
care of my voice. I mean, they'll be disappointed, because I really do very
little. I don't believe in paying too much attention to my voice. I don't
pamper it, I don't use humidifiers or special sprays, I don't vocalize, and I
don't sing in the shower.

I have a mixture of feelings about performing live. In the beginning, I
guess I enjoyed concerts as a forum for expressing myself. I could use the
moment to convey different nuances in each song. Each time I sing a song
it's different.

But truthfully, I would rather do something in private, like a movie or a record and then share it with an audience when I am done. I must add, however, that in the past twenty years I have performed live for free and for charity and have gained a great deal of personal satisfaction because of those appearances.

I believe that art is a very living process, that as we grow, our art grows, as we expand, our work expands. I'm very grateful to have the opportunity to live life and be able to express my feelings through my work.

Joe Smith

○ ○ ○

I think I was a very good disc jockey. I had a late-night show at Yale where I really started roasting people. I took on the campus heroes. William F. Buckley was the editor of the Yale newspaper, and every time I referred to him on the air, I played "God Save the King." Even then I knew he thought of himself as American royalty.

The first time I had any inkling of payola was when I was out of Yale and working for a small station in Johnstown, Pennsylvania. This promotion man came in with a box of Glenn Miller records. I said, "What's this for?"

He said, "It's a gift." A gift? I didn't understand what he meant. I couldn't believe someone would give me something, just like that. Soon people started inviting me to the nightclubs. I became very popular in Johnstown. I had a TV show, a radio show. I would get invited to all the openings in Pittsburgh. The record company would pick up the tab. It was an eye-opener for someone like me who was making no money.

But I was a good disc jockey because I listened to the music. Rock 'n' roll was just starting by the time I got back to Boston. Rhythm and blues records were just starting to cross over. Suddenly the kids didn't want to hear Perry Como anymore. They would write me the most intimate letters about how they went to bed with their radio under the pillow.

Radio is an aphrodisiac for a young disc jockey. You can't imagine the thrill of sitting in a control booth and saying, "You want me to play something, call up," and all the lines instantly light up. Or, "Hey, if you don't like the way they're doing such-and-such, toot your horn," and someone comes in and says, "Wow, they're tooting their horns all over town."

Frankly, I didn't understand Elvis Presley. I had no background to understand Elvis Presley. But I could instantly sense the impact this guy was having, so I figured I'd better play his records. I had been at smaller stations in Virginia and Pennsylvania, but when I got a job in Boston, I knew I had to establish an identity. Boston had lots of stations. Some of those stations occasionally delved into early rock 'n' roll, but I wanted to be known as something else. I would play Nat Cole records, but I went for the younger share of the audience.

Rock 'n' roll was consistently ridiculed. You can't believe the paranoia around it. We're talking the 1950s and Eisenhower. Conservative America had grown up with the big bands and Sinatra

and Bing Crosby, and now we're giving them Little Richard, Fats
Domino, and Elvis Presley. I took heat from sponsors, from the radio
station, from the police. I took heat from parent-teacher
organizations. Consider the morality here, and now translate that to
Boston of all places, absolutely the most conservative of all urban
centers. Enormous Catholic influence, and here comes this guy playing
this vile, suggestive music.

There was Alan Freed in New York, Jocko Henderson in
Newark, George Lorenz, or "Hound Dog," as he was called, in
Buffalo, Mickey Shorr in Detroit, Bill Randall in Cleveland, Howard
Miller in Chicago, and me in Boston. I was on in the afternoon from
two to six, and then at night from seven-thirty to eleven. The
afternoon was the key money-making drive time, but at night I could
get away with anything because there were no adults listening, just
kids.

I gave myself the name "José." I had a theme song. I rang bells
and banged on the telephone book. I talked back to the record:
"Hello, Fats. Is that you?"

And he'd sing, "Yes, it's me and I'm in love again."

I would get on the phone with Elvis Presley, Fats, every rock 'n'
roll star, all live. I gave away autographed pictures. I was opening up
New England to the record companies, booming up the coast of New
England at night. I was a hero.

I used to tape the night show in the morning from my mother's
house, then go in and do the afternoon show, then do a record hop
while the show I taped was airing at night. Kids hung out outside my
parents' house because they knew I was in there taping.

I remember getting a Chuck Berry acetate, "School Days," from
Leonard and Phil Chess in Chicago. I played it seventeen times in a
row on a Friday, and on Saturday the distributor, the late Cecil
Steen, called me and told me he already had orders for a hundred
thousand on "School Days." Every dealer in New England was
ordering it. I went crazy over the record and I wanted to test my
impact. We started the Joe Smith Record Club and gave out coupons
so kids could buy records at a discount at any store in New England.
It was a circus.

I did record hops constantly, many of them in churches. I'd bring
in Freddy Cannon, or Billy Ward and the Dominoes, anyone who was
in town. Even if they were playing at a club somewhere, I'd make sure
the record company brought the act over to the hop in between shows.
They would lip-sync some songs, sign a few autographs, give out

pictures, and I made anywhere from $150 to $500 a night. Guys wrote me checks, gave me wrinkled-up cash. I was the biggest drawing card on the Catholic Youth Organization circuit.

Cardinal Cushing used to come on for ten minutes during my show and do a rosary from the chancery. He sounded like a Chicago hood. The ratings soared when he came on. There was a reception for him one time when he came back from the Vatican, and I was on the receiving line. He'd go, "Whattaya say, Smitty?"

And I would say, "See what happens when you get on a good show? Now they know you in Rome."

There's a big charity in Boston called the Jimmy Fund. Cardinal Cushing was on the committee, along with Joe Cronin, who was president of the Red Sox, Ted Williams, myself to line up the entertainment, and the then-U.S. senator from Massachusetts John F. Kennedy. We'd meet every once in a while, and this one year I'm trying to get Ed "Kookie" Byrnes, who was very hot at the time on "77 Sunset Strip," to be on the show we were doing at Fenway Park. The Boston Braves, who had already moved to Milwaukee, were coming back to play an exhibition game against the Red Sox, and right after the game we'd do a show.

I lined up Paul Anka, Connie Francis, all the stars who were happening at the time, and now I'm trying to get Kookie. But Warner Brothers is giving me all this crap about Kookie being on a promotion tour in Baltimore. I said, "Switch him to Boston. I have every disc jockey in New England plugging the show."

Jack Kennedy even arranged to have an Air Force jet fly Kookie from Baltimore to Logan, so a helicopter could then take him and drop him down right on the pitcher's mound at Fenway. And still Warner's gave me a hard time. So I go to a meeting, and Cardinal Cushing says, "Well, Smitty, what about the creep with the comb? Is he going to be here?" Cushing was so powerful. The church was so powerful. I always wanted them on my side, and that's why I made sure that at least once a week I did a hop for them. I needed the church because the police were always on my case. They claimed I caused trouble wherever I went. Kids couldn't get in, riots outside. Then the big headline: "Venereal Disease on Upswing. Police Chief Blames Elvis Presley and Rock 'n' Roll Disc Jockey Smith."

It was very flattering. The record companies were kissing my ass. They'd tell you how great you were, they took care of you, you never picked up a tab anywhere. Some guys gave you $100 or $200 a month. Nobody ever thought about the morality of it all. When I got to the

Boston station, one of the disc jockeys took me to lunch and said, "This is how it works. Some guys take money. Some don't. Do whatever you want. Don't be ashamed. Just don't start undercutting anyone else."

It was never a case of, "Here's $500. Play this record." If I didn't like the record, it didn't go on. Mob guys who had artists would want to give you a jukebox or put a swimming pool in your backyard, but it always came down to the record. There was too much competition to play a bad record.

But people did give me money, and I took the money. I declared every cent of the money, figuring this was just the way things happened.

It was clear when the payola investigation came along and my picture was on the front page of the paper that they weren't really after us, the disc jockeys. It was simply a matter that we were pushing rock 'n' roll on these kids. They thought that if we didn't load the kids up on rock 'n' roll, maybe they'd still listen to Frankie Laine. We were loading them up on rock 'n' roll as a reaction to their wanting it.

The payola aspect of the investigation was over the minute the hearings in Washington started. It was over that quickly. We all went back to doing what we had been doing. It was a great overreaction for about ten minutes. Alan Freed got into all kinds of trouble because he didn't declare his money. Certainly he got a lot more than I ever did. My touch in Boston was petty cash compared to what Alan was taking in. But Alan was the best deejay in the world. The man had a sense of tension, urgency. It didn't matter which acts did his shows as long as he was there. People took care of Alan Freed because why not? He was the best and he was in New York, where all the record companies were. You would see Alan Freed in a bar or at a music hangout surrounded by people all hoping the king would just look over at them.

Bo Diddley

○ ○ ○

Bo believes he's been had by the music business. He poured out his frustration over the kitchen table in a San Fernando home, itemizing the mistreatment by record companies who didn't pay him and rockers who stole his music.

○ ○ ○

Kids gave me the name Bo Diddley in school. I got the nickname because I took up for little guys who couldn't defend themselves. I was raised in Chicago and you either had to learn how to be a fast runner after school, or either be fast with your hands. Be fast on your feet, or have a good gift of gab.

Later, when I got old enough to go into the gym, I started hanging around and learning boxing. We'd all beat up on each other, and it was good.

Anyway, they started calling me Bo Diddley. Don't ask me why.

I was playing guitar on the street corners at twelve, thirteen years old. I played violin mostly in church, classical music. But you never found any black people playing violins, and that kind of worried me a bit.

When I made the record "Bo Diddley" in 1955, it turned the whole music scene around. It was just three of us originally—Roosevelt Jackson, Jerome Green, and me. Later we added Clifton James on drums. He was the man who did the original Bo Diddley beat on drums.

We went to Chess Records and they liked it, but they didn't like the original title, which was "Uncle John." In Chicago at that time, they couldn't deal with words like that, so we changed the title to my name.

Muddy Waters had everything all sewn up, man. If you couldn't play like Muddy Waters, you might as well go put yourself back in the rack. Muddy was an idol of mine. I loved what he was doing, but I couldn't play blues. And Muddy couldn't do what I did, which was that real sanctified rhythm. When I want to make people sweat, I go into a sanctified bag on them, put that religious beat on. Don't ask me where it comes from because I don't know that either.

It was like I did the "Bo Diddley" song by accident. I just started beating and banging on my guitar. And then I fooled around and got it syncopated right, where it fit the dirty lyrics that I had. And then it just seemed to fall right into place.

Then I put maracas in there, because at the time we didn't have a drummer, so we needed something that sounded like drums. First, we started out with just two great big old shopping bags. I mean, a guy would sit there and slap on these bags.

We never had any money, man. I mean, the money was never right. I was never good at figures because I dropped out of school at an early age. But you don't have to be good with figures to know you've been had. When you look around and say, "Wow, the record is selling all over the United States of America. How many people are buying it? Two hundred thousand? One hundred thousand? Fifty thousand?"

And then you ask, "How much money does that mean for me?" And you begin to wonder, "Wow, that's a lot of pennies, you know. Where's mine?" And when you don't see any pennies, that's when you know you've been had. I didn't make any money.

But I made the record in '55, they started playing it, and everybody freaked out. Caucasian kids threw Beethoven into the garbage can. Kids were hollering, "Hey, I like that. I want to play a guitar, mama."

Parents were freaking out. They had piano players in the family for hundreds of years. "Your uncle was a great concert pianist, and you want to play a guitar?"

"Yeah, mama. I want to play a guitar. I want to sound like that cat."

And the parents say, "We don't want that black music in this house. We don't want that junk in here."

So the kid sneaks off, gets a guitar, learns how to play it. So here they come. But in the meantime, I can't get my stuff played.

So Leonard Chess and the others say to Alan Freed, "Hey, what do you think about us getting some white kids who can play guitar, kids who sound a little bit black, and let them cover the record?"

Somebody says, "I got the right kid. He's country. Let's try him out." So here they come. They record the song and the white stations start playing it. It's the same song, but they call me "rhythm and blues" and they call the white boy "rock 'n' roll." Just so long as it was separate, they could make believe it wasn't a black record anymore. But it was written by a black dude—me.

We are the originators of all this stuff, but nobody ever pays us any attention when one of us dies. I'm worried about when I kick off. Will anybody notice it? That's something to think about, you know, will anybody notice when Bo Diddley ceases to exist?

I mean, if I stay here, I have to get old, and if I get old, I got to die, you understand? Will anybody recognize that the man who started rock 'n' roll, the very same rock 'n' roll that Alan Freed named at the Paramount Theater, will they know I'm gone? I won't want praise, just some recognition that a good dude has gone to rest.

It hurts me sometimes when I think about it. I look at myself and say, "What am I killing myself for? I'm not making any money." Maybe one day when I'm deceased, they'll wake up and realize they lost me.

Little Richard

○ ○ ○

He hit with a bang and it lasted less than two years, but the memory has lingered on for over three decades. Richard built his image and he continues to live by it.

○ ○ ○

When I was a boy, people would go from city to city looking for work. They called it "following the seasons." When the fruit was ready, they would be in that area. The people who didn't do that type of work were either cooks or entertainers.

I was so skinny. I was ashamed of my size. I would wear shirts that would hang over my pants because I was so small. In the south, there were two names we called each other, bro and 'lil. I really don't know how my name came about other than people saying "'lil bro" or "'lil sister." Since I was the middle child in my family, it was always 'lil Richard. After a while I was hearing it so much that it became a part of me.

I remember the first time I heard a record of mine on the radio. I was lying in bed and I heard "Tutti Frutti." I didn't know it was a hit. In fact, I didn't think it would be a hit. It was too far for me to touch or reach. The call was too distant for me. But that night, lying in bed, I heard the record and it was strange hearing myself on the radio. I had recorded before, twice before, and it had killed my desire because I didn't hit with those records.

When you're a young artist, and you want a hit real bad, it's easy to get discouraged. It makes you mad, but you don't ever tell anybody that you might want to give it up and do something else. But when I heard "Tutti Frutti" on WLAC in Nashville with Gene Nobles, the disc jockey, I woke up my family. It was eleven o'clock at night. Then I called my friend Sam from Macon. He was a Jewish guy, so we called him Jew Sam. His family owned a store and we got everything we needed from Jew Sam. Then we called the radio station and Gene Nobles said it was the number-one most requested record. He said, "Whoever Little Richard is, he's taking over." I heard "Awop-bop-a-loo-mop alop-bam-boom," and I felt an electric charge go over my body.

When I started out singing, we didn't have much money so I would take my mother's brooches and pin them on my "Monday" jacket and my "Tuesday" shirt and my "Wednesday" pants. I didn't want everyone to know how poor we were. I would go out onstage with a ring on, and whenever I was singing I would stick my finger up in the air so you could see the ring. I kept it on until my finger turned green.

I met a singer in Atlanta called Billy Wright, who was working at a club called the Royal Peacock. It was Billy who made me realize I wasn't dressing. I wasn't truly professing and I wasn't contesting because I really didn't know what I was doing. Billy had on green and gold shoes and green suits and I thought this guy was fabulous. I wanted to compete with him.

If I had the money, I felt I could have done more than what he was doing, twenty times more. He knew how to make up and I didn't. So I started to copy him. He became my idol, and finally I got some flash shoes, and Billy gave me my first suit, my pretty suit. That's when I started to sing at the Royal Peacock, singing with Jimmy Witherspoon, Ruth Brown, Roy Brown, Willie Brown. I was in the Brown family.

I remember being out on tour with Ruth Brown, Fats Domino, Jimmy Witherspoon, LaVern Baker, and Chuck Willis. By the time the tour was over I was the one that was headlining. I was the one starring. "Long Tall Sally" and "Slippin' and Slidin'" was out. Then "Jenny Jenny" was released, and now I was the hottest thing on the show. And I was unpredictable. When they called me to come on the stage, I would go up in the balcony and hide. When they called my name, the spotlight would go searching for me and they couldn't find me. I was outrageous! Then I'd jump down from the balcony in a split and the promoter would hold his head and scream, "Oh, Lord!"

When I went to Specialty Records and met Arthur Goldberg, who later changed his name to Art Rupe, he didn't like the songs. He wanted me to sing like B.B. King, but I didn't feel it. I love B.B. King as a person, but it wasn't me. It was all too slow. Then they wanted me to imitate Ray Charles. The only way I got a chance to sound like Little Richard was after a session one night. We were in a studio in New Orleans, which wasn't bigger than my kitchen, and I went over to the piano. Nobody even knew I played. They were shocked, but they listened to my song. They wanted to add a writer to clean up my lyrics, but my lyrics weren't dirty. They were sort of how Prince's lyrics are today. But they would bring my lyrics on a piece of paper and I would name it on the spot and make up a melody. But I never actually knew a long tall Sally or an Uncle John.

Then Pat Boone started covering my tunes while they were still hot, and the pop stations would play his version and kill mine from ever having the chance of crossing over. You'd go into the record shops and there would be his version but not mine. Arthur Goldberg came to me and he said, "We have to do something about Pat Boone covering our records." And he was covering them so fast. But remember, Pat was also covering Fats Domino and many others. As a person, I've always loved Pat, but at the time I didn't like what was happening because he was cutting off my sales. Now, when I look back on it, it was really a blessing and a lesson because he opened the doors for us by making white kids more aware of me. From then on, it was always my version they wanted.

I had only been famous for a year and a half, selling all those records in such a short period of time, when I walked out of the business. I had been a flash of lightning for two years. You could have called me "The Living Flame" for that period. But when the Russians put *Sputnik* up in the air, I felt that God was speaking to me. I wanted to be closer to God. I was in Australia with Eddie Cochran, bless his soul, and Gene Vincent, and I was afraid to come back on the plane. I was at the height of my career, but I took a detour and it gave me a beautiful exit.

When I came back in the sixties, it was shocking for me to realize how many other artists I'd influenced. I met the Beatles and introduced them to Billy Preston, who was fourteen years old and my organist at the time. The Beatles became my buddies. They used to love to hear me talk. They thought everything I said rhymed. If I had known how big they were going to become, I would have hung on to their coats and gone on with them.

When I met Mick Jagger, who was opening my show, he was in a room with Bo Diddley, sleeping on the floor. When I met Eric Burdon and the Animals, Tom Jones, the Swinging Blue Jeans, David Bowie, Cilla Black, Elton John, it was amazing to see so many people who were inspired by me. Before I had felt unworthy, but later I felt blessed and thankful that God had given me something to contribute back to mankind and to be creative in the world that God had placed me in. While I'm passing through life, I'm able to pass something along to others that will never be forgotten. I'm glad to have done what God permitted me to do. I give all the glory to His name.

Jerry Lee Lewis

o o o

Talk about a life and a career—Jerry Lee hit with such force in his few years at the top that no recounting of the beginnings of rock is complete without his story. He sounds contrite after all these years, but nothing the man does would surprise anyone who's followed his story.

o o o

In this business, whatever you do you answer to the public. The public has a right to demand answers from you, and I don't care what it is, if you do something that is even semiwrong in any kind of way, you are going to pay for it.

When I married my cousin, I paid. God, I didn't know the hole could be that deep. She was a good ole gal. We were married for fourteen years, but it didn't work out. But I knew even before I married her that I was going to pay for it. Everybody warned me—Sam Philips, Judd Philips. They said, "Oh, Jerry Lee, you are going to ruin the greatest career in the world if you marry her."

Even Elvis. He laughed. Elvis Presley said, "You're not going to marry this little girl, are you? This is a joke, isn't it?"

I said, "No, I'm going to marry her."

And he said, "Well, God bless you, Jerry Lee. You just saved my career." We were just cutting up, joking. But he knew what he was talking about because I did pay.

I remember the first time I met Elvis. He came up to Sun Records to meet me, and I wanted to meet him. Carl Perkins was doing a session, which was a flop, as usual, and Johnny Cash just happened to be there, too.

Elvis started in '53, and I started in '56. Elvis was something else. He was my main man. First time I heard an Elvis Presley record I was living in Louisiana, eighteen miles out of Monroe, where I met my first wife. I married her when I was fifteen. Shows you what sense I had. But I heard Elvis singing, "Blue moon of Kentucky, keep on shining," and I said, "Wow, looka right here. I don't know who this dude is, but somebody done opened the door."

Success for me started with "Crazy Arms," my first record. "Whole Lotta Shakin' Goin' On" was my second record, and it was banned for eight months. No one would have any part of it. Then we got it on the Steve Allen show, and it broke nationwide.

That's right around the time when I met Alan Freed. Looking back, I didn't know how to deal with success. I was a kid. I didn't really know what was going on. Probably I still don't. I never was the smartest person in the world. I just played my piano and sang my songs and left the business to people like Sam and Judd and Alan Freed. Brainy people. Without the disc jockeys, people like me couldn't have made it. We created payola through Alan Freed and Dick Clark by giving them money. They did it. I was only a kid.

I was raised Pentecostal, and I guess it's how you are raised that determines how you grow up. You learn that God is a big God. You don't put him in one corner. He spreads himself out.

I got a cousin, you know, Jimmy Swaggart. I was at his house recently, and he wants to know why I don't do what he's doing. And I tell him real quick, I don't do what he's doing because he can't do what I do. I was a preacher before he was. But I started growing up and realizing that I couldn't carry the whole world on my shoulders and tell everybody they had to be exactly like me, or otherwise they were going to hell. That is not right.

I went to Bible college in Waxahatchie, Texas, and I preached for three years. I was probably one of the best. A lot of people were saved under my missionary. A lot of people are missionaries now who were saved under my missionary. They come to see my shows, and they knew me when. But I don't try to tell Jimmy Swaggart what to do. What he's doing is right for him.

All my life I've tried to open doors. I was a stylist, and no matter what I did people related. They took notice of what I did. Whether they liked it or not, accepted it or not, dismissed it or not, it was all OK. Of course, if they dismissed it, they lost.

You make your bed, and then you have to lay in it. We learn from our mistakes. We're not perfect. I don't believe that Jerry Lee Lewis was a stupid enough person to have gotten married as many times as he did, but there had to be some reason for it. It's nobody's fault but mine.

I was lucky to have great people around me like Sam and Judd, and Jack Clement, who made the records. Jack's still in Nashville. Great ole boy. Sure could drink. Still can. I once went to a party at Jack Clement's house, me and Elvis, and we got naked and rode our motorcycles down the street. Buck naked. And this policeman on a horse sees us. It was two-thirty, three o'clock in the morning. It was awful. If anybody would have seen us, they never would have bought another record. If that cop would have arrested us, we never would have gotten out of jail.

Back then, down South where me and Elvis came from, that time of the morning all the lights are out. We didn't know there'd be a policeman on a horse. Otherwise we wouldn't have done it. It was only for thirty-five or forty seconds, 'round the corner and back. How it ever happened I will never know. We were just kids. Jack was a kid. Me and Elvis were kids. Actually, I think Elvis had shorts on. You could say Elvis was nearly naked. But it was funny.

I was very honored to be the first performer inducted into the Rock 'n' Roll Hall of Fame. Rock 'n' roll went through a lot of hell, man. People have put it through a lot of pain. But it's carried its own load, and it's come through. You are not going to beat it.

Roy Orbison

○ ○ ○

A genuine piece of rock 'n' roll history. The voice has never wavered, and the mood Roy could create in three minutes of music was and continues to be powerful enough to rate him superstar status.

○ ○ ○

I am blessed with a terrific voice. It's a God-given thing, but I sang a lot as a teenager and there were no barometers around. I was the only guy singing and playing guitar in my area. If you learn to play different songs for dances and presentations and you get a band together, you just naturally get better. By the time I started recording, they would say to me, "Do you read music?"

And I'd say, "Not enough to hurt my picking." In my case, I hadn't studied enough. Didn't have any more training than in the Glee Club in high school. If I wanted to write a high note, I just wrote it in the piece and sang along with it. That was the metamorphosis. It was letting the songwriting lead the singing.

On "Running Scared," most of the high notes were falsetto. We had thirty musicians on "Running Scared," and we did the ending with Fred Foster, and he said, "How come I can't hear the ending? We're going to lose the record if you can't give us a little more."

He said, "Run it by us one more time," and I did it in full voice. I didn't even know I could do that at the time. I didn't know there was a difference between full voice and falsetto. I could feel the difference, but I didn't understand the technical differences. Then the power of the voice came. It was a gradual thing, and it came with confidence.

I came around at a time when there was a new excitement. It wasn't pop and it wasn't country. It was a place that needed to be filled. It was rock 'n' roll, and I think, had it not opened up, Jerry Lee Lewis would still be playing Honky Tonk Joe's and singing at schools. We all would have remained back there. But the rhythm had as much to do with us getting ahead as anything. The drums. I had drums from when I was fifteen. Elvis had drums. We went to the Grand Ole Opry, but they wouldn't let us on.

When I was on tour in 1956, '57, with Eddie Cochran and Gene Vincent, in Scranton, Pennsylvania, all around on these big packaged shows, there would be acts with only one song. Maybe the song would be "Bad Days," and the next act had "Good Days," then "Lonely Days," and then "Happy Days," and then oblivion. I never wanted to be in the position where the only thing I could do was something I had already done. So I started writing songs. The first song I wrote turned out to be a big hit down the line for Jerry Lee Lewis. The second one was "Claudette" for the Everly Brothers. I didn't know if the songs were good, but the artists were good.

Sun Records had the mystique then. Johnny Cash and Elvis Presley were performing all over. I think you can point to Bruce Springsteen and U2 today. They're on the road all the time, just like Cash and Presley and the rest of us back then. It's not just the music. It's bringing the music to the people. Sun Records used to send all these people out on tour. I headed off to Sun Records because Presley did and Carl Perkins did. I had sent a demo of "Oobie Doobie," which was made at Norman Petty's studio. When I got to Sun, we started recording everything we could get our hands on. Sun was near enough, and I was young enough, and it was all superexciting. Little bitty studios, really small. But being there with everybody working actually made it seem like a workshop.

And Sam Phillips had some success under his belt. He had just sold Presley for $40,000, which is what he said—I think it was closer to $35,000—and Carl had just had a hit with "Blue Suede Shoes." Sam had to go to another pressing plant just for that record. But what Sam did was bring out these records like "That's All Right, Mama" and "Mystery Train," big thick 78s, and he said, "Sing like this." He meant "with enthusiasm and energy." Sam was exploring, going with the flow.

The technology of what made those records sound great was that they were two-track recordings. Everything would be on one track, and then you'd put echo on the second track. One track for me and the band, the other for echo. Sam was pretty much full of himself. He seemed to know what he was doing. As it turned out, I don't think he did. But he may have lived his life the way he wanted.

Elvis was bigger than life. His success was documented and laid out for him. He came to the first show I had in Memphis, and it was very nice. He sort of treated me like an equal because we were both fresh in the business. We got to be great friends and kindred souls. We both sang pop and rock 'n' roll as opposed to country, so we were sort of battling for the same chart positions. We both had Number 1 records. We both sold in the millions. We already knew we were OK in our own right. Actually, I think what kept me from being threatened by Elvis were his great records. He made great records. I didn't like them all, but I liked a lot of them. I would have resented him had he not been delivering the goods. But he made great records.

I was in New Mexico when I was with Sun Records, and I met a guy named Slim Willet who wrote "Don't Let the Stars Get in Your Eyes." He said, "How's your BMI running?"

I thought he was talking about a foul note. I didn't know what he meant. So he says, "When they play your song on the air, they pay you."

I said, "Bull." Then he told me how much he made on "Don't Let the Stars Get in Your Eyes." I told Carl Perkins, "They pay you to play those songs."

He said, "Roy, you're not telling me the truth." So we floorboarded the car all the way to Memphis to talk to Sam about it. You know, earlier on occasion Norman Petty wanted to get me on record. I put down a couple of demos, and then when I signed the contract, he had his name on it. He got half the writer's share and all of the publishing. When you're young and enthusiastic, contracts are not the main thing in your life. I don't think I was manipulated back then. Maybe a little constricted.

The image, like the voice, also came in stages. I never sat down with anyone and said, "Let's design an image." I started using sunglasses in Alabama. I was going to do a show with Patsy Cline and Bobby Vee, and I left my clear glasses on the plane. I only had the sunshades, and I was quite embarrassed to go on stage with them, but I did it. Then I took the shades with me to England when I opened for the Beatles. Going to England to open for the Beatles was not like going into Pittsburgh and trying to find out where you're going to play, do the show, and leave. Everybody was in England—the record companies, the artists, the entrepreneurs, all the media. It was an opening night to end all opening nights. I walked on stage with my sunglasses on, and all over Europe we were an instant success. Big time. I probably also wore something black that night, and that's how come the black outfits and dark sunglasses stuck.

James Brown

We spoke with James the day after his arrest for allegedly possessing seven grams of PCP. The turmoil within him might account for what was certainly an unusual interview. He lets you know that he is *the* Godfather of Soul, just in case you questioned it.

∘ ∘ ∘

When I was growing up, I wanted to be Louie Jordan. I used to see him sing in movies. This is what I looked forward to, growing up in Macon and Augusta. I wanted to sing like Louie Jordan—and be in movies and play the organ as well. I also used to sing in the choir in the Baptist church.

I had no problems growing up black, because I'm color-blind to that. I was called everything and taken advantage of, but I overlooked it. I just wanted to sing, play, be in the movies, and dance. I never took any lessons. There was a big music community in Macon. I knew Little Richard, who was a little older than me.

I never felt like I had it made. No one has it made. I never had any money, but I was able to put a band together and we started to play music. I recorded an acetate that was played on the air and someone called me to record in Tampa, Florida. It felt good to hear my music on the air. I said, "God bless me and smile on me."

I got ripped off, but I can't do anything about that. I didn't even know it was happening. I just worked hard. They call me "the Godfather of Soul." That is not tough to live up to. I just pray to God and deal with it. None of the new generation can ever be the Godfather. The only people that qualify are myself and Sinatra. It's God's business that nobody can fill my shoes.

Everything I do is God's business. I'm still out on the road, and it's still the same kick that it's always been. I just want to keep on living because each day is better.

Dick Clark

○ ○ ○

The man is an encyclopedia of rock, and during the fifties and sixties he was a parent's ultimate dream of how a disc jockey should look and act. Talented, ambitious, and with a great instinct for what sells, he's still a star thirty years later.

○ ○ ○

"Bandstand" went national in August of '57, and it took all of twenty minutes after we went off the air that first day for us to know we had a monster on our hands.

The phones started ringing off the walls, and suddenly we had this extraordinary concentration of power. Radio program directors and the disc jockeys who were on in the afternoon against us were getting slaughtered.

Every kid in the country was watching the show, and as a result, program directors had their secretaries watching the show to copy down the records we played. In other words, whatever we played, everybody else had to play because a kid, say, in Keokuk, would call a station and say, "I heard it yesterday on 'Bandstand.' How come you're not playing it?"

I was twenty-six at the time, and all of a sudden I found myself going into the music publishing business, artist management, record pressing, every conceivable angle of music I could get into. I don't remember the budget for the show, but it was so low that there was relatively no money for any of us.

So the record companies worked a kickback system with us. Artists would come on the show, and the record company would allegedly pay them for their performance. We'd pay for maybe half the people who came on, and when our money ran out, we'd say to the record company, "We'll book them and you'll pay them." It wasn't illegal, nor was it immoral. In fact, NBC was doing exactly the same thing with the Mormon Tabernacle Choir, so it was quite common.

There were two of us in the office, Tony Mamarella and me. We had seven women answering mail. The promotion men came in and out at will. We had no hours. We worked in a tiny office with two desks facing each other. The office was so small we could reach out and touch all four walls.

I never gave a moment's notice to the impact we were having on people's careers. I was too busy with my own life, trying to figure out how I was going to do the shows and also do fourteen record hops a week.

We made seventy-five cents a head on the record hops. We used to buy rolls of quarters, take in a dollar from each kid, and then give them a quarter back. The dollars we would stuff into a 45-rpm record box.

Eddie McAdam, may he rest in peace, worked with me at the time. He used to sweat profusely. Literally, he would perspire all the time. By the end of the night, the sweat would drip off the end of his tie and into the box with all the money, which was coming in hand over fist.

We'd take the boxes of money and stick them in a spare bedroom. Two or three weeks would go by and then my wife and I would try to straighten out all these crumpled, sweaty one-dollar bills.

It was a cash business and we kept immaculate books. As a matter of fact, we reported that income. Friends of mine would say, "You're what? There's no way in the world anyone's going to know where that money came from."

But I was terrified. I was making a killing, racing around trying to get all the money I could. My tentacles went in every direction. I didn't want to let an opportunity go by.

We just made things happen. One story I'll never forget was when Nat Goodman, the manager of the Diamonds, walked into the studio one day, and I said to him, "The kids are dancing something called 'the stroll' to a Chuck Willis record, 'C.C. Rider.' They line up like they're doing a Virginia Reel, and then they do this sort of stroll where they peel off down the middle."

And I asked Nat, "If we could have another stroll-type record, you'd have yourself an automatic hit."

And Nat said, "I'll have one for you next week." And bam, he goes out and does a thing with the Diamonds called "The Stroll." We stick it on the air and it's a smash.

Same thing with a combination of the cha-cha and the calypso, called the chalypso. Commissioned a guy to write a chalypso song, which turned out to be "Lucky Ladybug," with Billie and Lillie. Another hit.

It became that every single human being in the record business wanted to be on "Bandstand." I remember Tony Bennett vividly. Here's Tony Bennett, a legend, slipping behind a little bit because this newer, avant-garde music is coming along with the kids. And he'd say to me, "You got to put me on the show. I have to have another hit while I'm renegotiating my contract with Columbia." That's how big the show was.

We kept our bookings in a diary. We would book, on the average, two acts a day, fifteen a week total. One of the reasons why we used so many Philadelphia acts was because if somebody fell out, say there was a snowstorm or last-minute cancellation, we'd just pick up the phone and call somebody in South Philadelphia.

It was such an exciting period. Things seemed to happen overnight. You found a record breaking in Cleveland or Columbus, and you'd charge in there and find some guy who didn't have the wherewithal, and you'd lay a few dollars on him, take the master, give him a piece of the record, put it on the air, and the next day it would explode all over the country.

At the time, I was a 50 percent owner in Swan Records. And we used our own acts, which people looked at as a conflict of interest. I always found that amusing because I'm certain that Lawrence Welk, the biggest music publisher I knew, was using some of his copyrights on his show. But we got criticized for it.

And that led to what was not such a terrific period for me. I remember having to go to the corner drugstore, to a phone booth, to call my lawyer, because I knew our phones were tapped. Government agents broke into my house. They were a tough bunch of cookies.

And I took it on the chin a little bit, I suppose, because I was so highly visible. But I never just took money to play records. Again, it goes back to bookkeeping. With all the companies I had, we had a budget for paying guys to play records. That doesn't necessarily make it morally right, but the minute the government saw that I was an entrepreneur—the payer and not the payee—they said, "Well, he's not so bad."

There was only one man in all of my life who ever offered me money to play a record. I have no idea who he was, or what the record was, but he wanted to give me a hundred dollars to play his record. I said, "Sorry, I don't do that." Hey, I was making over half a million dollars anyway. I didn't have to bother.

Of course, making all that money didn't necessarily mean I was right all the time. For example, I remember the first time I heard a Beatles record. My friend, Bernie Binnick, played it for me. I said to him, "I don't know what the heck you're so excited about. It's highly derivative. It sounds like Buddy Holly and the Everly Brothers with a little Chuck Berry thrown in. Why are they so excited in England?"

And Bernie says, "Well, they have this different look."

I looked at their picture and said, "You're absolutely insane. It'll never fly."

But Bernie was persistent. He wanted me to play this new Beatles record on our "Rate-A-Record" portion of the show. So we did, and it got a seventy-three. The kids said they weren't terribly excited. I asked this one kid later on if he thought the Beatles would be around for long, and he said, "Oh, yeah. A long time."

I asked him, "How long?"

He looked at me and said, "Oh, about a year or two."

Hank Ballard

o o o

A seminal figure in rhythm and blues, Hank and his Midnighters made some of the most basic and influential music of their time and helped lead black music into the hip young white community. And he's still going strong.

o o o

This is going to sound strange, but Gene Autry inspired me to want to be a singer. When I first heard him sing "Back in the Saddle Again," I was turned on. I used to play hooky from school just to hear that singing cowboy sing while he was riding his horse. I'd go to the farm every summer, and I'd rattle through the wooded areas on horseback pretending I was Gene Autry.

The man who had the guts to believe in me was Sid Nathan. He was a gambler. He would take a chance on anything. I wrote this song called "Sock It to Me, Annie." The FCC says, "No, no, no." So I change it to "Roll with Me, Annie." They say, "Forget it. Another no-no." OK, it becomes "Work with Me, Annie." See, "work with me" in Detroit, in the ghetto, was the same thing as saying, "Let's get down with some sex, babe." Like, "Say, man, did you get some work last night?"

We figured the rest of the world would know what the hell we were talking about. People used to call my wife and say, "Helen, your husband must be a sex fiend. Everything he writes is about sex."

Then came the song, "Annie Had a Baby," and I knew it was going to be a smash. We did it with one microphone, cut it in the afternoon, and Sid had the record out on the street the next day. Within a week it was Top 5 R & B. The lyrics created a lot of excitement. The stockholders would come through Sid's place and want to know when I was going to write another one of those dirty ones.

I remember how the Catholic Youth Organizations would pull my records off the jukebox. Most of the complaints came out of Boston. They'd come in and snatch my records off the jukebox.

It was different with "The Twist." We were in Miami, and I was watching the Midnighters going through some routines, twisting their bodies, and the title just came to me. Then I started thinking about a track and some lyrics. In the beginning, nobody heard it but me. I put new lyrics on it. I changed the track, took it to a neighbor, and he didn't like it. But Henry Stone did. Henry was working with Sid. So Henry and I sneaked down and did a new track. When Sid Nathan heard it, he picked up my option, but he still wasn't crazy about "The Twist." In fact, they made it the B side of "Teardrops on Your Letter," which went to Number 4 on the R & B charts. But I still had that gut feeling. I said, "The hit is on the other side."

So we're out on tour, and we're in Baltimore, and we're doing "The Twist," and the kids are dancing to it. Buddy Dean calls Dick Clark and says, "The kids are going crazy over some song Hank Ballard and the Midnighters are doing."

Dick Clark replies, "I don't even want to hear it. I'm sure it's a dirty song."

Freddy Cannon was there with his manager. He might have done the song if it hadn't been for the fact that his song "Palisades Park" was climbing the charts. Freddy probably still wants to blow his manager's brains out for not letting him do that song.

Once Dick was convinced the lyrics were clean, he called in Chubby Checker. Dick auditioned a lot of guys before Chubby, but Chubby sounded pretty close to me.

Dick Clark made "The Twist." He was a teenage god. He could sneeze on a record one day and it would be a hit the next day. Dick started out playing my version of the song, then he switched to Chubby's. Since Sid was the publisher of both versions, I knew he had sold me down the river. But that was OK. A lot of people had tried to catch Sid in some of the things he was doing. The only people who ever caught him were his own stockholders. They caught him bootlegging his own records in Cleveland, Ohio.

I was in Miami another time, taking this swim, and I hear "The Twist" blasting across this pop radio station. I said, "Goddamn, man, I am getting popular now." But it wasn't me, it was Chubby Checker. I actually thought it was me. They went and did a clone of my record. But that was OK, too. It was the best thing ever happened to my career. Suddenly, I'm being booked all over the place. I think it was a blessing in disguise, too, because if I had that kind of fame and money during that time, I probably would have ended up strung out on some kind of drug.

Paul Robi

o o o

The Platters were another of the key record makers of the fifties, and Paul was with them from the opening shot. They toured the world, took more than their share of bumps, but can still claim title to some of the best records of their day.

o o o

The five Platters were the most compatible group of people you could imagine. We loved each other dearly. It was always us against the world. There was a lot outside the group to fight, like prejudice. We couldn't go in the front door at most places. And we were also at the mercy of people like our manager, Buck Ram. But musically, at least, we were smart enough to arrange around the vocal.

We first started out in '53, '54, and we were playing clubs up and down the coast of California. We rehearsed in Los Angeles and we played the so-called black clubs on Central Avenue. Black people from Hollywood and everywhere else came to see the black acts perform.

Earl Grant was a good friend of ours, and he would allow us to come in and sing on his show. That's how we got our start, on a high level of show business, not singing the blues.

The first time we went to Vegas was from the Slim Jenkins supper club in Oakland. We played in Vegas on the black side of town in a club called the Moulin Rouge. When other things started closing for the night in Vegas, people would start coming into the Moulin Rouge at one o'clock in the morning. We were just starting out. We didn't have a record out, nothing.

One night this group called the Honeytones drops out, and this guy says, "Hey, why don't you use the Platters." Benny Carter was the bandleader, Dinah Washington was one of the headliners, all the greats. They had a black chorus line, Buck and Bubbles, authentic people, the greatest of all time.

When our first two records hit, "Only You" and "The Great Pretender," it was like we were getting away with murder because people in the South did not know we were black until we got on "The Ed Sullivan Show," and by that time it was too late. People had been having babies to "Only You." They played it at wedding ceremonies.

We went to Europe and played a command performance at the Palladium in London. We met the pope, just the Platters and the pope. Never in the history of the Vatican had that happened with a group of singers, but we had become that popular.

And after we finished in Europe we got a call that said we'd be going to Vegas for a second time around. We came back to the States and bought these Thunderbirds with the little wheels in the back, beautiful clothes, gifts for friends. We were so pleased to be going back to Vegas. Never did we think there were going to be any problems. We had been sailing along, working together, and things had fallen into place.

But when we drove to Vegas, to the Flamingo where we were scheduled to work, the guy in front asks me if he can help me, and I say, "Yeah, can you take these bags?"

And he says, "Oh, no. You have to go around the back."

I couldn't believe it. We had just come back to the United States and now we gotta go through all that crap again. Everyone in the group said, "Let's get out of here. Forget it."

And I said, "No. The best thing for us to do is stay here and just be better than anybody else."

So we stayed. They gave us a little room right by the kitchen. It was such a blow because it was happening to us at a very vulnerable time in our lives—at a time when, had we been white, we could have done things like Wayne Newton or Bobby Vinton. I look back on it now as though what we got was a good deal. It just made me fight that much harder.

Pat Boone

o o o

The name alone represented a genre of music in the early stages of
rock. Pat's scrubbed looks and boy-next-door manner made the songs
much more palatable to millions who couldn't quite get Little Richard,
Fats Domino, and others. Pat doesn't apologize but provides a
rationale for his approach to the music.

o o o

I thought I would be a high school teacher who had once upon a time made
a couple of records. Little did I know that by the time I graduated from
college—Columbia University, 1958—that I would have four children, a
million-dollar television contract, and a million-dollar movie contract.

Hugh Cherry was a very prominent disc jockey in Nashville, and he
helped a lot of people. Hugh took an interest in me, and brought me to
Randy Woods' attention. Randy liked what he heard. Some of the songs
Randy heard me sing on shows like "The Ted Mack Amateur Hour" and
Arthur Godfrey's show were "I Believe," "I'm Walking behind You," a Perry
Como ballad, "No Other Love," and a song Kay Starr was doing, "Side by
Side." Why Randy thought I could sing a rock 'n' roll song like "Two Hearts,
Two Kisses," I really don't know.

At the time Randy was having some success with the Fontaine Sisters
and a couple of other pop acts who were doing cover versions of R & B
songs and turning them into what we people were beginning to call rock 'n'
roll.

Anyway, Randy and I shook hands over a hamburger in Gallatin, Tennessee. He said, "You go back to Denton, Texas, give me your phone
number, and when I find the right song, I will call you within six weeks,
and we'll go to Chicago and you'll record it."

Well, six weeks came and went. Then, two months, three months, six
months, nothing. I just assumed he'd forgotten. He finally calls me in
February of '56, and he plays "Two Hearts, Two Kisses" over the phone,
and he says it's going to be a smash. Randy's favorite word.

I'm imagining a Perry Como or Eddie Fisher sort of ballad, in three-
quarter time, and Randy puts on this little R & B thing by the Charms, and
I hear, "One heart's not enough, baby. Two hearts'll make you feel crazy.
One kiss'll make you feel so nice. Two kisses'll take you to paradise. Two
hearts, two kisses make one love."

I said, "Randy, do you have that thing on the right speed?"

He said, "It's a smash, an R & B smash, and you're going to make a
hit record out of it."

Randy didn't just get the thing recorded, he constantly called DJs, rack
jobbers, distributors, and kept them aware of what was happening in every
other part of the country. He felt he had to because there were other covers
of "Two Hearts, Two Kisses"—Frank Sinatra, Doris Day, the Ames Brothers,

the Lancers. There were at least ten records out of that song, and here I was an unknown.

Hearing a record of mine on the air for the first time was the closest I ever came to being drunk. Probably my most exciting moment came after I recorded "Ain't That a Shame." I was on a side street in New York City. It was late August, I think, real hot. I had the windows down and I was driving. I pulled up to a traffic light and a car full of kids pulls up right next to me. They didn't recognize me, but they had the radio tuned to WINS and Alan Freed was playing my record. These kids were bouncing up and down in the car, and they looked right at me and had no idea that I was the guy they were listening to. It was the headiest feeling I ever had as an entertainer.

Regarding this thing about covers, everybody was aware that the original artists were not going to get played on 90 percent of the radio stations in America. They were not going to play an R & B record by Chuck Berry, or Fats Domino, or Little Richard. In fact, the original artists hoped and prayed their records would get covered by someone who could get airplay because it meant their records were going to get even more recognition in their own field. It would change later on, and the cover record would become virtually nonexistent, but we were sort of like catalysts who helped R & B become rock 'n' roll. It was not until after the covers died that I became aware of how people had looked down their noses at us.

See, I had already met Little Richard and Fats Domino, and they told me what it meant to them for me to record one of their songs. I went to see Fats Domino at Al Hirt's place in New Orleans. When he heard I was in the audience, he called me up on stage and he said to the crowd, "I want you all to know something. You see this ring?" He had a big diamond ring on every one of his fingers, and he pointed to the most prominent of his diamond rings and he said, "This man bought me this ring with this song," and the two of us sang "Ain't That a Shame" together.

I felt a great sense of camaraderie with the original artists. I knew I was benefiting them as writers. I had to change the lyrics to several of Little Richard's songs. The changes were minor, but they were important to me. And they didn't seem to bother him. Part of "Tutti Frutti" went, "Boy, you don't know what she's doing to me." I just couldn't sing that, so I sang, "Pretty little Suzie is the girl for me." It worked just as well. The kids didn't care. I mean, they weren't listening to the words much anyway.

Del Shannon

○ ○ ○

**More than a one-hit wonder, but the one big song will be his
trademark as long as oldies are played. Del had his troubles
personally and professionally but finds the impact of "Runaway" can
still keep him in the trade.**

○ ○ ○

All I ever wanted as a kid was respect, and I never got it.

My father worked as a truck driver. He drank a bit, and he moved us
out to the country where there was nothing but farms and Dutch Hollanders.

After I grew up a bit, I wanted to prove to everyone in town that I could
be somebody. I never went to church that much 'cause I didn't fit in.
Everyone would always laugh at me. I used to pick strawberries, and one
day I said, "Someday I'm going to be in the movies." And of course they
all laughed at me.

And then I picked up a guitar, and they all loved that, except that when
I got out of high school, everyone started saying, "Yeah, but when's this guy
going to get a job?" You know, like nobody just plays a guitar. But I had
that drive in me to just play a guitar and sing.

I wanted to be a country singer. I grew up playing in a bar in Battle
Creek, Michigan, called the Hi-Lo Club. Worked there a lot in '58
under the name Charlie Johnson with a band called the Big Little Show
Band.

One of the guys I worked with, someone who was a country singer, he
was a real drunk, and I was his guitar player. Doug Demont was his name,
and he started doing a little rock 'n' roll like Elvis' "Heartbreak Hotel." So
I started learning those licks.

Then I got into Jerry Lee Lewis, and Paul Anka, and then I started
writing songs with my piano player, Max Crook.

Max is out somewhere in the middle of the desert. He is into religion
now. He records religious groups. But back then Max was this amazing guy.
His father was a big brain surgeon in Ann Arbor, and Max was going to
college and he got nearly to the end of eight years but he quit because he
loved music so much.

Max used to record under the name Maximilian, and I would say to
him, "If either one of us ever makes it," you help the other guy.

In three hours one day, Max and I cut "Jodie," the B side of "Runaway,"
"Runaway," "The Snake," and some other song he wrote. Max's record
came out and it didn't do too well. "Runaway" took off.

It all started at the High-Low Club one night when Max and I were on
stage. Max hit an A minor on his piano, and then he went to G.

I said, "Shit, what was that great change?" 'cause all we were doing
was C, A minor, F, and G chords. And then I said, "Well, shit, play that

again, and follow me." And I just played the chords and sang any words I could think of.

The next day, I sat down at the carpet store where I worked and wrote the words. That night, I called Max and said, "Bring your tape recorder to the club, and when we're on stage and I point to you, play an instrumental. And he played an instrumental that he never changed a note of after that, and that was how we wrote "Runaway." I always wanted to run away. I think everybody wants to run away, which is why the song still grabs everyone, even today.

Anyway, the song took off, and I was thrilled. I called up my manager and I said, "How's 'Runaway' selling?"

He said, "Oh, about 80,000 records a day."

I didn't know whether he was lying or what, but I said, "I don't know how much that is, but it sounds pretty good. What does it mean?"

He said, "It means you're going to open on Broadway next week."

So now I'm on Broadway, in one of Murray the K's shows with Jackie Wilson, Dion, and Bobby Vee, and I'm real nervous. My manager says, "Forget the guitar. Be like Sinatra. You'll wear a tie and cuff links," and hell, I'm from out in the sticks, and all I want to do is kick ass, and he takes my guitar away and I don't know what to do with my hands. I'm a nervous wreck.

I'm doing five shows a day, doing my one hit, and then I'm back in this tiny dressing room and Dion walks in and says, "Look at this guy's clothes! Red socks, red tie, black suit. Where'd you get this stuff?"

And I'm saying to myself, "Who is this guy from New York? He sounds like a thug, like so many guys I've heard in the movies." I was scared to death, and even though he sounded as if he belonged in a cage, Dion and I got to be great friends. He even took me across the street to buy a pair of black socks to go with my black suit.

I had a tough time handling the success. At times, I wished I was back in the strawberry patch. The fear was unbearable. I didn't know what the hell I was doing.

And then I started to drink. That made it easier.

There was such a gigantic pressure on me to deliver. I'd go out on a Dick Clark tour and I'd run into a lot of other artists who were just pissing around at parties. They had songwriters writing for them, and I always envied that. Like Bobby Vee. He never partied much, and he's a great guy and a great friend of mine, but he had all these Carole King songs, and I'd think, "God, how easy."

And I'd be in my dressing room trying to clunk out a few songs. My manager always used to say to me, "You're only as good as your last hit." Or, "You know, you only have five years left in this business, so you better get off your ass. Quit the partying and get into writing some songs because you're a writer."

And I said, "Call Carole King and get her to write me some great songs so I can have time to party." But he never did.

So I had a few hits, and then I fell off. It's too bad I was such an obsessive person. I became obsessed with having hits. It isn't so bad now because I don't drink anymore and I can deal with it. But when you get into the position where you're obsessed with having hits, then you truly do become as good as your last hit.

Marshall Chess

o o o

A member of a royal family of R & B and rock 'n' roll, Marshall gives us some great insights into the workings of the recording company founded by his father and uncle, who signed most of the great Chicago blues artists, and others like Chuck Berry.

o o o

My father, Leonard Chess, and his brother Phil came to America from Poland. My grandfather had already been in Chicago for ten years. Typical case, where he came here by himself to earn money and then send for the family.

My grandfather had a scrap metal junkyard in a ghetto neighborhood in Chicago, so my father's first exposure was to black people. Eventually, my father opened up a liquor store in the ghetto. Then he progressed to a few different taverns. Then, in 1945, he had a club called the Mocambo Lounge. Live entertainment. A big, black nightclub that specialized in jazz music and was a hangout for musicians, whores, and dope dealers.

My father would see live recording equipment being brought in. He began to talk to people, and it didn't take him long before he realized there was a market for race records. Then he met a man named Art Sheridan, and they started Aristocrat Records. One of Aristocrat's first artists was Muddy Waters.

Chicago was the center for Delta musicians. They'd come up from West Arkansas by the hundreds. They came right off the plantations of Mississippi to Chicago. They'd ride up the Illinois Central from Memphis.

My father knew what these people wanted. He knew there was a market for their records.

Soon he found out that his partners were cheating him. Within two years he was able to buy them out and change Aristocrat to Chess. Chess was spelled with a z then, but was changed to an s on Ellis Island.

My own experience in the record business began when I was very young. I had a real father hangup. I never saw my father. He had records during the day and the club at night. He was home very little. I found early that the only way I could see my father was to go to work with him, so I began very young.

I was in the shipping room. I loaded trucks. One time I asked my father what my job was. He got pissed at me and said, "Your job is watching me."

I went on the road at thirteen. I drove the car for my father in the South. I'd sit on pillows, making those little stops with him. We would go to see the disc jockeys, and we'd have records in the trunk of his car, a '53 Cadillac, two-tone blue, the first car with air conditioning.

We'd go into these little towns and stop at the radio stations. We would see the disc jockey, most of the time pay him off. Sometimes we'd stay in a motel without the disc jockey knowing about it, listening to see if the guy really played the record or if he was pulling one of his tricks.

Payola was how you got your records played. It was how you did business. Nowadays it's a whole other kind of sleazy style, but back then it was totally open. "You help me, and I'll help you."

My father developed a way to feel, I think, by osmosis. If he liked it, it usually sold. He definitely knew what black people wanted.

Muddy Waters was our first really big artist. He was the biggest of the Delta blues singers. His was the first electric band. Muddy Waters was like a king. He had tremendous presence. You never treated Muddy Waters with disrespect. He was a leader, always in control, always a gentleman. He liked women and Cadillacs.

In a way, Muddy was an immigrant, just like my father. Muddy came from a farm where you made fifty cents a day. He came to Chicago, just like my father, and what's an immigrant's big dream? To make money. My father and the blues singers were there to make money, not to make great music. It was never a head trip of, "Let's make great music. Music is art." That wasn't it. The main reason was to make money.

We heard about Muddy when he was still driving a truck. My father called him up and said, "Come to Chess." He came by and we recorded him.

Chuck Berry was the first artist that crossed over for us. Chuck came to Chicago and he went to see Muddy Waters. That's like, when you're in London, you go to see Mick Jagger. Muddy was Chuck's idol. Berry was a blues singer. The B side of "Maybellene" is "Wee Wee Hours," a twelve-bar blues song in the Muddy Waters style.

Anyway, Chuck went to see Muddy, and he walked up to him after the set and said, "Look, I have a band. I have music. Where should I go?"

Muddy said, "Go see Chess."

Chuck Berry came in with a song called "Ida Red." My father listened to it and said, "You've got something here that's different, but I don't like the lyrics. Come back with some new ones."

One week later, he came back with "Maybellene," and my father instantly recorded it. My father used to say, "If Chuck Berry were white, he'd be bigger than Elvis Presley."

But that whole period—'54, '55, '56, '57—it wasn't just Chuck Berry.

We were flying. We had Chuck Berry, Bo Diddley, Howlin' Wolf, Sonny Boy Williamson, Muddy Waters, Little Walter, Memphis Slim, John Lee Hooker, Etta James. In doo-wop, we had the Moonglows and the Flamingos. In comedy, we had Moms Mabley.

I remember going to the first disc jockey convention in Florida. It was the first time I tried marijuana. Artie Ripp turned me on.

My father died in '69. He was 52. I stayed on as president of Chess under the GRT Corporation, but I hated it. GRT had no understanding of black music or a family-owned business. One day I called Mick Jagger up and said, "This is Marshall Chess."

He said, "Oh, Marshall, how are you?"

I said, "I'm out of work. I quit my job and I'm wondering, is there a chance we could have a relationship?"

He said, "That's exciting, but I can't come to America right now, I was just busted for amphetamines." That's what he told me. He said, "Can you come to London?" Two weeks later, I hopped on a plane, went to London, and that's how Rolling Stones Records began, and with it came more drugs.

It was very difficult for me to kick drugs. I stopped with the Stones in '77, and I was off drugs in '78. I had been strung out on heroin, coke, quaaludes. Spent a half a million on drugs, took nineteen drug cures. Everytime the Stones had another project, I would wind up in some other drug clinic trying to get well.

Phil Everly

o o o

Phil and his brother, Don, influenced almost every vocal group in rock 'n' roll. Their sound was one of a kind. While one might not be able to "go home again," their recent reunion reminded us of what an unbelievable lineup of monster hit records they had—and how sweet they all sounded.

o o o

Basically, every rock 'n' roller is a hybrid of some very diverse influences, and we were no exception. But our most direct influence was Dad and all that Kentucky heritage.

Chet Atkins knew of Dad and they corresponded every once in a while. When we got to Nashville, Dad asked Chet whether he'd be able to do anything for the boys. Chet had this publishing company, so we went over there and showed him some songs. Donald had written this one song called "Thou Shall Not Steal." Chet got Kitty Wells to cut it and it went Top 10.

Now you gotta remember, I'm fourteen at the time and Donald is sixteen, and he writes this hit, and it gets us into the union and provides us with enough money to buy our first cowboy suits. It also puts tires on the Chevy, and gets Donald several pair of suede shoes.

Then we got signed to Columbia, and they put a record out. It's still the funniest story of my whole life. We cut four sides in twenty minutes, and I still don't believe they would have signed us but for this one lady. We auditioned up in a hotel room, and this lady was there and she said, "Oh, they're so cute." And we were signed.

Don and I got a $200 publishing advance from Hill and Range. Well, Columbia released the first side, and we spent the entire $200 on 2,000 fold-out promotional copies of the second release, which never came out because the first one had died so miserably.

So our $200 was gone. And that was major money at the time, the difference between living and dying.

We hung around borderline broke for the next two years. We auditioned for every label in the United States, were turned down at least ten times. Then we got this girl we knew to talk this guy into giving us the use of a studio to make a tape. God knows what she promised him, but he gave us some free time. While we were in the studio recording, our car was towed and we had to get the girl to borrow twenty dollars from the studio guy so we could get our car back.

Well, when we finished the tape, we sent it to off to Archie Bleyer at Cadence Records and he turned it down.

Six months later, we were still borderline and hanging around Nashville, just about to give up and go North to find a job, when a friend of ours suggested we show our songs to Acuff-Rose, the publishers. Wesley Rose thought we were pretty good. Even though Archie had turned us down previously, Wes said he'd talk to him about us.

Acuff-Rose is where we got "Bye Bye Love," a song written by Boudleaux Bryant. The intro, which is the major innovation on "Bye Bye Love," came off a song Donald had written called "Give Me a Future." We cut the intro off Don's, put it on "Bye Bye Love," and it worked.

Another big break was when we were hired to do one of those Grand Ole Opry tent shows, the ones that moved all over the South, and the only reason they could get away with calling it the Grand Ole Opry was because Bill Monroe was headlining it.

This thing was a real carnival operation. It cost fifty cents to get in and another quarter to sit in the segregated seats. And it cost still another twenty-five cents to see the rock 'n' roll portion of the show.

The show was playing in Hattiesburg, Mississippi—a very rough town—and the radio station in town was playing "Bye Bye Love." We were sitting somewhere with Mel Tillis. It seemed like whenever Mel put out a record, Webb Pierce covered it. Webb had, like, twenty-four Number 1 records in a row.

Well, word comes to us that Webb has covered "Bye Bye Love." We tell Mel, and I'll never forget his reaction. He didn't say a word. He just dropped his head in his hands, like it was all over for us. He knew Webb's power, and so did we. Donald then got on the phone and called Archie Bleyer and said, "Archie, I got some terrible news. Webb Pierce has covered our record."

And Archie said, "Webb who?" Archie didn't know who Webb was.

It didn't really register with me how big "Bye Bye Love" was until this one time when we were playing Buffalo, and a jock there started playing the record at a sock hop. All the kids would sing along. So the jock recorded his version with 2,000 kids singing it, and he played it over the air. That's when it hit me how big the record had become.

With our next record, "Wake Up Little Suzie," which was another Boudleaux Bryant song, we still didn't have any idea what we were doing. But Boudleaux seemed to have an understanding of what we were up to. His idea of how to guide you was to show you twenty songs, and not tell you the ones he liked or didn't like. He'd sort of let you make the decision.

We went through almost every song he had, and we kept saying no. But when he got to "Wake Up Little Suzie," he left holes in the intro for us, which was creative thinking on his part, but then Boudleaux was a very brilliant man.

Well, we went on to cut "Wake Up Little Suzie" twenty-eight times with Archie, and we got into a huge hassle over it. He went back to New York, and we came in the next day and got it in about three takes.

It's common in the record business that after a few records people begin saying, "You're only as good as your last record." But I learned a lesson when I was eighteen years old, back in the days when we were doing the Alan Freed shows in New York. The audience would scream for us, and I'd think, "My God, they love us. They're never going to quit." And then they would announce the next act and the screaming would get louder.

You always have to have a realistic attitude. You never expect that your popularity will last forever. It's like a foot race.

When Donald and I split up, I did basically nothing for the next ten years. During that period, people would ask me what was wrong with me, and I'd say I was suffering from an acute case of stupidity. You get at odds, and Donald and I were both very opinionated.

It was nothing you could really lay you finger on. Frayed nerves, maybe. Frayed times, divorces—regular life struggles. So we quit, got off the treadmill, put it all aside.

During our time apart there were always people around trying to get us back together. But it was up to us to settle it, or not.

When Dad got sick, we talked. We hadn't talked for years, maybe five or six years, until we met at the hospital, and then again at Dad's funeral. And when we did talk, we never talked like anything was wrong. We never snarled at each other.

And then Donald finally gave me a call. You know, when you get older, you start thinking you might die. And we didn't want to end things like that. It wouldn't have been right.

For what it's worth, I believe if they ever had a singing Olympics, Donald and I would get Top 3, if not win some gold. If you put us all together and let us have a sing-off, we could hold our own with anybody from any era. That maybe sounds a little prideful, but it's what I believe.

Of course, if I had it all to do over again, if I had known Donald and I were going to last, I would have laughed in their faces and probably had a better time.

Dion

Dion's life reads like a novel. He hit the top with a succession of record triumphs, then dropped to the bottom with a monumental drug addiction. His subsequent return to the human race and his dedication to religious music make for a marvelous Act III.

∘ ∘ ∘

Back in the old days, in my neighborhood, we spent all day listening to songs like "Earth Angel" by the Penguins. Rock 'n' roll was in its infancy, the jukeboxes were going full blast, and we were singing on street corners.

I knew a few guys who could just hang by a jukebox and fall asleep standing up listening to it.

For me, music was a ticket out. I was very intense and real confused as a kid, so I grabbed on to music and got a guitar because I wanted to make the same sound I was hearing on the radio.

I come from a rough neighborhood in the Bronx. They were born animals on Belmont Avenue, and a lot of kids I knew died from zip guns. At the time, gangs were happening, and I belonged to a gang, but something deep inside of me knew I was acting when I punched someone in the face. Something inside of me was saying, "Hey, this isn't you." So I found that I could get recognition through playing a song.

We sang on the beaches, or on rooftops, or in hallways of tenement buildings. We must have been sensitive artists, even back then, because we always looked for the hallway that had the best sound.

But it was never part of my psyche that there was a music business, or that I could get into it. One Valentine's Day, though, I took the Sixth Avenue D train down to Manhattan. A songwriter from my neighborhood had told me where I could make this record for my mom. It was called "Wonderful Girl." The flip side was for my father, and it was called "Bopping the Blues," a Carl Perkins song. When I gave the record to my parents, they told me about someone else whose friend's friend knew a guy who was starting a record company.

It seemed this guy was looking to make the transition from recording crooners to a more modern sound. So they heard this record of mine, and they liked it. I went down to see them, and they played me some tracks, and I said, "You wanna hear some rock 'n' roll? Let me bring in these guys I've been singing with." That was the beginning of Dion and the Belmonts. I was seventeen.

The first thing they told us was that we sang flat. Listening back to all those old records—"I Wonder Why," "Teenager in Love," "Lonely Teenager"—I guess I have to agree with them. We really did sing flat.

Flat or not, though, we were good. When I think back to four kids with spaghetti stains on their T-shirts, singing and snapping their fingers, I can remember how great it felt. I mean, we were hot stuff. Music gave me an identity. All of a sudden I was the kid with the record on the radio.

It became an entire neighborhood experience. On Saturday nights, either Alan Freed or Murray the K would start counting down, and they would say, "Number 1 this week—Dion and the Belmonts," and the whole neighborhood would open their windows and yell to my father, "Hey, Fred, that's your boy."

We felt so hot that we traded in our T-shirts and went out and got these cardigan sweaters. We were so tacky that we got paint and squeezed out "The Belmonts" on the sidewalk like whipped cream.

We'd walk down Belmont Avenue and every radio in the neighborhood had us on, and you'd hear these voices across the alleyways and in the backyards of the tenement buildings. As soon as the record was over, the people would begin wheeling in their clothes from the clothesline and talk about us to their friends in the next building.

The music just turned inside of me. I got into this business because of Chuck Berry doing "Maybellene," and Fats Domino doing "Blueberry Hill," and all those early Phil Spector records. I sensed back then that I had the gift, this ability to put across these little, four-minute-long motion pictures.

My Phil Spector experience is a book in itself. I'm getting ready to make a record with him much later on, and I'm in his mansion with a lot of dogs and an electronic fence, and Phil comes downstairs and we start talking about music. All of a sudden he gets a phone call that George, his bodyguard, has just had a heart attack.

Phil says, "C'mon, we're going to the UCLA emergency room." The next thing I know, he runs upstairs and throws $100,000 in cash into a paper bag.

We get to UCLA, and he throws the money on the counter and says, "I'm Phil Spector. I speak seven languages. My friend George has just had a heart attack. I don't care if you have to fly in the greatest specialist in the world, you get him here right now."

The people in the emergency room look down at all that money, then at him, and they say, "No, Phil, you don't understand."

I was a kid from the Bronx with a limited education, and I was lucky to get out. But I also can remember how easily it could have ended. I was on that tour in 1959 with Buddy Holly, Ritchie Valens, and the Big Bopper.

Buddy and I had Fender guitars and Ritchie Valens and I would compete to see who could make the guitar ring the loudest. Buddy had asked me to fly with them because, he said, the more people on the plane, the less it would cost. I didn't go because I was cheap. I didn't want to spend anything extra.

When that plane went down, it was like having a carpet ripped out from under you. It was so baffling. Here you are, on the greatest high of your life, playing for packed arenas everywhere, and then something like that happens.

I started asking myself, "Who am I? Why am I here? Is this all there is?" And then the telegrams started pouring in from all over the country—Bobby Darin, Frankie Avalon, Paul Anka, Jerry Lee Lewis. That's what got us through. Our friends were encouraging us with their prayers. It helped us to know we weren't alone.

Jerry Leiber and Mike Stoller

o o o

It's difficult to separate them, though they are truly individual talents. Their writing and producing inspired many of the hit writers who followed them, and their presence in every music hall of fame is indicative of the respect they command among their peers.

o o o

My parents were Polish-Russians, and the neighborhood we lived in in Baltimore was mostly Polish Catholic. But my mother's grocery store was right on the edge of the black ghetto, so it was a dual culture.

Of the two areas, I dug the ghetto more. That for me was where it was happening. For everyone else, though, there were race wars going on. There were a lot of problems in that neighborhood, but my mother's store was untouchable. It was the only store within four miles that extended credit to black people. Nobody else did. Consequently, I was a welcome character in the black neighborhood.

Being exposed to the black culture like I was, I began picking up the idiom. My neighborhood was really anti-Semitic, and most of the kids didn't like me. Naturally, they didn't like black people either. I identified with the blacks. I felt very sympathetic to them, and they were sympathetic to me.

I imitated black cultural attitudes for so long as a child that it became second nature to me. When we moved to Los Angeles, I started going to

John Burrows Junior High, an integrated school. In Baltimore, I was used to segregated schools, and then a whole separate group of black friends who talked street talk. In L.A., I was surprised to find that the black kids in school spoke much better English than I did.

I started writing lyrics when I was about sixteen. The lyrics came out of the blues I was listening to on the black stations. "Hound Dog" comes out of that experience. Also, the kind of "playwriting" songs I wrote for the Coasters, a lot of that stuff was influenced by what I heard on the radio, programs like "The Shadow," "Gangbusters," and "Amos 'n' Andy."

I just wrote and it came out the way it did. I was looking for a form to put my stories in and Mike Stoller played the piano a certain way, and that's how it turned out. I played all the roles. I was an actor. I would play the heavy, or the girl, and Mike would have to score all that shit.

I don't know where ideas come from. I read the papers, I overhear people talking. I don't research something that I think may be interesting to write. I believe that stuff gets shaken up somewhere that you're conscious of, or not conscious of, and then it just floats to the surface. One day you pick it up and you get the signal. Sometimes it comes out in rhyme and other times it comes out in bits and pieces. I play with it, I don't even write it down right away.

"Hound Dog" just came leaping out. Mike played and I yelled. Same thing with "Kansas City," although that took a little longer because Mike created a melody that was not the traditional twelve-bar blues. But those songs were spontaneous efforts.

When you get down to constructing a song that is mapped out with dialogue, like "Along Came Jones," or "Little Egypt," where you have characters speaking lines and a narrative, then it becomes more complex and a different kind of effort.

Not all our songs were like that, of course. I first sketched out the song "Is That All There Is?" in 1966. We tried it fifteen different ways. Nothing. I rewrote it again in 1968 for Georgia Brown, and still it was wrong. In '69 we did it with Peggy Lee and it was an enormous smash. We felt, "OK, we've hit our stride for our adult years. We can write adult material for adult audiences." It was fun, but not as much fun as writing jokes for the Coasters.

Peggy is one of the great singers. My two favorite singers were Billie Holiday and Lee Wiley, and then of course there's Ella Fitzgerald and Sarah Vaughan. But Peggy is definitely up there with the greats. She's also a first-rate songwriter and has a marvelous sense of humor.

We also could fight like hell. In 1961 I tried to tell her how to sing, and she told me to mind my own business. I fought with her over "Is That All There Is?" We did thirty-six takes of that song. Peggy said she had never done that many takes in all the years she'd been singing. The most she goes, she said, was two or three takes.

But we did thirty-six takes of "Is That All There Is?" at my insistence. She was ready to kill me, she was so hoarse and tired. But I was unrelenting.

Stangely enough, the technician erased the best take. I never told Peggy.

With most of the acts we worked with, I almost always directed the singers, especially the ones we wrote special material for, like the Coasters and the Drifters and the Clovers.

With Elvis Presley, no direction was needed. He always knew what to do. He learned the songs from the demos we had given him, and then he'd imitate the demo singers. If Jeff Barry was the singer on the demo, Elvis would imitate Jeff Barry.

But the few times we made records with Presley—"Loving You," "Jailhouse Rock," "Treat Me Nice"—once the rhythm section started to cook, he would just start singing. And the man never made a bad take. One was better than the other, and different than the other. He was like an Olympic champion. He could sing all day.

Of the guys who came along later, Randy Newman is first-rate. He was probably influenced a little bit by our work. Randy did the arrangement on "Is That All There Is?" with Peggy Lee, and that was before Randy ever did arrangements. I heard his early work and I said, "He's great. Let's get him."

Billy Joel is awfully good, too, but he's a straight pop writer. I consider Randy a more important writer, a more serious writer. A poet, actually.

Lionel Richie and Stevie Wonder write great-sounding instrumental records, but if you're talking songwriting, Burt Bacharach is a great songwriter and a great composer.

Ultimately, the Beatles are second to none in all departments. I don't think there has ever been a better song written than "Eleanor Rigby."

o o o

When I was about thirteen, fourteen, or fifteen, I had these aspirations to be a jazz player, which was OK except for the fact that I had to take stock of myself and say, "Hey, I'm not Art Tatum, I'm not Bud Powell." And even though I loved Rodgers and Hart and Gershwin, I really had no use for the so-called "let me take you in my arms and thrill to all your charms" kind of songs. They were fabrications, superbland. And while I have a great deal of respect for Mitch Miller and Tony Martin singing "Kiss of Fire," I frankly believe that a lot of those songs were bullshit and funny at the same time because they were so terrible.

My partner, Jerry Leiber, felt very much the same way. Our taste for the blues was what became our common ground.

We responded to black records and to white people who lived a black life-style, like Johnny Otis, who was white of Greek extraction. He lived pretty much of a black life. His band was all black, he traveled the black circuit, he was married to a black woman. All that was highly unusual.

It was working with Johnny Otis that led to our unofficially taking over the reins as producers. And that was with Big Mama Thornton on our song "Hound Dog."

The entire process can be a funny thing. Sammy Cahn says the writing process begins when you get the phone call. When Jerry and I started writing, it was a kind of spontaneous combustion. I'd sit at the piano and start playing something. And the words would just start coming out of Jerry's mouth. "Hound Dog," for example, was written in about ten minutes after we'd met Big Mama Thornton at a rehearsal at Johnny Otis' house. And "Kansas City" was probably written in no more than an hour. Others took longer, of course, but the original concept, the premise, came almost automatically.

Still, Jerry and I would fight like cats and dogs—over syllables, or a note, or a phrase. It never came to blows, but it could get rough. Naturally, the next day we'd make up and that would be the end of it.

In 1956 Ahmet Ertegun and Jerry Wexler at Atlantic started asking us to write songs for some of their artists—Ruth Brown, the Coasters, the Drifters, and so forth.

And '56 was also the year Elvis came out with his version of "Hound Dog." I'll never forget this, I was on the *Andrea Doria*, and when the boat finally arrived in New York after everything that had happened, there was Jerry standing there on the dock with some clothes for me. And the very first thing he tells me is about Elvis doing "Hound Dog." I thought that was nice because I had heard of Elvis Presley.

A year later, Jerry and I decided to move to New York for good. We had gotten a taste of New York, and there seemed to be more action there. It was the hub of everything, and of course, that's where Atlantic Records was located.

We moved into 1650 Broadway, where people like Don Kirshner and Carole King and Gerry Goffin and Neil Sedaka and Cynthia Weil would eventually come. These people were always referred to as "Brill Building composers," even though they weren't in the Brill Building, which was 1619 Broadway. We moved around between both buildings, and also Atlantic, which was at 157 West 57th Street, just across the street from the Russian Tea Room.

We did most of our writing, though, either at Jerry's apartment, or at my apartment, or in Atlantic's waiting room, which had an upright piano in it.

The only social thing we ever did was a drink at Al & Dick's, which was where all the song pluggers and company A & R heads met after work.

In a way, we functioned as kind of senior advisers to a wonderfully talented group of writers that included Carole and Gerry, Doc Pomus and Morty Shuman, Barry Mann and Cynthia. We would ask for them for songs, we would criticize, we would suggest—all primarily out of a sense of our being producers. If we wanted to make a record and we felt the song could be strengthened, we contributed, frequently without taking any credit.

By '60 or '61 we started our own record company, Redbird. We took in a partner, a master promoter by the name of George Goldner, and our first release went Number 1, "Chapel of Love" with the Dixie Cups, which was written by Jeff Barry, Ellie Greenwich, and Phil Spector. In the first nine months of our company, we had eight Top 10 singles with big acts like the Dixie Cups and the Shangri-Las and the Jelly Beans. We were hot.

Phil Spector was a kid then. He wanted to come to New York and hang out with us. We sent him a ticket and he arrived from Los Angeles without a place to stay, so we let him stay in our office on 57th Street. We then signed him to a writing and producing contract, and he wrote a song with Jerry, "Spanish Harlem," which Jerry and I produced for Ben E. King.

I remember how we used to put Phil in these guitar sessions as a way of keeping him in money. Anyway, after a year or two of once in a while dropping in and playing rhythm guitar for us, we passed him one day on the street on our way to the studio, and we said, "Come on in, bring your guitar."

The record we were doing that day just happened to be "On Broadway" with the Drifters. The electric guitar solo on the record was Phil's. "On Broadway," with a Phil Spector guitar solo, went on to become the first record on the Atlantic label to sell over a million copies.

Ben E. King

o o o

Proof that a great group singer can be a successful solo star, Ben is associated with some of the classic black records that crossed over into the mainstream during the fifties and early sixties.

o o o

I started singing in church, and then on street corners with groups challenging other groups. Our role models were the Clovers and the Drifters, the Flamingos, Spaniels, Penguins, all these bird names. We heard their songs on the radio and found out how they did it by listening very closely.

We were all of the same mind. We found something we enjoyed doing a little better than baseball and stickball. And besides, our singing attracted girls. They heard the music and they came around.

I was a baritone-bass singer who never considered himself a lead singer. It wasn't until I ended up with the Drifters, which was by accident, that I became a lead singer. Jerry Wexler was in the control room, and I was teaching the Drifters a song I had written called "There Goes My Baby." The lead singer, Charlie Thomas, was having trouble with it, and Jerry came out and said, "Look, he's having trouble. You know it. You do it." That's how I became the lead singer.

Then I got a little cocky. I went back to my neighborhood with a little success under my belt and I couldn't miss being cocky. I thought I was the best thing in the world. And then I bumped into Frankie Laine and suddenly all my cockiness was gone.

I got a chance to go to San Remo to do a festival, and I was sitting there, waiting to perform, when a bunch of kids ran in. I got up and ran away, looking for a safe place. Frankie Laine had been watching me. He said, "Whenever someone approaches you for an autograph, I don't ever want to see you running away again. Don't ever run away from someone who appreciates you for being talented." I never forgot that.

The guy who started the Drifters, George Treadwell, had us sign a contract whereby we received no royalties. To this day, I have never received performance royalties. Luckily, I was a songwriter so I got my share. George just put us on a salary and everything else belonged to him.

The group was happy. They were even somewhat contented with the salary. But not me. I was unhappy with the salary. We were on the road, and when we got back to New York, we planned on going downtown to have a meeting with George Treadwell to discuss the fact that we were on terrible wages. The group elected me spokesman. I said my bit to George, and he pulled me aside and said, "You are not speaking for the group. If you're unhappy, speak for yourself."

So I did. I told him I was just married and how I needed more money to survive on the road, and he said, "If you're unhappy, you can leave." So I went out the door assuming the others would follow, and they didn't. Only Grover Patterson, who had been with me from before the Drifters and was now a road manager with the Drifters, he followed me out of the office. He stayed on my case. He told me we'd make it.

And then one day I got a call from Leiber and Stoller. They wanted me to come down and do "Spanish Harlem" with the Drifters. At the end of the session, Jerry asked me, "What are you going to do now that you're no longer in the group?"

I said, "Probably work with my dad."

Jerry said, "Have you ever thought about a solo career?"

I said, "Not really."

He said, "Well, let Mike and I talk to Ahmet Ertegun and Jerry Wexler." And they did. They could have easily finished up the session and said, "Thank you very much," and continued on with what they were doing.

Suddenly being solo was a frightening experience. Nobody to depend on. All of me, or nothing. I was so nervous. I'd sweat on stage. And then my manager at the time told me to open my eyes when I'm singing. I hadn't been aware of it, but my eyes were always closed when I sang. I'd hear the applause and think it was all right. I took lessons on how to keep my eyes open when I sing.

I'd also stand in the wings and watch other singers. I'd collect bits and pieces from singers like Brook Benton, Sam Cooke, and Lloyd Price. I loved the way Brook dressed, so I dressed like Brook. I loved the way Sam conducted himself on stage. He was a gentleman, and I adopted that. I loved the way Lloyd Price's personality bounced all over the place, and so I snatched a piece of that.

I wrote "Stand by Me" for the Drifters after I left the group because I knew they liked the things I was writing. Even though I was no longer in the group, I would call the guys together and rehearse them. Charlie Thomas was singing lead then, and he liked "Stand by Me." He said we should talk to George Treadwell about it. So I went down to see George with the song, and I don't know if he was still angry with me, but he said, "It's not a bad song, but we don't need it."

I walked out with the song and brought it to Leiber and Stoller. They changed the whole thing around, and suddenly it had an identity, a magic. The introduction alone was well worth their share.

Barry Mann

○ ○ ○

Together with his wife and collaborator, Cynthia Weil, Barry was a key figure among the hotshot New York writers who made the Brill Building the class of the sixties.

○ ○ ○

I don't know what it was about Brooklyn, but I went to Madison High, and so did Carole King. Our rival high school was Lincoln High. Neil Sedaka went there. Hank Medress of the Tokens went there. And Neil Diamond went there before he transferred to Erasmus, which is where Barbra Streisand went. A lot of talent sure came out of Brooklyn, and right around the same time, too.

I signed with Donnie Kirshner in 1961. How I got there was through a friend, Jack Keller. I had been working as a busboy in the Catskills to make tuition for college. Jack was in a band up there, and we struck a friendship. I ended up at Pratt studying architecture, but it didn't seem like the right profession for me. But I had held on to a lot of the names of the people I had met in the mountains. One was a publisher at Lowell Music. I went up to play the guy my songs and I bumped into Jack Keller. This was in the Brill Building. He told me he was with a publisher named George Paxton. Jack helped me out. He gave me advice. He told me to bring some of my songs to George Paxton, which I did, and I'll never forget that. I was jealous that Paul Anka started to make it before me. He made it at sixteen with a song called "Diana," so I wrote some song called "Eileen."

I was real excited about "Eileen," and I wanted to play it for George. I went up there. He had a secretary that was sort of surly. She told me he was busy, and I said I'd wait. It was something out of a grade-D movie. I waited for an hour, and then George walked in with the Ames Brothers. I said, "Mr. Paxton, you gotta hear this song." There were the Ames Brothers, looking like giant redwoods.

But I just kept meeting people, hanging around writing, cutting demos. I bumped into this guy named Donnie Kirshner as he was coming out of

Phil Kahl's office. About a year later, I found that Jack Keller was signed to Donnie's company. Jack was getting $200 a week. I thought that was great, so I went up and met with Kirshner, and he signed me for $150 a week against royalties.

I was there almost a year when I went to play a song for Teddy Randazzo, and I saw this girl who was writing with Teddy. I presumed she was his girlfriend. Basically, she wound up following me to Kirshner. She knew Eydie Gorme's secretary, and she asked her, "Who is that cute kid?"

The secretary said, "Barry Mann. He's with Donnie Kirshner." She ended up gertting in to see Kirshner, and that is how Cynthia Weil and I started writing together.

Donnie was like the father/mother figure to us, and Donnie was only two years older than me. All we wanted to do was please Donnie. If Donnie loved our songs, our day was made. We were like sibling rivals. The energy was incredible.

All of us—me and Cynthia, Carole King and Gerry Goffin, Neil Sedaka and Howie Greenfield—were so insecure that we'd never write a hit again that we constantly wrote in order to prove we could. We never thought the songs we wrote were going to be standards, or talked about twenty years later. We never thought in terms of history.

The way we worked was, Cynthia wrote the lyrics and I wrote lyrics and melody. Take an example like "Uptown," which the Crystals did. Cynthia was walking in the garment district, and she saw this great-looking black guy pushing one of those hand trucks. So she started thinking that downtown this guy is nothing. When he goes uptown, he must feel like something. So the song was written based on that imagery. When we finished "Uptown," we loved it. But Donnie didn't quite understand it. Donnie always kept saying, and it became a running joke, he'd say, "Write another 'Little Darlin'.' "

Each song has its own story. We brought in "Only in America" to Leiber and Stoller for the Drifters. It was originally written, "Only in America, land of opportunity, do they save the seat in the back of the bus just for me? Only in America, where they preach the Golden Rule, do they start to march when their kids want to go to school?"

I really loved it, but Jerry Leiber said they'd never play it if we wrote it like that. So we rewrote it, for the Drifters, who recorded it. But it's basically about a little white kid. Only in America you can grow up to be president. That wasn't about a black kid. And when the Drifters recorded it and it was sent around, the R & B disc jockeys wouldn't play it. So Jerry and Mike ended up cutting it with Jay and the Americans.

I remember when Phil Spector said he wanted to write with us. We flew out to California, stayed at the Chateau Marmont because they allowed dogs and we had a German shepherd. Phil told us about the Righteous Brothers, this group out of Orange County. He said he wanted a ballad.

"You've Lost that Lovin' Feelin'" was triggered by "Baby, I Need Your Loving," and somehow it evolved into "Lovin' Feelin'." Cynthia and I went back to the hotel. We rented a piano, and we wrote the first verse through the first chorus. We were using "You've Lost That Lovin' Feelin'" just as a dummy title.

I wrote the opening line, "You never close your eyes anymore when I kiss your lips," and then Cynthia took it over from there. Then we played it over the phone for Phil. When we got to the part that says, "It makes me just feel like cryin', because, baby, something beautiful's dyin'," he said, "That makes me want to cry." I didn't like the title. Phil said, "You're crazy. It's a great title."

There's a story told about me that says a lot. I once bumped into Paul Evans on the street. I was rushing, and he said, "Congratulations."

And I said, "For what?"

And he said, "Well, you have something that just came on the charts."

I said, "Oh, yeah? But shit, the other song just fell off." Our lives were dominated by the charts. By hits, not the money. It was being successful. And the funny thing was, outside the office there was no competition. We didn't think about Jeff Barry and Ellie Greenwich, or Leiber and Stoller, or Otis Blackwell. Outside the office we were just people.

Gerry Goffin

○ ○ ○

Married to Carole King, Gerry is yet another member of Don Kirshner's all-star songwriting team in New York. Pop memories of the 1960s include a number of Gerry's songs.

○ ○ ○

I think I'm a corny guy, and I want to stay corny because I think the corn accomplishes more than the tax on someone's head. I would have loved to have written twenty anti-Reagan songs since he became president, but I can't. I'm almost doomed to write these clichéd, soap opera kind of lyrics.

I once wrote a song to castrate Nixon, and I played it for Bob Dylan. It was very embarrassing. The lyric was filled with all sorts of atrocities. I played it for Dylan, and he said, "That's what people are expecting from me, so I can't do it."

I tried for a while to imitate what Dylan had been doing. And then, as the years went by, I laughed at myself for envying him because I realized he couldn't help being what he was any more than I could help being who I was. So I gave that up and continued trying to write popular songs.

In the beginning, it was Don Kirshner who had a lot to do with our early successes. He would say, "Write a song for the Shirelles," and we did. He was a very good publisher. He would say, "I got these kids, and they know what's happening. Give me the artist, and I'll give you the song." And he was right most of the time.

Everyone likes to talk about how writers like Carole King and myself wrote songs in cubicles. It was really nothing. When you're young, you can accept a lot more. If I told you that you had to go into a cubicle right now and write a song, you'd say, "Fuck you." But back then we were hungry. It was competitive, but it was an honorable competitiveness.

The truth is, we went home and wrote a lot more often than we went into a cubicle.

Steve Lawrence was one of Don Kirshner's pets. The song, "Go Away Little Girl," was originally written for Bobby Vee. Some great American work of literature. It should have died in the closet, but it didn't. I was never happy with the song, but I am happy for the money I received on it.

It's sort of a shame, though. "Go Away Little Girl" was our biggest song. Donny Osmond and Steve Lawrence. Took a half hour to write.

Songs sometimes happen under very strange circumstances. I was walking on Sixth Avenue in New York and Jerry Wexler spotted me from a limo. He said, "Hey, I got a good title for you, 'Natural Woman.' Why don't you go home and write it with Carole." We went home and wrote it in ten minutes.

The Kirshner years were really good for about a year. And then I started thinking, "Am I going to have to write this shit until I'm thirty-two?" By the time I was thirty-two, Dylan had come out, and so had the Beatles and the Rolling Stones and Joni Mitchell. So at thirty-two, I couldn't have written that shit because the market for it had dried up anyway.

I keep thinking that God is going to get on my ass any minute because this isn't a fit occupation for a man. It really isn't, but it's better than working.

Duane Eddy
o o o

His trademark twang sound influenced thousands of youngsters, many of whom made their own records later on. The legendary player is hanging in there looking for the golden ring again, but rock 'n' roll isn't easy.

o o o

A lot of the business people when I was starting out thought rock 'n' roll was a fad. They thought, "Why should we give the money to these idiot kids who come out of the sticks when we're in the business to stay?"

There'd be these big sacks of mail for me that they'd put in the back room of the record company, and I never knew about it. They'd go through it, or burn it, and it was my mail. I'd get bags and bags of fan mail. I guess they didn't want me to see it for fear that I'd start thinking I was a big star.

Early on, I worked for $35 a week, and I loved it because I was playing my guitar in a country band in Phoenix. Then we built it up to a couple of hundred a week, and then suddenly I'm making several thousand a night. I'd get a check for $50,000, $60,000, and think, "This is wonderful," when it should have been twice that much.

In those days, there were no such things as groupies. You couldn't get them into the hotels. We were lucky to get into the hotels ourselves. Everybody frowned on rock 'n' roll—the establishment, parents, and hotels.

I remember one time we checked into this motel, and the guy had me sign autographs for his daughters. He treated us like family. Well, that night we went to our show, and when we came back, the bass player liked to stand under the shower for a long time after a show and let the steam build up so he could stand there and really enjoy it.

Somehow this motel owner came around and saw all the steam coming out, and he thought it was smoke. He must have thought we were smoking dope or something.

He called the police and had us thrown out. It was three o'clock in the morning and I was in a nice hot bath myself, and the police came knocking on the door. So this motel owner who had been so nice, who had offered us dinner, which we had to turn down because we needed to get ready for the show—signed autographs for his kids—threw us out in the middle of the night.

We did a lot of those bus tours with other groups, eight or ten acts—Buddy Holly, the Platters, Bobby Darin. I became close with Bobby. He was a sweetheart, very cocky and brash on the outside, but a mellow person on the inside.

Bobby had his sights set high. He wanted to break out of rock 'n' roll and get into the mainstream of pop, which a lot of people in those days did. With "Mack the Knife," Bobby succeeded with what he wanted to do. He put on a tux, went to Vegas, and became a young Sinatra-type.

Because I just played an instrument I was like an odd man out. My background was more country than pop. There are two types of guitar players, the players who have developed their skills to a point where they can play anything in any style, and me. I can't do that. I've never been one to jump in on a jam session. I found a sound, the so-called twangy guitar sound, and I stayed with it.

Nothing was going on for me at the start of the seventies, so I did a tour of the Orient. I went to Vietnam and entertained the troops. Took a band, and the guys over there were at the right age to like what I did.

One of my more unusual experiences in Vietnam was when I was signing autographs after a show, and a guy comes up to me and asks for an autograph, and he says, "Can I get mine first because I really have a problem?"

"Fine with me," I said. So I signed it, and these MPs took the guy away. I said to someone, "What happened? Is he being arrested?"

The guy said, "No. The silly sonofagun got shot down today in a jet fighter. He bailed out and the helicopter picked him up and he's cussing all the way back saying, 'Can't you go any faster?' "

Soon as this guy gets back, he rushes over to my show and sits in a front-row seat he had reserved for weeks. After the show, he gets the autograph and the MPs take him to debriefing so he could answer to his superiors about what he did with their $20 million airplane.

Al Bennett

o o o

We included Al to give a picture of what the independent record company looked like and accomplished in the fifties and sixties before the corporate world took over. Liberty Records was a key player on the West Coast.

o o o

I went from Dot to Liberty in the late fifties. I had gotten $165,000 when Dot Records was sold. That's how much my 10 percent was worth. I put it in my savings account, so I wasn't hurting much. I knew my family wasn't going to starve.

The first record I put out at Liberty was "Witch Doctor," by David Seville, who created the Chipmunks. But at the time David Seville was a studio orchestra. They were making mood music more than novelties. David Seville was really just a name.

I thought "Witch Doctor" was a crazy record, but crazy enough or novel enough to happen. I hadn't even started at Liberty yet. Two weeks before I go there, though, I was making decisions. There wasn't a great deal going on there before I put out "Witch Doctor," so there weren't a whole lot of sales decisions that needed making.

I released "Witch Doctor," and it started to happen. Now I find myself without credit. Not enough credit to get the records pressed. I went to RCA because they had been doing our pressing, but Liberty already owed RCA $800,000, and half of it was for pressing. The first thing I did was go to Harry Fox, God bless him, who already had us on statutory licensing, and then to Herman Starr, the toughest dude in the world.

I had never met Harry Fox, and I said, "Mr. Fox, I don't know if I'm going to make it. But if I don't, you're not going to get anything. If I do make it, you're going to get your 100 percent. If you don't give me some cooperation and relief, I have no choice but to go bankrupt."

He said, "Have you been to see Herman Starr?"

I said, "No. I'm going there after you."

He said, "He's never going to go with you, but if he does, I'll go with you." So I went to see Herman Starr. Goddamn, I was frightened to death. He was the toughest son of a bitch in the world. So I laid my story on him. I told him I needed this relief.

He said, "I don't think you're going to make it. You ought to go out of business. None of you people pay your royalties anyway." That was his attitude.

I said, "Mr. Starr, I'll tell you this. There are no guarantees, but this is my deal. I'm going to make $15,000 a year, and I'm going to get a 10 percent override, and I'm going to break my ass. Whether we're going to make it or not, I don't know."

He said, "I like the way you talk, young fellow. You've got your credit."

Then "Witch Doctor" did about a million and a half and every dime in profit had to go to pay somebody. The government gave me four quarters to pay them the $80,000 we owed, and I paid it as soon as I could.

A few months later, I didn't have a damned thing to sell. Now I'm scrambling, I'm looking. I don't have any hits, and none of the things we're releasing sound like hits. We had Julie London. She was selling some, but she hadn't had a hit since "Cry Me a River" in '55. I had Martin Denny. I had Patience and Prudence, but they hadn't had a hit since '56. I also had Eddie Cochran, who I finally had a hit with, but it took me a year to get that. Eddie Cochran, Martin Denny, David Seville, those were the acts we had.

In the meantime, I have my ear at the radio like crazy. Anything that's good that's on a smaller label I'm looking to make a deal for. A guy had a song called "Western Movies" on the Demon label, by a group called the Olympics. I went and made a deal to distribute it. Nobody had done that before. The guy wouldn't sell his master, wouldn't lease it, but if I took the label, then he'd make a distribution deal with me. I said, "Shit, that gives me something to sell, gives me a reason to talk to distributors."

I did the same kind of deal with the Ventures, out of Tacoma, on the Dolton label. I'm basically a salesman, you know? And I became a pretty damned good administrator out of necessity.

That fall I hit with the Chipmunks, and by Christmas we'd sold about 4.8 million Chipmunk records. Five or six albums later and we'd sold about 18,000,000 or 20,000,000 albums of the Chipmunks. It was the Chipmunks that enabled me to find an underwriter and take the company public.

Little Anthony

○ ○ ○

Another story of stardom, exploitation, and memories. Little Anthony had hits and a few years of the good life but never saw all of the money or the long-term security he was looking for.

○ ○ ○

George Goldner was unique. Guys like Morris Levy would stay in their offices and be like big executives, but George was more of a record man, like a promoter. He didn't know he was president of a record company.

George would really go on the road. I mean, this guy would get in his car and go. I'd be up in his office and he would call in three or four times a day.

I remember when he said to me, "Kid, you got a hit." I didn't even fathom what a hit was. A hit record to me was always when your friends heard you in your neighborhood, or heard your record on Doctor Jive. If Doctor Jive played your record for more than a week, you were in. That's all that interested me, that the guys in my little world in Brooklyn heard it.

George was very close to the radio man, Georgie Woods in Philadelphia. Georgie called one day when I was in the office and I couldn't hear what Georgie was saying, but George seemed very happy. The Chantels were doing something around the office, and we were sitting and waiting to do something, when George ran over to me and said, "We got a smash, kid." I had never even heard the word smash.

About two weeks later, "Tears on My Pillow" was everywhere we turned. Before we knew it, we were taking trips to Washington, and I'd never been on a train in my life.

Never saw any money, but you're talking about a new entity, something no one really understood. If you played jazz, or were a big-band dude, you were respected, you had this sort of air about you. But rock 'n' roll was like noise. "They can't sing. That's not music." Really good lawyers didn't want to handle that sort of thing. We had lawyers from the garment district, and they didn't know anything about the music business. They were just as ignorant as we were.

My parents kept saying, "Where's the money?" So we started asking questions. People said, "You don't want to be asking questions. You'll be blackballed." It was a form of slavery.

We were so young. My parents weren't rich people. They used to say we were on the edge of poverty but not poor. We'd always get something for Christmas, but there was always a struggle to get it. So here I am running with girls and traveling. I was way better off than I'd ever been. It didn't take much to please me.

Mike Douglas was probably the first guy on television to introduce rock 'n' roll people in a different light. He'd sit us down and talk. Johnny Carson didn't do that. None of them did. They were too scared their ratings would drop. But Mike gave us a shot. We did his show in Cleveland, did a lip-synch of "Tears on My Pillow."

People from William Morris saw us, and suddenly we were thrown into a different world from anything we'd ever known—Vegas. Now we're rubbing shoulders with the Vegas crowd, learning from them, meeting other people. The Checkmates were there, and they were really hot. We were across the street working at the Flamingo.

Despite ourselves, we grew by leaps and bounds. Pretty soon we became one of the highest-paid lounge acts in the history of Las Vegas.

Introducing us to Vegas in '66 was a killer. It was so exciting. There I was, in a room with Sammy Davis. There I was, talking to these people, people I was influenced by as a kid. To become very good friends with the Treniers, a group I used to watch dance on Ed Sullivan's show, to become their friend and be invited into their homes was something. To be accepted by Dionne Warwick and Jack Carter and Mel Torme and all these people who used to hang together at night, I wouldn't give that part of my life for nothing in the world. It was better schooling than any college or university on this earth.

Artie Ripp
∘ ∘ ∘

**A street guy who made some great and some not so great moves in
running record companies, artists, and whatever else was available.
Artie gives you a feel of the New York state of mind as it worked in
the music business.**

∘ ∘ ∘

In 1956, I had this singing group called the Four Temptations. We did a single for ABC/Paramount. Don Costa ate pizza, drank scotch, and produced our session. I listened to the record when it was finished, and then when it was on the radio, and I said, "Boy, that's great."

And it was great. I got my rocks off. I started getting laid regularly and I was signing autographs. But as a singer, the truth was, I sucked. I was no Elvis Presley, and I wasn't a writer. I figured, if I was going to stay in the music business I'd better find a job.

So I started walking around Broadway and I'd see these kids who were making records and not getting paid. They could have a Number 1 record on the charts and end up owing the record company a half a million dollars.

I thought, "This business has some system."

Every party was charged to the artist. "I've got a hundred hookers. Charge them to the artist."

Here I was, out of high school, no diploma, wasn't going anywhere. The music business seemed terrific, so I decided that I needed to learn absolutely everything I could about it—A & R, promotion, sales, publishing.

And then I woke up one morning and said, "I'll be 153 by the time I finish serving my apprenticeship. Forget this." So I looked to find that one guy who owned his own company, who produced his own records, someone who was a creative, entrepreneurial kind of hustler. And that's how I got to George Goldner, owner of Rama and Gee Records.

I watched him work. The man was unbelievable. Everything was "snap, snap, snap."

And I said to myself, "Now that I don't have a real future as an artist, I want this guy to hire me."

Every day I'd hang around, watching, waiting. And then one day he grabbed me by the ear and said, "All right, you little motherfucker. I can't get rid of you, so tell me, what do you want from my life?"

I said, "Mr. Goldner, you're the greatest. I have to work for you. I want to be the next George Goldner. I need twenty dollars a week. I'll come in from Queens. I'll work seven days a week, twenty-four hours a day, whatever you want." He must have had pity for me. He gave me fifty dollars a week.

A year later, I had a car and I was the third-highest-paid person in the company. And learning. All the time learning.

What can I say about George? He was loving, caring, energetic, very self-assured, willing to take chances, an insane gambler, passionate, classy and at the same time classless.

George was a father. I was a child. None of his children at that point were in the music business. His girls, Linda and Barbara, were interested in being girls, so I had the opportunity to be a son.

He was a genius in the studio. He could come up with these lines and arrangements. He never wrote any of it on paper, he just knew exactly what he wanted to get. He was like a great artist.

I met Leonard Chess, who was very smart. I met the Erteguns and Jerry Wexler, who were like diplomats. George was different. He was a high school dropout, a very emotional and caring guy. You could always borrow money from George. Give him a story, and he'd give you some money.

I would go on the road with George, which meant I had to get the broads to the hotel and then make sure the disc jockey who had just finished with the redhead knew that the blonde was down the hall.

Back in those days I saw bags of money going out and bags of money coming in. You could sell 100 records over the table and 1,000 records under the table. Guys at radio stations got money, of course, but the interesting thing was that most of them were taking money to play records they would play anyway.

The incredible thing was, the majors at that time—Columbia, RCA, Decca—were not in the business of selling kid music by kids to kids. The independent guys, like George, discovered that kids actually had creative value. And what's more, you could put that value on record. It was a brand new industry, and it didn't require a thirty-seven-piece orchestra to make the music happen.

People like Alan Freed allowed that door to come open, and little entrepreneurs like George Goldner walked right on through.

When you look back at who had hits with George—the Cleftones, Frankie Lymon and the Teenagers, the Valentines, the Flamingos, the Chantels—it was an incredible period for music, it was an incredible time for George.

George would open up a record company, and then go across the street and open another one, and then go back across the street and open another company and it turns out to be Redbird Records with Leiber and Stoller.

George Goldner effectively introduced the concept of one record company distributing another record company. Up until that point only record distributors distributed records.

Most guys would consider it an unbelievable career to have found a couple of real stars along the way. For a guy to start out in one place, then go across the street, start again, go back across the street and start again, and actually come up with classics everywhere, well, that's just beyond extraordinary.

The guy had a mind like Einstein and ears like a teenager. To have done those classic arrangements, like George did, of black guys singing "I'll Be Seeing You" and "I Only Have Eyes for You"—forget it.

But that's what New York was like then. Manhattan was like a nuclear test site. Everybody was coming into the record business. Every kid had a group. And it didn't cost you anything. All you had to be able to do was hit a chord and sing. You didn't have to have a piano, or a guitar, or anything. You just needed to be able to sing.

It was an amazing, energetic time. People hustling, bustling. Hearts being broken. With so many people getting into it, it got to a point where you had to think like a piranha and act like a snake, just to survive. Suddenly, being artistic and creative wasn't enough.

Jimmie Haskell

o o o

For twenty-five years he's been writing arrangements for almost every kind of popular music. His touch and style are familiar to a generation of artists, and his perspective is vital to an understanding of the music world.

o o o

There was a girl who worked for Lew Chudd at Imperial Records named Anita Steiman, and her mother knew my mother. Anita ran Lew's publishing company. I kept telling her I was an arranger, and finally one day she called me and asked if I could do lead sheets. I said, "Of course I can do lead sheets."

She said, "I've got a lead sheet here on a Fats Domino record."

So I copied the lead sheet, but kept saying, "I'm an arranger."

Finally, Lew Chudd said to me, "Are you a good arranger?"

I said, "Of course, I'm a good arranger."

He said, "OK, let's do a session Friday night." So we did, and Lew liked it very much. It was for a group called the Spiders, or something like that. Totally unknown group, then and now. Those were the days when Lew was doing race records. Lew had two ways of working. He would get demos of songs that he liked, and I would copy the demo and enhance it in some way. And then, because he was friendly with so many disc jockeys all over America, particularly in Detroit, New York, and Chicago, places where records would start, his friends would call him up and tell him about a record. And if Lew liked the description of it, he'd ask them to send it to him.

Then he'd call me up and say, "Jimmie, I'm going to have a record here tomorrow morning at eight. You be in by then, take the record down, and we'll do a session at noon."

I'd listen to the record, take it down, and maybe improve it a little. Lew would say, "What are you doing?"

I'd say, "I'm improving it."

And he'd scream, "Don't improve it. Copy it."

And I'd say, "Is that ethical?"

And Lew would say, "Of course it's ethical. They copy me every day, don't they?" And he was right. Everybody was copying Fats Domino. By the way, when I joined Lew, Fats had already had twenty-three gold records. And I never heard of Fats until I joined Lew. So that's what Lew had me doing, copying records. And that's how I learned about producing.

Lew sat in the booth with me for my first few sessions. He was nasty, ruthless, and rude. But he knew how to make hit records.

About a year and a half after I joined Lew, I heard about how Ozzie Nelson was unhappy with the first record Ricky made at Verve. At the time, my wife, Barbara, was working at Verve, and that's how I knew Ricky hadn't even signed a contract with them. So Ricky was brought over to Imperial, and Lew said, "You're going to produce Ricky Nelson. Go in the booth and make hit records with him."

Ricky knew what he wanted. He couldn't analyze it, but he knew. He had a good ear and was a good musician. Most people aren't aware of that. He sang in tune. Most people aren't aware of that. He felt very embarrassed when he made a mistake. Most people aren't aware of that either.

Ozzie never believed Ricky had good breath control. We made a point of singing the verse, skipping the bridge, singing another verse, skipping the last verse, coming back. That way he wouldn't have to sing all the way through. After a while Ricky said, "This is ridiculous. Can I sing it all the way through?" But whatever Ozzie said went, which is why we set it up the way we did.

But Ricky prevailed, and he began singing his vocals all the way through. He turned out to have amazing stamina. He could start a session at seven P.M., and still be going strong at seven the next morning. We had a drummer named Richie Frost. During playbacks he'd sleep on the floor while I listened to the tape with Ricky. And Ricky would say, "One more take." They still didn't believe in editing in those days. It had to be a perfect take.

So I'd start walking over to wake the drummer, and just as I got close to him he'd open one eye and say, "One more?"

And I'd say, "That's right."

I was Ricky's producer for umpteen records. We had nine gold records in a row. Unfortunately, they didn't put credits on singles very much in those days. Same with most of the albums. I remember Ozzie saying to me, "Jimmie, we want people to think Ricky produced these records. We'll give you name credit on the back of the album for arranging, but not on the singles." I don't know if that was his way of keeping me from charging a producer's fee, or not. I didn't even know about producer's fees until I was already in the business for ten years.

Tom Jones

○ ○ ○

**What great records he made early on. Later a Vegas sex symbol, Tom
doesn't seem to mind the lack of respect from the rock world. His
career pays him plenty, and the women scream just as loud as ever
when he makes his onstage moves.**

○ ○ ○

The problem in Wales was that there were no record companies, no local
radio station. Everything came from London, the BBC was everything. You
had to go to London to do anything.

People in Wales would say to me, "Jesus Christ, you're a great singer.
You've got to make it."

I'd say, "Who do I talk to? There's nobody around Wales to see." I just
didn't see myself going to London and knocking on doors. I didn't know
anybody. I was waiting for somebody who knew something about music to
come around and realize my talent, and that person turned out to be Gordon
Mills.

A friend of his that he grew up with in school used to knock around
the pubs with me. He told me that Gordon was coming home to visit his
mother. He said, "Do you want me to try to get him to come have a look
at you to see if he can do something?"

I said, "By all means."

So he came and saw me, and he said, "You should be in London."

I said, "I understand that, but who do I see?"

He said, "If you want me to introduce you to people, I will. I know
people in business." Gordon wrote songs for Leeds Music. He said, "I know
publishers, I know agents, I know people in London. If you come up there,
I'll show you around, as a favor," and that's what he did.

Gordon had written some songs for Cliff Richard and Johnny Kidd and
the Pirates. Gordon wrote a song for Johnny Kidd called "I'll Never Get
Over You," which was a big hit in England. So I knew he knew what he
was talking about.

So I went to London with my rhythm section because Gordon had said,
"I'll try to get you some auditions, try to get you some gigs, try to get the
ball rolling," waiting for a song. I knew I had to have a song.

I became the demo man, the singer for Leeds Music. Then one day
Gordon wrote this song with Les Reed for a girl named Sandy Shore. The
song was "It's Not Unusual."

When I did the demo, I said to Gordon, "This is the song. This is the
bloody song."

He said, "Oh, I can write another one like it."

I said, "I hope you can, but this one is definitely the song."

Les wanted Sandy to record it because she was already established. She
had two hit records. I hadn't had anything yet. Les was pushing for Sandy

because he knew that if she recorded it, it would go somewhere. I said, "If you give this song to Sandy Shore, I'm going back to Wales."

Well, they gave the song to Sandy Shore anyway. They went over to her manager's place with the record, my demo. Sandy Shore said, "Just put it down over there, and when we have time, we'll listen."

Well, while she was finding time, we went into the studio and recorded it.

Bob Marcucci

o o o

They couldn't have made the movie *The Idolmaker* without Bob because it was based 100 percent on him. As manager of both Frankie Avalon and Fabian, Bob was part of a skyrocketing story that ended almost as quickly as it began.

o o o

I just knew the idols were going to come in. Presley was very, very big. He and Ricky Nelson were really the two big artists, and I felt that if I could find kids like that and put them on my label, I could have some big stars, too.

None of the other big labels were thinking like that. RCA had Presley, but no other big labels were doing it. Remember, the business was still coming off that big beautiful sound of Patti Page and Perry Como and Kay Starr. That was fading away and the new sound was taking over. I wanted to be part of that new sound.

Frankie Avalon was a trumpet player. He was a protégé of Ray Anthony's. Frankie was well-known in Philadelphia. Sweetest little kid, ten or eleven years old, playing the trumpet. My partner, Pete DeAngelis, was very close to Frankie and his family. Well, we opened the first teenage nightclub, first of its kind, big beautiful ballroom, and different record stars would come down on weekends. Our first act was Tony Bennett. And then Frankie Avalon and his band would play. It was the hottest spot. *Life* magazine came down and wanted to do a piece on us. It was going great.

But we were right underneath a dry cleaner. They had a big fire and it closed us down. To this day I think the cleaner started the fire. They hated us being up there. After the fire we were closed down. Frankie went his way and I went mine.

Later on I said to Pete, "We need some idols." I called Frankie up and asked if he knew a great singer, and he said he had just the guy, Andy Martin, who was singing in his group. I went to one of their afternoon jam sessions and Andy Martin came out and sang. Blond, blue-eyed, good. But he didn't

BOB MARCUCCI / 141

impress me. I'm just about to leave and who comes up on stage but Frankie. I thought, "Oh, he's going to play his trumpet." But he started singing, and he had everything it took. When he came offstage, he asked me if I thought Andy was great, and I said, "No. You're the one I want."

He said, "I'm not a singer."

I said, "You're great. You got personality," and so forth and so forth, and that's how we signed him. We took him in and cut two songs with him. They both bombed. But everybody loved Frankie. No matter where he went, people loved him. I went back to Pete and said, "We've got to write him a hit song."

Pete, who didn't like rock 'n' roll, said, "I'm not going to do it, Bob. Those other two records embarrassed me."

I said, "You've got to do it. This kid is going to be the hottest kid in the country."

In the meantime, Dick Clark was the only way to get your artist to be seen throughout the entire country in the matter of one day. I didn't know Dick Clark that well, but I sent him a little gift when he played something of mine. When his son was born, I sent him a little diamond ring, a twenty-five–dollar ring for his son, and he sent it back to me and said, "Who the hell is this guy, Marcucci?" I sent him parakeets, which he sent back to me. Finally, someone arranged for me to get Frankie on the show. The day Frankie was on was his birthday, and I arranged for a birthday cake for him, and Dick Clark said, "Who the hell is this man, bringing in a cake? Who does he think he is, telling me what to do on my show?" But Frankie was a Philadelphia boy, so they let it go, and we made a big deal out of Frankie's birthday, and from that point on he became very hot. And I became very loyal to Dick. From then on, anytime Dick wanted Frankie Avalon, Frankie Avalon was available.

So we wrote a song for Frankie called "DeDe Dinah." We released the record on December 5th, 1957, during a Christmas season, and by December 12th the thing was a smash.

Things were going very well with Frankie, and I decided I needed a star like Presley. Frankie wasn't that star. He didn't have that kind of look. He wasn't in that genre. Ricky Nelson was very hot. Sal Mineo was very hot. I did a search throughout the country. Big search. I had disc jockeys do promotions. I asked for people to send me pictures. But I couldn't find him. I couldn't find that look, the look I wanted.

I received a lot of tapes from the South. Good singers, but they didn't have the look. So one day I'm driving home, and I go past the street where my best friend lives and there is a big red devil, a police ambulance, in front of my friend's house, and I became very concerned because my friend's wife was pregnant. Turns out the ambulance was for the house next door, and out walks Fabian. He had the look. I went up to my friend and asked him if he knew whether that guy could sing. My friend said he had no idea.

Fabian

○ ○ ○

A created star, he now knows what happened and wonders if it was worth it. A teenage idol carries a lot of baggage into later life, and Fabian doesn't hesitate to talk about it.

○ ○ ○

I was fifteen when I got into the business. My father was very ill at the time. He was being taken out to the ambulance and Bob Marcucci asks whether I'd like to get involved in the business.

I said, "No. Go to hell." I was worried about my dad. But Marcucci kept bugging me, and the guy next door gave me some records to listen to.

There was no way my father could make any money. He was getting forty-five dollars a week in compensation. I had two younger brothers and my mother. I was making six dollars a week, plus tips, as a delivery boy at a drugstore. When Marcucci came up with the suggestion of recording, the combination of the enormous need and the excitement of possibly being a part of the business was like ramming two shifts.

I went to see Frankie Avalon at a record hop, and people were screaming. It didn't faze me because I was very shy, very insecure. I was also very young, and this was like taking me to Ethiopia to plant coconuts. I mean, I didn't know anything about what was going to happen. I was frightened, but I had to swallow it because of this overpowering need to make money.

I never had a pompadour, but they said, "You're going to have a pompadour, and then we're going to pluck the middle of your eyebrows out, and then we're going to dress you in a certain shirt and pants." And white fucking bucks. I hated those things.

The strategy was for me to be a male teen performer, but the big problem was songs. They put me together with Doc Pomus and Mort Shuman, and they gave me "I'm a Man," which was a medium hit. Got me on the charts. After that I had "Turn Me Loose," and that one did a lot better.

Performing terrified me. People were screaming, and I had no idea why. Bob would say, "Move this way, move that way," until it became second nature. Bob was the guru. The only thing he couldn't do anything about was my face. I had my face. Bob always wanted to be a star himself. He kind of lived through Frankie and me.

I'd be out on tour with the Drifters, the Coasters, Frankie Lymon, Chuck Berry, Little Richard, and while most of them were very nice to me, they'd be thinking, "Where the fuck did this person come from, this white, good-looking teenage idol?" In retrospect, I totally understand where they were coming from.

Touring was a blur. All I remember is doing, like, ninety shows in maybe ninety-six days, eating hamburgers at White Castle, sleeping on buses. I remember the dread of somebody catching a cold on the bus and then everyone else getting it.

I also remember drinking with the guys, and all the girls. I loved that part immensely. Being with them, that is, not waving at them.

Even my family started treating me differently. Instead of saying, "Get your foot off that fucking table," it would be, "Why don't you put the other foot up."

Disc jockeys treated me well, too. We all washed one another's hands. The standing joke in the business was, "Of course payola exists. How else would a man like this make it?" I am afraid that is part of my legacy.

If I had to change one thing, it would be the age I started. I would want to be older if I were starting all over. Unfortunately for me, there was no such thing as a school for teenage idols. Nobody ever told me it would end. When it started to go, I was very confused. Nobody ever said, "Well, gee, shit, man, this might end."

Jeff Barry

o o o

He wrote for Phil Spector and for a number of sixties pop stars. He gave Neil Diamond a shot early on, and he has consistently written in-the-pocket pop songs for twenty-five years.

o o o

I went to Erasmus Hall High School in Brooklyn. I'd get out of school, run home, hide under the bed, and wait for the future to get here.

But I wrote songs, did so since I was a kid. My mother has a song of mine I wrote when I was seven. It wasn't a bad song. It's about my favorite things, girls and horses. Growing up in Brooklyn, a little Jewish kid, you had to be a lawyer or doctor or something along those lines. If you could make $10,000 a year, that was the goal. Ten thousand a year and you were a made guy.

Well, a friend of the family knew this one person in show business, and he was Arnold Shaw, a publisher. He said he'd listen to me sing. I thought maybe I could be a singer because I only knew two chords, G and C. I couldn't play anybody else's songs, so I wrote my own. I sat down for Arnold Shaw and played a few songs, all in G and C, and he says, "You sing OK, but what are these songs you are playing me?"

I said, "This is what I write."

He said, "Got any more in G and C?"

I played him all kinds of songs, all in G and C. He said, "You mean, you don't know any other chords?"

I said, "No. I don't know what I'm doing."

He said, "Do you want to be a songwriter?"

I said, "I never occurred to me that I really could." To this day, I can't spell Juilliard.

He said he'd pay me seventy-five dollars a week, which was almost half my life's goal. So I quit college and within four or five months I had the Number 1 record in the world, "Tell Laura I Love Her."

Along the way, Ellie Greenwich and I got married, and we were a team. We had this group called the Raindrops. Several chart records. One called "That Boy John," which had jumped on the charts in the sixties the first week and looked like it would go on to become a smash. That week John Kennedy was killed. Suddenly no one would play a song called "That Boy John." Boom! Off the charts.

Normally, when we went into the studio with the Raindrops or anyone, we went in with one song, one A side. A three-hour session to make one smash. Well, this one time with the Raindrops, we finished the session in two hours. We had a perfectly good hour left with the band, so Ellie and I went out into the hall and wrote "Hanky Panky." Our thinking was, "Let's put this silly, stupid song on the B side."

Tommy James, who was a fan of ours and would always listen to our A sides, turned the record over this time, heard "Hanky Panky," and said, "This is a hit song." He goes into the studio, records it, and has his first hit, with a song we wrote in a hall.

I was signed to a firm called TM Music that Bobby Darin was in the process of buying. Bobby brought me out to Los Angeles, wined me and dined me, gave me the corner office, the whole thing. I met Tony Curtis, Hugh Hefner. It was fabulous. I was a kid.

Leiber and Stoller gave me one room with one speaker and half the money. The difference is, at TM I would have been the most knowledgeable guy. I could play you a napkin and make it sound like a hit, but I needed people around me that I couldn't knock out that easily, which is why I turned down TM and went with Leiber and Stoller.

Honestly, I don't know how we did it. I wish I could say, "I did this to accomplish that." I didn't do anything. Ellie would sit down at the piano, and basically there were three parts to the song—the words, the melody that the words were hung on, and the chord bed. You can't teach someone how to write words, you can't teach someone how to write melody, but you can teach someone about chords and chord progression. Today I know more than just the G and C.

In all that time, though, during the early years, I never met the consumer on any grand scale. OK, fade out on the midsixties, fade in on the midseventies. I'm in L.A., single, living in Bel Air, driving tricky cars, and having a great time. There I am at the bar at Le Dôme saying, "Hi, can I buy you a car?" Real glib.

We chit-chat, and someone says, "What do you do?"

I say, "I'm a songwriter. I wrote 'Be My Baby.' "

They say, "You wrote that?" Now I'm meeting the consumer as an adult. It never occurred to me what those songs meant to those people. All

I was trying to do was entertain them, give them some fun. I didn't think beyond that, nor was I intending it to be more than that. I never once thought of those songs as works of art. They were more like ear candy.

Ellie Greenwich

o o o

The other half of the Barry-Greenwich team from that magic time in New York in the sixties. They eventually split, but the discography is amazing—with a lot of hits in very little time.

o o o

In the early sixties, the music business was much smaller, and there was a lot more room for songwriters to be heard and seen and listened to. And there was atmosphere, especially in the Brill Building, which was almost all writers, producers, publishers, and musicians.

It was so exciting. We'd write songs in the elevators, or while we were eating next door at Jack Dempsey's. It didn't matter where we were when we wrote. The atmosphere was just very conducive to writing songs.

I met Jeff Barry at a Thanksgiving dinner at my aunt's house. Jeff was married at the time, and he was my aunt's cousin through marriage. All the two of us did all night was eat and talk music.

One of the things he told me that night was about a song he had coming out by a guy named Ray Peterson. He didn't want to tell me the title of the song for fear of jinxing it. But he did have a feeling that the record was going to be a real biggie. The song was "Tell Laura I Love Her."

Jeff was on the brink of being not happily married, and I was still in college at the time. He was on his way to getting an annulment and he just started calling me. He said if I ever wanted to come into the city, I could hang around the office where he wrote songs. Every now and then I did, and I'd say to myself, "Boy, I can't wait until I can do this, too."

Right after I graduated from college, Jeff was already annulled, and we started going out. We had the most musical relationship imaginable. It was terrific. We never got to know each other, but we sure could sing harmony and write.

Jeff and I began to get edgy with the people we were working with— Jeff had been writing with a guy named Artie Resnick, who co-wrote "Under the Boardwalk"—so we decided to speak to our respective people and say, "We're going to have to stop this. Jeff and I are going to put all our efforts into working together." Which is exactly what we did.

I got to meet Phil Spector when he cut one of my songs, "(Today I Met) The Boy I'm Going to Marry," with Darlene Love. Phil was so weird.

He would come up to the office in his ruffles, and he'd walk around and make these garbling noises and look in all the mirrors.

Our input with Phil normally took place before we went into the studio. Once in the studio, Phil had total control. We'd discuss things sometimes in the control room, but never in front of the musicians. Phil was the boss, and you were invited into one of his sessions. You didn't just go to a Spector session. You had to be asked in.

My original dream in music had been to make a hundred dollars a week. That was my big dream. I never even thought beyond a hundred dollars during the first months of my being in the business.

But as soon as people started making money, the first thing the guys would do was go out and get motorcycles. Jeff had one, Shadow Morton had one, Brooks Arthur had one. It was the "in" thing.

I remember saying, "We've got to do something with motorcycles."

And Shadow said, "Ah, yes. Wheels!"

We knew we needed a great title and sound effects. We thought immediately about the Shangri-Las, because they had a nasal sound. So I said, "Let's write a song about the head of the gang." But "the head of the gang" didn't sound quite right, so we just bounced things around and came up with "Leader of the Pack."

I've been involved in a lot of songs, but there have been only two songs that, walking out of the studio, I knew for certain would either sell nothing or go to Number 1. The two songs were "Leader of the Pack" and "Chapel of Love." They were the kind of songs you either loved or forgot about altogether.

"Chapel of Love" was written initially for the Ronettes. And the Ronettes did record it, but Phil didn't want to put it out. He just simply refused. So it sat in the can, and it sat in the can.

After I don't know how long, we called Phil and said, "Listen, if you're not going to put it out with the Ronettes, Joe Jones is up here from New Orleans with a load of people, male and female, and maybe a few of them could do "Chapel of Love."

Phil said OK, and we said, "All right, we need some girls to sing 'Chapel of Love.' " Three girls stepped forward, and they became the Dixie Cups.

Jeff and I lasted as a writing team about as long as we lasted as a married team—a little less than five years. We tried to write together right after we split up, but it was awful. We couldn't sit and write "baby, I love you" with divorce papers sitting right next to us.

I remember in the early seventies going to do a session at 1619 Broadway, the Brill Building. I looked around and nothing was the same. The theaters were gone, Dempsey's was gone, and I just stood there and I felt defeated. I thought, "Look what's happened to this place. It's not alive like it used to be."

Back then, it really was the "music" business. There was a camaraderie that was incredible. Maybe it was because there seemed to be room for all of us. It's nice to be able to feel good about somebody else's success. It's nice to be able to do somebody a favor and sing on their session. It's nice to be able to turn people on to other people. I mean, it's a struggle enough.

Writing songs is so nebulous. It's like, "Who knows? I love it. You hate it. You like it. Can you use it? Well, no, politically we can't." You just never know. Every ounce of you is going into this intangible thing.

Not too long ago I spoke to Cyndi Lauper, and all she wanted to know from me is what it was like back then.

"What was it like back then?" I said. "It was terrific."

George "Shadow" Morton

○ ○ ○

Producer and writer, Shadow hails from that period when a group of young people from Brooklyn crossed the bridge into Manhattan and led the pop music world for a decade.

○ ○ ○

Jeff Barry nicknamed me "Shadow" for the obvious reason—I would never show up, and nobody ever knew where the hell I was.

My success in the music industry was an accident. I had no desire to be in it and no idea what I was doing. I was nineteen years old, floating around. One day a high school friend of mine said to me, "Would you believe Ellie Greenwich, the girl we went to high school with, has written hit songs?"

I said, "What hit songs?"

And he said, " 'Da Doo Ron Ron' and 'Be My Baby.' "

I said, "You gotta be kidding. You're putting me on." I thought it was a joke. Well, we go into a record store and I go through the records and I see her name. I got a dollar to my name, but I call her up and I say, "Ellie, I'm coming into the city from Long Island. Can I see you?"

She says sure, and I tell her I'll be there tomorrow.

The next day I show up at her office, and there's this guy sitting at the piano in her office and he never once turns around to look at me. He just keeps tinkling on the piano. Turns out to be Jeff Barry. In a way, he does me a favor. By insulting me so badly I lie to him. When he finally turns around and asks me what I do, I tell him I write songs.

He says, "Oh, yeah? What kind of songs?"

And I say, "Hit songs."

And he says, "When can you bring me one?"

I say, "When do you want one?"

He says, "How about next Tuesday?"

I say, "OK." The next day, I call up this friend of mine, George Sterma, who's involved with bands and musicians, and I say, "George, listen, I got this record company, they want to hear my songs. I need a band."

He says, "OK, I'll put four or five guys together."

Then I call another guy, Joe Monica, who owns a studio in Hicksville, Long Island, which is nothing more than a basement studio, two-track. It was nothing. I say, "Joe, listen, I got a record company interested, I got a band. I need a studio."

He says, "No problem. You got it."

Then some friend tells me about these three girls who are singing in Queens. I go see them, and afterwards I go to their dressing room and I say, "Girls, listen, I got a record company, I got a band, I got a studio. All I need now is a group."

They say, "Sure, we'll sing."

I say, "All right. Sunday afternoon. Two o'clock." On the way over to the studio that day it dawns on me that I have everything going except a song. I don't have a song. So I pull the car over on South Oyster Bay Road—I'll never forget—and I start to write.

I get to the studio, the people are there and they're saying, "You're late, you're late."

I said, "Don't worry about it. Piano, you play this. Girls, you sing this."

On Tuesday I bring the song to Jeff, and writing to me at this point is a joke, and Jeff, who has no love lost for me, plays my song, and then says, "Can I play it again?"

I say, "Certainly."

He plays it again, and he says, "Can I play it one more time?" Now I'm getting nervous.

He plays it again, and then he says to me, "Can I play it for someone else?"

I say, "Certainly."

Jeff disappears, me and Ellie stay in the room, and suddenly this man opens a door, sticks his head in and asks, "Did you write this?"

I say, "Yes."

He says, "Did you make this record?"

I say, "Yes."

He says, "Would you like to work for me?"

I say, "Here? No way."

He says, "You can work wherever you want. You can work at the beach. I don't give a damn. You can go to Mexico or Canada."

I say, "How much will you pay me?"

He says, "Three hundred fifty dollars a week," which was a lot of money at that time.

I say, "OK, I'll take the job."

He says, "Oh, by the way, I'm putting this record out."

I say, "The one I just made?"

He says, "Yes, it'll be out in three weeks."

Three weeks later, the record comes out and it goes to Number 1. It was "Remember (Walkin' in the Sand)," by the Shangri-Las. The man's name was Jerry Leiber. He had one blue eye and one brown eye. I loved Jerry Leiber then as I love him now.

B.B. King

○ ○ ○

From the cotton fields to Memphis and eventual stardom, B.B. hasn't found the town he hasn't worked in. With his guitar and his sense of what the blues are really about, he continues to spread the word to succeeding musical generations.

○ ○ ○

In the early years when I was starting out, if you said you were a blues player, you weren't always welcome in a lot of the clubs. People—and this is still true today—usually have preconceived ideas about blues music. They often feel it's depressing, that the lyrics aren't even planned. They think a guy just comes out, sits on a stool, grabs a guitar, and starts mumbling.

There's an old saying, you know, about how you had to have experienced hard times to play the blues. It's not entirely true. But it helps. Hard times, of course, doesn't necessarily mean being poor. I've known people with money who've had problems with their families, with their love life. Really, that's how the blues began, out of feeling—feeling misused, mistreated, feeling there's nobody to turn to.

I've always tried to defend the idea that the blues doesn't have to be sung by a person who comes from Mississippi, as I did. People all over the world have problems. Maybe not the same kind of problems. But a problem is a problem. You got a problem, it's a problem. And as long as people have problems, the blues can never die.

I always try to present both sides of the blues. For instance, if a guy is jealous and blue he sings, "I don't want nobody hanging 'round my house when I'm not at home."

On the other hand he can sing, "I got a sweet little angel. I love the way she spreads her wings."

Both ways the feeling can be exactly the same melodically, but it's the words that make the difference. When I was growing up, boogie-woogie was the thing. Eight beats to the bar. Well, gospel music had the same feeling. The only difference was the words. Gospel singers sing about heavenly bodies, and we blues singers sing about earthly ones.

Growing up on a plantation, my aunt used to buy records by such people as Blind Lemon Jefferson, a great guitarist who was born blind, and Lonnie Johnson, a guitarist who was associated for a time with Duke Ellington and Louis Armstrong. Lonnie was kind of contemporary for his time. I like to think I'm a lot like him.

My aunt, when I was a good boy, would allow me to listen to her windup Victrola, or whatever it was called at the time, and the two people I liked to listen to the most were Blind Lemon and Lonnie.

It was only when I got to be older, like just before my preteens, that I really started to make sense out of what they were doing. I got a feeling from their music that I couldn't describe to anyone. It just seem to go inside me and stay there.

Later, when I started hearing jazz, I began listening to Charlie Christian, who was playing with Benny Goodman at the time.

Then, in the late thirties when I heard T-Bone Walker playing the electric guitar, man, that did it. I did everything anybody asked me to do just to make enough money to buy me a guitar. From that time on I knew what I wanted to do.

When I first left Mississippi and was hitchhiking to Memphis, this truck driver saw me, stopped, and picked me up. I helped the guy deliver his groceries all the way to Memphis.

When I got to Memphis, I heard Sonny Boy Williamson on the radio over in West Memphis. It immediately reminded me of when I was a boy in the fields. Sonny Boy would come in over this Arkansas station, KFFA, every day at twelve-fifteen. This was about the time of our noon break. We'd rush home from the fields just to be able to catch Sonny Boy on the radio. He'd be on for fifteen minutes playing blues. And he was sponsored by a company called King Biscuit Flour.

Well, now I get to Memphis, and he's got his own radio program in West Memphis. I just knew I wanted to go see him. So I did. I told him I wanted to sing a song on his program. He thought about it for a few minutes and wound up putting me on the radio that very day.

After I played, he called a woman, he called her Miss Annie, over at the 16th Street Grill, the place he'd been playing at. And Sonny Boy says to her, "Did you listen to that boy who played a while ago?"

She said, "Yeah, he was all right."

And he said, "Well, I'm going to send him in my place tonight." And she said OK.

He hadn't even asked me if I wanted to do it. He just said, "You're going to go down and play for Miss Annie tonight. And you better play well because if you don't, you're going to have to answer to me."

Well, I was thrilled. I didn't even ask how much money it was going to pay, anything. I didn't even think about it. Remember, it's the early fifties, and I'm just coming in from Mississippi, where I'd been making twenty-two dollars a week driving a tractor.

OK, I go down to the 16th Street Grill that night and I find out that

Miss Annie has a gambling room in the back of her place. My job, says Miss Annie, is to keep the gamblers happy.

Well, Miss Annie liked me. She says, "B, if you can get yourself a job on the radio, same as Sonny Boy has, I'll give you a job here and pay you twelve dollars a night, six nights a week, plus room and board."

Man, I'd never heard of anything like that in my life. So I said, "Yeah, I'll get a job on the radio, just you see."

Well, as fate would have it, I heard about this new radio station opening up in Memphis, WDIA. I walked over there on Union Avenue, where the station was, and I saw this black guy sitting there at the microphone. I knocked on his window, got his attention and told him that I wanted to make a record and get myself on the radio. He laughed. His name was Professor Nat Williams, but everybody called him Nat B.

So he gets all the people at the station together to size me up. I looked mighty homely, the way I looked when I was back at the plantation.

They wound up giving me a job singing a commercial for a competing product that Sonny Boy was selling over the air in West Memphis. His sponsor was a tonic called Hadacol. Our station was starting a similar tonic called Pepticon. I remember writing my own little jingle: "Pepticon. Sure is good. Pepticon. Sure is good. You can get it anywhere in your neighborhood."

Well, I became very popular. Eventually, they upped me to ten minutes every day, then fifteen minutes a day with a little trio. Then they trained me to be a disc jockey, and they still let me play live every day. Pretty soon I had a fifty-five-minute segment, Monday through Friday, with twice that on Saturday. National sponsors like Coc'-Cola and everything.

A year later I graduated from the radio station, and Miss Annie's, and I guess you can say I was on my way.

Harold Leventhal

o o o

He worked for Irving Berlin and managed and promoted acts like the Weavers and Woody Guthrie. Through that politically active and tumultuous time, he managed to be labeled subversive by the infamous House Committee on Un-American Activities and came through a winner.

o o o

It was the late thirties, and I was just out of high school, and I got a job as the errand boy at Irving Berlin's company. They promoted me very rapidly, and soon I became what was called a "counter boy," which was the first person someone would see when they came in asking for sheet music. Soon after that, they made me a song plugger.

Irving Berlin was in the office pretty much every day, but he remained aloof from everybody. Once a week there would be a meeting of all the "contact men," as we were called, and Charlie Warren, the brother of Harry Warren, the songwriter, would head the meeting, and he would say, "OK, you take care of Benny Goodman, you get Charlie Barnet," and so on.

Being the youngest, my job was to find the new guys coming up, and then get them to play our songs. If someone played your song over the radio and people heard it, they'd come in and buy the sheet music or a lead sheet.

When the war broke out, Irving started writing war songs. He comes into this meeting one day and plays a war song he's just written called "Arms for the Love of America."

He said, "Everybody's got to get out there and get airplay on this." Well, the song wasn't worth much and nobody liked it.

But I went out with it, to a guy I knew who was a band leader at the World's Fair in Queens. He had these leftist leanings, and I had leftist leanings, and I asked him to do me a favor and play the song on the air. Well, he did, and it was the only time any one of us got an air plug on that song.

At the next meeting, Berlin pointed to me and said that I was the only patriot in his company.

I was there when Berlin wrote "God Bless America," and Kate Smith came into the office to hear it. I was there the first time he played "White Christmas." He would write these songs and then get on the phone and call big stars and have them come to office to hear it. Irving Berlin was the one writer who never had to go out to meet anybody.

I went into the army in '43, and when I got out of the service, I called a song plugger friend of mine, Juggy Gayles, a great Damon Runyon character. Juggy had started his own company, United Music, and I joined his company. It was at that point that I met up with Pete Seeger.

Pete was singing with the Weavers down at the Village Vanguard, and I went down to hear them. After they finished playing, Pete came up to me and said, "How would you like to manage us?" I said I would. Pete and I got along great. We were both leftists.

I was a communist then, the whole route, but I kept quiet about that in the music business. But politics aside, when I heard the Weavers' music and how the audience reacted to it, I felt their songs could make it. So I became their manager. I knew nothing about managing, but I was a good organization man. I knew how to follow through on things, and if I didn't have the answers, I knew where to go to find the answers.

Of course, the Weavers did want someone who saw politically eye to eye with them, and that was me.

It was the late forties, and folk music was just beginning to happen in the small Greenwich Village clubs. It took almost ten years for folk music to become a big national thing, but in the meantime there was enough interest in the Weavers for all of us to make a living.

Folk purists looked down on the Weavers because they were singing songs like "Goodnight, Irene," songs you could hum and remember.

Pete was a driving force in the group. He and Lee Hays wrote "If I Had a Hammer" and "Kisses Sweeter Than Wine." Both songs were innovative for their time because they represented a moving away from the Tin Pan Alley "moon-and-June" kind of song to a tradition that had been laying untapped for hundreds of years.

The Weavers were very politically conscious people. At first, they began digging up labor songs that no one else would do. Then they dipped into Negro culture, to those gospel and blues songs that had some social meaning behind them.

Unfortunately, we were coming into the McCarthy period and things started getting pretty rough.

The Weavers were singled out in New York by a group called the Red Channels, which began listing communist groups and communist singers and actors.

At one point, the Weavers were about to be signed for a network television show. When word about them got out, the show was canceled. And then, for example, we played the Strand Theater, with Yvonne DeCarlo on the bill, and there were pickets outside protesting the Weavers as being "Reds."

And then some people came to us and said, "Look, we can get you off this list. All you have to do is get on your knees and say, 'Hey, we're sorry we did this.'"

Then the Weavers were called before the House Un-American Activities Committee. Some of them took the Fifth Amendment. Pete didn't take anything. He just didn't answer questions. No matter what they asked, he didn't answer.

But the fallout was that the group couldn't get any more work. Decca pulled their records. Wouldn't sell them. Too many complaints from the distributors, they said.

As it turned out, the Weavers were the only musical group to be hit by the blacklist. It forced them to disband for a few years. When they disbanded, Pete started going out and singing before little groups—colleges, churches, labor organizations—and they'd pay him twenty-five or fifty dollars a night, and he managed.

That's the thing about Pete—no matter what, no matter how rough it got, Pete faced it. He always found a way to survive.

Pete Seeger

○ ○ ○

His name conjures up campfires, union meetings, and all the seeds of the social change that brought the folk music of the thirties and forties to prominence. Pete still writes, sings, and performs—and brings a wave of nostalgia to audiences throughout the world.

○ ○ ○

I remember when Woody Guthrie was blacklisted from being on the air. Couldn't sing "This Land Is Your Land" on the air. Couldn't get a job on radio. But it didn't bother him one little bit. He sang for people who liked him, whether at the local bar, or at a friend's house, or at an occasional union meeting or rally.

Woody took himself seriously in the same sense that Charlie Chaplin took himself seriously. Woody was always ready with a grin and a joke. He loved to tell jokes, and when he heard a good new one he would start embellishing it and telling it everywhere he went. Woody wasn't a down-in-the-mouth character at all. He knew that the reason he was a musician was not to distract people from their troubles, but to help try to help people understand their troubles. At best, he helped people do something about their troubles.

Woody and I were once part of a group that called itself the Almanac Singers. We walked down the aisle one night at a union meeting, about 1,000 longshoremen there, and some of them are turning around and saying, "What the heck are these hillbilly singers coming in here for? We have work to do." But the head of the union introduced us as the Union Singers, and he asked them to please listen to us. We sang a couple of our songs, "Oh, You Can't Scare Me Out" and "Take It to the Union," and they were cheering and up on their feet. When we walked back up the aisle, they were clapping on our backs so hard they nearly knocked us over. I don't think I will ever forget that.

I was about seven years younger than Woody. I was very proud that he put up with my New England ways. He couldn't quite understand me, but we got along well and he liked the banjo.

Like the Almanac Singers, the Weavers also hoped to sing for peace and civil rights. We never expected or intended that the Weavers would be a commercial success. The Weavers were about to break up. We couldn't make a living. Couldn't get five dollars here, or ten dollars there. The Cold War was closing in and organizations were folding. Union leaders were in jail.

Well, we're about to split up, and as a last resort we got a job at the Village Vanguard. I had once worked there for $200 a week, which was not bad pay for one person, and I went to the owner, Max, and he said, "Pete, I don't know this group, but I will pay you $200 a week."

I said, "I don't want to work by myself. I want to be in this group. Pay us $200 a week."

He said, "I can't very well turn you down, I guess." It wasn't much money for the group, but he gave us free hamburgers. About a month later he saw the size of the hamburgers, and he increased us to $250 a week, but no more free hamburgers.

We stayed there for six months. Sometimes there were only ten people in the place. We would sit at the tables because there was no sense in us standing up. It was like a little party. We started in late December, or January, and by March or April the audiences started picking up. By May we were getting big crowds. That was when Gordon Jenkins came in and said, "You guys are great. I have to record you." He got us on Decca and we recorded "Goodnight Irene." Suddenly we were finding ourselves in big nightclubs like the Waldorf Astoria in New York and Ciro's in Hollywood.

In 1950, the blacklisters must have looked at us in astonishment and said, "How did we ever let those so-and-so's slip through our fingers?" They had been aiming at big fish to blacklist, like the Hollywood Ten, and we were unknowns. Then we zoomed up to notoriety, and it took a year or two to chop us down. In the summer of 1950, "Goodnight Irene" was selling 2 million copies. It was the biggest hit record since the end of World War II. We were offered a coast-to-coast network TV program sponsored by Van Camp's Pork and Beans, half an hour a week. The contract came in, we signed it. The next day, when they were supposed to sign, an outfit called the Red Channels came out with an attack on us. Called us "commie fellow-travelers," and Van Camp's never signed the contract. The jobs started vanishing, and pretty soon we were down to singing at Daffy's Bar and Grill on the outskirts of Cleveland.

After the Weavers were blacklisted, I went from college to college telling young people that there once was a guy named Leadbelly, that there once was a guy named Woody G, and that they made some great music, and that others would pick up where they left off. I sung in Palo Alto once for the local Democratic club and a college student there writes me a letter and asks for a mimeographed copy of my banjo book. Dollar fifty-nine. I sold a hundred copies in four years. A year later he writes, "Dear Pete, We're putting that banjo book to good use. I and two others have formed a group called the Kingston Trio."

A twelve-year-old girl was at the same concert in Palo Alto. After the concert she went back and looked in the mirror and made faces at herself, pretending she was onstage. Her name was Joan Baez.

I was once called "the high priest of folk music," then "the dean of folk music," and now I am an elderly folksinger. But I was lucky after the Weavers to get a little job teaching at a private school that didn't care if you became a political radical. You learn to live with the consequences. You have to face it that sooner or later you're bound to lose a job. Some people got beaten up and killed. Some were sent to jails. But I learned that trying to stay away from an argument is not necessarily a good idea. People are out there being killed, and if you say, "Oh, no, I am going to remain neutral," and take the safer stand, that to me is rather immoral.

I came to this way of thinking early. My father's younger brother was a poet who wrote a famous poem about World War I. "Have a rendezvous with death. At midnight in some flaming town. And I to my pledged word am true. I shall not fail my rendezvous."

Alan Seeger was his name, and my father wrote Alan and said, "You're a damn fool volunteering." He volunteered for the French Foreign Legion. And my father said, "I don't expect to see you again," and he didn't.

My father ended up getting fired. He was the head of the music department at Berkeley. He realized that if you're going to be open about your opinions, you might just get fired. On the other hand, you have certain wonderful advantages by being open about your opinions. You don't hide anything, and by not hiding anything, you lead a much more relaxed life. Maybe a little more broke, but my kids have always had clothes to wear. We live in the country, where we built our own cabin. Never owed a bank a whole lot of mortgage. I've done OK.

Joan Baez

○ ○ ○

Joan registers some bitterness about the wind-down of folk music, but her voice, along with Bob Dylan's and one or two others, served as a beacon for a generation. She is a quality woman with a remarkable music history.

○ ○ ○

I was the right person in the right place at the right time. I could have popped up in the eighties with this voice and nobody would have given it the time of day.

I fell in love with folk music at a time when folk music was beginning to boom. I'm a Quaker, very socially and politically engaged. Before I even sang I was involved.

I wasn't part of the New York folk scene. I was more Harvard Square. I had been to Greenwich Village a couple of times, and I was awed by it. I wandered around with black eye-makeup on, did all the appropriate things. I remember some extraordinary things, like going in and ad libbing wordless notes to Hugh Romney, who is Wavy Gravy now, one of the West Coast's more appealing lunatics, an absolutely extraordinary and wonderful lunatic. Back then he was an extraordinary and wonderful comedian.

I heard about Bob Dylan before I heard him. Somebody invited me to

Gerde's Folk City in 1961, and that was the first I heard him sing. He knocked me flat. Everything everyone said was right. I thought he was brilliant, amazing, a scuff ball. He sang a song to Woody Guthrie, and then sang a song he was making up as he was sitting there singing it.

Pete Seeger was an early influence. He came to my high school and sang. I must have been sixteen, seventeen, and all my relatives were sitting with their fingers crossed, hoping I would be interested. Up to then I had been singing rhythm and blues to the ukulele. I never thought I would be a singer. I didn't plan it. It simply happened.

I was afraid of it, afraid of show business, afraid of the industry, afraid of being commercial. At the beginning, I limited my concerts to twenty a year. People thought I was being clever, that I was saving myself to make more money the next year. That had nothing to do with it. I just thought it wasn't healthy to be on the road.

Actually, I was completely overwhelmed by my success, and it took its toll. I certainly bought into my Madonna image. It was very flattering. I thrived on the attention. I loved it.

It was easier for me politically in the sixties than it was musically. Politics came more naturally to me than music. I remember seeing Mick Jagger dancing around with handcuffs on, and people trying to levitate the Pentagon, and a lot of the Merry Pranksters on their bus, and all the love and drugs. And I thought, "Gosh, where was I?" And I was in jail. I took a much more serious Quakerly approach to politics. In a way, I missed out on all the playful politics. I was too serious. When everything was happening in San Francisco, I was singing in the deep South. Or I was in jail for draft resistance, or aiding and abetting.

And that's how people remember me. When someone is as visible as I was, doing what I was doing at the time, that is how you remain in most people's minds. Unless, for example, you're talking about Tina Turner, who will forever have two images, Tina in a short skirt and Tina with the lion hair. She surpassed her earlier image as far as mass media was concerned, and I never did. Maybe I never will, and it can't concern me. Because of the kind of society we are, we remember people for who they are at their pinnacle. To them, I'll always have long hair.

It was disorienting after the sixties when everything changed. A lot of what I went through had to do with personal ego. I have heard people lie about it, and I have heard other people be straight about it, but it is an ego bashing if you have been a superstar and then you go on an eight-year period when record companies are no longer interested, when you come to terms with yourself and figure out what you do. What do I do with my gift? What's the best way I can use it here and now? How can I cut away all the trash around it?

I remember many years ago, singing in Salt Lake City. I was picketed by the Young Americans for Freedom outside the hotel. So I went out and talked to them. I said, "What are you guys picketing about?"

So we started chatting, and I said, "You've never even heard me. Tell you what, I will give you guys complimentary seats, and afterwards we'll talk." After the show we became great friends. They may not have liked some of the things I said, but I enjoyed being able to meet new people and having a chance talk about nonviolence and my ideas. Some people, of course, are so sure I'm a communist that they'll never be able to listen and talk, but that is pretty hardheaded stuff.

Some stations in the South would not play my version of "Brothers in Arms." They said, "Ha-ha, antiwar songs. That old commie. Are you kidding?" I was floored when I heard about that, but there is still plenty of that around. I think as long as I'm attacked by the KGB and the CIA, then I'm probably on the right track.

John Stewart
o o o

John looks like an Ivy League professor. His years with the Kingston Trio and some subsequent success on his own have kept him in the business for more than a quarter century. Still making music in Malibu, he wants one more crack at it.

o o o

I wanted to be Elvis Presley. He changed my life forever. Radio had been sort of in the background for me. I was aware of it—"Old Cape Cod," Frankie Laine, Johnnie Ray—but just aware of it. It was like wallpaper to me. Growing up on the race track where my dad was a horse trainer, country music was there, and Hank Williams was there, but it wasn't important to me. Then I heard "That's All Right, Mama" and "Heartbreak Hotel" within the same two weeks and it was as though I'd been hit by a bolt of lightning. It was a shock to me. "What is that sound? What is that?" It was as though I had taken a drug.

Then I went out and bought a guitar. Sort of did an Elvis impression. Then, as soon as I learned three chords, I started writing songs. I immediately found two guys in school who played electric guitar, and we started doing Elvis Presley's songs, Buddy Holly's songs, and my songs. I said, "This sounds like something that should be on the radio," so I went down to a little studio in Pomona and cut a demo and brought it to Marty Melcher's label. They had Jan and Arnie, which is who they were before they were Jan and Dean. Marty liked the demo.

At the same time I was going in and recording in Johnny Otis' studio with Johnny's people. I was the only white guy in the whole place. They couldn't figure out what the heck I was, but they were kind of interested in it. I was sort of doing folk music at this point. I had wanted to be Elvis.

That was my dream. But Ricky Nelson got there first. I was very jealous that Rick got to be Elvis and I didn't.

The first song of mine that was recorded was "Molly Dee," by the Kingston Trio. It was the audacity of youth hanging around the dressing room. I felt, "Hey, I play these guys all the time. I play guitar. I sing, too. Of course they are going to like me. Why shouldn't I be here." I said, "Hey, can I play you a song?"

And they'd go, "Yeah, yeah, sure." So I played them the song, and they went, "Wow. Got any more?" Every time they came to town I played them songs. One day they were at the Coconut Grove at the Ambassador Hotel in L.A., and I walked in and they were in the big showroom. The waiters were getting ready for the evening. The Trio had their guitars and banjos. They were in their shorts and sweatshirts. This to me was the epitome of making it, guitars and banjos in a posh room like the Coconut Grove.

So I played them this song, "Molly Dee," and they said, "Yep, we like that one. Who is the publisher?"

I said, "What is publishing?"

All three of them went, "Frank, Frank," for Frank Werber, their manager. They said, "Sign here, son." They recorded the song and it went on their next album, an album that went to Number 1 in about two weeks. There I was, my name on a Kingston Trio record.

I was still going to junior college. Then the first royalties came in— $10,000. I said, "That's it. Why am I going to school to be an accountant?" At that time, 1958, ten grand was a year's wages. That was more than my dad made in a year.

I dropped my rock 'n' roll band and formed a duo called John and Monty. Exciting name. Exciting group. And then Frank Werber, the Trio's manager, called and told me that Roulette Records wanted a folk trio and could I put one together. Morris Levy had called Frank Werber and said, "We want another Kingston Trio." So I called my high-school choir teacher, and he left his family of four, and we got on an airplane and rehearsed in the first-class section. We went in and auditioned for Roulette Records and we were signed.

And when Dave Guard left the Trio, the others knew I was tall and played banjo and guitar and wrote songs. They asked me to come out and audition for the Trio. It was a great lesson for me, because once I passed the audition and they said, "Congratulations, John. You are going to be one of the Trio," a great feeling of emptiness came over me. It was not quite depression, but it was an empty feeling. I remember going into rehearsal and playing those songs I knew by heart. I thought, "Where is Dave? Wait a minute, you are Dave. But I am John. Dave should be here."

I remember putting on the shirt for the first photo session. There I was, wearing the striped shirt, the uniform of the day for college kids at that time. It was the Kingston Trio's famous striped shirt, and I looked in the mirror and I felt like Danny Kaye in *The Inspector General*. I felt like a fraud. That feeling never left me the entire seven years I was with the group.

Mary Travers and Peter Yarrow

○ ○ ○

They're two-thirds of the group that brought Bob Dylan's songs to the charts and made folk music fashionable in the sixties. The trio had a look, a sound, and an impeccable taste in song selection and delivery, and it continues to prosper to this day.

○ ○ ○

I grew up in the Village as the daughter of two liberal journalists. And folk music was a very integral part of the liberal Left experience. It was writers, sculptors, painters, whatever, listening to Woody Guthrie, Pete Seeger, the Weavers. People sang in Washington Square Park on Sundays, and you really did not have to have a lot of talent to sing folk music. You needed enthusiasm, which is all folk music asks. It asks that you care. Even if you're playing spoons, have a good time doing it.

So for me it was a social mechanism. I would go to the White Horse Tavern and sit in the back room with the Clancy Brothers. I've never been a drinker, but I would sit with them. They drank and I had a wonderful time with my Coca-Cola.

When we started the group, it was very clear that we needed a musical director. Enter Milt Okun. Milt came over to listen to us, and he really did not have much faith in the process, but he felt he'd give us a little hand, maybe stay on board for a while and get us started and polished up. You know, sort of straighten up the kid, put her on the street, but you really don't want anything to do with her.

So Milt asked us to sing, and as soon as we started, he grabbed me. We were standing in a V, with me standing behind the boys. Milt took me and pulled me forward, and he said, "For starters, let's invert the V."

We were untrained singers who didn't write music. I had a tendency to sometimes go flat, Peter had a tendency to sometimes go sharp, the guitars would go out. In other words, from a professional point of view there was a lot wrong. Milt fixed it.

Don Graham was someone else who was very important for us. He was crazy—I don't mean crazy—but he was tremendously energetic, a great salesman, willing to do anything. We knew absolutely nothing about the record business, so in essence Don had three willing bodies, valuable and untutored.

Don would hire students to hang signs on underpasses. Peter, Paul and Mary were literally grafittied on underpasses. Milt Glazer designed a typeface for PP&M, and Don Graham would plaster PP&M stickers all over the elevators in New York, including the ones at Columbia Records, which was funny since we recorded for Warner.

The success was like champagne bubbles. It was fantastic and mind boggling. When you're successful and you don't understand why and deep down inside you have a sneaking suspicion that you really don't deserve it, when success hits it is absolutely mind boggling and exciting.

Suddenly, you're going to the White House and you can't believe it. You're in your long dress, the boys are in rented tuxedos, and you're going, "My God, four weeks ago we had cockroaches in our apartment."

The first time we were invited to the White House it was to sing at John F. Kennedy's celebration of his second year in office. We were to sing at the party afterwards at Vice President Johnson's home. That afternoon, me, the child of the Village, was in the Washington, D.C., equivalent of Saks buying a long dress and discussing with the sales lady the protocol when shaking hands with the president of the United States. "Do I take my long gloves off? Do I leave them on?" This was the big question of the day.

So we're in the limousine, and the boys are in their first tuxedos. I'm sure Peter had never worn one in his life. Mind you, we're in the back seat of a limo, being shepherded by a motorcycle policeman who is clearly breaking the speed limit, and we're laughing so hard we're falling off the seat. We were laughing because it was so ludicrous. Here are three kids from the Village with not a suit between them on their way to touch the president of the United States.

If I had to pick one song, my softest spot, it would be "Blowing in the Wind." If you could imagine the march on Washington with Martin Luther King and singing that song in front of a quarter of a million people, black and white, who believed they could make America more generous and compassionate in a nonviolent way, you begin to know how incredible that belief was.

And still is. To sing the line, "How many years can some people exist before they're allowed to be free?" in front of some crummy little building that refuses to admit Jews in 1983, the song elicits the same response now as it did then. It addresses the same questions. "How many deaths will it take till they know that too many people have died?" Sing that line in a prison yard where political prisoners from El Salvador are being kept. Or sing it with Bishop Tu Tu. Same response. Same questions.

o o o

I instructed a course in folk music at Cornell. I did it for the money because I wanted to wash dishes less and play guitar more.

But as soon as I started teaching this course, something happened that altered my life. I saw these young people at Cornell who were basically very conservative in their backgrounds opening their hearts up and singing with an emotionality and a concern through this vehicle called folk music. It gave me a clue that the world was on its way to a certain kind of movement, and that folk music might play a part in it, and that I might play a part in folk music. By the end of the year I was catapulted from a degree in psychology to Greenwich Village.

My primary reason for wanting to be a part of folk music was to see

162 / OFF THE RECORD

activated what we still see activated by folk music today—a sense of community that appears almost inevitably when people feel they can reach out for one another and care for one another. It's a confirmation of a mutual feeling about something, whether personal or political, that seems to happen whenever traditional songs are sung. It doesn't always have to be "Blowing in the Wind."

When I came to Peter, Paul and Mary, I found another person who understood that exactly in the same terms I did. It was Mary. She lived it.

I thought Mary was gorgeous. I looked at that face, I hadn't heard a note, and I said, "That's it. Who is she?" Albert Grossman said she would be good if I could somehow get her to work.

Albert had been my manager for about a year, and while Mary and Noel (Paul) Stookey were getting to know each other in the Village, I was traveling around the country, playing clubs like the Ash Grove. Albert was seeing me enchant audiences opening up for Odetta, or fall on my face, depending on what I was reaching for. If it was a comedic moment, sometimes I fell on my face. If it was a ballad about suffering, I was usually in good shape.

The strategy of Peter, Paul and Mary was simple—absolute understanding of who we were. Had the Weavers not been blacklisted, I don't think Peter, Paul and Mary would have happened in terms of the explosion we all saw.

In the beginning, clubs never had much money to pay us. I would go on and do the first portion of the show as a solo. Noel would then come on and do a comedic portion, and then the group would come on as a whole and sing.

It was Albert's edict that Mary should not speak. His premise was for her to maintain a mystique. In today's terms, this would be insufferable chauvinism, but it looked good then. Mary was the sex object for the college male. She was "the" woman in America when Peter, Paul and Mary were the Number 1 recording artists in the country. To be with Mary was like being with Brigitte Bardot, she was so desirable.

In the meantime, I did all the serious introductions and Noel did the comedic ones. It took years for Mary to become that which is now apparent—a musical ambassador to the left-wing orientation of political investigations.

It was Bobby Dylan's writing that put us on another level. A big controversy started when Albert brought in the acetate of Bobby's new solos. Albert thought the big song was "Don't Think Twice." That, he said, was the hit. We went crazy over "Blowing in the Wind."

We went into the studio and released "Blowing in the Wind" as a single. We didn't wait for an album, we just put it out. Instinctively, we knew the song carried the moment of its own time.

We first met Dylan in the Village. Noel was the friendliest with him initially. He and I were somewhat friendly. At a certain point I felt sorry for him. He was in the city and it was hot, and my mother had a little country home in Woodstock, and I invited him to come up with his girlfriend. This was before Albert was in Woodstock.

I remember Albert asking me if I thought he should manage Dylan. We were walking in the Village, and I said, "Yeah, I think so."

And Albert said, "Yeah, I think so, too. He's too good not to happen."

You know, in the beginning, Bobby was a Woody Guthrie imitator. He did not have his own identity. Albert really shepherded him through those early years.

I remember Bobby's first concert at Town Hall. There was a party at my mother's house afterwards. My mother didn't know what was going on. At the party, she asked the scruffiest kid she could find to go out and get more ice. Of course, that was Bobby. He answered my mother by asking her to marry him.

Bob Dylan

o o o

Bob changed the nature of songwriting like no other individual. His impact on what was happening and what was to come is incalculable. And he remains as major a pop star as there ever was.

o o o

Little Richard, Carl Perkins, and Jerry Lee Lewis were the people I listened to before I got into folk music. But their scene wasn't happening anymore. It was over. The Kingston Trio and Harry Belafonte stopped having hits in the late-fifties. I heard Leadbelly somewhere and that's what got me into folk music, which was exploding. To me, it seemed like the only thing to do. I had never heard much of it growing up, except the country stuff like Bill Monroe, the Stanley Brothers, and Hank Williams.

New York was the center of activity for folk music, the mecca. Everything was coming out of New York, but I didn't go there as quickly as I could. I managed to get there in a roundabout way. It was all that I ever thought it was supposed to be. It was happening. It was a learning process because there were so many people there who knew more than I did. I picked up on what I could and I worked at it. When I got to New York, there was a small crowd of people my age, but most of the people I met were five to ten years older than I was. As far as I could remember, the scene there stayed that way until the middle-sixties when things started to turn toward more professional-type things.

When I began to record, with the early records, there used to be people in the hallways with songs for me to record. I never used any of them, but I met people who could just sit down at a piano and bang out original songs.

I already had my own material, but people were always surprised to find that I was doing only folk songs and my own songs. At that point, I didn't even consider myself a songwriter. Back then I was just carrying on.

All those early songs were first drafts that I never even sang other than when I began to record. Recording was so new to me that when the sessions were scheduled, you had to deliver. You couldn't go into the studio without songs. So whenever my sessions were scheduled to happen, I would just hole up and write songs on the road, or even at the sessions themselves. Today you write a song and think about it and change a few lines. In the old days, you wrote them up in ten minutes and that was it.

I felt passionate about all those songs because I had to sing them. They were written for me to sing. To stand in front of people and sing, I have to care about the songs. As I remember, I cared about all that stuff I wrote about.

I would meet the Top 40 people when I was out on the road, and it was surprising to me that they knew my work. All the club singers who had hit records that I knew of in the late-fifties or early-sixties crossed paths with me, and I knew my work was being perceived out there. To what degree I never knew. I knew my work was appreciated on a pure level, but I didn't know how long these songs would be around. I never really could imagine way back then that I'd still be singing the same songs in the eighties.

I wasn't surprised by the reaction I got in 1965 at Newport. Going electric was a natural progression. I had been hanging around with different people, playing different material in small gatherings and at other festivals. Newport got more media attention because it was larger than the other festivals. The way people reacted was nothing I could have prepared for, but by that time I knew pretty much what I was doing onstage.

Anytime there's a change there's a reaction. I'm conscious of criticism. It always bothers you when you think you've been treated unfairly, and I felt I received a lot of unfair criticism from the so-called rock music press. It hurts, but I always managed to get through all that and come out the other side. You get used to it after a while. Music isn't one thing or another. With most good performers you can hear all kinds of music in their music. Most performers who are rock solid you can hear country or gospel in their voices or their instruments. I don't feel that anybody is really bound down by one thing, unless you're George Jones.

People think they know me from my songs. But my repertoire of songs is so wide-ranging that you'd have to be a madman to figure out the characteristics of the person who wrote all those songs. I don't bother much with how people view me. It's hard sometimes to live up to their expectations. I like my audience a lot, and whether it's 50 people or 50,000 there's immediate feedback on both sides. So I've never really been bothered by preconceived expectations because right there that night the truth always comes out.

Some people want to lock me into the sixties, and that's OK. It's like Paul Kantner of the Airplane said, "If you can remember anything about the sixties, you weren't really there." And that's pretty much correct. I can't imagine people making such a big fuss over the sixties unless things are so dull now that they have to think of some time when things were better. If you think back, it really wasn't that much better. It was tougher in so many ways. I'm not really a nostalgic person so I don't buy into the sixties thing like a lot of people seem to do.

People ask me if it's hard being me. I answer, "To a degree, but it's not any more difficult than being George Michael." You can't really complain about who you are, whoever you are. You just have to make the most of it, and that's all that can be expected of you.

Smokey Robinson

○ ○ ○

A pivotal player as an artist and a driving force in the Motown story, Smokey has written or performed or produced at least one of your all-time favorite songs. He's going into the nineties with the same style and verve he showed during the Miracle years.

○ ○ ○

I started out so young, seventeen years old, and I guess I just happened to be at the right place at the right time. I should say *the* right place because Berry Gordy, who was just starting out himself, was at an audition we were doing. At the time, we were called the Matadors, but we changed the name to the Miracles because we had a girl with us.

At the audition, we sang all these songs I had written in high school, and the songs impressed Berry. Because he was also a songwriter, we were able to strike up a relationship. It turned out that the people we auditioned for didn't like our group, but Berry and I developed a relationship. It was shortly after that Berry started Motown.

Motown was started very precariously. Berry was the first black trying to break into the record business, and for many years we struggled. We started with five or six employees. We would mail out the records, take them to the shops and radio stations. But we loved what we were doing.

A lot of talk is made about Motown being a family. It all started with family money. Berry borrowed money from his family to start Motown, so it started with a family atmosphere. We were all young black people from the same neighborhood, and we all had one goal in mind—to make good records.

We never dared to dream, but there was a point where we became aware of what was happening in the music business. A great awakening for me was when I began receiving letters from white kids who lived in the Detroit suburbs, places like Grosse Pointe, where blacks couldn't live at the time. And we would get letters from the white kids who would say things like, "We love Motown. We have all your records. Our parents don't know we have them. If they knew, they'd take them away."

People look at the Miracles and they think, "God, they had all those hits." But people don't remember the misses. When you're part of it, you remember the misses. You remember the lean times as well as the good times. Which is good. We were common folk and we never got bigheaded. We never said, "Hey, we're the Miracles." We remained pretty levelheaded. A lot of talent and luck goes into making a successful recording career.

If you start to believe you're something special, that because you're onstage and the chicks are screaming and trying to tear your clothes off, you are in trouble. You are doomed. If you somehow can remember, "Yeah, they're doing this, and it's wonderful that they're reacting in this way, but I'm just a guy who sings," you'll be OK. The cabdriver's daughter is out there, the grocer is out there, people like that. I need them, really, more than they need me.

I know that I have a voice that when people hear it, they know who it is. I enjoy singing, but I don't consider myself a great singer. I think I feel songs, but I don't consider myself a great singer like, say, Aretha Franklin, or Luther Vandross, or Jackie Wilson, people who can just sing. Basically, I'm a song feeler who has sung some of his songs thousands and thousands of times. But each time is a new time for me.

As a writer, I'm a song lover. All my life I've been a song lover, from the time I was a little kid. With what money I had, I bought songbooks. And I had a great teacher in Berry Gordy. He was the one who showed me how to turn my songs into little stories. I could always rhyme stuff, but I wasn't a good continuity person. My songs didn't tell a complete story from beginning to middle to end. I would go off on several subjects in the same song. But everything always rhymed. I am a songwriter who takes my songs very seriously. I have many songs I'll never reveal because I know they're not right yet.

From time to time I've thought, "Hey, maybe that's it. Maybe that last hit was it. Maybe it's over." But I don't think like that anymore. I just know I have a God-given gift, and if I apply myself, then probably I will come up with something else.

When I look back at my life, the thing I'm most proud of is that I'm still here. I have been doing this for thirty years, and I have a hit album. Right now. That makes me feel real good.

Little Richard, 1985
(Photo by Leo Jarzomb)

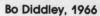
Bo Diddley, 1966

Jerry Lee Lewis, 1984
(Photo by Henry Diltz)

Roy Orbison, 1979
(Photo by Chris Gulker)

Left to right: **Hank Ballard, Lawson Smith, Norman Thrasher and Henry Booth, 1958**

James Brown, 1981
(Photo by Paul Chinn)

Dick Clark, 1986
(Photo by Henry Diltz)

Paul Robi

Muddy Waters *(left)*
with Marshall Chess *(right)*, **1966**
(Photo by Jeff Lowenthal)

Pat Boone, 1961

Del Shannon, 1986
(Photo by Mike Mullen)

The Everly Brothers—Phil *(left)* **and Don, 1986**
(Photo by James Ruebsamen)

Dion, 1988
(Photo by Leo Jarzomb)

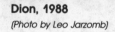

Mike Stoller *(left)*, **Elvis Presley, and Jerry Leiber, 1957**

Gerry Goffin, 1986
(Photo by Ellen Minasian Goffin)

Ben E. King
(Michael Ochs Archives)

Barry Mann and Cynthia Weil, 1975
(Photo by Henry Diltz)

Duane Eddy
(Michael Ochs Archives)

Al Bennett

Little Anthony

Artie Ripp
(Photo by Bob Green)

Jimmie Haskell and Rick Nelson, 1959

Tom Jones, 1980
(Photo by Anne Knudsen)

Bob Marcucci

B.B. King, 1982
(Photo by Chris Gulker)

Harold Leventhal

Fabian, 1959

Left to right: **Ellie Greenwich,
Jeff Barry, and Brooks Arthur, 1963**

Pete Seeger, 1984

Joan Baez and Bob Dylan, 1982
(Photo by Henry Diltz)

John Stewart, 1971
(Photo by Henry Diltz)

Noel Stookey *(left)*, **Mary Travers, Peter Yarrow**
(Photo by Dean Musgrove)

Martha Reeves and Smokey Robinson, 1983
(Photo by Anne Knudsen)

Mary Wilson, 1986
(Photo by James Ruebsamen)

Lamont Dozier
(Michael Ochs Archives/
Photo by Don Paulsen)

The Four Tops *(left to right)*: **Duke Fakir, Lawrence Payton, Obie Benson, Levi Stubbs** *(Michael Ochs Archives)*

Jan Berry and Dean Torrence, 1964
(Photo by Jill Gibson)

Mike Love *(left)* **Carl Wilson, 1980**
(Photo by Rob Brown)

Eddie Kendricks
(Michael Ochs Archives/ Photo by Don Paulsen)

Burt Bacharach, 1967

Lester Sill

Herb Alpert, 1987

(Photo by Henry Diltz)

Bones Howe, 1986

(Photo by Sandy Gibson)

John Tropea and Bob Crewe
(Photo by Popsie)

Neil Diamond, 1986
(Photo by Leo Jarzomb)

Bobby Vinton, 1964

Frankie Valli, 1984
(Photo by Dean Musgrove)

Chubby Checker, 1961

George Martin, 1975
(Photo by Henry Diltz)

Paul McCartney, 1984
(Photo by Anne Knudsen)

Mick Jagger, 1978
(Photo by Chris Gulker)

Dave Clark

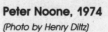

Peter Noone, 1974
(Photo by Henry Diltz)

Roger Daltrey, 1969
(Photo by Henry Diltz)

Peter Asher, 1970
(Photo by Henry Diltz)

Mickie Most

Cliff Richard
(Michael Ochs Archives)

Mark Lindsay
(Michael Ochs Archives)

Lou Adler, 1986
(Photo by Sandy Gibson)

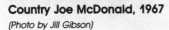

Country Joe McDonald, 1967
(Photo by Jill Gibson)

Mike Nesmith, 1967
(Photo by Henry Diltz)

Donovan, 1984
(Photo by Mike Sergieff)

Bill Graham, 1982
(Photo by Paul Chinn)

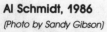

Al Schmidt, 1986
(Photo by Sandy Gibson)

Paul Kantner, 1971
(Photo by Henry Diltz)

Jann Wenner, 1985
(Photo by Chris Gulker)

Mary Wilson

○ ○ ○

A Supreme who's full of vivid memories of the group's success and definite opinions about the lead singer. Diana gets mixed reviews from Mary.

○ ○ ○

I am a Supreme, so it is very difficult for me to say, "Oh, it was just us, just our combination." But I really think it was our combination.

Holland-Dozier-Holland had a formula for music, and the proof is the Four Tops, the Temptations, and Martha & the Vandellas. The Supremes were different. The producers had their way of producing, and the other artists were really R & B artists, very soulful. Like Martha was really soulful. But when Holland-Dozier-Holland applied the same technique to the Supremes, who were really not soulful . . . And regardless what anyone says about the Supremes selling out and having a white sound, that is not truth. We wanted to be soulful, but we could not. It was not Diane's [Diana's] style. Florence and I were a bit more soulful, but with them producing us, their technique had to be turned around and applied to another medium.

What that brought out was a new philosophy, a new sound. And that's where the magic came in. We couldn't sing R & B, so the R & B came out a different way, and everyone kind of grasped it, and we crossed over. We were black, and we were singing, but we weren't singing black. And maybe that's what sparked a new creativity.

But the producers had the clout, and that kept the artists begging. The producers treated us not very kindly. They received more money than the artists. We were broke for years before we became stars. The producers ran Motown, the producers and Berry.

My first impression of Berry Gordy was, I was not impressed. You hear about people, and in your mind they become very big, and here comes this little guy hopping in and grinning. We kind of looked at each other, and I thought, "This is the big man we are supposed to impress?"

I felt there was a lot going on behind the smile. There was something at work back there, in his head. Being so young, I could not figure out what it was. In retrospect now I know. That man had something he wanted to accomplish. I don't think he was very different from a lot of other people in Detroit at the time, con men and hip people, but Berry was different because he had a goal, a vision.

Motown was like walking into a dream world. Everyone there had a dream. We pestered Berry, we pestered Holland-Dozier-Holland, and we pestered Smokey Robinson—to make our dream come true.

The one time I remember complaining was in 1968 when I went to Berry and said, "You know, we have been working for years, and I have not had a legitimate vacation. I really want one."

And he wouldn't give it to me because Holland-Dozier-Holland had left, and everyone was fighting to get the records. Berry said to me, "You have to stay here with us. You have to be a part."

I said, "I don't want to be a part. I want a rest." Florence had left, which devastated me, and I needed to get away from Berry and Diane, and he wouldn't let me. He said, "You'll see, one of these days you're gonna wish you were here."

Diane may choose to pretend that the Supremes never existed for her, that the happiness was not there, and Florence may not have gotten all the beauty that was there because of her own problems. I chose to enjoy it, and enjoy it I did. So I had many romances. One romance, perhaps the most beautiful one in my life, was with Duke Fakir of the Four Tops. He and I were known as the sweethearts of Motown. We lived together for three years. I was in my late teens. He was a star, and I was a star, and we'd come home from the road and we'd share experiences. Then he'd call the guys from the Temps, the Miracles, and they'd all come over and we'd sing. I don't think any other man, except someone who was a star in his own right, could understand a woman being on top like that. Duke understood.

The Supremes were in England when the first rumors came out about Diane leaving the group. I think it was the *Daily Mail* that said, "What about Diane leaving the group?"

We were sitting there going, "Ahh." Florence and I were becoming very angry about Diane being pulled out. We were never consulted, and suddenly Diane was slowly moving forward and the Supremes were being pushed back. I knew once Florence left the group that it was over. It was then we knew for sure that Diane was eventually going to leave, too.

Diane and I talked a little, but we never took our problems onstage. Once we were onstage, everything was beautiful again. Once we were off-stage, Diane and Berry went one way, and Florence and I went the other.

I don't blame Diane, and I don't blame myself. We were both too young to know how to communicate, too young to know how to cope with people coming in and building you up, people tearing you apart. Diane was thrilled that it was happening for her, so in her mind I am sure she was just caught up in it. Stars get caught up in those things, which is too bad because all you're really in it for is to sing.

Most of the bitterness was during the time Florence was leaving and shortly thereafter. Diane and Berry had to deal with me being there, knowing I was not happy because of what had happened to Flo. Eventually I was told Diane would be leaving, too. At that point it got a little better for me because I saw the chance for me to start the group over and continue it. Not because I was taking her place, but because it had grown ugly, and it had all been too beautiful to become that.

In the end, I learned a lot from both women. Florence gave it up because she couldn't stand what was happening in the name of being a star, and I know I don't want that to happen to me. So from Florence I learned a lesson.

And I also learned something from Diane. Diane went on to make it on her own, so I know it can be done. I am where I want to be because I planned it that way.

Lamont Dozier
o o o

Lamont is probably fated to have his name forever sandwiched between two Hollands. However they list him or them, the trio carved out a piece of American history with their Motown music. Incredible songwriters, the best of the English wave acknowledge their debt to the records they produced.

o o o

We punched a clock, literally punched a clock, nine o'clock in the morning. That was the procedure at Motown. Berry Gordy had worked at Ford, so he ran Motown like a factory.

We'd come in and right away we'd start banging away. It was like, "OK, turn on the creative machine."

I first met Brian Holland when Berry suggested I team up with him to write and produce. I had seen him around town, but we'd never been formally introduced. I would cut sheets of paper out of brown shopping bags. I'd have these stacks of brown paper with song titles and lyrics, like "Come and Get These Memories" and "Heat Wave," little things I'd scratched down or started.

My first collaboration with Brian was for the Marvelettes, a song called "Locking Up My Heart." It went Top 20, and I went straight to Berry and asked him for an advance so I could buy a Cadillac. He said, "Wait a minute. Slow down. You're not even together yet, and you want to take all your royalties and buy a car? You don't have a decent place to sleep. Did you think you'd sleep in the car?"

Brian and I got a little bogged down after that. We were writing for the Marvelettes and nothing big was happening. Then Eddie Holland decided he didn't want to sing anymore. He never wanted to be a singer anyway. So he came in with us as a lyricist and we became Holland-Dozier-Holland.

Eddie was very quiet, very businesslike. The guys never drank. They were milk drinkers. The dope and the drinking was for somewhere else, but not at Motown. Motown was clean. Motown was image conscious. Berry kept a tight hold over the girls and guys. I had a saying that went, "Motown could stumble and fall, but it would always come up smelling like a rose."

It was important that we gave a song character or definition, or a feeling.

We would often use the same chords for more than one song. For example, "Where Did Our Love Go" by the Supremes and "Can't Help Myself" by the Four Tops are actually the same song because they have the same bass figure. Take the bass figure out of one and you can easily sing the other.

The studio at Motown was a very small room, like a family room or a billiards room in someone's house. You had to step down two or three feet to walk into the room. It was made of cinderbrick, not what you'd call the perfect recording studio.

Brian was basically the recording engineer, melody man, and producer. Eddie wrote lyrics, and he would sing the demos for the artists. My function was melody, lyrics, I'd sing backgrounds on the demos, and I produced with Brian.

If I started a song, like "Heat Wave" or "It's the Same Old Song," I'd give it to Eddie to finish up. Down the line somewhere Brian and I would get together and produce it.

Berry Gordy felt Diana Ross was going to be a big star. I have to admit, at the time I didn't agree. All I heard was a very high voice that most of the time sounded like a cat. I always liked Diana's tone, but I felt she needed to cut down the register to give her voice more body.

"Where Did Our Love Go" was originally cut for the Marvelettes. When we gave it instead to the Supremes, Diana said to me something to the effect of, "You're always giving us the crap."

My reply went something like, "You ought to be glad to get what you're getting."

When the song hit, Brian and I went to the airport to pick up the Supremes after they came back from touring with Dick Clark, and their whole attitude was "star time." No apologies, no nothing.

Everybody was sheltered at Motown. If we wanted to take a vacation and go to New York or L.A., Berry would say, "Why don't we all go together?" He wanted everybody to come to him, he wanted to stay in touch with everybody. What he didn't want was the outside world coming in and snatching up one of his people. That's why he kept it like a close family for as long as he could, until the company just got so big that it got out of hand.

Levi Stubbs

o o o

**The lead singer of the Four Tops, whose distinctive sound and style
made the group one of the best of breed from the Detroit school, Levi
remembers it all. He's out there on the road again, savoring the
memories himself while exposing them to newer audiences.**

o o o

The Four Tops originally recorded for Chess Records, and nothing ever
happened. Prior to Motown we were searching for an identity. We had been
working in supper clubs, singing songs like "Paper Doll," whatever it took
to put some bread on the table.

By the time we got to Motown we were pros, but not pros as far as the
record business was concerned. We were not great dancers, but we thought
about dancing a lot because all black groups danced. We were working one
time in Palm Springs at a place called the Chi Chi, and after the first show
the owner, who liked us, asked us whether we were singers or dancers. We
decided right then to be singers and forget about all the crazy steps.

So we come to Motown and we're at a place called the Twenty Grand
watching the Temptations, and Brian Holland comes up to us and says, "I
think we have a song for you guys." It's one-thirty in the morning and he
says, "Listen to it tomorrow."

We said, "Why don't we go into the studio tonight?" He said OK, and
after the show we went back to Hitsville and recorded "Baby I Need Your
Loving" that night, our very first record on Motown.

That was one of the unique things about Motown. There were no set
hours to do anything. If you came up with something creative at three in
the morning, you called everyone up and said, "Hey, man, I got something.
Do you want to listen?" And everybody would get in their cars and ride down
to the studio on the spot and do it.

So the song comes out and it's a hit. The first thing we did was go out
and buy cars, long before we had any money, mind you. That was one of
the foolish things we did, but it was a dream come true. When you come
from the ghetto, man, you just can't believe that something like that is going
to happen to you.

When we recorded "I Can't Help Myself," I felt there was nothing to
the song. Eddie Holland sat me down and said, "Levi, sing the song. I
guarantee it will be a big song for you." I didn't believe him. Shows you
what I know.

We went down to Georgia once. We'd never been in the South professionally. We knew about the racial stuff, but we hadn't experienced it. We
get off the bus and go into a white waiting room, and this big cop comes
in, seven feet tall with his gun out, and says, "I don't know where you niggers
are from, but down here segregation still exists, so get your black so-and-

so's back into the colored waiting room." And then he grabs us by the back of our necks, just to make sure we go where we're supposed to go.

Another time we were performing in Alabama, and the people loved us. We did an hour and a half on stage, and we were exhausted. The people kept screaming. Two sheriffs came back into the dressing room and told us, "If you don't get back on that stage, we're going to confiscate your clothes."

In the end, the Four Tops were extremely fortunate. We had a lot of hits, and we managed to keep our heads above water. By the time the calm came—like Billy Eckstine says, "All of a sudden it gets calm"—we accepted it and went with the flow.

Eddie Kendricks

o o o

Eddie was a key man and a great voice in the Temptations. They made so many records that still live for the *Big Chill* generation and beyond that it was difficult to find a starting place for our talk.

o o o

The Temptations wanted to look good, because when you look good you feel good, and we wanted a bebop kind of charisma, the whole nine yards.

We were a group already, with a look and the choreography, before we ever met Berry Gordy and Smokey Robinson. Our sound was unique, and mainly because we had more than one guy who could sing. That was one of our claims to fame, and not a lot of groups could duplicate that. So the looks, the sex appeal, the dress, and numerous lead singers was a combination Mr. Gordy saw. And obviously he liked what he saw because he sure knew what to do with it.

As we became successful—and I'm only speaking for myself—it didn't take me long to realize that when I get out of that limousine, I had better be me. Can't get too used to that kind of car because there's no telling the kind of car I'm going to have to get into in order to get home. And my car may break down, and someone may have to pick me up in a truck. Just as long as I get home, and just as long as I'm me. That's the point.

I don't know how the other guys looked at it, but I always tried not to let my feet get too far off the ground. You can really get spaced in this business. I always tried to remember that yesterday's news is yesterday's news. It's today's news that feeds you. And because my feet were on the ground most of the time I never got too tripped out on the big houses and the big cars.

In this business, anyway, you only make enough money to afford you to go get more money. So it winds up costing you more to get more, which means you got to maintain a cornerstone for yourself if you ever want to build a nest egg. And it's hard to build a nest egg because you're always working for somebody else. And when you work for somebody else, that's it. You work for them. Who you are is something you better have a handle on.

Martha Reeves

o o o

A fabulous voice who let it fly during her days on top, Martha's another Motowner who has something to say about the Berry Gordy empire and how it treated her.

o o o

I started singing at the age of three at my grandfather's church in Alabama. My role models were gospel singers like the Caravans and Mahalia Jackson. I saw Lena Horne when I was three, and I fell in love with her. Dinah Washington's was always the voice I thought most beautiful of all jazz singers. And I greatly admired Ella Fitzgerald, too.

If there was a party, I was always made to get up and sing. I started out trying to please my mom and dad. If we did what they told us to do and made them proud, they'd give us ice cream and cake.

I was making five dollars a night singing when I met William Stevenson from the A & R department at Motown Records. He approached me and said, "You got something. Come on to Motown." He gave me a card. I was not smart enough to wait a week or so and get me a fur coat and a dog and go in like a big star. I went in nine o'clock the next morning and became Motown's first A & R secretary.

When I first arrived, I was taken to an office in the basement where they used to usher in all the writers. All these guys were working under adverse conditions. They had a piano and maybe a desk, but no clock, no file cabinets.

Everything was done to satisfy Berry. Whatever he said was right. During the early days, when we'd be rehearsing, he would sit in the audience and critique us and gives us pointers, things I still use today. The man did know what he was doing. Everybody who did well at Motown owes it to Berry Gordy and his taste.

I get misty every time I hear our first record, "Come and Get These Memories." The record typifies the Motown sound, which was derived from using Benny Benjamin on drums, Jamie Jamerson on bass, and the Funk Brothers.

I was there when a lot of the great Motown songs were written. I would be sitting at the desk, and someone would come over and say, "Martha, write this down," and it would be a rhyme and they would dump it out on the piano. The next thing you know it would be on a lead sheet.

Of the Martha & the Vandellas records, "Heat Wave" was good, but "Quicksand" came too soon after it. It cut into the sales of "Heat Wave." Same with "Live Wire." It jumped the gun, too. As far as I'm concerned, we never had a real hit until "Dancing in the Street." That's when we really made our mark.

Although we were mistaken a lot of times for Freedom Riders when we were out on tour, we crossed color lines without much difficulty. I never really considered myself a black artist. Just a good R & B singer. We did play some places where they had segregated audiences, but by the time the music started to gel, people got together and mixed much easier.

On the whole, no one who sings is ever treated fairly. In the beginning, you don't get paid. You might get a hit and achieve some kind of financial success, but the time and effort that it takes to retain a voice and keep yourself under control and attend to the different things you need to do to be a performer, it never ends up being fair.

I didn't leave Motown. Motown left me. I was in Detroit when they moved the whole works to Los Angeles. I was one of the people who had to face the people in Detroit who said, "What happened? Why did they move?"

Motown made a decision to get out of town right away, and some people were able to make the move and some weren't. I was one of the ones who was not informed. I heard about it, like the song says, "through the grapevine."

Mike Love

○ ○ ○

The Beach Boys are a national treasure, and Mike Love has been in from the start. But as Mike points out, it wasn't always fun in the sun for the group.

○ ○ ○

When the Beach Boys started, the rock business was still pretty new. Chuck Berry, Little Richard, Jerry Lee Lewis, and Elvis were the guys who established rock 'n' roll music, and we sort of came right before the Beatles and the Rolling Stones.

As a group in the early sixties, there was not much around to pattern ourselves after. And the business at the time, especially the business of one-nighters, was funky. We'd play in a ballroom in the Midwest, and a bunch of rural people would come in on Friday and Saturday night to dance. And the microphones would look like those big round things from the forties.

And there was always inadequate sound. And the lighting, nobody gave a shit about that. Most of these places were built for basketball. The acoustics were rotten. This is how rock groups taking their own sound and lights on the road evolved. We were a vocal group as well as a rock group, and we would die out there without the right microphones and amps. For that reason, I think we may have been the first rock act to spend a fortune on sound.

In the beginning, Murry Wilson was our manager. We fought with him, we disagreed with him. Even though he was my uncle, and Brian and Carl and Dennis' father, the natural thing between young guys and their parents is to argue. Murry was rough. He would not listen to another guy's side of the story. But in the time that he was our manager, he was a genius when it came to promotion. He was a tireless promoter. In fact, when he got tired he would lay in his bed and call another radio station. He'd light up his pipe, pick up the phone, and dial a station in Salt Lake City, or Fresno, or San Bernardino. He knew all the call letters and all the program directors.

In addition to being nice guys with talent, the reason the Beach Boys were so successful was that first, we had a concept—surfing, cars, girls, all the stuff about growing up. The second most important thing was Murry. He promoted us like you would not believe. I can't even count how many DJ hops and teen hops we did. I remember once how we stood on the roof of a radio station in Fresno in 110-degree temperatures. We were playing on the roof, and the kids would drive around the station. We'd get our hundred bucks, and then we'd drive to San Gabriel, or Riverside, wherever we could, just to play for another DJ. And the DJ would have these little dances, and he'd get his hundred bucks for being at the dance. It was like a little taste for the DJ, which was a legal form of payola that they called an "appearance fee." You do that three or four times a week, and you can buy that little extra something for your girlfriend.

But we played for nothing, or next to nothing, or for expenses. The DJs and the program directors were making a thousand dollars, and we were making a hundred dollars. But we owned every radio station we played at. The DJs and the program directors always knew we'd come back. So they played us and played us and played us, and the kids loved it.

We got to the point where we were so successful that people, certain collectors, would buy anything the Beach Boys put out. During our peak years, we could burp in unison, and people would buy it, just to have it as part of their collection.

The flip side is, the Beach Boys were definitely affected by that success. Some were hurt more than others. Dennis unfortunately ruined himself. And Brian was so vulnerable and so naive. He succumbed to the people around him who were giving him drugs. Some people can smoke a joint, some people can take a pill, or do whatever up their nose, and seemingly not be hurt by what they do. They can still function. Then there are others, like alcoholics. Once they take that drink, they can no longer control themselves.

To some people, pot is no biggy. To other people, it gives them psychotic episodes, makes them paranoid, or schizophrenic, and they go completely nuts. With Brian, he became clinically classified as a paranoid schizophrenic. To this day he still has a lot of paranoia.

Dean Torrence
o o o

He's the Dean of Jan and, who had a remarkable run and led the way for California in pop music. Jan's tragic accident and their subsequent return to touring the world is a dramatic twist in the pop world.

o o o

It happened so darn fast. We struggled doing music for, oh, a good four months before we had a hit. I tell you, it was terrible. Living at home, going to school, going to the beach on weekends. I mean, we had real rough lives. Jan was pre-med at UCLA, and I was in the school of architecture at USC. We thought of music as something to do on weekends and holidays and after school.

Jan was schlepping a tape around in '58 of a song we had done called "Jenny Lee." We had done this tape in Jan's garage and we wanted it put on disc so it would look like a record. Basically, we wanted to play it at parties so we could tell everyone we had a record and really get the chicks interested.

So Jan found a studio that would transfer the music to disc, and right around the same time I get this bright idea to go into the army. Jan says, "Come on, I found a studio."

I said, "Jan, this is my last day before the army. My girlfriend, Cindy, is sad that I'm going in. We're going to take a drive." Off I go for this drive, and Jan goes into the studio.

As he's in the process of transferring it to disc, the proverbial record producer walks through the studio door and says, "Give me that tape. I'll add some instruments, and then I'll put it out, and you'll be bigger than the Everly Brothers." Jan gives the guy the tape.

Later that night, Jan tells me that we got this record deal. Jan says we're going to be bigger than the Everly Brothers. I say, "Yeah, sure, that's very nice, Jan, but I'm leaving for Fort Ord in the morning. Call me if anything happens."

Well, the sucker comes out on this little label, Arwin, which was a write-off label for Doris Day and her husband, Marty Melcher. And it's a hit. I'm in the army and I hear it on the radio. At the end of it, the DJ goes, "And that was 'Jenny Lee,' a new boss hit out of L.A., by Jan and Arnie."

I go, "Arnie? Who the heck is Arnie?" Actually, I knew who Arnie was. He was Arnie Ginsberg, a guy who helped us write the song. He also sang backgrounds on the tape.

I call Jan. I say, "I heard the record. It sounded pretty good, but my name wasn't on it."

Jan says, "I couldn't find you. I called your mom and she said you were busy with the army and stuff."

Some time after I came out of the service, Arnie decided he'd rather be surfing somewhere, so I rejoined Jan and it stayed that way from then on.

Lou Adler came up with "Baby Talk." Jan had known Lou, who had been working with Sam Cooke. Lou and his partner, Herb Alpert, were a couple of years older than we were, and they seemed like knowledgeable guys.

"Baby Talk" was already out by someone else, but it didn't do so hot. We took home the 45 and worked on our own arrangement, two vocals and a piano in Jan's garage, and we gave the tape to Lou. Herb Alpert arranged the rest of the record, and "Baby Talk" became a reality and a Top 10 record.

We worked with Lou and Herbie for maybe two, three years. Herb functioned more or less as our musical director, and Lou was pretty much our personal manager. And then one day Herb took Lou into another room and said, "I think Jan and Dean are about at the end of their rope. This is the next thing." And Herb plays Lou this trumpet thing with a mariachi band called "The Lonely Bull."

Lou says, "What the hell is this?"

Herb says, "It's the trumpet. Pretty soon everyone is going to be into trumpets."

Lou says, "I believe in Jan and Dean. I'm going to stick with them." Herb believed in what he was doing and the two parted company. We dug into our savings and cut "Heart and Soul." It went Number 1 in L.A., and we're thinking that Herb is hearing this somewhere and kicking himself. As it turned out, Herb didn't do too badly for himself.

I wouldn't say Jan was a reckless driver, but he did like to drive fast. He would be driving and all of a sudden he'd come up with a musical part that he wanted to remember. So he would have me hand him a notebook, and I would steer as he wrote it down. I would say, "Why don't we pull over?"

He'd say, "Nah, we don't have time."

About a week before Jan's accident in '66, we were on a road someplace in the Midwest, driving fairly late at night in a brand-new rented Thunderbird. Jan wants to see how fast the car will go, so he opens it up and we're going a hundred. We drive right by a couple of cops. We were going so fast that it took them ten or fifteen miles to catch us and pull us over. These guys are ready to put handcuffs on us, and Jan is telling them who we are and that we're late for a concert for crippled kids in Chicago.

These guys don't have a clue as to what he's talking about, so Jan starts pulling out our albums and hands them to the cops. In five minutes, we were best buddies. We signed the albums for their kids and they left. It was eleven o'clock at night, and yet they believed us about this concert for crippled kids in Chicago. As soon as the cops were out of sight, Jan stepped on the gas and we were off again.

I heard about his accident at school. Someone came up to me and asked whether Jan was going to be OK. I said, "OK about what?"

Jan was in a coma for about twenty-one days until he finally came out of it. But that was it. Jan crashed and it was over. As quick as it had begun for us, one crash in the time it takes to snap your fingers and it was gone.

Bones Howe

o o o

A pioneer engineer and producer from the days when California became a force in the pop music business, his work with the Association, Fifth Dimension, and other L.A. acts kept him jumping. He now does motion picture music with the same skill.

o o o

Lou Adler was hanging around Keen Records with Sam Cooke when I met him. I didn't work with Lou right away because I was a staff engineer at United, and Lou was more or less independent. I would do a pop artist like Sinatra one day, and then rock 'n' roll the next day. This was '61, '62, a time of tremendous transition in the music business.

Around '62 I decided I wanted to be an independent engineer. I no longer wanted somebody telling me what time I had to come to work, or who I had to work with. I wanted control over my life. I kept saying to myself, "I don't see why I can't work for a record company on a session-by-session basis, and be paid the same amount a musician is paid." Certainly my services as an engineer on a recording session are just as valuable as the fiddle player or guitar player.

So I went independent, and within four days the studios were hiring me back at an hourly rate that was twice the money they were paying me before. I was off and running.

Amazing, but guys like Lou Adler, who had never used me before, started calling. Because they were independent producers they wanted to work with somebody who worked for them, not for the studio, and that's what started my working relationship with Lou.

We did an Everly Brothers record together, "Don't Ask Me to Be Friends." We did the mix and Lou took the dub home, and he called me at home and said, "You know, this is the best mix I've ever heard on any record." The record was a minor hit, nothing major, but it was the beginning of our relationship. Lou was still at Nevins-Kirshner at the time, which was the publishing company he worked for. But he was producing, on behalf of them, becoming a producer under their auspices.

Lou and I had a good working relationship. He had a good sense of songs. He knew how to cast particular songs for particular artists. He wasn't technical minded and he wasn't a musician, but he knew what he wanted a record to sound like. Our working relationship was so good that we hardly spoke. And this extended through Jan and Dean, Johnny Rivers, the Mamas and the Papas, right up until the time I started producing on my own.

In Jan and Dean, Jan was always in complete control of everything. Dean just sort of came in, sang and went home. I think he resented that a lot, but that's the way things were. Lou started out as Jan and Dean's producer, but then Jan really took over and became the producer. Once Jan learned the studio, he took over. Jan and Dean had started recording in a garage, and once they started working in a real studio, Jan got very, very smart about the technology. He had all these ideas about overdubbing, and making sounds with two drummers, all kinds of things that weren't being done at the time. Little by little, Lou backed out. He became like the executive producer of Jan and Dean, and then he wasn't involved at all.

With Rivers, Lou was very involved. Like the time we recorded "Memphis." Lou decided to cut it and make it sound like it was a live recording. He had what he called "go-go girls," which were just a bunch of high school girls, neighbors' daughters, come to the studio, a dozen of them, and they'd just sort of talk and mill around, and we'd play the record back into the studio and pick up the sound of their voices. And they'd clap along with the record. We mixed that in and the result was it sounded live. "Memphis" started a whole chain of go-go records.

The Mamas and the Papas weren't even called the Mamas and the Papas. They were called the Magic Circle, which I thought was great. When they changed it to the Mamas and the Papas, I said, "The Mamas and the Papas? What kind of name is that?"

They sang in the studio for us, and Lou said to me, "What do you think?"

I said, "If you don't sign them, I will." The day we met them, Lou gave them twenty dollars to go have dinner. They were absolutely broke. But their music was alive. Vocally, they were doing something that hadn't been done before. They were light years ahead of their predecessor, Peter, Paul and Mary.

Burt Bacharach

○ ○ ○

Grammys, Oscars, and platinum records fill his Los Angeles home. He brings a touch of class to pop music and has been doing so for twenty-five years. Along with a few others, Burt represents the Kerns, Porters, and Gershwins of the modern era.

○ ○ ○

When I got out of the army, I got a job working for Vic Damone. I had no intention of becoming a songwriter. It was just a chance to play piano for Vic Damone and maybe conduct for him.

When I got fired, which I did, I went to work for the Ames Brothers. The songs that used to come in for them were so deceptively simple—songs like "You, You, You"—that I thought, "Geez, I ought to be able to write four or five of these a day."

So I'm out on the road with the Ames Brothers thinking, "Just write five of these a day and you'll be very successful." Well, I went a year without getting anything published.

What I learned, of course, was that it was not so simple. In fact, it's the hardest thing in the world to write a simple melody that's fresh and doesn't sound stolen.

Songwriting, at least when I was young, seemed like such a chore. I didn't even like playing the piano. I would like to have been an athlete, like an All–Southern Conference fullback, or something, but I was short and music seemed like a good access road to some kind of social contact.

I was the smallest kid in a high school that had the tallest basketball team in the city of New York. I just could never find a girl as short as me. Then I had some shots of peanut butter, or whatever it was, and I started to grow, and I found that by playing in a little band, or knowing how to play the piano, girls would speak to me, and some of the shyness would go away. That was the tap-in for me. Music was never a burning desire.

I also knew that you don't make much money as a musician, and you don't get fresh orange juice in the morning. In other words, I knew it would be a hard road.

When I began writing, it seemed everyone was bouncing around. It was almost incestuous. I'd write with Hal David three times a week, and then I'd switch off and write with Bob Hilliard in the morning, and then in the afternoon Bob would write with the same composer Hal had just finished with. And on and on like that.

Ultimately, I settled in with Bob and Hal. Bob wrote the Chuck Jackson hit, "Any Day Now," one of my very favorite songs.

With Hal, of course, it became quite successful. And fun, both of us sitting in a room staring at each other. I'm a very slow writer. I've always been very slow. I can really labor over something. And Hal wasn't extremely fast either, so we were a good match.

But I must say, that first year it was very hard. A lot of rejections. Playing a song and somebody stopping you after eight bars! I remember going in to see Connie Francis, and she lifted the needle off the demo.

I've always thought, there must have been a lot of people who, had they been able to stick it out and have the stomach to be rejected repeatedly and beaten up by the whole process, might have become very successful. But I guess there's a point where you just can't take it anymore.

Luckily, that didn't happen with Hal and me, and that's probably because we met Dionne Warwick.

Jerry Leiber and Mike Stoller were doing a date with the Drifters, and we had two songs on the date. We came into Jerry and Mike's office and there were these three girls, background singers, rehearsing for the Drifters' session. One was Dionne, another was her sister Dee Dee, and the third was Cissy Houston.

They sounded really great, but Dionne had a very unique look—pigtails and sneakers, just a certain quality about her.

She contacted us a little later on about maybe coming in and doing some demos for us. We said OK, we did the work, and the demos sounded great. We played them for Florence Greenberg at Scepter Records, and she said, "Why don't you produce her."

So we did, and when we brought the record into Florence's office and she heard it, she cried, and not because she loved the record. Florence cried because of how much she didn't like it.

The record we're talking about, by the way, was "Don't Make Me Over."

Well, needless to say, we were all highly taken aback by Florence's reaction. Eventually, Florence came around. Not because she finally realized how much she liked the record. Not at all. Florence started loving it because she watched it go up the charts.

People don't always hear the same thing in the same song. A perfect example is the song, "What the World Needs Now Is Love." I didn't believe in that song very much. I wrote it, I guess I must have liked it a little, so I finished it and played it for Dionne—who didn't love it either. And when she said she didn't love it, then I really didn't love it.

Well, when we were getting ready to cut Jackie DeShannon, Hal said, "Play that song, 'What the World Needs Now Is Love.' " Hal's really good like that. He believed in the song.

And then I heard Jackie sing it, and the rest, as they say, is history.

You just never know what is going to happen when a song of yours is recorded. The feeling can be terrific, especially if somebody is whistling one of my songs and they don't know you're standing nearby. That's the greatest.

But there's the other side, too. I used to be terrified every time a new record of one of my songs came out. I'd hear it on the radio, be hearing it for the first time, and I'd get totally freaked out. Almost like I didn't want to hear it. I didn't want to be disappointed because I knew it wasn't going to be as good as I wanted it to be.

I could get very crazy about it, too. Like I'd go out to the pressing plants just to see what they were pressing on, to actually see what kind of garbage they were using. I'd scream at the quality-control people. They'd say, "What are you talking about? We sold 7,000 records in Philadelphia today."

And I'd say, "Yeah, but if it had really been pressed right, man, you could have sold 11,000 records in Philadelphia today."

Jerry Ragavoy

o o o

You might not know him, but he produced and wrote some of the best rhythm and blues of the sixties—and he's not black. He's a man with a sense of soul.

o o o

Mo Ostin called and asked me if I wanted to produce Miriam Makeba. I said to myself, "What the hell do I do with her?" I've written songs for Garnet Mimms and the Enchanters, "Time Is on My Side" that the Rolling Stones recorded, "Piece of My Heart" that Janis Joplin and Big Brother recorded, but only thing I had ever heard of Makeba's was "The Click Song."

But I met with her. She said she wanted to do American songs. Ballads, whatever. Very pleasant, nice lady. I said, "Let me see if I can find some material for you."

I called a number of publishers, they submitted material, and I picked what I thought were the best ten or twelve songs. During that time, Miriam was performing down at the Village Gate, and she had asked me to come down and see her. I had never seen her live. The woman was amazing, dynamic. I thought, "How can I capture this on record?"

Two days after seeing her live, I had a meeting with her to show her the songs I had picked out. She came in with two of her buddies, a very stout South African with the turban and the whole thing, and a girlfriend. I said, "Miriam, I've gathered these ten or twelve songs, but I know I've gone in the wrong direction. You told me what you wanted to do, but when I saw your show the other night I realized that everything I picked out was wrong. You're incredible. You shouldn't be singing this stuff. You are what you are. Trying to make you into anything else is a mistake."

I said, "Miriam, what about some of the folk songs you grew up with in South Africa? Sing me some."

Her eyes lit up. She said, "You are the first one who has ever asked to hear these songs." So she and her girlfriend started singing. The both of them, a cappella, no piano, no nothing. I turned on the tape recorder. Got an hour of them singing one song after another.

I said, "This is fantastic. Do me a favor, Miriam, let me figure out what's going on with this tape, and I'll get back to you."

So I listened to the tape and picked out two or three things which I thought maybe, maybe, had commercial appeal within the context of Miriam Makeba. One of the songs was "Pata Pata." I felt it needed some English translation to get it across, so I wrote some lyrics that pretty much defined, in a rhyming pattern, what this song was all about.

We made the record, and it was like, "Well, that was fun." If someone had told me it would become a smash hit record, I never would have believed them. If someone had brought it to me as a master, I would have turned it down. I would have passed.

Shortly after "Pata Pata," Miriam married Stokeley Carmichael. I went to their wedding. It was at some African consulate up in Vermont. I think there were maybe two or three white people there.

Subsequently, we started another album, and Stokeley started coming to all the sessions. By now Miriam is starting to talk to me about politics. I said, "Miriam, I just produce music. Politics is singularly the most boring subject I can think of. I have no interest in it whatsoever. It's an exercise in futility. If we're going to have a relationship, please, don't bother me with politics."

Obviously, she passed this on to Stokeley, and I didn't want to hear about him because he was probably a target, and here I was hanging out with him all the time.

One night we were all in the studio recording this African album. I think it sold two copies. Anyway, after one of the takes, Stokeley jumped up and said, "What a smash! What a smash!"

I looked over at him and said, "Hey, Stokeley, do I write your speeches?"

Herb Alpert

o o o

Take a sound and an idea and have the public ready for it. From then on, it's only a question of how well you execute the game plan. Herb took the Tijuana Brass and his record company to the limit, eating up the early sixties with his own particular sound, and is now an active recording mogul.

o o o

When I was in the army, I started listening to jazz—Miles Davis, Louis Armstrong—trying to find my own identity. I was Louis Armstrong for a day, Miles for a few moments. And then, when I heard Clifford Brown, I realized he was doing everything I had hoped to accomplish with a horn. That's when I knew I had to find out who I was as a musician.

I met Lou Adler after I got out of the army. He was working for an insurance company at the time, and he was also married to my ex-wife's best friend. He sold me a $10,000 life insurance policy that I didn't need. But I liked the guy. He had a lot of style. He wrote poetry on the side. I put some of his poetry to music.

It was 1956 and I wasn't sure what I wanted to do. I was playing weddings and bar mitzvahs and parties on weekends, whatever I could pick up. Lou wanted to get out of the insurance business, so he wanted to start taking our stuff around to publishers. We wrote about three or four songs together, and we took them to Ray Stanley, who had an office right next to Nickodel's on Melrose. They got us one recording with Sam Buttera and the Witnesses. We couldn't wait to hear the song on the radio, but that never came because nobody played the record. But it was fun just seeing our names on the label.

We wrote a couple of songs for Sam Cooke. One was "Wonderful World." Watching Sam record, just seeing his attitude in a studio, was an important learning experience for me. Sam was a real instinctual, gut musician. He didn't know a C chord from a head of lettuce, but he had a feeling. He would come up with lyrics that didn't seem poetic enough. He'd have these verses that on paper didn't look right. But whenever we asked him to pick up the guitar and play the song, he'd turn the words into something magical. He had motion, he had a rhythm concept, he was feel-conscious. He'd listen to a record with his eyes shut. He also always dressed in great clothes. Color coordinated. I loved him.

I used to work on my trumpet in my garage in West Hollywood. I was intrigued with the sound of Les Paul and Mary Ford, the way Les would double his guitar and stack Mary's voice. I started doing the same thing with my trumpet at home. I had two tape machines, and I'd go from machine to machine, back and forth, seven, eight times. It started sounding interesting. I felt I was on to something. It was just a matter of finding the right material.

I met Jerry Moss in New York. He had been the most successful promotion man on the East Coast. He said he wanted to live in Los Angeles. So we got together when he moved to L.A. He started talking about doing a record with this friend of his, Charlie Robinson, an actor from New York. Jerry wanted to see if he could produce a record and then put it on the street. In those days, for a couple of hundred bucks, you could make a record, have it pressed, put a label on it, and put it out. If somebody bites, you either turn it over for distribution, or you try to hold it for yourself and get paid by the distributors, which was pretty impossible.

At the time, I was in the studio experimenting with a song I had written with my next-door neighbor called "Tell It to the Birds." When Jerry started talking about recording his friend, Charlie, we decided to pool our records together.

So we put out "Tell It to the Birds" and this record Jerry produced called "Lemon Twist." We released it locally on a label called Carnival. Suddenly, "Tell It to the Birds" started selling. In Los Angeles, it got to Number 16 on KFWB because of B. Mitchell Reed. He loved the record, so he played the hell out of it. It also didn't hurt that he was a friend of mine.

Then we released it in San Francisco, and it started happening there. We didn't have the funds to see how far we could take it, so we turned the record over to Dot Records for distribution. With that money, I recorded "The Lonely Bull." Jerry and I never had this master plan of starting a record company. It just sort of happened.

"The Lonely Bull" was one of those rarities. It took off. From city to city, country to country, it was just one of those records. It was a word-of-mouth record, and we were so busy trying to organize our scene and hold on to the record that we never gave any real thought to the future. Basically, we were just trying to hang on.

It was September '62. Distributors were crying for us to put out *The Lonely Bull* album, which, obviously, we were more than willing to do. However, before a distributor received one album, Jerry made sure they were all paid up on the single. That gave us operating cash, and essentially that was the beginning of A&M Records.

Lester Sill

o o o

You may not have heard of Lester, but he provided the money and opportunity for Phil Spector, Leiber and Stoller, and a number of other young Californians to go on and hit it big. A premier music publisher, he recalls his moving and shaking days with relish.

o o o

When I was selling records for Jules Bihari's company, Modern, one of the stops I would make was on Fairfax Avenue in Los Angeles, Norty's Record Shop. Everybody knew Norty's. I walked in there one day and I was mesmerized by this clerk. He had one blue eye and one brown eye. It was Jerry Leiber. He said to me, "I love the records you sell. I'm into this kind of music, and I'd like to play some songs for you."

We set up a meeting and he came to my house with his partner, Mike Stoller. They played me a song called "That's What the Good Book Says." I called Jules at Modern and I told him it was a pretty good song and it rocks. He said, "Bring those guys up here." So we go to Jules, and someone who works for Jules is producing Jerry and Mike's song, and right away Jerry and Mike start to make suggestions about what the guy is doing. Jules says, "Hey, go ahead, take over." The record came out. It was never a hit. Done by a group called the Robins.

But later on, after I left Jules and I was now working at Norbert Sales Distribution Company on Pico, Jerry came to work for me as a shipping clerk. He would write in the back room. One day Johnny Otis called him and asked if a particular song was finished. Jerry said to me, "I have to take off. I'm going to run a song over to Johnny Otis. He's cutting this act, Willie Mae Thornton—Big Mama." The song he was working on in the office, on his lunch break, was "Hound Dog."

In the meantime, I go on the road, and I come back, and I sit down with Mike and Jerry and they tell me that the song came out but Don Robey didn't give them any writer's credit. So I called Robey and I said, "We're going to sue you if their names are not on the song. They're the writers. They didn't sign the song over to you." So he corrected it, and sent us an affidavit to the effect that Leiber and Stoller wrote the song. But their names did not appear on the original copyright.

Mike and Jerry said, "Why don't we start a company? Why don't we get into business and start a publishing company?"

I said, "Fine," so we opened up a small office on Crenshaw between Wilshire and Pico. One little storefront. We had a piano in there, and we started a record company called Spark Records. We ran everything from that office—accounts receivable, accounts payable, the whole thing. When things started getting good for us, we moved to a larger place on Melrose, a long thin office.

After some more hits, I sold out my share to Mike and Jerry at a ridiculous price. I owned 25 percent of the copyrights. I'm talking about some big songs—"Black Denim Trousers," "Motorcycle Boots," "Red Ruby Lips," "Young Blood," "Searchin'," "Smokey Joe's Cafe." And I sold it out for a pittance. Why? Because I didn't know any better.

Even though we were very close—Jerry lived with me for a couple of years—when it came to business, both Jerry and Mike—Mike quietly—they were ruthless when it came to business. Absolutely business, all the time. Mother, father, it didn't make any difference who it was, they would kill them. That's just an expression. They wouldn't actually kill, but I made the mistake. No one forced me to sell.

By the very early sixties I had already been involved with Leiber and Stoller, and then Phil Spector, and now I was looking for other things to do. I was working with a kid up the street named Hal Wynn, and we were putting little packages together for Trini Lopez, and then selling the masters overseas. In the meantime, I don't have any money, and the money I have I'm running out of. My son, Chuck Kaye, is working for Donnie Kirshner, and Kirshner's got a couple of records coming out on the West Coast, so he calls me. He says, "Look, Les, will you help me? I got six records. Can you do something for me on the West Coast?"

I said, "Sure," and he sent me six sweaters, one for each record. The records break, I'm getting friendlier and friendlier with the writers, and Donnie calls me one day after he sold the company to Columbia Pictures, and he tells me that his writers are upset. They never knew he was going to sell the company, and they resented him treating them, in their words, like meat.

I went to New York to talk with Donnie, and he offered me a six-month consultancy to work on the writers. I set up an apartment in New York. I started with Barry Mann and Cynthia Weil. They said they would sign, but only if I could promise them I'd be there for a while. This was right around the time that Donnie fired Lou Adler. Lou was on the West Coast, and I was in to see Chuck, and Lou was on the phone with Donnie saying, "Donnie, you're ruining my life."

A few years later, I said to Lou, "He didn't ruin your life. He saved your life."

Eventually, Barry and Cynthia came around, as did Gerry Goffin and Carole King and Neil Sedaka and Howie Greenfield. They were all pissed at Donnie, and now they were deciding to stay with him because of me.

So now Donnie wants to talk to me about a three-year contract. I said, "Fine." We talked. I took it to my lawyer. He said it was OK. Not thrilling, but OK. So I took the job at Screen Gems—Columbia. It turned out to be a twenty-one-year gig.

Neil Diamond

○ ○ ○

A true superstar, Neil has crossed demographic lines for twenty years with his personal and special songs. He still packs concert halls, makes great records, and maintains his position among the musical elite.

○ ○ ○

Neil Sedaka had a very big impact on me. My senior year I went to Lincoln High School, and Sedaka was at Lincoln, and he was a professional singer. He had records out and you could hear them on the radio. Back then, you judged yourself against Sedaka.

In the back of my mind, I suppose I thought I could sing as well as Sedaka. Otherwise, I wouldn't have had the nerve to get together with my friend, Jack Packer, who lived around the corner and was a trained operatic singer. We'd rehearse in my basement and try to be my idols, the Everly Brothers, which is hard if you're from Brooklyn.

After a lot of years of being a nobody writer, I had my first couple of hit records, "Solitary Man" and "Cherry Cherry," and I'd go out on tours.

Whatever dates they offered, I took—bowling alleys, ski lodges, bars in Florida. Anything to get out of Brooklyn.

I don't know how prolific I was, and I haven't always been hot during my career, but when you get your first taste of success, you don't want to drop the ball. And I was intent on not dropping the ball.

So my agent calls me—he wasn't even my agent, he was a friend of mine—and he says he's got three dates for me in Florida. He said they'd pay me $750 to go down for the weekend.

"My God," I said, "seven fifty!"

Of course, I didn't figure that the plane was going to cost so much, or that I would have to buy a new suit in Greenwich Village, and a new strap for my guitar. Or that I'd have to go down there and rehearse with a high school band, and then have to carry them around with me to six different locations.

Developing a stage technique during all this was difficult. I'm not a very good mimic. I realized after a few times on stage that I didn't know who I was.

I tried to be Sammy Davis, and soon realized I wasn't Sammy Davis. I tried Elvis. No, Elvis is very unique, you can't be Elvis. I tried Harry Belafonte.

What I found, of course, was that it just had to be me alone. I realized I couldn't imitate anybody. I had to figure out who I was, and then hope they would like me.

In a sense, I discovered myself on stage, discovered myself as a person. And that's all I've done ever since. Everything I've done on stage since my very early years is development, an enlargement of that whole thing.

I find it very hard to watch what I do as a performer because every couple of seconds I see something I do that I hate. I look terrible, or the shirt is horrible, or I sang that note wrong, or why didn't I direct myself to the audience, or why are my eyes closed.

Still, I remember a lot of performances, and most of the ones I remember are the early ones. I did a show at the Hollywood Bowl in 1966 with about twenty other acts. It had a revolving stage. I walked on—I didn't know who I was yet—and I had on a big black cowboy hat, black shirt, black pants, black boots, and black guitar.

I sang the only three songs I knew, my hit record and two songs I learned at summer camp, "La Bamba" and "If I Had a Hammer." Fortunately, they only wanted me to sing three songs.

The band thing was funny. You had twenty minutes to rehearse with them, and twenty seconds before I went, some guy comes up to me and says, "I'm the new bass player. The old guy left." This is the Hollywood Bowl! So I cranked my guitar very loud and hoped that everybody in the band would start with me and end with me. That was the best I could hope for.

I also remember Broadway, which was more than a little scary. In '68, maybe '69, I played Carnegie Hall, which was a little too early in my career to be playing Carnegie. Although it was sold out, no critics showed up. Not a single critic, which pissed me off and also caused me to fire my PR guy. My wife had taken the train in from California with a sick baby, we stayed in somebody's apartment, and no critics show up.

Three years later, I had some success under my belt, so I thought I'd come back to town and play the Winter Garden and really kill them.

There was a certain attachment I had to the Winter Garden because I knew Jolson had played there. I loved him when I was a kid, and I loved his singing. I could feel his ghost there.

Also, *West Side Story* was at the Winter Garden, it was New York, so there was a sense of that excitement.

So I come back, and I'm at the Winter Garden and my picture is up on a billboard. It was scary, but I think I was probably too dumb to know how I had to act or how really important it was.

Opening night, I came out on stage, I looked at the audience and they didn't look like a regular audience to me. They looked older, they looked like people who were there to stare as opposed to participate. So I said to the audience—my first remarks—I said, "Hello, my name is Neil Diamond and I intend to own you tonight."

There was a gasp from the crowd, an audible gasp. You don't own these people. It was not the right foot to start out on. I should have been a little more humble and said, "Love me," or something.

Well, they gasped and I heard it, so I said, "I'll settle for a long-term lease." There were some laughs, and we went into the show.

It took me a while to recuperate from that line. About half way through the show I started kibbitzing with somebody in the audience. Some girl started yelling requests. It was a small theater, and I had this whole conversation with her. She was just going on, and finally I said, "These Jewish girls are just impossible to control."

And she yells out from the back, "I'm not Jewish." The audience fell down, and that broke the ice. I was actually saved by a shiksa for the first time in my life.

Bob Crewe

○ ○ ○

Crewe wrote marvelous pop songs and made less-than-marvelous records. But he had the touch and the feel for what could be a hit for others, and became a top record producer for over a decade.

○ ○ ○

I learned a lot from Jerry Wexler. Jerry always said, "If you want to know how much promotion is being done on your record, just consider how much you're doing and then cut that by 90 percent. That's how much promotion you're getting."

He'd say, "You have to get on the phone, you have to be in contact with people, keep the dialogue running." He taught me so many things, like how the business was based on relationships between people. There sure was a lot of stuff going on at the time about payola, but I never got into it. I gave parties instead, and everyone had a grand time.

The first success I had with the Four Seasons—and it was a tiny bit of success—was a record called "Bermuda," which came out on George Goldner's label. It was a minor hit out of Philadelphia. But Frankie Valli was getting a little restless because nothing was really happening beyond Philly.

One night I went down to Point Pleasant, New Jersey. My mother and father lived in Ocean Beach, New Jersey, and I went to see the Seasons, Bob Gaudio and the guys, who were appearing at this dive in Point Pleasant. But Frankie did a thing that night that blew me away. He put a bandana over his head, took two maracas and stuck them under his coat, and began singing "I Can't Give You Anything but Love" like Nellie Lecher with that high voice.

I had a lot of other things happening at the time, but I said to Bob, "Go write a song for Frankie with that chi-chi voice and jump it an octave. I don't care if you call it "Bananas," just jump it an octave, and we'll make a record of it, whatever it is."

He came up with several ideas. One was a song called "Jackie," inspired by Jackie Kennedy, who was the darling of the world at the time. But the song didn't work out. It was then that Bob wrote "Sherry."

At the time, I'm living in a duplex on 50th Street, which looked like it cost a billion dollars but was put together with Scotch tape. I was confronted with the choice of either paying the rent or going back into the studio to make one more record with the Seasons. By now I was calling them the Four Seasons. I decided to go in and make it because I really believed in what we had.

We had five songs on that date, and "Sherry" was one of them. Now for years I'd been working with this guy, Paul Marshall, who would make deals for me by selling my masters all over the place, so I was able to stay afloat and keep going. Paul and I went down to the NARM Convention in

Miami and played the record for Henry Stone, who was a great friend of mine, and Joyce Monroe, who was at WFUN.

Henry heard the record and said, "Don't say a word. You got a Number 1 record here, and we're gonna get this thing going." During the next two or three days, the buzz around the pool and the lobby was that I was carrying hot gold.

Then the bidding started, and we wound up making a deal with Ewart Abner at Vee Jay. On paper, it was one of the largest deals that had ever been made on a record, sixteen cents a record. Later down the line, I realized that we probably should have made a deal with CBS for five cents a record because maybe we would have gotten a better count. There were times when Ewart could be found in Vegas, blowing a quarter of a million bucks a night at the crap table. But I loved the guy.

None of that matters now. We had a great run with the Four Seasons. And although the line of hits with the group—"Big Girls Don't Cry," "Walk Like a Man," and the rest—were all by Crewe and Gaudio, my favorite record during that entire time was Cole Porter's "I've Got You under My Skin."

Frankie Valli

○ ○ ○

The high end of the Four Seasons sound. Hits came easily to this group for more than ten years. Frankie had success on his own and is out there looking to get it rolling again.

○ ○ ○

Bob Gaudio was the major creative force behind the Four Seasons. Bob had his first hit record when he was sixteen years old. At the time, he was in a group called the Royal Teens. I met him on the road. We exchanged telephone numbers, and I found out he lived in Bergenfield, New Jersey, and I was from Newark. We got together and he played me some songs, and I said, "This kid is definitely going to make it."

We went into the studio, cut some demos, and brought them around. Coming out of Larry Uttal's office at Madison Records one day, we met Bob Crewe. I had known Bob Crewe from some earlier things, and we said hello. I introduced him to Bob Gaudio, and Crewe said, "Whatever you got, give me a shout, let me know what you're doing." That's how we got connected with Crewe.

Our first successes were on Vee Jay. We had "Sherry," "Big Girls Don't Cry" and "Walk Like a Man," but there was very little money, maybe an accumulation of $30,000. Later on, we found out that there was a lot more money, but we never saw any of it.

The nice part was, Crewe and Gaudio were writing together, and everything they did seemed tailor-made for us. The most important thing we wanted to establish was a sound that would be uniquely ours, and as soon as you heard the radio, you would know who you were listening to. And we did developed a sound before there were any hit records, very much like the Beach Boys consciously patterning themselves after the Four Freshmen.

I remember as a kid my mother taking me to New York, to the Paramount Theater to see Frank Sinatra. Something amazing happened to me that day. I was mesmerized. I looked up him on the stage, and I said to myself, "Someday I'm going to be up there, too." And in the early sixties we worked the Paramount Theater, just before they tore it down.

Right at the beginning, we had three Number 1 records in a row, and then "Ain't That a Shame," which was a cover and not a big hit, and then "Candy Girl," which went to Number 3. Well, you never saw four more depressed people in your life. A Number 3 record and it felt like it was over.

The first house I bought was a two-family house because I was afraid it was all going to go away. This is the way it was with me since childhood. My father would come home and ask me, "So when are you going to get a real job?"

Nobody thought rock 'n' roll would last. Everybody was ripping everybody else off. No one was concerned with anyone's career. The music was supposed to be around for a couple of years, and then it was supposed to fade away.

For us, things began to erupt after the first two years. All of a sudden things were happening that never happened before. It's strange, but when people are struggling for success together, it's amazing how close you become. Everybody sleeps in the same bed, everybody drinks from the same cup. And then, as soon as success comes, everybody needs his own limousine, everybody wants his own suite in a different hotel. I think it's sad that people drift away from one another.

The first eruption with us happened between Tommy DeVito and Nick Massi. They were at it constantly until one day Nick couldn't take it anymore. He walked out saying he didn't want anything. He just wanted out. And he's never done anything since.

It's frustrating knowing you had earned a certain amount of money, sold a certain amount of records, and now you're not going to get paid for it. Someone was cheating us. We were beginning to spend more time with lawyers, accountants, and business managers, and that was not fun. That was another thing Nick couldn't handle.

He said, "You go to the meeting. I don't want to hear how much they owe us. It makes me sick." That's where his head was. Fortunately, for me, I had some street sense. I grew up in a poor environment and I spent a lot of time on the street. So I learned how to deal with it.

But talk about being mishandled and mismanaged, I can remember one time we had a guy who was managing us, and he convinced us that he should take care of all the bills. We give him power of attorney, we went out on the road—Boston or Connecticut, I don't remember which one—and we're on stage doing a show when all of a sudden we're surrounded by police. They take us offstage and right to jail on charges of defrauding an innkeeper. Could not have been more than fifteen or sixteen dollars a night per room, maybe the entire bill was seventy or eighty dollars, but our manager never paid it.

We got crazy with this guy. We climbed all over him. He says, "Oh, it was a terrible mistake. Don't worry, it won't happen again."

OK, now we are in Columbus, Ohio, doing a state fair, and right in the middle of the show the paddywagon pulls out onto the field. The police come in, we're surrounded again, and they bring us down to the local jail, and we're booked for defrauding an innkeeper again.

We finally get back to New York, and I am so embarrassed. I tell my lawyer, "Look, I want you to get in touch with every Holiday Inn we've ever stayed at, go over every contract for every date we played over the last two years. I want to find out whether there is anybody else out there we owe money to, because I do not want to get arrested in every city I go to."

We had another problem in the early days. Not just problems with money. We would go through different parts of the country, and we'd see an awful lot of racial tension.

We were on a tour once with Jackie Wilson. It was an all-black tour, and we were the only white act. It was heavy duty through the South. We had to stay at a different hotel, and I never knew from any of that. I never saw any of that growing up in New Jersey. But now it's really heating up, and we are the only white act on the bill, and we're in Jackson, Mississippi, in a National Guard–type of complex. We're doing the show inside, and people are protesting outside with signs and all that crap. We get out of the bus, and they are calling us "nigger lovers," and all this shit.

I go for a hot dog at the refreshment stand before the show. Someone from the Orlons walks over. I order a hot dog, the guy gives it to me. The guy from the Orlons orders something, and the guy looks him straight in the face, and he says, "We don't serve niggers." I started to choke.

Bobby Vinton

o o o

He's had a dozen lives. Always when you counted Bobby out, he came back with another Number 1 record. A shrewd businessman, he spoke with us at his sprawling Malibu ranch.

o o o

When I did "There! I've Said It Again," I walked into the studio, the session started at 7:00 P.M. I sang the song at 7:15, one take, and I said, "Goodbye, everybody. This is a Number 1 record. We could stay here all night, but all we'd do is mess it up."

That record was done live, all at the same time. Today it's tough for me to get a hit because of all the overdubbing. I'm a master at performing live. When they took away that style of recording, I lost the magic. Tony Bennett had the magic, Johnny Mathis had the magic on "Chances Are." When that magic of recording live was taken away from the recording process, my kind of recording artists got into trouble.

Burt Bacharach wrote "Blue on Blue" for me, so I was not that excited to record "Blue Velvet" when I heard the song. But Al Gallico was there in Nashville, where we were recording at the time, and he said, "Why don't you do 'Blue Velvet'? I'll send a girl out for the lead sheet." I did the song in ten minutes. I had no idea it would be one of the biggest records of 1964.

I really wasn't a singer. I was a musician. I made two band albums. I led the NBC staff when I was twenty years old. Doc Severinsen was my trumpet player.

I was an arranger then. NBC brought me in to do a show because ABC had Dick Clark. NBC wanted something similar, but they didn't have a young guy who could write arrangements, so that was my function—arranger, saxophone player, leading the band.

Jim Foglesong found me at Epic. He wanted to bring back the big band sound, which had died, and I had two more sessions to do on my contract, and then I was going to be dropped from the label. I found "Roses Are Red," which was a reject. Epic was throwing that out, and me out, when I heard it. I said, "Now this is a song anybody could sing well enough to include in a big band album."

I didn't even know I could sing. I made records. I fit in, understood teamwork. I was like a fair quarterback on a great team. I called the right plays. I knew how to win. In other words, I figured out how to make hit records. Voice wasn't important. Half the songs today won't be around in ten years because of the overemphasis on performance. The performance in so many of these cases is better than the material, and songs last because of the songs, not the singers.

When "Blue Velvet" was Number 1, I went to Vegas. I went to the health club, and Dean Martin was there. He was one of my idols. I said,

"Dean, I'm Bobby Vinton and I have the Number 1 record in America, 'Blue Velvet.' "

He said, "Never heard of it, and I don't know you."

I said, "I just came in first in a big singing poll. Frank Sinatra came in second, and Elvis Presley third."

Frank was getting a rubdown next to Dean, and he didn't know me either. They cared about a Bobby Vinton about as much as I care about the guy who has a Number 1 record today.

But I did have a very good run. I sold an awful lot of records and I didn't change when the Beatles came in, like a lot of performers did. Allen Klein was my manager at the time. I'd be up in his office and the Beatles would come in, the Rolling Stones would come in. I'd joke with Allen. He'd say, "Are we still friends?"

I'd say, "Sure. You've eliminated all my competition." The English groups were so strong that only a few male performers were left alive. I was so big at the time that the Beatles pushed me from Number 1 to Number 10, which isn't so bad.

Everyone wanted to be English, with long hair and sound like the Beatles, to be a part of this new musical explosion. I continued doing what I always did, and as a result, I didn't change. I may not have been Number 1 anymore, but at least I was alive for the next twenty years.

Chubby Checker

o o o

The twist came on strong and disappeared. Chubby hasn't disappeared, but the instant success and the size of it was a mixed blessing. It's tough recapturing the moment and all that goes with it.

o o o

When I was four years old, my mother took me to a show in Andrews, South Carolina, where I was born. A little kid named Sugar Child Robinson was performing. He was a child pianist, and he wore a white tux and tails. He was about eleven, twelve years old. Well, this kid did a boogie-woogie piano, and my life was never the same.

By the time I was a teenager, I was working in a poultry market in Philadelphia. The people in the market could never get me to shut up. I would sing everybody's songs all day long. Just working and singing, that's all I did. I'd call up my friend when there was no one else around, and we'd entertain each other.

Well, through the grapevine, my boss at the poultry market, Henry

Colt, heard that Dick Clark needed someone to do impressions while singing a Christmas card for him. My boss said, "Why don't you go over to Cameo-Parkway Records and do this little record for Dick Clark? He's making a Christmas card in the form of a record and they need someone to do impressions."

I showed up doing my Fats Domino and this lady walks in the room and she said, "You're Chubby. Chubby Checker, like Fats Domino." She said that and then she walked out of the room and that was the end of it. That lady was Mrs. Dick Clark, and that was the start of my record career.

My boss had been calling me Chubby ever since I started working for him. I said, "I don't like that."

He said, "You're working for me, I am the boss, and your name is Chubby. That is it." I've often said that the public gave me everything, even the name.

In 1959 Kal Mann called me from Cameo and said, "We got this record called 'The Twist.'"

I said, "Hank Ballard and the Midnighters did that tune."

Kal said, "Yes, I know, but I think we can put a little dance to it, and then you can show the people how it's done." I said OK.

I already knew the tune because Hank Ballard was a favorite of mine, one of the great X-rated singers of the fifties. He did songs like "Annie Had a Baby" and "Work with Me, Annie." You couldn't sing songs like that. People thought they were smut. Radio stations didn't play Hank's songs, but the kids loved them.

So I went to Cameo-Parkway and we did "The Twist" in three takes. The problem was, how do we explain it to the audience? How do we explain the movement to them. I truly don't know who came up with it, but somebody said, "It's like putting out a cigarette with both feet, and wiping your bottom with a towel, to the beat of the music." That little formula literally changed this planet.

God bless Zsa Zsa Gabor. She was the spark that lit the fire that flamed "The Twist" on an international level. She did the Twist at the Peppermint Lounge, in New York. The columnist, Earl Wilson, was there watching Joey Dee and the Starlighters on stage. My record came on, Zsa Zsa started dancing, Earl Wilson wrote about it, and suddenly everyone in the world was doing the Twist.

Timing had a lot to do with it, too. Buddy Holly had gone down. Elvis had gone into the army. Chuck Berry had been ostracized for transporting a minor across state lines. Jerry Lee Lewis had married his cousin, and he was ostracized. Little Richard had gone to the seminary. It was a down period. It was like rock 'n' roll had died.

In a way, "The Twist" really ruined my life. I was on my way to becoming a big nightclub performer, and "The Twist" just wiped it out. It got so out of proportion. No one ever believes I have talent.

There were times when I stopped and thought, "Is it worth going on?" In the back of my mind I'm saying, "Chubby, these people don't even know what you're about. They have no idea that a guy like you, from where you are from and what you represent, could be as great as you are."

And right to this day, a little voice inside me tells me, "Keep doing what you're doing. The people will come around again. You are directly responsible for dancing as we know it at this very moment."

And I do believe that. Before "The Twist," people touched while they danced. "The Twist" caused people to dance apart. And they're still dancing apart all these years later. In Hong Kong, or anywhere, right now, people are dancing the Twist. And the only way they know how to do what they're doing is because of a guy named Chubby Checker.

Brooks Arthur

o o o

He talks about the acts he's worked with from behind the control board and in the production seat. His track record in motion picture music and in making hits, along with his sense of history, establishes him as a necessary participant in anyone's musical review.

o o o

Mira Sound Studios was owned by a guy named Bob Goldman, and it was located in a little funky sleaze-bag hotel called the America Hotel, on West 47th Street. Nipsy Russell lived there, Sammy Davis' uncle, Will Mastin, lived there, Lenny Bruce lived there. They all had little rooms. Calling them efficiency apartments would be stretching the point.

Most of all, though, the America Hotel had hookers, and more often than not the place was being raided by the cops. You'd see the sign, "These premises raided," hanging on a chain that stretched across the doorway.

The studio was on the ground floor, in the back in what had once been an old dining room. The control room was probably the old kitchen. But the studio was wonderful. Phil Spector recorded a lot of his hits there. Leiber and Stoller worked there. Ruby and the Romantics cut a lot of records there. It was a most unlikely place, but it had a great sound.

In 1963, I was booked into Mira Sound to engineer an Eddie Fisher session. Eddie was not exactly at the height of his career. His "Oh My Papa" days had long been over. He was booked into Mira to do a vocal overdub on "Sunrise, Sunset." The tracks had been done elsewhere, and now he wanted me to finish his vocal and mix the record.

I got to the studio at about six, six-thirty P.M. for a seven o'clock date, and as often was the case at the famous America Hotel, a "These premises raided" sign was hanging across the doorway. So I climbed over the chain, and I walked through the studio door, and I was met by this gigantic CIA type who asked me for ID. He checked for my name, which was on a list. I walked inside. Eddie was there, and the control room had already been set up for a buffet supper—wine, cheese, corned beef sandwiches on rye bread. I asked Eddie what was going on, and he said president and Mrs. Kennedy would be stopping by along with Mrs. Kennedy's sister, Lee Radziwell, her husband, Prince Stanislas Radziwell, and Mrs. Kennedy's secretary, Pamela Turnure.

Everybody was on guard. Every exit had a guard. I was there, Eddie was there, Bob Goldman, the owner of the studio, was there. My assistant engineer, Bobby Bloom, a great singer-songwriter in his own right who had a hit record called "Montego Bay," and who wound up dying years later because of drugs, he was there. Linda Goldner, George Goldner's daughter, who worked at the studio, she was there. The nighttime studio manager, Nancy Cal Cagno, who later married Jeff Barry after coming between Jeff and Ellie Greenwich, she was there, too.

Now Eddie is singing his heart out, and little by little people begin showing up. Pamela Turnure gets there and sits on a director's chair, in the seediest control room, in the seediest hotel in the city. Then the prince and princess arrived, and they started drinking wine and eating sandwiches. Eddie kind of noticed, and he took a break and everyone started schmoozing and hugging.

Then a hush fell over the room and the Kennedys walked in, after, I assume, stepping over the "These premises raided" sign just like everyone else did.

The Kennedys were there maybe four or five minutes. They were gracious, they met everyone, everyone shook the president's hand. Eddie chatted with them, and it was all very social and very nice. Then the president and Mrs. Kennedy left as quickly as they had arrived.

But the prince and princess and Pamela Turnure stayed, and they continued to drink, and it got a little randy there for a while. The kisses got a little more serious, and now it was getting interesting. It wasn't turning into an orgy, mind you, but it was clear that Pamela and Eddie liked each other, and that the princess and Eddie liked each other. I'm not sure who liked whom, but the prince got a little drunk and he walked out. Now it was just the three of them trading kisses, and I'm busy trying to do a session.

Finally, by two or three o'clock in the morning the wine was gone, the food was gone, and Eddie, Pamela, and the princess disappeared into the night, and everything evaporated as quickly as it had begun. It was awesome.

A week later, I saw Jackie Kennedy on Fifth Avenue, and I was about to say, "Hello, remember me?" when I was prevented from getting near her. Suddenly, I was just a face in the crowd. I was nothing.

Cut to later that year. Jeff Barry and Ellie Greenwich had a studio group signed to Jubilee Records called the Raindrops. The group had a hit with "What a Guy," and then another hit with their next record, "The Kind of Boy You Can't Forget." Now they needed a follow-up. Jeff and Ellie were masters at going into the studio in the morning and then coming out later that day with a hit song. Well, the song they came up with for the Raindrops was called "That Boy John."

I remember the record so clearly. It came out on the charts in the nineties with a bullet. Then it went to the eighties, then the seventies, then the sixties, and then President Kennedy was shot. I was working with Gerry Goffin and Carole King and Little Eva when we heard the news. Like everyone, I cried like a baby.

And then, early the next week I saw Jeff and Ellie, and the normal thing to ask them was about the record and how it was doing. I asked them, and they told me that the record had been pulled, that it was over. The president was dead and a song with John in the title was no longer acceptable on the radio.

The record was over, the Raindrops were over, Eddie Fisher was over, the entire era of early-sixties songwriting—New York, the groups, the Brill Building—it was all over. The president was dead, and everything was changing.

Paul McCartney

○ ○ ○

Sitting in his country home in southern England, Paul told how he wrote songs with John, how fame became so burdensome, and how he keeps going, carrying the legend along with him.

○ ○ ○

When I wrote "Yesterday," I was aiming to impress people who knew music, rather than just get the teeny-boppers. We'd be around musicians who played in dance orchestras up in Manchester. They were the kind of hardened guys that Sinatra would have played with if he ever got that far north. We hung out with a lot of those people and we wanted to be respected by them. We had the kids, but we wanted their parents to like us, too.

Just like a song is an immovable object and an irresistible force, so too were we the irresistible force that was not going to be stopped. We had captured Liverpool, we had captured London. It was like a military campaign. We were out to capture the world.

My dad was a musician. He had a little band in the twenties called the Jim Max Band. Because of him, I knew many of the songs that the older crowd knew. John, too. One of John's favorite songs was "Don't Blame Me." People think of John Lennon as a peacenik, or a crazy man, or a great man, but they never associate him with the kinds of songs his mum taught him. His mum was a musical lady. She taught him banjo chords. I had to change him to guitar chords. We used to love "Little White Lies," "Don't Blame

Me." I was a big Fats Waller fan, a big Peggy Lee fan. In the very early days, we used to do all sorts of stuff that no one would have suspected of us, so that when we did get to the level of "The Ed Sullivan Show," we were real and not just some little schmucks from out of town.

The cheekiest thing the Beatles ever did was say to our manager, Brian Epstein, that we didn't want to go to America until we were number one. Cliff Richard, Tommy Steele—big British stars—would go to America and be third or fourth on the bill to Frankie Avalon, and then they'd come back and we'd read in interviews that although they had a wonderful time over there, they never became big hits. We thought surely the Americans were going to buy their records, but what they proved in the end was that they were little European acts who got a bit too out of their depth.

The four of us brought different things to the table. John brought a biting wit. I think I brought commerciality and harmony. My dad used to sit me and my brother down and say, "This is harmony," so when it came to the group, I'd say to them, "Let's do a harmony on that one," and we gradually worked our way into things like that.

George was serious, always very good on the business side, and always very good on his instrument. Ringo was simply the best drummer in Liverpool. Ringo also had native wit. He didn't know when he was being funny. The three of us went to grammar school, Ringo didn't. Ringo said he only went to school for three days because of this bad operation he had when he was a kid. Ringo had peritonitis. His stomach has a lot of scars on it. His parents were told that he died at age three, so with Ringo everything was always a bonus.

He would say to us, "God, it's been a hard day's night." We'd say, "Say that again."

"Tomorrow Never Knows" is also one of his. Ringo talked in titles. We had to follow him around with a notebook and pencil. You never knew what he would say next.

Everybody thought we were an overnight success. We started off in Liverpool as nothing, just as a crummy little band, and we got this opportunity to go to Hamburg. The very first club we played in Hamburg was the Indra, which was German for India. The first night we played, I think there were two people there. But it was there where we started learning our show-biz skills.

The club was in a tourist area. When people stopped by the door, the first thing they would look at was the price of the beer, you know, to see if they wanted to come in and have a cheap drink and hear this band. As soon as we saw them at the door, we would change the number, do a better song as a way of enticing them in. Our role in life was to make people buy more beer. That's how we actually started off. The more beer they bought, the more likelihood of our pay going up.

When we finally happened, we were in Paris. A telegram came through from Capitol Records saying that "I Want to Hold Your Hand" had gone Number 1. We just jumped on each other's backs and screamed the whole place down. We knew we were off for the fame. In a funny way, we expected it.

And then older people like Benny Goodman wanted to know, "Who are these guys?" He was told, "Oh, they're nothing. They'll be over to-morrow." You know, like, "Don't worry, gang. This won't last long."

But then the kids started telling mum and dad about "Yesterday," and this "Michelle" song, and "Here, There and Everywhere," and people began saying, "Not bad."

The anchor that always held us was our musicality. We were pretty good musicians, in a smallish way, perhaps, but we were a good little rhythm section and a good little band.

I remember hitting upon this idea and saying to the group, "OK, for this one album we won't be the Beatles. This is going to be our safety valve. We're going to think of a new name for ourselves, a new way of being, a new way of recording, everything fresh, and by the way, I've written a song about something called Sgt. Pepper's Lonely Hearts Club Band."

And we agreed that we weren't the Beatles anymore. When we went in to make the record, it wasn't "John" singing on this or that track. It was anyone John wanted to be. And it was quite good. We did stuff on that record that we had never done before. I think John and I were the main influences on it. George took a lesser role. He was into his Indian music, so he did his Indian track, and Ringo, as usual, came along for the ride.

There were three ways that John and I would write. We would sit down with nothing and two guitars, which was like working with a mirror. I could see what he was doing, and he could see me. We got ideas off each other. In fact, it was better than a mirror because if he was plunking away in D, I could see where his fingers might go and then I could suggest something.

So, that was like writing from the ground up. "She Loves You," "From Me to You," "This Boy" were all written that way, as were most of the earlier songs.

Another way of writing was when one of us had an idea. I used to drive out to John's house. He lived out in the country, and I lived in London. I remember asking the chauffeur once if he was having a good week. He said, "I'm very busy at the moment. I've been working eight days a week."

And I thought, "Eight days a week! Now there's a title." So when I got to John's house, I said, "Eight Days a Week." So that was the second way. One of us would have an idea, and then we'd both sit and write together. "Norwegian Wood" was like that. John had the first idea. He said, "I once had a girl, or should I say she once had me." And then we finished it together. It always got a bit more bizarre when the two of us got going.

The third way was when one of had an idea, and we weren't going to be seeing each other for a week, and the idea was just too hot to stop. I wrote "Yesterday" that way. Most of the ballady stuff I wrote on my own. "Yesterday," "Michelle," "The Long and Winding Road," "Let It Be," "Eleanor Rigby," although I did bring "Eleanor Rigby" to John for help with the third verse. John could always spot a bum line.

No matter how we did it, we were just as happy working together in the accepted way of writing as we were keeping it loose. Just as long as there was never a formula.

I do miss it, and him. It's very hard to replace someone like John. I should say impossible. I have worked with other people, and I've had some fun with other people, and I've done some stuff since the Beatles, like "My Love" and "Maybe I'm Amazed," which I think stacks up with the Beatles, but the co-written stuff has not been anywhere near as good as the songs I wrote with John.

Of my writing partners since John, Denny Laine was obviously nowhere near as good as John. Stevie Wonder is very good, but not lyrical. He's not a lyricist. Michael Jackson is not as good of a writer as he is a performer. And Eric Stewart was good, but again, not as good as John.

John and I as writers, and the Beatles as a whole, we were virtually an impossible act to follow. Ours was quite a rich time. Meeting the queen for the first time. Coming to America for the first time. It was incredible, unbelievable. I mean, I would not be impressed going down to Florida now and seeing a motorcycle cop ride by and wave. But then, it was like heaven. We would be riding along and a motorcycle cop would breeze by on his bike and take photos of us. It was magic.

George Martin

o o o

George is the tasteful intellectual who corralled the talents of the Beatles and put them on tape. Long on tradition, talent, and respect from his peers, he turned what some thought was another comedy act into the most popular group of all time.

o o o

I was a comedy producer in the late 1950s. I guess I always had a funny sense of humor. So I started rooting around, mixing with some friends I knew, and I struck up a friendship with a couple of young radio performers called Spike Mulligan and Peter Sellers. They had just started a radio series called "The Goon Show."

I started recording them. Peter was just about to start his film career. I also made a record with Peter Ustinov which my bosses had so little confidence in they ordered 500 to be pressed and that was it. Those 500 sold out in the first day.

The first album I made with Peter Sellers I arrogantly titled, *The Best of Sellers*. Again, my bosses didn't believe in it. In fact, they didn't believe in it so much that they wanted me to make the record in ten-inch and not in twelve-inch.

Then I secured the rights to *Beyond the Fringe*, with Jonathan Miller, Peter Cook, and Dudley Moore. I became known as the comics producer, a thorn in the side, if you will, of EMI.

I would always be telling EMI about how our studios weren't good enough, that they should be better, like American studios. EMI offered to send me to America to have a look at the scene. I went over and I was invited to a number of recording sessions, one of which was Frank Sinatra's *Come Fly with Me*.

Sinatra was there with Lauren Bacall. He sang live. Billy May was the conductor and arranger. They started at seven in the evening and finished by eleven. In that entire time they had cut five titles, and I was overwhelmed. Sinatra sang beautifully, and almost invariably the first take was the master.

I went back to England so enthused with America and saying that we needed to do something with our studios because they were so dreadful.

And then one day, Brian Epstein walks into my office with a disc of this group he had in Liverpool. I must admit, I didn't do a handstand and say, "This is the next coming." I said it was OK, interesting, and that I'd like to meet the guys, spend an afternoon in the studio with them, and we'll see what we can do.

I spent the afternoon at Abbey Road with them, fell in love with them, and signed the Beatles immediately.

The very first record I made with them was "Love Me Do." Nobody wanted to hear it, particularly the people from EMI. When I announced at a meeting that I was issuing a new group called the Beatles, they all fell around laughing, particularly because of the way it was spelled. They said, "It's another one of your funny ones, George, isn't it?"

I said, "No, it's not funny. It's rock 'n' roll."

They said, "You doing rock 'n' roll? But you're a comedy producer."

We reexported American music back to America. A lot of things John and Paul did were dead copies of the things they'd heard. Paul's falsetto singing and the way they shook their heads was a takeoff of Little Richard. They would listen to American records, lift phrases, and work out how they'd want to do it. If George Harrison mastered a Chuck Berry riff, he would come home very proudly and play it ad nauseam.

When we had our first Number 1 hit, which was "Please Please Me," I knew we needed an album very quickly. I listened to all the other stuff of theirs, which was mostly other people's songs like "Roll Over Beethoven," and I said, "Let's take all the stuff you know and come down to the studio and we'll do it in one day," which we did. We started at ten in the morning and finished at eleven that night. We got the album out in three weeks. That was the Beatles' first album. We made it in one single day.

I was working my guts out making Beatles records, and Brian Epstein wasn't satisfied. He kept bringing me new groups, saying, "George, it's a Liverpool scene now. It's all happening." I got access to Gerry and the Pacemakers, Billy J. Kramer, Cilla Black. Brian said, "Record them all. We'll keep everything for ourselves."

I said, "Brian, there are only so many hours in the day."

I was very much in charge because I was a kind of school master teaching them everything. They had to do everything I told them. They brought me a raw song and I'd tell them, "This has got to last two and a half, three minutes. You just played me about fifty seconds of music, so let's make a little more out of this."

I would structure it for them. I'd tell them, "Two chords here, the second one needs a guitar solo. We need an introduction and an ending."

"Can't Buy Me Love" is an example of that. The original song started with the verse. I felt "Can't Buy Me Love" worked better as an introduction.

Of course, as the songs became more interesting, and more complicated, and as the boys got to know the studio better because they were very canny boys, it became much more of a democratic team.

Gradually, things changed. The boys went into their little spheres and there was more of a rivalry brewing between John and Paul. In truth, they were never great collaborators in the sense of sitting down and writing together. They were never Rodgers and Hart. One would have an idea for a song and he'd go to the other guy and say, "I need help on a line. Can you give it to me." That was how John and Paul collaborated.

Generally speaking, their songs were pitched against each other. One would say, "OK, you've written that. Now listen to mine." It was competitive collaboration. In fact, Paul misses it terribly now. He misses that spark of John being rude to him, saying, "You can't write that, Paul. It's awful." Paul needs that, and John was the only one who could really say that most effectively to him.

I was amazed it lasted so long. I mean, it lasted eight years. It was 1962 when I started with them, and we made the last record in 1970. That's a hell of a long time for four people to live in one another's pockets.

I thought it was all over during the *Let It Be* time because it was so uncomfortable with John and Paul and George all fighting. They hated each other's guts, and the women were doing the fighting for them, and money entered into it. It was a messy scene. I was unhappy about it, but I was just a bystander.

I was very surprised when Paul rang me up after *Let It Be* and said, "Will you come back and make another record with us?"

I said, "Well, not *Let It Be*."

He said, "We want to do a good record. Will you produce it?"

I said, "If you allow me to produce it."

He said, "I promise you, we will."

So we went back and we made *Abbey Road*. The boys were wonderful on that. I think they knew it was the last record. They all tried to make good. Even John tried to settle his differences with Paul.

Dave Clark

○ ○ ○

The man made a lot of money and outstripped even the Fab Four at the outset of the British attack on the American charts. The songs might not have come down through the years, but their impact was immediate. He's a promoter and hotshot businessman now, but he loves to recall the glory.

○ ○ ○

The English explosion was a bit like the old Hollywood star system where, bang, everybody takes off. Somebody would ask you how you felt on television, and you'd tell them exactly how you felt. If the camera shot you up the nose, and the lighting wasn't great, it didn't matter. It was live, raw, and magic, like the records were.

The Dave Clark Five was basically a live band. We failed a lot of record auditions, but we packed them in at the clubs and dance halls.

But we still needed a record. I thought, "Well, why not go out and make one ourselves?" I didn't have any money, and I wasn't that educated. I left school when I was fourteen, and I crashed cars in a film doing stunt work. I was an extra. People would say, "What have you done today?" and I'd tell them, "Oh, I've been working with Elizabeth Taylor and Richard Burton, but if you sneezed, you missed me."

Because we came from a suburb in London called Tottenham, we were suddenly the Tottenham Sound. Like the Beatles, who were the Liverpool Sound. And really, all it was was a commercial sound. The American press pitted us against the Beatles, but there was no rivalry between us. I often laughed about it with John and Paul. There was no rivalry at all. The press made it up. The magazines in America made a war out of it.

I think my background helped me to keep my sanity through that entire period. I come from a working-class family. At home, I was always treated like Dave Clark, person. If they didn't like something I did, they told me, which was lovely because as soon as you start believing your own press, or believing that you are a star, that's when the downfall comes.

For us, there wasn't a downfall. It just gradually wound down after our sixth world tour. We were at our height with our own plane, the *DC-5*. I mean, we had been arriving at airports and getting a key to every city in the States. We'd have two Cadillac limos and six motorcyclists escorting us. It was like being president, or king for a day. It was wonderful.

But after a time it got to be like the only thing we ever saw was the airport. We'd get whisked off to the hotel, we'd enter through the back entrance or kitchen. We'd have a suite on the top floor, or the entire top floor, and we'd be locked away.

Somebody would go down to the arena for us and tune up our instruments. We would arrive secretly at the intermission, go on, take a forced bow, and then rush off back to the hotel. After three years of answering the same questions and people only wanting to hear our hits, I turned around to the guys and said, "Let's stop while we're ahead. Let's retire gracefully while we're still in our twenties."

In the seventies, I grew a beard and I auditioned at the Royal Academy of Dramatic Arts because I wanted to study drama. I went under an assumed name. They had no idea who I was until they called out my name. I felt myself changing color. I didn't answer. After a while, it didn't matter who I was. They accepted me as just another actor.

I've been called many, many times to go out on those nostalgia tours. One time even at three o'clock in the morning. This guy woke me up and said, "Look, we want to put you on at Madison Square Garden. We want to put you on at the Hollywood Bowl. Only the major cities." He said, "You've already turned down two million dollars. How does three million sound?"

I said, "It's not the money. It's just that I don't think one can recapture the past."

He said, "Look, son, everybody's got a price."

And I said, "Well, I'm afraid I don't," and I hung up.

You can't go back. It is like going back to a place where you spent your childhood with your favorite aunt. You go back and it's never as good the second time. I wouldn't want to do that. Even if I didn't have a penny I'd rather go and get another job outside of the industry, or within the industry, but I wouldn't go back on tour. Not that I'm ashamed of it. Not that I feel we couldn't do it. We could do it easily, but we'd never do it any better than we did.

Mick Jagger
o o o

One of the world's most recognizable faces and leader of the baddest group in rock history, Mick has been analyzed and dissected by the world's press for over twenty-five years. We discussed the darkest side of stardom in a London flat when news of the Stones breakup first surfaced.

o o o

I remember other bands saying, "Oh, we can play Howlin' Wolf, but we can't play Bo Diddley." Or, "We can play Muddy Waters, but we can't play Jimmy Reed."

We said, "Well, we like rock 'n' roll as much as we like rhythm and blues, so even though we call ourselves a rhythm and blues band at rehearsals, we'll do anything from Elvis Presley to Buddy Holly to Ritchie Valens."

Keith and I were more into rock 'n' roll than, say, Brian, who particularly liked Elmore James. Brian learned to play in that style. I'm not saying that we didn't like that style, but but I don't think we would have played it if it hadn't been for Brian.

In the very beginning, before we made a record, before we signed a deal, before we had any contracts with management, I didn't have any idea of image at all. It didn't cross my mind. It may well have crossed Brian's mind, but no one ever brought it up. The first time I remember talking about anything that could be remotely connected with image was when I was wearing some kind of layered look, at one of these clubs, and either Brian or Keith said it was too effeminate. I didn't understand why I couldn't be effeminate, or be whatever I wanted, but I hadn't really thought about it. But I think Keith and Brian had thought about it. It just was something we didn't talk about.

Look what happened to Brian. The pressure obviously got to him. He didn't like it, couldn't live with it, and it just became very sad. I think eventually Keith suffered that way, too.

Of course, I was not able to distance myself from it either. I suppose it has to do with what success does to you. We started out simply to be a good R & B band. A few years later, things got a little twisted. The road to success is a very slippery one.

Every band did outrageous stuff on the road, but we were always singled out. We did stupid things, but we also did do-goody things, like going to hospitals and visiting sick children. That's not what I set out to do. But there you are. England has such a small show business community that if you don't become a part of it and join the Variety Club and do charity work, then you're looked upon as some kind of weirdo. I don't think I'm a part of it now, and I tried not to be a part of it then.

Eventually, of course, I do think the image stuff contributed to Brian's cracking up completely, and to a certain extent, with Keith becoming a junkie.

To use a cliché, the sixties never really ended until later on in the seventies. I sort of remember the album *Exile on Main Street* being done in France and also in the United States, and after that going on tour and becoming complacent, and thinking, "It's '72. Fuck it. We've done it."

We still tried after that, but I don't think the results were ever that wonderful. Maybe some people liked *Goat's Head Soup*, *It's Only Rock 'n' Roll*, and *Black and Blue*, but basically, those albums did not represent the best of the Rolling Stones. But on the nice side, we did decide at that time that we were definitely going to stick together. After all, we'd signed this big contract with Atlantic Records, and we were quite happy with being a band. But we were complacent, which is what critics were saying, and while I didn't believe that at the time, looking back, I can accept the fact that we were coasting.

It's hard to make it every night. I mean, lots of people don't move around much onstage. Even with young bands, it's amazing how little work they do. The only guy that I've seen lately that works very hard is Paul Young. I mean, I went to see this band, INXS, from Australia. They were an OK band, very much like a version of the Rolling Stones, but not as good. The singer is good and he looks great, but he doesn't really move. He can't be expending much energy. He can't really be tired when he comes offstage. And he's, like, twenty-three. He must be able to sit there and be recovered in three minutes. But who cares, really?

Lots of rock 'n' roll people are boring. There are lots of musicians that are dull as hell. Duller than a hound, some of them. I enjoy socializing and meeting people. If I don't enjoy it, I leave. I'd rather be out and about on my own than in the middle of some entourage creating attention.

Although I have never met him, I would imagine that Frank Sinatra enjoys being the center of attention. Maybe he likes walking into a room with bodyguards and friends and women and people who work for him, but I don't.

I don't have bodyguards, and I don't particularly enjoy being the center of attention. I'd rather slide into a room and observe the room, and then if I want to make some point, make it. But I don't like people in show business to do that whole number. I don't particularly want to be noticed above anyone else, and I don't want to be less noticed than anyone else. I mean, I don't want to be ignored and stuck in a corner and not given a drink. It's just that I'd rather not do things in a show-bizzy way.

In London, you can't ever be rude. People don't like it if you have an attitude. You've got to be one of them. It's the same in New York. People say hello, they don't stop you or gape. Same in London, and that's how I like it. You always have to be a little like a local politician. You can't just say, "Fuck off." Do that and people will pull you right back down to earth.

How does Frank Sinatra go out and buy a newspaper? How does Barbra Streisand do it? Do they wear fur coats? Do they always go in a limo? I'd rather just walk down to the store myself. I can send someone out to buy my favorite magazines, but if I do, maybe I won't see that cover of a magazine I didn't think I wanted but now I do. Maybe I've forgotten to tell someone about *The New Yorker*, and that one will be on the stand. I can send someone out for clothes, but how will they know that I really like that green shirt? I like it when I'm on the same level with other people. I'm not saying that I spend my whole life doing this stuff, but it's nice to be able to do the same things everyone else does.

Mickie Most

○ ○ ○

He was as key a player in the first wave of English rock in the sixties as anyone. Mickie knew how to make pop records for very little money, and along the way he became a star.

○ ○ ○

I returned to England from Africa in 1962. The British music scene was very sad then, very pathetic. The American stuff was pretty much the same. There was a lot of Bobby Vee and Del Shannon, which was all quite pleasant, but it really didn't have the depth of, say, Elvis Presley, Chuck Berry, and Little Richard. The early sixties were a down time.

So I return to England looking for bands. I traveled all over and all they were doing were American cover records. In '63 I started to see movement, and the movement was R & B. Instead of playing American chart records, the bands were starting to play more obscure R & B stuff out of Chicago. I saw the Rolling Stones, and their manager, Andrew Oldham, had already decided to take them into the studio himself. In Newcastle I met the Animals. They were playing in a club, and I signed them as an independent producer.

I paid for the production of the records. Of course, in those days they weren't that expensive. You'd take the finished tape to the major label, and you'd say, "Will you release this record?" Fortunately with the Animals they did. But you made the deal with the artist first, then you went to the record company, and the difference between what you paid the artist and what you got from the record company was your profit. In a lot of cases it was hard to make a profit because the record companies in the early sixties weren't too flush with their royalty rates. But when the Beatles broke internationally, the floodgates opened.

The Animals' first record was "The House of the Rising Sun." They had been playing it onstage. You'd have to be deaf not to hear that as a hit record. But no one had picked up on it, and it took me a bit to get them to record it as a single. It was six minutes long, and they thought it was too long and a bit dreary. But it was magic, and we made the record.

They had been on tour with Chuck Berry, and they took an all-night train, and we picked them up at seven-fifteen in the morning. Took their equipment and them in a truck around to the recording studio. We started recording at around eight o'clock in the morning, and by eight-fifteen "The House of the Rising Sun" was finished.

The studio cost eight pounds an hour, which was about twenty dollars in those days. And we recorded the song in fifteen minutes, so you're talking about five dollars. And because they were scheduled to catch a twelve-thirty train to Southampton to continue with the tour, I said, "Let's do an album." We finished the album by eleven, and they made their twelve-thirty train.

I took the single to America. People were nice but nobody was really interested. When I got back to England, "The House of the Rising Sun" came out and it went from Number 30 to Number 10 to Number 1. Representatives of MGM happened to be in England at the time, and they were saying, "Why don't we have the Beatles? Why don't we have Gerry and the Pacemakers?" EMI distributed MGM's product in England, and Len Wood was looking through the charts and sees the record by the Animals. He says to MGM, "You can have the Animals," and that's how they wound up on MGM in America.

There was a rawness to the Animals' records, to the Beatles' records. It was very basic. There was no schmaltz about it, and it hit young people. Young people wanted a change, and the change came at the right time.

With Herman's Hermits it was different. I just saw a young John Kennedy in Peter Noone. That's what I actually saw. I saw his picture on a postcard and I made a mental note. I wrote on the back of the postcard, "Good for the U.S. market. Young Kennedy. Have to find them a song."

I went to Bolton, where they were playing, and I listened to all their songs, which were pretty awful, really. And then I found one song, and one song led to finding other songs, and of all the acts I worked with, Herman's Hermits had a good run in America. They really sold a lot of records. I think they had six Number 1 records in one year.

But we were making records for the States, not for England. Maybe it was MGM's greed, I don't know. All I knew was that I'm two years back from living in Africa and I'm being told on the telephone that MGM needs a new Herman's Hermits album by Friday. And it's now Thursday evening. I was so involved in feeding the machine, feeding them the flavor of the month, and it was fun. It wasn't premeditated. You just made records. You said, "I've got twelve now. Let's put out an album."

You can't computerize this business. It's all done by feel, and once the feel goes, you lose touch, you lose the communication with kids. Kids get into buying music during their preteen years, just about at the time when boys and girls vaguely become interested in each other. You say to a girl, "Hi. Have you heard the latest album by so-and-so?" That goes straight into some dialogue. It's communication to those kids, and culture. Kids spread Elvis Presley the same way they spread Duran Duran. If a boy looks at Elvis Presley or Simon LeBon or Bruce Springsteen, he models himself after them. With girls it can be a sexual thing. Try to put that into a computer and it probably will not work out.

Peter Noone

○ ○ ○

Quite simply, Herman of the Hermits. His is a story of achieving too much too soon and keeping his young head about him during some rather hysterical success.

○ ○ ○

Until I met Mickie Most I was busy trying to be Bobby Vee meets the Everly Brothers meets Roy Orbison. It was Mickie who came up with the song "I'm into Something Good." I was supposed to play piano on the session, but as soon as Mickie heard my piano playing, he called in another piano player.

Mickie wasn't sure about the record after he finished it. He played it for a few people around the business, and they all went, "Nah." But then Chris, his wife, heard it, and she said, "This is a Number 1 record. You've got to put it out." A week after it was out it was on the airwaves.

I was very anti-English. It's amazing I was even part of the English invasion. The Beatles did American rock 'n' roll very well. They played Little Richard songs, and Chuck Berry, and they played them better than any other band around. So I didn't want to be in competition with those guys. In fact, I idolized them. John Lennon drank Bacardi and Coke and smoked Lark cigarettes. For five years after I found that out, I only drank Bacardi and Coke and smoked Lark cigarettes.

I remember, we were sitting in a bar watching cartoon shows, trying to come up with a name. The Bullwinkle show came on, and we said, "That's it—the Bullwinkles." Then we came up with Sherman, then Herman, a little cartoon character. I thought that would be great. Everyone was going for a Bobby Rydell image, and I'd come up with a real nerdy character.

Then a guy who hated the band walks through the bar and says, "Call yourself Herman and the Bloody Hermits," and wow! We thought we could dress up in sack clothes, how embarrassing.

The following day we had a date at the Plaza in Manchester. We would do these lunchtime dates for secretaries. We were kind of hot with secretaries and Woolworth's working girls—a real working-class band. So we get on stage in our potato sacks, and it was a disaster.

There was a television play called "The Lads," which was written by Trevor Peacock, who wrote "Mrs. Brown, You've Got a Lovely Daughter." And he'd written it to introduce the play. It was the kind of piece you could do at bar mitzvahs, and we learned it. We would joke and change the words to "Mrs. Silverman, You've Got a Lovely Daughter." What it was was a successful stage song.

Now we make an album for EMI and MGM. Essentially, the album amounted to "I'm into Something Good" and eleven other songs. After ten songs we were struggling. So we did "Mrs. Brown," as a joke! In the English album version it's well hidden—track four, side two.

All of a sudden some disc jockey in America starts playing it, and amazingly enough it's a hit. It hadn't even been released in England.

We were never comfortable with the recording. It was done in one take. The bass is slightly out of tune with the guitar. We never thought it would see the light of day.

We came to the States and it was unbelievable. I was very interested in meeting girls—the more the merrier. I took care of myself. I avoided the drugs. I would go to parties with other rock 'n' roll musicians, and they would all sit in one room smoking dope with the blinds closed, being very serious and talking about the war in Vietnam, and in the meantime I was in another room with all their girlfriends.

Herman's Hermits was a singles act, and in the future it was all to be album acts. We were not prepared to be an album act. We didn't write songs. I didn't want to write songs. I figured, let Carole King or Neil Diamond write me a song. Even their demos sounded like Number 1 songs. How could we fail? All we had to do was copy what they did, and with my voice we'd have a hit.

San Francisco basically blew Herman's Hermits out of the water. In '66 we did this date at the Cow Palace. We were on the top of the bill. The other acts were flower-power acts, and they surely didn't like us. They didn't want to lend us any equipment, nothing. They were down on Herman's Hermits because we were a pop act and we didn't know where Vietnam was.

Back in England, I could do shows as Peter Noone, have twenty musicians with me, do nothing but Herman's Hermits' hits, and be accepted by the audience.

And then Mickie got this David Bowie song, "All You Pretty Things." Herman's Hermits weren't even invited to the session. It was called a Peter Noone record. It was a hit in England, and that was the end of Herman's Hermits.

Tony Stratton Smith

o o o

Shortly after our wonderful talk in his Covent Garden office in London, Tony passed away. He was a man who came to the music business from the sports world relatively late and made an enormous impact as a record company executive and as a manager of Genesis.

o o o

I had spent a lot of time in Brazil and the only experience I'd had with rock 'n' roll—you couldn't even call it rock 'n' roll—was Cliff Richard and

Tommy Steele at the old Two Eyes in Soho. I'll never forget that sweaty little sewer. Extraordinary place, which, oddly enough, was owned by two wrestlers. One was an Australian. The place had begun as a sportsman's hangout. They were all Australian cricketeers, rugby and all the scum.

But the place also had a cellar, which they had no use for, but they rented it out. I can't remember the man's name who first rented it out, he deserves some praise for being one of the early promoters, but he started putting bands in—Lonnie Donegan, Tommy Steele, Cliff Richard.

Then the Beatles happened. I remember Jimmy Young who had a little TV show that came out of Bristol. Had the Beatles on for their first-ever television appearance. And Jimmy Young apologized for the Beatles in advance. I'd only seen that once before, in the fifties when the late, lamented British disc jockey, Jack Jackson, totally misread Elvis Presley. Jack used to play Elvis' records in '55, '56, and he'd put the words up on a board and use a pointer. Totally misread Presley's quality. I remember being angry about that and even more angry about Jimmy Young and the Beatles. The song was "Love Me Do," and he was apologizing in advance.

But their performance was electric. They were exactly what the business needed. I'm not knocking Cliff Richard because he's a marvelous professional, an admirable person, and a damn good artist. But the Beatles were it. They had style, material, and everything coming together in one incarnation. Presley was style. The Beatles were style plus material. The Beatles had the hearts of the kids in a way that no other artist at the time had.

I went to see Brian Epstein about possibly doing a book on the Beatles. If I had taken the job, people might never have heard of Derek Taylor. I say that as a joke because Derek is an old mate, but I was flown to Amsterdam to see Brian. We were supposed to talk for a few hours, and the few hours became a weekend. I said, "I'd really love to do the book."

Brian said, "All right, we'll start next week."

I said, "Hang on a minute. I have a commitment on another book that's going to take me another four to six months." He went mad, he went potty. He wanted it out right then, like a record, like next week. But I got on my high horse. I said, "I'm sorry. I'm committed to do *The Rebel Nun*, and if you don't make any other arrangements, I'll be available in six months' time."

I realize now with hindsight that it was arrogance on my part. Probably a little stupid, too. The first of many bad decisions on my part. Derek Taylor got the assignment and the book was quite successful.

But I got to know Brian, and I learned a lot about rock 'n' roll management from him. Rock 'n' roll management in England was invented by Brian Epstein. It was through his success that people saw real money being made. Other people of entrepreneurial bent started moving in.

My generation in England was lucky. We had three mentors. One was Brian, who was shy in many ways but a thinker. He thought a long way ahead. A lot of people attack him now for what they say were poor commercial deals for the Beatles during the very early days. What these people forget is that he was doubling the existing deals that people at the time were being forced to take. In the context of the time, Brian Epstein was a hard cookie.

Andrew Oldham was another mentor. I had a very ambivalent attitude toward Andrew. I think Andrew's career was arrested by a rather childish streak. He had a kind of willful-child thing that made him very uncomfortable to deal with.

The other mentor was Kit Lambert. Similar kind of person to Andrew, but infinitely nicer. Of the three, I would say Kit was the model in those days. He made it with the Who, but he could have made it with any good band. Before he started running off to Paris and drinking too much and drugging too much, before all these things ruined Kit's life, he had a fine mind. If he could have controlled himself, he could have become the best manager in the world.

Cliff Richard

○ ○ ○

He was an enormous success in England and in much of the world, but the failure to transfer that success to the U.S.A. has him bitter and still wondering. The fame across the ocean is so deep-rooted and pervasive that he can't spend too much time thinking about why it didn't happen here.

○ ○ ○

Elvis was about four years older than me. He's the reason why I became a singer. He was the best, the prototype. I don't suppose there will ever be anyone like him again.

I had a chance to meet him once. It was in the States. He was not well. He'd put on a lot of weight, and I decided to keep my earlier memories of him intact. The Elvis I remember was the Elvis of "Heartbreak Hotel" and "All Shook Up," classic hit after classic hit. I was not interested in Elvis' music from "Crying in the Chapel" on. He lost me after that.

But in the beginning all we did was copy American music. America is still the fatherland of rock 'n' roll. I don't think America has control of rock 'n' roll, nobody does. It belongs to the world now. But America gave it to the world and therefore holds a private place.

This is why I've always desperately wanted something to happen for me in the States. I've cracked it everywhere but where it started, and it irks me. The Shadows and I always seemed to represent the rest of the world, and it was the rest of the world versus America. When the Beatles came in, they came in on the backs of what we had done around the rest of the world. Of course, it was about that time that England looked like it was going to take off anyhow. But the Beatles broke in 1963, five years after us. And the Beatles had to leave England to make it.

I read this article once about how John Lennon "took off his glasses." It was *my* guitarist that took off his glasses, not John Lennon. They left the country because we had it all sewn up. There wasn't anything for them in England. Of course, at the time they really weren't the Beatles as we know them. I mean, I've heard some early recordings and they were diabolical. The singing wasn't good, and the tuning was duff, and there was no original material. When they got to Germany, somehow the magic got into them. Somehow they became McCartney and Lennon and the Beatles. I mean, there's no doubt that they took pop music into another realm. It had to happen, someone had to do it, and they did it. It couldn't have been us because we started too early. But we were pioneers, and they came after the pioneers, built upon that foundation, and took it soaring away.

People forget what everybody else was doing because of all the media attention heaped upon the Beatles. In 1965, a poll was taken either in *Billboard* or *Cashbox* or one of the trades. The Beatles were the biggest record-sellers in the world. And who was the biggest solo artist in the world? Me. And I didn't sell a record in America.

Peter Asher

o o o

Peter's career ran from teen idol to great producer to brilliant manager. Among the whole panoply of managers, he has linked possibly the most solid relationships with his artists, as James Taylor and Linda Ronstadt will testify.

o o o

I think Gordon and I just wanted to be the Everly Brothers. I remember us getting an audition with EMI. We did a folk song, "500 Miles." They liked the way our voices sounded and they signed us.

Right around the same time, Paul McCartney had met my sister, Jane, and they started going out. That's when I met Paul. He and I got on very well. At some point later he played me this song he'd never finished. It was "A World Without Love." He'd written it for Billy J. Kramer, who turned it down. I thought we could sing it. I told Paul to write a bridge and we'd do it. And he did.

It was fantastic. When we first came to the States in June of '64, we played the World's Fair. The whole thing was amazingly exciting. When we landed at the airport, there were crowds of screaming girls with signs, jumping all over us. And then, to get into this incredibly long black limousine, which by English standards is, like, a hundred miles long, was all so stunning.

I'll never forget that World's Fair because there was this body of water out in front of us. And all these girls jumped in the water fully clothed and swam across just to climb up onstage and be near us. It was a terrific time to be in the music business and a terrific time to be an English rock 'n' roller, and have girls tearing your clothes off. It was wonderful.

Gordon and I got along pretty well. As duos go, we probably got along admirably. We disagreed about some things, and we used to get into arguments. As the years progressed, I supposed we got along less well.

Peter and Gordon broke up sort of gradually, as these things often do. Gordon wanted to do a solo record, and this friend of mine, Paul Jones, who eventually became the lead singer of Manfred Mann, he knew I was interested in production, and he asked me if I'd like to produce some records with him, which I did.

Paul McCartney heard the stuff I was doing with Paul Jones, and he asked me if I'd produce something for Apple. I'd already known about Apple at that point because we'd all hung out at Paul's house quite a bit, and we'd all sit around and smoke dope and explain our plans for changing the world.

Anyway, Paul asked me if I wanted to produce something for Apple, and I said, "Great, I'd love to." A little later on, he asked me if I wanted to be head of A & R for Apple, and I said, "Great." I didn't quite know what the head of A & R did, but it seemed like it would be a good job.

With all the accounts of the madness at Apple, one tends to forget that for two or three years it was an effective record company. There were so many lunatics and weird people hanging around that you get the impression in books that the whole Apple thing was one amazing party. In fact, there were a lot of people who came in every day, did their jobs, and got everything done.

But there was a lot of lunacy. We had an A & R meeting once a week with a sort of quorum of Beatles in attendance. They tended to be more interested in their own projects than in anything else. George was more concerned about the Jackie Lomax record, and John was more concerned about the Plastic Ono Band.

You really didn't get the feeling you were dealing with a board of directors who were terribly concerned with the corporation as a whole. Everyone was sort of running in different directions. So, while the responsibility was mine to decide whom to sign and whom not to sign, signing anyone who didn't have a couple of Beatles as supporters was a futureless prospect.

It was very hard for any of us to imagine what it was like to be a Beatle. Whatever degree of success or adulation any of us have ever been subjected to, it's incomparable to what they went through.

They used to have a lot of arguments among themselves about one thing or another. Especially after Brian Epstein died. Brian ran things a certain way. It later dawned on the Beatles that Brian didn't know much more than they knew, but he was so well-meaning, so honorable. Without him, they argued a lot more. Normal questions could easily become an argument, and often did. Sometimes we'd be having an A & R meeting, playing tapes, and they'd start arguing about something else. Or one of them would moan to you at dinner about one of the others.

Paul was the one I knew the best. He sometimes moaned to me about how unreasonable John was being. I'm sure if John had been my friend, he'd be moaning to me about one of the others. I think Ringo said the least. But he would get very upset sitting at his drums waiting for the others to stop yelling at each other.

Roger Daltrey

o o o

The Who occupy yet another special niche musically and theatrically in rock 'n' roll history. Daltrey's good looks and demeanor and his much publicized squabbles with Peter Townshend only added to their mythology. What a group!

o o o

There was a strange chemical makeup to our band. It thrived on friction. We were very aggressive. In some ways, we were probably the first male-focused rock 'n' roll band. Before us, groups were popular first with girls. The Who was more popular with men, basically because we were so aggressive. Men like a good rugby song, and that was the atmosphere the Who created.

How we were and what we turned out to be just happened. When we first started out, we did like all bands did, we copied what was in the Top 20. Then we started to develop more obscure kinds of music, like blues and the Motown sound, which was unheard of in England. Boredom with what we had been hearing led us to experiment. And the more we experimented—Keith Moon, for example, used to do these incredible things on his drums—the more positive the feedback we got. And it grew every night.

It was extraordinary. We were playing seven nights a week, and you could see the progression from week to week. The Who was never planned. It just grew, and that is probably why it was so successful.

It was the same with Pete Townshend's guitar smashing. It just happened. When his guitar broke, as it did onstage one night, it made this incredible noise, like an elephant in heat. Now Pete, being the kind of showman he is, decided after he saw the neck of the guitar break—he just started smashing the rest of it. Well, the crowd went bananas. And because Moonie didn't want to be upstaged, he started thrashing at his drums a hundred times harder that he usually hit them, which was hard enough in the first place.

Our Mod look was engineered by our first manager, a very bright boy named Peter Meaden. At that time in England, 90 percent of the bands resembled either the Rolling Stones or the Beatles. If anything, we were similar to the Stones. We had long hair, and we played a scruffy kind of blues music. It was Peter who made us aware that the whole thing was more than just music. It was about image, too.

He said, "Everybody has long hair. Get yours cut." That was an incredibly dangerous thing to do because kids with long hair over their collars were dying to get thrown out of school. To walk in with short hair was taking a very big chance, but it worked.

The Mod look was very clean-cut, Ivy League, fashion conscious, which was exactly opposite from the Stones. Peter told us to do it, and he was right. Our personalities didn't change, we were still a bunch of rotten, dirty-boy rock 'n' rollers, but kids began identifying with our short hair and Ivy League clothes, and it just took off from there.

When we hit with "My Generation," which was a statement—an anthem, really—it showed the public that we were a lot more than just another pop group. The only trouble was, it was very hard to top "My Generation." I don't know if we ever did.

We were a weird mixture. I believe Pete and I aimed for the same thing, only from different angles. Pete was either the angry young man or the seeker of truth. I think I was more down to earth. John Entwistle was always the quiet one. He never said much, but he added a lot of humor. And Moon was our comedy, and also very creative in the studio. He would come up with the wackiest ideas, and somehow they came off.

The idea for *Tommy* actually began with Kit Lambert. He had it in his head that we should do a rock opera. Kit's father was a conductor and very well-known in classical music circles. Kit had this thing about rock not being belittled or downtrodden. Kit was "from the other side," as we used to call it. He was proud of rock 'n' roll, and he wanted it to be accepted as an art form. And one of the ways to break that barrier, he said, was to do a rock opera.

So Pete came up with a song called "Amazing Journey," which was about a guy going through life deaf, dumb, and blind. All his experiences were through his sense of touch. *Tommy* grew from that one song. But most of the pushing was done by Kit. He had a hell of a lot to do with it.

It was shocking when Keith died. In a way, though, it gave us a lot of strength because we had been fraying at the edges before he died. His death had a kind of pulling-together effect. It made us determined not to let the band die. If we had let the band go then, it would have made two tragedies out of one. We got through it. We probably made a lot of mistakes, but

Keith's death gave us an incredible amount of freedom, which I think we threw away.

And then Cincinnati, with people getting trampled to death, was an unbelievable thing to live through. I don't know if people outside the business are aware of what happens when a group like the Who goes out on tour. Your whole life is magnified, and yet you are trapped in this little insular group. Everything is out of proportion. You become more important than you are. You can't see anything other than the Who. When you're in the papers, or shown on the telly, it's like being in never-never land.

And then you walk away from a tour six weeks later, and you suddenly realize that it wasn't important at all. But when you're doing it, it's like Third World War.

Maybe the only way to beat it is to not give a shit about it, but we were never like that. If anything, the Who cared too much, and it made things very hard. Touring was no longer much fun. That was what was so great about Keith. He could always pull the light switch. If there was too much pressure, there was Moon taking the top off the lid and letting the air out. But once he died, it was very difficult.

I am not bitter. I had a great time, and I'm proud of it. We were a great band. We were lucky, we tried our best, and I think in most areas we succeeded. We washed our laundry in public, and people liked that. We wore our hearts on our sleeves, and people could identify with that. Mostly, we tried, and I think we gave people through the seventies a lot of optimism for the future.

Donovan

○ ○ ○

Flower child at the right time, Donovan had to shake the "British Dylan" tag and managed to do so, writing another chapter in music that translated so well to the rest of the world.

○ ○ ○

I was fourteen, I think, when I had a group called the McCarbs. We were silly kids dressed up in hoods with slits cut out at the eyes. I was the drummer, but I wasn't really a drummer. I just was able to pick out rhythms and such because I used to hang out in the jazz clubs.

We jigged and we danced and we played bohemian. And in bohemian circles, there was the American folk music of Woody Guthrie, Pete Seeger, Joan Baez, and of course, Bob Dylan.

I had a great love of acoustic blues as well. I would be in the record store—hanging out, smoking dope, reading Buddhism, and going down to the record store to hunt for rare albums, like the finger-picking albums of Ramblin' Jack Elliott. One time when Dylan came to England, the press asked him, "Have you heard Donovan? He's ripping off your style."

Dylan said he hadn't heard me and asked if they'd play him my record. When they played it, they waited for him to say, "Yeah, he's ripping me off." What he did say was, "He doesn't play like me. He plays like Jack Elliott."

They said, "Who?"

I remember walking up my mother's stairs to her home. I'd run away a couple of times and police would bring me back. So I came back this one time, and I walked up my mother's stairs, and there playing on the radio in the kitchen—one of those black and white things with a grill on it that looked like the grill on a Cadillac—was this tune "Love Me Do." I didn't know who the Beatles were. I just heard a harmonica playing. I had already been playing the harmonica, and here was this band playing harmonica, so I listened. I was stunned. I remember saying, "I want to do that. This folk scene is limited."

Then I listened to Buddy Holly and the Everly Brothers. Every week I'd work at the local fruit market selling fruit and reject cakes, and every Saturday I'd take my money and buy an extended-play record of Buddy Holly. The Beatles were influenced by the harmonies of the Everly Brothers. I was solo, so I went for Buddy Holly.

The problem of my always being compared to Dylan began with a television show in England. The guy who introduced me said, "You know what happened in the States with Dylan. It looks like this young man is going to appeal the same way in Europe." There followed this whole spate of comparisons with Dylan. It got on my nerves. It bothered me. But it only served to strengthen my resolve and my own work. I spoke out against it, I said I never ripped him off. He said I never ripped him off, but that didn't stop people from comparing us.

I remember seeing Dylan at the Savoy Hotel when he was in England doing a show. I remember arriving, and Bobby Neuwirth, Dylan's roadie at the time, quietly bringing me into Dylan's suite. The hubbub had died down, and they said, "He's through the back." I went into a little television room, creeped in and shut the door. It was dark in there. Dylan was just a shadow. He was looking at the ice skating championships from Austria on a television in a darkened room. He didn't say anything. We just sat down. Neither asked the other a question. There was nothing to say, nothing to ask. Slowly my eyes got accustomed to the dark, and I realized there were other figures in the room sitting on the couch. Slowly the figures became more real. It was John, Paul, George, and Ringo. I must say I felt a little out of my depth.

Much later on, I taught John Lennon the finger-style guitar he wound up using to compose five or six songs on *The White Album*. It was simple to teach him. He picked it up very quickly, and I felt that in a way I had returned something to them that I had gotten the first time I heard "Love Me Do."

Mark Lindsay

o o o

If there is one act that typifies the lighter aspect of pop music in the sixties, Paul Revere and The Raiders is it. Mark was the leader of the group, which is remembered more for what they looked like than for what they played.

o o o

I'm not sure any of us in Paul Revere and the Raiders will ever score well in the *Down Beat* poll, but we were enthusiastic players and we had fun. From the Headless Horseman in Portland, Oregon, to the Coliseum in Los Angeles, it didn't make any difference. Nobody could hear us anyway. There was always too much noise.

There was this band in the Portland–Seattle area that was a big local group called the Wailers. I remember reading in the paper that they'd played at some organizational function for $300, and that was their price. I said to Paul, "Gee, if we can get our price up to $300 a gig, we'll have arrived."

Our manager, a guy named Roger Hart who was on a Portland radio station, went to California to meet a secretary of Dick Clark's, and somehow Roger finagled us onto the bill as one of the 1,000 opening acts for the Rolling Stones at the Long Beach Auditorium.

So we got up and did our thing. I got up and danced on the piano in my three-cornered hat, and people loved it. The ridiculous outfits started in Portland. We had been wearing these hip, colorless La Jolla blazers—our Beach Boys look. And then one day we passed a costume shop in Portland and there are all kinds of costumes, including this Revolutionary War outfit with this guy in a three-cornered hat. I said to Paul, "Do you know what'd be fun? How about if we rented these things for the guys, and just after intermission tonight we'll come back out onstage looking like this?"

The gig was at the Lake Oswego Armory, and we come out wearing these costumes, and all of a sudden I look over at Paul and he's a clown playing the piano. It was, like, suddenly you can do anything. It was a total removal of all inhibitions.

People went crazy. They loved it. Every time you looked over at the guy next to you, you couldn't help but laugh. And the enthusiasm spread. At the end of the gig, Paul and I are backstage in the dressing room feeling like Gorgeous George must have felt when he realized, "Hey, I think I got something going here."

We felt like the costumes were a gimmick, like the Beatles had their look. We felt sort of like the answer to the Beatles. We were Americans, it's tied into the Revolution. "We're going to fight those guys." The outfits gave us a totally unique look. Nobody, but nobody, was dressing up then like idiots.

Rolling Stone magazine said, "The Raiders have arrived," and they gave our album, *Collage*, a glowing review. And I've seen *Rolling Stone* pan the Beatles, right? I thought, "Well, this is it." Of course, it sold nothing.

About that show in Long Beach with Dick Clark's secretary, I didn't know if people were hooting at us or cheering for us, but we brought the house down at that concert. Dick Clark's secretary went back to Dick and said, "Do you know the show you want to put on the air? Well, I found the perfect band for you."

So Dick hired us to play backing tracks. He must have thought, "Well, these guys will be OK until the show takes off. When it does, I'll hire somebody's who's worth something."

Luckily, wherever we played live people loved us. And now we're on television getting national exposure, live everywhere, in everyone's house every afternoon. Within three or four weeks we were getting 50,000 letters a week.

When it came time to re-sign, somebody from the show called us up and said, "Come down and get your mail." I wandered down thinking there'd be three or four pieces. The person said, "No. Here are these sacks."

So Paul goes back and talks to Dick. Paul says, "Hey, Dick, let's re-sign something here."

Michael Nesmith

o o o

Remember the Monkees? Michael was a driving force in that strange band that entered pop music through a side door—a truth that he readily admits to and actually seems proud of.

o o o

The Monkees were not a musical act. We had very little to do with the music business, and absolutely nothing to do with rock 'n' roll.

There is this idea that the group was put together, manufactured, and put onto television for the sole purpose of creating hit records. That simply was not the case.

We were a very visible part of pop culture, formed by a combination of creative people from movies and television.

For example, the man who wrote the original screenplay for the Monkees was Paul Mazursky. Burt Schneider from Columbia Pictures produced the show, and Bob Rafelson was the director. On the periphery of the Monkees you had people like Jack Nicholson, Harry Dean Stanton, Peter Fonda, Dennis Hopper. These are not musical people. Who knew from the music business? We were actors and writers and filmmakers. None of us had any concept of making records or writing music or playing in a band. All we knew was that we needed a certain stream of music for the show.

So we went to a junior executive at Columbia's publishing by the name of Don Kirshner. Burt Schneider called him and told him we needed some music. Don said he had a stack of writers—Gerry Goffin and Carole King, Barry Mann and Cynthia Weil, Neil Diamond—some of the hottest, most important popular songwriters in the world.

So Kirshner put together this stack of songs, including a song called "Last Train to Clarksville." Lo and behold, and much to everyone's surprise, the thing was an absolute, walkaway, smash hit record. When I say it caught us off guard, I mean, it blind-sided everybody!

Who knew? We'd go down there, sing a little background vocals, decide that Mickey Dolenz is the best guy to sing, and that maybe I'll play a little guitar here and there, and that was it. We were so busy making a television series. The music wasn't important.

Well, we're driving along and we turn on the radio and there's "Last Train to Clarksville"—the Number 2 record in the country. And we didn't even realize that was us.

The whole thing was utterly bizarre. Suddenly Kirshner got it in his mind that he had created the group. Don Kirshner had nothing whatsoever to do with the Monkees. He was a junior executive at a publishing company who got together some writers to find some songs for us to use as soundtracks.

What made Don's pronouncement that he created the group so troublesome was the simple fact that we were not a musical group. It was a television show, for Christ's sake! But Kirshner kept insisting that we were a rock 'n' roll band that somehow ended up with its own television show.

The idea became so insidious and perverse and twisted that none of us stood up and said, "Hey, wait a minute, Donnie. One, there is no rock 'n' roll band, and two, you didn't find us." Nobody stood up and said that. Everybody sort of went along with the notion of "OK, if we have to be a rock 'n' roll band, then we'll do it. But we better be ourselves and not lie about it."

The entire time was a mixed blessing. It opened a lot of doors and closed a lot of other doors.

There were a few incredibly unusual side effects to the Monkees, not the least of which was the strange case of Jimi Hendrix and the Monkees.

It is a little-known fact that Hendrix was introduced to the United States by the Monkees. Actually, he was discovered by Mickey Dolenz in a small club in London.

I can't remember why we were in London at the time, but I was hanging around the London pop scene with John Lennon. The Monkees were due to start an American tour and we needed an opening act.

So Mickey comes to me and says he heard this trio in a club the night before, and the rock 'n' roll they played was unlike anything any of us had ever heard. At this point, we had enough control of our tours to demand who we wanted.

Mickey says he wants the trio, and I say fine, OK. Later that night, I trundled off to a club and met Lennon and McCartney and George Harrison and Eric Clapton. This was like me being with the Vatican, the pop priests of the time.

Lennon says, "Listen, you guys have to hear this." And he pulls out this little Sony tape recorder and plays "Hey Joe," by Jimi Hendrix, the same guy Mickey wants for the tour.

The table all of a sudden gets very quiet. It seems as though we're listening to a guy who has invented a new kind of music. I'm talking a real leap forward in musical thought. OK. Fade out.

Fade in. Raleigh, North Carolina. A Holiday Inn. We're on the first leg of our tour and Hendrix is coming to join us. I've never laid eyes on the guy, OK?

So we take over a wing of the Holiday Inn, and there are lots of police around who are doing their best to keep the screaming girls away from us.

It's late at night, and I'm standing around with a serious case of the "road rummies," as in bored. And then I look down the hall and I see two uniformed policemen standing there, arms akimbo, on each side of the door.

Then the door opens, almost as if by magic, and there stands Jimi Hendrix in all his colors. Mitch Mitchell and Noel Redding are standing on either side of him. Jimi's hair is standing straight up. He appears backlit. And he begins to waft down the hall with these long, flowing, multicolored paisley things. He has pinwheels for eyes. And I'm thinking, "Who is this?"

And he walks up to me and says, "Hi, Mike. I'm Jimi Hendrix."

I say, "Oh." That was all I could say. I was totally blown away by this man's presence. He had a very peaceful countenance about him. I thought, "Well, I want to hear this guy live."

Going to the arena early posed some security problems, so I disguised myself. I'm standing there, and he comes on, and the first song he does is "Purple Haze." I can remember being moved back, physically back, about two feet. I had never heard such music in my life. I thought, "The man has plugged into some celestial outlet."

It was most exhilarating, the most majestic, the most entertaining, the most fulfilling music I'd ever heard. It was neither too loud, nor too soft. I could hear every single nuance. Mitch and Noel seemed to be driven by the one central, single vision that emanated from a spot in the back of Jimi's head.

I listened all the way through "Purple Haze," and at the end, I broke into this shrieking, yelling, cheers of applause. I was the only one of 10,000 people shrieking and yelling, and I suddenly realized that I was calling attention to myself, which was dangerous to some degree.

I looked around at this sea of faces. Pink, clean-cut, fourteen-year-old girls, and they were absolutely nonplussed. They had no idea of what had just gone on. I ran backstage and listened to the rest of the set.

From Raleigh to Forest Hills, and four to six dates in between, things went downhill. The girls would start calling out, "We want the Monkees," somewhere in the middle of one of his songs, and it was very depressing to Jimi. Devastated him. Here was this guy, a musical giant, opening for four guys who are trying to duplicate a reasonable facsimile of their television soundtracks.

Finally in New York, at Forest Hills, the yelling for us got so bad during Jimi's set that he walked offstage. He was in the middle of a number. He threw his guitar down, flipped everyone the bird, said, 'Fuck you,' and walked off the stage.

I was standing with Mickey Dolenz, and I turned to Mickey and I said, "Good for him."

Johnny Rivers

○ ○ ○

The Sunset Strip in Hollywood exploded in the sixties with Johnny Rivers at the Whisky A Go Go. One of the great live performers, he consistently produced hit records for ten years.

○ ○ ○

I came out to L.A. in the fifties from Baton Rouge, Louisiana, because James Burton, the guitar player from Shreveport, was a good friend of mine. James had been playing guitar for Ricky Nelson, who was the hottest thing next to Elvis at the time. I had written a song and given it to James, thinking that it might be good for Ricky. James called me a couple of months later and said, "Ricky's gonna cut your tune."

I said, "Hey, I'm gonna come out," and I did, just to check out the scene. It was around '59 and there wasn't much going on in L.A.

I knew Jimmy Bowen, and he and I and Glen Campbell were hanging out at American Music, a publishing company on Sunset. I was just kicking around, doing a few gigs here and there. Gazzarri's was on La Cienega. It was like a late-night spot with a little jazz trio and a little teeny dance floor. I'd go in there late at night and hang out.

One night Gazzarri says to me, "Hey, I know you sing and play. Can you help me out? My band's leaving. I can't find another band."

So I called Eddie Rubin, a friend of mine and a jazz drummer who played with Don Randi at PJ's, and we went into Gazzarri's and started playing the songs I'd played in junior high. With nothing else happening in town it caught on. Guys like Andy Williams had been dominating the charts. It was just before the Beatles hit. There was no place to go to hear rock 'n' roll, so I guess we were in the right place at the right time. Within two weeks you couldn't get near the place. It was packed. The movie stars were coming in and hanging out.

That's when I started hanging out with Lou Adler. He knew Elmer Valentine, who had gone to Paris and had seen the Whisky A Go Go, which was just a disco. Elmer said to me, "If we can get this place going here, will you come in and sign with us for a year?" I said OK.

In the couple of weeks in between my deal ending at Gazzarri's and opening the Whisky, I was approached by these guys who had a place in San Francisco called the Condor. So I went up there with Eddie for two weeks. I asked them if I could have a bass player and they brought in a guy who was the DJ in the club. His name was Sylvester Stewart. He came in late one night and I fired him. Funny that he turned out to be Sly Stone.

The Whisky was a smash from the moment it opened, which was in January 1964. It was a major thing. Jack Paar came in and did a television special out of there.

After about six weeks, Lou and I talked about doing a live album out of the Whisky. I borrowed some money from a guy downtown and we got the Wally Heider recording truck, and recorded everything we did for two nights. It cost all of $1,200. "Memphis" was one of the songs we did.

I was making about $300 a week then, so it wasn't like I was rich or anything, but I knew something was happening. You could feel the energy. The electricity was there. Trini Lopez had had some success with a live album out of PJ's, so Lou and I said, "Let's try to put our live album out, too."

We went into the studio and mixed it down and then took the album around. No one wanted it. I shopped it everywhere in town. And then finally Bob Skaff, who had been hanging around the Whisky and was a fan, talked Al Bennett into putting the record out. Al put it out reluctantly. The bottom line was, we had a Number 1 single in "Memphis," and a Number 1 album in about three or four weeks.

Two years later, someone brings me a tape with about ten songs on it and says, "Here's a kid I think is a really good writer." Normally you listen to one or two songs, and if they're not great you stop the tape.

But I listened to these songs and there was something interesting about them. Nothing knocked me out, but the last song on the tape was "By the Time I Get to Phoenix." So I called Jimmy Webb and told him I wanted to meet him. That was the start of a relationship. I bought his contract from someone who had it at the time, and Jimmy did an album with me called *Rewind*.

One of the songs I recorded for that album was "By the Time I Get to Phoenix." But I'd just come off the charts with "Poor Side of Town," and Lou and I both felt "Phoenix" sounded too much like "Poor Side of Town." So we put out "Baby I Need Your Loving," and it was a lucky thing for us that we did.

Lou Adler

○ ○ ○

A premier mover and shaker, he produced monstrous hits, keyed the Monterey Pop Festival, and walked away with his money, reputation, and mind all intact. On the beach in Malibu he told us what it was like.

○ ○ ○

I produced Barry McGuire's record "Eve of Destruction," which went to Number 1. We were in the studio, Western Recorders, working on his album, when he brought some friends down from San Francisco that he wanted me to hear. Friends of Barry's were always amazing looking, but that day even more so. These people looked down and out, like they had just come off every trip imaginable.

Well, they sang me five songs. I recorded one of them, "California Dreamin'," with Barry, and Cass Elliot, John and Michelle Phillips, and Denny Doherty singing backgrounds. It was one of those musical moments you're forever thankful you were a part of. I remember looking at the engineer, Bones Howe. We were both smiling from ear to ear. I knew this was it. And that was the very first time I ever heard the Mamas and the Papas through a speaker. I asked Barry if I could take his voice off the record and make it their record, and he said OK.

The Monterey Pop Festival started with a call I got one day from Alan Pariser. He said he wanted to hire the Mamas and the Papas to do this show he was planning in Monterey. He came to us through Derek Taylor. We met at John's house. Alan said he wanted to pay the group $10,000, which at the time was a real good fee. He said it was a commercial venture, he said he had a concept. He said he wanted blues groups, rock groups, folk groups, a sampling.

Alan was involved with Benny Shapiro, who had a background in jazz. Neither one of them were very rock 'n' roll minded. Anyway, the meeting evolved into a heated discussion, and Benny said, "If you want to do it, buy it from us." We asked how much, and he said $50,000 to buy them out, so we could then take over the fairgrounds in Monterey and get it started.

I put up $10,000, Johnny Rivers put up $10,000, John and Michelle put up $10,000, Paul Simon put up $10,000, and Terry Melcher put up $10,000, and we bought the date, took over the place and most of their staff. Benny Shapiro left and Derek Taylor stayed on.

John and I directed the festival. I called Andrew Oldham, the Stones' producer, asking him for suggestions about English acts. It was through Oldham and Paul McCartney that we came to contact The Who and Jimi Hendrix. Neither had played before a major American audience. So we just started calling people. A lot wanted to do it but couldn't. Some just canceled out. We ended up with thirty-three acts.

It was tough. We actually said at one time in a hotel room in San Francisco, "Let's forget the fucking festival and just fight." The San Francisco acts were the toughest to deal with. We called the Grateful Dead the Ungrateful Dead. We fought with them over everything. To the San Francisco groups, I represented Los Angeles and everything that was slick about the record business. They looked at John like he was a traitor, that he was ignoring the plight of San Francisco's street people. They threatened to stage a free festival down the road.

As it turned out, it went well with the San Francisco groups, and that was mostly through the efforts of Bill Graham. We had the social consciousness and free spirit of San Francisco combined with Los Angeles' broader musical tastes and business sense, and it worked. It got down to a point where they saw we were going ahead with it, no matter whether they were in it or not. The publicity started to mount. We made a TV deal with ABC. Tom Moore was the president of ABC at the time. Later, when this southern gentleman saw the footage of Hendrix banging his amplifier and balling his guitar, he said, "I'm sorry, ABC cannot be a part of this." He gave the project back to us, and that is how *Monterey Pop* became a film.

Nobody got paid at Monterey. Only Ravi Shankar, not because he wasn't going to do it unless he got paid, but he had a contract with Shapiro and Pariser. But no one else was paid. Our philosophy was, do everything for the acts that the acts and their representatives have been screaming about all these years. We provided the best sound system, first-class transportation, good food twenty-four hours a day, good rooms, everything for the artist. There were no promoters involved. We were setting standards for the future conditions and treatment for artists. All the money went into the concert and making the acts comfortable, both artistically and in every other way. And what was left would go to charity. There was no greed involved.

I stopped working in '68 and '69. The Mamas and the Papas split up, and I hadn't found any music that interested me. I was tired of saying, "More bass." I had been in the studio since 1958, without a stop, eighteen hours a day. I recorded one album with Peggy Lipton, who was my girlfriend at the time, and I continued doing Spirit. But I no longer felt energized. I wasn't searching out new music and I wasn't excited by the music I was doing.

But I had known Carole King since 1961, and her demos were always great. In fact, you could never get her demos back. The A & R men and producers that were serviced with Carole's demos for songs never wanted to give them back.

So Carole cut an album for my label, Ode. I had been distributing Ode through CBS. Spirit, Peggy Lipton, Merry Clayton, Scott McKenzie, and Carole King were the artists on Ode. I wanted to get out of my CBS deal, and to do that I had to come to some sort of agreement with the president of CBS, Clive Davis. The deal was, he kept Spirit and Scott McKenzie and I could leave with Peggy, Merry, and Carole King.

I went back to Herb Alpert, whom I had started out with. We hadn't been together for a long time, but when we'd see each other, he'd say, "What are you doing?"

And I'd say, "I'm just lying around."

And he'd say, "Why don't you do some records over here?" So I took Ode to A&M, and Carole put out one album, *Writer*. About a year later, she played me some of what ultimately became *Tapestry*. That was the album that excited me enough to want to go back into the studio.

Tapestry maybe cost $15,000, but I doubt it was that much. I remember the first ad, "Honesty Is Back." The album stayed at Number 1 for fifteen weeks. The timing was right. Suddenly, the singer-songwriter was in.

Country Joe McDonald

o o o

A brief flash across the pop music scene, Joe was part and parcel of the San Francisco move that came and went in the mid sixties. He didn't make the cut when the music changed, but his is an inside look at what Haight-Ashbury and all of that was like.

o o o

For me it starts when I was fifteen, growing up in southern California. When it came to music, I was like a sponge. There was cool jazz happening at the time at the Lighthouse in Hermosa Beach. There was good-time jazz with Frank Bolan on the radio, and folk music at the town hall in Baldwin Park. And then I would also go to see Fats Domino, the Platters, and the Penguins. Plus, I was even playing some semiclassical music.

I came to the San Francisco Bay area in 1965, just after the free speech movement. I came essentially to be a beatnik after having served in the navy for three years. I liked Berkeley. It was a small town, close to everything, and political. Very political.

You might say there was this revolution in songwriting that took place in the sixties, and I just happened to pick the Vietnam War to write about.

Well, when I got to the Bay Area, I made what turned out to be the first of an endless series of self-produced small records and tapes that I just sort of stuffed into manila envelopes and sold. It was truly folk-rock, an ad hoc kind of thing. Putting out these records, though, meant coming up with a name for the group, and that's how Country Joe and the Fish was invented.

The name itself comes from Mao Tse-tung and his philosophy of the Chinese revolution that says that revolutions move for the people like fish through the sea. I became Country Joe because I was the only Joe in the group.

Anyway, by 1967 we were riding on a wave. I didn't have much of a chance to feel a lot then because it was happening so fast. I mean, there we were at the Monterey Pop Festival in the middle of that whole community scene. It was like an entire new West Coast music industry was created in a month. I mean, they just shoved us out there with everybody else, like we were part of this new childhood Zen.

I don't know, but somehow the whole thing drained us. Sucked us dry. Maybe it was the pressure and hysteria and reality of Big Business versus the Aquarian Age. Whatever it was it was a bummer.

It was also like the birth of recreational drugs as a national pastime. Up until that point people had just been consuming alcohol and falling down from that. But the new idea became, "Hey, take drugs and act crazy." So everybody took drugs, different kinds of drugs, whatever kinds of drugs they could find. Never with any sense of danger.

Mostly it was marijuana, mushrooms, and other psychedelics. People were smoking a lot of pot and acting silly. That's about what it amounted to.

None of this stuff was happening with any sense of danger because something magical was going on that was hard to explain then, and is still hard to explain even now. An innocence, I guess.

Ultimately, though, we found out the hard way by having our innocence smashed out of us. Lots of things happened, mainly political assassinations and the war. You can't separate the era from that, from all those caskets. Ours was an era of extremes, unbelievable extremes. And inside that era we were like this little dreamland.

Turned out to be frustrating, really. I thought other things would happen. If I could go back and do it all again, I don't know if I would do it all the same way, but it's too late to speculate anyway.

I think back fondly on that period, but I don't romanticize it. I mean, I don't think I'd want another generation to experience the negative things we experienced—mostly I mean the war.

But there were the positive things, too, that sense of community, of communication. We developed family roots that were just wonderful. I love to think about that, walking down Haight Street in San Francisco and saying hello to everybody. It was a rare moment for those of us who made music, being in this really happy environment full of really intelligent people who were all doing some very heady stuff.

Bill Graham

o o o

The ultimate promoter for the rock generation, he battled his way to the top of the competitive business with ingenuity and courage, founding the Fillmores and putting together some of the biggest shows ever.

o o o

In 1961 I met a theater group in San Francisco called the San Francisco Mime Troupe. They were doing free shows in the park, radical shows, political satire. I worked for them for $125 a month arranging shows, getting permits, doing the trucking, putting up lights, talking to the law, doing the business. Three years later, we were arrested in Golden Gate Park for using four-letter words.

We had a loft at 5th and Howard, behind the *San Francisco Chronicle*. I had gotten to know a lot of musicians and painters and poets and I said, "Let's have a fund-raiser for ourselves." We needed money for legal matters. That fund-raiser was on November 6th, 1965. I invited a group that used to rehearse in the hall—the Jefferson Airplane. I invited Allen Ginsberg, who knew Frank Zappa. That night was by far the greatest theatrical night of my life. We raised $4,200 and the place was jammed. It was the first time I saw the undercurrent of San Francisco—long hair, short hair, pants, no pants, signs, tattoos, light shows, film. It was the only pure communal gathering of its sort. You turned over all the rocks, took all the worms, and put them in one place.

These were all people who wanted to express themselves, and they all had something in common. It was Vietnam, and all these people were doves. I never heard anyone say, "Let's kill those gooks." The glue was always, "What are we doing there?"

The Mime Troupe was a good life, but very hard at $125 a month in 1965. I got to meet Ralph Gleason. I had been running around town looking for a larger place, and Ralph suggested the ballroom at the corner of Fillmore and Deery called the Fillmore Auditorium. I went to see it. It was run by a black gentleman named Charlie Sullivan. He was running R & B shows there, and I rented it from him for a night. On December 10th, 1965, five weeks after the first benefit, I did Mime Troupe Benefit II at the Fillmore with the Jefferson Airplane and a group called the Warlocks, which became the Grateful Dead. The setting was four walls, liquid glob, slide and light shows, but all the people there had something in common. They were all doves, and they all believed in "Be and let be."

It cost two dollars to get into the Fillmore, but what I saw was an adventure. I'd have a clipboard and I'd check off security, advertising, posters, sound, lights, and I'd still be dealing with a lot of the artists and the public. It was as if life filled out the form of how I could express myself. I didn't want to be an office manager and be behind a desk. I couldn't take regimentation. I had trouble in the army, and I wanted to be independent, but money was never a great object. But more than anything else it was a means of expression, being totally in charge.

We weren't just dealing with people who were coming to see an act on stage. They would come in to the show, paint one another's faces, or talk about their travels. There was an openness that never existed before and has never existed again to that extent. "I am peaceful, you are peaceful. Do you want to dance or talk or make love?" The whole thought of people adopting one another as cousins for a few hours would fascinate me. Some of the people coming in were inhibited, and I'd say, "Let's put balloons on the floor, put a barrel of apples at the door, or paintings on the wall," and they'd drop their inferiority problems. And maybe by the fifth or sixth time they came, they'd feel more relaxed.

As time went by, we opened in New York and it became more and more difficult to retain the artists' services. In other words, they'd say, "We loved you, loved your work, but now we want to play a bigger place." So we moved to Winterland, and then they wanted to go to the Cow Palace in Oakland, or Madison Square Garden, and from a business point of view they had that right. I always looked at the Fillmore as the white man's Apollo. We appealed to everybody, but the audience was predominantly white. I had this thing about mixing artists, white with black, and as an example I had the Grateful Dead with Otis Redding. But big in rock 'n' roll then was playing to 15,000 people. Today rock 'n' roll consumes all mankind.

For me, though, I got very angry and disillusioned with managers and agents. The youth and the artists of that era extended from the late teens to early twenties. I was in my late thirties, and I had been in the real world. I had made some mistakes, but I was making money from the psychedelic scene. Rock 'n' roll was the umbilical cord of the alternative society, and people perceived my position from strange angles. Generally speaking, during that time there weren't enough practical leaders. Timothy Leary and Jerry Rubin were not practical leaders. Some of them had wonderful tricks, and some of them were assholes. I am convinced that I was extremely fortunate to be in the right place at the right time.

There were some tremendous high points for me. The 1974 Dylan tour, from a touring standpoint, was the most exciting thing I'd ever experienced. This man created a one-on-one with every person in the audience. During a song like "Just Like a Woman," I would cup my hand around my eye like a telescope and go from row to row. People would excuse themselves from who they came with to go one-on-one with Bob. He was the man, far more than anyone else.

In 1981 everybody in the Rolling Stones felt good, and we all decided to kick some ass. These guys rehearsed strong. We started in Philadelphia with outdoor shows, and my goal was to build a great stage and make it a great event. They are an awesome rock 'n' roll band. There are a lot of flaws, but those guys are a great mix. They also had a physical attitude—a jungle-cat attitude—that prevailed. For me, the most sensual lines in rock 'n' roll, the lines that define rock 'n' roll, are the opening lines of "Honky Tonk Women." Every city they went into became the rock 'n' roll capital of the United States for that one day. When the Stones performed, every man felt like a man and every woman felt like a woman. And they all wanted to take the Stones home. I think with Dylan they wanted to give him a bowl of soup.

But there is also the other side. The price of a ticket goes from two dollars to twenty dollars, the act doesn't do an encore, someone has to stand in a long line, and it's all my fault. In the sixties, they called me "a capitalist pig," the man who kept it from becoming a free concert. Then they want to know why I'm putting shows in stadiums. The guys on stage are their heroes, so I can't be the hero. They say to me, "We'd rather see Simon and Garfunkel in a club, but you, schmuck, would rather put them in a stadium."

People get a picture in their mind of how they think it's supposed to be, and when it's not that way, they can't handle it. I was once walking through Golden Gate Park with my son. It was very festive—congo players, kids playing ball, the bandstand—and the tie-dyed guys would say, "Hi, aren't you Bill Graham?"

"Yes."

"Who's that with you?"

"My son."

"You got a kid?"

"Yeah, I fuck just like you." They were flabbergasted that I took the time to have a child.

Paul Kantner

o o o

**A founding member of San Francisco's first major-hit group, Paul
went the route with the Jefferson Airplane, Starship, and several
other configurations. He saved his money, and we met at his beautiful
home overlooking the Pacific and discussed the impact of drugs on his
music.**

o o o

The sixties were like science fiction. Some people say the CIA introduced
LSD into society to thwart the civil rights movement. Some people say the
sixties represented a generation gone awry. I think it's probably a million
factors.

All I know is that I was in the middle of it. We did what came naturally.
I remember even back in grammar school thinking, "What a bleak society!"
I mean, the total sort of American suburban reaction—teenage reaction to
the postwar period, nuclear bombs hanging over your head. I thought I was
either going to have to commit suicide or become a bank robber. I got into
folk music and it probably saved my life.

San Francisco, like most seaports, attracts crazy people. It's like a last
refuge for malcontents, noncommercial kinds, and in terms of the music
business, the sort of people who don't really expect to succeed, or even
become noticed.

I just lived here. I didn't go to L.A. My friend, David Crosby, was in
the Byrds, and he and I had a house in the Fillmore District, the black
district, and we just sort of considered ourselves folk musicians gone off a
step rather than rock musicians gone down a step.

We took drugs and ran away from authority and the institutions that
didn't necessarily deserve our respect. I suppose it was that our generation
didn't grow up, didn't accept the world as it was. You know, "This is the
world. You're not a child anymore. Be a man."

Well, none of us did those things. When we were children, we were
taught all about Santa Claus. And then somewhere from five to ten, you
learn that there is no Santa Claus, and you have to accept that. For some
reason, I guess, we didn't.

Everybody I knew had this pretty independent way of progression. And
the strength we drew upon was when we all sort of combined to do it together.
Hard drugs played a big part in pushing everyone away from that. Cocaine
especially. The first time I saw cocaine was at the Monterey Pop Festival.
Made everybody ruder and nastier and colder and badder. Bad drug. Great
drug on the surface. Cool. A cool drug. So cool that you're dead.

As for the Airplane, I think we were all rude characters right from the
beginning. Maybe not rude, but feisty, individualistic. For example, even
before Grace was in the band, we were probably the first group to start the
button craze, the "Jefferson Airplane Loves You" button and bumper stickers.

Grace's band, the Great Society, came out with a button and bumper sticker that said, "The Great Society Doesn't Like You Very Much at All." And it's been like that ever since. It was never just peace and love, particularly in the band.

Part of being in a band is recognizing that all of us are going to be assholes at some time or other. You've got to allow your mate to be an asshole, and when you want to be an asshole he'll go along, and you'll make a great band. A band is like a family. Maybe not the Ozzie and Harriet kind of family, but a band still has to be something that all its members can sort of hold up as an ideal.

In the early seventies, all that began to change and we started breaking apart. Marty Balin left first. He was severely affected by Altamont and that whole semi-quasi-religious, naive hope for mankind. It was all dashed at Altamont, if anyone was still naive at that time. And Janis' death, that was probably the final "Whew!"

In the end, we did what we did for the ride, really, for the thrill of the energy. Some people are in the music business to become famous and make a lot of money and then retire and buy Oahu and live there for the rest of their lives. But a lot of musicians, especially in San Francisco, are there just for the ride. It's like a river ride. You're holding on and you're not thinking three turns around the road. That's the way it was with us.

Al Schmidt

o o o

Al engineered and later produced records for a variety of major hitters. His ability to capture the feeling on the tape kept him in great demand.

o o o

I started in this business in 1950, in New York, at a little studio called Apex Recording. The engineer there was Tommy Dowd. He was just breaking in himself. I was doing voice and piano things, little demos. I'd been there all of three months, and it was a Saturday. They had a demo booked for a half hour, and no one was there. I didn't know how to repair equipment. I just knew how to operate it. The next thing I know all these musicians start coming in. It was a session for Mercer Records—Mercer Ellington and Leonard Feather. And in walks Duke Ellington. His band, without his name, the piano player is Billy Strayhorn. And I start to sweat. I said, "Listen, I've never done anything like this before."

I tried to get people on the phone. It was Saturday. And Duke Ellington pats me on the leg and says, "Don't worry. We'll get through this." I tried to remember how Tommy set things up. Duke Ellington sat next to me and we did this record for Mercer Records. It was mono. No tape machine. Direct to sixteen-inch transcription disc. That was my first real experience in the business.

I made coffee and I hung onto Tommy's coattails. I worked there for two years, and then the studio went bankrupt, so I followed Tommy to another studio called Coastal Recording Studios. We did a lot of Atlantic's stuff.

When I came to Los Angeles, the recordings appeared archaic as opposed to what we had been doing in New York. Nobody in L.A. was using condenser microphones like the ones we were using in New York. Maybe they'd use one on a vocal, compared to our using eight or nine. So I started working in L.A. Bones Howe was there, and we got to be friends. He started to do the first "Peter Gunn" album, and then he had a problem with the producer, so I wound up finishing the album. I did a lot of work for MGM. I did "My Happiness," which was a very big record for Connie Francis.

The producer wasn't even there when we did "My Happiness." David Rose did the arrangement and conducted, and I engineered. Because there was no producer there I became kind of like the producer. That's what got me interested in producing. I did "What Kind of Fool Am I" with Sammy Davis, Jr. The producer forgot about the session. I said, "Wait a minute, I can do this. I have good ears."

You can really tell the difference from one studio to the next. Certain rooms are spectacular for string sounds. Others are great for big bands. Harry James loved the RCA studio. I did a bunch of his records. He just loved the brass sound in the room. Back in those days people went into a certain studio because of the live echo. Tommy and I did so many things at Capitol just because of its echo chamber. We would listen to a Columbia record and compare it to ours, check for the differences in sound. Inevitably, Columbia's were a little brighter, a little crisper.

I'm talking all mono, two-track stuff. We used to do an album in seven hours. I've done Henry Mancini albums in nine hours. And they were finished when you were done. You just edited them together, put a sequence together, and that was it. I did a Ray Charles country and western album in four hours. Full orchestra. Done.

I can remember the days with Bobby Shad. He was a madman. He was fun. I liked him. He would get these guys in there and pay everyone in cash. Ten, fifteen bucks. Nobody ever got any royalties. They used to bootleg their own records in those days. Bobby would sit down at the producer's little desk, pull out a little .32 automatic, and place it on the desk. He was dealing with crazies out there, and this was his way of saying, "OK, I'm going to be the boss."

I wound up producing the Jefferson Airplane. This was bizarre. They were bringing motorcycles into the studio. They had a tank of nitrous oxide, laughing gas. They would call up at a quarter to eight and say, "Are we working tonight?"

And I would say, "Yeah, we start at eight."

And they would say, "Oh, well. We'll be there as soon as the plane leaves." They were calling me from San Francisco, and they would show up four hours later. I was used to people getting to the studio on time, and getting through on time. The Jefferson Airplane didn't care. I could never understand how they could work, doing the drugs they did. But they were evidently so used to working that way that they could do it. A lot of people in the sixties could smoke grass and work.

I did the first Hot Tuna album, which was a spinoff of the Airplane. We were working live, at a club in Berkeley, and we had Wally Heider's remote truck. I got some apple juice at the bar, and I was talking and getting everything set up, drinking this apple juice, and I went out to get in the truck, and as soon as I got into the truck, the truck expanded. They had spiked me with LSD, which was a horrible thing to do. But that's what they did. They spiked the wedding cake at Tom Donahue's wedding. Little old ladies were walking out into Golden Gate Park. You could never tell the Airplane to stop using drugs. They would simply say, "Screw off."

Jann Wenner

o o o

Sitting in *Rolling Stone*'s hustling office in New York, you can relive the excitement and tumult of the role it played during the musical and social explosion of the seventies. Jann started it with Ralph Gleason and carried on after Ralph's death. The magazine remains the key reporter in rock 'n' roll.

o o o

Bill Graham might never have existed had it not been for Ralph Gleason. I'll give you an example. I first saw the Grateful Dead at a Rolling Stones concert in San Francisco. I think it was '66. I drove there with a friend of mine. This was around the time Mick started wearing this little jacket, and he would tease the audience as if he was going to throw them the jacket.

After the concert Ken Kesey was having one of those acid tests at someone's house in San Jose, and I went to it. The Dead had just changed their name from the Warlocks, and here they were in the living room at someone's house playing, and it sounded great. I was staggered, and I was taking drugs at the time, too. I remember going, "What do you guys call yourself?"

And they said, "The Grateful Dead."

And I went, "Wow!"

But about Graham and Ralph, the police wanted to shut Graham down, and actually did shut him down until Ralph, who was a columnist at the *San Francisco Chronicle*, brought the *Chronicle* around to Bill's defense. Ralph was the one who told Bill about the Fillmore. He counseled Bill. Without Ralph, Bill could not have continued.

I met Bill when I was writing a column for the *Daily Californian*, when I was still in school at Berkeley. That was also where I met Ralph. The column consisted mainly of what I did over the weekend, which dances I attended, which concerts I went to. So I would write about these concerts, and one day I went to Bill and said, "This is what you have to do," and it infuriated him. I mean, he flipped out. He was going around Berkeley stapling concert posters around the campus, and that's where we had our first fight, and our first reconciliation. I would say, "Bill, I just saw this band, the Grateful Dead, and I think you should book them."

And he would go, "Nah, nah, they're terrible."

Ralph truly loved the music. He loved the people, and the scene. He was a forty-eight-year-old who couldn't make up his mind whether he was twelve or sixteen. But he loved people, and he sort of took me under his wing, this schleppy kid who didn't know much about anything. Ralph saw what rock 'n' roll was about, and he saw it before anybody started writing seriously about it. He saw the value and the joy in rock 'n' roll.

He taught me the basics of journalism. He gave me a list of concert venues around San Francisco, with all the attendance figures. He insisted on good reporting. The truth is, I couldn't have started *Rolling Stone* without him. The Roxy in L.A. wouldn't have survived without Ralph. The whole scene might never have happened without someone like Ralph J. Gleason reporting on it.

He was the most delightful man. And I was lucky enough that he decided to see to my music education. I would go on and on about how Mike Bloomfield was the greatest guitarist in the history of mankind, or how wonderful Jerry Garcia was, and Ralph would take me to a jazz club to see Wes Montgomery. Ralph loved telling his friends about how he just took his nice young friend to see someone who really was truly great.

Joe Smith

○ ○ ○

I came to California and all I knew was that I wanted to get into the record business. My last three months in Boston, I would get up in the morning, go to a distributor, and work for nothing packing records in the back. I thought, here I am, a graduate of Yale, married, about to have my first baby, and I don't know how to do anything except be a disc jockey. I didn't want to do that my whole life.

A lot of people in L.A. already knew who I was from my half-assed reputation in Boston. I interviewed with a lot of people and told everybody I could be a major promotion person because I knew the lingo. George Hartstone, whose family was from Boston, had a distributorship, one in L.A., another in San Francisco. He called me up and said, "While you're looking around and deciding what you want to do, why don't you come to work for me as a promotion man?" He had Liberty, Dot, London Records. He said he'd give me $150 a week, car, expenses, for as long as I wanted to do it. It wasn't big, but I wanted to get in.

But people kept asking me to do radio shows. Alan Freed was already in L.A. He came out two months before me, and he was doing an afternoon show on KDAY. In the bright sunshine of California, Alan's show sounded silly. He clicked on a winter's night in the east, not in L.A., with the beach and surfboards. But he was doing a show. The government had attached everything, and he needed bread, so he started blatantly asking for money from the promotion guys. He put one price on the Pick of the Week, another price on the Pick of the Day. I said, "Maybe you should devise a Pick of the Ten-Minute Period."

He said, "What do you think I can get out here?"

I answered him by repeating the old Lenny Bruce story: A guy is stranded in Mexico. His car has broken down. He's trying to call California, and the operator says, "That will be three dollars and forty cents."

And he says, "I only have a dollar eighty."

And the operator says, "Put it in, put it in."

I said, "Alan, just ask someone what they have on them, and that will be how much it costs."

So I started doing some radio while I was working for the Hartstones. Incredible how easy it was for me to get my own records played. To my knowledge, no one had ever worked both ends of the business—radio and records—at the same time. The other promotion men knew I had an edge, but they never complained. It was a very close-knit community, and they knew I was fair.

I probably worked for every radio station in L.A., and still did PR and promotion at the same time. When Hartstone opened in San Francisco, George's brother, Lee, asked me if I would become the promotion man in both cities and maybe go to San Francisco one day a week, or whenever I felt I should. I picked up the record "Monster Mash," by Bobby "Boris" Pickett, and then they wanted me to find talent for them. So now I'm doing promotion, radio, and A & R. I signed Wayne Newton, picked up a couple of records, and then up in San Francisco I met Tom Donahue, who would later be called "the father of FM radio."

San Francisco was virgin territory. Tom was on the radio there, as was Les Stein, who became Les Crane, and I was offered the night show. "There's a ton of money up here," they said.

I said, "No, I don't want to do this anymore. I moved 3,000 miles away to be in Los Angeles, to be in the record business." They understood and accepted that, but they knew I used to run live shows in Boston, so they asked me if I'd help them get some acts. Beach Boys, Shirelles, Chubby Checker, every early-sixties act imaginable.

For this one particular show, I went up to San Francisco for the rehearsal. Phil Spector was the bandleader, and Sly Stone was the keyboard player. I was helping emcee the show. I'll never forget the night. A young fellow named Cassius Clay had just made a record reading his poetry, "Float Like a Butterfly, Sting Like a Bee." He was on and the kids were booing him. Donahue says to me, "You have to get him off."

I said, "I beg your pardon?"

He said, "You gotta do it."

So I walked to the center of the stage and I said, "Thank you, Cassius."

He says, "I'm not through."

I said, "Yes, you are." And we cut the mike.

I started becoming a high-profile, hotshot guy. Jerry Moss was a local promotion man, Russ Regan was a local promotion man. We were all hotshots. And if you were in L.A., working for any eastern labels, it was wonderful. You could quit at three in the afternoon because everybody had all gone home in the east.

So I get this call from Mike Maitland, who had just left Capitol and was now president of the record division of Warner Brothers, and he says, "At Capitol I couldn't afford you. Now I can. What would you like to do here?"

My father-in-law said, "God, Warner Brothers." There was such an aura to it. Warners up to then had been managing with Bob Newhart, the Everly Brothers, and a lot of television people—Bob Conrad, Troy Donahue, Connie Stevens, Dorothy Provine, Kookie— and Maitland says I can be head of promotion and look for acts. This was a serious job, so I left my radio gig, and I got down to work.

I remember standing around on the top floor of a machine shop in Burbank, and this was the record company. We didn't even have a bottom floor. We had about twenty-eight, thirty employees, and we're going to have this Christmas party, and Maitland says, "Make some jokes, make some jokes, get something going fast."

Which was essentially what I had to do at Warners, make something happen fast. I had no idea that what Warners really wanted was to get out of the record business. The better I did the better the chance that we could convince the studio to stay in the record business.

My first act was a guy named Saverio Saridis, a New York policeman who patroled the front of the Plaza Hotel. He sounded like Mario Lanza. He made a record, "Love Is the Sweetest Thing," that I managed to get to the twenties on the charts, but it probably didn't sell more than ten copies. Well, Jack Warner got so excited when he heard it on the radio that he made a movie deal with the guy. Saverio was never heard from again.

I had a hit with Joanie Sommers, "Johnny Get Angry." Alan Sherman happened. Then we had Peter, Paul and Mary. After that was when Warners really committed to the record business.

Then in '63 Warners buys Reprise, which was Sinatra's company. Besides Sinatra, Reprise had Dean Martin, Alice Faye, Phil Harris, Dinah Shore, Lou Monte, Trini Lopez, and of course, Mo Ostin, who was running it. He and I were neighbors in Encino. We used to see each other all the time at Gelson's supermarket. He had offered me a job at Reprise, and now four months later, we buy the goddamn thing. Maitland was in charge of both labels. Mo ran Reprise, and I ran Warners. Recording studios were opening up all along Sunset Boulevard. Sunset Strip started to happen, kids out in the middle of the street surrounded by sheriffs' cars, wall to wall. The Whisky opened. L.A. was alive, and that's when my career as an executive really started.

We knew we would have to begin taking San Francisco seriously after RCA signed the Jefferson Airplane. The act we started hearing about was the Grateful Dead. Well, my wife and I are in San Francisco and we're having dinner at Ernie's, a rather well-known, established restaurant. I was in a dark blue Bank of America–type suit and my wife was in basic black with pearls, and I'm paged to the phone. It was Tom Donahue. He said, "The Dead want to talk to you now. They're at the Avalon Ballroom."

I said, "We're dressed up."

He said, "No one will notice."

So we go to the Avalon Ballroom and we walk up the stairs, one of the most dramatic moments in my entire life, and we walk into this gigantic hall where people are lying everywhere on the floor painting each other's bodies. A light show was going on on the walls, the smell of marijuana was in the air, and somebody was playing a droning guitar solo. It was the Grateful Dead, but it was more like Fellini.

Somebody asked my wife to dance, and I told her, "You know, maybe you should sit out of the way somewhere." The Dead come off the stage, and I sit down with them at a table at the back end of the hall. Donahue introduces me to everyone. I started telling them what I thought, all the standard things about the relationship between the label and the artist, and it was like talking to a wall. I said, "You go on tour. We support the show."

They said, "We don't want to go on tour."

I said, "We'll put ads in the magazines."

They said, "We don't want ads in the magazines."

Finally, with no great trust between us, we agreed on a deal. Now they're going to come down to L.A. to record, and they arrive en masse—families, babies nursing on their mothers, Owsley was there to provide the drugs. It was quite a scene. Everyone was lying around on the floor of the studio. Avalon Ballroom, Part Two.

The Dead used a lot of acid, and the fallout from that was this instantaneous switch from reality to fantasy. We'd be talking about the most pragmatic thing, and suddenly they were on Saturn. We were talking about recording, and one of them said, "What we ought to do is record thirty minutes of air in the summertime, when it's hot and smoggy. Thirty minutes of heavy air. Then we could go to the desert and record thirty minutes of clean air. Then mix the two together, get a good sound, and record over it."

I looked around expecting someone to laugh, but there was

complete agreement that that was the thing to do, record the air because no one had ever done it before. I told them the American Federation of Musicians wouldn't allow it, and we moved on to the next subject.

Jerry Garcia
o o o

He's the heart and soul of the Grateful Dead. His loose approach to life and his remarkable ability to play guitar in many forms—along with the dumbfounding longevity of his band—set him apart from most of the rock world.

o o o

I started out when I was fifteen years old. My father was a professional musician, and I had taken piano lessons all my life, which I learned nothing from. At fifteen I fell in love with electric guitars, mainly Chuck Berry's, and I just wanted to make that sound in the worst way.

But by 1959 I didn't think it was cool anymore to play rock 'n' roll. It was getting to be unfashionable. Somebody turned me on to folk music and I heard that sound of a bluegrass banjo, and that completely copped my attention. So that was a three-, four-year excursion into that world.

Bobby Weir and Pigpen were both in the jug band with me. But Phil Lesh was a guy I knew from Berkeley. He was the first guy I ever knew who was a total music lover. He was also the first guy I ever knew with perfect pitch. He had the best musical education, a music major. He took me over to his apartment at Berkeley, and there he was with a card table and no piano. He's writing a piece for three orchestras out of his head, with no piano. I couldn't fucking believe it. He turned me on to all sorts of music. He was also a jazz trumpeter with an incredible background in classical music. But he wanted to join a rock band because it was during that period that everybody was looking for something neat to do. The Beatles movie *A Hard Day's Night* had just come out, and it looked like fun.

Sounded like hell, though, for the first few gigs. But pretty soon, because of Pigpen's solid ground in blues, we got to be a pretty fair blues band. When we played the bars, we had to play Top 40 songs. We played Rolling Stones songs, the Chicago/Chess Records sound. Basically, we got our first gigs because we were a blues-oriented Rolling Stones–style band.

We started taking acid when we were still the Warlocks. We didn't do it at shows. But we were playing these divorcee bars up and down the peninsula. We had a booking agent named Al King who booked dog acts, magicians, and strippers. Between him and the Local 6, that's how we worked. We worked six nights a week, five sets a night, the standard bar thing for about a year. After that, you're ready for anything.

A guy named Page came to one of our late sets, and he told us about the parties every Saturday night up at Ken Kesey's place. Page said, "You guys should come up there." Luckily, the following week we got fired and we had nothing to do. Saturday comes around and we went to one of those parties that later became known as the Electric Kool-Aid Acid Test.

After a while they moved the party out of Kesey's place and started sending guys out to rent bigger rooms. We just set up our equipment and everybody would get high. Kesey and his Pranksters were doing this for a long time, so they knew how to set up these kinds of things. Mostly it was completely free. There were no real performances of any kind. Everybody there was as much the performer as they were the audience. We plugged our gear in, which looked like space-age military-nightmare stuff, we played for five minutes, and we devastated these people. They begged us to come back to the next one, and we did. The neat thing about the acid test was that we could play if we wanted to. But if it was too weird, we didn't have to play. That was the only time we ever had the option of not playing.

Drugs were always around. I had my own personal bad run-in for about ten years with hard drugs, but the rest of the band never really agreed on drugs. There were always guys in the band who would take anything.

Luckily, our first record was not a huge success. It did OK, hit a little bit, and gave us national exposure. So now we got to play in New York and other places, but that we weren't immediately successful helped us in a huge way. It gave us a chance to be slow and deliberate about our own development. It kept us interested. Hell, we had to keep on working, which is really what we wanted to do anyway. We would have loved it if our first record went gold, but since it didn't, no major loss.

So now someone comes along, Lenny Hart, and he burns us for a couple of years, no problem. It was like having someone working in your scene working against you. The thing that made me mad about Lenny was that he wasn't smart enough to exploit us the way we would have exploited ourselves, if we had cared to. Lenny was like a dumb crook, and we're still here.

I haven't the slightest idea why we've been able to continue doing it twenty-three, twenty-four years later in front of audiences who weren't even alive the first time around. You'd think most of today's Deadheads would come into it with some sense of history, but they don't. They haven't read Kesey. To the kids today, the Grateful Dead represents America—the spirit of being able to go out and have an adventure. It's like the thing to do, go out and follow the Dead around. You can trade stories. It's like a traveling Woodstock that can be shared with your friends. That's what motivates audiences now. We represent something like hopping railroads or getting out on the road. It's not supposed to be done anymore, but being a Deadhead means you can get in your van and cross the U.S.

We ponder the thought of these people daily. It's become our life, really. How the Deadheads deal with us and each other is a matter of basic concern to us. These people are from today, not the past. They are their own people, self-designed, and they're a big reason why the band continues to hang in there every day.

Mickey Hart

○ ○ ○

He drummed and still drums for the Grateful Dead. Their story is long and strange, and Mickey has seen it all unfold from his San Mateo base in Northern California.

○ ○ ○

We were playing our asses off for $3,500, $5,000 a night. I don't remember what our price was at the time, but it wasn't exorbitant. We were a working band, and all of a sudden some people come in and repossess Pigpen's organ. That was our first inkling that something was wrong, when we were playing four, five nights a week, and they're coming in an repossessing our equipment.

So Phil Lesh and I asked Lenny if we could see the books. We met him at a hamburger joint, and he wouldn't give us the books. Then I knew something was wrong. I mean, it was amazing. Not only was he stealing from the Grateful Dead, which was like hitting Santa Claus over the head with a club, but he was also stealing from his own son! I had no idea it was going on. I had no idea that Lenny Hart was a liar and a thief.

He left when I was an infant, so I never really knew him growing up. And then we met again. He was a world champion regimental drummer. I'd even seen his picture in a brochure. I looked him up when I joined the air force in '59, '60. We became friends. When I got out of the service, we started hanging out. He had a drum store in San Carlos, and he asked me to join him. That's how I met the Grateful Dead.

Looking back, not only was Lenny disgraced for almost ruining the Grateful Dead, and myself personally, and our relationship, he actually made it possible for the Grateful Dead to be the Grateful Dead. If you look at it in a bigger way, Lenny was responsible. In a certain kind of bizarre, off-the-wall way, Lenny got us all together. I would never have been in the group had it not been for Lenny. It wouldn't have been the Grateful Dead, as we know it, without him.

Never mind that I contemplated suicide because of his stealing from the band. What a disgrace. But the Grateful Dead never blamed me. They stuck by me like brothers. But at the time I was in a giant funk. I was so embarrassed and humiliated that my father would steal from the Grateful Dead, and that it would happen right under my nose.

Lenny thought we were just a bunch of hippies taking LSD. That's all he saw, and I guess he tried to take advantage of that in the worst way. And I couldn't face anybody. Not that they were blaming me, though. I laid it on myself.

Lenny took between $75,000 and $200,000. We never found out exactly how much. But $200,000 then is like $2 million now. We never got any of it back either. We're not cops, we're not collection agencies, and if there's no money, where do you get it from?

Lenny wound up spending six months or so in jail. We couldn't stop that. Didn't even try to stop it. The D.A. simply got ahold of it and prosecuted him and put him in jail. Jerry Garcia went to court during the trial. I couldn't go. I never saw Lenny again until the day he died. He was in his coffin and I buried him. I drummed on his coffin. I gave him a drummer's burial so he could go out the way he should go out. But he was a dog, an absolute rotten human being. I'm ashamed that he was my father, but he was a superb drummer. For no other reason will I remember him.

Robbie Robertson

○ ○ ○

A cerebral and private talent, Robbie was the drive for The Band and occupies a unique spot in the history of the time. The group's records were almost always critically worshiped, and their immediate acceptance by the elite of the rock world was unusual. He's gone on to films and other ventures, but the recollections are fascinating.

○ ○ ○

When we were kids playing in clubs, everybody played cover songs, and we never wanted to do that. We'd do something else, like playing with Ronnie Hawkins. We never wanted to play what club bands were supposed to play. We had to separate from the pack. Trying to be different was part of the nature of our group.

When we first started playing with Bob Dylan, we did not know a whole lot about him. We knew about these folk songs, and that he was a folk singer, and that he could write good songs. And then we started playing with him. It was a disaster. Our job was to travel to the place, go out and play, have people boo at you, then pack up, leave and go to the next place, where again they'd boo. This happened all over the world. We said, "This is an odd way to make a buck," let alone make a musical mark.

People were always saying to Bob, "Let me give you a little advice. Get rid of these guys. They're killing you." We didn't know, either, if it was such a good idea. Except when we played. It was like thunder, with this Elmer Gantry speaking, going on, talking these words, singing them, preaching them. He was no longer doing this nasally folk thing. He was screaming his songs through the rafters, and it was like thunder. It was very dynamic, very violent, and very exciting.

We thought, "Great," but everywhere we played people threw things at us, night after night. It's very hard to keep your chin up all the time, and you want to say, "Yeah, fuck them. They don't know." And we'd go and listen to the tapes of the concert and we would say, "What is so bad about that? It sounded pretty good." The tapes, of course, went on to become classic bootlegs.

But at the time, people were pissed off because they had this purist attitude about Dylan. We did not see what was wrong musically. We were treating the songs with great respect. We had no idea whether we were having a great impact, or whether this entire thing was going to go up in smoke.

Dylan had every opportunity to say, "Fellows, this is not working out. I'm going to go back to folk music, or get another band where they won't boo every time." Everybody told him to get rid of these guys, that it wasn't working. But he didn't. That was very commendable.

Being out with Dylan put us more in touch with what was going on in the world. We had come out of the swamps, and these back-roads clubs, and suddenly we're stuck out on the world with this attitude we brought with us, and now people want us to come back in and find a cute name for this group. The whole thing seemed very childish to us. Names were really goofy at that time. Everybody was thinking up very psychedelic names, and just to go against that we said, "We are not going to name the group."

The record company went crazy. They said, "You have to have a name. Call it Number Seven, anything, but you have to think of something."

We said, "OK, we will call ourselves the Crackers."

And they said, "That's a cute name." They were thinking soda crackers, or biscuits. Then they came back and said, "No, you can't call yourselves the Crackers. That means something else altogether."

From playing with Dylan, and this little neighborhood we lived in called Woodstock, everybody called us The Band. That was about as anonymous as we could get.

We had the record company over the rail. They were printing up our first album, *Music from Big Pink*, and we came in that afternoon and said, "Well, we're The Band."

They said, "That's not a name."

And we said, "Right."

I thought of a band as like a little workshop. This guy fixes the furniture, this guy takes care of the glass, this one does the plumbing. Everyone has his own little job. That's the biggest reason why I chose not to sing. I was into being the director. I enjoyed saying, "You know, why don't you try singing this in here. When we get to this section, you go up. Then we'll sing the melody, and the characters will change, and you over here come in on the second line." That became a part of the style of the group—voice interchanging.

I enjoyed being the director, but I wasn't the captain of the ship. Everybody did his part, and that is what made us a true band. We were a unit. John Fogerty and Creedence Clearwater Revival were not a true band. It was really John Fogerty and some backup guys. The Band was a true band.

John Fogerty

o o o

This is a voice you can identify immediately if you listened to any pop music during the Creedence Clearwater run. A powerful personality, John broke up the group when he felt it had served its purpose, waged legal war with his record company, and made an amazing comeback after nine years with a Number 1 record.

o o o

Creedence was different from a lot of the other bands in San Francisco. We may have looked a lot like everyone else in those days, but I was antidrug, which was a weird stance to be taking then. I did my very small share of dabbling with marijuana, but that was as far as it ever went.

I think I was antidrug because I was paranoid about getting caught. But I am also one of those people who do not like to be out of control. When I got stoned, I'd become paranoid and I'd stare at the wall and not be able to do anything.

Creedence was also different from the others musically. My roots were in Memphis. My idols were Howlin' Wolf, Elvis, Jimmie Rodgers, all in a way traditionally American.

When you hear "Proud Mary" and "Bad Moon Rising," it sounds so all-American. People forget that it came out right in the middle of the acid period and the Strawberry Alarm Clock and Grateful Dead. That's what was all around us, and yet I was preserving my own vision of what I thought rock 'n' roll should be.

But I never thought we were good enough at the time. We were young and not particularly good musicians, including myself. "Suzie Q" was recorded when I was twenty-two, "Proud Mary" when I was twenty-three, "Bad Moon Rising" when I was a baby. I was a pup and I never felt we had the soul of a band like James Brown's. But what I did not realize at the time was that James Brown may have been young in the fifties, but the guys in his band weren't even a band, they were older session guys, which meant they had a lot of experience. What I failed to understand was how really young we were.

It's taken me all these years to be able to say we were awfully good. Very, very good. During our time, when we were at our peak, I don't think anybody could top us. I have always said that the best rock 'n' roll band of all time was Booker T. & the MG's, and I still believe that. But we had material they did not have, and we had a singer that they did not have. It's like measuring a baseball team, position for position. Maybe they had us beat, but as a team, we were probably the World Series champs.

But the success became a nightmare, a wonderful love affair gone sour. Looking back now, I wish we'd had an outside manager instead of me. If we'd had a Brian Epstein, maybe we could have all been screaming at him, which would have taken the burden off of me. I know now that it would have been wiser to have a fall guy.

The end of Creedence was like what Will Rogers said about real estate. "They ain't making any more of it."

Now, our records just sit there in a time warp. I'm really proud of them. They are a testament to what people can do with no one to help them other than themselves.

We were four guys from a small town called El Cerrito, totally outside the mainstream of the record business. We did not have a Hollywood manager. We were not even on a Hollywood label. We were basically a P.O. box, distribution-type deal, a rocket ship built in the basement that just exploded.

Every day we went into our little room and rehearsed and rehearsed. We wanted to be the best in the world. It could have gone on for fifteen years. It did not have to die because of one shortsighted individual who shot the goose that laid the golden egg. He wanted the eggs and he poisoned the goose.

The great ones are always able to go on, but the tragedy with us is that we weren't ready to hang it up, and I feel like the rug was pulled out from under us.

What followed was me reaching the stage where I could not write anymore. Creatively it went away, and I knew it was gone, and that was a terrible thing for someone who had been doing so well.

In the entertainment business, you can be a genius at eighteen and the very best in your field at twenty, twenty-one. A young Michael Jackson, or a young Brian Wilson, or a young John Fogerty are all kids who absolutely understood what a pop hit record was.

But by the time I entered my thirties, I was slowly drying up. I kept trying, and it kept coming out lousy. Suddenly, I began to feel like I could no more make a hit record than the guy out in the street running a jackhammer. It went away, I knew it was gone, and I also knew I would get it back if I worked hard at it. I always had the faith, but while it was gone, I was miserable.

Basically, I am like all those artists who died and then become legends after they die. And in a way I did die. The miracle is that I did find my way back again.

Creatively now I can compete. I don't want to be an oldies act. Ricky Nelson said, "If memories were all I sang, I would rather drive a truck." I agree with that, but I also recognize that millions of people know me for "Proud Mary."

When I'm registering in some hotel in Arizona, and the guy behind the desk looks up at me and says, "You look familiar," I always go "Proud Mary." And no matter what his age is, he goes, "Oh, yeah, 'Proud Mary.'"

Robby Krieger

o o o

He gave us an insider's look at a group that haunts us still. The Doors never were your average teen favorites and seemed to reflect something dangerous. Here's one report on what it was like to work with Jim Morrison.

o o o

It was probably at our very first rehearsal that I saw the shape of things to come. Right at the end of our playing this guy walks in the room and Jim jumps on him and starts hitting him for no apparent reason. It was about a dope deal. They told me Jim Morrison was crazy, but I never believed them.

At that time, drugs weren't playing too much a part of it. Oh, Jim was into psychedelics, which was fine, but later, when he turned to alcohol, that's when things really went downhill.

We rehearsed for about a month, sometimes at my parents' house or at Ray Manzarek's house. Then we started getting a few gigs. One was at a friend of my parents, a doctor, and we played at his house. Then we got a gig at the aircraft company where Ray's mother was working. You know, little parties here and there.

Jim wasn't very musical. He could pound around on the piano pretty good, and he could fake playing a harmonica, but you'd never say to Jim Morrison, "OK, Jim, hit a B-flat."

Well, when we became the house band at the Whisky, back in the days when we were playing with such acts as Them, Buffalo Springfield, the Turtles, B.B. King, Otis Redding, and John Lee Hooker, we started knocking on every record company door in town. But nobody wanted us. Columbia signed us, and then let us out in six months. Frank Zappa wanted to produce us. Terry Melcher wanted to produce us. But we didn't want a producer. We wanted a record label.

Finally, Jac Holzman came in from Elektra and he liked us. His wife had seen us at the Whisky, and she probably talked him into it.

Some pretty weird stuff started to happen—like at the Swing Auditorium in San Bernardino, Jim kicked a light off the stage and it slashed some girl's eye open.

That kind of stuff was hard to deal with. The three of us would always be saying, "Goddamn Jim. Why did he have to do that?" It was always the three of us against him.

On our first album with Paul Rothchild, Jim was so strung out on acid when we were trying to do "The End" that he got totally out of hand. He threw a TV set through the control-room window, and he was into this Oedipus-complex trip and saying, "Fuck the mother, kill the father," and he would just rant on like that for hours. When we finally managed to get him in to record the song, he started doing it great.

Then we decided he was too high to continue, so we closed the session. But by now Jim didn't want to stop, so he climbed back into the place and started having fun by hosing down the place with a fire extinguisher, including all the instruments. Paul jumped in and dragged him out.

It was always nerve-racking with Jim. One day we were supposed to be rehearsing and we get this call from Blythe, California. And it's Jim. We said, "Jim, what are you doing in Blythe? Don't you know we have a rehearsal?"

He said, "Come on, you guys. Come up to Blythe, take some acid, and we'll rehearse out here."

"Can't do that, Jim. You gotta come back."

When he did come back, he had a black eye, like he'd been in a fight. Jim tended to make people beat him up. He'd push people into doing it.

And when we played live, it was usually baby-sitting time with Jim. He would just go off with anybody and get drunk, and we would always be in the position of having to wonder if he was going to show up for the show. Somehow he always did.

I loved the guy when he was straight. I disliked him immensely when he was drunk.

You know, we did real well for a while, but Jim never thought we were big enough. He thought we should be at least as big as the Stones. It was never fast enough for him. He kept saying, "Why isn't it faster? Look at the Beatles—swoosh!—straight up." I think Jim had a sense that he wasn't going to live all that long, like he had to do it in a certain space or else.

Another reason why he was getting drunk so often had to do with the size of the halls we were playing. As we got bigger, the places we played got bigger, and Jim felt he wasn't reaching the audience. It frustrated him. He was never geared to a large hall, and he felt the only way he could reach them was to get them totally crazy.

I remember this one instance in New Haven, right before we were supposed to go on. Jim's in the dressing room with some bimbo, and a cop comes in and thinks Jim is some hippie and he tells Jim to get out. Jim starts arguing with the cop, and then the cop maces him. After a while they shake hands and it's over.

We get on stage, and for some reason Jim feels compelled to tell the story of the cop and the mace, right during one of the songs. Well, the cops didn't like that, so they came onstage and hauled him off in the middle of the show.

Riots became normal. There was a pretty big one at the Singer Bowl in New York. Jim felt he had to push himself more and more as the crowds got bigger. I felt sorry for him. I remember Paul Rothchild saying, "We better get him in the studio to record everything we know because we may not have him around much longer."

Miami, of course, was the real crusher. Jim was late for the show, I think, because he had seen this theater piece with all this nudity the day before and he was obsessed with taking it all off onstage. But he never did whip it out like they said. It was so stupid. He yelled out, "Do you want me to take it all off? Do you want to see it?" But he didn't actually do it.

The crowd was writhing around. There was no air-conditioning, the building was overfilled, the people were all standing and packed together. Somehow Jim got thrown off the stage and all I could see was this this big snake of people following Jim around.

I said, "I'm getting out of here." Just before the stage collapsed, I jumped off and made it up to the balcony.

Not too many promoters wanted us after that, and I think in a way that's what Jim wanted. He didn't like his image anymore. He was getting fat. He looked more like a pool player than anything else.

The last time I saw Jim Morrison was right before he left for Paris. He was very sick when he went to Paris. He was coughing up blood. This is my own theory of how he died, but I think it would have been very easy for him, after a night of drinking, to take a couple of snorts of something and not know what it was. Jim could do that, take a big snort. And then just maybe go into the bathtub, fall asleep, and drown.

Paul Rothchild

∘ ∘ ∘

He produced the Doors records along with some other key folk and rock acts of the sixties. The look at Morrison _et al._ from this side gives us more background into that mysterious crowd.

∘ ∘ ∘

I always sought out the creative edge, so looking back it shouldn't surprise me that I worked with artists like Paul Butterfield, Jim Morrison, and Janis Joplin, three individuals who lived on the edge, both in their music and in their personal lives.

Paul Butterfield was traveling with his good buddy, Nick Gravenites, who wrote blues songs. They were both from Chicago, and I heard their acoustic stuff, and I said, "Yeah, it's nice. Nice to have met you. In case we ever need anybody, I'll let you know."

Cut to Cambridge, Massachusetts, two years later, 1965. I'm at a party at John Cook's house. John would later become Janis Joplin's road manager. Fritz Richmond, one of the original members of the Jim Kweskin Jug Band, is at the party, having just come off the road, and he says, "Hey, Paul, you remember that harmonica player, Paul Butterfield? I gotta tell you, he's playing the best music I've ever heard in my life. He's playing at a bar in Chicago, and he's got a full-on electric blues band. You should go see him right away."

I said OK, and I went out to Logan, got on a plane, landed in Chicago, walked into Big John's at three in the morning, just in time for Butterfield's last set. It was the most amazing sound I ever heard in my life. Over pizza, I told him I wanted to make a record with him for Elektra.

He says, "Great, but first let's go hear my buddy at this after-hours place on the South Side, Pepper's Lounge." I walked in, Muddy Waters was playing. It was that kind of era. Those guys played the clubs every night.

Now it's dawn and Paul says, "One more stop." That's the way it always was with Paul. "One more stop."

So we walk into this luncheonette kind of place, and there's another band playing, a pale reflection of Paul's band, but there was a guitar player in the band that tore my mind apart. About four songs into the set, I turn to Paul and ask, "Who is that guy?"

He says, "Oh, that's Michael Bloomfield. That's his band."

I said, "How would you feel if he were in your band?"

Paul said, "It'll never happen. I've tried twenty times."

I said, "Mind if I give it a shot?" And Paul says no. Michael comes down, sits at our table. We shake hands, and then do a half hour of intense intellectual Jew at each other, and I found a kindred soul. I ask him if he would consider leaving his band to join Paul's band, and he says OK. Paul is sitting there with his jaw on the table.

It was with Butterfield's band at Newport that Bob Dylan did his first electric set. I was at the mixing console. The scene backstage was colossal. There was this polarization at Newport. On one side you had Pete Seeger, George Wein, the old guard. Pete is backstage, pacifist Pete, with an axe saying, "I'm going to cut the fucking cables if that act goes on stage." Pete, my childhood hero, and he's talking about my act.

On the other side is Jac Holzman, Peter Yarrow, Albert Grossman, myself. There were about eight people on each side of the cable, one group trying to defend it, the other trying to cut it. Finally, Pete's group calmed down. We said, "Look, this is an aspect of the American folk process. You've got to let it happen." And they did let it happen.

But then it gets to be Dylan's set, and there's no defense for this, no historical precedent, just a young Jewish songwriter with an electric band. I was the only one on the grounds who had ever recorded electric music, so I said, "I'll mix the Dylan set."

Everyone says, "Great." So there I am at the console, in the middle of the field. Dylan hits the stage. I could barely hear the music because of the furor in the audience. From my perspective, it seemed like everybody on my left wanted Dylan to get off the stage, and everybody on my right wanted him to stay on. I turned up the sound so you could hear the music. Here comes Pete with the axe again.

Peter Yarrow sees this, and he comes running over to the console and says, "Here comes trouble, man, but I'm with you, Paul. Just keep the show going." Peter Yarrow and Pete Seeger went nose to nose, screaming at each other. I'm mixing the set, and more people are gathering around. It was the turning point. The old guard realized the world was changing, just as they had participated in a change some years before.

As to Jim Morrison, he was two people, a true chemical schizophrenic. When he was sober, you wouldn't want a better friend. Dear heart, sensitive, an aware human being. Well-read, wonderful person, you could take him anywhere. You could take him home for dinner with Mom, take him to Ahmet Ertegun's party for senators and princes.

But don't give him a drink. If you do, you wind up with a little kid, a taunting kid, looking to find your darkest weaknesses at all times. Jim Morrison was a guy who tested the edges endlessly. When he was drunk, he tested them cruelly, with everybody. No exceptions, none.

Janis Joplin was the rough-hewn model for every feminist that walks the planet today. She insisted on driving the band car. She wouldn't take any bullshit from anybody backstage. She was also soft, loving, and loyal. But like Morrison, she was an expert in guerrilla warfare.

She aggressively sought out mates. I remember one night at the No Name bar in Sausalito. We were sitting there talking, and she says, "Hey, man, see that dude at the bar? I want his hat, and I want him, too. Ask him to come over."

And I did. I walked over to the guy and I said, "That girl over there wants to talk to you." The guy turns around, sees that it's Janis Joplin, and his knees go out.

Bobby Neuwirth tells this great story of when Janis met Joe Namath. She goes to meet Joe Namath, who she thinks is the hottest dude on the planet. She wants to see him at his club, Bachelors Three in New York.

Well, Joe is holding court. He's got two bimbos on one side, three on the other. The table is covered with goodies. Janis bullies her way past the front guards, charges in, stands at the front of Joe's table, cackles the way she could cackle, and says, "You're Joe."

He looks up and says, "Oh my god, it's Janis Joplin. I've wanted to meet you for years."

She says, "Me too." And with that she gets on the table and walks across it. She has nothing to do with the bimbos, and she's shattering stuff everywhere. She sits on his lap, they hug, huge kiss. He then picks her up and carries her out. They disappear for four days. But that was her aggressive style. She went out after what she wanted and she got it, all the time.

John Sebastian

o o o

The Loving Spoonful reflected flower power coupled with memorable hit records. John was the drive and later had his solo success for a time. We talked about the difficulties of recapturing those moments.

o o o

I met Cass Elliott while I was accompanying a man named Valentine Pringle, who was a protégé of Harry Belafonte's. Val was a big man, six feet, five inches, 230 or 240 pounds. He had this tremendous Negro baritone, a distinctly black and rich operatic voice.

I had been helping Lightning Hopkins, carrying his guitar and speaking for him in certain situations. Lightning was playing at the Village Gate and the show included Valentine Pringle. Val was having problems with his accompanist, a fellow who was masquerading as a flamenco guitarist but was really a local guy. Several Jewish guys with Spanish names used to do that.

Anyway, I was eighteen and a little cocky about my guitar playing, and after the show I went back to Valentine and said, "I can play anything this guy can play." Lightning told him I was OK, and I began working with Valentine. On one of our first gigs in Washington, we opened for a group called the Big Three. Cass was in the group. I walked into the dressing room and she immediately started a light banter with me. She was an absolute dream at that kind of humorous wisecracking. In between shows, we became friends.

The Mugwumps—which I was probably in for all of two weeks with Zally Yanovsky, Cass, and Denny Doherty—came together after the Big

Three started losing momentum as the commercial folk boom lost momentum. Self-contained groups were suddenly in, and even though the Mugwumps weren't exactly self-contained—songs came from here and there, Roy Silver and Bob Cavallo managed us, Felix Pappalardi was our arranger—there was this feeling of community.

The main gist of what I was doing in the group was transporting a half a pound of Jamaican pot to Washington so that the Mugwumps could continue having a good time.

Roy eventually fired me because he thought I was a bad influence on Zal. I would play this little lick on harmonica across the stage, and Zally would answer it with his guitar. At that time, we weren't all that great as musicians, so this little move of ours was not always successful. So I got canned. I wasn't unhappy about it because I was just starting to become known in the New York studio scene as a harmonica player. So I came back to New York and dug in and continued to work as a studio musician.

When the Mugwumps disbanded, Zally and I quickly got together. We knew Cass would be all right. But we were worried about Denny. He'd turned the heat in his room at the Albert Hotel up to eighty-five, and he wasn't doing anything except living off the money he'd made from the Mugwumps. We didn't have to worry about him all that long. Within six months, the Mamas and the Papas materialized.

Me and Zally, meanwhile, were forming the Spoonful with Steve Boone and Joe Butler. The Spoonful, I believe, had a little bit of a drop on everybody as far as pushing some of the idioms together, making electric jug-band music and drawing from rural music to make modern rock 'n' roll.

I was a songwriter out of necessity. We had simply run out of jug band tunes to renovate. Like the Stones and the Yardbirds, we were also doing Chuck Berry, but in a slightly different way.

The fourth song I wrote was "Do You Believe in Magic?" I had this idea that if I electrified an autoharp, I would come up with an instrument that nobody else on the rock scene was playing. Once I put a ukulele contact microphone on the back of an autoharp, I realized a shuffle was something that would sound good. The instrument dictates that you write in C. There's so many things about those first few tunes that came out of necessity. It's like it says in the book *If They Asked Me, I Could Write a Song*, great songs are often inspired by great need.

The Spoonful had a kind of New York savvy about it. We looked pretty cynically at the West Coast rock scene. Everybody was talking about all these West Coast psychedelic bands, and we'd go and watch them rehearse and they were all loaded. I could never fathom how they even came up with the twelve tunes they needed for an album.

The Spoonful had its down side, as well. I used to be real frustrated with the teenybopper side of things. As a songwriter, I felt the Spoonful had a lot to offer. We weren't matinee idols, but the country had already been preprogrammed to scream in response to four men with long hair and guitars. It had already happened and there was nothing we could do about it.

Towards the tail end of the Spoonful, I remember actually swinging my instrument at girls who were enveloping the stage. I couldn't take that mindless admiration. I wanted it to be for a musical reason.

That said, it was still wonderful to be able to go over to England and have a dialogue with the Beatles within forty-eight hours of getting there. I remember lying in my hotel room and saying to myself, "John and Paul came to see us last night, George wants me to come over and look at his sitar, Brian Jones wants me to go take drugs with him, people are handing me obscure hashish." It was all tremendously exciting, but it was also before the effects of some of those things were known.

Clive Davis

o o o

One of a handful of leaders who shaped the look and the future of the music industry, Clive zoomed to the top at CBS, went through an excruciating time, and reemerged at Arista with touch and style still intact. One of a kind.

o o o

If I were to be honest and accurate about it, I would have to say that I lucked out by going to the Monterey Pop Festival.

I went to Monterey not for any business reasons, but because my friends, Abe Somer and Lou Adler, said to me, "Why don't you come out for the weekend?" I really thought I was going for a social weekend. I knew some established acts would be performing, like Simon and Garfunkel and the Mamas and the Papas, but I never knew there would be unknown talent there or, literally, that it would mark the creative turning point in my life.

Monterey was like being hit over the head with something whereby you feel the knock and also see the light at the same time. It was clear that a social revolution was occurring, clear that a musical revolution was occurring. Listening to Janis Joplin, seeing that charismatic, whirling dervish of a figure, seeing the Electric Flag and Jimi Hendrix and all the great new artists that appeared there, it was so dramatic. I said to myself, "This is the time for me to make my move."

Well, I moved to sign people, but I did it quietly. I didn't want other record companies—my competition—to know what I was doing. So I quietly negotiated the purchase of Janis Joplin's contract. Then I signed the Electric Flag. Then Blood, Sweat and Tears and the Chambers Brothers, and I said to myself, "I'm onto something hot, and I know it."

Then Bill Graham called me about Santana, and it just kept mushrooming and exploding. And that continuity of success gave me the confidence I needed to keep going.

Mind you, these deals were not big deals—$10,000, $15,000. The most, $25,000.

I was not a rock 'n' roller, by any means. I came into my position at CBS as someone who loved Broadway, someone who loved songs. I was a lawyer, and I wore my suits and ties in New York and I never tried to be "with it" or put chains around my neck, although I did wear Nehru suits and white slacks when I'd go to the Coast. But it took several years to break down the barriers of suspicion that existed against lawyers and people who couldn't read music.

I looked for uniqueness and originality. I started honing my ear for the Top 40 singles. I began editing singles in my office. I'd bring in one of Columbia's studio engineers and we'd edit out all the extraneous parts. If the hook to the song was not repeated at the end of the record, I'd bring it back by artificial means.

I edited "Black Magic Woman" for Santana, "Peace of My Heart" for Joplin. Those artists never knew what Top 40 was. They never even remotely understood it. The late sixties were the days of the extended, amplified virtuoso sections of music, so you really had to edit, not only for the artists but for their producers, who were usually engineers who also didn't know the first thing about Top 40.

Joplin was my first original signing at CBS. Here I was, essentially a representative of the establishment at a major company on the New York Stock Exchange, signing nonestablishment-thinking artists whose great appeal was almost inherently based on eschewing materialism.

Janis marked CBS's first confrontation with nonestablishment thought. When she and the group came to the CBS Building to sign the contract, they went to the tenth-floor conference room, and I was in my office on the eleventh floor.

Janis asked to see me alone. She came upstairs and we chatted. She was genuinely moved by the fact that she was signing. With her shy but very genuine cackle, she said, "Just to sign in this building, it's so corporate, so establishment. It really would not be meaningful enough just to put our signatures on a piece of paper. What I would like to do, unless you think it's out of order, is for you and I to go to bed together."

She didn't use the word "fuck," but she thought if we went to bed together, our lives would be intertwined. She was serious.

I said, "Well, we shouldn't mix business and pleasure," and I laughed because it was funny.

We wound up going right back downstairs, and we're having drinks in the conference room, getting ready to go to a party where we would take pictures to celebrate the signing, when all of a sudden one of the guys with the group takes off all his clothes and is standing there nude—in the CBS Building—and this guy is walking around nude.

For some reason, it was not untasteful. It was just a different kind of thinking by someone from a different background.

Of course, the idea of trying to translate to a CBS board what it was like living as the representative of this establishment company in a nonestablishment world is something I never made a major effort to do because they never would have understood it.

A few years later, I took over the Ahmanson Theater in Los Angeles for a week of concerts, and I mixed and matched people like Loudon Wainwright with Miles Davis, Bruce Springsteen with the Mahavishnu Orchestra, putting these acts together on different nights, with Bill Cosby and Richard Pryor emceeing.

In the case of Bruce Springsteen, he had such lyrical imagery, the first of that kind to come along since Dylan.

But at that time, Springsteen was not especially charismatic in person. He was a lox, he stood still, didn't move for years. When I put him into the Ahmanson, he never moved around the stage.

I never knew what Springsteen would develop into. I never knew he would become the best living rock 'n' roller. But I did know that his lyric content, the imagery in his songs, was so unique that I went on closed-circuit television to every Columbia branch and read Springsteen's lyrics just prior to the release of his first album, "Greetings from Asbury Park." I was concerned that the branch people wouldn't listen to the words because his music was so pulsating.

That same kind of feeling carried over into Arista Records with Patti Smith. It was her lyric content, her poetry, the uniqueness of what she was doing.

Today, virtuosity ain't enough. Neither is lyric ability. If it's not heavy metal, where an act can break through live performances, you've got to have hits.

When I signed Billy Joel to Columbia, after he had not made it on Paramount, or Boz Scaggs after he had an album out on Atlantic, it was because I listened to their material and I knew they could write hit songs.

There is a great thrill in establishing someone. Whitney Houston, for example, is this generation's Lena Horne, but with far more commercial impact.

With Whitney, I not only signed her to Arista, but I pick every song and every producer. We work as a creative partnership, just she and myself, like the way Quincy Jones is with Michael Jackson. That's the difference for me now, working with people like Whitney and Dionne Warwick and Aretha Franklin. I am very much on the creative firing line. I am no longer just a signer.

Still, if I had to pick one time, it would be Monterey. It changed me as a person. For me, a Brooklyn lawyer, to be able to reach out in musical terms and find nonestablishment, original, unique talent that the public would go on to endorse—that was tremendously exhilarating.

George Harrison

○ ○ ○

A complex man with many talents, George was actually the hardest Beatle to solve. He survived the fame and fortune to produce films and solo records and has pulled together his musical mates to get it on for a variety of good works and high ideals.

○ ○ ○

I don't go around from day to day thinking, "I am George Harrison from the Beatles." I try to balance my life with peace and quiet because the other side of it is real rowdy. I'm a Pisces. I am an extreme person. One half is always going where the other half has just been. I was always extremely up or extremely down, extremely spiritual or extremely drugged. Now there is a bit of maturity. I have brought the two closer to the middle. I don't get too far up or too far down, and that feels good.

I started out at fourteen, fifteen. I met Paul and John, and we played in little events until 1960, when we started to do better and sought to do it professionally. Then we had the mania, and I had a solo career. Actually, I had little careers going on on the side, like my involvement with Indian music and Ravi Shankar. I have lots of hobbies. I love gardens. The Beatles was such a big part, but I didn't want it to be the end of my life. "In 1964, we came to America. We went out in 1969, and that is the end of the story." Actually, it is a continuing story. "Here today, gone to Maui."

There is a lot of renewed interest in the Beatles because of the CD releases, and this "Twenty Years Ago for Sgt. Pepper," but there will always be periods when the Beatles sell again. In the seventies, there was a period, and now another one in the eighties. I think it happens with each generation. I saw it happen with my own boy. I didn't tell him anything about the Beatles, and then one day he suddenly said, "Hey, Dad, can you show me the piano riff to 'Bulldog'?"

I thought, "How the hell did he even hear such an obscure tune?" And then I realized that when all kids get to be five and six, they watch *Yellow Submarine*. As they get older, they somehow discover the Beatles. It has an everlasting quality.

There was a magic chemistry that happened between us and somehow it got into the grooves on those records. Not every song we ever did was brilliant, but a lot of them are timeless, great songs that happen to have a chemistry in the grooves which appeals to each generation as it comes up.

It was sad when we broke up because we had been so close for so long. Mick Jagger said at the Rock 'n' Roll Hall of Fame dinner that the Beatles were a four-headed monster. We never went anywhere without each other. We shared all the miseries, and the isolation of limos, hotels, planes, and concert halls, which is all we ever saw for years.

Like Jagger said at the Hall of Fame dinner, "I would like to think we

are all still friends because those were some of the best times of my life."
And that is true.

The saddest thing was actually getting fed up with one another. It's like
growing up in a family. When you get to a certain age, you want to go off
and get your own girl and your own house, split up a bit. At the same time,
for me it gave me the perfect chance to do my own records. I didn't have
many tunes on Beatles records, so doing an album like *All Things Must Pass*
was something I had been eager to do. I had been feeling a musical con-
stipation, and *All Things Must Pass* was like going to the bathroom and
letting it out.

Some of my solo records didn't do so well, which was OK. Paul feels
more like he has to be a success all the time, but for me I had such ego
satisfaction through the Beatles period. We had more fame than anybody
could imagine, so when some of my solo records didn't sell, it didn't really
matter to me. As an example, Ringo once said to me, "I have to have a
Number 1."

I said, "You don't have to have a Number 1. You want to be number
one. The record is second." I say, if you set yourself up looking for success,
when you have a failure, you fall much deeper. I say, bring the two together.
As Bob Dylan said, "When you find out you are at the top, you are at the
bottom."

The *Concert for Bangladesh* happened because of my relationship with
Ravi. He is such a humble person. He said, "I am going to do this show.
Maybe, if you or Peter Sellers or both of you can come on and do something
or announce something, maybe we can make $25,000 and do something
about this terrible war."

I said, "If you want me to be involved, I think I'd better be really
involved," so I started recruiting all these people. It was difficult at first, but
once it got closer to the show I had commitments from so many people that
some had to be turned down. Everybody wanted to be in it.

Mainly the concert was to attract attention to the situation that was
happening at the time. The money we raised was secondary, and although
we had some problems because Allen Klein had not been handling it right,
they still got plenty of money, even though it was a drop in the ocean. The
main thing was, we spread the word and helped get the war ended. Little
Bengali waiters in Indian restaurants still come up to me and say, "When
we were fighting in the jungle, it was so great to know there was someone
out there supporting us."

The *Concert for Bangladesh* was just a moral stance. These kinds of
things have grown over the years, but what we did showed that musicians
and people are more humane than politicians. Today people accept the
commitment rock 'n' roll musicians have when they perform for a charity.
When I did it, they said things like, "He's only doing this to be nice."

Writing with Jeff Lynne is really the first time I've ever written with
anyone. I wrote one tune with Dylan back in '69. I wrote one with Eric

Clapton. I've helped Ringo finish songs. But I'm not the type of songwriter that says, "Let's sit down and write." Every Beatles album that had a song of mine on it I wrote alone. John and Paul had been writing so much together. Once in a while I got a line from John when I was stuck. But at the same time I gave them lyrics. I helped out on "Eleanor Rigby." I wrote some of the lyric to "Come Together."

Of my songs, "Here Comes the Sun" and "Something" are probably the biggest. Frank Sinatra, who sings it with his "Stick around, Jack," says "Something" is the greatest love song of all time. He used to say it was the greatest love song of the year. Then the decade. So what he's saying now is very nice. At last count, which was years ago, there were 140 covers of "Something." Sinatra, Smokey Robinson, Ray Charles. My personal favorite is the version by James Brown. It was one of his B sides. I have it on my jukebox at home. It's absolutely brilliant. "Taxman" was done not too long ago by Berry Gordy's son, so I've done all right.

You can take the Beatles separately and analyze all their energy, but when you put them together astrologically and chemically, something stronger takes place that even the Beatles never understood. As Dylan said, "To understand you know too soon there is no sense in trying." Dylan is so brilliant. To me, he makes William Shakespeare look like Billy Joel.

Yoko Ono

○ ○ ○

Yoko resents the accusation that she broke up the Beatles, but her individuality and intense focus could never have worked in a community effort. She is a figure in one of the great stories of our time.

○ ○ ○

I did not know very much about the Beatles. Nobody believes that. People say, "How dare she say such a thing? Of course she must have known." Well, I did know the Beatles, but as a social phenomenon, just like I know about Elvis.

I remember reading the newspapers about these long-haired kids. I was in Japan. It was a small article that said these boys with strange haircuts were becoming extremely popular. I also remember scanning another article in Life magazine which had something to do with Brian Epstein, this clever guy who made this group happen, and one of them was supposed to be very intelligent. That was John.

I met him when I was doing a gallery show. He entered the gallery on opening night, about an hour before the opening. I was very busy trying to make sure everything was all right. Busy and very nervous. And then John Dunbar brought this guy in, but he definitely did not properly introduce me to John, who was just looking around independently. And then John asked me a question about one of the paintings. He asked if he could hang a nail on it.

I said, "No, not now. Not before the opening."

And he said, "Well, could I hammer an imaginary nail in and give you imaginary money?"

I thought, "Oh, that's pretty good." You meet so many people at a gallery show, and a lot of very interesting people came, but I did remember John because he had a very gentle, warm look.

There was so much misinformation, to put it mildly. In England, they started saying, "Well, John said that when he went into the gallery he was totally drunk, up all night, unshaven." And he wasn't. I hate men who drink. I am very good at smelling their breath. He did not have a drink. I know that. He was well shaven, looking his best.

There was another gallery opening two weeks later, and I met him again, and this time, yes, John looked like he had been up all night. I don't know what he was doing, but he looked like a totally different person, unshaven, looking very sort of angry. I was amazed that he was the same person I had met two weeks before.

Once we were together, and the Beatles were breaking up, for Johnny it was like a divorce. He felt good about the group breaking up, like a big weight was off him, but at the same time he was very proud of the group. He knew there was nothing that compared with the Beatles. He also had an extremely high opinion about each one, which might seem surprising. He used to say, "They were very intelligent kids, and the fact that they came from Liverpool, you would think they would not understand these things, but they do." He was always protective of them in that way.

I don't think he ever voiced anything about how he missed being in the Beatles, but that was because I was the other party that he got the divorce for. And I suppose I fell into that trap right away, that he divorced them to marry me. But that doesn't mean I broke up the Beatles. I didn't break up the Beatles. The Beatles were getting very independent, each one of them, and Johnny was not in fact the first one who wanted to leave the Beatles. Ringo and Maureen came to John and I one night and said, "Well, he wants to leave."

George was the next, and then John. Paul was the only one trying to hold the Beatles together. But then again, the other three felt that Paul was trying to hold the Beatles together as his band. They were getting to be like Paul's band, which they did not like.

There was an incredible period of unpleasantness for John, so in fact he was delighted he was out of it. In a funny sort of way I felt the weight of the breakup because he had been communicating and having an extremely intense and stimulating exchange with three very intelligent, very quick guys, and now he expected all that to be replaced by me.

Booker T. Jones

○ ○ ○

Cool and controlled, Booker T. gives us a look into the scene in Memphis when it sparkled with a combination of new and old blues styles. His MG's were the house band for Stax Records, and every rock star knew their skills.

○ ○ ○

I remember when Otis Redding came into Stax Records as a valet for Johnny Jenkins and the Pinetoppers, who were auditioning in '63 or '64. Otis would say, "Let me sing a song, let me sing a song." That is how he got in. He was so dynamic. I miss him still.

Otis was excited about music all the time. When we did "Dock of the Bay," we were in the studio until two or three in the morning, and then back at ten A.M., recording all the time during that last week. Through it all he was electric. Otis was head honcho, but he was also very temperamental when it came to his music. That was all he cared about. It was the only thing he ever lost his temper about.

Otis taught me a lot about the rawness of music and about working live and getting people excited and creating a feeling. But I can't say he was my favorite because I really did enjoy working with everybody. Wilson Pickett, for example, was a wild man. He would have made a good boxer. And Isaac Hayes, who couldn't play piano but stood there watching me and taught himself to play, he had his own ideas and he made great music.

The important thing always was to be fresh. You can't redo "Green Onions." That was a new sound.

I don't know what it was exactly, but certain talent seems to develop around places like Memphis, New Orleans, and Chicago. Look at Memphis—Roy Orbison, Elvis Presley, and the many people who came out of that city. Not far from Atlanta, but you never saw that in Atlanta.

Maybe it was the physical location. Maybe it had something to do with the water, or the temperature. Who knows? They made cars in Detroit, and Motown came out of there. Maybe it takes that one guy, that one executive, who says, "Go ahead, make me a record."

Isaac Hayes

○ ○ ○

**The voice and the attack were trademarks of some powerful music
from Memphis during the seventies. A big sexy man, he set the style
for a run of black male vocalists to follow.**

○ ○ ○

When you're a sharecropper and you're poor and have no shoes, you think
of that pair of shoes you want to wear. When you have no clothes, you
think of the wardrobe you want. When you have no roof over your head,
you think of the fine home you want to live in. Somewhere in the back of
my mind I knew I would not spend the rest of my life as a sharecropper.

The people I was around all the time in the cotton fields would call
me a daydreamer and a good-for-nothing. I simply was not motivated to pick
cotton, but it was how we made money. You'd make enough money to go
to the fairgrounds, or you'd go up to the cafés and beer joints and get drunk.
I said, "This is not for me."

I used to hang on the corner with the fellows singing doo-wop, and
we'd sing in the cotton fields. But even then I'd stand there and watch the
planes and say, "I'm going to be on one of those planes, wherever it's going."
I always thought beyond my immediate environment.

When I was a ninth grader in Memphis, I won a talent contest. I was
a raggedy kid with holes in his shoes up onstage singing the Nat King Cole
song, "Looking Back." All of a sudden I win this contest and I'm signing
autographs and the pretty girls are noticing me.

Black kids didn't have much access to entertainers. The only entertainer
I came remotely close to as a kid was Sam Cooke. I was singing with the
Teen Tones and Sam Cooke was hospitalized in Memphis from a car accident
in Arkansas. We sneaked up the fire escape, into his room, and he had a
thermometer in his mouth. The nurse looked up and saw us and said, "Get
out of here." We had to sneak in to see him, but Sam Cooke was the closest
guy we ever got to.

When I graduated high school, I had seven scholarships in vocal music,
but I didn't pursue it because I got a job at a meat packing house in Memphis
slaughtering hogs and cows. But still my mind was on music. In my yearbook
people had written, "See you on TV, Ike. Good luck."

I did a lot of playing in a lot of small clubs and then Jim Stewart,
president of Stax Records, heard me play and said, "Hey, would you like a
job?" Booker T., of the MG's, had gone off to school, and Stax needed a
keyboard player and a staff musician. I said OK.

I had been to Stax a few other times—with a blues band, a rock 'n' roll
group—and they always turned me down. Now, here I was in this big old
empty theater where they had cut "Gee Whiz (Look at His Eyes)," "Green
Onions," and "Walking the Dog."

My first session was an Otis Redding album. I was scared to death. Otis was incredible. He was dynamic, exciting. There were times he made up lyrics as he went along.

Then David Porter, who was going under the name Little David, came in one day and said, "Why don't we hook up? I write lyrics, you write music. Let's be a team like Holland-Dozier-Holland, or Bacharach-David." I said OK, and the first thing we wrote was a thing called "How Do You Quit Someone You Love" for Carla Thomas.

And then Jim Stewart came in and said, "Look, we have Sam and Dave, these two guys Jerry Wexler sent down from Atlantic. They'll need some writers."

David and I wrote a thing called "I Take What I Want," which was our first Sam and Dave single. Then we followed with "You Don't Know Like I Know," "Hold On, I'm Coming," and "Soul Man." We had no idea how good we were. We were just doing something we felt, and the stuff was catching on.

Stax was a family atmosphere. Everybody knew everybody else. Jim was a banker. He'd come in evenings, after banking hours. Pretty soon we were revving it up and doing well, so Jim resigned from the bank. He was a quiet and unassuming, almost introverted. We used to tease him. His instrument was the flute.

I had been bugging him about cutting an album, and he'd say, "Isaac, your voice is too pretty."

And then Al Bell, who was head of promotion, and I locked the door one day and downed two bottles of champagne. And Al says, "Ike, let's cut a record."

I say, "When?"

He says, "Right now."

I say, "Sure. I ain't feeling no pain." So we get a few of the guys together—Al Jackson on drums, Booker T. played a little organ, me on piano—and we do an album. I didn't take Al seriously because I was drunk, full of champagne. Well, we do "Misty," "Stormy Monday Blues," "Goin' to Chicago," "Rock Me, Baby." We finish it, play it back, and I'm still half high, OK? And then we go our separate ways.

About three weeks later, Al says, "You got an appointment with a photographer."

I say, "What for?"

He says, "For the album cover."

I say, "You're kidding?"

Well, he wasn't kidding. I show up at the photographer. They put me in a tux, top hat, tails, and a cane. I was so embarrassed, but a lot of critics liked it, and it served as a prelude to *Hot Buttered Soul* and *Shaft* and all the incredible things that happened for me later on.

Al Green

o o o

An amazing singer, Al's passionate songs in the seventies turned on
women around the world. His movement toward the church and his
departure from the popular music scene are genuine, and he explained
why when we talked in Memphis.

o o o

I started in Memphis during the Stax era. Back then, it seemed like everybody
and his brother was on Stax—the Staple Singers, Sam and Dave, Otis
Redding, Steve Cropper, Booker T., Margie Joseph. Stax had everything
going for itself, and Hi Records, where I was, was like the ugly duckling
across town.

People would say, "Who is this Al Green?" I was just a little fish in
the pond.

I looked up to Sam Cooke, Brook Benton, Jackie Wilson, and Otis
Redding, definitely. I never got to meet Otis, but I did get to see his car and
I heard half his show once standing behind the Royal Theater in Chicago.
I had no money to get in. I was a nobody, a guy who comes over from
Grand Rapids to Chicago to see Otis Redding. I hung around the stage door,
and it was great. I got to see his red and silver suit. I stood there speechless
for an hour thinking, "Wow, this is fabulous."

I never got to meet Sam Cooke either, but he was the artist I most
looked up to. It's twenty-three years after his death and it's still hard to
comprehend how good Sam Cooke was.

I started writing songs in Grand Rapids. The first song I wrote was
something called "What Am I Going to Do with Myself." I moved from
Grand Rapids to Detroit and I was staying with the singer, Laura Lee. I
wrote "Tired of Being Alone," my first million-seller, because of her. This
lady used to leave me all the time. She was the busiest woman I'd ever seen.
Always had something to do—her nails, hair, shopping. Consequently, I
was alone a lot, and that's why I wrote that song.

Things changed drastically for me around '73. I'd be onstage doing a
concert, singing "I'm Still in Love with You" or "You Ought to Be with
Me," and I'd feel the spirit of the Lord. I'd be in Liverpool singing and I'd
get that feeling and I'd say, "This is strange."

Then I'd be back in the Latin Casino in Cherry Hill, New Jersey,
singing "How Can You Mend a Broken Heart," and I'm saying to myself,
"I don't know the scriptures. I've been to church. I was raised in the choir.
I've heard the preacher preach, but I don't know this stuff."

So I was born again in '73, in Anaheim, California. From that moment
I knew it I couldn't sing "baby baby" anymore.

It took me three years to dissolve contracts, liquidate deals. In '76, we
started a tabernacle. A lot of my people found it difficult to stay on the ship.
It wasn't a problem for me, but there was a real division with the musicians.

On one side there were the guys who preferred hanging out with chicks and smoking pot, and another group of guys who would say, "I believe the guy. He feels like he's been forgiven for his sins. He feels like living a cleaner, purer life. We support him."

Then there were the people in the record industry who said, "I need to get these records out. I got 50,000 I need to move, OK?"

You see, I made a commitment to do what I'm doing. There are a lot of people who did not make a commitment and now they're no longer with us. We lost Otis Redding, Sam Cooke, Jackie Wilson, Jimi Hendrix. I think maybe some of them didn't know where or when to get off. The important thing is to be here. A buck is important, but you need to consider where you come from and what you are doing in order that you may possess your own soul.

Al Kooper

∘ ∘ ∘

A musical gadfly who appeared here, there, and everywhere for over a decade, his Dylan stories and proficiency as a musician kept him either in the spotlight or in the immediate background.

∘ ∘ ∘

I was this nerd from Queens. Simon and Garfunkel come from the same neighborhood. Before they were Simon and Garfunkel, they were Tom and Jerry. Paul's dad was a society band leader, Jerry Simon. In '63, around the time of "The Twist," Paul's father hired Paul and I for some of these society gigs. We would sit up on the stand with our guitars, with our volume turned off, and they would be playing "Laura" and "Stardust," and we would be sitting there in our tuxedos, strumming along.

Every forty-five minutes, Paul would jump up and sing a rock 'n' roll song, and I would play guitar behind him. We would make fifty dollars each, which was good money. We did a whole string of debutante parties, and it was during that time that Paul played me a Dylan record. I didn't get it because I was into rock 'n' roll. Then Paul played me "Baby Let Me Follow You Down" on the electric guitar. That I got. That I understood loud and clear. It was fantastic hearing this folk music, this finger-picking, on electric guitar.

It was through Tom Wilson, a producer at CBS, that I met Dylan. Tom had a Harvard education, and he produced a lot of jazz. But somehow he wound up as a staff producer at CBS, and they gave him Dylan. I don't know why they gave him Dylan. It's, like, beyond my comprehension why he got Dylan, but they gave him Dylan, and the two of them got along pretty well.

I had the kind of relationship with Tom where I could walk into his office, go through his things, and steal Dylan acetates. Finally, Tom invited me to a Dylan session, which was like the end-all for me.

I practiced all night. I brought my guitar with me. Showed up an hour and a half before the session was scheduled to start. I went in, plugged in my guitar, and when the musicians came, I was already there, which wasn't unusual for me. I used to sit in on a lot of dates when I was never actually booked for the session.

Well, Tom Wilson hadn't shown up yet, and I was in there looking good. I figured when Tom got there, everyone would say, "Cool," and I'd be playing on the session.

Dylan walks in. It's the dead of winter. The guy with him is Mike Bloomfield, and he's carrying a Fender Telecaster, no guitar case. The guitar is just slung over his shoulder like Johnny Appleseed, covered with snow and rain.

They just came in, got a towel, toweled off, sat down, and started warming up. Bloomfield was my age, and I was floored with his facility. I thought I was a good guitar player because all these people had been hiring me for my stupidity. But this guy could really play. I thought, "I don't have a chance."

So I packed up my guitar and went into the booth and started watching the session. About halfway through the session, they still hadn't started recording yet, they had Paul Griffin move from organ to piano. I went to Tom Wilson and said, "Hey, why don't you let me play the organ? I have this great idea for a part." Tom didn't really say no, so I sat down at the organ when he took a phone call.

Now I had played organ before, but just on my own demos. All of a sudden they started recording. The song was a very long one, and the band was playing so loud I couldn't hear the organ. I put my hands on the keyboard, and not hearing what I was playing but knowing enough about music to know that if I played a C it would fit into an F chord, I waited for the band to make a chord change before I played.

It was the first complete take of the day, and when they went to play it back, Dylan said, "Turn up the organ."

Tom Wilson said, "That cat's not an organ player."

Dylan said, "Don't tell me who is an organ player. Just turn up the organ."

That was the take of "Like a Rolling Stone," and that is how I became an organ player.

You couldn't help being influenced by Dylan. And he couldn't help being influenced by the Beatles and the Stones. He would go to England, and they would come to the United States to see him, to pay homage to him. They were influenced by him, and he in turn was influenced by them.

They kind of cross-pollinated each other. You never would have had a "Like a Rolling Stone" without Dylan being into the Beatles, just as you never would have had "I'm a Loser" and "You've Got to Hide Your Love Away" without Dylan.

Tom Wilson was there again for me when I joined the Blues Project. During those years, Tom was responsible for everything good that happened to me. He was a great guy, very articulate and intelligent, hilarious, and virtually unsung. He was the guy who signed Simon and Garfunkel. He cut an acoustic album with them, and then after they split up, Paul moved to England and Artie was teaching math or something, Tom overdubbed the electrical instruments on "Sounds of Silence," without them being around or even knowing about it, and put it out.

My joining the Blues Project started with a phone call from Tom Wilson wanting me to play on a session. When "Like a Rolling Stone" came out, I was swamped with calls to play on sessions, and this was one of them. Tom Wilson called and said he was doing an audition tape on a band for Columbia. So I went and played on the session. It was not a spectacular day for me. There really wasn't much room for me to play. But the band and their manager invited me to lunch the next day and really surprised me when they asked me to join the Blues Project.

I thought, "This is a great idea. These guys play in bars, in clubs, and maybe I can get my keyboard chops together by playing with them." Suddenly I was a keyboard player. Everybody was calling me to play keyboards, and I didn't know what the fuck I was doing.

Van Morrison

o o o

One of the most inpenetrable figures in rock music, Van never seemed comfortable with success. He's managed to remain aloof from the trappings of stardom while making some of the most acclaimed records of his time.

o o o

There were two branches of rock 'n' roll when I was brought up—the Elvis Presley branch, a straight commercial thing that included Presley, Ricky Nelson, Roy Orbison. The other branch was Jerry Lee Lewis, Little Richard, Fats Domino, people who were a little less commercial than Elvis. Jerry Lee seemed to have a lot more going on. He covered a lot of territory, so I used to listen to him.

Then you had R & B people like Slim Harpo and Harmonica Fats. And then also Ray Charles at Newport. There seemed to be something happening between the horns and the way Ray was singing and the harmonies. So I keyed on that. And I also listened to Gerry Mulligan, and people like that who really like to blow. I remember getting a saxophone and going to a teacher to get lessons. I also played some folk guitar, and that turned into working with rock 'n' roll bands.

I started out playing parties and local dances where people would jive a lot, jump around and sweat. I liked it.

Then there were the obscure blues things I liked. John Lee Hooker, Muddy Waters. I was listening to that stuff since I was two or three. I had it in the back of my head that I wanted to do more of a blues thing. To me, blues seemed better than rock 'n' roll. I remember, I was in London playing in a show band, and I went to this club and a band came on, and all they played was Bo Diddley and Jimmy Reed. I said, "Well, if they're getting away with it, I can, too."

So I went back to Belfast and started an R & B club at the Maritime Hotel, which had been a dance hall for sailors. But we turned it into an R & B club, and somebody showed up from Decca and we made a couple of singles. That was with the group Them. The song "Gloria" came from listening to those old blues records.

I got to the States by complete accident. This guy called Bert Berns came over. Phil Solomon was managing us at the time, and he brought Bert over to produce Them. He produced a few tracks, and then he had to go back, so we finished it on our own. But before Bert left he said, "I would really like to work with you guys again," and that's how we left it.

A couple of years later, somebody saw Bert and he said, "Oh, yeah, if you see Van, tell him I have my own record company, and I'd like to do something with him."

At the same time I was trying to get a solo thing together, and basically the interest from Bert was the first thing that had come through. I was waiting on someone else from another company to make up his mind when Bert said, "Why don't you come over and we'll cut a few things," and that was it. Six months later, Bert said, "Let's do some more," so I ended up somehow in New York working with Bert.

I was in Ireland when "Brown-Eyed Girl" started to happen. I never wanted to be commercial, and suddenly "Brown-Eyed Girl" was making me even more commercial. The people I was listening to never sold a lot of records. John Lee Hooker was never on the charts, so I was never in it from a commercial point of view. Other people expected things from my records, but I never did.

Like with *Astral Weeks*. I had been working on some songs just prior to that record, thinking that I wanted something different this time. I actually recorded some of the songs that eventually wound up on *Astral Weeks* for Bert. I did one album for Bert, and then for a second he said, "You know we have to get you back into the studio," that sort of thing. So I played him a tape, me on guitar, and he said, "Great, this is what we should do." Just like that. He said, "We'll fill out a little here, put that there." Well, I showed up for the session, and forty people are there—four guitar players, four keyboard players, five singers, four entire rhythm sections. It was bizarre.

We struggled through that one, but the songs just didn't work out. *Astral Weeks* became what it was because everything was stripped away. Just me and guitar, and we went from there.

There is one thing I don't understand about *Astral Weeks*. Of all the records I have ever made that one is definitely not rock. You could throw that record at the wall, take it to music colleges, analyze it to death. Nobody is going to tell me that it is a rock album. Why they keep calling it one I have no idea.

People think I'm eccentric, cranky. If I'm eccentric because I've never been into mainstream things, then I am eccentric. I've never been comfortable working live, and I'm still not. I was never able to adjust to it because when I started and we played dances, you would finish a couple of songs and just walk through the audience and say, "Hi, how you doing?" No stuff about being a star.

When I played clubs, same thing—you walk through the audience, have a drink with some people from the audience. Nothing about you're up here, and they're down there. So this is the environment I came from, where everyone was the same. I was always more music-oriented and less star-oriented, which is why I've never been comfortable on big stages in big halls.

I always related more to what the jazz people were doing. Louis Armstrong said, "You never play a thing the same way twice." That's me, but people expect you to play it the way they know it, and I can't do that. I'm not the same way twice. If I just had a hassle with somebody, there is no way I'm going to paint a smile on my face and say, "Good evening, ladies and gentlemen. And now for my latest record." That is not where I'm at. If I had a hassle, I'm not going to be feeling good. The next night I may be happy. I just take it as it comes. I can't turn it on.

It is like how people perceive me. It's all an illusion, all about how others project an image on you. John Lennon said it in his last couple of interviews. He said, "This is a load of shit. This is not how it really is. I will tell you the way it was, but nobody wants to hear it."

I don't think I will ever mellow out. I think if you mellow out, you get eaten up. You become like a commodity. So I don't think I will mellow out. It is not in my blood.

Alice Cooper

○ ○ ○

The kid from Arizona opened the door for every shock rocker everywhere. Alice faced hostility and indifference, but he showed that theatricality could work in pop.

○ ○ ○

The weirdest thing about our band was that it was made up of athletes. Alice Cooper, the sickest band in America, we were all four-year lettermen.

We lived on Kool-Aid and Wheaties that we stole from stores. And then we'd mix the two together. We all lived together, seven guys in one room. One guy in the band was really good-looking. He would invite a girl over, and when he took her into the bedroom, the rest of us would go through her purse and take, like, five dollars. We weren't major thieves. We just took enough to keep the band together.

The thing that really turned it all around for us was when we realized we were not into peace and love. We were more sensational. We were the *National Enquirer* of rock 'n' roll.

We finally got an audition with Frank Zappa, and we showed up at his house at seven o'clock in the morning. We got there, set up outside of this log cabin he had, and we started playing. We were dressed like we dressed every day—chrome pants, hair, makeup, everything—and Zappa liked us. He was our hero. Knowing him was like knowing the Beatles. He was so straight. It was shocking. When Zappa said he was going to sign us to Bizarre Records, we were just elated.

Then we met Shep Gordon at a party at the Landmark Hotel. Everybody was living there—Hendrix, the Airplane. Shep had just moved out, and he said, "I'm a manager. I'll be your manager."

We said, "Great." I knew immediately that Shep was the guy. He was as outrageous as we were.

The night that really did it for us was the night of Lenny Bruce's birthday party at the Cheetah. There were 6,000 people there. We went on last, after the Paul Butterfield Blues Band. Everybody was on acid, everybody was into peace and love, and here we come looking like *A Clockwork Orange*. We started out with the theme from "The Patty Duke Show," and we scared everybody out of the building. It was as if somebody said, "There's a bomb in the building." We cleared the building in three songs.

I guess we represented something people hadn't thought about for years. Even hippies hated us, and it's hard to get a hippie to hate anything. But the next time we played, there were maybe 1,000 people there. It became the "in" thing in L.A. to come see Alice Cooper and then walk out.

Our official "coming out" party at the Ambassador Hotel was totally outrageous. Nobody knew who Alice Cooper was. The Ambassador thought Alice Cooper was a debutante from Pasadena.

"Eighteen" became our license to kill. Probably the most dangerous thing anybody ever did in the business was give Alice Cooper a single. It gave us confidence.

We played the Toronto Peace Festival with John Lennon, Yoko Ono, and the Doors. While we were on, somebody from the audience threw a chicken on stage. I'm from Detroit, I'm not a farm kid. I figured a chicken has wings, it'll fly away. So I took the chicken and threw it and it didn't fly. It went into the audience. Blood everywhere. The next day, everybody's reading, "Alice Cooper rips chicken's head off, drinks blood." Zappa called me. He said, "Whatever you did, keep doing it." To this day, wherever I'm booked the ASPCA is usually there, too.

I used to be terrified of snakes. One time someone had a boa constrictor backstage. I realized that the snake is perhaps the strongest image in the world. I thought, what if I bring it on stage and sing a song with it wrapped around my arm? The next thing you know, the snake is fifteen feet long, the biggest snake anybody's ever seen.

We lost the snake at the Marriott Hotel in Knoxville, Tennessee. They had barely finished the hotel, and we were staying there. I put the snake in the bathtub to let it swim, and I closed the door. I got up the next morning and the snake was gone. There was no lid on the toilet, and the snake had gone into the toilet and down into the pipes.

I called the manager. "My snake is gone." Workmen start tearing down walls, and they don't even want to find this snake. Well, they couldn't find it, so I had to go out and buy another one for the next show. I knew the snake would survive for a while in the pipes. They only eat once a month.

Well, now it's two weeks later, and we're in another town, and I pick up a paper and I read about how the snake came up in Charley Pride's bathroom. Apparently, he walked into his bathroom at the Marriott and there was a boa constrictor coming out of his toilet. He must have turned white.

One of the best things that ever happened to us was getting banned in England on our very first tour. They hadn't even seen us and they banned us. On the flight over I sat next to an old woman, probably eighty-five years old. She says to me, "I've been traveling from Beirut. I want to go to sleep. Please don't wake me when the food comes." I said OK.

We land in London and I go to wake her up. She doesn't wake up. She's dead. Died in her sleep. I get off the plane, they pull the body out, and the people say, "We understand that a lady died sitting next to you."

I said, "Yes," and they go, "Wow," and start checking for holes in her throat.

Robert Hilburn

o o o

One of the most respected and long-lasting music critics in America, he excites delight with the raves and anger with the slams. Bob manages to deal with reactions to both.

o o o

I went to the *Los Angeles Times* and told them they had nobody writing about pop music. At the time they had a guy who was a publicist writing a Sunday column, and they finally got rid of him because he really didn't know about music. He did a review of Alice Cooper that said, "She can't sing."

Pete Johnson took over the column and at the same time worked on the copy desk. I went to Pete and Charles Champlin and asked if I could do some stories they might not be interested in doing themselves. I did Joe South and Gordon Lightfoot and some country stories, and I got tagged a country writer. Chuck once asked me to do a story on a rodeo performer because he was country and western.

But I felt real secure about pop music. Once I started writing, it was real humbling to think people were going to read this review. What if I'm wrong? There would be bands I'd go see and people would be applauding, and I didn't think they were so good. So who was right? There were two things that helped set up my philosophy. One was getting phone calls from publicists every day asking me to do stories on certain people. How do you decide who you do a story on? They'd tell me the person has a Number 1 record. Does that mean I only do stories on people with Number 1 records?

Secondly, I always tried to write about people who mattered, not only now but far into the future. I used to go see bands that really left no impression on me, but the audience loved it. So I told it how it was, and I was always nervous about giving a negative review because what happens if I'm wrong? I'd be unfair to the artist and I'd look like a fool to the public. But after my reviews came out, the sun still shone, the radio still played, and the records still sold.

There is still some fan inside of me, to support certain acts. I try not to get to know acts because then you can get emotionally involved. I try to keep as few friends in the business as possible. I try never to go backstage. There are some you invariably get to know down the line, like John Lennon and Bruce Springsteen, and you want to know more about them. If you are convinced that they are great artists, it's OK to sacrifice some of the objectivity.

A review is entertainment for the person who is a regular reader. If you go to a concert, it's fun to pick up a newspaper the next day to find out what this jerk in the paper said about the show. It actually amazes me that someone won't buy a record because of a review I've written.

Then you have managers that say, "You're killing my artist with your review." It's really the artist that has to kill the career. If you're a fan, you're a fan no matter what the guy in the paper says. Music is more passionate than movies. You live for a certain artist and grow up with that artist. The review may have tremendous effect on the ego of the artist, and maybe somebody in the industry gets upset, but what I'm doing is trying to respond to the music and have a certain integrity.

Record companies call me up and ask if I have a vendetta against their artists. I'm not even conscious of what label the artist is on. It does upset me, though, when there's an artist I like, for example, Elvis Costello, who played four nights at the Beverly Theater and got annoyed with my review for the first night. It was supposed to be a "greatest hits" show, and I said in my review that it wasn't very different and I was disappointed that he didn't do more material. Of course, he comes back with, "Well, if it isn't Springsteen, you'll never get a good review from Hilburn."

I'm just a guy who likes music and writes for a newspaper. In a strange, strange way I'm trying to pay back these artists who make this music I love. I'm trying to be fair to them. I'm saying, "These guys are important and what they're doing is meaningful."

I think what gave me confidence about being a critic was in the fifties, when I first heard Elvis on a Mexican station doing "Baby Let's Play House." This was before "Heartbreak Hotel." I said, "Who is this guy?" I came from Louisiana so I liked country and blues. So then I hear this guy on a country station doing blues. To me, he was the best thing I'd ever heard in music.

After I became a writer, Elton John and David Bowie were the two artists I was hip to way before everybody. I really underestimated Billy Joel commercially. I thought he was a copy of Elton. I thought Billy Joel's "Piano Man" was a copy of Harry Chapin. John Cougar Mellencamp was arrogant in the beginning, but now I think he's found true nerve within himself. Maybe he was influenced by Springsteen. But his has been a big turnaround for an artist.

John Prine was always one of my favorites before anyone knew him. Unfortunately, he never really made it big. I remember calling Paul Colby at the Bitter End in New York to tell him about an act I thought he should book at the club. He holds the phone out and I hear John Prine playing onstage. Paul then gets back on the phone and tells me I'm not the only one who recognizes talent in the early stages.

If I were writing in the fifties, I would want to write about Elvis and Jerry Lee Lewis. I wouldn't want to write about Georgia Gibbs and the Crew Cuts. I'm trying to find those five, six, seven people for each generation. Springsteen has gotten bigger and bigger as the years go by. What I try to do is point out who the artists are going to be ten years from now. U2 and Springsteen are bands that will be here forever. There's a purpose and a philosophy behind my reviews—to find the artists that will be around for a long time.

Russ Regan

○ ○ ○

A great promotion executive, A & R man, and finally a pretty good record company chief, Russ championed the California sound and has been doing it for twenty-five years.

○ ○ ○

In 1959 I teamed up with Bobby Plaisted, probably the dirtiest man I have ever been around. He never bathed. But I put up with him because he was talented. We wrote a song in '59 called "Happy Reindeer" by Dancer, Prancer and Nervous. Big Christmas record. Probably the last big Christmas record.

I started moving along, label to label—Shasta, Canadian American, and Linda Scott with "Every Little Star." Lots of little labels and then I got the chance to work with Berry Gordy. Big opportunity for me, a really great turning point in my life. Berry is one of the few geniuses in this business. The guy was no accident. But the guy who really broke me into being a promotion man was Sonny Bono.

Let's not kid ourselves, the promotion man has a lot of power. I would say, "These six suck, these four are potential hits." You had to work the entire station, all the jocks, which meant a lot of hanging out. I hung out a lot. I was a bachelor. No hours, long hours, no time limits, no boundaries.

I didn't get directly involved in payola, but I did take guys to Vegas. I would fix them up with girlfriends. I was a bachelor so I had a stable of girls. But I was never given any money to give money. My payola was more like dinnerola. Maybe, if a guy was short at the crap table, I would say, "Here's fifty," something like that. But that's not payola. Let's face it, payola has always been around in our business. But you hear about payola in Congress, too.

I learned the record business at Warner Brothers. I knew the street record business from my days in distribution, but I didn't know the basics about running a record company—corporate, administrative-type things—until I got to Warner's.

It was during my time at Warner's that I found "That's Life" for Frank Sinatra. A guy named Kelly Gordon, who got busted and since then died, brought the song to me. He was a co-writer and he wanted a record deal. I listened to it and I said, "My God, this is a hit for Frank Sinatra." I looked at Kelly and I said, "How badly do you want to sing this song?" He wanted to know what I meant. I said, "What if Frank Sinatra records it?"

He said, "Here it is. Take it and run." Then he said, "But I do want you to know it's already been recorded by O. C. Smith on CBS." I told him it didn't matter, and I took the record into Mo Ostin. Mo listened to it, called his secretary in, and said, "Thelma, get ABC Messenger and send this over to Frank."

Three days later, Mo buzzes me and says Frank loves it, he's going to record it. I freaked out. I don't give a damn who Sinatra punches out. I loved him then and I still love him. And it was a big thrill for me when "That's Life" became a hit. It went to Number 4 on the pop charts, and Number 1 R & B.

Mo and I and Sonny Burke flew up to Vegas to see Sinatra, and God, was that a great night. I lost $600 at the blackjack table. We had a ringside seat. We were sitting with Frank's then-wife, Mia Farrow, and his daughter, Tina. He came out and did "That's Life." People literally stood up and cheered. What a thrill.

Elton John will always be an interesting story for me. I used to hang around Martoni's, an Italian restaurant in Hollywood. I was single and there was a lot of action there. Martoni's was a place to promote records and pick up girls. But later on, when I became general manager of Uni Records, I couldn't go to Martoni's like I did. So I started having breakfast at the Continental Riot House, which is how we referred to the Hyatt House.

I was eating breakfast there with a bunch of guys one morning when my boss, Ned Tannen, called and said, "You won't make a quarter of a dollar at the Continental Riot House. Get your ass into the office." He knew where to find me.

But I was having breakfast with a guy named Lenny Hodes, who worked for Dick James, and Lenny says, "I have some masters on a guy. I really love him. Will you please listen to him?"

I finished breakfast, took the tapes, went into the office, and didn't listen to the tapes until about five that evening. Elton had a thing called "Lady Samantha" that I loved, but I didn't think Elton John was a superstar. *Empty Sky* was the first album I took on, but it's not one of his greater albums. Before we could put out *Empty Sky*, here comes the *Elton John* album produced by Gus Dudgeon and arranged by Paul Buckmaster. It was a work of art. Everybody loved it except Mike Maitland whose comment was that it was overproduced and too slick. Definitely took the wind out of my sails. How am I going to launch the artist if the man who controls the bucks doesn't like it?

Luckily, I had developed a relationship with Lenny, and I asked him if he could get Dick James to put up some promotion dollars for Elton John to come to America. I said, "I would like to bring him to America and launch him at the Troubadour, which is where I launched Neil Diamond. And I will get Neil Diamond to introduce Elton John."

Lenny asked how much it would cost. I said, "Probably about ten thousand dollars." My plan was to get another $10,000 from my own company, shame them into it. Lenny said he would let me know.

The next day he got a telex from Dick James saying, "You got the money."

I called Mike Maitland and said, "Dick James is willing to put up ten thousand dollars to promote Elton John. We've got to match it."

Mike said, "Do you really think so?"

I said, "I really think so." It cost $20,000 to launch Elton John. We brought him here, Neil Diamond introduced him, and the rest is history. Elton exploded out of the Troubadour, but initially only in Los Angeles. He drifted into San Francisco, but the rest of the country didn't know anything about Elton John.

I went to San Francisco with Elton. I went to New York with Elton. I get to Philadelphia and someone calls me and says, "Do you have any idea how many records we've sold nationally? Eleven thousand."

I said, "Well, man, we're growing. It takes time."

He said, "Do you know what they're calling Elton John at the MCA tower? 'Regan's Folly.' " I turned purple.

I went to Elton's room and told him what was happening. He looked at me and said, "Tonight we're going to burn down the city of Philadelphia." He had a song called "Burn Down the Mission." Drove the audience hysterical. It was scary. People were hyperventilating. Elton practically had an orgasm on stage. A couple of days later "Your Song" came out. We put "Take Me to the Pilot" on the back for insurance. "Your Song" was a hit, Elton took off, and all of a sudden I was a hero.

Elton John

○ ○ ○

A great songwriter and even better performer. In the mid-seventies no artist was hotter on record or in arenas. The leveling of his popularity took its toll, but the man is one of the best.

○ ○ ○

I remember going to see Guy Mitchell once at the London Palladium. They used to have Saturday night shows at the Palladium, and Guy Mitchell was starting this one show, and at the end of his set, he took his sock off and whirled it around his head. I thought, "What a funny guy."

You know, I never forgot that, and maybe it accounts for why I would get so outrageous on stage, I don't know. I've always said that what I do on stage is a direct result of the mood I'm in. I mean, I get ovations because of the stage clothes I wear. Hopefully, I haven't been trapped by that because, really, there are so many other strings to my bow.

I've done talk shows in England, and they'd like it if I came on in an angel outfit. It's OK for the stage, but when sitting down talking to someone, you feel like a bit of a prat.

I never thought the outfits got in the way of the music. I did live my teenage years through my success years in my twenties. I never had the freedom to do that before, so I did it. With me, I'm afraid, I'm very excessive. If I do it, I do it to extreme excess.

I remember doing "The Henry Mancini Show," which was filmed at the Santa Monica Civic Auditorium, my segment of it, anyway. There's a very famous picture of me from that filming where I'm horizontal in the air, and I have on mauve tights and silver boots with stars. I had taken off eight outfits during just this one song, and the faces on the people in the audience were, like, "My God."

Of course, I wasn't always that way. That famous first night of mine at the Troubadour, the only thing I can remember is shaking hands with Quincy Jones's family. On the second night, Leon Russell was in the audience. Leon was my big idol at the time. With that silver hair of his, he was a startling-looking man. I knew he was in the audience, and I was petrified. I lost my voice during the next day, and he invited me up to his house, and I thought he was going to tie me up to a chair and say, "Listen, motherfucker, this is how you play piano."

But he was so nice. He gave me this gargling potion that I continue to use to this day. It's great for the voice.

Every artist who makes it big goes through a period where it seems they're invincible. We've seen it with Phil Collins, Bruce Springsteen, Madonna, Prince. It just seems like they can't fail. And then suddenly everything levels off. I knew it when it started happening to me. I was real tired. The *Blue Moves* album, which I think is one of my finest albums, certainly one of my most sophisticated albums, was not one of my most successful albums. I knew I was peaking. I knew it was time for someone else to take over. You have to be realistic about these things. I didn't want it to end, but I knew it had ended because I was physically drained. And because I was already involved with a football club in England, I didn't sit behind my locked gates at Windsor and sulk because Peter Frampton was selling 20 million albums.

It came at a time when people were fed up with me anyway. When Jim Croce died, John Lennon said to me, "You sell more records when you die than when you live. And with you, I hear so many of your records on the radio now that if you die, it will get so ridiculous I'll have to throw my fucking radio out the window." Very sick world we live in.

Looking back, though, if anybody ever said to me that I would make seventeen albums in six years, I'd tell them, "That's fucking ludicrous."

And for most of that time, we would go into the studio and not have any idea of a single. We never had any idea of a single. There was never any pressure to get a single out. We just went in and did an album, and the singles would emerge. Now, there's so much pressure to have a single that it changes your writing. I find it much harder to write under these circumstances. I don't think I was ever good when I went in trying to write a hit single.

But a lot of hit singles did come out of it, and a lot of them are lasting. "Your Song," I think, will always last. At least I'm not fed up with playing it. It's hard for me to choose the ones I like, because the ones I like aren't always the most popular.

I am only just beginning to realize how songs affect people. Stupid that it's taken me so long. I've always had periods in my life where certain records at certain times played a very strong role. The times when I'm really miserable, or not in love. Or times I was in love with someone, and it was really disastrous. I will play a particular song for that moment probably a million times. At certain times, "How Sweet It Is (to Be Loved by You)," "My Sweet Lord," and "Brown Sugar" have meant a great deal in my life. But for so long I never thought songs could be like that. And I'm a songwriter.

I guess I just want to be remembered as a good musician and a good writer of good songs. I'd like to keep improving my writing. When Frank Sinatra sang one of my songs at a concert—it was "Sorry Seems to Be the Hardest Word"—it was, for me, one of the highlights of my life. Good songs should last. A good one should last forever. "Just the Way You Are," by Billy Joel, is that sort of great song.

I have been incredibly lucky, really. I am a very happy man. I can't remember too much from 1970 to 1976 because there was so much stuff going on. The years just run into each other. But I think from 1970 onward, when I became Elton John, my life changed. I became much happier as a person when I took on Elton John. It became my real name and I could do things I wanted.

I am Elton John full-time now. I don't even think of myself as Reg Dwight anymore. But Reg might be surfacing again, I don't know. Maybe Reg will make an album, and he'll be the one putting songs out. There is still a lot to come out of me, and I do desperately want a platinum album again, but for now, I feel very fortunate to have lasted so long.

Paul Simon

o o o

Brilliant, intellectual, and sensitive, Paul's been universally admired for over twenty years. With Art Garfunkel he gave the world indelible memories. On his own he continues to surprise and win. He strummed and sang at his New York office during this talk, and he focused on the early influences.

o o o

My clear recollection of the first time I ever heard rhythm and blues was when I was listening to the Yankees, sitting on my father's lap. I'm a New York kid, so I am a Yankees fan. When I was at the peak of my passion for the Yankees, I was twelve years old. I would score the games as I listened to them on the radio. Ball one, strike three—that kind of thing.

The game would come on in the afternoon, and I would be on the back porch of my house in Queens getting my score card all set up. Pencil ready. I didn't want to miss a thing. The radio would be on a half hour, twenty minutes early, game wasn't on yet, but on that station was Martin Block and the Make-Believe Ballroom. The kind of popular music he was into I couldn't stand. It wasn't rock 'n' roll and I didn't like it. It was corny, grown-up music, but one day he says, "Now here is a record I'm getting lots of requests on, but I have to say this record is so bad that if it's a hit, I will eat it." And that record was "Gee," by the Crows. And I'm filling in Rizzuto, Coleman, and I realize, this is the first thing I've ever heard on his show that I liked. He said it was bad, but I liked it.

New York was a pool of sounds, but only one station was playing rock 'n' roll, the station Alan Freed was on. But he wasn't on every day of the week, only six days a week, so on Sunday, I would look for rock 'n' roll on the radio and the closest thing I could find to it was gospel, a church station. I had never heard gospel music, but it sounded kind of close to what Alan Freed was playing. It wasn't as good as the rock 'n' roll station, but with no other choice on Sunday it was good enough.

On the way to searching for it, I found a country music station coming out of New Jersey. The first country tune I remember hearing was "Jailhouse Now," by Webb Pierce. Hilariously funny and corny song.

Early rock 'n' roll drew from a lot of different elements, situations you would never find today with the rigid programming they have on radio. Today, if you have Johnny Cash, the Everly Brothers, and Elvis Presley, they'd be on a country station. Back then, those things were mixed into Top 40—Roy Orbison and Gene Vincent with groups like the Platters and Ruth Brown. Fats Domino, Jimmy Clanton, Frankie Lymon, it was all called rock 'n' roll, which made for a very rich musical era. Different sounds, different cultures.

Folk music was part of it, too. Pete Seeger singing in Spanish, the pure country of Woodie Guthrie, Joan Baez singing in different languages. So folk was another overlay on top of my first exposure.

Also, my father was a band leader. He had a band at Roseland for twenty-five years. He played on Saturday nights and Thursday afternoons, and the band that was on before him was a salsa band. So I was always interested in and exposed to a lot of different sounds.

I was in Paris in 1965, right before Simon and Garfunkel broke. I was roaming around Europe by myself, doing folk stuff. It was there I met Los Incas at a concert. I was booked, and they were booked, and that was the first time I had ever heard South American music. They gave me an album of their stuff, and "El Condor Pasa" was on the album. The Simon and Garfunkel record of "El Condor Pasa" was recorded over that preexisting track. So that's where it all comes from, and the notion was, if I liked the music, if it sounded good to me, it was popular. For me there was really no distinction between one culture and another.

I write in my head. I hear it all in my head. I think in terms of textures and sounds first. It has taken me all these years to realize that I don't get into writing a piece of music until it sounds right in my head. When I put those sounds down on tape, I begin rearranging them into some kind of harmonic pattern. Once I have the harmonic pattern, I improvise on it. I might go to the guitar to technically work out what scale I'm in. When everything is right, it comes out musical. If something is off with the harmony or the scales, then maybe the premise is off. Either I'm putting in an inappropriate melody, or I haven't constructed my textures properly.

Every time I've made a record that hasn't been a good record there is usually considerable lying going on. I think something may be wrong, but then I get misinformation. Other people whose opinions I have faith in say it's good. And because I don't know how to solve the problem I think I feel in my head, I keep going. Then I find out when the guy in the street says, "Boy, that is bad."

A lot of my lyric writing is instinct I can't explain. The truth is, I don't know why "Losing love is like a window to your heart" came out the way it did. I can't tell anyone why it comes. It just comes.

When I started doing music, music was in real danger. It's still in real danger. My theory is that every time the industry gets powerful and corporate thinking dominates what the music is, then the music really pales. There was a great burst of music in the mid-fifties, and it came from unknown artists and tiny labels. Columbia and RCA didn't want any part of it. They didn't think there was a market for it. They were thinking corporately. The people who were making the music weren't thinking about what was going to sell. And then, the first time the industry started to get a little cynical about it, that's when you had Fabian and Frankie Avalon. That was about teen idols, it wasn't about music, it was about image. The reaction to all that was the Beatles. Folk-rock came out of Greenwich Village. It was anticorporate, left wing.

I knew the minute I wrote, "Like a bridge over troubled water I will lay me down," that I had a very clear image. The whole verse was set up to hit that melody line. With certain songs you just know it.

When I was working on *Graceland*, I was thinking, "If I don't make this interesting, I will never get my generation to pay attention." They are not paying attention anymore to records. They were at a certain point, certainly around the time of *Bridge over Troubled Water*, but they no longer look to records to have their lives illuminated. They look to movies, or literature. I said, "Here is a group of people already attuned to the language of rock 'n' roll. They are used to listening to information, but they've stopped listening to the music because in their minds it's no longer saying anything to them." I thought, "If I don't make this record interesting, nobody's going to listen to it."

Of the people I know, no one says, "I can't wait for so-and-so's next album." It used to be people couldn't wait for the next Beatles album, or the next Stones album. So with *Graceland* I thought, "This is really it. If I don't make this really interesting, then, well, maybe it will sell a half a million albums, but I won't have any effect on the thinking."

Lou Rawls

○ ○ ○

A street boy with a seductive style, Lou ran a series of talk-along, sing-along hit records and remains a cabaret favorite, with some highly identifiable commercials as well.

○ ○ ○

I lived down the street in Chicago from the 430 Club on 43rd Street. The 430 Club was one of those joints that had a window that you could look in, and as a kid that's exactly what I would do. B.B. King played there, Muddy Waters, Johnny Otis, Little Esther Phillips, Dinah Washington.

If they didn't play the 430, or if they got bigger, we also had the Regal Theater, which was over on 47th Street. The Regal had live stage shows, five a day. I would go there on a Saturday morning and stay all day.

I started out singing gospel music with Sam Cooke. We formed our first teenage quartet in Chicago. He got his inspiration from people like Bill Kenny of the Ink Spots, people with high falsetto voices. Mine were more on the order of Joe Williams, Billy Eckstine, and Al Hibbler, guys with the rich, deep voices.

I was a religious singer, and I didn't sing any blues when I first started out because if I did, my mother would have killed me with a brick. She raised me, and she was the boss. You either danced to her music, or you didn't dance.

In the late fifties, I was on the road with Sam in a traveling show he had put together. He was hot then with "You Send Me." I was doing backgrounds for him, as I had been doing on all his records.

One of the great music trivia questions has always been, "Who was that other person singing on 'Bring It on Home to Me?' " It was me.

So I'm on the road with Sam and Bumps Blackwell. Bumps was this man with a golden finger for finding talent. He discovered Little Richard, he discovered Quincy Jones and Johnny Otis. He was a great guy, and we had put this revue together, and Sam and I were leaving St. Louis after a show one night, heading to Arkansas or Mississippi or one of those places, and we were on a narrow road, and it was raining, and Eddie the driver was speeding.

I'm in the back seat sleeping, and we come over this hill, and there's this big truck sitting in the middle of this road. Eddie hits the brakes, the front end dips and goes around the back end of the truck. The bar on top of the convertible catches me across my head and gives me a brain concussion. I was in a coma for five days. I was even pronounced dead.

When you're in the business of traveling around with other black acts, you get to know everybody on the R & B circuit because all of us traveled the same roads, the same circuit, stayed in the same motels 'cause there weren't that many we could stay in.

In some towns, they didn't have any hotels for us, so we'd call up the local minister and we'd have him say that we were members of his church so other members would open up their homes to us. And that was nice because you would wake up in the morning and smell those fresh biscuits and bacon.

After the accident, it took me about a year to get myself back together. I started going into small jazz joints around Los Angeles, like Pandora's Box, the coffeehouse on Sunset.

Preston Epps, the guy who had a hit with a thing called "Bongo Rock," had me come over there to sing. The guy who owned Pandora's then asked me to do some singing on weekends. He said he'd give me ten dollars a night plus all the pizza and cappuccino I could eat for free. The pizza was terrible and the cappuccino tasted like dish water, but I was making thirty dollars over a weekend, so I figured, "What the hell."

One night Nick Venet, the producer, comes in. And then Herb Alpert and Lou Adler. I'm beginning to meet people. Nick tells me he wants me to do an audition. He says he thinks he can do something. So I went out and cut an audition tape and about a week later Nick and a few other people took me to dinner at the old Villa Capri on Selma.

We sat in a booth that they tell me Nat Cole used to sit in all the time, and I'm sitting there answering all these questions about my aspirations and what not, and I wind up signing with Nick, and that's how I started making records.

After a while, I began spending time with Sam Cooke again at an office he had at Warner Brothers. And there was this place right near Warners called Aldo's, where the hot disc jockeys, like B. Mitchell Reed, and all the promotion men would meet during the day.

It was nothing for the promotion men to keep the disc jockeys in cars and deep freezes and televisions, and fur coats for the little lady.

That was the way business was done, and all of them did it until the Man stepped in and busted Alan Freed for payola.

Sam died in '64, and it was two years after that that I broke through with "Love Is a Hurtin' Thing." Because of that, I was suddenly opening for Judy Garland in Vegas. I played the Latin Casino in Cherry Hill, places like that.

Then in '65, I started doing my monologues and that brought on a whole new thing for me. The years of working in small joints, singing my butt off, I would always try to think of ways to get the audience's attention. So I got on stage one night and instead of singing, I started talking and making up stories that related to the song. Funny thing, everyone got quiet. They were listening.

The first one I made up, and I made it up on the spot was "South Side Hustler Blues." It was all about pimps and hustlers and Cadillacs and silk suits and people with patent-leather hairdos. It was easy for me to talk about those things because I knew the subject so well. My hometown, the South Side of Chicago, where I was born and raised, was loaded with people like that.

Jac Holzman

o o o

He started Elektra Records with a love for the music and an IQ very high on the charts. The company's origins and success make for textbook reading in the music business.

o o o

Elektra Records started with $600 of my bar mitzvah money and another $600 that I got a friend to put up. His $600 bought the records that were eventually returned, and my $600 went for the Magnacord tape recorder. I had one Magnacord and an old hammerhead style Electro-Voice microphone. That was my recording studio, a tape machine and a microphone strapped onto the back of my motorscooter. I would go off and record in people's homes. The cost for a recording session was limited to tape, and that was generally around twenty dollars.

The company was a storefront on Bleecker Street in the Village. One of the reasons why the company started with an *E* was because of a lesson I learned from my uncle who was in the scrap materials business. I had worked for him one summer in Cincinnati, and I noticed when the accounts payable were done we started with the A's and worked our way back. If there was any money left by the time we got to the W's, maybe they got their money. I mentioned this to my uncle one day, and he said, "That's why we're called AA Cincinnati Waste Materials, because it gets us up there first." I decided that was a lesson worth holding on to.

I never expected any money out of the record business. Nobody did. I mean, you never paid advances. The first five years of Elektra it never cost me more than forty-five dollars to make a record. If we sold 500 or 1,000 of them, it was OK. We never printed more than 250 at a time anyway. And we hung on, we just hung on, and we were able to generate enough money to keep going. Plus what I was earning by installing hi-fi systems. I picked up money wherever I could. I had a little record shop. Whatever I took in went right back into Elektra.

For the first five years the company consisted of nobody but me. The music in the early fifties was bland beyond belief. Nothing really lasted from that period with the possible exception of jazz and Johnny Mathis.

Then in 1956 my wife, Nina, joined me. I got her to leave *Dance* magazine, where she was earning all of fifty-five dollars a week, and come with me for no increase in pay. After that at least she didn't have to ask me what my day at the office was like.

I never had a plan. The only thing I had was a hope for the future and the thought that if I'm observant, intelligent, and energetic, one day I'm going to be lucky. I'm going to be standing in the right place at the right time.

I guess I was fairly horrified at Elvis Presley in 1954. I mean, in those days the choice was either to watch the army–McCarthy hearings on a TV set I trotted into the office, or listen to the radio, which was filled with a lot of Elvis Presley, and I didn't much like him at the time. It took me another two or three years before I got religion on the subject of Elvis. For a long time it didn't seem like real music to me.

Eclectic folk music was more my music of choice. In 1955 I ran across Josh White, who had been blacklisted for years. In talking with Josh and going over his history it was pretty clear he was having a twenty-fifth anniversary, only there wasn't a twenty-fifth–anniversary album because nobody would record him. So we put together an album called *The Story of John Henry*, which was a collection of a lot of different songs with similar stories under a light narration, and it did really well. It sold about 10,000 copies, which gave us enough money to pay ourselves and some of our bills. It also helped move us into the pop/folk era.

And then came Theodore Bikel, who was introduced to me at a party. He was an actor who was doing his first play on Broadway, a man with a rich vocabulary and material in many different languages. He had spent many years in Palestine, and I always wanted to do an album of Israeli folk songs, so we did just that, an album of Israeli folk songs sung by Theodore Bikel. Theo was Elektra's first major artist.

As we got into the sixties, there was an excitement around that hadn't been seen before. Suddenly people were hanging out at places like the Kettle of Fish, which was somewhere you'd go to find out where the action was. Albert Grossman would be there, Richard and Mimi Fariña, if they were in town. Or you'd go check out the Gaslight, and then the Bitter End. And you would attend all these places hoping to find somebody. Of course, you were there and so was every other record company person. The thing was, you just tried to get there first.

The big advantage in those days, or just prior to those days, was that you could find somebody like Judy Collins in 1960 and watch her a bit before signing her. You could talk to her, but you didn't have to make a commitment right away.

I was told about Judy by Bob Gibson, who was one of those pivotal figures in popular folk music. He was connected to a lot of people, and in his together moments he was as sweet a man as you could find. He was at Newport in 1959 when he brought an unknown Joan Baez to the stage and watched as she caused a sensation. I missed out on Joan. Grossman got a hold of her quickly and made a fast deal with Maynard Solomon at Vanguard. I always felt somewhat disadvantaged and second-class about not having somebody who I thought was as exquisite a singer as Joan Baez.

So, I was looking around for my Joan Baez, and it turned out to be Judy. I produced Judy's first album, and then co-produced with Mark Abramson for a period of years, until the third album. The third album was when Judy moved away from the traditional songs and into the area of the singer/songwriter. That was a marked departure for her and the company, and it was really the beginning of Elektra breaking out into the big time.

Judy Collins

o o o

She's been a lady of great style with a devoted following for many years. Never a rocker and somewhat on her own track, she possesses a crystal voice and impeccable taste in song selection.

o o o

I came to folk music from a background of classical music. I was trained as a classical pianist so that by the time they were singing "Earth Angel" and "Rock around the Clock" at my high school dances, I was at home playing Mozart.

The other thing that called to me was theater music. My father's favorite songs were songs that I eventually recorded with an orchestra, along with "Send In the Clowns," "City of New Orleans," and "Houses." I began in 1966 to make those eclectic combinations that continue to be the thing people remember about me.

In a way, it's made it tougher for me to be identified as a certain kind of singer. I'm harder to define in terms of songs because I'll do a Broadway song, a Steve Goodman song, one from a classical writer, and a country song from Hugh Prestwood, all in one album. Eclectic groupings please me the most.

I am fortunate because a number of very fine writers have crossed my path at a time before they became famous, writers who have written songs which seem to fit me like a glove. Case in point would be Joni Mitchell's song "Both Sides Now," which nobody would call a folk song if they looked at it musicologically.

Also people like Randy Newman and Leonard Cohen. I was fortunate enough to hear one of Leonard's very first songs, "Suzanne," an extraordinary song that has almost a meditative quality to it. Leonard brings in that European influence, which is part of my background. He reaches for lyric ideas and musical ideas that are unusual for an American singer.

And it's largely because of these fine writers that people, remarkably, started answering my phone calls.

Of all the stories about all the songs I've recorded, "Send In the Clowns" offers the most interesting example of how one can sing a song differently every time without ever fully comprehending the true meaning of the lyrics.

The song was about two years old when a friend of mine said, "You have to go see this Hal Prince show, A Little Night Music, because there's this great song in the show, and maybe you should think about recording it."

My problem was, Sinatra had already done it, and when Sinatra does a song, it automatically becomes his version. I think he has "the" version of almost every song he's ever recorded. But when I heard him sing "Send In the Clowns," I knew immediately that it was OK for me to do it. I don't know, I just sensed that there was a space for me in that song. I felt it, and so I did it. And it's funny, the song was passed on by a couple of people who used to look for songs for me. They said, "A song from a show? Oh, Judy will never sing that."

But as soon as I put the needle down on that song, I never bothered playing the rest of the score. I just called Hal Prince and told him how in love with the song I was.

I had no idea what the lyrics meant. Every time I sing it, I sing it differently. Stephen Sondheim's idea of it is equally puzzling. He doesn't know why it works, nor do I think he thinks it's a very good song.

"A Horse with No Name" is another example of a song coming to me in a strange way. A friend of mine called me, a woman who lives in England, a wonderful writer, and she said, "I was driving down to my house in Bridgehampton and I heard this song on the radio."

She repeats part of the lyric, and says it sounds like Neil Young, and it's a hit. I say, "It was a hit." This is years after the song was a hit here.

And she says, "Well, you should do it anyway." And it piqued my interest in the song again. It's a feminine song, you know. I think "Send In the Clowns" is a feminine song, as well. I can't tell you why I say that, but I do believe both of these songs have a mysterious feminine quality about them.

You have to have a certain sense about a song, almost a chemical interaction with the piece of material. Another writer I have that with is Hugh Prestwood. Another one is Amanda McBroom, who wrote "The Rose." I was always indifferent to Bette Midler's version, so the time has probably come for me to do "The Rose." It's a very strong piece of material.

People often ask me how I find writers. I dig, I ask, I listen, I look. Sometimes they come through people I hire to find them. Sometimes someone will say, "Have you heard about so-and-so?" When I get to know a writer, I'm never bashful. I get on the phone and ask, "What have you written lately?"

Mostly I listen. And because I do, I think I've been lucky. I would love to be called a renaissance singer, a fortunate woman who has been unique enough not to fall into any one particular category.

Bill Medley

○ ○ ○

Bill's the Righteous Brother with the deep voice, the one who opened the sensational "You've Lost That Lovin' Feeling." They sounded black and had some classic hits.

○ ○ ○

In my high school choir I was the first tenor, the highest male voice in school. I was also five-three, and in one year I grew seven inches and went from a legitimate first tenor to a legitimate baritone/bass. The combination of what my voice became and my love for Little Richard, Chuck Berry, and Ray Charles probably accounts for me singing the way I do.

I've always said, "If my sinuses ever cleared up, I'd probably be out of the business."

I grew up in Orange County. So did Bobby Hatfield. In the fifties, Orange County had two black radio stations, and Bobby and I would always be trying to get them in without the interference.

Orange County was ultra-white. Pat Boone and Gale Storm were having hits with Little Richard and Fats Domino tunes, which really upset me and Bobby. Even though Pat Boone is a friend and a wonderful guy, in my opinion he wasn't a rock 'n' roll singer. Little Richard was a rock 'n' roll singer, in my opinion the greatest singer I had ever heard in my life.

Later on, when Bobby and I were doing the TV show "Shindig," Little Richard was on, and I can remember being freaked out when I ran up to him and told him he was my idol, and he said, "Are you kidding? I listen to all of your records."

Anyway, I was raised in Santa Ana, Bobby was raised in Anaheim. He had a little combo and I had a little combo, and eventually we got together. Now in Orange County, no white kids sang R & B, much less sounded black.

We idolized Don and Dewey, who were real big in California. To us, they were like two Little Richards. So we ended up doing a lot of their songs and a lot of Ray Charles songs in this one club where we worked called John's Black Derby.

A friend of mine out of Garden Grove, Ray Maxwell, who had started Moonglow Records, came into the club one night and heard this one song I had written called "Little Latin Lupe Lu." He said, "Why don't you go and record that?"

Ray was just a local guy, he didn't have anything happening, and we said OK. We were going to do it under the name of the Paramours, but some black guys from the El Toro marine base always referred to us as the Righteous Brothers, which meant we were their good friends. So we became the Righteous Brothers.

Well, we recorded "Little Latin Lupe Lu," and it didn't become a hit. We're then working over at the Rendezvous Ballroom in Balboa, fronting a band, making fifty dollars a week, thinking that maybe somehow we'd get to Las Vegas and become a lounge act, when some kids start coming up to us and telling us how much they like "Little Latin Lupe Lu."

We told them to go to their record store and buy it. But the people in the record store didn't even know what it was, so we took the record and put it in record stores ourselves, and then sent the kids out to buy it. We weren't trying to make it a hit or anything, but then in one of the stores in town, like 1,500 kids went in and bought the record.

Now KRLA calls the store and wants to know what's happening. The store says, "Well, we sold 1,500 copies of this song by the Righteous Brothers."

Of course, KRLA never heard of us, but they ask for the record, and they begin playing it as background music while they're plugging some record hop. Suddenly people start calling in wanting to know the record they're playing in the background.

I remember KFWB not playing it because it was too hard-rock. Of course, what they really meant was that it sounded black. Today, radio stations play those kinds of songs to soothe the elderly.

As a result of "Little Latin Lupe Lu," Phil Spector said he wanted not only to produce us, but also he wanted to lease the remainder of our contract on Moonglow. And he had a song he wanted us to hear.

So we went to the Chateau Marmont in Hollywood, and there was a piano, and Barry Mann and Phil Spector sang "You've Lost That Lovin' Feelin'." They had these little high, thin voices. To me, they sounded like the Everly Brothers.

I said, "Man, that's a great ballad, but it's for the Everly Brothers. We're rock 'n' rollers."

But Phil insisted that he teach it to us anyway. All we did was lower the tune to accommodate my baritone voice and it became like another song.

We were young, dumb, and full of cum. Twenty-four-year-old, very basic "Happy Days" kind of guys with regular families, and suddenly 10,000 and 12,000 are coming to watch the Righteous Brothers perform. The good news was that it was happening so fast and we were so busy that we didn't have a clue as to what was going on.

Our first indication of how big we were getting was when we actually got caught in traffic on the way to our own show.

We had no idea until maybe 1980 the kind of impact the Righteous Brothers had on other singers, or for that matter, the impact "You've Lost That Lovin' Feelin' " had on people's lives.

We always felt like we were the tool. "Lovin' Feelin' " was Barry Mann and Cynthia Weil's song, which Phil produced and we sang. We never felt like creative geniuses. We just felt like pretty good rock 'n' roll singers who could get a point across and have a good time. The Righteous Brothers didn't have a lot of hit records, but our main strength was that the records of ours that were hits weren't just hits, they were killers.

Jimmy Webb

o o o

A great songwriter for a concentrated period, Jimmy then had a long dry spell. Fresh into Los Angeles from the Midwest, Jimmy's music was in demand by almost any artist not writing his or her own material.

o o o

Jim Messina was a year ahead of me at Colton High School. He had a band, Jim Messina and the Jesters, and I wanted so badly to have my own rock 'n' roll thing. Eventually, between my last year at Colton and my first year at San Bernardino Valley College, I got a group of four blond girls together called the Contessas. I don't know how we got the money together, but somehow we raised $3,000 and cut a record. I knew some guys at Motown, Hal Davis and Frank Wilson. They helped me set up the session and encouraged me to do arrangements. I did my first one in pencil on the living room floor.

My training was about listening. I listened to Teddy Randazzo's arrangement of "Goin' Out of My Head," in my opinion the greatest record ever made. That's how I learned to write, by listening.

My colleagues don't particularly approve of the way I go about it because I'm a song-title man. Give me a title and I'll give you a song. People sometimes perceive that as shallow and insincere, but it's my handle on the form.

My first royalty-paying song was a song I wrote for Motown, for a Supremes Christmas album. It was called "My Christmas Tree," which wasn't the most unique title in the world, but it did deliver $360 that semester, and it did prove to me that I could actually turn a song into the green stuff.

Johnny Rivers was sort of like my mentor. He took me under his wing when I moved to Los Angeles from Oklahoma. I stayed at his house for a while. He took very good care of me. Later on, David Geffen bought that same house, and Jackson Browne sort of developed under David's wing. It was almost like an apprentice system. It was nice to be able to have an older brother in the business, as it were, and Johnny was that for me.

My problem was, I loved rock 'n' roll. I really loved the Rolling Stones. I'm one of their top fans ever. When I did the Thelma Houston album *Sunshower*, I did "Jumpin' Jack Flash." Right in the middle of the song I put in a Stravinsky string passage. This is the kind of thing that drives my friends crazy. They say, "What are you doing?"

And I say, "Exploring music. Taking it as far as I can." I really don't like to repeat myself. If my life has any story, that's it. Certainly my life would have been more financially rewarding if I'd just done what I was supposed to do all the time, or what was expected. A Stravinsky string passage in "Jumpin' Jack Flash"—those are the kind of mistakes I like to make, important ones.

You see, I had created a kind of middle-class, middle-of-the-road, middle-America persona for myself because those were the kinds of acts that were covering my music. When I realized what was happening to me, I panicked. I remember a deal I could have had at Caesar's Palace. They were going to pay me $40,000 a week to play "MacArthur Park" and "By the Time I Get to Phoenix." All I had to do was come out onstage before the headliner, play a couple of songs, and they were going to pay me $40,000 a week. That was a lot of money then, and it's a lot of money now. I thought about it for a while, and then I called my agent and told him I wasn't going to do it. I just couldn't play Caesar's Palace. That would have been the final nail in the coffin.

When I found out early in 1968 that KHJ had been forced into the full-length version of "MacArthur Park," that was probably the best moment for me in the sixties. They had originally said they wouldn't play it unless we edited it. We said, "OK, don't play it." We stood firm, and three or four days later they started playing it, all seven minutes and twenty-one seconds.

The song is about a girlfriend of mine. It's really simple. You associate a place with a person. You spend a lot of time there with that person, and when the relationship ends, you do a lot of thinking about that place. That's what "MacArthur Park" is all about. I used to go there and have lunch. That's where the cake comes from, "Sitting in a park on a bench eating cake." The image is, the rain comes and the whole thing is going, or melting, and then it's gone.

Richard Harris jumped right into the song with both feet. I hadn't seen him in years because of a misunderstanding. I never understood particularly why we stopped talking to each other. I think it was over a Rolls-Royce he was supposed to give me if "MacArthur Park" went Top 10 in the United States.

He promised me a Phantom 5 Rolls-Royce that had once belonged to the queen of England. Well, when the record went Top 10, he didn't want to give me the car. He wanted to give me another Rolls-Royce. But I didn't want another Rolls-Royce. I wanted his Rolls-Royce. I loved him, I adored him so much. To have had the other car just wouldn't have meant as much to me. I wasn't coming from greed, but from me wanting to covet something that belonged to him because of this tremendous admiration I had for him.

Anyway, I don't know if that was it, but I suppose that started it, and for years we didn't speak. But we did get together not long ago, and we did hug and kiss.

Graham Nash

o o o

He's been part of music history with two of the best bands ever—the Hollies and Crosby, Stills and Nash. Through it all, Graham seemed to radiate dignity and style in an era when neither was much in vogue. Socially conscious, he spurs others on to participate in his causes and beliefs.

o o o

I remember going to a school dance and listening to the Everly Brothers do "Bye Bye Love." It paralyzed me. I had to stop what I was doing, which was walking across the dance floor. And I stopped because I was so shocked musically. Right at that moment, something inside of me said, "I want to make people feel what I feel at this moment."

Jumping ahead to the Hollies' music, it was, of course, a lot lighter than Crosby, Stills, Nash and Young. And the pressures were totally different. In fact, I can't remember much pressure with the Hollies. We were having too good a time. We were five guys who escaped from Manchester, in the north of England. We escaped from the cycle of doing what our fathers did, and what their fathers before them did. You know, work forty years, get a gold watch, and then die. Music saved our ass, so we never really succumbed to the pressure of "What do you do after you've had a Top 10 record?"

But in the late sixties, I changed as a person. In '67, in America, I met Mama Cass. She turned me on to grass. I started smoking a lot, I started to get more introspective, which was one of the reasons why I was attracted to Crosby. He didn't live under the surface. He was right out there, on the surface, telling you exactly what he felt, even if you didn't ask him.

But it was partly through David that I began to realize that there was much more to music than creating a three-minute pop hit, which the Hollies were brilliant at. And so my experiments with dope opened my eyes to the fact that life was serious, that there was more to talk about than moon, June, and spoon in the back of the car. One of the reasons I left the Hollies was so I could play deeper music, deeper than the fluff the Hollies were doing. Naturally, the Hollies had their biggest hit, "Long Cool Woman (in a Black Dress)," after I left. Pissed me off, but it didn't surprise me. They had an uncanny knack at finding hit songs.

When I told people I was leaving the Hollies, they said, "You're leaving fame, fortune, and all these hits? Are you crazy?" But they didn't know one vital secret, I had sung with David and Stephen. I knew what it sounded like. I wasn't crazy at all.

When I met Crosby, it was at his house in Laurel Canyon. He was prone, on his back, rolling a joint. He had no idea who I was.

David was with the Byrds, and Stephen was with Buffalo Springfield, and one night we're riding in Stephen's Bentley. I'm sitting in the back, Stephen and David are in the front, and suddenly they look at each other, point to me in the back, and David says to Stephen, "OK, which one of us is going to steal him." Little did they know that I had totally had it with the Hollies by then.

I was very different from Crosby and Stills. Crosby was volatile, and Stephen was crazy. In our first year together, we spent probably eleven months together, twenty-four hours a day. We could sing our entire first album with just a couple of guitars. We would sit people down and we would say, "Listen to this," and we would rip off these ten songs, do them brilliantly and floor people. People would fall down. People like Paul Rothchild, Peter Fonda, Cass, John Sebastian, and all the Hollywood folk-rock people were knocked right on their ass.

But when we went out to play live, Stephen soon realized that David and I didn't play guitar well enough to play lead with him. So Stephen schemed with Ahmet Ertegun and Elliot Roberts to get Neil Young involved. Neil had just put out a solo album, and it wasn't exactly burning the charts down, and that's how we formed Crosby, Stills, Nash and Young.

Joni Mitchell and I were an item right around the time of Woodstock. We were in New York, and she was going to be doing "The Dick Cavett Show." Rumors about Woodstock kept multiplying and multiplying. First, we hear 20,000 people will be there. Then, my God, we hear 100,000! Joni wanted to go, and I said, "If you go, I can't guarantee that I can get you out of there and back to do the Cavett show," which was an important show at the time.

So Joni didn't go to Woodstock, and she was able to sing "Woodstock" based on information given to her by us and Sebastian.

I still wear a button on the lapel of my jacket that says, "I Do Not Remember Woodstock." Talking about Woodstock is like talking about the

Second World War. It was the first time I had ever been in a helicopter. About twenty or thirty feet from the ground, the back rotor blade stopped, the body of the helicopter started spinning, and the pilot wound up having to slam the thing into the ground. That's how Woodstock started for me. It was overwhelming.

I get a kick when people tell me how different *Deja Vu* sounds from our first album. David, Stephen, and I were in love with each other during the first album. Musically, we ate, drank, and slept together every night. I was with Joni, and that was flowering. Stephen was with Judy Collins, and that was flowering. David was with Christine, and that was flowering. Within a year, it had all changed. My relationship with Joni had turned sour, Stephen had stopped going with Judy, and David's girlfriend, Christine, had been killed. We were knocked for a loop. We were all romantic people, and our love-lives were in shambles. Then bring in Neil and plug into his insanity, and it's amazing *Deja Vu* ever got recorded.

I remember one night at the Fillmore East in New York. We were playing, and Dylan had come to see us. Our live shows usually would break down to an acoustic first half, followed by an intermission, followed by an electric set for the rest of the night. Within that structure, we would all have acoustic solos. I would do two songs, David would do two songs, Stephen would do two songs, and Neil would do two songs.

But on this particular night, because Dylan was there, Stephen goes out and does five songs. It pissed everyone off righteously. We all wanted to impress Dylan, and yet Stephen takes it on himself to go overboard. Well, we were all so infuriated by the time intermission came that I started talking to Stephen and telling him exactly what I think about him. And while I'm doing it, he's holding a can of Budweiser in his hand, and he's slowly gripping it, crushing it. Stephen is an immensely strong man, and with this maniacal energy of his he crushed the can flat, and now beer is frothing all over the carpet, and all over his pants.

And right after that, we went out and played the greatest electrical set we'd ever played. So go figure.

The incredible thing about my relationship with Stephen and David is that I can be screamingly mad at both of them, and they with me, but all of us have the knack of saying, "OK, while you're screaming at me, just listen to this new tune I wrote." No matter what is going on, someone plays you a song that knocks you on your ass. Now I ask you, how can you stay mad at someone who has just played you one of the best songs you ever heard?

Robbie Robertson, 1978
(Photo by Chris Gulker)

Mickey Hart, 1982
(Photo by Henry Diltz)

Jerry Garcia, 1971
(Photo by Henry Diltz)

Paul Rothchild

John Fogerty, 1969
(Photo by Henry Diltz)

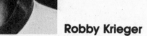

Robby Krieger

John Sebastian, 1967
(Photo by Henry Diltz)

George Harrison, 1988
(Photo by Chris Gulker)

Yoko Ono

Clive Davis, 1979
(Photo by Dean Musgrove)

Al Green, 1983
(Photo by James Ruebsamen)

Booker T. and the MG's
(clockwise from top):
**Donald "Duck" Dunn,
Steve Cropper, Booker T. Jones,
and Willie Hall, 1976**
(Photo by Henry Diltz)

Isaac Hayes
(Photo by Rob Brown)

Alice Cooper, 1979
(Photo by Chris Gulker)

Van Morrison, 1986
(Photo by James Ruebsamen)

Al Kooper, 1986
(Photo by Sandy Gibson)

Robert Hilburn

Elton John, 1979
(Photo by Anne Knudsen)

Russ Regan

Paul Simon, 1987
(Photo by Javier Mendoza)

Lou Rawls, 1981
(Photo by Rob Brown)

Jac Holzman, 1986
(Photo by Sandy Gibson)

Judy Collins

Bill Medley (left) and Bobby Hatfield
of the Righteous Brothers, 1967

Jimmy Webb, 1974
(Photo by Henry Diltz)

Graham Nash, 1970
(Photo by Henry Diltz)

Stephen Stills, 1982
(Photo by Ken Papaleo)

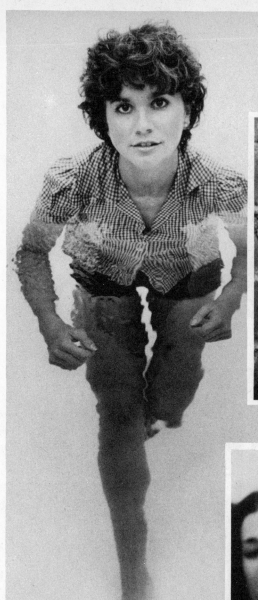

Linda Ronstadt, 1978
(Photo by Henry Diltz)

Joe Cocker, 1986
(Photo by Henry Diltz)

Mama Cass and David Geffen, 1971
(Photo by Henry Diltz)

Joni Mitchell with David Crosby, 1969
(Photo by Henry Diltz, California Rock, California Sound, A Reed Book)

Carly Simon
(Photo by Pam Frank)

James Taylor, 1969
(Photo by Henry Diltz)

Jackson Browne, 1973
(Photo by Henry Diltz)

Ry Cooder
(Photo by Susan Titelman)

Nick Ashford and Valerie Simpson, 1986
(Photo by Henry Diltz)

Kenny Gamble

Teddy Pendergrass, 1978
(Photo by Dean Musgrove)

Randy Newman, 1986
(Photo by Sandy Gibson)

Richard Carpenter, 1973
(Photo by Henry Diltz)

Al Jarreau

**Kenny Rogers and
son Christopher Cody, 1985**
(Photo by Henry Diltz)

Herbie Hancock, 1984
(Photo by Anne Knudsen)

David Gates
(Michael Ochs Archives)

George Benson and stepfather, Tom Collier
(From library of George T. Simon)

Bob Seger, 1986
(Photo by Michael Edwards)

Robert Plant, 1985
(Photo by Anne Knudsen)

Walter Yetnikoff, 1980

Chris Wright

Ian Anderson, 1987
(Photo by Henry Diltz)

Rod Stewart, 1981
(Photo by Mike Mullen)

Stephen Stills

○ ○ ○

A veteran of Buffalo Springfield, Crosby, Stills and Nash, and a number of solo appearances and records, he's a great guitarist and a charismatic player in the golden age of rock 'n' roll.

○ ○ ○

I have some marvelous tapes sitting in a box of me and Jimi Hendrix—waiting to find out exactly who is in charge, so I can get permission to finish them the way we intended.

We got to be good friends. I'm a southern boy who was taught to play music by the same people who taught him. We wound up being in England at the same time. In England, I was called a "gray" because I had some soul, and I ate at the best soul food restaurants, and I was a part of the black community.

Jimi had a hard time relating to anyone, but he could talk to me. We formed a deep bond. We would play clubs. I would play bass or rhythm guitar, and he would play lead guitar. I sort of followed him around like a little puppy dog waiting to learn how to play guitar. He always thought that was silly because he was actually learning acoustic guitar from me. But he was so shy, so impossibly shy. If you weren't playing real close attention, you would swear he didn't like anybody.

But I was a good rhythm guitar player, and I could sit there and play idiot guitar all day, and all the while Jimi was teaching me how to play lead.

Neil Young and I had a similar approach to folk music as it related to rock 'n' roll, and in Buffalo Springfield Neil and I would imitate each other on guitar the way Jimi and I imitated each other on guitar.

Buffalo was a happy band. However, when we got to our first session and we went into the studio and cut this one song, the voice came over the talk-back saying, "No, that's too long. Play it faster."

Neil and I looked at each other and said, "We better learn how to work this shit ourselves." So from then on, it was a race to see who could learn the most about making records, about electronics and engineering, the whole nine yards. He worked on one aspect, I worked on another aspect, and Ahmet Ertegun was there to finance the studio time.

But the band lasted for such a short time. I remember we were headed back east to do the Johnny Carson show, the first rock 'n' roll band to be on the Carson show, and Neil quits the night before we're supposed to leave. We fell prey to the whole entourage system. Everybody had to have his own entourage, and it got stupid. We forgot the initial brotherhood.

I remember David Crosby and I doing a concert for one of the free clinics. The Kingston Trio, Peter, Paul and Mary, and God knows who else was there, and we all ended up at Alan Pariser's house. I will never forget the conversation. We were all sitting around and I said, "You know, we ought to do one of those things with a whole bunch of the new rock bands."

And Alan looks at me and says, "Where would you do it?"

And I say, "Oh, where they hold that jazz festival, in Monterey."

He says, "That's interesting," and we continue to party. The next day he calls me up and says, "Will you come and talk to Ben Shapiro?" I walk into this little place in Hollywood and Alan says, "Tell him what you told me the other night."

So I say, "I think there should be a pop-rock festival up in Monterey."

And Ben says, "Who would you have?"

So I rattle off some names, and I say, "Who knows where it can go? It could be just like that damn jazz festival, or the other one in Newport."

They say, "We'll get back to you." Two weeks later, I'm in the office begging Andrew Oldham for a spot on the bill. We get to Monterey and Lou Adler is telling me maybe we'll get to play on Saturday night. But Neil's not in the group, so I get David Crosby to come and sit in with the band, so at least there's somebody sitting in, and probably that was the only way that Buffalo Springfield, which was this unimportant little band, could get a spot on the bill.

After the band split up, I got myself a little place in Topanga and tried to keep my associations open, keep the door open. I was invited to join Blood, Sweat and Tears, but the thing with David and Graham Nash was just starting to pull together.

There was a time when I thought Crosby, Stills and Nash could rule the world. But I never said we could save it. I just said, "There's something happening here." I suppose I just tried to keep things open-ended. I tried to do what I was doing in the best spirit of the troubadours.

Joe Cocker
o o o

I had to drive into the hills above Santa Barbara to find this sometime tragic victim and survivor of the rock world. No voice is quite like his, no stage presence quite the same. Joe's life is a great chronicle of the excesses of the day.

o o o

I was a drummer originally, but I never thought I was that good. Trying to sing and drum was difficult. I remember the band saying, "You have to do one or the other, and we'd prefer it if you drum because we'll never find another drummer." And we had this horrible kid singer.

At the time we were called Vance Arnold and the Avengers, and we were playing the pubs, which was a great upbringing. We'd go to these pubs every night after our day jobs and drink a lot of beer and play until the pubs closed. Kept us in beer money. We weren't in that big a hurry to be successful.

After the Beatles, the scouting rush was on. People came north and saw the Avengers and said, "We don't like your band," as usual. I remember doing an orchestrated version of "Georgia on My Mind," which was never released.

Then they had me go in and do a cover of the Beatles' "I'll Cry Instead," which died a death. I was still living at home at the time, and my parents said, "OK, you had your shot. Now grow up and go out and get a proper job." My older brother, Victor, turned out to be an economist. He did really well on the straighter side of life.

I never smoked pot when I was young. I was a very late bloomer in that I sort of made up for it after. I always swore I'd be a drinker to the end. But then, when someone turned me on to some black hash, musically speaking, it was such an opening to the ears and senses.

When I got popped, busted, in 1968, it was an incredible sensation to find yourself on the evening news busted for pot. It was almost like the fuss they made over Boy George, the kind of fuss now over heroin that smoking a joint was then.

Those early tours of the States were the greatest. Like the gig at the Atlanta Raceway with Spirit and Janis Joplin and Hendrix. I remember going on at, like, six in the morning, and all these kids acid-blazed. It was a very warm occasion.

And the hotel, too. One of the floors caught on fire, four days' wait for room service. But they were great times, hippie times.

After Woodstock, I laid low. I did an album with Delaney and Bonnie, but there was nothing much for me until I heard Leon Russell. Leon came up with the idea for *Mad Dogs*. We all lived up at Leon's house. We all ran around in the nude and had some pretty wild times. But it was strange. Leon was into this revivalist sort of thing. He'd always have to have a meal before a show. We'd all sit down and he would say a little prayer.

Having come out of the *Mad Dogs* tour with no money never really bothered me. Back then, the feeling was, it was a crime to have money anyway. We were into this trip of stripping off our worldly goods.

I remember giving money to various people—$70,000 here, $40,000 there, to people that I had known for years who wanted houses. I said, "If you ever make it back, you can pay it back." Of course, I never heard from them. But five years later I did hear from the tax people who demanded I come up with all the money I thought I could give away like the Magic Christian.

This thing about me being spastic is something I can't seem to get away from. I did "The David Letterman Show" not long ago, and he is still going on about me being spastic. I can't talk about anything else when I go on those shows.

During the time of "You Are So Beautiful," I was working at Village

Recorders, in Los Angeles, and someone comes into the studio and says, "Joe, we've got this video to show you that you're not going to like." I don't know how long "Saturday Night Live" had been on the air, because I never watched much TV, but when I saw this video of John Belushi doing me being spastic and pouring beer, I became hysterical.

Everyone else said, "Joe, you're not supposed to find this amusing. You're supposed to find this gross and offensive."

I said, "Oh, come on. You can't not laugh at this." I didn't even know who Belushi was.

Moving my hand around is subconscious with me. A lot of time I'm more or less conducting the band, just keeping a feel. I don't know why I do it. It's just one of those things.

I didn't know where I was by the time Jim Price came around to my house asking if I'd be interested in making another record, which turned out to be "You Are So Beautiful." After we finished the album, Jim booked the Roxy for me in L.A. Everyone was there. Somebody should have kept an eye on me, but some dealer found me backstage and filled me up with cocaine. I hadn't performed live in a couple of years. I drank a whole bottle of brandy, and then went out there and got through about two songs, and then I sat down on stage with a total mental block to all the words. It was rather embarrassing. Everyone just sort of closed the curtain and said good night. That was supposed to be my return.

The worst feeling in the world is to lose your voice before a concert. Happened to me in Germany. We were doing this show for, like, 90,000 people, televised all across Europe, and that morning I wake up with no voice. So I go to this doctor and he gives me a shot so powerful I thought he'd turned me into a woman. It was that big a dose.

That night, I opened my mouth and I couldn't believe it. I sang like a bird. I was so scared of the power coming out of me that I realized why people are so afraid of drugs.

I get called a fossil, which is OK when I start thinking of some of the musicians I've know who are dead. People talk with morbid fascination about who is most likely to die next. I'm sure I've been talked about as the next potential dead candidate.

Linda Ronstadt

○ ○ ○

**She has shown a musical curiosity and a willingness to take risks with
her career for almost seventeen years. Her talent is so versatile that it
seems natural she's handled rock, country, Latin, and Broadway—all
with relative ease.**

○ ○ ○

The Troubadour was like a café society. Everyone was in transition. No
one was getting married, no one was having families, no one was having
a particular connection, so our connection was the Troubadour. It was
where everyone met, where everyone got to hear everyone else's act. It
was where I made all my musical contacts, and found people who were
sympathetic to the musical styles I wanted to explore.

We all used to sit in a corner of the Troubadour and dream. I remember
one night, I was on my way to the bathroom, during a hootenanny, and
this band, Shilo, starts doing my exact version of "Silver Threads and Golden
Needles." I was flabbergasted. Shilo ultimately became the Eagles.

We would all sit around motel rooms together, and they'd be working
out harmonies. They were so good. When I heard them sing "Witchy
Woman" in the living room of J.D. Souther's house, where I was living at
the time, I knew the Eagles were going to make it.

The Eagles backed me up, but I was the one who was inconsistent
onstage. I could do a real good show in one town, and the next night would
be like the first time I'd ever gotten up onstage. I was never comfortable
repeating what I'd done the night before.

But I got tougher being on the road with the Eagles. I walked differently,
I became more foulmouthed. I mean, I swore so much I sounded like a
truck driver. But that's the way it was. I was the only girl on the road so the
boys always kind of took charge. They were working for me, and yet it always
seemed like I was working for them.

I could never quite get used to being a celebrity, or the idea that people
were looking at me and I was up there with all the responsibility. It made
me so uncomfortable that I would have preferred standing behind the am-
plifiers.

Years later, I'm doing *Pirates of Penzance* on Broadway, and Jerry
Wexler comes to see the show. He invited me out to his house on Long
Island, and he started playing me all these different kinds of songs. Pop songs.
Non-rock. He said, "You could sing this kind of stuff."

I said, "No. You really have to be a singer to do that." But the songs
affected me so completely that they became the way I dreamed.

My roots are folk roots. I remember in 1964, an actor friend of mine
played me Frank Sinatra's *Only the Lonely* album. I said to my friend, "That
guy sings in Vegas." But I listened to the record and knew it was one of the
best records I'd ever heard.

But I never got any real encouragement to do that kind of music, maybe a couple of friends lurking here and there, but it wasn't until I met with Nelson Riddle that I really started believing I could sing those songs.

I always think I'm not a very good singer, and I feared that Nelson wouldn't want anything to do with me. I was afraid he'd go, "Linda who?" Or, "She's jive. She's not a singer, I don't want to waste my time." I didn't even know if he was still alive, or whether he had retired. But I did know that he was the only person besides Randy Newman that I'd ever heard write stuff with an orchestra that I thought was right.

I like the stuff I did with Nelson Riddle better than anything I've ever done. My entire life, the accumulation of all my experience as a person, went into the work I did with Nelson. Those three records summed up everything I knew to that point. Everything I'd read in books, everything I'd ever seen, everything I'd ever learned from talking to people, every feeling I'd ever felt went into those records.

All my life since I've been making records, I always tried real hard, but I always thought I failed. "You're No Good" and "Heat Wave" are good records, but I still feel like I didn't sing very well on them. I was always very disappointed in my contribution to them, even though I turned myself inside out with effort.

But with the Nelson things, I feel differently. I don't think they're as good as Frank Sinatra or Billie Holiday, but they're different. They're a different statement from a different point of view in a different time. I feel like they were authentically mine, my statement, an authentic representation of the amount of effort and thinking I put into it. To me, it was like floating on ecstacy.

To be able to sing Nelson's arrangements was like floating in pure musical ecstacy and emotion. It was so heavenly I hated for it to end.

Now I know it's ended forever. I know Nelson will never write those charts for me again, and I'm never going to have that exquisite pleasure of having him come over with his briefcase, and hearing him grumbling about whatever he was grumbling about that day—his dog, his kid, the weather outside. We would sit down at the piano, we'd put the music out, we'd start to talk about it, then laugh about some stupid thing, and then go in and do it.

David Geffen

○ ○ ○

**It appears that the term wunderkind was invented for this dynamite
record, film, and theater impresario. His career as an agent, manager,
and entrepreneur is one of the great stories in rock.**

○ ○ ○

I was working in California as an usher at CBS and they fired me. I was a
bad usher. So I go back to Brooklyn because I don't have any money, and
I'm trying to get a job that will earn me enough money to fly back to California
when somebody suggests I go to the Ashley Famous Agency.

I didn't know what an agent was, and they explained to me that an
agent is somebody who advises people on their careers. I thought, "Gee,
that sounds like a good way to make a living." So I went to Ashley Famous
and I filled out my application honestly.

The personnel director reads the application and says, "You've dropped
out of two schools, you've had four jobs, you were fired from CBS as an
usher after six months—hardly a recommendation to hire you as an agent
here. I'm sorry."

I learned my lesson. I look in the Yellow Pages for the biggest agency
ad and it's William Morris. I go over and fill out an application. I write that
I graduated UCLA, was a production assistant on "The Danny Kaye Show,"
and they hire me. I'm now learning to deliver the mail at the William Morris
Agency with this guy who's been there for four months, and all of a sudden
he's fired. I want to know why, and he says, "Well, you know, they check
your references." My heart dropped.

I started coming in early every morning waiting for a letter to come,
saying they never heard of me at UCLA, never heard of me at "The Danny
Kaye Show." I came in early for the next six months. I sorted every piece
of mail that came into the agency looking for the letters. I couldn't be sick,
I couldn't be late, and I turned down promotions. I couldn't get out of the
mailroom until the letters came, and finally they did. The funny thing is,
I had to forge a letter saying I graduated from UCLA, and today I'm on the
Board of Regents at UCLA.

I eventually did get a job at Ashley Famous. I had no desire to be
involved in the music business, but I saw that Jerry Brandt, who was the
head of the music department at William Morris, had a limousine, and he
was hanging out with Mick Jagger. I asked him, "Jerry, how do you get a
limo?"

He said, "Schmuck, you're twenty-four years old. Do you think Norman
Jewison is going to sign with you? Does Irene Dunne want you to be her
agent? You better get in the music business with people your own age." I
thought that was the best advice I'd ever heard, and that's how I got into the
music business.

I went to management in the late sixties, first with Laura Nyro, then with Crosby, Stills and Nash. Steve Binder, who was a friend of mine at William Morris, was directing "The Steve Allen Show," and he told me he wanted to book Laura Nyro on the show. I had never heard of Laura Nyro, and he said, "Don't you remember? She was the girl who bombed out at the Monterey Pop Festival." Steve played me one of her tracks, "Wedding Bell Blues," and I was hooked.

I called Artie Mogul, who was her manager, and I said I wanted to represent her as an agent, and he said, ' "You don't want to represent her. She's a dog." He put her down terribly, but I had to meet her. So he took me over to her apartment on Eighth Avenue. She lived at 888 Eighth Avenue in this one-room apartment filled with cats. It was a nightmare, but she and I became instant best friends.

She was a very strange girl. At that time, she hadn't cut her hair in twelve years. She had hair down to her thighs. She wore purple lipstick, Christmas balls for earrings, strange clothes. But very talented. She is among the most talented people I've ever seen in my life. It was because of my belief in Laura that I agreed to manage her and give up my career as an agent.

And then Crosby, Stills and Nash came along. They didn't have managers, but they had record contracts with different companies that needed to be consolidated. I remember the first time I went up to Atlantic Records. The only name I knew at Atlantic was Jerry Wexler, so I went to see Jerry to ask him for a release for Stephen Stills so I could make a deal with Columbia Records and Clive Davis, and Jerry physically threw me out of the office.

The next day, Ahmet Ertegun calls me to apologize for Jerry. Ahmet asks me to come up and see him. He was the most charming person I'd ever met in my life. He just sucked me right in. Because of Ahmet, as soon as I got Crosby, Stills and Nash free of all their other contracts, I signed them to Atlantic Records.

After being a manager for a year, I realized I didn't like it. I didn't like being called in middle of the night, I didn't like being so closely involved with their personal lives, so I called Elliot Roberts, who was already managing Joni Mitchell, and I said, "You manage them. I'm going to go back to being an agent. I'll be their agent, you be their manager."

So Elliot became the manager for all those artists, and I went to CMA where I worked for David Begelman and Freddie Fields. But I didn't like that either, so I said to Elliot, "Let's go into partnership. We'll start a management business together."

Elliot wasn't thrilled with the idea. He'd had them all by himself. He said, "Why should I do this?"

I said, "Trust me. It's better to be in business with me than without me." He agreed. Our first client was Jackson Browne.

I went to everybody in the business trying to make a record deal for Jackson, and everybody turned him down. I went to Ahmet again and I said,

"I'm telling you, this guy is good. I'm the guy who brought you Crosby, Stills and Nash. I'm doing you a favor."

And he said, "You know what? Don't do me any favors."

I said, "You'll make millions with him."

And he said, "You know what? I got millions. Do you have millions?"

I said, "No."

He said, "Start a record company and you'll have millions. Then we can all have millions."

I thought, "Fuck him. I will start a record company." So I started Asylum Records and Jackson Browne was our first artist. Within a year or so, I had signed Linda Ronstadt, Joni Mitchell, Jackson Browne, John David Souther, and Glenn Frey.

As it happened, Souther and Frey were living upstairs from Jackson Browne in a duplex in Silverlake. They were broke. Jackson came to me and said, "I want you to sign them. They're really good and they're broke. They can't pay their rent." So, to be a hero to Jackson Browne, I signed them. I encouraged John David Souther to be a solo artist and I encouraged Glenn Frey to put a group together. Glenn would come to me with each new member, and he would say, "Can I make a record now?"

And I'd say, "No. Not good enough yet." Finally it was, and that was the beginning of the Eagles.

Joni Mitchell

o o o

This Canadian lady turned the folk world into something else with her notable records over a fifteen-year stretch. She continues to be revered as one of the finest songwriters and musicians.

o o o

I was in the industry for a long time before I had any idea of what drugs people were doing. I mean, I'd say, "Geez, he looks awfully skinny. Why doesn't he have an appetite?"

I was very, very sheltered by Elliot Roberts and Crosby, Stills and Nash, when I first entered the business. Even in my early teens, in Canada, I was always protected. People always looked out for me in that way.

In high school, I was kind of like the school artist. I did backdrops for school plays, I was always involved in illustrating the yearbooks. I designed a UNICEF Christmas card for a guy who was like the school leader, the senior watchman. He reimbursed me with a Miles Davis album.

Friends of mine who were older than me and in college began talking about Lambert, Hendricks and Ross as the hottest new sound in jazz. Their record flipped me out, but it was already out of print. I had to finally buy it off somebody and pay a lot, maybe fifteen dollars, which was unheard of at that time. But you couldn't get the record anywhere. Lambert, Hendricks and Ross were my Beatles. In high school, theirs was the record I wore thin, the one I knew all the words to.

When I was nineteen, I went to art school. I had six months of playing baritone ukulele under my belt, so I was sort of a novice folkie when I got there. There was the one folk club, and some of the people from the art school frequented it. I got a weekend job working there. Sometimes, on my way up to Edmonton, I would pick up some pin money. But it was just a hobby. Art was still my serious direction.

When I went to Toronto, to the Mariposa Folk Festival to actually see Buffy St. Marie, I still didn't have an image of myself as a musician. I found I couldn't work, and I didn't have enough money to get into the union, which was $160. So I worked in women's wear, in a department store. I could barely make ends meet.

And then I finally found a scab club in Toronto that allowed me to play. I played for a couple of months. Then I married Chuck Mitchell, and we moved across the border. We still scrambled for work. As a couple, I think we were making fifteen dollars a night.

In Detroit, we had a fifth-floor walk-up apartment with some extra rooms, and so when Eric Anderson and David Blue and Tom Rush and people like that passed through Detroit, they would stay with us.

Eric started teaching me open tunings, an open G, a drop D. For some reason, once I got the open tunings I began to get the harmonic sophistication that my musical fountain inside was excited by. Once I got some interesting chords to play with, my writing began to come. But still, I was pretty much a good-time Charlie. I was a bad student, I failed twelfth grade, I did my book reports from classic comics.

I was anti-intellectual to the max. Basically, I liked to dance and paint and that was about it. As far as serious discussions went, I found them boring. To see teenagers sitting around trying to solve the problems of the world, I figured, all things considered, I'd rather be dancing.

My husband was different. He had an education, a degree in literature. Chuck always said that you couldn't write unless you read. He considered me an illiterate, and he didn't give me a great deal of encouragement regarding my writing. But Tom Rush did. Tom would say, "Do you have any new songs?" I'd play him a batch and he'd say, "Any more?" I always held the ones out that I felt were too sensitive, or too feminine, and those would always be the ones he chose. Because of Tom, I began to get noticed.

I liked playing in small clubs the best, still do. I really like holding the attention of thirty or forty people. I never liked the roar of the big crowd. I could never adjust to the sound of people gasping at the mere mention of my name. It horrified me.

And I also knew how fickle people could be. I knew they were buying an illusion, and I thought, "Maybe they should know a little more about who I am." I wanted to believe that the attention I was getting was for me. I didn't want there to be such a gulf between who I presented and who I was. David Geffen used to tell me that I was the only star he ever met who wanted to be ordinary.

I never wanted to be a star. I didn't like entering a room with all eyes on me. I still don't like the attention of a birthday party. I prefer Christmas, which is everybody's holiday.

I went to the Newport Jazz Festival. Judy Collins called me up. She was supposed to take me. Al Kooper had put us in touch and we were supposed to meet and go. Well, Judy stood me up, and she was my hero. It was kind of heartbreaking, I waited and waited and waited and she never came to pick me up to take me to Newport.

A day went by and I got a phone call from her and she sounded kind of sheepish. She said somebody had sung one of my songs in a workshop. It was a terrible rendition, she said, but people went crazy.

Judy really felt I should be at Newport, so she gave me instructions on how to get there. When I played there, I got that large roar and it made me incredibly nervous. That night, my girlfriend Jane, who was road-managing for me, and I went to a party at one of those old mansions. Standing at the gate was like being at Studio 54 in New York. People all over the place who couldn't get in. A guard asked us for credentials. I kind of waxed passive and backed down. Jane, who was always trying to get me to use my existential edge, said, "Do you know who she is?" Well, she said my name and these kids standing at the gate went, "Aaaah," and sucked their breath in. My heart started to beat like crazy. I turned around and ran in the other direction like some crazed animal. I ran, and I ran, and I ran. I must've run about five blocks before I realized how strange my reaction was.

Speaking of strange reactions, right at the time I made *Court and Spark*, which was my most successful album, David Geffen was trying to sign Dylan for what turned out to be the *Planet Waves* project. David and I were sharing a house. I'd been working on *Court and Spark* under his nose, and maybe he heard it through too many stages, but I knew I was making something special.

I was so excited the night I finished it. I brought it back to the house to play it. There were a bunch of people there, including Dylan. I played *Court and Spark* for everyone, and Bobby fell asleep and snored all the way through it. When the record came to the end, the people went, "Huh?"

Then they played *Planet Waves* and everybody jumped up and down. There was so much enthusiasm. Now, *Planet Waves* wasn't one of Bobby's best projects, and I hadn't expected it to be a competitive situation, but for the first time in my career I felt this sibling rivalry. It was an ordinary record for Bobby, a transitional piece, and yet everybody was cheering. Finally, one of the women took me aside and said, "Don't pay them any attention. Those boys have no ears."

James Taylor

○ ○ ○

His success at the outset of the seventies set a tone for the singer-songwriters that followed in great numbers for the next several years. James' fame and troubles and marriage and everything else about him made for great media fodder.

○ ○ ○

I came out of the scene that Waddy Wachtel calls, "The great folk scare of the sixties." It was a period of time that formed me. I listened to other music, mainly country, rhythm and blues, the white and black gospel they played on the radio down south, and whatever my older brother, Alex, exposed me to. But the music I connected with most was coffee house music, the folk scene.

Folk music was a very portable music. It didn't use piano, just guitar, maybe banjo. I remember spending long hours playing guitar in North Carolina. I felt relatively alienated. Maybe it was adolescence, maybe it was a combination of the way I was, and just being in North Carolina, but I knew how to isolate. And when I did, I turned to the guitar.

At the time, I didn't think my songs were personal. Generally speaking, the songs to me seemed like love songs. "Fire and Rain" is a very personal song which drew a lot of attention, and therefore people connected me with that kind of song, but I didn't think of my songs as being particularly personal or autobiographical. Years later, I don't deny it. The stuff I write does come from an autobiographical place.

I suppose it was my good fortune to be in London just after Brian Epstein's death, when Allen Klein was taking over Apple, and the place was wide open. The Beatles were listening to everything, doing everything they could. A lot of it was misspent and wasted time, but the idea of what the Beatles wanted Apple to be was still fantastic. Peter Asher became the head of A & R, and he listened to everything that came across his desk.

I had made a demo tape and was trying to take it around to various people. Peter heard it and liked it. He played it for McCartney, who said he liked it, and suddenly I was signed, and now I'm up in their offices with them, sharing time in the studio with them. I even tried the studio where the Beatles recorded *The White Album*.

It was amazing to be around that, and have all that available to me. And then acceptance by the public on top of that, which leads to public scrutiny, which then changes what you do and how you think of yourself. It changes your motivation, it shifts your focus. In my case, I went from the very interior kind of process of making music and finding a personal outlet to thinking of how best to prepare for a huge audience. That process can be very disruptive, especially to musicians and songwriters who in many cases are ill-adapted to that kind of public life.

In a way, that is why we've seen so many burnouts. You can count the people who went down. I'm not saying it was because they were popular and successful and commercial and marketable and incorporated into a larger capitalistic system, but it certainly couldn't have helped them. It is very hard to make that shift. That is another one of the miracles about the Beatles. In spite of the fact that everything they did was accompanied by wave after wave of public and press onslaught, they continued to come up with more and more meaningful stuff. That's amazing to me.

I turned to a lot of things. I got into drugs extremely heavily for a long period of time. That is something of its own progression, and it's also familiar, but it has happened to a lot of people in this kind of work. Drugs were always around. Being a musician and working late hours in a lot of bars, you're going to see a lot of drugs consumed. It started out recreationally, the rule rather than the exception. At least where I was.

When you give somebody millions of dollars and millions of fans, and amazing press, and incredible support from all areas, when you're twenty years old, you feel as though you can have everything you want. At that age, you haven't necessarily figured out how to find it. You just expect to be able to feel good and have what you want. It is never about finding peace of mind, or serenity, or just finding your proper place in your own skin. All that takes a long time. It doesn't happen overnight just because a celebrity machine turns its powerful glance on you. So it's easy to want to buy a pill or a vial or a syringe, or twist up a joint.

At that age, you're looking for instant gratification, instant life, instant arrival, instant feelings. You're out there thinking, "I can buy it all." After all, the music business had always been a maverick choice to take. It wasn't an acceptable profession. It wasn't acceptable to be a DJ, or in record promotion, or managing a rock 'n' roll band, or promoting a rock 'n' roll concert. Just as it wasn't acceptable to want to play rock 'n' roll or blues or folk or whatever. If your parents had any aspirations for you, they did not run in those directions.

I didn't meet with a whole lot of resistance from my folks when I left school and went to New York City. But I am sure it caused them a lot of deep concern. It wasn't exactly what they had in mind.

As to the years I was with Carly, ours was a very public marriage, and in that sense it suffered because it was so public. I think I dealt with it mostly unconsciously. We just took it as it came. Carly had her own agenda to follow, and her own feelings on how she wanted to deal with the publicity and the press. I feel she was more comfortable and more capable to deal with it than I was.

But I'm remarried now, and I'm in the time of my life when things become real. When you're twenty, there are lots of possibilities. Everything is wide open. No matter if they're romantic feelings or fear or enthusiasm or anxiety, when you're in your twenties and thirties, there's always a conceptual view of what your life is going to be like.

By the time you're forty and fifty, your life is largely what it is going to be, and I think that's a crushing blow to a lot of people once they find that out. Your job is what it is, your kids are who they are, your home is where you made it, you have a mortgage, and you became what you were going to be. Physically you may be losing your hair, slowing down a little bit, and in need of some major dentistry, but basically a lot of the mystery doors have been opened and the contents are clearly there. Unfortunately, a lot of people look at that and fold up.

I look back and say, "Well, they were hot days, but they couldn't last forever." Sometimes I wish I was less conflicted about the past. I wish I was more capable of just saying, "Look at this," and enjoy it because it is a flower.

Carly Simon

o o o

A lot of guys keep her album covers in their memory books. She also happens to sing and write with great skill, and her former marriage to James Taylor adds another dimension to the story.

o o o

Odetta was my idol. I wanted to sing like her. Then I listened to Joan Baez, and it didn't seem possible that I could ever sound like her. Then I heard Judy Collins. I was a senior in high school. When you think you're a singer yourself, the people who influence you are the people you can sound like, people you can imitate, and Judy Collins I thought I could sound like.

It's still unbelievable to me that I had success doing this. I heard a song of mine on the radio the other day followed by the Paul McCartney tune "Yesterday." The DJ called both songs "classics." I find it so amazing I'm even on the airwaves, and I'm not being humble. I have a very good memory, and I remember what it was like to wish for that or to imagine myself as a star. I had a pipe dream, and then I had reality, the reality being that I wanted a middle-class life like my mother had. I wanted to be around great artists and great writers, and then be a great hostess. So today when I hear a record of mine on the radio, it's just incredible.

James taught me a lot about how to behave after achieving some success. He got it before I did, so I just followed what he did and went along with him. If James bowed his head down rushing through a crowd, I did it, too. I learned a lot from him in the way he dealt with things. James is extremely generous. He doesn't like to say no to anybody, which sort of confirmed my instinct to do the same. So very often we were at the mercy of people who wanted to do things. Even though James has an image of being aloof and cool, he is really very kindhearted. He could be a pushover.

I felt that any success I had on my own was a fluke. I didn't say, "Well, how come I'm not being treated like Neil Young?"

I think we change our opinions of ourselves so often. What the outside world thinks is only a small part of our image. With some people, public persona is the only thing that matters. I do fool around with that to a certain degree, but a lot of it is unconscious. I can manipulate like Boy George or Madonna, but I don't change my hairstyle or my costume very much. I think people have a feeling of who I really am.

Maybe another persona comes across because of the artwork on my albums. My personality in front of a camera is quite playful. When I get in front of a camera, video camera or still, that's when the ham in me comes out. My father was a good photographer. When he took pictures of me, it was a way for me to get across because the other girls in the family had a much easier time getting his attention. I felt I had to be a clown. I was always a clown in front of my father's camera. I was always very on. It was a habit formed early. So now, when I'm in front of a lens, I get turned on in the same way I used to with my father.

I think that's why my album covers are sometimes talked about as much as the albums. Even though I feel a freedom to play in front of the camera, people are not seeing the outtakes. I've done many album photos that have nothing to do with sex, nothing to do with sensuality. Art directors always choose the ones that do have something to do with sex, and those weren't always necessarily my choices. I would give them a wide variety of images, and the sexy ones got the most number of votes. I had veto power, but I thought most of those pictures were fun, too. I don't think there was ever one album cover that was lewd, rude, or crude.

The songs I write come from so many places. Largely from problems I'm trying to solve. If I'm having emotional problems—and it's usually an emotional problem, often having to do with a crisis of the heart—it motivates me to try to figure out how I can get that into a lyric or a melody.

Sometimes it comes from stimulation from the outside. A number of times it's come from a magazine article or a TV show, or a movie or conversation about a particular subject. I recently read an article on Jerry Brown, and it made me write something just one second after I read it. I wrote a song called "The Summit" about an ideal summit meeting. So something from the outside can affect me. I wrote "A Legend in His Own Time" after reading an article on Hank Williams.

"Loving You Is the Right Thing to Do" came from a line in *The Last Picture Show*. It can come out of a phrase I hear. I heard something in that dreadful movie *Falling in Love*, with Meryl Streep and Robert DeNiro. A line Meryl used was, "Everything else seems wrong." I thought that was a nice title for a song. "Everything else seems wrong, everything but you." Song titles themselves can really be an idea for the developing of an idea.

Jackson Browne

○ ○ ○

Jackson has been the embodiment of the California singer/songwriter. His good looks and sensitive, personal songs gave him a great run through the introspective seventies—a run that shows no signs of diminishing.

○ ○ ○

The summer I was out of high school I got busted for pot. But I got out of it because I paid a lawyer to tell the judge that I was a nice boy and that this was the first and last time I would ever be in trouble.

I had this $500 publishing advance from Elektra's publishing company, Nina Music, and it all was used to buy off some smarmy judge who had the same twinkle in his eyes as my lawyer.

There were 200 black and Chicano kids in court that day and it was an inescapable fact that they were all going to the slammer, while the other three or four clean-cut kids like me whose parents had paid a lawyer to stand up and say how "upright" we were—well, you just knew we weren't going to jail. I mean, I was glad not to be going to jail, but it was pretty obvious that whoever had the bread was gonna be all right.

I graduated high school in '66 and hung around Hollywood and Orange County for about six months. And then in January of '67, some of my friends and me drove across the United States in a Rambler station wagon. It was the dead of winter and it took us less than four days. We never stopped, we just barreled straight through.

I remember listening to the Clay–Liston fight while we were driving across the Texas panhandle. My hair was down to my shoulders and I had people genuinely mistaking me for a girl in places like Missouri. We'd stop for gas, and I'd ask for the restroom and this old guy dressed like a sack of potatoes says, "Right over there, dearie."

Being from Orange County where people were normally hostile to anyone who looked like a freak, I was used to it. But this old guy had really directed me to the women's restroom. When I came back and asked him for the key to the men's room, he got real embarrassed. He really did think I was a girl.

In New York, I lived for a while on the Lower East Side. New York was such a fascinating place. I was there in the spring of '67 for the first be-in. They had a be-in in New York and a be-in in San Francisco and a love-in in Los Angeles, and it all happened on the same day. It was some sort of synergy going on, people heading for these places with this wild understanding happening between everyone. It was really amazing.

Tim Buckley was in New York at the time and I went to see him play at this place called the Dom. Dom was mod spelled backwards, and there was always this carnival of people around. Andy Warhol with his entourage, a film loop of Lou Reed eating a Hershey bar, Nico sitting at one end of the bar in this Dietrich pose singing these incredible songs, and Tim Buckley as opening act.

When I got hired to play, Nico was being accompanied by various members of the Velvet Underground. They'd trade off. Lou Reed would back her one night, John Cale the next, and so on. And she was getting crazy about not having the same guy backing her up every night. So she asked Tim to do it and he said no. Then she asked me. First thing they asked me was whether I could play an electric guitar. I said yes, but I didn't have one. They said if I could get one, I could have the job. So I borrowed a friend's.

But I wound up leaving New York shortly after the spring. Back home I was all set to have this group, the Soft White Underbelly, as my backup band. I spent a week trying to figure out some arrangements to my songs that would fit this band, but it didn't matter because they later became Blue Oyster Cult.

They were great musicians, they really were. And they played my songs really well. I'm afraid I was the least proficient musician among them.

And then I remember hearing "A Day in the Life" on the radio. It was off a Beatles acetate, before the *Sgt. Pepper* album even came out. Nothing before had prepared me for this incredible song. It was a milestone, and it changed everything.

The Troubadour was the big thing then, but I'll tell you something, I don't really think there was ever songwriter's scene around the Troubadour. It was like Bob Dylan said: "You probably call it folk music, but it's not."

It wasn't folk music at the Troubadour, and nobody thought of it as folk. People came in with a full band. They'd come and they'd get record deals and they'd go. A lot of them were really corny. And flashy, too.

If you hung out there long enough, you could almost chart someone's progress. You'd see them one day by themselves, and the next day with two or three people and they'd be forming a band. Like J.D. Souther and Glenn Frey began playing there as a duo, and eventually you'd hear J.D. go up there by himself. And then a couple of weeks later Glenn would be in rehearsal with these other guys and they'd become the Eagles.

A lot of people hung out at the Troubadour, but I used to be wary about it. I wanted to be taken seriously, and I would show up with my guitar, and I would sing or I wouldn't sing, but I couldn't really hang there in the bar.

I think back now on that time and I wish I had been in a band in high school. One of my best friends, Eric Brow, he loved the Righteous Brothers, and he used to stand on his bed and just howl. Eric wound up joining a group.

And another guy from our class was the guitar player. They played at all the school dances, and I wish I'd done that. It took me until making my fourth album before I realized how cool the drums were.

The truth is, I don't even know what I do, and I don't quite know how it's supposed to be done. My songs are the residue of my life. When everything else is done, the songs are what's left. Generally, it tends to be sort of looking in the rearview mirror. The songs are about a time that is past, or a resolve about the present that in some way relates to the past.

I've never been able to collaborate with others. Another person with an idea is a problem for me. I'll be thinking of something, and then another person will say, "Hey, how about this?" And I won't even know what they're saying because I've been off in my head thinking of something else.

Valerie Simpson and Nick Ashford

o o o

The pint-sized lady and her rangy husband talked with us in their New York apartment while Valerie was extremely pregnant and they were trying to get a new album done. These top writers remain just a hit away from major record success.

o o o

Nick and I hooked up right in that church. One day someone came in scouting for writers. Apparently, they heard this church had a lot of good singers. And so they scouted us to write love songs.

Our first hit wasn't a love song, though. It was "Let's Go Get Stoned" for Ray Charles. I always wanted to thank Ray Charles for getting us going.

Soon after that, Motown contacted us and said, "Come on out. Let's talk." We had no idea what that meant. We drove up in a taxi. The sign on the front of the little building said "Hitsville." I said to the driver, "Well, this is a little house with a homemade sign, but we want the main building."

He said, "Sorry, this is the only Hitsville I know," and he put us out.

When we first had a song on the charts, we couldn't do anything but sit and watch the charts. We stopped working because we had gotten so caught up in what it meant to have a hit.

After a while we started begging for a production contract, and finally we got it. And there we were working against other producers like Johnny Bristol and Harvey Fuqua. The first song of ours we produced was "Ain't Nothin' Like the Real Thing." Everybody started walking into the control room. Smokey Robinson, Norman Whitfield, the very people we were competing against. Everyone stood around while we stumbled through our first production.

We learned right away to produce three songs in three hours. If you went a half an hour over, there was hell to pay. There was something about the Motown banner—you couldn't get out from under it. Everything was Motown. The individual was very far down the totem pole, like they wanted to keep everyone a secret. Who the musicians were was even a secret. If you chose it, your entire career could be a secret at Motown.

But I will say that it was very interesting to have a president of a company who could sit down and talk songs with you. Berry Gordy was not just an executive. He would argue about whether this verse should go here or that chorus there.

I remember when we were recording "Ain't No Mountain High Enough" with Diana Ross. Berry loved the record so much. He called us in for this meeting and he said, "I think you ought to put the chorus, which you have in the back, at the front." We disagreed and we argued violently about it. Berry didn't want all the slow talking in front because it took so long to get to the singing. We were very sensitive about the song. We said we wouldn't change it. Consequently, they didn't release it. It became popular not because Motown put it out but because the disc jockeys started picking it up.

Over the years I've grown to love performing for its instant gratification, the way you immediately know. I love that getting out there onstage and having it hit you. Recently we did a two-day festival at Madison Square Garden, and on the second night we did a version of "Reach Out and Touch Somebody's Hand" that proved to be the best moment we've gotten from a crowd ever, and we don't know why.

It was like thunder and lightning. Something caught on and Madison Square Garden would not let go. It was unbelievable. I didn't know what was happening, but I felt it. We weren't singing any better, but the applause would not stop. Then they started with those wolf whistles. It went on and on, the best reaction we've ever had.

And with all that, the most wonderful moments are when we've just completed something, right upstairs in our room when we say, just the two of us, "This one is a hit." I'll always like that feeling the best, before the song gets out, before the record company starts telling us how they feel the public will react.

o o o

My story is like a fairy tale. I came to New York with fifty-seven dollars in my pocket and ended up sleeping in the parks.

Once a week I'd go up to Harlem, to get a meal in this church. That's where I met Valerie. She was singing with three girls. I'd be there on Sunday, get my meal, and then I'd disappear mysteriously. They never knew where I was going, but I'd be going back downtown to deal with life.

Motown for us was like going to school to sharpen our instincts. Motown was a very competitive situation. It was like a quality-control board. You didn't just write a song. It had to be voted on, it had to be screened, and they didn't want you in the room when they voted.

All the staff writers felt the competition. You'd have your own little music room, and you could hear hit music coming out of all the other rooms, and it sure sounded good. And you'd be in your own little room saying, "What am I going to do?"

But Val and I were unique. Valerie was the only woman at Motown who would go in and talk to the musicians. She was skilled and they respected her. And they could be very cold. But they had never seen another woman being so expressive in the studio. Because of Val I could lay back and be cool. I realized what worked, so I kept my mouth shut and let her do the talking.

Motown at that time was the place for a black writer to be. Just to be able to say "Motown staff writer" was an incredible credit. We never thought of ourselves as artists. We concentrated on writing songs, either at random or projects they would assign us. Anything to get ahead.

And, of course, we worked with a lot of very talented people. For example, Marvin Gaye. There was something about him you couldn't put your finger on. Very elusive person. He liked to tell jokes as a way of screening his personality from you. In the beginning, I was so overwhelmed by his talent in the studio that I didn't try to seek out his friendship. I could sense he was screening me out. Terrible jokes, bad punch lines, worst jokes in the world. But that was his way.

Diana Ross was always a hard worker, sometimes moody, very self-absorbed, but in a positive way. Even then she was very conscious of her image.

Stevie Wonder made me nervous. Something about his power. It was intimidating, like he knew something I didn't know. We'd be walking down a hall at Motown, and he'd be in a room somewhere, and we'd go stand in the doorway, and he'd say, "Hi, Nick. Hi, Val." Had no idea how he knew it was us. Scared the shit out of me.

My greatest moment at Motown had to do with one of those quality-control meetings. Smokey Robinson was there, Holland-Dozier-Holland, everybody. It was my first time at one of those meetings. Val was not there. Finally, our record comes on. It's "You're All I Need to Get By," by Marvin Gaye and Tammi Terrell.

When they finished playing the record, everything was quiet for a while. And then Berry Gordy said, "I don't think we need to vote on this one."

I had been so nervous, so tense, thinking, "Who's gonna like it, who's not? How many people are gonna vote for it?" And then there was no vote. It was, like, the greatest moment of my life.

Ry Cooder

○ ○ ○

There aren't any platinum records in his trophy room, but there's a whole body of stars who call for his slide or straight guitar on their sessions. Ry is both a consummate film scorer and a dedicated proponent of the blues.

○ ○ ○

This friend of my dad's gave me a guitar when I was four. I would sit and listen to Woody Guthrie and Leadbelly, even some classical guitar records, never knowing that what these people were playing was not impossible. So I played along with records and music became a part of my daily life.

Now blues wasn't exactly the music of West Los Angeles, or Santa Monica. We're not talking about a blues community here, or the hillbilly experience. But in the fifties, there were some old guys in Los Angeles who had come up from the South.

It was obvious to my parents that musicians were poor and could barely sustain themselves. As a result, I never thought about making any money playing music because I never saw any of these guys who had a nickel and a nail together. They were always scuffling, always at the mercy of club owners. This one old guy, Sleepy John Estes, would come out on stage, blind and infirm and barely able to walk, and you'd think, "This is the music business? Look what it's done to this guy."

But then I would say to myself, "Yeah, but it sounds good, it feels good, and I like it."

And then a club owner, Ed Pearl at the Ash Grove, hired me as an accompanist. I was fifteen, in high school, and he paid me a few dollars a night and got me into the musician's union. It was certainly a break from school, which was boring. I mean, if anybody at Santa Monica High School even thought about music, they probably thought about surf music and the Beach Boys because that was the music that was happening then. We were the Pepsi generation. We had surfing and records and dances and a certain style of clothes. Kids were acknowledging that music existed, but I could see it was a low-grade experience for them.

I really knew something about music. I could play it, I had seen other people play it. It was very real for me. To them, it was accompaniment, something you listened to while you ate lunch.

After playing for a while at the Ash Grove, I started to see that if you played good enough, you wouldn't be laughed off the stage and people wouldn't get up and leave. And then it finally occurred to me that there was money involved—a small amount, but something. And then I got lucky and got to doing record sessions, and all of a sudden the door opened.

Here were these guys playing guitar, bass, or whatever, and they owned Cadillacs and airplanes and boats—the pre-Manson high living.

I thought, "Look at this. These guys aren't broke-down, blind, and peg-legged." So after spending a year in college it became obvious to me that I really did want to play music for a living.

I went to one of my teachers and said, "Look, a guy wants me to play sessions for two weeks in L.A. I'll come back, I won't miss any work, I'll be OK."

And he said, "How much do you make on these sessions?"

I said, "Somewhere between $5,000 and $8,000 for the two weeks."

And this guy just shook his head and said, "If you can make that kind of money, why in the world are you going to school?"

Well, I listened to him. I went straight to my sessions, and I guess along the way I was very lucky. I had nice people like Terry Melcher and Jack Nitzsche helping me. I started playing on Paul Revere and the Raiders dates, the Byrds—the same sessions everyone played on. I waited, I learned, I was patient, and I had fun.

No one ever actually told me what to play. The aesthetics were a bit limiting. I mean, what's a Paul Revere and the Raiders record about anyhow? In other words, I could see there were plenty of other things to do. Nitzsche thought I should make instrumental records like Duane Eddy.

And I thought, "No, that's boring. It'll wear out in a couple of years."

I started making my own records for Warner Brothers, but in an abstract kind of way, Nitzsche was telling me that what I really should be doing is scoring films. I had never thought about that before, so I went with Jack to see this picture *Candy*. It was the stupidest thing I've ever seen in my life. But after spending some time with Jack, I could see right away that there was a place for me in this area.

Well, we did the film and the producers hated the score. They didn't understand it, they thought it was insane. So they threw it away, which was OK, because the score became the model for the Mick Jagger film, *Performance*. What we did for *Candy*, we did for *Performance*, only more so. Because of Jagger, the film could take some interesting music because the imagery was so vivid. Let's just say it wasn't quite as trashy as *Candy*.

For years, I was subsidized by Warner Brothers Records to improve my concept and get better at what I was doing, which is exactly what happened.

Film, as it turned out, proved a good way for me to go, from *Performance* all the way to *Paris, Texas*, which was easy to do because it wasn't so much talk and noise and other technical things to deal with.

High Noon is the perfect example of music and film because it seemed like such an amazing accomplishment to tell an entire story in just that little song.

Just to watch that film is a trip. It's a very simple film, not much to it. It's just a song and this guy, Gary Cooper, and what he's going through. The script was incredible. So symmetrical, everything just locks in over and over again. I love that. If you didn't have the picture, the song would never be quite as real. And if you didn't have the song, there would be a hole in the picture a mile wide.

My mind has always remained on the music and on the development of music. It's like Dizzy Gillespie said, "You don't learn your instrument. You advance on it, but you never finish." Great players develop, they're not hatched. The idea that I'm some guitar hero who looks a certain way, plays a certain way, and is a certain way has very little to do with the people who seriously pursue music and their instruments.

I think we've come around now to the point where the reaction to what I call "haircut music" has to take place. I mean, how much of it can you stand? Teenagers will buy virtually anything you throw at them. If you promote it right, they'll go for it.

There are very few of us dinosaurs that can get up on stage and, by God, "play" it. These "haircut" guys can't just play it. They need their cartridges and programs and tape to make their shit work.

So, there's still no substitute for a guy who can get up and really play. That's one thing people will always respond to.

Randy Newman

○ ○ ○

While talking to Randy at his Brentwood, California, home it became clear that there was no defining what he does. His lyrics have been praised, his voiced panned. And he wrote "I Love L.A.," the theme song of the Los Angeles Lakers Championship basketball team.

○ ○ ○

Los Angeles has had an enormous influence on my music. I can't tell exactly why. Maybe it's because film music was in Los Angeles, and my family was in film music. Or that I've always liked living in L.A., or the obvious examples, like "I Love L.A.," or "God Song," where the god I'm writing about is sort of a California god because of all the yucca trees out in the desert.

Los Angeles has probably affected my work habits in an adverse way in that it's a difficult town to bear down in. I never learned to work—in school or anywhere. Eastern kids, like Paul Simon, now there's someone with a good work ethic.

I've always tried to say something. Often it was a joke. Eccentric lyrics about eccentric people. I would plead guilty on the grounds that I prefer eccentricity to the bland "I love you, you love me, we're as happy as we can be, let's go party under the tree." If I wrote them like that, we'd all be in the same business.

I've been called pungent. I prefer pungent to satiric. But I never pay attention to that stuff because it can't do me any good. Either it makes you self-conscious, or it depresses you.

There was one song I wrote that I thought was cruel after I wrote it. I didn't think "Rednecks" was cruel, or "God Song," or "Davey the Fat Boy" because it was obvious there was something wrong with the protagonist in the song, the narrator. In "Short People," it's the narrator that's the untrustworthy guy, not the short person.

But the song I wrote called "The Blues," the one I did with Paul Simon, that one almost made fun of sensitivity. It made fun of a kid who had trouble, a kid who would rush to his room to play the piano. That was wrong. I can't think of another song of mine that I regret in the slightest, but I do regret that one.

I'm not very careful. I've written things that I didn't think were all right, and I let them go. I wrote a song, "Half a Man," about homosexuality as a contagious disease. I got some letters and some calls on it, but I thought it was funny. It was a song about the lack of understanding of homosexuality, but it hurt some people. Some gay people said my doing the song wasn't worth it, but it was to me.

I once played "Rednecks" in Lafayette, Louisiana, and they'd all stand up, which is not the right reaction but it's the one you get in the South. I get this letter from a black kid who was there, and he says, "I don't know where you're coming from, but I am sitting in a room with 1,500 white people, and there's this white guy up on stage saying "nigger," and these people are standing up, and you know, it disturbed me." I called the kid, and I think I explained it to his satisfaction, but I don't feel that I've ever been guilty of bad taste.

There's more allowed now. I mean, Prince is as interesting a writer as Cole Porter was. They're a lot alike. In the videos, you can see the similarity.

The first thing I ever did I was the B side of "Lovers by Night, Strangers by Day," by the Fleetwoods. Mine was a summer song called, "They Tell Me It's Summer." I was trying to capitalize on the season. And I kept that up. Every season I'd write, "Oh, it's fall, look at the leaves."

I don't think I was ever hungry for success. I was talking to my mother about that just the other day. She told me I never wanted anything. There was this motorscooter I wanted one time, but I didn't seriously want it, because I knew if I got it I'd die. But I wasn't really hungry because I was never really poor. It wasn't that I was disdainful of success, but it didn't tear me up when I didn't get it. Except after "Short People." When I finished the album right after "Short People," I didn't want to fly in a small plane. I didn't want the plane going down and me not knowing how the record did. As it turned out, I should have flown in the small plane.

Whatever success I've had as a songwriter, I guess I have to trace back to my friendship with Lenny Waronker. His father played in the orchestra at Fox when my Uncle was there, so I know Lenny since I was one. He's two years older than me. I remember when I was four or five, he would tell me stories. I would be the audience. He would say, "Let's ride on this tricycle." He'd get on the back and I would pull him, and we'd fall off. I would get hurt and he wouldn't. I still have scars from that tricycle. He'd say, "We can do this, we can do that," and I would be the one who ended up getting smashed. And it was that way with songwriting. I was studying classical music, and Lenny said, "Why don't you try writing some songs?"

Lenny tried to get me to sign with Warners for no money. I said, "I can't believe that. You're my friend. A&M is offering me $10,000, and Warners is offering me nothing? Fuck you."

He got so pissed off at me. He had a terrible temper as a kid. We'd play football, and he'd get mad and walk off the field. Of course, I do remember getting the $10,000 from Warners.

Warners would love me to write more hits. I'd be interested to know how many people who say they're going to try to write a hit song actually do. I've never done it. Maybe I should try. It would certainly be a nice thing to do for the old record company, but I don't think I'm capable of saying, "Gee, I'm going to try to write three hit singles on this one." I just write what comes out. Like "Short People." It just came out. I had no idea it would be a hit. I just looked at it as another one-twelfth of what I have to do to get my half a million.

But "Short People" was the worst kind of hit anyone could have. It was like having "Purple People Eater." I'd try to watch a ball game and the band would play the song and the announcers would make jokes about it. It was too noisy. I prefer quiet money.

Teddy Pendergrass

o o o

Teddy delivered some of the most sensual, intense records and personal appearances ever heard or seen. His fateful accident left him somewhere between bitter and hopeful. It was difficult seeing this terrific talent so restricted by his injuries, but he forged on, an incredible example of guts and courage.

o o o

Harold Melvin was the kind of person who thrived off making sure he had the authority. He was never a sharer, he never designated anything. He never said, "Let's do this together." He always came first, no matter whether he had anything to do with a particular situation or not.

We had a strange relationship. He is a very intelligent person, a genius when it comes to working the stage. He taught me a lot about how to work a stage, how to deal with people, how to bring people into what you're doing, how to work the audience.

If someone said it was red, he said it was pink. Even if the color was green, he had to make it blue. And he was never one to want to go further than nightclubs. That is all he knew. I wanted more.

The decision to leave Harold Melvin and the Blue Notes wasn't a hard decision. I just didn't feel I was getting all I could out of everything around me. We ended up with an album called *Wake Up Everybody*. I sang that song every night and finally I said, "God, I'm singing it, but I'm not doing it." I was telling everybody, "Wake up, pay attention, watch out, do what you have to do to make things better," and I was staying in the same rut.

Eventually, the people I was involved with convinced me it was time to go. I had to go. I had no money, no nothing. I was in California, 3,000 miles from home. I stayed up all night one night, and the next morning when it was time to go to the next job, I said, "I'm not going. See ya. Have a good time, enjoy yourself, God bless you."

The record company said, "You can't leave, you can't do this, we have a business going on here."

I said, "I am not intending to leave the company. I just need to make things better for myself. I can't stay where I am staying, I can't do what I am doing."

I don't want to sound contrived, but this thing about women finding me sexy was something that was formulated way before the Blue Notes. I never had a problem with attractive ladies. Girls always came around and sat on my steps and talked to me. We'd just sit and pass the time, and I suppose it carried over into my work. I took advantage of the situation, and the attraction became a major part of my relationship with the audience.

But there were bunches of problems, a lot of unnecessary charges. Someone was always accusing me of something. God knows, there were threats from women, threats from men. Some women said, "If you can't be mine, you can't be anybody's."

This presented a very serious problem. You go from one place to another, and a lot of times you feel you have to look over your shoulder. Could be a jealous husband who wants to jump you and blow your brains out just because his wife said something.

When the accident happened, it was devastating but it helped me to not take myself too seriously in terms of what my image had been.

But it was devastating, devastating to the max. For one thing, you find out who your friends are.

It's been very trying since the accident, but you do what you have to do to keep going. I don't mean to sound like some damned hero, but after a while your life does become normal again.

I am not worried about the wheelchair. I don't see any problems in it. I don't think I'm chained down one bit in terms of me being a nice man who is a good, hearty, total person.

Kenny Gamble

○ ○ ○

Along with his partner, Leon Huff, Kenny created the music of Philly International—dance, funk, and successful. A musician and a businessman of great talent.

○ ○ ○

I was born and raised in Philadelphia. I was working at Jefferson Medical College in cancer research, going to school trying to specialize in endocrinology, and working in music on the weekends. I was in a group called the Romeos. We worked weekends at the Hyatt Club in Jersey for six, seven years. The crowds were unbelievable. We packed the place.

This was in the early sixties when Motown was the epitome of R & B music in America. The Romeos played a lot of Motown songs, and we played a lot with Motown groups. We'd play on shows with Marvin Gaye, Smokey Robinson and the Miracles, Junior Walker, Lloyd Price.

When I heard Marvin Gaye sing, or David Ruffin and Eddie Kendricks, I said, "Now these guys are singers," and the Romeos were basically a show band—good harmonies, excellent musicians—but not great singers. It was then I started thinking about writing and producing records.

Leon Huff, Thom Bell, and myself used to talk all the time about how we hoped one day we'd be able to make our living in the music industry. Thom worked in a fish store, and Huff and me in the hospital. Like performing, we wrote songs on the weekends, late at night, and we dreamed of the day when we could wake up and come to a piano and a tape recorder and write all day long, every day.

I used to watch "American Bandstand" every day on television. I went down there a couple of times trying to get black kids in. They wouldn't let too many black kids on "Bandstand." Every now and then you'd see a few black couples dancing, but not often. "Bandstand" was basically a white show that featured a lot of black acts. The thing that attracted me to "Bandstand" was the entertainment, not the dancing. But it's funny that when black dancers came on and they showed some willingness to demonstrate new dances, somehow you wouldn't see them on anymore.

The thing about Philadelphia is its location. It's only an hour from New York and ninety minutes from Washington, two major concert cities. And there's always been plenty of talent in Philly.

For Gamble and Huff, and then later with Philadelphia International, we have tried to follow the Motown pattern of establishing a home away from home for writers and producers.

We have fifteen writers' rooms and we've turned out hits by Harold Melvin and the Blue Notes with Teddy Pendergrass, Billy Paul, the O'Jays, Patti Labelle, Lou Rawls, and many more. We have guys who, like I did, go to school and then come in here after school and write for two or three hours a day. That's what Motown did. They supplied equipment and a presence for songwriters, producers, and artists. That's what Huff and me are doing in Philly. We write, produce, and above all we teach.

Richard Carpenter

o o o

He talked about the days with sister Karen with sadness and joy. Together they fashioned some of the loveliest pop records of their time.

o o o

The Carpenters were criticized a lot, and we took it, but every now and then I would open my big mouth to someone during an interview.

I didn't feel the criticism was deserved. The thing is, it had to do with what we represented, middle America and all. We weren't trying to stamp down rock. I like rock. We just made the records we wanted to make, and it so happened that radio was ready for it and it clicked.

But they would throw these barbs at us, clawing at us. I'm not saying everyone should like it, but no one can ever tell me those records weren't well made.

One reviewer, I'll never forget, was writing about our album *Now and Then*, which ended with a Randy Edelman tune called "I Can't Make Music." And this guy writes: "The album finishes with a tune called 'I Can't Make Music,' to which, regarding the Carpenters, I can only add, 'Right on.' "

And I'm thinking, "Wait a minute! You may not like the style of our music, but don't tell me we can't make music."

Karen and I were meant to work together. Her singing and the way our voices blended and the fact that I could write and arrange was meant to be. And the songs are there to prove it.

But Karen and I both pooped out in 1975. It had been nonstop everything—world tours, recording, guest shots, photo sessions, interviews. It was also right around that time that Karen's anorexia started to manifest itself.

It really hit her in Vegas during the summer of '75. She had to go into the hospital. That girl could walk out on a stage and sing like she had never sung before. We all marveled because she was down to eighty-five pounds at the time. In between shows, she'd be flat on her back. But when she walked out onstage she was fabulous.

I still have no idea what caused her anorexia. The disorder is a mystery.

Personally, I don't believe her career had anything to do with it. Karen loved singing and recording more than anything in the world.

In '75, we had to postpone two international tours. The whole rest of the year we did nothing. Then we started back up again in January of '76. We were hoping her situation was temporary, but it was up and down.

Then the singles stopped happening. Without a doubt, I picked a couple of duds. We felt frustrated. We were still selling a lot of records, the company, A&M, was still behind us, and we had the two of us. We always felt that the next one would be it, which is every recording artist's cry. So we kept on.

And Karen was still battling with her problem. She didn't want to admit it. I remember quite a few talks with her. I said, "I'm going to kick back. Why don't you take this opportunity to seek some help, while I'm just relaxing and recharging and getting ready to start a new decade? We'll come back and start over in the eighties."

But still, she did not want to recognize, or could not recognize, that she had a problem.

By 1980 I was all set and ready to go. Karen's solo album was ready to be mixed. Then she got married and started getting thinner again. Then the marriage didn't work out. By the time we came back from our promotional tour for *Made in America*, she realized she needed some help. She came back for a couple of weeks in '82, and we cut a few tracks, but that was it.

Karen was unique. I really think we were unique, I really do. We made good records, the songs were great, and Karen was a fabulous singer. The public knew. Maybe they couldn't articulate it, but they knew.

Al Jarreau
○ ○ ○

They said his music was not black enough, not jazz enough, and not pop enough. What he did was persevere and prove that his talent was enough to get him Grammys and the recognition as an artist of quality.

○ ○ ○

I grew up during the time when rock 'n' roll was really bursting out of the seams. The people I sang with in school—"shoo-be-doo" street-corner stuff, tile-bathroom rhythm-and-blues singing groups—they would say, "Rock 'n' roll, rock 'n' roll." But thinking back on it, I see myself standing outside of myself and thinking, "OK, there are some nice songs in here, but no, I'm not fascinated by this."

I had been listening to Sarah Vaughan and Billy Eckstine and Count Basie and Stan Kenton. Probably the biggest influence on me as a singer was Jon Hendricks. Another was Johnny Mathis, who was, for me, an extension of Nat Cole. So rock 'n' roll seemed like a step backwards. Occasionally it peaks, and some wonderful things have come out of it, but for the most part the music is mediocre bullshit, you dig?

I really liked the rhythm and blues of the time, and I sang a lot of it, but I never got this Bill Haley stuff. I never got the Elvis thing. Years later, I intellectualized about what it had meant to me over the years, but I never got it musically. On the other hand, I am so happy that somebody got it because if nothing else, four guys from Liverpool heard that stuff and because they did the world was really changed.

But I was busy singing "Mood Indigo" and bebop songs with a jazz quartet, and wondering what all the fuss was about. I have an historical appreciation for "I Want to Hold Your Hand," but there ain't anything redeeming in it for me musically.

I wanted to sing a solo and improvise like a horn player. Or stand back and let someone else do it, but while they are doing it, I'm going to make "goonga" sounds, and add to it, embellish it, accompany myself.

Suddenly, sounds just started flying out of my mouth. Just me and a guitar player. Or me and a piano player, and that is how it happened for me.

But my way had its price. Maybe I should have said, "I just need a good song. One song that is going to be a hit." I'm an OK songwriter, but I always needed, and still need, that one song that will go through the roof. I haven't had it. People speak my name in the same sentence with hugely successful recording artists, and I'm glad for that, but I haven't had the kind of success in terms of sales as, say, Lionel Richie, Stevie Wonder, and Aretha Franklin.

Al Jarreau simply hasn't had that really big-selling album. I'm one of those guys who got real sacred about writing and wanting to write my own songs, when I really should have been out there looking for a great song.

Kenny Rogers

○ ○ ○

**He's had several cracks at a career and his name represents a genre
of music and appeal that brought him enormous financial and musical
rewards. Kenny carved out an audience that remains loyal and, at
times, even fanatic.**

○ ○ ○

I remember back during the First Edition, we'd put out songs, and boom,
they'd go right up the charts. I thought, "This is so easy. We've stumbled
onto a magic formula. Amazing how stupid everyone else is."

Then I remember the day the First Edition broke up, and there were
no more hits, $65,000 in debt, and I'm thinking, "What happened to that
magic formula I was so sure I had?"

The way I see it, I just want to be in the Top 10 every so often. I'd like
to know I'm capable of being more than, "He was great one time."

If anybody in this business tells you they don't have an inflated ego,
they're either lying to you or lying to themselves. You get to where you
thrive on the high, that rush at night, that one hour on stage. I can walk
down Sunset to the front of the Roxy, and it's amazing to me that the kids
in their pink spiked hair know who I am. Of all the places in the world,
that's the one place I wouldn't think anyone would know me. They might
not like my music, but they don't laugh at me. That's important to me.

I think my favorite time was when "Lucille" came out. My manager,
Ken Kragen, and I had plenty of strategy time. We'd meet for hours in the
day, and we'd say, "OK, if we can pull this off, and then do this, maybe
they'll let me sing a song on the American Music Awards. Then, if you do
that, maybe they'll let you on the 'Tonight' show. If you get on the 'Tonight'
show, maybe they'll let you host it once or twice." It was a little ladder we
planned, and we pulled it off. And in this business, once it happens for you,
you become an order taker. You take the best orders that come in, the best
requests.

I guess I really hit my peak in '79, '80, when I was winning a lot of
awards and everything I was doing was going right to the top. They were
comparing me to Elvis Presley because I was breaking house records he had
held for years. I said, "Wait a minute. Elvis was a very special man. He
changed the course of music. I didn't. All I did was have some hit records."

I have always believed that if you build yourself up, others are going
to tear you down. If you tear yourself down, they will build you up. It's
really diffusing in an interview with a reviewer who plans on tearing you
apart, and you say to him, "Hey, I know I'm not a great singer." What can
he say? You've already said it. All he has to do in his review is reflect what
the audience did. It's a mechanism, and it works.

Something happened to me right before my throat operation which I
will never forget. It was one of the most touching things that ever happened

to me. I was in Salt Lake City struggling through a show. The next day we were to be in Eugene, Oregon, and I told the guys we needed to cancel Eugene because I can't sing.

Anyway, we went to Eugene, and I said, "Look, I'll try. But if I can't do it, I'm going to quit."

The Gatlin Brothers and Lee Greenwood were with me, and they do their sets. I go out and the first thing I do is, I start squeaking. Forget singing, I couldn't talk. I tried to do the first song and couldn't. I stopped the band and said, "This is not what you paid for. I can't do this to you. I want you to know I will give everybody their money back, and the first two acts were on me. I will come back when my throat is better."

They said, "No, no, we don't want you to go."

I said, "But I can't even talk." Well, I did an hour and ten minutes that night. I couldn't talk. I couldn't sing, and the worse I was the more we laughed. I'd screw up notes, and the audience would break up. I did "Lady," and it was terrible. Lionel Richie would have died, but the people loved it. I realized at that point that people really do care about me.

Everyone thought I was crazy when I went to work with Lionel. They said, "He's an R & B singer, an R & B producer," and that is exactly what I wanted. One of my favorite albums ever is one of Ray Charles' country records, the one where he does "Georgia on My Mind," and a bunch of country songs. What he did was, he took country tracks and he sang them R & B. All I did was take R & B tracks and sing them country.

There is a very fine line between country and R & B. Country music is the white man's R & B. The beauty of both country and R & B is that if it hurts, they say it hurts, "Goddamnit," they say, "it hurts." That is why country and R & B will always reign.

David Gates

o o o

The sounds of Bread were mostly David's creations and performances. His soft style and sentimental lyrics combined to sell millions of records in the seventies in America and Great Britian.

o o o

I was playing night clubs and dances for sororities and fraternities, and my parents wanted me to finish college, but I was losing interest. My grades were slowly slipping. At the end of my junior year I told my father I'd like to leave Tulsa and go to California to give it a try. I said, "Let me go out for the summer, just to see what happens."

He said, "Take two years and give it a shot. If it doesn't work out, you can still finish college." So I saved my nightclub money, which was all of $10 a night at the time. I was married with a one-year-old and a six-week-old, we lived with my parents. I had an old Cadillac that I'd bought from a friend of my dad's. When I'd saved $200, my wife, the kids, and me took off in the Cadillac for California.

I had a nightclub job waiting because of some friends who had already made the trip from Oklahoma. I go out there, and on my third night in the club we get fired. And the $200 is gone—first month's rent, gas deposit, phone deposit, groceries. And nobody to help me except my uncle who lived in Whittier. He couldn't give me any money, but he brought me food.

We drove from club to club, three a night, auditioned for everybody until we finally got a job and got rolling again. And then on Saturday nights, after hours, musicians from all over the city would meet at a place called the Crossbow, in the Valley. It was at the Crossbow that I met guys like Steve Douglas, Glen Campbell, James Burton, Leon Russell, Chuck Blackwell, Jerry Cole. Slowly they were getting into recordings, mostly demo sessions, some union jobs. By jamming with these people, I got more work. All of a sudden, I was being asked to play on demo sessions and then on recordings.

Then I began submitting songs, which got me fired up about writing because, hey, I could work at home and I didn't have to spend all night in clubs.

It was Roger Gordon who then suggested, "Why don't you sing your songs? I mean, you're already singing on demos. Why don't you go for a deal on a label?"

I said, "I really don't want to go on the road. I'm happy being behind the scenes." But I felt like I should be doing my own stuff, just to see if I could do it better than the people who were recording it.

So with that motivation in mind I went to Columbia to see Jack Gold. I'd done a lot of arranging for Jack's artists, so I asked him, "Will you sign me?"

He said, "You don't want to do that. That's hard work." He didn't take me seriously.

At about the same time, I had produced a small group called the Pleasure Faire. One of the guys in the group was Robb Royer, who was writing with James Griffin as a team. Rob suggested one day that I come over and meet James. And I did. They played me two or three of their songs, and I played them two or three of my songs. Then we decided to form a group and look for a deal collectively because we thought we'd do better as a group than independently. That's how Bread started in late '67.

A bread truck came along right at the time we were trying to think of a name. We had been saying, "How about bush, telephone pole? Ah, bread truck, bread." It began with a B, like the Beatles and the Bee Gees. Bread also had a kind of universal appeal. It could be taken a number of ways. Of course, for the entire first year people called us the Breads.

Herbie Hancock

o o o

**He's so literate, so musical, and appears to have discovered the
fountain of youth. A much respected jazzman who moved into another
arena, he has piled up Oscars and Grammys to prove he can handle
it.**

o o o

I would go back to Chicago every summer during college and work as a
mailman. I'd play gigs, too, but working at the post office was how I supported
myself.

When I finished college and the next September rolled around and
there was no school to go back to, I was lucky enough to get a gig for ten
days with Coleman Hawkins. It was for ten consecutive days, which is
supposed to be illegal, according to the musicians' union. But they billed it
as a show, like a Broadway show, and they got around the union. I played
four sets a night, five on Saturday, for ten straight days, and I was still
working for the post office during the day.

After three days of trying to keep this pace, I got very sick—fever, head
cold, hardly slept at all. On the third day, I tried to deliver the mail. I was
a carrier, and I was thumbing through the sack at somebody's house, looking
for this woman's mail, when I fell asleep standing there. I almost fell down
a flight of concrete stairs. After that, I said, "This is it," and I quit the post
office.

All the guys at the post office said, "If you quit the post office, you're
gonna regret it the rest of your life." They also said I'd be back.

A few years ago, they had a big jazz festival in Chicago. They even had
a Herbie Hancock Day. I'm in the dressing room and the maintenance man
walks by and he says, "I know you won't remember me, but I used to work
with you at the post office."

I said, "Really?"

He said, "Yeah. We said you'd be back, and you never came back."

I said, "No, I never came back."

Three months after I left the post office, Donald Byrd came through
town, and I got a gig with him. Donald took good care of me for a long
time after that. I shared an apartment with Donald. And then in '63 I started
getting calls from people saying that Miles Davis was looking for me.

Donald said, "Look, if Miles calls, tell him you're not working with
anybody and take the gig."

I said, "Donald, after all you've done for me?"

He said, "Just do it. I will not stand in the way of you making the most
out of this opportunity."

And that's exactly what happened. Miles called and he said, "Are you
working with anybody?"

I said, "No."

He said, "Can you come to my house tomorrow at one o'clock?"

I said, "Yes," and he hung up. I didn't even know where Miles lived. Thirty minutes later, I got a call from Tony Williams, the drummer. He had gotten a call from Miles, too, and Tony knew where Miles lived.

Well, I showed up at Miles' house scared to death. Tony was there, Ron Carter, considered the greatest bass player, had already been with Miles for a couple of months, and he was there. An awesome saxophone player by the name of George Coleman was there. And we're all in Miles' basement. And Miles doesn't show up. He was in the house, upstairs, and when I came in he just told me to go downstairs. George and Ron were kind of conducting. We went through some new tunes, and after a couple of hours Miles came downstairs, stayed there for about a minute, and then went back upstairs. A half hour later, he came back with his horn, played three notes, said, "Shit," and threw down his horn and went back upstairs. I didn't know what was going on.

What I didn't know was that Miles had already decided that I was in his band. I thought I was auditioning. After three days of doing this, Miles comes downstairs again and says, "Two-thirty tomorrow, Columbia Studios, the big studio on 30th Street."

I was so scared. I said, "Miles, does that mean I'm in the band."

And he said, "We're making a record tomorrow."

We get to the studio and Miles starts playing these tunes we hadn't rehearsed. We started playing a song called "Seven Steps to Heaven." Miles had kind of rehearsed the melody, but he'd never taken a solo off it. Not until the record date. I learned later just how Miles works. He is so honest about music that he wants to catch the kernel of creativity as it's being created. If you rehearse too much, you're not going to get it. He'd rather have the mistakes on record just to get the spontaneity. Pretty risky, but very honest.

George Benson

○ ○ ○

**When a great jazz artist hits the mainstream of popularity, his jazz
pals call it selling out. The public calls it amazing, and George has
been just that with great pop and R & B hits along with the brilliant
guitar technique he's had for years.**

○ ○ ○

A lot of jazz people ate me up when I started doing pop songs. I was the
pop star who changed from jazz, and a lot of people got very hostile. I made
a statement about how jazz musicians need to think with a new mentality,
and Oscar Peterson said something like, "Speak for yourself."

I think of all the people I came in contact with over the years, a meeting
I had with John Hammond was the most effective of my career, in the sense
that it gave me an identity. He realized I had other music in me, that I
could play rhythm and blues and some rock 'n' roll. But he said, "Be known
as a jazz musician first. It will be more lasting." And the two albums I did
for him at Columbia gave me a base that will last me a lifetime. John was
also a lover of the guitar.

I came to play the guitar quite by accident. I didn't even own a guitar
when I was learning to play, for years. After my initial start as a ukulele
player, I had a guitar from age nine to eleven. But then my stepfather got
rid of it, and I didn't own a guitar for maybe the next four years. Then,
when I was fifteen, he made me my first electric guitar because we couldn't
afford to buy one at the pawn shop. He said, "I think I can make that." He
had never made a guitar in his life.

But he managed to muscle up about twenty-one dollars' worth of sup-
plies, and he chopped apart my mother's hope chest. I designed the guitar.
We traced it on brown paper, on top of the chest top, then we sawed it out.
It took the whole day because it was made out of oakwood. We used formica
to cover it. When I came along, those corner bars that used to hire bands
in the thirties and forties and fifties were all closing up. Whatever the
reason—lack of business, or they couldn't afford to pay the bands—they
were closing and jobs became harder to find.

Artists like Dizzy Gillespie, who had always been popular because he
was an entertainer with a great personality, he was moving on to another
category, to the more elite places. I was working the leftover places, and I
was stuck in the middle musically because the new audience wanted to hear
what they were hearing on the jukeboxes, which wasn't the jazz they heard
on the jukeboxes years before. The new musicians didn't accept me either.
They were playing straight contemporary stuff, and I was out there somewhere
in between, trying to tie these audiences together. How do you play "Everyday
I Have the Blues" to an audience that wants to hear tunes by Jackie Wilson
and James Brown? That was my challenge. I mixed the music and never
really made one audience happy.

But it was just enough. Somebody would have their head out the door, and we'd be playing something, and they might stop for a minute and listen to it, or they might come back the next night and say, "Man, play that tune you played as I was walking out the door last night." It was a terrible era.

My guitar playing started to get popular among the young players, but I was playing in places where they wouldn't dare come. For years I was doing that and not knowing it. We would play in, say, Boston, at Estelle's on Tremont Street, right in the heart of the ghetto, and sometimes two brave guys would come over, take a chance and come to the club. One day they stayed over and they said, "George, do you know that if you were playing down at such-and-such street, or at Lenny's on the turnpike, do you realize the place would be packed every night."

I said, "Is that right?" and I went back and I told my manager, and he being from an old school and not knowing anything about crossover audiences, he would make statements like, "George, the people love you. They will go anywhere to see you."

And I said, "Wait a minute now. You wouldn't put Glen Campbell in the Apollo Theater, would you?" Wouldn't mean anything.

Same story in L.A. I was playing in a black club in L.A. once, and the club owner didn't pay me, and I was stuck. These two young boys, white guys, came over to me and said, "George, we're taking a chance seeing you here. We're scared to death, and we don't know if we're going to get out of here."

And I said, "Oh, ain't nobody gonna bother you." But the bottom line was, I looked around and I saw other jazz musicians who were limited, guys who wouldn't compromise their talent and wouldn't search for an audience. I don't think I ever compromised my talent, but I did search for a newer audience.

Walter Yetnikoff

o o o

**One of the record industry's high-profile executives, he led the
juggernaut CBS record company through its greatest growth,
continued to forge ahead, and eventually got CBS to sell it to Sony.
Definitely not a shrinking violet.**

o o o

I was working at a law firm, and they sent me over to CBS around Christmastime to do a file search. Very boring. But CBS was having a Christmas
party. Lots of girls around, music, lights being turned off. I thought, "This
looks like a fun place."

About a week later Clive Davis offered me a job to be his assistant at
$1,500 more than I was getting. He gave me my own secretary, and the
most exciting thing, a telephone with four buttons on it.

Rock 'n' roll was becoming a big business, and there were very few
people around who understood the deals. Records were not something artists
historically did to make money. It was more of an ancillary thing. And then,
all of a sudden there is this giant business. All these young bands with
eighteen-year-old guitarists coming in and asking for $1 million, which
shocked a lot of people.

"The kid wants one million dollars."

"What's his name?"

"Quicksilver Messenger Service."

"I never heard of such nonsense."

I think I can tell a hit record as good as the next guy. It's from listening
to the radio, not because of some musical ability. I'm kidding myself if I
were to think I had creative talent. In fact, I'm in awe of it because I can't
do it. We had a dinner for Michael Jackson. A lot of retailers at his house.
Very gracious, very nice. Someone had to say something to the retailers,
and Michael says, "I can't do that." He turns to me and he says, "How do
you do things like that?"

And I said, "Are you kidding? How do you do the kind of things you
do?" I'm in awe of artistic talent. I said the same thing to Springsteen. I
said, "I'm jealous of you." He sits down and plays a song, and I want to
know, "How do you do this?"

CBS has always been a broadcasting company first. They got interested
in the record business when we started making a lot of money, but they
never treated us with the same dignity as they did the broadcasting division.
After Goddard Lieberson and after Clive Davis, I was running the international division and Irwin Siegelstein was running domestic, and it was a
question of which one of us, or an outside person, was going to get the
Fuhrer's job. I got it because Arthur Taylor's assistant, a lady, liked me. I
think that's why I got the job.

I was walking into this title which was a little scary. I said, "I can't step into Goddard's shoes. He was a very special guy." When he died, I was very angry at him because he left and he didn't beat the system, which no one beats. He was one of the most elegant guys I've ever met. So now I have the job, and I'm scared shit, and I have no one to talk to. Whatever one thinks of Clive Davis getting fired by CBS in retrospect, we all agree it was a badly mishandled situation by the company.

So I have to follow Clive and Goddard. Terrific. I have to develop my own image. The first thing I did was take a piece of yellow paper and write down everything everybody thought I should do. I would then go home at night, look at the yellow paper and choose what I wanted to do. How do you forge your own image? Difficult. Unconsciously, I picked a fight with Warner Brothers. So now I have a big flag out that says "Fuck Warner Brothers." I have all the troops rallying around the flag, using the excuse to go in and steal artists under the banner of "Fuck Warner Brothers."

It was like I'd created a nation. Follow Walter? No one knew who I was. So unconsciously I made a war out of it. I believed in the cause, and now I had an army behind me. Years later, I realize that Warner Brothers wasn't trying to do anything to me. I did it because I didn't know what else to do, so I created a rallying point. Today I feel sort of stupid about it. Why was I fighting with Warners? What did they ever do to me? They didn't do anything to me. It was a way to make an image, a way to create an army, a rallying point for a company that was floundering a bit at the time. I was never mad at anyone, but it worked.

At that time, though, I turned to Clive for advice. I knew what he was going through, but still I needed his advice, and I think he gave me bad advice because unconsciously he still couldn't let go of what he had been at CBS. Once you work for someone, it is very hard for that someone to accept you as an equal. To them, you are always their employee. I think Clive gave me very bad advice. He said, "Don't sign this artist. Sign that one." Exactly the reverse of what proved ultimately right. He was pretty pissed off at CBS, and with good reason, but he didn't help me very much.

But still, the record division was always looked upon as a stepchild. At one point when Barbra Streisand was going through a bad time—this was around the time of *Yentl*—she wanted a plane because she was going to Utah. She wanted to go skiing. If she had said that to Steve Ross at WCI, he would have sent nine planes to take her to Utah. I went to the guy upstairs and I said, "Can I have a plane for Barbra?"

He said, "That's not what the plane's for. It's to take six sales reps to a seminar in Georgia."

I said, "It doesn't matter. They can walk. The plane should be for the talent."

He says, "You tell her that the plane is not available."

Well, I'm not going to lie to her. My point is, this was not very helpful. Better off we didn't have a plane, which we don't now. But Sony has planes.

With CBS I always felt like an orphan. They never cared, even when we started making a lot of money. It didn't get serious until all the talk started about CBS selling the record division.

I know I have the reputation of having a big mouth. I don't think I could stop yenta-ing and yakking. In this business, you play your own ego. Whatever the public image is, it's foolish to try to change it. This is not the easiest job in the world. It's very scary. Who really knows what the people are going to like out there except Clive.

Bob Seger
o o o

The man from Detroit powers his rock across America and has done so for many years. His tours are electric, his songs are gutty, and his persona is low-key for a man who's had so much success. He tells why.

o o o

In a sense I'm like Paul Simon. Seldom does he listen to his records. When he is done writing and recording, he listens to whatever turns him on and gets him going. It's that admiration for other artists that gets us to the point where we seek out stuff to inspire us.

I was born in Detroit, but I grew up in Ann Arbor, and the R & B I listened to more than Motown, which was really good, was the R & B they played on WLAC out of Nashville. I would hear James Brown, Wilson Pickett, Solomon Burke, the Falcons, the stuff that was really gutsy, urban R & B that hit me harder than the Top 40 Motown factory beat. Motown was cool, too. But I found that I was appreciated best when I sang real hard. Those guys—Wilson and James and guys like that—sang their brains out. Those were the guys who got me going.

I don't write about my own life too much. I find that when I do it tends to be melodramatic. I try to write about other people's lives, people I'm close to, people in the band, a guy in the crew, or someone I just met. I listen real hard to get things from them. I went up to this actor friend's ranch in Montana, and I wrote a song about Montana called "West to the Moon." It was being there for three days. The place was just so beautiful.

I really like the level of celebrity I have. I feel sorry for people like Michael Jackson and Bruce Springsteen. The first thing that happened when Bruce got huge, I called Roy Bittan, his keyboard player, and I said, "OK, ask him where he goes for a hamburger now." Bruce always loved to, after the gig, go and find the best hamburger in whatever town he was in. Just go out and drive and find it. I'm glad that I can still do things like that. I try to stay off TV. I like to be able to observe. I stayed off my album covers for seven years, just for that purpose. I don't mind my 2 million fans or whatever knowing it's me. That's a level I'm comfortable with.

I've kind of patterned myself a little bit after Peter Townshend of the Who. In spite of them being together for twenty years, they did not put out that many records. But the records they did put out were always good. I've seen a lot of artists putting out too many records. Record after record after record, and their popularity gets diluted. The basic thing for me is to make sure that I wait until something I have is good enough to release rather than just making an album because I'm hot.

Early on, when I didn't know any better, my manager said, "Look at the Beatles catalog. Look at what they did in six years." Makes you kind of feel like you're lazy. But then I happen to know. For instance, Jimmy Iovine is a very good friend of mine. He worked with John Lennon. Jimmy said how easy it came for John. I mean, the guy could sit down in the studio and write a great song, just like that. Some people are more gifted. I'm slower. I'm not as talented, nor as inherently gifted as John Lennon. I'd be the first to admit it. For me, it's more of a workman's effort. I have to keep at it. It's like Thomas Edison said, "It's 98 percent perspiration, and 2 percent inspiration."

I was a poor kid growing up. Looking back on it now, I really felt like I didn't deserve to be among the big guys. Eric Clapton is my age. Peter Townshend is younger. But yet they made it ten years before me. It took me a long time to begin to feel like I deserved it. Because I'm not gifted, it took me a much longer time to learn how to really write a good song. I used to go out and play 250 nights a year. Drove all over the country in a station wagon from '65 to '75. I didn't believe I deserved it until probably '78. And that's in spite of *Night Moves* and *Live Bullet*. It wasn't until *Stranger in Town* that I really knew that, "Hey, I do deserve this."

Robert Plant

o o o

Led Zeppelin was the first and perhaps the all-time best of what we now call heavy metal bands. They blazed a trail across the world, and Robert doesn't mind talking about that wondrous decade when they shone. Now a solo star, he admits to a wish to get the band together again.

o o o

The prolific quality of the late sixties could take an average or a just-above-average musician to incredible heights simply because of all the changes in the air. I really thought when I first heard the Buffalo Springfield and "Forever Changes" by Arthur Lee that I was listening to anthems. I really thought the whole social structure was going to shift, naive little boy that I was.

I wanted to be a part of that great ambiguous movement, that kind of fanfare of change and responsibility. I look at some of the lyrics now, and perhaps they were a bit embarrassing, or naive or cute or quaint. The fact that I thought I was going to contribute to something that was going to make some sense and take us out of the period of early-sixties confusion and actually bring on another kind of confusion later on was enough for me. To be a part of all that made us all raise a little bit higher than we expected. Whatever limited qualities or capabilities we had, certainly we found a real hotbed of enthusiasm to absorb whatever it was we were doing.

My singing voice came out of the loins of a civil engineer. I didn't ask him too much about it. He was a bit embarrassed about me being around at all. Seriously, I don't know where my voice comes from. I listened a lot to Ray Charles. I wanted to be Ray Charles. I also liked to listen to Mose Allison, Oscar Brown, Jr., Maurice Williams & the Zodiacs. I loved the way Maurice Williams' voice used to sort of trail around and leave you high up in the clouds, and then swoop down again.

I was like a middle-class kid. My dad used to drop me off at the club where I used to play, and at that club I was exposed to the black man and his music. I could sit there and listen to King Pleasure, even though I was far too young to know who King Pleasure was.

It was very spontaneous most of the time in Led Zeppelin. Things were created virtually as a four-piece band. It was Jimmy Page bringing in cassettes or ideas that were then created on the spot. Sometimes John Paul Jones would contribute the main leading part of a song, and then it would be a pretty quick arrangement of bits and pieces so that the thing fitted together rather quickly.

We set standards for ourselves that we knew we couldn't ever dip away from. The first album took thirty-six hours and cost £1,700. The enthusiasm quality was such that we could actually turn up when we were ready, really hot, and do it. The longest period of time that ever elapsed between creation and a piece of music being there to smile at and brag about was the time it took to design the album cover. Looking back at it now, it's quite hilarious that we followed everything meticulously right down the line. You could lose more sleep worrying about an argument with Atlantic Records about having no print at all on the cover of *Houses of the Holy*. Generally, we just fucked around with the previous order of things.

I didn't even know what we had. I was nineteen when I heard the tapes of our first rehearsal. I mean, it really wasn't a pretty thing. It wasn't supposed to be a pretty thing. It was just an unleashing of energy. But it felt like it was something I always wanted.

I had a couple of bad knocks which, no matter what happens, will always have taken their toll on me. I know that my kind of vision, or the carefree element I had, disappeared instantly when I had my automobile accident in 1975. That kind of ramshackled "I'll take the world now" attitude was completely gone.

But I never stopped singing. I just played a gig in the Potteries, a district in England where they make porcelain. I played in a hall that I hadn't played in for fifteen years, and I sang better than I had ever sung in my life. I don't view life in terms of singing in front of 60,000 people at the Pontiac Silverdome. It's such a fine line between having a great night and having an average night. My enthusiasm and my capacity to give is more important than the magnitude of the reception.

The satisfaction today is great. It's important because I'm trying to make some kind of move on my own terms, without the hysteria that was common only to that great epoch. I mean, David Gilmour of Pink Floyd is having the time of his life right now. He'd be the first to say how wonderful it is. Pink Floyd is merrily dancing along. But right now I don't want to hang onto the name Led Zeppelin and say, "Here it is again. We better get the keyboard player on a diet." I'm not Led Zeppelin. I'm just this character who keeps saying, "I'm not Led Zeppelin."

But I really, really would like to be in Led Zeppelin again. Whether or not time allows that to happen, I don't know. Led Zeppelin would have to be a combination of what is was and what it should be. It's something that would take quite a lot of work. That work would be quite painstaking. Led Zeppelin would have to come out with all the pride it had initially. I'm afraid there are a lot of bands reforming for the hell of it, and I find it all a little bit forward. I believe that the power is still there between Jimmy and myself. Led Zeppelin doesn't need to be encouraged to become Led Zeppelin again. It'll happen or it won't.

Chris Wright

○ ○ ○

Chris teamed with Terry Ellis in the seventies to shake up the British music establishment by forming Chrysalis Records. They spawned a host of stars and are proof that small can make it.

○ ○ ○

I found Ten Years After when they were called the Jaybirds and they were backing a group called the Ivy League. The Ivy League was a big act in England that went to San Francisco and recorded a song about San Francisco and wearing flowers in your hair. They put out a record under the name the Flower Pot Band, and the Flower Pot Band proved to be a one-record wonder. When they went back to calling themselves the Ivy League, Ten Years After was backing them.

I was working up in Manchester, straight out of university, and I was booking a lot of colleges up there, plus I was running a blues club on Thursday nights. There was not too much work for blues groups and Ten Years After played blues. They would do "Woodchopper's Ball" as a playout number when the Ivy League went offstage. It was quite something for a rock group to do something like "Woodchopper's Ball." They knew I did booking on the weekends, and they persuaded me to book them. Then they persuaded me to manage them when they got up to Manchester.

The name Ten Years After meant we had a problem finding a name. We spent weeks looking for a name, and then someone came up with something stupid and that was it. Somebody was reading the paper and the story said, "Ten years after the Russian revolution." It was just at that point where they were ready to give up hope of ever finding a name, and so it became Ten Years After.

Management is like being in the trenches. I will always be a record man, but my business was built on management. You're always managing. "Which number goes where?" "How many encores tonight, guys? Four?" I still think in those terms, but I made a conscious decision to give up management when I started having children. I couldn't deal with the baby waking up in the middle of the night and, at the same, time, the four A.M. phone calls from someone in a band. My partner, Terry Ellis, and I had been sidestepping into the record business anyway. I wanted to get out of the management end and just be a record company. It was a conscious decision, based on life-style.

Jethro Tull was not a troublesome act to manage because I did not deal with their troubles as much as Terry. Ten Years After, which I did deal with, was a nightmare. I had a vested interest in keeping Ten Years After together, and if it were not for my emotional commitment to Ten Years After making it, they would have broken up before they ever made it.

The things they went through, the fights, were outrageous. It was ridiculous. They did a number called "Good Morning, Little Schoolgirl," an old blues number. The keyboard player dropped out, and the drummer dropped out completely, although he might have done just a little high-hat to keep the rhythm going. But the guitarist, Alvin Lee, and the bass player, Leo Lyons, would stand next to each other and fight, making these noises at each other in front of 20,000 people. It gets worse. They would also throw bottles at each other. There was many a night I did not think we were going to get through the gig. The minute I stopped managing them, it was over. That quickly. I suppose deep down inside all groups are a little difficult to manage.

I was very happy to get out of management and into the record business full time. Of course, that doesn't mean Chrysalis always made the right decisions. I remember how we hemmed and hawed over the Sex Pistols. I was prepared to sign them until their lawyer wanted us to up the deal by ten grand, claiming he had an offer from EMI, and that he would go to them if I didn't come up with the additional money.

I could not believe they would sign with EMI so I called his bluff. I sent one of my blokes to EMI to see if Malcolm McLaren and the lawyer were there for a meeting. The guy came in the next morning and said they never went to EMI.

The lawyer called me and said, "It's yours, but you have to come up with the extra ten grand or we're going to EMI."

I said, "No. That's my deal. I'm going to stick with it."

They said, "We'll, we're going to EMI."

I said, "OK, go with EMI," thinking he would call me back and say they've changed their minds. Unfortunately, my espionage agent fucked up. He was watching the wrong door because the Sex Pistols did sign with EMI.

Ian Anderson

∘ ∘ ∘

He was and is Jethro Tull. His hopping on one leg while playing the flute excited the audience but belied a serious mind with other interests besides rock 'n' roll.

∘ ∘ ∘

Jethro Tull was always a band that went out like Led Zeppelin. We went out to clean up, to work six, seven nights a week, and make money.

We didn't go out like the Rolling Stones and rent two floors of a hotel and have bodyguards and a vast entourage of people that ate up every cent of profit. We went out with the guys in the band and two or three road managers. Everything was done low-budget.

We came in during the progressive-rock era, which coincided with a boom in FM radio and the whole idea that you could do something that didn't have a catchy chorus, and you didn't have to wear a suit on stage. You could break all the rules that had ever been written, never even release a single, and still have a Number 1 album.

I was always seen as a bit of an eccentric character on stage. People thought I was forty when I was twenty. On our first album, *This Was*, we all appeared as old men, as a spoof. We couldn't believe anyone would take it seriously. But when we arrived in America for our first tour, people said, "We thought you guys were old—forty, fifty, even sixty." They were really let down when they found us to be twenty and twenty-one.

Our image wasn't carefully thought out or manufactured. I was never particularly outgoing as a child. When I got into music, I wasn't a showman. I found it easier to hide behind an image. I wasn't trying to create a gray impression. I was actually hiding from the world by wearing a long overcoat and pretending to be eccentric. I just wanted to be totally outside my peer group, and that's how I covered up my basic insecurity. By becoming another person onstage, it lets the private individual off the hook.

I never could have lived the life-style attributed to me. I can never be the character I portray on stage. I'm always surprised when people think I should be a lot crazier than I am.

I chose the flute because I wanted something unusual in the context of a rock band and yet very portable and pocketable because I literally left home with a carry bag containing a few belongings and that big overcoat. That's all I had when I went away. The flute was nice because when it was disassembled it fit very nicely into a small box in my pocket. I really liked the idea that I could produce something from my pocket and make music on it.

From 1971 onward, I began telling everybody that our next tour would be our last tour. By everybody, I don't mean the public or the press, but the guys in the group and management. I'd say, "Look, this really is it, guys. After this tour, that's it. I can't do it anymore." Of course, after the last tour, we'd say, "All right, one more tour, one more record." It just never petered out.

I started to see that I didn't actually have to stop playing music completely. I saw that I could carry on with music, but at a level that would be fun, where I didn't have to be Ian Anderson, the rock star, or Ian Anderson, from Jethro Tull, to everyone I met. I could be Ian Anderson, salmon farmer, and not have to talk about music all the time, which was very exciting.

Outside of music, my life is a strange mixture of academic science, biology, husbandry, and entrepreneurial flair. That's what fish farming is all about. The people in that industry no longer say, "Oh, he can't be serious. He's just some pop musician who made a few bucks and is now trying to lose it quickly doing something else."

I've been fish farming for eight years. Relatively speaking, I'm one of the early starters in the industry. I have respect from people in that business now, and I don't find the idea of being a musician as getting in the way, except when I have to say, "OK," to the people who work for me, "you're on your own for a few months. I'm off to make another record."

Rod Stewart

o o o

You hear that voice on the radio and you know it immediately. Rod's music has ranged from plaintive ballads to disco rockers, and his popularity is universal. Also, his ability to attract some of the world's loveliest women is a matter much discussed by his contemporaries.

o o o

Al Jolson was a strong influence on me. I do a lot with my hands, like he did. My family used to collect his records. Even now, at Christmastime, we still go through a Jolson routine. My brother does an absolutely marvelous Jolson impersonation. The whole family is into it. I was brought up on Jolson.

Then I got into folk music, listening to Woody Guthrie, Jack Elliott, Leadbelly. Then into black music—Sam Cooke, Otis Redding—and some Eddie Cochran. But I didn't start out in music. In 1964 I had just left a job in the cemetery. Me and my mates, we all had long hair, so we couldn't get jobs. I wasn't in the music business. I remember seeing the Stones before an audience of twenty-eight, thirty people. I will never forget that. Ron Wood says to me now, "Why don't you come to see us?"

I said, "I did in 1964. I don't want to see you again."

It was a tremendous time. The Yardbirds had Eric Clapton and Jeff Beck at that time, and I knocked around and listened. I fancied myself as a singer, and I would be at the railway station singing with a bunch of guys, playing harmonica and singing while waiting for the train. One night, and this is absolutely true, Long John Baldry heard me singing at the station. He was on the other platform, waiting to go the other way. This is after Cyril Davies died of alcohol poisoning, which I thought was a very heroic way to go.

Baldry says to me, "Why don't you join the band?" which was called the Hoochie Coochie Men. This is '64, just after the Stones' first record came out. Baldry was taking a piss. He said, "I will pay you £35 a week," which was a good wage for singing three, four nights, three songs a night. I thought, this guy has got to be mad.

We did our first gig at Manchester University. We had one rehearsal, one single rehearsal. I said to John, "What am I going to do? I only know one song, 'The Night Time Is the Right Time,'" the Ray Charles thing.

And John says, "Don't worry. Just get up there and sing." One of the guys in the band gave me a pill. It was a black pill, a black bomber. I didn't know anything about drugs, but I took it. It made the song last for almost an hour. I just kept singing the same verses, over and over. That is how I got started.

I never thought any of this would happen to me, are you kidding? All I wanted in those days was a £300 sports car, an Austin-Healey Sprite. The only thing I wanted out of the music business was this car.

But it was an amazing period when I started. I never liked the Beatles or Herman's Hermits. Rock 'n' roll for me was the Stones and the Yardbirds. It was that kind of music that put me in touch with Jeff Beck. We were all out of work. I had been fired from Steampacket, which was Brian Auger, Long John, and Julie Driscoll. Brian thought I was earning too much money. I was getting 10 percent off the gross, but it was just an excuse. He wanted me out, and he wanted John out. So he got rid of me, and then he fired John. So I was out of work, Woody was out of work, the Byrds just folded, and Beck had left the Yardbirds. I think we all bumped into one another at the Cromwellian Club one night. It was a little place on Cromwell Road. I think we had been there to see Jimi Hendrix.

Beck's was a miserable fucking band, horrible. Beck is a miserable old sod, but I do love him as a guitar player. But he can be miserable. Me and Woody, though, had a lot of fun. To this day we are like blood brothers. I am actually thinking of asking him to do this tour with me. Everyone tells me he's straightened himself out. He really has survived. There was a time he didn't see daylight for seven years. I went to his wedding. You've never seen such chaos in your life. All the Stones except Jagger were there. The Who was there. And Woody leaves his brothers behind. Just forgot about his brothers. Left them in his mom and dad's house. His brother was supposed to be best man. They get to the church, and Woody says, "Oh, where has my brother gone?" He does bumble through life, but he has such a lovable nature that you can't be cross with him for very long.

Me and Woody had a lot of fun in the Faces. It was the ultimate heavy-drinking band. Not because we had a mission in life to be a load of boozers. We were scared shit, and we didn't think we were very good. We were all big drinkers, so that is how we got our image. The truth is, I can't listen to those records. People must hear something I can't hear. The Faces sound so out of tune, so out of time. We never had the musicianship. Individually we were good, but we did not come together as a band. Don't get me wrong, it was a great band to be in. We did so many things. We were the first band to trash a hotel. We were womanizers. We came along at a point when everything was extremely serious. Marc Bolan was topping the bill at a big outdoor festival, and everyone was taking music extremely seriously. Marc's head was down as he played. Then we came along, blind drunk and laughing.

The friction came when promoters starting putting up signs, Rod Stewart and the Faces. Billy Gaff used to have to get into a town early so he could make sure they took those signs down. He didn't mind it as long as the boys didn't see it. One night a promoter didn't take the sign down and there was hell to pay, quite rightly. We had all started together, and I had no intentions of leaving the band. But there you are. Woody went with the Stones, then we lost Ronnie Lane. For me, Lanie was the Faces. He was to the Faces what Keith Richards is to the Stones. Once Lanie left, it took the ass out of it for me.

Joe Smith

○ ○ ○

Mo and I were real upset in '68. We had no contracts with Warners, no stock, and not much money. But we were hot. We were the ones signing people, and we had nothing to show for it. Suddenly Ahmet Ertegun gets involved. By now Ahmet was a major stockholder in Warners–Seven Arts. They had bought his company, Atlantic, for stock. So Ahmet says to them, "You can't let these guys go. They're the best in the world. Make sure Maitland signs them."

It was very dramatic. Maitland was supposed to be on his way to Greece for an anniversary vacation, and instead he's locked up in a hotel room on the phone with us. That's how Mo and I got our contracts.

OK, fade to black. Mo and I are continuing to produce, and 1970 comes along and our contract with Warners is up. Some companies are talking to me, others are talking to Mo. We each had several opportunities, and we let it be known that we were both going to leave. Not as a team, but that's the way it probably appeared. Maitland was a terrific guy, great boss, but we wanted our own operation. Ahmet went crazy again. And he got Steve Ross at WCI crazy. And WCI fired Maitland and gave us the company. They said, "You guys run it together," and that's what we did for the next six years.

During that time, I had relationships with a lot of artists, of course, but with Van Morrison his career got to be a very personal thing for me. Even more so because he was such a hostile, difficult guy. He really didn't get along with anybody, but he got along with me less bad than with the others. I had to pay off a guy with the mob who had a piece of Van's contract. I helped Van move to Woodstock. I helped him move to California. I advanced him monies. Soon I became his only contact at the company.

He was so self-destructive professionally. He would tour six, eight months after his record came out, and then he wouldn't make another record for a year after the tour. The tour never helped the record, and the record never helped the tour. But finally, in 1975, I believe, Van made a record, and he was about to go on tour. We're now going to seize the opportunity and break him wide open.

Van had certain demands. He wanted someone from the company to travel with him. Fine. He wanted Jon Landau at *Rolling Stone* to do an interview with him. Fine. He wanted a bunch of other things. I said OK to everything. I said, "Look, I have to go to England next week. I'll be away for eight days. I'll follow the progress of the tour when I get back." His first stop was Dallas. Everything went well. Van said he was thrilled with the guy we sent with him, and now I go to England. But I'm not there for eight days, I'm there for a month, tied up with a Rod Stewart lawsuit.

I come back on a Thursday, the day before Christmas Eve. The office is closing at one P.M. that day. I'm jet-lagged and I haven't bought any Christmas gifts. I get a call from Van's agent, Peter Golden, and he says Van wants to meet with me.

I say, "Can't this wait until after the holidays?"

And he said, "No. It's an emergency." Van and Peter arrive with Van's lawyer, Bob Gordon, at one-thirty. The building is closing down. Van comes in and sits in front of my desk. Peter and Bob sit on a couch alongside the desk. Van's in a suit and tie, very dignified. He picks up a trade paper and begins going through a litany of things that didn't go right on the tour. The local promotion man in San Francisco didn't show up. Someone else didn't show up here. Jon Landau didn't do the interview. Ben Fong-Torres did it instead. I say, "Time out. I've been away for a month. Everyone's gone home for Christmas. Can't this wait until after the holidays?"

As I'm talking, Van stands up and screams at me, "You fucking liar! You're just like everybody else. I didn't think you were a liar, but you're just like everybody else." He's screaming, getting red in the face.

So I scream, "Stop yelling at me and sit down. I have Christmas shopping to do. I promise you, after the New Year I'll find out what went down." Van stands up again, and he's screaming again. But now he takes the trade paper and slams it down on a set of Cross pens I have on my desk. I'm clumsy. Every month I break one of these pens. Big joke around the office. But I hadn't broken a pen in six months, and now Van has broken both pens by slamming the trade paper down on the desk.

Normally I'm not a violent person. But I'm jet-lagged and aggravated and I blew it. I grabbed Van by the tie and collar and I yanked his head down onto the desk. I picked up my broken pen set, and I started screaming, "You broke my pen set, you broke my pen set." Out of the corner of my eye I see that Peter and Bob have gone slightly ashen. Van is a little pale, too. I pushed him. I screamed, "Get out of here, all of you. I don't ever want to see you again. I don't ever want to talk to you again."

They're all scurrying backwards, Van knocks over a chair. As they get to the door, Van turns around to me and says, "Merry Christmas." I pick up the pen set and I throw it at him. It crashes into the wall and gets stuck. I left it there for the next eight months, until we moved into our new offices. I cherished the memory of throwing it.

A little later on, Van gives an interview to someone in Canada. During the interview he says the only man who really understands him in the record business, the only man he really likes, is Joe Smith.

The changes for me when I moved from Warners to head up Elektra/Asylum had a great deal to do with numbers. I had less artists on Elektra/Asylum, but we made a lot more money. This was happening to the industry in general. Instead of watching an album top off at three hundred thousand copies, you sold three million. It was the start of the cassette phenomenon, and more people were becoming interested in music.

Irving Azoff, who managed the Eagles, had a lunch for me the day I started at Elektra. Linda Ronstadt was there. Carly Simon and Judy Collins came in from New York. Joni Mitchell was there. All the artists came. The next day Irving came in to renegotiate the Eagles' contract, which was an ongoing thing. Every time they put out a record Irving renegotiated. The record business had become big business.

But I still had to deal with the crazies. And as some of the superstar artists I had got increasingly crazier, it was nothing for them to really exert some economic clout on the label. The Eagles holding back a record might represent $35 million, $40 million in lost billing.

David Geffen had left me a good roster. I wanted to expand. But in order to do that, I needed the artists who could sell a lot of records to make records. The Beatles used to knock off three albums a year. Four Eagles albums could take ten years. My line about Jackson Browne was that he'd make a record every time Halley's Comet comes around.

A perfect example of how artists exerted their clout was the Eagles' live album. I spent a year trying to convince them to do it. They were having problems internally, and this was probably going to be their last hurrah. And while they agreed to do the live album, they did so reluctantly. For me, it meant enormous billing—8 million to 10 million albums worldwide meant between $40 million and $50 million in business. But as Henley and Frey and the others were getting further and further apart personally, the thought of having to spend more time in an editing room together, and maybe even coming up with a new song or two, scared them to the point where they were now on the fence about the project.

We had four dates scheduled in Southern California, and the day before the first night I get a call from Irving Azoff, who tells me we have a problem. The problem means I'm not getting the album. In my mind I'm trying to explain to Steve Ross at WCI why he's not going to get the $40 million to $50 million I promised him.

Irving says, "The guys want to tell you themselves." Glenn and Don get on the phone, and they say, "Look, we really don't want to do this. We really don't want to spend that much time with each other. We could do a short tour and not record and be finished. But we promised you we'd do this, so we're going to give you a chance, if you can answer one question."

I said, "What's the question?"

They said, "In 1971 the Baltimore Orioles had four twenty-game winners. If you can name them, we'll do the album."

God must have opened a recess in the back of my mind, and I named them—Dave McNally, Jim Palmer, Mike Cuellar, and Pat Dobson.

Glenn and Don said, "OK, we'll do the album and we'll see you tomorrow."

I said, "What would you have done if I didn't answer the question correctly?"

They said, "We'd go on tour, and you'd never have the live album." They weren't kidding.

Don Henley

○ ○ ○

The serious Eagle, Don is the writer of some of the group's more intense songs. He provided steady drumming along with a husky vocal style and has been brilliant in his solo career as well.

○ ○ ○

The Troubadour was the first place I went to when I got to L.A. I had heard about how legendary it was, and all the people who were performing there. The first night I walked in I saw Graham Nash and Neil Young, and Linda Ronstadt was standing there in a little Daisy Mae kind of dress. She was barefooted and scratching her ass. I thought, "I've made it. I'm here. I'm in heaven."

I really didn't know anybody. I just hung around the Troubadour by myself. It was kind of pathetic, really. But one night Glenn Frey invited me over to his table and bought me a beer. He said, "What's going on?"

I said, "My group's not doing anything. Things are a drag. One of the guys left to go play with the Burrito Brothers."

And Glenn said, "Me and my partner are breaking up, too. And there's this guy named David Geffen," who I didn't know from Adam, "and there may be a deal in the works if a band could be put together."

I said, "That's nice."

And he said, "In the meantime, do you want to go on the road with Linda Ronstadt and make 200 bucks a week?"

I said, "Sure, fine, I'd love it." I'd never really been on the road before. So Glenn and I became good friends and we started plotting and planning. He told me about Randy Meisner and Bernie Leadon, who had been with Poco and the Burritos, respectively. Glenn said we needed to get those guys because they could play the kind of country rock we were all so interested in. So when we got back from being on the road with Linda, we recruited those guys. We didn't all agree on things from the beginning, but we were so enamored of one another that it was OK for a while.

Then Geffen talked Glyn Johns into listening to us. Glyn said that although we needed a lot of work, he'd produce us in London. So they packed us off to England and stuck us in this little apartment, picked us up, took us to the studio, and then we'd go back to this little apartment and drink ourselves to sleep. Then we'd get up the next day and do it all over again.

As we got into making more albums, Glenn and I would go through a series of moving in together and then moving out. We'd have girlfriends and live with them for a while, and then we'd get ready to do an album and we'd move back in together. Dudes on a rampage.

By '76, '77, Glenn and I were living in a big house that belonged to Dorothy Lamour, up in the hills with a 360-degree view. Glenn and I were the odd couple. I was sort of the housekeeper, the tidy one. He was the lovable slob. All around the house he'd leave these little cigarette butts standing on end. They looked like miniature cities. Burns all over the furniture and carpet, coffee cups all over the place. We would get up every Sunday, watch football together, scream and yell, and spill things. It wasn't my house, I didn't care.

During the "One of These Nights"/"Hotel California" period, I lived in Irving Azoff's house on Benedict Canyon, and Glenn lived on Coldwater. I was in an upstairs corner bedroom in Irving's house. This was before Irving was married, and we were bacheloring it pretty good. It was during this time that I had my brief affair with Stevie Nicks. I remember the Eagles were on tour, and so was Fleetwood Mac. These were the extravagant days. One time I chartered a Lear jet and ran her to where I was, and for weeks I got a lot of shit about that from the band. If she had a couple of days off, she'd come over and go on the road with us for a while, and then I'd fly her back in time for wherever Fleetwood Mac was supposed to be. The affair with Stevie lasted off and on for a year or so, and we remain good friends today. But back then we coined the phrase, "Love 'em and Lear 'em."

Hey, Lear jets were a lot cheaper then, and when I speak of sending one for Stevie, that kind of thing did not happen every week. Once in a while we would do something completely over the top like that, and it was simply our way of coping with the absurdity of making so much money and being so famous at such an early age. We had to do absurd things sometimes just to be able to put it all in perspective. We would feel silly about it later, but we would laugh it off because we knew one day it would end. That's what the *Desperado* album was all about, how you get hung sooner or later, or hang yourself.

As we became more and more successful—the Eagles, Jackson Browne, J. D. Souther, Linda—it seemed to take us all away from one another. In a way, success separated all of us. In our hearts we were still good friends and mates and all that, but the salad days were gone.

Glenn Frey

o o o

Glenn was more the pop writer in the Eagles, and between him and Don Henley, they seemed unstoppable. Glenn is a wild personality and a fine vocalist who has also carved out a solo stand with more of the same.

o o o

Thinking back over the nine-year period of the Eagles, it amazes me how single-minded Henley and I were. We could be in the studio for weeks at a time—eating and sleeping and breathing what we were doing, the same way a kid who's infected with Little League baseball can't get it out of his system.

The Eagles were propelled by more than just ambition. At times, we were propelled by whatever we could get our hands on. Which means that some of those nine years went by in a blur. But in the beginning, we were the underdogs. That's how we thought of ourselves. We'd always say, "This guy is a better singer. That guy is a better guitar player. These people write better songs than us."

Being around David Geffen, and in close proximity to Jackson Browne, Joni Mitchell, and Crosby, Stills and Nash, this unspoken thing was created between Henley and me, which said, "If we want to be up here with the big boys, we'd better get our game together and write some fucking good songs."

We were also like a keg of powder, waiting for someone to come in and light the fuse. We were serious about becoming successful, and we were serious about being taken seriously as songwriters.

The band was like a fake democracy. Henley and I were making the decisions while at the same time trying to pacify, include, and cajole the others. There was always so much turbulence around our band that it made us serious all the time. There was never a day when all five guys felt good. I'd think, "Who is gonna blow it today? Who's gonna want to fire everybody."

I will never have the patience to deal with all those kinds of personalities again, but at the time it was necessary to get to where we had to go, even though we didn't always get along.

You knew it when you were in a room with the Eagles. There was a certain intensity. Perhaps a lot of it was all bluff because we were really just a bunch of skinny little guys with long hair and patched pants and turquoise.

I was never tough, but I sure was mad. I think I was more for entertainment, and I think Henley was more for trying to get more out of your entertainment dollar. But underneath it all, we were best friends. We talked every day for seven or eight years. Every day, like roommates.

Splitting up the Eagles, though, was not because of a rift between Henley and me. There was a rift and that didn't help, but we had come to a point where we were running out of gas artistically. We had gone from being a band that could make an album in three weeks to a band that couldn't finish an album in three years.

In some ways, the success took a lot of the fun out of it. Putting pressure on ourselves also took a lot of the fun out of it. I think Henley took some of the fun out of it for me, and I'm sure I took some of the fun out of it for him. Looking back, I think the band lasted a couple of more years than I thought it would.

You don't want to be in a band in your thirties anyway. At least I didn't. It's like being a doctor or a lawyer. You come out of school with some knowledge and talent and you start working with other people. Then you get your legs underneath you, and when you get to be thirty or so you want to take a shot at having your own practice.

The Eagles had its best chemistry when Don Felder and Joe Walsh were both in the band at the same time. Don and Joe were both tremendously gifted guitar players. Walsh is like an almanac. I could sit down at a piano at any given moment and play every song the Drifters ever recorded. But Joe can do the same thing with Jimi Hendrix, Jimmy Page, and Eric Clapton. I mean, every single blues lick.

But it was rare when everyone in the band got along. We used to joke around and say we were like the Oakland A's—as long as we got along on the field, it didn't matter what happened behind closed doors.

I really felt that when it came to getting people to play with, you didn't go around picking the nice guys, you found the guys who could play blues and rock 'n' roll, the guys who could take the Eagles up from a country rock band to a serious stadium filler. And it took the combined guitar talents of Joe Walsh and Don Felder to help us achieve that.

Unfortunately, what happens when you really make it is that you begin looking at your career in terms of how each album sold. The next one is always supposed to be bigger than the last, and so on. It's like Dylan said, "They deceived me into thinking I had something to protect."

Someone once asked Bob Seger why the Eagles broke up. He answered them in two words, " 'Hotel California,' " because it was impossible to top.

For me, it ended in Long Beach, California, at a benefit for Alan Cranston. I felt Don Felder insulted Senator Cranston under his breath and I confronted him with it.

So now we're on stage, and Felder looks back at me and says, "Only three more songs till I kick your ass, pal."

And I'm saying, "Great. I can't wait."

We're out there singing "Best of My Love," but inside both of us are thinking, "As soon as this is over, I'm gonna kill him." That was when I knew I had to get out.

Irving Azoff

○ ○ ○

One of music's most controversial managers and executives, Irving now heads all the MCA music activities, and he talked about the style that takes no prisoners and the smarts that got him where he is today.

○ ○ ○

I was working at Geffen-Roberts Management all of three weeks when Elliot Roberts calls me. He says, "I'm sick. Neil Young's tour starts tomorrow at Queens College. I can't go. You go."

I ask Elliot, "What do I do?"

He says, "Go to Queens College, find Neil, he'll be rehearsing. Hook up with him on the phone, and I'll explain to him what's happening."

I rushed to the airport. I had never met Neil Young. I'd never even spoken to him. Neil hadn't worked a date in three years, since his *Harvest* tour. So I walked up to him, told him the story, and he looks at me and says, "Are you trying to tell me you're my manager?"

I said, "No. Elliot's your manager. I'm just here because Elliot is sick."

He says, "Would you mind standing in the corner?" Neil Young is telling me to stand in the corner. Mysteriously, during the day my bags were stolen. I'm sure Neil had the crew throw them away. I'm out there on the road, no baggage, I have a head cold, and I'm calling Elliot every ten minutes, and I can't find him anywhere. I now find out that Elliot has neglected to hire a road manager. The crew is coming up to me and asking for money. Now it's show time, and Neil, who hasn't said two words to me all day, comes over to me and says, "So, Mr. Manager, do you have any advice for me before I go play this important gig?"

He had recorded an LP called *Tonight's the Night: Live at Studio Instrument Rentals,* which was basically a bunch of songs he had written after the death of someone in his band. So he opens the set with "Tonight's the Night," plays the entire LP, and closes the set with "Tonight's the Night" again. I'm standing with promoter Ron Delsener, one of the great comedians of life, and Neil walks offstage, comes up to me, and says, "Well, Mr. Manager, do you have any advice?"

I said, "Yeah, go back onstage and play something the audience knows."

He says, "Good idea." He goes back onstage, plays "Tonight's the Night" for a third time, and leaves. True story. To Neil, this was one of the greatest practical jokes of all time.

Another time, before I was at Geffen-Roberts, when I worked at the Heller-Fischel booking agency, Jerry Heller sent me with Lee Michaels to Stockton, California. I had just arrived on the West Coast from Chicago. I was about nineteen, twenty years old. So I fly to San Francisco, rent a car, go to Mill Valley to Lee Michaels' home, and he's walking me through his backyard, and the guy's got lions, cheetahs, and all sorts of crazy shit. I'm scared to death. We get into his Ferrari and drive to Stockton to play this gig. Now it's him and Frosty the drummer—it's a two-piece band. About fifteen minutes into the set, he comes offstage and asks me if we've been paid. I said, "Yes. In cash."

He says, "OK, let's leave."

When I worked at Heller's, I had driven out to Clairmont College to see the Eagles play. They were my absolute favorite band. I had never met them, didn't know them. When I went to Geffen, the first thing I wanted to do was meet the Eagles. So I was in the office one day and the secretary tells me I have to take a call from this raving madman, Glenn Frey. Geffen had just signed America to manage, and Warner Brothers paid for limos for them to run around town in, and the Eagles are leaving for the airport and they're upset because we didn't send limos. Elliot wants me to tell them to take a cab. So my first experience with the Eagles was being yelled at by Glenn for fifteen minutes on the phone about limos.

I immediately made the Eagles my business. We were all just a bunch of punk kids who were the same age. Other than Bernie Leadon, who didn't think it was funny when I crashed into the back of his rental car, everybody thought everything was hysterical. The first three, four days I thought I died and went to heaven. These guys were out there with 400 girls. Here was a band with a terrible image, but it was the first time I was ever exposed to real rock stars. They were fabulous singers, but not a great live stage performance. But the songs were very much on the cutting edge of what was going on.

I stayed out on the road with them for ten days. Immediately they came to me because Jerry Rubinstein, their business manager, was also the business manager for Geffen-Roberts. Jerry had taken all the money from the tour to pay back commissions to Geffen-Roberts, so there was a war from day one that I was trying to mediate. They were very unhappy with the *Desperado* LP that Glyn Johns produced. I thought the album was poorly produced, too.

On the road I'd been playing them some tapes that Joe Walsh had been doing with Bill Szymczyk. I was sort of an obnoxious young kid then, as opposed to an obnoxious old kid now, and I played the Eagles these tapes, and I said, "You need to go back in with someone like Szymczyk. We need to hear some more guitars." Geffen was furious. That led to scrapping most of the LP, hiring Bill, and having Don Felder, who had been playing with CS&Y, sit in on a couple of tracks. Joe Walsh went out on the road with them. Et cetera, et cetera. That was the turning point. I'm not taking any credit for the turning point in their music, but it had turned.

About six months later, David and Elliot reneged on my compensation and I said good-bye. When they figured out that several acts would be going with me, they said, "No, you have to stay." I went back to all the acts and said I was going to stay, and Henley and Frey talked me out of staying. They said they were going to leave, even if I didn't.

The Eagles were breaking up from the day I met them. The first day I met them, in Kansas City, Missouri, we were driving to Springfield, and Bernie and I were feuding. There was talk of breakup on that tour. At the end of every tour they broke up. So there is no date as to an actual breakup. One day they just kind of drifted into a divorce. I still believe that someday they'll collaborate once again. Many other bands have come back for reunion shot after reunion shot. They take the money and run. Glenn and Don don't do that. That should tell you something about their integrity.

David Bowie

o o o

An innovator and an icon for rock followers for almost twenty years, he tells how he needed the alter egos to write songs and how the characters came and went in his life. A major league star.

o o o

I had a very reserved, respectable childhood. Nothing really happened to me that one would consider freaky. I went to one of the first art-oriented high schools in England, where one could take an art course from the age of twelve, thirteen, as opposed to waiting until seventeen when you go to art school. So there was a strong bias toward art from when I was quite young.

I had a very excellent art teacher, Peter Frampton's father, who was an inspiration to all who were involved with him. It was an experiment for him to try to get us involved in art at a younger age. I think three-fourths of our class actually did go on to art school, which is a hell of a proportion. Some of us went straight into street jobs because we didn't really believe in ourselves as painters/artists, and I was one of those. I went into the visual side of an advertising agency. I was doing paste-up jobs and small designs for raincoats. It was awful. If all this goes down the drain, I can be on Madison Avenue with the best of them.

A lot of people have tried to analyze me in print, and it just gets in the way of my own conception of what I do and what I want to do. Early in the English period, when Tony Palmer decided the Beatles were art, the whole ball started rolling for home philosophy and the psychoanalysis of artists. It was far too ridiculous. I'm just a popular musician, and that's how I view myself.

But a lot of us in England did try to bring another dimension to rock. Roxy Music, T-Rex, Marc Bolan. In America there was Iggy Pop, who is radically different than the person he projects on stage. Also David Johansen from the New York Dolls, who was a pretty hip guy during that period. But up until that time, the attitude was "what you see is what you get." It seemed interesting to try to devise something different, like a musical where the artist onstage plays a part. Like the Ziggy Stardust character. He was half out of sci-fi rock and half out of Japanese theater. The clothes were simply outrageous, and nobody had seen anything like them before. The clothes were the brainchild of a well-known designer, at least he is now, Kansai Yamamoto. Extraordinary designer. He did all the early Ziggy clothes. He contemporized the Japanese Kabuki look and made it work for rock 'n' roll.

I moved out of Ziggy fast enough so as not to get caught up by it. Most rock characters that one creates usually have a short life span. I don't think they're durable album after album. Don't want them to get too cartoony. The Ziggy thing was worth one or two albums, so after *Aladdin Sane* I had to start thinking quickly about what I wanted to write, which came out as an abortive attempt to do *1984*. Abortive because we couldn't get the rights from Mrs. Orwell. She saw her husband's work through a far more serious pair of eyes than I imagine we did. I got half the thing written before I thought, "I better go and ask her if I could continue this."

So I sort of did a quick turnaround and it became *Diamond Dogs*, which was sort of a piecemeal attempt at forming a postnuclear kind of society with this rather shabbily disguised form of *1984*.

From the *Diamond Dogs*/abortive *1984* thing, which did produce one excellent tour, I brought everything I ever wanted to see on the rock 'n' roll stage. Needless to say, it was a huge financial disaster. But it was a terrific bit of stuff to have done.

It was on that tour that I met Toni Basil. She had been working with a group of black dancers called the Lockers, who were, I guess, the progenitors of the street dancers. Toni worked hard in the early seventies to make street dancing something people would know about. It wasn't until the eighties that street dancing itself became break dancing. Toni choreographed the *Diamond Dogs* tour. I won't say we waved any banners for street dancing, but it certainly was evidence of what was to come.

I've always found it easier to write for other people. I feel terribly inhibited about writing for me. It's only in the last few years that I've resigned myself into believing that I'm a moderately good singer. I can interpret a song, which is not quite the same thing as singing it. I had no problem writing for Iggy Pop or working with Lou Reed or writing for Mott the Hoople. If anybody wants a song, come and ask because I can do it in fifteen minutes. But I find it extremely hard to write for me.

I never had much of a relationship with the Beatles or Rolling Stones, but I did with individuals like Mick Jagger and John Lennon. Mick is ambivalent with his likes and dislikes. He's actually quite conservative when it comes to making his own records. He's aware of who's doing what and what's happening, but he's a rootsman to this day, and the music he plays more than anything else is the blues. He's never deviated from that. That's one thing you can say about Mick, he has absolute perfect integrity to the music he wanted to start playing when he first started playing. He's bemused by all the other things that go on, whereas I'm more of a sucker, more of a fan. If it's wearing a pink hat and a red nose and playing a guitar upside-down, I'll go and look at it. I love to see people being dangerous. Mick, I think, is more of an onlooker.

John was the only one I got to know from the Beatles, and unfortunately it was toward the end of his life. I first met John in the middle seventies when I was doing *Young Americans*. It was an inspiration to work with him, but it was one of those associations that last about the length of the recording. We didn't see each other for another year. Then we started to pick up on what was becoming a very instructive and deep relationship. Having gone to art school, a lot of the stuff we talked about went into the world of art, why an artist wants to do things in the first place, and all of that. It gets very melodramatic, but it's the kind of relationship that one savors, and it's something you don't forget easily.

But I never really felt part of the other stuff, not from an elitist stance, at least. I knew I played as well as them, and I always felt a little out of my element, which is a ridiculously hifalutin' way of looking at it. From my standpoint, from '72 to '76, I was the ultimate rock star. I couldn't have been more of a rock star. Anything that had to do with being a rock 'n' roll singer was what I was going for. I was it for all that period. I kept myself away from all the supergroups, or maybe they kept themselves away from me. Who knows?

On the whole it's been quite kaleidoscopic. It's been quite a rich, colorful affair over the last fifteen years. It's all been rather terrific. I feel very lucky to have been able to do it all.

Roger Waters

o o o

The writer in the almost faceless but internationally celebrated Pink Floyd, Roger is a quality man whose views on the band's position in the rock spectrum are surprising.

o o o

In the very early days of Pink Floyd, Syd Barrett was the center of everything. He was the only one of us who was writing any songs. He was very zippy in that way, very creative, in a way that people who are in danger of going over the edge sometimes are.

Syd was terrific to be around, and great to be in a band with. He's still alive. He lives with his mother in Cambridge. But he was a casualty. After a while, he became completely impossible, so we approached Dave Gilmour to come in and play guitar and sing, which he did. And we were all fine for a while. Syd even did a couple of gigs with us. But he was becoming crazier and crazier. I remember the final straw, and that was when Syd one day suddenly decided that the answer to the band's problems was to introduce two saxophone players and a girl singer. We said, "Yeah, yeah. Good idea, Syd."

Syd moving out meant that we just had to start writing. In fact, his leaving made us pursue the idea of the extended epic and a more classically constructed idea of music. "A Saucerful of Secrets" was fifteen minutes or so long, and that was considered rather outlandish at the time.

From the early seventies on, I'd say, from *Meddle* on, I made all the decisions—how often we're going to tour, how long the tours should be, which cities, when should our next record be, those kinds of things.

And my writing was such that I could never make anything up. *Dark Side of the Moon*, for example, in terms of its construction and lyrical content, as well as the music, is simply how I was feeling in 1972. I found that the more direct I've been with my feelings, the better I felt about work at the end of the day. Even up to the last Floyd album, *Final Cut*, which was almost more direct than anything I had ever done because it was about my father, was about how I was feeling.

And although it wasn't a huge commercial success, I could say, "So what?" It's very easy to become trapped into the thing of, "Well, what's important is selling a lot of records and filling a lot of stadiums and making a lot of money." Of course that's important to anyone who's gone into rock 'n' roll. But that can't be the most important thing. And it's not the most important thing to anybody who lasts a long time in this business.

At the end of the day, whatever day, I knew that *Dark Side of the Moon* was a well-structured album. I listened to it recently, for the first time in maybe ten years, and it holds up very well. It's interesting that people are still buying it. It takes a long time to arrive to its point all the time, and there are meandering passages. If you took it to an A & R man today, he'd say, "OK, we've got to tighten this up. Nobody's going to stand for this. Take these sixteen bars out here, please. They'll never play it on the radio." I mean, if that record were made today, it would be dismissed out of hand as a no-hoper.

But *Dark Side of the Moon* is very easy to digest. It's easy listening, and yet it feels different, and somehow serious.

When you go through the list of bands that came out of England, the so-called important bands, people always talk about the Beatles and the Stones and the Who because they all played the game in one way or another. We never did. So we never get mentioned in that context. But I feel if you're talking about Mick Jagger, Pete Townshend, and John Lennon, you should be talking about me, as well. Sometimes I get a bit niggled and miffed by that. What's interesting, I think, is the fact that we will always be remembered for the number of weeks *Dark Side of the Moon* remained on the *Billboard* charts, and not for anything we did, because of what makes good copy and what doesn't.

I had to finally leave Pink Floyd because inevitably people change, and the way a band works changes. In the end, Pink Floyd changed in a way that was uncomfortable for all of us. Inevitably jealousies and things crept up, and at the end of a day they start to outweigh the pleasures. The battles get a bit tougher, and there's a bit more backbiting. In the end, you just have to say, "Well, let's do something else." I never wanted to be the longest-lasting band in the history of rock 'n' roll anyway. I think we'll leave that to the Stones or somebody else.

Richard Branson
o o o

Another wunderkind whose odyssey through music, transportation, and other avenues makes him one of Britain's treasures and a bane to the financial world of London. His office is on a houseboat on the Thames and on a windy day we rock-'n'-rolled in fact as well as in story.

o o o

There used to be no such thing in England as a discounted record. I had a magazine, and I took an ad in my own magazine offering from 10 percent to 60 percent off on any album on any label. In the ad, I listed a bunch of rock records.

Some of the people I was working with, we liked certain records, and we listened to them a lot, and we called them "virgin" records. I knew nothing about the record business. But immediately, because of the flavor of the ads, we built up an identity.

But I didn't actually have any records. So when the orders came in, we went down to the local record shop and said, "We'll buy more records. You sell them to us a little cheaper." The record companies wouldn't supply us with any records because they didn't want discounting to come to England. They had already seen it in America, and they didn't think it was a good idea.

In the end, we found a little shop in the East End of London, and we made an arrangement whereby they would buy all the records for us. Suddenly in that little shop they were turning over $8 million. The building was 200 feet long and the records couldn't fit into the shop. It was then that the record industry decided this was a farce, that they might as well start selling to us directly.

The other shops also refused to discount. They thought discounting was a dirty word. We sold our records fifty cents cheaper, and the others wouldn't discount. Before the others knew it, we had thirty shops open. By then it was too late. When they started to discount, we already had the image. The kids liked us, they knew the name, they knew they could get a certain kind of record from us. They knew we had headphones in the shop. They knew if they came in and smoked dope we weren't going to throw them out. There were pillows on the floor. It was the sixties, and Virgin Records was indelibly stamped on their minds.

Virgin became synonymous with something alternative which had good value for the money. Still, moms and dads would look in and run the other way.

Simon Gray must get a lot of the credit for helping build Virgin. He had a record collection of about 4,000 records. He was a cousin of mine from South Africa. He turned up one day knocking on my door. He said, "I'm your cousin from South Africa, and I used to buy all these records from your mail order company." I didn't know I had a cousin in South Africa, but I took him out to lunch. We became the closest of friends. He had something I didn't. He spent his entire life listening to records.

In the seventies, we bought a place in the country and converted the barn into a studio. Since the day we bought it we've never had an empty den. The McCartneys have used it, Cat Stevens, everyone. It was a lovely place. We put a lake in.

One day Mike Oldfield came to the country with a tape. He played it for one of the engineers, who liked it, and then played it for Simon, who loved it. Simon played it for me and I liked it, too. But at that point we didn't have the money to sign him so we gave him the names and addresses of record companies and A & R people and sent him off to try to get a deal elsewhere.

About a year later, we rang him back and said, "We assume you got a deal." He said he hadn't. I remember, we copied the contract of Sandy Denny, the English folk artist. Mike Oldfield and I typed it out together, word for word. And that's how we got our first artist. Mike then lived at our facility for the next year, where he learned. He engineered bands, and he recorded "Tubular Bells" in between sessions, basically to fill a gap. Then we put "Tubular Bells" out, and it was a gigantic hit. That was our first record.

Robert Lamm

○ ○ ○

One of the keys in the long-lived success of Chicago, Robert overcame his own chemical problems and is now riding the group's great second wave of success.

○ ○ ○

We were aware of two things. One was the stuff that was coming out of Memphis—"Knock on Wood," "In the Midnight Hour," Sam and Dave. All with rhythm sections, horns, and guys singing. That was the ensemble size we envisioned.

Then there were the knockout club bands which always had three horns, a rhythm section, and a guy down front singing. Groups like Jimmy Ford and the Executives; the Mob, out of Chicago. They worked college dates, they worked teen clubs, big clubs. That's what we wanted to do. We were all in college, and we thought we could put together a band that could eventually go to Vegas during our summers off from school, earn a lot of money, and then come back and pay our bills. Basically, we just wanted to play rhythm and blues.

Then we heard what the Beatles were doing on *Sgt. Pepper*, writing songs that weren't rhythm and blues. No longer was it just guitars, bass, and drums. They were doing orchestrations, which we thought we could do, too. So I guess we just wanted to be the Beatles with brass. That's really where we were coming from.

The founding members of the group were Walt Parazaider, Danny Seraphine, and Terry Kath. I was like an employee who was called in. Somebody called me up and said, "Hey, we heard you play keyboards and sing. Would you be interested in joining a band that we're putting together with brass?" On the South Side of Chicago, where I was from, that was a novelty.

Terry and Danny probably would have been in street gangs on the North Side of Chicago, except they were musicians. I was just this sort of South Side guy, studying music at Roosevelt University, playing gigs at night.

Looking back, it was so strange. I'm not an outgoing person. At the time, I didn't take risks, especially if it meant going to the North Side to meet with a group of musicians. But I got this phone call asking me if I would be interested, and I said yes. I don't know why I said yes, but I did.

We all met at Walt's mother's house because she had a big basement. We all brought our stuff, started playing, and it was magic. We were playing "Papa's Got a Brand-New Bag," "In the Midnight Hour," "Knock on Wood." It was a thrill. I had never played in a band that big.

After *Chicago Transit Authority* was recorded, we went on the road, and all of a sudden we're opening for Jimi Hendrix, Janis Joplin, when they were at their absolute height. We were exposed to arena-sized crowds, and we were moving so fast that we didn't even realize how successful we had become until we started recording our third album. We turned around and said, "Hey, you know, we're big. People love us. They're buying our records. I mean, really!"

By the time *Chicago VIII* came around, the magic was beginning to go away. The band started getting into drugs, and the two things went hand in hand. I couldn't see it then, but I see it now. The more we got into drugs, the less productive we were. It started out as something recreational and then became prime time.

And then we did the unthinkable. We fired our producer and manager, Jim Guercio. It was like firing Hitler. You don't just fire Hitler. You either assassinate him, or let somebody else assassinate him. But we fired him.

And then a high-powered coke dealer got into Terry's ear. He wanted to go into business with Terry. He was the most divisive factor I'd ever seen. When Terry died, he went away.

I wasn't there when Terry died, but I know his death was drug-related. Drugs hampered his judgment. Nobody in the group talks about it too much. A close friend of mine was there when Terry shot himself, and he swears to this day that it was an accident. It was just two guys sitting across from each other. But Terry had been up for a couple of days, and he was playing with a gun. That's like drinking four six-packs of beer and then walking along the edge of a building expecting to make it.

Olivia Newton-John
○ ○ ○

A terrific woman who came from Australia to become an American sweetheart. Along the way she starred in a couple of motion pictures and racked up a number of hits. Living in Malibu, she's raising a family and trying to get back on the professional track.

○ ○ ○

When I was fifteen, I won a talent contest. The prize was a trip to England. I didn't really want to go, but my mother kind of took me by the ear and said, "We need to broaden your horizons. You should go to Europe." I didn't want to go. I didn't want to leave my boyfriend. I was very young and I thought Australia was everything.

I had to wait until I was eighteen before I could go to England, but I went. My friend Pat and I were a double act, and we worked on a bill with the Shadows, who were Cliff Richard's backup band. I started going out with one of the guys in the Shadows. Cliff heard my voice and he wanted Pat and I to sing with him on one of his B sides. That's kind of how my career started.

My boyfriend in the Shadows was a friend of Paul McCartney's. We went round to Paul's house one day and he said, "I have just written this song," and he started playing "Lady Madonna." At the time, I didn't even realize what I was hearing. I was thrilled to meet Paul and all, but I had no sense of what was really going on at the time. When I look back, I know it's amazing that I was there when he wrote that song.

I guess you could say I was detached. We had our own little group of people—Cliff and the Shadows, Pat and me and a few other musicians.

I was never really an ambitious person. A lot of other people were ambitious for me. My sister believed in me, my mother believed in me. I entered that contest for fun. I never thought I'd win. But before I knew it, I had indeed won, and I was still in school with choices to make. I suppose everything just fell into my lap. In the beginning, I have to admit it, that's the way it was. Soon I realized that things were not going to continue falling into my lap forever. You have to work to get further.

My favorites growing up were Dionne Warwick, Ray Charles, Joan Baez, and Nina Simone. More than anyone else, they were the four people I listened most to in Australia. I listened to the radio and I knew every pop song. I sang all the time for my family and friends, but if they asked me at school to get up and sing, I was always too shy.

I had my first hit record, "If Not for You," in 1971. It was a hit in England and it began to get some airplay in America. I was asked to come to America to do "The Dean Martin Show," and I did. When I got here, Helen Reddy and Jeff Wald took me under their wing. They said, "If you want to have a big hit in America, you have to be here. You have to concentrate on this country."

When I decided they were right, I moved into the Sunset Marquis Hotel in West Hollywood. When I arrived to check in, there was a dozen red roses waiting at the desk for me. They were from Glenn Frey. The card said, "Welcome to America." I wasn't even sure who the Eagles were, but I've always had a soft spot for Glenn because it was such a nice thing of him to do. It's very hard, you're a stranger, you're from out of town, and you're not about to call someone up and say, "Excuse me."

Helen and Jeff were important to me at another time of my life. I was in Miami, and I went to see Helen's show, and they invited me for dinner one night, and Allan Carr was there. He was goofing about at the table, and he started talking about me doing *Grease*. I had seen the show in London with Richard Gere as the lead. When Allan asked me to do it, I got very nervous, but I did it.

My image had been so white bread, so milk shake, and *Grease* was a chance to do something different. I didn't want to be forty years old and still be the girl next door.

Critics can get vicious sometimes. If they don't like you, there isn't much you can do about it. I can't pretend it doesn't irk me because it does. You want everyone to like you. The reason you go into show business in the first place is to be accepted. But when they call you "a singing air hostess," that's cruel and vicious.

At least when *Grease* hit, I was accepted. *Grease* proved to be so important for me. It meant I could have a hit movie with hit songs and a new image. Suddenly, if I wanted to be outrageous, I could. If I wanted to sing rock 'n' roll, I could. Had it not been for *Grease*, I don't know if I ever could have gotten away with "Let's Get Physical."

Justin Hayward

o o o

No one seemed to know who made up the famous Moody Blues, but the group dazzled record buyers and audiences for years. Justin has been one of the creative sparks, and our talk in London took place while another Moodies record was being readied.

o o o

With the Moody Blues there was never a "Moody Mania Week." There was never a record company spending $2 million trying to establish the Moody Blues. The Moodies were something people discovered for themselves. We were never rammed down anybody's throat. We worked and toured with every album, and you had to care enough to want to discover the Moody Blues. Once you did, it was long-lasting. We believed in making albums that you could put on at the beginning and have a complete experience to the end.

The album *Days of Future Passed*, which established us as a band that could make albums as opposed to just singles, came about completely by accident. What happened was, we didn't have a recording contract to make albums, we had a contract to deliver four singles a year. We owed Decca some money, so they came to us and said they wanted the group to record a rock version of Dvorak's *New World Symphony*, as a demonstration record to demonstrate that stereo could be as interesting for rock 'n' roll as it was for classical music. When stereo started, it was confined to classical.

So we said, fine, we'd do the demonstration record if we could just have five days alone in the studio without any record company executives coming in and telling us what to do. Decca hemmed and hawed a bit, and then finally they said OK.

We went into the studio and recorded our stage show. "Forget Dvorak," we said, and we continued working out a little rock opera we had already been doing on stage. We were performing "Days of Future Passed," with "Nights in White Satin" and "Tuesday Afternoon," a long time before we recorded it.

In the studio, we worked on the album from a Monday to a Friday, then we mixed it on Saturday, and gave it to Decca in time for their regular music meeting on Monday. They took one listen to it and they said, "This is not Dvorak. But it's good. Let's put it out anyway on our demonstration label," which meant "full-frequency stereo album at a cheap price."

Soon it was January, when we would be playing at MIDEM, the music convention in France. The Supremes were due to go on. The show was supposed to be an hour of live Eurovision television, and something happened. The Supremes' backing track didn't turn up, and it was complicated by the fact that something was wrong with the entire tape system. Everybody that was miming had a problem.

So the producer of the show came rushing around saying, "We need an act to play live." Nobody was prepared to do that. None of the American acts could work without their backing band, but we said we'd do it. We went on and wound up with forty-five minutes of live Eurovision time. "Nights in White Satin" was one of the songs we performed. The next week it was Number 1, that fast.

We couldn't afford a press agent, and when we decided on our own not to put our faces on the cover of Days of Future Passed, we became— by accident, I suppose—an anonymous sort of band. It didn't help that we were anti-everything. We hated putting out singles. When we finally got powerful enough to say what we wanted and didn't want, we told the record company we didn't want a single out, which, if you're a record label, can be a terrifying thing to hear from a group.

We worshiped America because nothing else was really happening for us. Around the time of Days of Future Passed, we began making inquiries to America. We received a call from Bill Graham, who had heard about Days of Future Passed. He offered us two dates, the Fillmore East in New York and the Fillmore West in San Francisco. The only trouble was, the dates were ten weeks apart.

We came to America anyway, thinking, "This is our chance." We hired a U-Haul truck and we toured everywhere and anywhere. We did the Fillmore East gig, and then by word of mouth we started getting gigs at clubs that had names like the Psychedelic Factory and the Electric Supermarket. Then we teamed up with the Jefferson Airplane, and they had a truck where you could let the side down and play anywhere. So we did a few gigs with them, playing for nothing, and eventually we ended up in San Francisco.

Like all groups, the Moodies have had our share of personality problems. We actually did split up for three years, which I thought was total madness at the time because we were right at the height we had been working towards. We had been on tour for about two years, and none of us had any kind of life outside of the band, nothing at all. That in itself is what breaks up a lot of bands. So we split up for about three years, and looking back now, I think it was the best thing we ever did. It made coming back together that much more meaningful.

No one has the divine right to be successful, particularly in the eighties, and a lot of people were surprised when we came back with a Top 10 album and single. Everybody was surprised but the band. But then, we think even our flops were good.

Jon Anderson and Chris Squire

o o o

They are different in personality and style, but they form the foundation of Yes, a band that was among the leaders of the new rock that emerged in the seventies.

o o o

I met Chris in 1968, in a drinking club in Soho called La Chasse. The very first thing we talked about was the production on Simon and Garfunkel albums and whether we could make a few musical statements of our own.

The first actual show Yes did, half the show was a rendition of "Midnight Hour," a groovy "Midnight Hour," slowed down. The organ player at the time, Tony Kaye, would do a Doors sort of thing, and the guitars would start doing feedback stuff. Not heavy, more quiet and groovy. In a way, we were doing Motown-type songs, slowing them down, reinterpreting them our own way.

By the beginning of the seventies, after Steve Howe and Rick Wakeman had joined, we were on our way to becoming a very strong unit. I was learning how to motivate. My whole part in being in Yes was to motivate. I never wanted to just stand there and look like a singer, probably because I was always unsure about being the singer.

But it was relatively easy to motivate the others because they were all willing. It was only after we became very successful that it became more difficult. It seems to just happen that way. We moved into larger territory. We started playing longer pieces of music, music with more dimension, stage visuals when we went out on tour. We were going onstage and doing "Close to the Edge," a twenty-minute piece, plus another three ten-minute pieces. That was a new thing, a sort of quantum leap for a rock 'n' roll band to be performing a twenty-minute piece without a guitar solo. And there's no guitar solo in "Close to the Edge." It's a steady, structured piece of music.

I remember performing it in London for the first time. We were on a show with Elton John, and the twenty minutes seemed like two hours. We were so frightened of losing the audience, figuring they'd get bored and have to go out for a hot dog. How do you hold an audience without hitting them with a three-minute pop song? We didn't have a three-minute pop song, but we did hold them.

I suppose the fact that it was the early seventies had a lot to do with it. FM radio was really beginning to flex its muscles. They would play albums all night long, music without stopping for a commercial. That was heaven for a band like ours. It allowed us to play "Close to the Edge" and not worry about it.

I'll never forget this one radio station in Paris. I think it was called PFI. They would play David Bowie, then Sinatra. Then Beethoven, then Yes, followed by Frank Zappa and Cleo Laine. It was one of the world's great radio stations.

o o o

No one in my family was musical. When I was very young, I joined the local church choir because a friend of mine who lived on the block had a father who was a clarinet player, and they were a musical family, and the boy and I were the same age, seven or eight, and he let it be known he was joining the choir. So I joined, too. He was my mate, and I went along with him.

Amazingly, our little church choir then got a guy straight out of Cambridge University. This guy was destined for stardom in the English church system. As a matter of fact, he ended up at Charles and Di's wedding. But we got the guy when he was twenty-one and I was eight, and he made our little local church choir into the best choir in England. It was a great lesson for me.

I couldn't play an instrument. I would just sing. And that's how I learned music, through English church music. In fact, our church choir was so good that we actually ended up doing gigs as a unit. We would go from church to church, which seemed ridiculous. Then we'd do radio shows. We even got paid for some of the radio shows, which was unheard of. But I never thought music would become a career for me.

And then, when I was fourteen, my voice changed, and I began going to regular school. Of course, I had all that musical knowledge, and I would tell the choirmaster at school everything—which way to do things, how to arrange. He was always asking me because he knew I was one of the guys who had learned under that superstar from Cambridge. This was all very pleasant, but I still had no idea what I was going to be when I grew up. I wasn't thinking musician, or lawyer, or doctor. I had no idea at all.

Then, at sixteen, which was in 1964, the Beatles were happening, and there I was, sixteen, and a friend of mine got a guitar and said, "Oh, Chris, you're tall. Why don't you get a bass guitar and become a bass player?"

And that was it. I did. I had big hands, which meant I could play bass.

Gene Simmons and
Paul Stanley

○ ○ ○

**These two gentlemen painted their faces and went on to make Kiss the
shock rockers of their era. Here they tell us what the group was
supposed to be like and what it became.**

○ ○ ○

We used to practice in this loft in New York, on 23rd Street and Fifth
Avenue. That's where we started. Two hundred dollars a month, that was
a fortune. And then two years later we're playing Madison Square Garden,
headlining. I remember taking the subway, like I always did, after having
dinner at my mom's, and landing at 33rd Street, and then buying a ticket,
getting in and going backstage and into makeup and then onto the stage and
playing. It was two years later, but somehow it seemed like the completion
of a ritual.

The idea of us seemed so obvious. Nobody else besides Alice Cooper
had been doing it. You have to have real guts to get up on stage and look
weird. And that was our calling card. You get attention real fast, you know,
by walking down the street and pulling down your pants. In a sense, we were
willing to get up onstage and drop our pants, just to have people say, "My
God, look at that."

The premise of the band was that each one was going to be a star. All
of us trim, tall, white, dark haired, no blond guys. It was going to be very,
sort of, defined. Every guy had the same-length hair, very much in the mold
of the Temptations. In fact, a lot of our stage movements were ripped off
from the old Motown stuff, besides, of course, the bombs and the explosions
and all our madness. But there was a method to our madness. It wasn't just
chaos.

I remember when we did a showcase for Don Ellis, who was doing
A & R at the time at Epic Records. He came in to see us and we were
painted up. And he said, "What is this? I don't get it. You guys can't do
that." To make matters worse, our drummer's brother was drunk and he
threw up all over the floor. Needless to say, Don Ellis walked out.

But the kids liked us. They might have been flabbergasted and unbelievably stunned, and maybe they didn't know what the hell was going on,
but they went for it right away, in a big way. The first time we played in a
club there was nobody there. The next night there were lines around the
block.

And then Neil Bogart heard about us. He was in the process of leaving
his record company, Buddah Records, and starting a new company for
Warner Brothers, but he didn't know what he was going to call it. But he
heard a tape of ours and he signed us right away.

When Neil finally came to see us live, we were in makeup and he was shocked. He said, "I don't know about this. I think this kind of garish stuff is over. Forget the makeup and do it my way."

And I remember saying something like, "This is a chance of a lifetime, but we've got to do what we believe. If we can't wear the makeup, we'll go someplace else."

Neil turned around and said, "OK, if you guys really believe in it, I believe in your belief. Let's go."

By the time we played our first big show—New Year's Eve, 1973 into '74, at the Academy of Music in New York, we were the fourth act on the bill—I was already into breathing fire.

Of course, on this night when I breathed fire, my hair caught on fire. One of our roadies put it out, but everybody thought it was part of the act.

The mania happened so suddenly. We didn't have a chance to react. All of a sudden we're fucking our brains out every single day of our lives and doing 210, 230 shows a year. It was ten months on the road, four weeks to make a record, and then back out. And we did that for eight years.

It was like, we were Kiss. We could do no wrong. We were supermen. It was almost like a crusade. I think about those guys today who walk down the street with those ghetto-blasters. I'm sure someone says to them, "Don't you feel like a knucklehead, walking down the street and making a nuisance of yourself?"

But the very fact they're a nuisance is giving them a sort of power that nobody else has. And they're getting a response—whether it's hate or admiration or whatever—from the people around them. It was exactly the same way with us.

Hey, our music was modern folk music, and I'm obviously proud of it. Somebody bought those records, a lot of people. The songs are good. Now, I don't know whether they will last into the next century, but I don't really care. It was relevant for its time.

o o o

The first time I became aware of the potential of what you could do on stage was through the Who. The idea of smashing instruments was so beyond my comprehension. Why would anybody want to take their guitar and break it? That means you gotta go get another guitar. But I related to it because it was theater.

There was also Jimi Hendrix. The idea that this black man could do what he did in front of a white audience was incredible. I remember showing pictures of Hendrix to some of my classmates in junior high school, black classmates, and they were in convulsions, laughing. They never saw anyone so funny looking.

But I think it was Eddie Cochran who really turned me around. I remember being five, six years old, and seeing Eddie Cochran. He was much more intriguing to me than anyone else, and probably because of his bleached blond hair.

Hey, when the Beatles came out, people laughed at them, too. I don't think you can lead a parade and not have people stare at you. The idea of Kiss was to take that kind of thinking to its natural next step.

Initially, we promoted ourselves. We would rent a ballroom, very often at the Hotel Diplomat in New York, which was a hotel for hookers and junkies on 43rd Street, off Broadway. No club would hire us because of how we looked and how loud we played. We weren't ready to compromise, and as a result, most places wouldn't hire us.

I was an art major, so I would draw an ad for a paper like the *Village Voice*, and then we would put these ads up all over the city. We would find two other local bands that were willing to sign a contract with us agreeing when we'd all go on, and we'd do a mailing to everybody. That's pretty much how we started out.

After Neil Bogart signed us, we spent a year or so opening for virtually anybody who would let us open—Rory Gallagher, Savoy Brown, Manfred Mann—hard-core British blues bands. And every time we walked out on stage, if people weren't outright laughing, they were hitting one another in the ribs and snickering. I can remember on one occasion, on a show with Savoy Brown—Michigan, I think Flint. We walked on stage and everyone was just laughing. We were like sacrificial lambs. But when we played, the crowd went crazy. What we lacked in musicianship we made up for in conviction. We did a couple of encores, and after we left, half the audience left. From then on there was a lot more respect. We became like Reverend Ike with Marshall amps.

I remember one time my parents came to see us at Madison Square Garden, and there I am on stage playing game-show host to 18,000 people, and I'm wearing tights and high heels and playing with a guitar between my legs, stroking the guitar. I remember saying to myself, "My God, my parents are out there absorbing this." They're watching 18,000 people watching their son, and their son is in makeup and high heels and he's jerking off a guitar. Now, any one of those things would be enough to give them a coronary, but all of them together?

Later on, my father said to me, "I can't believe it. You really did it."

I said, "I told you I would."

But underneath everything, I was still their kid from Queens who was taught the difference between what nice girls do and what bad girls do. I was taught etiquette, I was taught manners. And then I'm out on the road, we finish a gig, go back to the hotel, and there's a line of women waiting outside my door.

I didn't know how to contend with that. It was so blatant. The fact that somebody would call your room and say, "Hi, what are you doing?"

And I'd say, "Uh, well, I've got somebody in my room."

And she'd say, "OK, I'll wait in the lobby. Let me know when you're done." I wasn't brought up like that. In fact, it took me a long time to get used to it.

Dan Fogelberg

○ ○ ○

A sensitive singer and writer who is consistently in the Top 10, Dan can charm you with his underplayed personality on- and offstage. His concerts play like love fests.

○ ○ ○

I met Irving Azoff in college, in Champagne, Illinois. He was booking REO Speedwagon and a bunch of people, and I was a folk singer in a coffeehouse, with moccasins and waist-length hair.

Irving heard some stuff I did, some of the local records I did, and he thought I was good. We were totally on opposite sides of the track. He was a businessman, a capitalist, and I was a radical musician. I was a little standoffish at first, but as soon as I met him, I knew this was the guy.

Irving respected me as an artist, and as a human being. He knew I wasn't a businessman. I was not the type of person who could deal with record companies all day long. I don't understand economics. I've got a good accountant and they tell me I'm doing fine. I ski and write music. My life was totally different from Irving's. He told me right from the beginning, "You make the music, and I'll take care of the business." I couldn't do what he does to save my life.

The first time we met was when an ex-girlfriend of mine dragged me out of bed and said, "Irving Azoff is out at this bar in Champagne, and he wants to hear you."

I'm going, "Are you crazy? I'm asleep."

She said, "He wants to hear you. Now get up." I'll forever feel gratitude for that woman. So I went out there, and Irving was there, and they brought out this little upright piano. The place was called the Chances Are. It was a fraternity bar, on a Friday night, and the place was going nuts. I'm in the lounge, and a band is playing in the main area. But Irving listened to me. I mean, people are throwing glasses. One guy smashed his head, and it was all bleeding, and an ambulance came. Police were throwing people in jail. Total fraternity madness, and I'm up there singing my sensitive little art songs at two in the morning. Irving was the only one in there who was listening. And he did listen. He heard every note and every word, and after I finished, he came up and said, "Yeah."

David Geffen had just formed Asylum, Bruce Springsteen and Billy Joel had just been signed to Columbia, and Irving was trying to sell me.

I was a big fan of Joni Mitchell's. She was a big influence on my songwriting. I'd seen that Geffen had set up this label for singer-songwriters, and I said, "What a great idea. This is where we want to be."

At the same time, Clive Davis had heard about me through Irving, and Clive was offering me a singles deal. I said, "No, I want an album deal, or we don't do it."

Geffen's label sounded like a haven for progressive artists, so I showed Irving an article about Geffen in *Rolling Stone*, and Irving said, "OK, I'll call the guy."

We got David's number and got him on the phone. He said, "I have no idea who you are, or what you're talking about, but if you send me a tape I'll listen." The rest is pretty much history. Irving went to work for David, and they hollered at each other across Sunset Boulevard.

But the ironic thing was, I didn't go with Asylum. It didn't feel exactly right, and Irving was saying, "Look, there are a lot of places to go here." He wanted to play all the record companies, and for six months he just made the rounds. Every day I'd be sitting out in the Valley, in this little apartment, eating chili and waiting for a record deal.

Irving would come home and say, "Well, it's A&M, definitely."

I'd say, "Oh, great. When do we start?"

And Irving would say, "We'll talk about it tomorrow." The next day he'd come home and tell me about another record company.

He did this to me for about six months. Finally I said, "I'll believe it when I see it." In the end, we went with Columbia and Clive, but for an album, not just a single.

Michael McDonald

○ ○ ○

A brilliant musician and vocalist, he hit his stride when he joined the Doobie Brothers. From there he proceeded right to the Grammy stage.

○ ○ ○

I was playing this casual job with Jeff Porcaro, a Christmas party on the Universal lot for the cast of the TV show "Emergency." I got the gig through a girl I was going out with. She was a bass player, and she had also been dating one of the guys from the cast of "Emergency."

Anyway, he asked her to put a band together for the Christmas party, and in the meantime, she gets a better job in Las Vegas, and she asks me to put the band together for "Emergency," and I tell her, "No problem."

I called everybody I knew. Jeff Porcaro, David Paich, Mike Porcaro on bass. It was the kind of thing where we had to double up on instruments because some guys just showed up wanting to sit in. Mainly I sang and played.

About a year later I got a call from Jeff Porcaro, and he tells me Steely

Dan is looking for a keyboard player and singer for a tour they're trying to get together. Jeff says, "Can you come down and audition?"

I couldn't believe it. Steely Dan was on its way to becoming the best band in pop music. I threw my Wurlitzer in the car, jumped in, and went down there to play. Well, Donald Fagen and Walter Becker were not crazy about my piano playing, but I could sing all the high parts and a few leads. I wound up getting a job.

Donald and Walter were funny people, eccentric in a very normal way. Temperamental, but never malicious. Musicians usually have an overblown opinion of themselves, but these guys weren't like that. But they tended to excite the environment around them.

I sang backgrounds with them, and they worked me very hard. But they were harder on themselves, and on the road they were reckless, Donald more than Walter. They were New Yorkers who weren't crazy about L.A. They would say, "If we're going on the road, it better be tight. The promoter better not mess up, or we'll walk." I toured with them in '72 and '73.

It was during my time with Steely Dan that I met Jeff Baxter, who had gone off with the Doobie Brothers. There seemed to be like a trail of dead bodies from Steely Dan to the Doobies. Everybody had played at one time or another with everybody else.

Jeff called me from New Orleans. The Doobies had just done the second show of the tour and Tom Johnston was having health problems and it didn't look like he'd be able to continue. Jeff asked if I could play organ. I told him I really didn't play organ, and he said, "Don't worry. Just come down. You'll cut it."

Two guys picked me up at the airport in New Orleans, and I didn't know if I was being hit or about to join a band. Everybody seemed like road-warrior types, war horses, an intense hard-core touring band, very different from Steely Dan's cast of characters.

So they took me back to the hotel, where the band had taken over the dining room. They were tearing it up pretty good, as I remember. Those were the days when a band that was bored stiff could do anything it wanted because it had the money to pay.

I fit in in an odd way. I was pretty shy, quiet, not a party person by any stretch of the imagination, but we all got along pretty well.

But Tom Johnston was tired. I don't think he ever believed he deserved what he achieved during his career, and if you get out there and get tired enough behind a machine like the Doobies were at the time—suddenly big business overnight—there may not be much consideration for human frailty. The pressure was on and it was relentless. If you don't take care of yourself in a situation like that, it can kill you.

It was the classic rock syndrome of a band going through an identity crisis after a successful stretch. It was a machine. "Feed the machine." No one knew how to react any differently. Everybody's jobs and lives depended on this huge monster they had created for themselves.

I had never made that kind of money in my life. I was offered a certain salary per week that I couldn't believe someone would ever pay me. I thought, "With my luck, the band will break up next week." But that, of course, didn't happen, and the run we went on for the next several years was a fantasy come true.

Lionel Richie

○ ○ ○

When he sang with his pals the Commodores, Lionel couldn't have guessed how high he would rise. A respected songwriter and a potent draw in concert, he continues to maintain his superstar status.

○ ○ ○

I was busy trying to dodge the draft, not sure whether I should be in law or accounting, even though neither one was fascinating me. It was my part-time band, though, that was getting more and more exciting every day. Finding Suzanne De Passe changed everything.

Suzanne said our first assignment at Motown was to go out with this group called the Jackson 5. We rehearsed very hard, went to Madison Square Garden for their opening date, and I saw more people looking in my direction than I'd ever seen in my life. It was terrifying to me, and they weren't looking at me, they were all waiting to see the Jacksons.

I watched Michael Jackson backstage as he and his father and a few of his brothers pooled their money together to pay for the limousine service that brought them to the back of Madison Square Garden. The driver said, "I'm leaving unless I get paid up front." To make a long story short, Michael and his brothers went onstage and played for forty-five minutes and they gave him a check for $108,000.

I said, "Wait a minute. This is a viable business." There were so many Rolls-Royces and limousines backstage and only one limousine for the group. The others were for the manager, the publisher, the publicist, sound and lighting company owners, building managers. I said, "There is a business in this music business."

It was a highlight and a struggle at the same time to arrive in Los Angeles and be the opening act for the Jackson 5 at the Hollywood Bowl. And for them to say to you that "Berry Gordy will be in the audience tonight. He is coming to see you"—you must know there was not enough air to breathe.

Naturally, we figured we were about to be plugged into the Motown machine, and tomorrow at four o'clock we're going to come out with a hit record. But it didn't work like that. It was two years later that we had our first hit record. When we signed with Motown, we were number fifty-eight on the Motown roster. In front of us you had the Temptations, Supremes, Gladys Knight and the Pips, Martha Reeves and the Vandellas. They were all in front of us. When we got ready to do our recording session, we were bumped because the Temptations had priority over us.

Over the next two years, acts started leaving Motown one by one. The joke at Motown finally got to be, "OK, Commodores, we've reached the end of the roster. Now it's your turn."

But that two-year period was good for me because I discovered my writing ability waiting around and hanging out with Norman Whitfield while he was recording. I watched Holland-Dozier-Holland. I watched Quincy Jones. I watched Berry Gordy one night dub in Diana Ross on a Marvin Gaye record, and it gave me the opportunity to study what these people were doing. When they finally asked me, "Well, what do you have in the way of material," I had a lot of material after two years.

But between the press and the industry, the age-old story says, "Single out one guy from the rest of the group," and they singled out me. I was not the only competent one in the group. The idea of leaving the group and going solo was never an issue. But things probably went the way they did because of Kenny Rogers. Kenny was very kind. Instead of standing in front of me taking all the bows, he said, "I owe it all to my dear friend, Lionel Richie." Every time Kenny made a personal appearance and I made a personal appearance it caused a strain within the group. I would join the group, and the press would be in the room, and as I walked in, the interviewers and cameramen would knock the other band members over just to start interviewing me.

I would say, "I'd be glad to do an interview, but first would you pick up that guy off the floor? That's my drummer." I started apologizing. I felt badly about what was happening. And then the next year, when "Endless Love" came out, it added gasoline to the fire. And then it got unbearable. I was doing a Commodores show at the Greek Theater, and I remember rushing to the newspaper the next morning to see the reviews, and there in the entertainment section was the headline, "Richie a Hit at the Greek." Needless to say, on the second night at the Greek it was real cold in the dressing room. I started apologizing. I said, "Fellas, I did not write this." I was apologizing for something I had no control over.

But the animosity and friction were there. And after the big success Kenny Rogers was having, Motown came to me and said, "If you're ever going to do a solo album, now is the time."

Natalie Cole

○ ○ ○

The bloodlines are great and her early career is a picture book of success. And then the bad times came. As we talked, she was out of the woods and on her way with more great hits, a powerhouse album, and a new life.

○ ○ ○

I grew up with people around me like Harry Belafonte, who used to swim in our pool, and Count Basie, Pearl Bailey, Ella Fitzgerald. They came to our house for lunch, they played golf with my dad, I went to their house, that sort of stuff. They were all like aunts and uncles.

And the kids I knew, too. Danny Thomas' kids, Bob Hope's niece, Phyllis Diller's son, Walt Disney's grandchildren. We all looked at one another like oddities. We all led very different lives.

My mother tried to keep us all normal. I was the first natural child. My sister is adopted, but she's really my cousin because her mom and my mom were sisters, and then mom's sister passed away and my mother adopted my cousin. My father wanted a boy, and my parents tried and tried. After they adopted a boy, my mother gave birth to twin girls.

I remember being very nervous when my dad found out I could sing. He was always bringing home jazz records. That was all I knew until I was fifteen. I knew every song Ella Fitzgerald ever sang. One day I made my father sit down in the living room and I sang him a tune Ella Fitzgerald used to sing called "Unsighted." He was so shocked to hear me sing that he found me a part in this show he was doing, "The Merry Young World of Nat King Cole." The show had already been running for weeks, and Dad had been taking it to different cities. I ended up doing it in Riverside and at the Greek Theater. Barbara McNair was also part of the show. She played me as a grown-up.

Then I started getting into other musical influences, like Marvin Gaye, the Supremes, and Stevie Wonder. Those were my big three. I met Stevie at a place in Hollywood called the Haunted House, which was a hot after-hours club. He was just getting started. He was still Little Stevie Wonder, and he was coming into his own. I remember how he would get up onstage and play piano and drums and there would be no one in the club. My girlfriend and I would look at him like he was crazy. We'd think, "Boy, is this guy wild."

Because my dad recorded for Capitol, and Capitol had the Beatles, I said to him one day, "Dad, please bring home a Beatles album." He was very upset with me, but he did bring the album home. Mr. Cole would not rock 'n' roll, and whenever he tried, it was funny. I remember laughing as I watched him dance. He was just not that type of person.

But he sure could sing. I would sit in the audience and watch him perform. He was great. He was the same easygoing guy on stage that he was at home. It was a great thrill for me to watch him mesmerize an audience.

When my father died in 1965, it just threw everything off kilter. No one in the family really knew what they wanted to do after that. It was such a sad, grief-stricken time for all of us. I felt like my arm and leg had been cut off. He meant so much to each of us. The twins never even knew him. They were three years old when he died. My brother was about seven. My sister and I are the ones with memories. He was only forty-seven years old.

Richard Perry

o o o

A world-class record producer for twenty years with a client roster ranging from Barbra Streisand to the Pointer Sisters, with lots of stops in between, Richard is a great song man who is enormously respected in the business.

o o o

If I didn't know Tiny Tim, working with him the way I did would have been beyond difficult. It would have been like trying to work with inmates in an asylum.

For openers, he had no conception of time whatsoever. He would suddenly skip a bar if he felt like it. If he didn't feel like going through the chorus, he would just jump right into the next verse. This became particularly difficult when I was conducting a sixty-piece orchestra at Albert Hall in London at a Tiny Tim concert. I think I sweated off ten pounds during that concert.

But right after he hit it big, we went back to New York to do the "Tonight" show. We were taking him home to see his parents, who lived on, like, 128th Street and Amsterdam Avenue. He was coming home for the first time, going back to the neighborhood where he'd been a bum for so many years. Finally, he was returning home a hero.

He wanted people in the neighborhood to know he was home, but it was ten o'clock at night. He wanted to knock on the building superintendent's door, the super's kid was a friend of his, but no one was home. He needed an outlet, he needed people to know he was there, but no one was home. I said, "Come on, Tiny. No one's home." But he's taking me through the back alleys.

I say to the limo driver, "Christ, let's get out of here." I opened the door to the limo, and Tiny was gone. I see him streaking down the block. I get in the limo and say, "Quick, follow him." His massive body was running at full speed, his hair was flowing in the wind. He runs to one corner where home plate must have been, and he pretends to hit a ball. He runs to first, and I can see what's happening. I jump out of the limo. He's on his way to second. I say, "Come on, Herbie." His real name is Herbert Khaury. He's on his way to third, really into it now. I say, "Come on, Herbie. All the way home." He streaks across the plate, and I say, "Yeah, Herbie hit a home run."

A few years later, when I had become an independent producer, I told Clive Davis I wanted a shot at producing Barbra Streisand. Clive put me to the test. He said, "OK, find some material for her," which I did. We sat down and listened to the material together and picked three or four songs we both believed in, and Clive set up a meeting with Barbra. People said, "How are you ever going to be able to work with her?"

I said, "Two Jews from Brooklyn. How far wrong can it be?" Immediately ours was a brother and sister type of relationship. But I was suggesting she move into contemporary music, which was a tremendous departure for her. She was totally not into contemporary music at that time.

At first she said, "This music isn't me. I don't get it." Then I get a call. "I want the new Van Morrison album, the new Randy Newman, new Marvin Gaye, new Joni Mitchell." Every week she had a list of new albums.

Barbra's a total pro, with finesse, like a jewel. She always did her homework. She always knew the song. But while we were rehearsing alone she was scared to death. She wanted to cancel the session, and I had to talk her out of it. This is the first session I ever did with her. The orchestra was there, the background singers, rhythm section, everybody. It started at seven o'clock at night and lasted until five-thirty in the morning. To most of those musicians, ten o'clock at night is late, but everybody hung in. Barbra's doubts were all before the session. The minute the session got underway with Nilsson's song "Maybe," all doubts left her. We did the Randy Newman song, "I'll Be Home," with Randy on piano, which excited Barbra. "Stoney End" was next, followed by "Just a Little Loving," which had previously been recorded by Dusty Springfield. We closed out the session with a fabulous Joni Mitchell song, "I Don't Know Where I Stand." Quite a broad range of composers. Quite a celebrated session.

Carly Simon was very difficult. Even though we continued to get closer and closer, we had major musical differences between us. She saw herself as more of a folk artist. Part of this, I think, was influenced by her relationship with James Taylor. We recorded her *No Secrets* album in London, from September to November in '72. She married James at the end of November. The album was kind of like her final days as a single woman.

James visited a couple of times during the making of the album. She wanted to do his song, "Rainy Day Man," which is a beautiful folk-oriented tune, but it really wasn't happening to our satisfaction. I said, "You want to do one of James' songs? OK, let's do 'Night Owl,' " which was a funky, bluesy kind of thing which we could turn into a rock 'n' roll song. That's a good example of the differences between us. I mean, "You're So Vain" was originally conceived by Carly as something she would do without drums.

In March of '73 I got together with Ringo Starr in Nashville, and I played him some songs. One was "You're Sixteen," which I felt he could remake. And then, Ringo and George Harrison had written a song called "Photograph," which Ringo played for me. As soon as we got to Los Angeles, we launched into the album. The first week we cut five tracks, three of which became hit singles. George arrived and did his thing. He was totally enthusiastic and supportive.

And then John Lennon came. It was a unique situation. John, George, and Ringo were all in L.A. at the same time because of meetings they were having with Allen Klein about the dissolution of the Beatles. When John heard Ringo's material, he went wild. Immediately he said he wanted to write a song for the album, which was incredibly exciting for Ringo.

The day came during the second week. John was coming in to do his song. George had been there and left during the first week. Well, the minute John walked in the air filled with excitement. He worked at an incredibly fast pace. He cut out all the fat. He was nonstop energy. No sooner did we finish one take than he was already counting off the second.

We all gathered around the piano because the song wasn't quite finished yet, and I'm saying to myself, "Can you believe this? I'm sitting at a piano with John Lennon, helping him finish a song for Ringo Starr."

In the middle of working with Lennon at the piano, the phone rings. Someone says George is on the phone, and he wants to talk to me. I get on the phone and one of George's men says, "We hear there's a session going on. Is it OK if George comes down?"

I say, "Hold on." And now Richard Perry is going to ask John Lennon if it's OK if George Harrison comes down to join in on the session. I thought I'd died and gone to heaven.

John says, "Hell, yes. Tell him to get the hell down here and finish up this bridge for me."

Ten minutes later, George quietly slips in, plugs in his amplifier. We're running the song down. No one tells George about the song, or what's going on, or how or what to play. He plugs in and immediately plays the perfect part. I mean, a typical George-Harrison-of-the-Beatles guitar part. I knew right then what the magic of the Beatles was all about.

Peter Frampton

○ ○ ○

The curse of a giant success early in the game saw Peter whipped and frustrated when the golden touch disappeared almost as fast as it came.

○ ○ ○

I do not have a clue as to why *Frampton Comes Alive* was so big, but it was, and at the beginning of all the success we went to a party for Electric Light Orchestra in New York. A table had been roped off for our band. There were, like, thousands of photographers there, and we walked in and sat down and just began giggling. The band was saying to me, "Do you realize that everybody is staring at you?"

I said, "Yeah, it's a funny sensation. What is it? Is my jacket dirty, or what?"

I didn't quite realize what was happening to me. I'd become the flavor of the month. People thought of me differently, not as a human being, which can be very disconcerting to deal with, especially when it happens so quickly and so big.

Somewhere along the way, my credibility as a musician got lost. I was overmarketed. The live album didn't need hyping, and yet it got hyped with me on the cover of *Rolling Stone* with my shirt off, which instantly turned off a lot of my musical fans.

I didn't realize what a split-second photo like that could do. It was only one shot by Scavullo. I let him take just one of me with my shirt off. The rest of the session was normal, you know, with a jacket on and everything. But the one with the shirt off was the one they used. It's the one of me everyone likes to use.

So it just got to the point where the image had totally overriden everything else. Suddenly, I was appealing just to teenage girls. Everyone forgot that I could play the guitar.

Later on, I remember turning up at a gig, and the girls were outside afterwards saying, "Oh, I didn't know you played the guitar," which was, like, alarm bells going off inside of me. But it was too late at that point. The damage had been done.

And then came the *Sgt. Pepper* movie. The last thing you want to do is copy the Beatles. I mean, that's an unwritten law. But at the time it looked good on paper—Beatles music, a Robert Stigwood production, George Martin doing the music, the Bee Gees, and the carrot: Paul McCartney playing the part that Billy Preston eventually played at the end of the film.

McCartney's name gave it all the credibility I needed to hear. I said, "Yes, I'll do it."

Of course, I arrive on the set the first day, and they go, "Paul who?"

There were maybe a half-dozen people involved that had made a movie before. I think we all should have gone to school. The director would say, "OK, you come around the corner in the car, you look at the balloon, and I want you to look amazed, surprised."

So you think about looking amazed, and you go "Ah," which on screen looks as if your mouth is four feet open. So ridiculous. All one needs to do to look amazed is raise your eyebrow just slightly. We didn't know any of this. I remember seeing myself in that scene and laughing. It was so ridiculous it was funny.

The next big thing in my illustrious career was a car wreck in the Bahamas. When I woke up, I was so glad to be alive that I started wondering, "What the hell is going on?"

It was not a nice time at all. My personal life had completely fallen apart. A lot of people were making a lot of money off me, but they weren't necessarily thinking about my career in the long run. They used what I had and sort of ran it dry.

My last album for A&M, *Breaking All the Rules*, was a valiant attempt to sort of get it back, but it wasn't in my heart. I'd lost the drive, the energy, and the excitement. I suppose I was bitter. By 1982, I was no longer with A&M. My management had gone two years before that, and I just pulled back from everything.

Barry White

ooo

Barry developed a style and a stage presence that was as difficult to define as it was successful, and it led to a short and sweet career on top.

ooo

I remember the day I decided to come to Hollywood. It was very unexpected. As a young man, I did not get along well with teachers. They never had all the answers, and still they tried to bully us into thinking they did. I went to school in southeast Los Angeles, and on my eighteenth birthday, as I was getting ready to go to school—my clothes had all been laid out the night before—something inside me said, "You're not going to school anymore. You're going to Hollywood."

I was combing my hair in the mirror, and my mother saw me, and I said, "I'm not going to school."

She said, "Are you crazy? This is your last semester. You're so close to graduation."

I said, "I'm going to Hollywood." And that's what I did. I hitchhiked to Hollywood. Landed where Rossmore turns into Vine. There is a statue there, and I stood there and looked at that statue for ten minutes before I finally turned around and started walking up Vine. I got up to Hollywood Boulevard, and I saw the Capitol Records building, which always represented Hollywood to me, and I stood there staring at the building for three hours. I was looking at the cars, at the people, everything. What can I say, it inspired me. I went home that night, and four days later some guy asks me to sing bass with a group called the Up Fronts.

I was concerned with rehearsing new dance steps, and unfortunately, the others in the group were more concerned with drinking wine. After that, I swore I'd never be in another group.

From 1960 to 1971, I struggled. I was the kid they saw coming, the kid with holes in the soles of his shoes. You could hear me coming two blocks away. That's how badly my shoes flapped.

Hal Davis at Motown used to give me clothes to wear. One of Stanley Goldstar's musicians once brought in a coat for me to wear that he said he wore in the war. I wore that coat, even conducted in it, and Stan said to me, "If you ever explode, Barry White, you're gonna scare people." He had tears in his eyes, he felt so sorry for me. Even my wife felt sorry for me.

In 1970, things started changing. I met three girls from San Pedro who didn't know a thing about the business, and I named them Love Unlimited. Nineteen seventy-one rolls around, and Larry Nunes gives me some money to begin rehearsing the girls. We make a master, we bring it to Russ Regan and he freaks. We put out an album, *Walking in the Rain*, and it's a smash. We go on the road and misery sets in.

I didn't mind the small clubs, and the lousy conditions, but I resented being in a club where pimps hung out. I thought the music I was creating would touch a higher intellect.

Well, the record was a hit anyway, and when we came off the road, I made a call to Sammy Davis, Jr.'s, office because he had expressed an interest in Love Unlimited opening for him in Vegas. A few days before my meeting with Sammy, I went into my office on Sunset, and I started fooling around with the intro to one of the songs. Then another song, and another song, and soon I canceled the meeting with Sammy. I was so excited when I went into the studio. I knew I needed to find a singer to sing these new songs. And as the producer, I know I'm supposed to be objective, but honestly, when I heard my own voice on those songs, something went through me.

What happened as a result of that was incredible. I suppose everyone has to pick their own subjects to talk about in music. Mine just happened to be about love. When a man is making love and about to climax, the last thing he thinks about is war, the last thing he thinks about is how he can blow up a nation. If there's one thing in this world we can all tune into, it's making love. Everybody does it. Fleas fuck. Flies, snakes, everybody is into lovemaking. It's the most powerful element that men and women possess, and for some reason, most of us don't know how to use that power.

But people did use my music to make love. Women used the music to get their man to relate to them better. "Talk to me, baby. Tell me what's on your mind."

Men used the music to get their women in the mood to make love. Either way, Barry White was the one artist who was actually in your bedroom with you at that sacred, sensuous moment of your life.

I've had guys walk up to me on the street and say, "Barry, I feel like you've been watching me get off." A lot of babies have been named Barry. If there was a Barry boom in '74, I was the one responsible for it.

Don McLean

○ ○ ○

The curse of the enormous hit and the constant association with it is Don's story. He keeps trying, but "American Pie" is one piece of history that is hard to duplicate.

○ ○ ○

I wrote the opening part of "American Pie" up in my little room where I used to compose. I started thinking back to when I was a paper boy, one of those experiences about growing up in New Rochelle, where I cut open this paper bundle and saw that Buddy Holly, the Big Bopper, and Ritchie Valens had been killed. I stood there and couldn't believe it. Holly was my favorite performer. So I started writing, "A long, long time ago," but I didn't know what to do with it.

Then I came up with the chorus, which was kind of catchy, but I left the thing alone for three months until finally one day I wrote this whole story about the day the music died.

The first time I played it was when I was opening for Laura Nyro at a concert in Philadelphia. I had a lady come out of the audience to hold the lyrics because the song was very long. People didn't know what the hell I was singing about, and I didn't get a very good reaction.

The record is where the song happened. I found a guy named Ed Freeman, who had done several records for Columbia. One of the reasons I liked Ed was because of a record he did with Tom Rush. Tom is a nice fellow, but not the most exciting singer in the world, but on this album he sounded wonderful, fantastic. I said to myself, "This producer must be someone special."

Ed spent a lot of time with me redeveloping my material. Over a period of months he did a lot of figuring as to who should be on the sessions. A little while later we rehearsed, and it was the worst. I mean, it sounded so bad. Suddenly this song, "American Pie," is the centerpiece of the whole record, and it sounded awful. The guys didn't understand the rhythm changes, and I had no idea how to communicate with them. I was getting very depressed.

And then this one piano player named Paul Griffin, who had worked with Bob Dylan, started running "American Pie" down, and he played the ass off that song. It just started bouncing all over the place. He really pumped the thing and drove it. And with my guitar in his ear, and him jumping around on piano, it came together. Once I put the vocal on, it became a very hot record.

I brought the same guys on "The David Frost Show" six months later, when the song was a hit, and they didn't play it well at all. I have no idea what happened. Maybe it was the length of the song, almost nine minutes. The record company said, "It's great, we love it, but why does it have to be so long?"

When the record started selling, it caused me to deal with a very boring subject, which was people asking me what the song was about. They would badger me to the point where I became quite frustrated. I thought their curiosity about this song was to the exclusion of dealing with the body of my work, which I felt was valid.

When the song turned into an anthem, some of the fun was taken out of it. Suddenly it became more of a struggle for me than it had been before. I don't know if people will understand this, but it can actually be harder after you've been successful. That's the way it was for me after "American Pie." The fact that "Vincent" was my follow-up to "American Pie" lessened that burden a great deal.

Not too long ago, I performed at an outdoor concert in Buffalo. Maybe eight, ten thousand people were there, and a lot of them were tough bikers, and I'm singing "Vincent," and the bikers are going, "Starry, starry night." Here were the toughest guys on the planet getting teary-eyed. "Vincent" never could have been a hit record had it not ridden in on the coattails of "American Pie."

But the record of "American Pie" did stillborn me a little. It prevented me from having the natural progression so important for an artist to have. As much as I don't like to admit it, "American Pie" did become a cross to bear. It's something I have to face. That's the way it is.

Don Henley *(left)*, **Glenn Frey** *(right)*, **and Eagles manager Irving Azoff** *(back to camera)*, **1980**
(Photo by Henry Diltz)

David Bowie, 1987
(Photo by James Ruebsamen)

Roger Waters

Richard Branson

Robert Lamm, 1986
(Photo by Henry Diltz)

Olivia Newton-John, 1987
(Photo by Mike Mullen)

Justin Hayward

Jon Anderson

Chris Squire

Paul Stanley *(left)* **and Gene Simmons**
(Photo by Mark Weiss)

Michael McDonald, 1986
(Photo by Javier Mendoza)

Dan Fogelberg, 1985
(Photo by Henry Diltz)

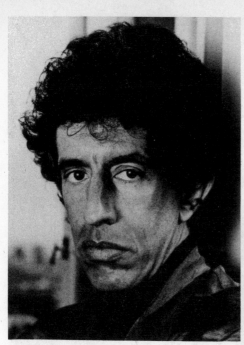

Richard Perry

Natalie Cole, 1985
(Photo by Anne Knudsen)

Lionel Richie, 1984
(Photo by Henry Diltz)

Peter Frampton, 1986
(Photo by Henry Diltz)

Barry White, 1981
(Photo by Mike Sergieff)

Boz Scaggs, 1980
(Photo by Rob Brown)

Leo Sayer, 1981

Don McLean, 1986
(Photo by Leo Jarzomb)

Donna Summer, 1983
(Photo by James Ruebsamen)

Tommy Mottola, 1987
(Photo by Ebet Roberts)

Anita Pointer, 1985
(Photo by Leo Jarzomb)

Lindsey Buckingham, 1980
(Photo by Anne Knudsen)

Christine McVie, 1980
(Photo by Anne Knudsen)

Tom Petty, 1981
(Photo by Rob Brown)

Michael Chapman

Tina Turner, 1985
(Photo by Javier Mendoza)

Steven Tyler, 1978
(Photo by Dean Musgrove)

Joe Perry
(Photo by Ron Pownall)

Pat Benatar, 1983
(Photo by Jeff Mayes)

Robert Palmer
(Michael Ochs Archives)

Dee Snider
(Photo by Mark Weiss)

John Cougar Mellencamp, 1986
(Photo by James Ruebsamen)

Billy Joel, 1984
(Photo by Paul Chinn)

Phil Ramone

Phil Collins, 1985
(Photo by Leo Jarzomb)

Sting, 1985
(Photo by Anne Knudsen)

George Michael
(Photo by Chris Cuffaro)

David Lee Roth, 1986
(Photo by James Ruebsamen)

Bono, 1987

(Photo by Leo Jarzomb)

Boz Scaggs

o o o

Boz couldn't get it together for years after breaking through with some fine blues-flavored records. His story winds through San Francisco, Europe, and eventually the Top 10 before he was struck by whatever afflicts rock stars.

o o o

I went to Europe in the middle sixties, and I began to hear white boys over there who were playing the blues. That was pretty alien stuff at the time. Outside of maybe Paul Butterfield, white boys in America just weren't doing that.

It was people like Georgie Fame, Chris Farlowe and the Thunderbirds, and Eric Burdon, who was doing Ray Charles and some Bobby Bland. I heard the Stones and Peter Green and John Mayall's group, and it started me thinking that London was the place I needed to be.

Sure enough, I get to London, walk into a club on my first night in town and there's Chris Farlowe doing a rendition of "Stormy Monday Blues" in Bobby Bland's style. I'd never seen white boys playing with such feeling, with such mastery. I'd never seen anything like it in the States.

Out of that movement, of course, came Eric Clapton, Cream, and Jimi Hendrix.

Pretty soon the Texas guys I had gone to London with split and went back to America, and I started traveling on my own. I based myself in Scandinavia and began working clubs as a solo. I played guitar, mostly blues, some rhythm and blues, even a little esoteric jazz. By the time I got back to the States I had been stretched in more than a few musical expressions.

In the States, I settled in San Francisco and continued writing some of the things I'd begun when I was with Steve Miller. But I had no real ambition.

Much, you know, has been made of the so-called music community in San Francisco, but to my knowledge there's never been a true music community there. It was never like Los Angeles or New York, where you can jump into a taxi and say, "Take me over to so-and-so's session." That scene never existed in San Francisco. It was always this group, or that group—Airplane, Grateful Dead—and I was never part of that scene.

In San Francisco, I lived across the street from Jann Wenner, the editor of *Rolling Stone*. It was Jann who supplied the encouragement that became the thrust for my next move, which was to become a real solo act.

Jann loves music, which is probably why *Rolling Stone* has been around as long as it has. We haven't seen much of each other in recent years, but the last time we did get together we got out the latest Al Green release.

Slow Dancer was the album that got me my foot in the door in Los Angeles. I looked around town to see the kinds of musicians who might be available. I needed to make a distinction between *Slow Dancer* and the album I was about to make. *Slow Dancer* was pretty much a session call.

So I looked around town and came up with guys I could feed off and be fed by—a wonderful young section made up of Jeff Porcaro, David Paich, and David Hungate, the nucleus of what would later become Toto. But at the time they were just hot-shot musicians with a lot of energy and ambition. I went into the studio with these guys, we took a shot, and they performed above and beyond the call of duty, with input that was invaluable. They gave me their "A" stuff, they didn't save anything for themselves, and that's a huge reason why *Silk Degrees* turned out as good as it did.

Leo Sayer

○ ○ ○

I found this young man years ago in a pub in Brighton, England. His subsequent fame in Europe and to a lesser degree in the States kept me personally involved. He never went as far as we all thought he would.

○ ○ ○

There was a blues boom in Britain in the late sixties, but I found it very hard to go out and sing about how, "I left a steel mill in Chicago," so I started singing about how, "I left my fish-and-chip shop in Brighton."

I started twisting the blues form into an English lyric. I spoke to Bruce Springsteen once about it, and he thought it was great. When he came down to Brighton to play, he said, "Show me these places, man."

Because I didn't write melodies, I took actual blues melodies and put my lyrics to them. I did that absolutely, unashamedly. I thought blues melodies were like folk songs in the public domain. I didn't mean to be screwing blues artists. I wasn't exactly making any money doing this, but it did seem to be a kind of answer for me. I mean, the Rolling Stones were singing about Route 66. All these guys—Eric Burdon, Mick Jagger, Paul Jones of Manfred Mann—I never believed they totally understood what they were singing about. It was like they were just issuing words like a bunch of Paul Oliver–type bluesologists with voices.

I thought, "What's wrong with my little town? What's wrong with the things we see here? Maybe I can romanticize it." So I kind of set out in my early songs to romanticize my own life. That probably sounds a little Harry Chapinish, or like how Billy Joel wanted to make Hempstead, Long Island, the center of the earth. I wanted to make Sussex the center of the earth.

I also had a brief foray into soul music. And I have a bump on my head from the time a bunch of black GIs hit me over the head for trying to sing like them. They said, "A white guy can't do this," and that was the end of that.

I was an observer, incessantly catching shows, seeing artists, learning from them. I remember seeing Paul Simon in the folk clubs. I followed him everywhere. I talked to him. I followed Donovan around, too. I used to bask on the London streets. A lot of folk clubs stayed open all night, and you just sort of hung around, stayed up, and caught hepatitis.

My big break came when I started doing my first album in Roger Daltrey's home studio. Pete Townshend had just done a solo album, and Roger kept walking around while we were rehearsing, saying, "Oh, I like your songs. I really want to do my own solo album." During our recording, he actually popped the question. He said, "I'm fed up. Pete's done a solo album. I want to better him." Typical band talk, one member trying to outdo another.

So Roger says, "I like your songs. Give me ten songs."

I looked at my writing partner, Dave Courtney, and we rushed home that night and found ten songs. We went through all our tapes, and we thought, "Well, we'll give him that one, we'll finish that one." One of the songs was "Giving It All Away," a song I dared not play for my manager-producer Adam Faith, because it was about me leaving him.

He kept saying, "Wait, kid. Don't worry, it's all going to happen. You've got to be patient."

I thought, "Well, I'm just a boy giving it all away. I'm throwing away my whole creativity to these people who keep telling me to wait."

When Daltrey heard the song, Adam turned to me and said, "That's incredible. What's that song about?"

I said, "Oh, it's about somebody walking out on his wife." Later on they found out what the song was about. It was interesting. We were halfway through my album, and Roger liked the whole sound of what we were doing. Not only did he like our songs, he took on Dave and Adam's production, as well. The entire team moved in on Daltrey.

And it all worked out nicely. "Giving It All Away" was successful on both the English and American charts. People had been waiting for Daltrey to do something special. They were also wondering if Roger would fail without the most important part, the writing of Pete Townshend.

Donna Summer

○ ○ ○

Talking with Donna at her ranch in California, we were a long way from the days of the Disco Queen and the supposedly difficult-to-handle prima donna performer. She tells how the title wasn't any great help and the reputation not really deserved.

○ ○ ○

Everybody in my family used to sing. We were the Supremes at home, or Dionne Warwick or Barbra Streisand or Aretha. Whoever was famous, I thought I sang like them. All I wanted to do was sing, and the first time I did, I really thought I heard a voice telling me I'd be famous. And I became famous, and by the time I was nineteen, I was singing in the same clubs with Janis Joplin. Janis' first time out in Boston was at the Psychedelic Supermarket. Back then she was braless and singing real raunchy.

I auditioned in New York with my two sisters for *Hair*. There were about three hundred people auditioning, and we were the last ones in line. I had a feeling I was going to be taken, but I also felt like I had nothing to lose. I had seen the musical two weeks before, and one of the kids in the show, Lamont Washington, walked over to me during one of the scenes in the play and he said, "You should be in this musical," and he gave me a flower. He later died in a fire.

Very peculiar things happened around my coming into success. I was walking through the streets of New York with a friend. We were on the Bowery giving quarters to the bums. I had never been on the Bowery, and as we were walking along, I saw this man coming toward me and he looked like Santa Claus. It was almost as if this guy had a light bulb in his mouth. His whole face lit up. As we got closer, this man put his hand on me and said, "Don't be afraid." He proceeded to tell me that I was going to take a trip to Europe, meet a man there, and that I would be more successful as a writer than a singer. That night I went home. I auditioned for *Hair* two days later, got the part, and within ten days I was leaving for Europe.

I did *Hair* in Germany, and right off the bat I became a star in that country because the musical was a hit. In the show I sang "Let the Sun Shine In" and "Aquarius." Being a star in Germany is more low-key than it is in America. It is more quaint.

I did other shows in Germany, too, and when I began singing backgrounds on records, Giorgio Moroder saw me and wanted to cut some demos with me. He released some things in Holland and we had a few hits there. I love Europe. I don't even feel American. Sometimes I feel like a foreigner here.

I remember the day I came up with the phrase "Love to love you baby." I had to go to Giorgio's office, and I said to him, "Listen to this line. Isn't it a cute line?"

And Giorgio said in a very deep accent, "I love to love. I love to love you." Two days later Giorgio's girlfriend came to my door telling me I had to come to the studio. I went in and sang "Love to Love You Baby," and Giorgio sent it to Holland. He played it at the MIDEM convention, and everybody wanted it. Somehow Neil Bogart was given the track, and he called Giorgio and told him the DJs were playing the shit out of it. But there was only one problem—it was too short. The story Neil Bogart used to tell is that he played it when he was being intimate, and if only he could capture this mood for an entire side of an album. So Giorgio sent Neil eighteen minutes of ooohs and ahhhs, and it sort of was history from that.

At the beginning I wasn't even in America and a few transvestites started using "Love to Love You Baby" as their theme song. It started a rumor that I was actually a man.

Nobody thought I could sing when I first did "Love to Love You Baby," probably because I was whispering. But that was good because when I finally opened my mouth and sang, people were surprised that there was a little bit of voice there.

It was a very trying time. Sometimes I feel like I was raped emotionally and didn't even know it. When I finally had time to regroup and look over all the facts, I felt like somebody took something of mine and didn't ask my permission. I'm one of those artists who feels like she's been taken advantage of, but I'm not bitter about it at all. I was royally robbed, but I don't care. I am richer than I was before.

Things back then were moving so fast. I had a chemical imbalance in my body, and with all the pressures of not sleeping and being on the go, it got worse. I became extremely depressed and I would have to do things to elevate myself. I felt like I couldn't fight anymore, to the point of being suicidal. I knew I had to get help. Neil Bogart had a doctor who put me on a drug for about two and a half years. During that time, I had my biggest records, did the most touring and had the most stardom.

After that period I bought a house in Hancock Park. I knew I couldn't keep up that pace. I wanted to have children. I already had one daughter and I felt like I wasn't a good mother. So I started to pray one day in my bed, and I asked God to help me make a new dream. Every day I prayed. I was doing it without even thinking about it. When I was taking the medicine the doctor had prescribed, I could literally stay up for days, and that frightened me. My medicine became my God. I would have stacks of this medicine hidden in places so I would always have it, just in case they stopped making it. I knew I had to get something "outside" of myself. But after I started praying, I stopped taking the medicine. I felt like something had been lifted off my shoulders. From that point on, I considered myself born again.

Tommy Mottola

o o o

**Although he achieved great success as a personal manager and
currently is the new president of CBS Records, Tommy looks and acts
like a street guy. Locked in with the Hall and Oates career, he gave us
a firsthand account of the management game.**

o o o

I played in local rock bands in New York City. I had a recording deal with
Epic Records. I recorded under the name T. D. Valentine, and when I
listen to those records now, I know why they weren't hits.

At the age of twenty, I began promoting records independently for some
of the labels in New York. My first job in the business was with MRC Music,
Mercury Records' publishing company. Six months later, the company was
purchased by Chappell, so I did my apprenticeship at Chappell. Mostly they
had old-time writers. They didn't have a clue about rock 'n' roll, so I ran
the contemporary division. Some of the people I ran across at the beginning
of my working there were Hall and Oates, who I signed, a group called Dr.
Buzzard's Original Savannah Band, and another group called Odyssey. Even
though we were publishers, I was working with these people on a day-to-
day basis, helping them set up record deals, helping them get bookings,
helping them promote their records. In essence, I was acting like a manager
out of Chappell and on Chappell's behalf because Chappell retained all the
publishing.

At a certain point I said to myself, "Gee, this is really crazy. I'm doing
all these details, I'm doing all this work." So at twenty-five, I left Chappell
and opened up my own management company that managed Hall and Oates,
Dr. Buzzard's Original Savannah Band, and Odyssey. Why I decided to
leave when I did had to do with Hall and Oates' first hit, "Sarah Smile,"
breaking. I had been making $25,000 a year at Chappell, and with "Sarah
Smile" going all the way to Number 1, I knew I could make more managing
these acts. Ken Glancy, who was president of RCA Records at the time, was
very friendly with me, and he was gracious enough to provide me with a
blanket production deal, like a talent scout for RCA Records, which then
also provided me with the financing to open an office and start a company.

I thought at the time that I knew it all. I had somewhat of a chip on
my shoulder. I was the street kid who thought he knew everything, but was
really wet behind the ears. When I look back on it, I made a lot of mistakes.
I did some stupid things, like opening my mouth when I shouldn't. I turned
off a lot of people. I was overly aggressive or pushy in certain areas. I thought
my run would never end. I thought my acts would never stop having hit
records. When I was around twenty-nine, thirty, I had a rude awakening.
The Savannah Band had broken up. Odyssey stopped having hit records.
And Hall and Oates, who had had three Number 1 records back to back,

"Sarah Smile," "She's Gone," and "Rich Girl"—their next four albums died completely.

The down side of management is that there are no thank you's. You're damned if you do and damned if you don't. There's a slight amount of gratitude, but basically you're the guy in the hot seat all the time. You are subject to the whims and emotions of your artist twenty-four hours a day. You're the guy who becomes the punching bag when things don't go right. You're in the middle of it with the record company, so you're getting beat up on the outside as well as on the inside. You're supposed to be on the same team with the artist, but sometimes they look to you before they necessarily want to look to themselves.

The up side is that if you love this business, and eat, sleep, and drink it the way I do, the rewards are incredible. I'm like a kid in a candy store who doesn't know which candy bar to pick. The things I dreamed about doing my whole life I'm doing in real life.

See, I think this business is great. I look at myself as someone who has come up through the ranks. I used to look at guys like Clive Davis and Ahmet Ertegun and all the big managers. It was all so intimidating. But my motivation was: Someday I'm going to knock those guys out of the box. Someday I'm going to be up there with them.

Lindsey Buckingham

o o o

When Stevie Nicks and Lindsey joined Fleetwood Mac, they transformed that troubled band into a world power with a few multi, multi-platinum albums. He provided the spark creatively and brought the group back for an encore in 1987 before leaving it for good.

o o o

It's very difficult having a love relationship with somebody you're working with. On the other side, one of the great pivot points of Fleetwood Mac was that you had two couples that were breaking up simultaneously. The kind of tension created by that also helped us keep our priorities in order. There was pain, there was confusion, and it all added up to make *Rumours* a soap opera on vinyl. What made us attractive to people was the feeling that you can hear those songs knowing we had these relationship problems in our personal life. You don't see a lot of that within one group in a rock situation, and I think that's part of what made us unique.

After Stevie and I joined the group, for the next several years I had to pretty much throw out everything I was about. Stevie had a different way about her. She had the freedom to create something of her own. Being the musician, for a long time I had to play Bob Welch tunes, Peter Green tunes—people who had left the group. In a sense, I was like a lounge player in a group, which was not an easy thing. Philosophically, though, it provided me with a slow progression. It wasn't an easy progression, but it was a solid one.

Throughout Fleetwood Mac, there was always a sense of division. It was very subtle, nothing you could really put your finger on, it wasn't even all that negative, but the fact that there were three English people and two Americans meant there were cultural differences. I want to put this in the least negative way, but the cultural differences almost guaranteed that we would get to know one another as friends only to a certain point.

I'm that way anyway. I've got maybe one very close friend. I keep my life as simple as possible. But a formality in the group did exist, and it probably always would have.

There was another thing that was different about us, and that was the road. When you're out on the road with a group of guys, your attitudes are going to be looser. You might even have the tendency to get more debauched on a general running level. But with two ladies on the plane it tends to make the gentlemen a little more gentlemanly.

Add that to the male–female tension, not necessarily in the way Stevie and I interacted, or John and Christine McVie, but as former lovers it was there.

Finally, there were the expectations that followed our tremendous success. There was a great deal of pressure to adhere to whatever the machinery wanted. Just look at the making of our *Tusk* album. The story is probably famous now, but the word was, when the people at Warners first heard *Tusk*, they saw their Christmas bonuses going out the window.

The whole idea of refuting the machinery can be viewed as more than a little awkward. You sell 16 millions albums, like we did, and you've set that machinery in motion for next time. *Tusk* was a good album, but the focus of that album tended to be more on the visibility of the group, and the phenomenon of our previous sales figures, than on the music.

Christine McVie

○ ○ ○

An earlier Fleetwood Mac member, Christine's relationships with others and her highly identifiable contribution make for a special view of the band.

○ ○ ○

I had gone to London and was working as a window dresser. On the weekends I played in some youth club. One day I get a call from one of the guys I'm playing with, Andy Sylvester, and he asks me if I really want to join the band full-time and go professional. I was earning eight pounds, ten shillings a week dressing windows for a bunch of fruits. I was totally broke. Of course I wanted to join.

We called ourselves Chicken Shack, and we had a few rehearsals. I was completely at a loss. I didn't have a clue as to what to do on piano. One of the other band members, Stan Webb, bought me a Freddie King album and said, "Listen to this. See if you can copy a few of the licks." I listened to the album, and that was the beginning of my absolute love for the blues.

Fleetwood Mac was my favorite band at the time. They were like a drug. They were so good—Jeremy Spencer, Danny Kirwan, Peter Green, Mick Fleetwood, and John McVie. They were an enigma. They had a real magic about them that was infectious. I went to see them at the Thames Hotel in Windsor one night, and John just asked me out. I went out with him. We courted for six months.

They did their first American tour, gone for six weeks, and I didn't hear from John once. When he came back, he proposed to me. Ten days later, we were married and I left Chicken Shack. As far as I was concerned, my music career was finished. I was quite prepared to be a housewife.

Then Fleetwood Mac went to Europe and the bombshell hit. Peter went off with the German jet-set and did way too much acid for his own good. He came back and said, "I don't want to be in Fleetwood Mac anymore. I don't want to do anything." He dug graves for a while, he worked in a pathologist lab, he wanted to get back to his Jewish roots. He left everybody high and dry, right at the point when they were supposed to make another album.

So, without Peter, the four of them did another album, *Kiln House*. The next thing we knew it was Number 48 on the American charts. No one could believe it. "OK," they said, "let's go on the road. Let's go to America."

Then they realized the sound wasn't full enough, so they said, "Chris, you know all the songs. Play piano." Ten days later, we were playing in New Orleans. I'd never been to America before, except when I visited John one Christmas.

We landed in Los Angeles just after the big earthquake. I remember the sky being yellow, and Jeremy saying, "I don't have to be here, I don't want to be here." No one thought anything of it. We got to the hotel, Jeremy went out for some magazines, and he never came back.

Jeremy did at least six songs in the set. Without him, we didn't have a long enough set, by any means. So we called Peter Green and begged him to come over and help us complete the tour rather than being sued. Peter came over, and the remainder of the tour was done without singing. A totally instrumental tour. We did a version of "Black Magic Woman" that lasted for forty-five minutes. Peter refused to sing, and that's when I really learned to jam.

The next step was Bob Welch, a good guitar player who was in Paris and out of a job. Soon as we met him, we didn't bother to talk to any more people. We liked him right away. We got on like a house on fire through *Future Games* and *Bare Trees*. But the strain was beginning to tell by *Heroes Are Hard to Find*. Bob was playing the part of our lawyer/manager, and it was taking its toll on him. We were out on the road and the halls were a quarter filled. Everybody was fighting. It was unpleasant and Bob left.

Meanwhile, the diehards—me, John, and Mick—were saying, "What now?" Well, Mick happened by a studio in the Valley called Sound City, and the resident engineer, Keith Olsen, played Mick a tape of this young couple, Buckingham and Nicks. We had them come over to Mick's house one night and asked them if they wanted to join the band.

We knew we were going to be sensational. From the first rehearsal, we knew it. Unfortunately, there were more problems after *Rumours*. John and I were split. Stevie and Lindsey had broken up. Mick was getting divorced. None of us were happy. You could not get all five of us in a room together. Somehow we managed to laugh through it all, even though it was awful.

Anita Pointer

○ ○ ○

Tall, perky, and cooking, Anita and her sisters resurfaced in the late seventies after being out of it for years. Their style is unique and they look smashing.

○ ○ ○

Mother kind of tried to lump the four of us together. I guess it was easier for her to buy one dress four times as opposed to getting everyone a different style. It seemed we were always in twos—Ruth and me were like a team, and June and Bonnie were a team. We were the two oldest, and they were the youngest.

But the four of us did do a lot together. We played together, slept together, went to church together. Like I said, it was easier for mother to keep us together.

We did manage to be individuals within the group. I consider myself more of the oddball. I was the fat kid, and I acted much older than I was. I liked hanging out with older people. In a way, I did resent always being lumped together with my sisters, having to share a room, my clothes, do everything with my sisters. The resentment was there. I guess that was one of the reasons why Bonnie decided to leave the group.

Bonnie just moved away. She remains very distant. I don't talk with Bonnie very much. I miss her a lot. I could definitely work with her again. When she did her most recent album, she came to Los Angeles from her home in Florida, and Ruth and I sang background vocals on the album.

I have always found a lot of security within the group. I would hate to be without the group, but at the same time I understand Bonnie wanting her freedom to do the things she wants. I want the freedom to do the things I want, too.

We sang backup for Dave Mason, and through that we met David Rubinson. He listened to our songs, and he introduced us to the music of Lambert, Hendricks and Ross, and Charlie Parker. Dave turned us on to nostalgia. We were kind of doing nostalgia, but we didn't know what we were doing. We'd get our clothes from thrift stores, pretty dresses that we couldn't afford, but we'd get them at half price because they were used. We'd buy them on layaway.

We were doing harmonies similar to what the Andrews Sisters did in the forties. I had heard of the Andrews Sisters, but I'd never really listened to their music. We were not allowed to hear that kind of music at home. No popular music at all. We'd have to sneak away to our friends' houses to hear Elvis Presley, Smokey Robinson, Jackie Wilson, James Brown, Aretha Franklin, Gladys Knight, Stevie Wonder. We did have one Elvis Presley record in the house, "Crying in the Chapel," but that was only because mother liked that one.

Our first big break was when we went to London with Dave Mason. That was our first trip outside of the United States. Everyone in the family went, "God, you guys are serious. You're getting out of the country." We got passports and everything. It made us feel like we were taking a very big step.

Our problem was, a lot of other musicians said all we were trying to be was white. People said we weren't soulful enough, that we should have been an R & B group like all the other black groups. But we wanted to do something that was outside of the norm.

I remember when we did our first thing with Atlantic Records. Jerry Wexler saw us at the Troubadour and he signed us to Atlantic. We did five songs, all R & B stuff. We wanted to sing a cappella, and they just laughed in our faces. They flew us to New Orleans and Jackson, Mississippi, and had us stand up in front of a roomful of strangers, and we sang a cappella.

They said, "You can't sing stuff like that. You have to sing R & B songs. Now, we have some songs that sound like Honey Cone and the Jacksons, and that's what we are going to give you."

We flipped out. June and I got real angry because we had some country music with us, and they thought that was just totally out of line. We ended up persuading them to let us do a country song with an R & B arrangement, and it made us stick out. Now people were saying, "You gotta see these girls. Their clothes are ridiculous, but their sound is phenomenal."

It was weird when we went to Nashville. They gave us a party at a big beautiful country mansion. Roy Clark and a lot of old country music people I had admired from Nashville thought we were the maids. We got there, and there were armed guards in front who made us go around to the back door. We didn't know it was the back door because the house was so huge. We didn't know the difference. We were the only black people there besides the butlers. David Rubinson had a fit. The owner of the home apologized, and it really turned out to be a great party.

I was so nervous I barely remember what happened. I do remember meeting Dolly Parton backstage, and I also remember one guy standing up in the audience talking about, "Goddamn, them girls are black."

Michael Chapman

○ ○ ○

A lot of hit songs, many of them forgettable, came out of England through the seventies. Michael produced many of those, along with some of the more memorable. The man always had an ear for the pop song.

○ ○ ○

I was working as a waiter in London in 1969 when I met Nicky Chin. I was a waiter. He was my customer. I used to bring my demos in and play them in the disco to hear what they sounded like, and one night he came in and heard this thing playing, and he said, "What's that?"

I said, "It's me. I write songs."

He said, "Wow, I'm trying to write songs, too." Basically he was just a rich kid who had nothing to do. We had a lot of problems during the eight years that our partnership lasted, and I think they all stemmed from the way things started. I was his waiter, and he was my customer.

We got together the next weekend and tried to write a song. I went to his apartment on a Sunday and we sat down and wrote a song. The third song we wrote together was "Funny Funny," which turned out to be a hit for Sweet. It was like a cute bubble-gum song.

But Nicky and I were never in synch. I needed encouragement. I needed someone to say, "Here's an avenue for you to achieve success." I couldn't make it as a rock star, so I had decided to be a writer or a producer. Anything other than a singer. Nicky claimed to be a lyricist, and I suppose he was after a fashion. The best thing about our partnership was that he was a terrific sounding board. He'd listen to what I was doing, and he'd say he likes this, doesn't like that.

He'd come up with a line and he'd say, "I've got this great line," and he'd rattle off a line that was really stupid. It would take me three hours to convince him that the line wasn't right. But we were writing hits, so that made it easier to continue working together.

Nicky and I worked with Mickie Most, who was a very successful record producer. This is around the time in England when glam rock started to happen with acts like Marc Bolan and Slade. Everybody had makeup on, and I'd see Mickie Most building his career, and I watched how he did it and how he got into the position where he could dictate his own future. I wanted to be able to do the same thing. I wanted to be out of my partnership with Nicky right from the beginning. But I figured I'd better bide my time, keep making records, bite my lip, and wait.

Mickie Most eventually sold his record company for nine or ten million pounds. He bought a house in the South of France. He had a boat. The boat sunk off St. Tropez. Mickie sat on the deck and drank a bottle of champagne as it was going down. True Mickie Most style. But he taught me the bare essentials of making a record. And he always told me what I was doing wrong. When I told him I was going to America to make records, he said, "Don't go there. It sucks." That made me more determined than ever to go to America and prove he was wrong.

It wasn't until 1977 that I found my place in the business in California. I had written a song called "Kiss You All Over," which was eventually recorded by Exile, but my big break didn't come until I cemented my relationship with Terry Ellis at Chrysalis.

I first saw Blondie in 1977. It was at the Whisky, and Tom Petty was opening for them. I saw them four nights in a row. At the time they were on Private Stock Records. When Terry Ellis signed them to Chrysalis, he came straight to me and said, "Go meet Debbie Harry and Chris Stein. Let's see if we can't get this thing happening." I produced Blondie's *Parallel Lines*, and we wound up having five Number 1's after that.

Debbie Harry was, and probably still is, one of the most extraordinary and unusual artists that you could hope to come across. She had this intense relationship with Chris Stein, her boyfriend, and the two of them were unbelievably talented. They did some incredible things during those three, four years. I'm sure it's all gone now. Drugs and what-have-you destroyed all that. She used to write all the lyrics in the control room while I was waiting for her to go in and sing. She wrote the rap in "Rapture" in about five minutes flat. Then she sang it in one take. She never thought she was a good singer. It took her two hours to get her face made up before she could go in and stand in front of a mike. She was singing a song and Ronnie Spector walked into the studio. Debbie was a big fan of Ronnie's. She got so nervous when Ronnie walked in. She called me over and said she didn't think she could sing in front of Ronnie.

I said, "Yes, you can." It took me three hours to convince her she could. Finally, she did it and she did a great job. But she was a terribly insecure person in the studio. She never thought she was that good. I thought she was brilliant.

It was after I had just finished a Blondie album that I started hearing a buzz about the Knack. As soon as I heard "My Sharona," I knew it was a Number 1 record. We made the Knack's album in two weeks. Made and mixed. I knew we were in for something big. Unfortunately, the group began talking about themselves as though they were the next Beatles. I didn't see that. That seemed a bit silly. But I felt theirs was going to be an enormous career.

Well, about a year after the Knack thing had happened, I was a guest speaker at a BMI dinner one night, and they were asking questions, and somebody said to me, "Is it true that the first Knack album only cost twenty thousand dollars to make?"

I said, "Yes, it's true—twenty thousand dollars, very easy to make."

Then they said, "What was the cost of the second Knack album?"

I thought for a minute, and I thought, the only thing I can say is that the second Knack album cost me my reputation.

I was as much to blame for the immediate downfall of the Knack as anybody. We all fucked up. We all made a dreadful mistake. We had just had a Number 1 record. We figured we could do no wrong. The group was burning holes through the radio channels. Everybody got so caught up in the Knack as "the next big thing" that we made a second Knack album and never even listened to it carefully. The songs weren't there, and the leader of the Knack, Doug Fieger, started getting weird. He started to think he was like Jim Morrison or Buddy Holly, that there was nothing he could do that wouldn't work, and I guess we all believed it. Doug was a great con man. A nut case. Doug blamed me when the first single from the album, "Baby Talks Dirty," bombed. It was not a "My Sharona," and I knew it.

Doug said, "You made the wrong record."

I said, "Well, fine, OK. Go make a record with somebody else." It was a great education. The act died a terrible death, and I'll never make the same mistakes again with anybody else.

Tom Petty

○ ○ ○

**He's a real rocker and a dedicated fan of others who preceded him.
Tom's success and his relationships with Bob Dylan and Del Shannon
tell you a lot about the range he covers.**

○ ○ ○

In 1974, when we came to Los Angeles from Gainesville, Florida, we heard
there were two places to play—the Starwood and the Whisky. But you needed
to have a record out to play those places, and we had no record. So we'd
go out to the Valley trying to find some little beer bars to play, and the
people in those bars, all they wanted to hear were the Top 10 songs of the
day, which was pretty awful music in the mid-seventies. It wasn't the kind
of stuff you could whip up with a combo and play. It was very frustrating.

After our first album came out, we got to go England, and we had big
success over there, opening for Nils Lofgren. We ended up staying in England
and headlining our own tour. When we came back, it was like coming from
success back to nothing. No gigs, nobody knows about us.

But we did get to play at the Whisky. Elmer Valentine at the Whisky
was kind enough to let us have a few shots in the beginning. We opened
for Blondie. It was a two-week stretch, two shows a night, us and Blondie.
By the end of the first week, there were tons of people lining up in front of
the club. Then the same thing started happening for us at the Starwood. It
was then that they started playing us on the radio.

I remember this one fellow, Jon Scott, walking up to me out of the
blue and saying, "You don't know me, but you're going to know me because
I'm going to get your record 'Breakdown' played on the radio."

And he did. It was, like, slow at first. Took almost a year, actually,
before stations really began playing it.

In '77 we went back to England, and all of a sudden we're seeing a lot
of people emerging—the Sex Pistols, Elvis Costello. And people were just
showing up. There was quite an excitement about it. You gotta remember,
this was during the time when disco was so huge, which none of us could
stand.

When I got back to L.A., Denny Cordell came around to my house,
and I told him how exciting things were getting in England, and he said,
"You're not going to believe what's happening here."

He took me Madame Wong's, which had just opened. We drove over
to the Troubadour and saw the Knack. Then there were the Go-Go's, and
all of a sudden every little place was a club. I thought, "Great. Things are
finally the way they're supposed to be."

As a band, the Heartbreakers had learned how to play a lot of different
kinds of music. We can play country, we can play folk, we can play rock
'n' roll. I think the reason Dylan gets along so well with us musically is that
we can kind of jump to whatever channel he wants to change to.

I think Dylan and I were among the first people Neil Young asked to do Farm Aid. We'd all done Live Aid, and that was the last time I'd seen Bob. I didn't know him, really. I had only met him a couple of times, you know, "Hello, how are you, what do you say?"

But after Neil called him, he called me and said, "I've seen your show. What do you think about us playing together at Farm Aid?"

I said, "Sure. Come on over to rehearsal and we'll see how it goes." Well, we wound up playing for hours. It was over at MCA, at the Universal Sound Stage. We stayed there for a week, and that week was the biggest thrill of my life. We would play way into the night.

Not only does this guy have so many great songs, but he also knows hundreds of cover songs that he could play at the drop of a hat. We'd be playing something, and then Bob would go, "OK, now let's play 'Tears of a Clown.' " And he'd just go right into it. For us, it was incredible. It was OK for him, too, because it'd been so long since he worked with a unit that plays together all the time. He said it was like talking to one guy. Well, by the time we got to Farm Aid we were beaming.

People talk a lot about Dylan because he's such a great lyricist. I've always had trouble with reviewers because all they tend to do is review lyrics. It's very hard for people to write about music. How do you describe music? Most reviewers, at least in my case, base their reviews on lyrics. When I read the reviews to *Southern Accent*, I thought I'd written a book. I remember saying to my wife, "I didn't mean to write a book." It was taken much more seriously and literally than I ever intended it to be. Part of me enjoyed that, and part of me was rather disgusted.

Reviewers can get a little snooty sometimes, condemning a whole album because of one particular lyrical idea. And it's fine, whether they like it or don't like it. I mean, lyrics are important. They have the power to lift people, or whatever they do, but the true spirit of rock 'n' roll is still in the music. "Shake, Rattle and Roll" was a great rock 'n' roll song. Same with "Whole Lotta Shakin' Goin' On" and "Tutti Frutti." Great songs. But I wonder what would happen if those songs were being reviewed today. Would they be dismissed as slight? I don't know. Records are funny things. You can't always write down the words to a song and read them as poetry. But they work perfectly fine within the record. I have never quite figured that one out.

Dylan told me recently I was a poet. Although I was impressed by what he said, I couldn't help feeling it was like being told you're an archer. Well, they may think you're an archer, but you know you don't own a bow.

Tina Turner

o o o

**She's been belting it out through good and bad times for thirty years
and has found peace of mind along with the success she's fought hard
to attain. Tina is energetic, dynamic, and always exciting.**

o o o

When I was a very little, little girl, way back to Knoxville, Tennessee, actually
during the war in 1939, I remember singing some of the McGuire Sisters'
songs. I had a little bank that I collected all these shiny coins, and it was
taken from me and I was really brokenhearted. That makes me remember
how long I have really been singing. But I had no voice training. This is it.

When I started to sing with Ike, I was basically patterning myself after
most of the male singers that I was around, like Ray Charles and Sam Cooke.
When I started singing, there were more male singers than female. I think
my voice is heavy because my mother's voice is quite low, as is my sister's.
I think the raspiness in my voice is the natural sound. But the style really
came from mimicking and copying my surroundings.

Mine is not a pretty voice. Actually, it sounds ugly sometimes. I don't
like to sing "sing" that much. The pretty way of singing is not my style. I
don't enjoy singing pretty songs. I like them rough, rocky, and rock 'n' roll
because it suits my type of voice.

Years ago, I think it was during the time Janis Joplin had some nodes
removed from her vocal chords, I thought maybe I had that because during
the sixties I was hoarse all the time. And I went to the doctor and he told
me that although my voice was overworked, it was strong. When I was a
little girl, we didn't have telephones and we would yell across the fields to
the next house to get someone's attention. That's how it is now. It takes a
lot to get me down, and when I have voice problems I just totally shut up.
I don't use any oils or sprays. I just don't talk.

In 1960, Ike and Tina toured England for the first time. Mick Jagger
told me that he was standing in the wings watching the show. He said that
basically after that was when he started dancing and moving around. I think
he was inspired by the performance because of the energy and the movement
the girls and I were putting out. Mick also liked Ike's sound and style because
English acts do like blues music.

I think through the years it's still that old cliché of R & B and jazz, the
roots of music, that were with me. That's how I grew up, and I'll never lose
that. It's there in every song. You'll always get a little bit of gospel/blues no
matter how many pop songs or rock 'n' roll songs I sing. All of that is also
in a lot of the music the Beatles and Stones made. And I think they were
attracted to us because of our energy and soul.

There were a lot of ups and downs, but Ike kept our act going because
he had a dream to have a certain amount of songs in the Top 10. He wanted
to be successful with charted music and be known for that and to receive

that type of recognition from the industry. As a producer/musician, I think that's what most people strive for. He worked for that. The more tracks they gave him in the recording studio, the more tracks he used. So he overwrote a lot of the music. Things sort of got lost due to the mixture of drugs and mechanics.

For myself, I knew I had to have my own band and be on my own to be successful. And when I went on my own, it was like working with Ike's band but without Ike. I got over my fears of going onstage and not being as good as I'd like to be. I knew that whenever I got my own musicians I would be better because I would be surrounded by people that I had chosen and I would be in control. There was no fear. Actually, it was a great time because I had really made the decision to leave, and I valued my freedom. I wanted to start all over again. I really felt the purge was worth it all and I think I grew from that.

Once you've experienced a type of bondage and then gotten free, you really learn what being free is all about, and it's about just being comfortable and free. So I didn't put any value on not having an immediate hit record or not being in the limelight. I was fine where I was. I watched myself to see what I could do with people. It was a studying time after I left Ike. Then, when I was ready, I said, "OK, I'm ready." I knew I was ready, I knew I could do it. Working with the Stones and Rod Stewart really helped me. It wasn't hard times; it was the beginning of great times.

What a lot of people don't realize about me is that I've never done drugs and I've never smoked. I became homeopathic nearly ten years ago, so that means I don't have any drugs in my system to tear me down. There's nothing in my body that pulls me down. I never drink when I'm working. I'm a strong, healthy person, and that comes from eating fairly well and being homeopathic and never abusing my body.

I enjoy my work. I'm an unusual person. I could get onstage right now and do a show. Had I abused myself during the early years, I never would have gotten as far as I got. But I'm healthy and in control.

Steven Tyler and Joe Perry

○ ○ ○

They were the founders and the creative drive behind Aerosmith, one of the biggest and best of the metal bands. They fought with each other and abused their bodies, but they eventually got back on the road again and have set out on another career.

○ ○ ○

I can remember the height of my oblivion, when I was doing things just because I could. I would think nothing of tipping over a table with a whole long spread on it just because there was turkey roll on the table and I had explicitly said, "No turkey roll." No mystery meat, please, just some real turkey, and I would come in after coming off stage, and I'd have twelve ounces of Jack Daniel's in me, a gram of coke, I was sweating profusely, and I'd see a tray with turkey roll on it. I'd just turn the whole thing right over. It felt good.

It was cool back then to have a $750 Porsche watch. I went through nine of them. I'd keep it by the side of the bed, and when I got pissed off, I'd wing it across the room. I was so far out on the edge that I felt I had to trash something quickly. There was a running joke about rolling over and dialing room service. I lived that way for ten years. It became so ingrained in me that even after I got home I would wake up in the morning and dial 0. That was the lunacy I was basing my life on. I was consumed with drugs, and how much toothpaste to get for the tour, and what room Joe Perry was in.

Joe was a guy I could sit down and make patty cakes with, like a kid you went to the park with and played in the same sandbox. Your mom brings you over, and within minutes you're playing and you're compatible. That's the way it was between Joe and me.

But I was just so selfish and one-sided. I would crawl into a little hole with whatever drug I was doing, and that was how I lived. It was OK to be drinking away my life. The manager would come backstage and say, "Fine. Drink all you want. Just go onstage." That was great for an alcoholic to hear. It was the perfect place to be. Liquor flowed backstage. Someone would say, "Give him what he wants from the bar."

I don't blame them, and I don't blame myself. Four rehabilitation centers for drug abuse later, I've been able to take a long, hard look at my behavior.

○ ○ ○

I remember this one CBS convention. They wanted us to come up and present all their sales reps with platinum records. They wanted Steve and I to be there. We said, "If we're going to do this, we're going to have a good time."

They wanted us for the weekend. They're all in Century City. Rick

Derringer's band is playing at the convention, other bands are playing, and the record company just wanted us to say thank you, and have others say thank you to us, and we said, "We stay at the Beverly Hills Hotel, or we don't come."

We get to L.A., everybody is staying in Century City but us. We're at the Beverly Hills Hotel with a liquor tab of $5,000 because all the bands are coming over from Century City and partying all night with us. The waiters were in a bucket brigade. We were on the phone with room service every twelve minutes. It was great. All we had to do was say what we wanted, and that was it.

I never thought this would be a career. I never thought I would make it past thirty. I look at some of those early Beatles interviews. Ringo wanted a hairdressing salon, if he could make enough money with the Beatles. That's really the attitude that prevailed. A lot of us were young high-school dropouts. Suddenly we were making a lot of money. The thinking was, "Who knows how long this is going to last. In the meantime, have fun."

So we drank to keep the vibe we felt. It was like, if we feel good, maybe the audience will feel good. If we're getting off on the music we're playing, maybe they'll get off on it. Of course, if you listen to our records down through the years, it definitely gets diluted. We started to lose sight of it, we started to see how screwed up we could get before we walked onstage, just to see if we could get away with it. There were times when we were on our knees, literally, trying to find blow. There were times when we would drink just to see how much we could consume. Really ridiculous stuff. It did suffer in the end, that little picture, that little window to what we thought we were all about.

Pat Benatar

o o o

She is a tough-sounding cocky girl singer, and that's the spot she created for herself. But as we talked, she was trying to work her way out of the image. She's made some fine rock 'n' roll, and she's still in the game.

o o o

My image is not something I do every day. I found this character I wanted to play, and it helped me to get over my lack of confidence, my nervousness, and my vulnerability. I never considered the character to be a sex symbol. I just was looking for extreme strength and self-assuredness.

I was always a little wild, but shy. I lived a very sheltered life. I grew up on Long Island, in a small town, and the most education I ever got was when I married at nineteen. I didn't know anything. My husband at the time got drafted, so I went through that whole scene. In '75, I moved back to New York, and that's where I got my real education. I was twenty-two, and it was fast and furious.

I listened a lot to male-dominated groups like the Stones and Led Zeppelin. There weren't a lot of women to emulate, no one female figure, so I took a shot in the dark and tried to figure out a way to do this without looking stupid and being victimized. People would say, "Why are you doing this? Rock 'n' roll is no place for you. Look how you look. You have a pug nose. Janis Joplin died. Isn't that enough?"

When I began playing live, the initial reaction to me wasn't very good. Mostly it was curiosity. People would come to see this girl for what she was wearing. Did I have eye liner on that night? What color was it? That kind of stuff. The minute I opened my mouth they paid more attention, regardless of how I looked or acted.

As soon as everything got out of control, I backed off. It was so overwhelming, and I didn't like it so much. I wasn't prepared for the stardom. I wasn't prepared for everyone wanting a little piece of me, literally and figuratively. The first year was so hard, going from a nobody to a somebody. I didn't like the fact that people were driving by and taking pictures of my house, calling out my name. It was a little strange.

Now it doesn't matter as much. Now, when I'm ready to go out, all dressed in my black clothes, looking real cool, I notice I have baby throw-up on my shoulder.

Dee Snider

○ ○ ○

Mr. Twisted Sister tells how a nice kid from New York grew up to carry out the wildest rock 'n' roll fantasies and then defend them before a Senate subcommittee in Washington.

○ ○ ○

When I was asked to join Twisted Sister, I had to choose between Twisted Sister and a fifties band called the Dukes, a group that was big locally on Long Island. It was a matter of cutting my hair and greasing it back or doing Twisted Sister, and I realized there was no future in being a second Sha Na Na.

Metal is a suburban, rural music. It is fantasy oriented. Suburban kids are stuck in their houses. They are frustrated by the tract housing, the similar middle-class or lower-middle-class existence. So they look for ways to escape. The black kids go for sports and the white kids go for rock 'n' roll. Rock 'n' roll is not exclusively for whites, but there is a certain white mentality about it.

Everyone focuses on the sex, drugs, and rock 'n' roll fantasy aspect of metal, the fire and brimstone, the devil aspect. Most of the bands I know who sing about it do it for the shock value. They're not real serious. If they ever came face to face with Satan, they would shit in their pants.

When Twisted was formed in '76, I was wearing the platforms and the makeup and the heels, and all that stuff was out. The glitter scene had died in New York. The city had gotten fed up with it, but in the suburbs they'd still never seen a pair of platform boots on a guy wearing lipstick.

Every night I'm having a fight in a bar. I'm standing there with my makeup on, and these people in the suburban bars are freaking out. I would be standing on stage in stockings and lingerie and someone would call me a queer.

I would say, "Queer? Fuck you." I would get pissed off, but really, what was he going to call me, "masculine"?

I used to jump off the stage, every single night. Bars are tough, and if you let one of them get away with something, it might spread like a disease, and soon you have the whole bar against you. What you do then is have some street training, hit the biggest one hard and fast, and stun the rest of them.

I would dive off the stage wearing six-inch heels, and I'm six foot, one inch. With my hair I'm six-ten, with lingerie. And I weighed almost 200 pounds. They didn't know what the hell hit them, they were so shocked. People used to think it was a movie screen up there. They would throw things and they expected the picture to be in 3D.

This one time we were opening up for Ronnie Dio in Massachusetts. Dio's album was charging up the charts, the show was sold out, and I'm standing on stage and I see this guy seven rows back, and he is looking at me with this bottle in his hand. He puts his hand up like he's going to throw a football pass, and I'm looking back in disbelief. He throws the bottle, I duck out of the way, but this is the first time I actually see someone throw a bottle at me.

So now, I climb off the stage and start crawling over the rows of seats towards this guy. No one could believe it. I punched the guy in the head and a big rumble broke out. The band was on the last chord of a song, and I'm out there for five minutes, and for five minutes they're playing the D chord.

The crew is out, the security is there, and I'm fighting with this guy. Then I climb back onstage, the band finishes the song, and we bring the house down, of course.

The next day I get a call from my lawyer, my manager, my accountant, and they all say, "Never again."

I say, "What do you mean?"

And they say, "Dee, you're not in the bars anymore. You're making money now. A little prat like that can sue you and take you to the cleaners."

But it keeps happening. One time a guy throws a bottle at me in a club with 3,000 people, and I start cursing him out. I say, "Come on up here, you wimp. Show me who you are."

Now I see the guy and I do a swan dive into the crowd. I'm thinking my loyal minions will catch me, but human nature says, when you see someone in silver lamé, six-seven and almost 200 pounds, and he's flying at you, you get the fuck out of the way.

Well, like the Red Sea they parted, and I hit the ground so hard I was dazed. When I lifted my head up, I see this wild-looking Bruce Lee–type guy hissing at me. His hands are spinning around, and I'm thinking, "Oh, shit."

I look around for my loyal minions and a couple of bikers I thought would come to my rescue, and they're making room for us to fight, moving everybody back. I'm in the middle of this room with this fucking Bruce Lee. My head is still spinning from hitting the floor, and I reverted back to high school football and charged the guy, plowing through the crowd. People are flying everywhere.

Security then dives on top and drags Bruce Lee out of the place. I climb back onstage, and the place is cheering. Everyone is shaking my hand. And then one girl pulls me aside and says, "That was staged."

I go, "Yeah, right."

Robert Palmer

∘ ∘ ∘

An odd combination of European style and hot rock 'n' roll, Robert emerged from the pack of respected but not commercially successful artists in 1986 with his Grammy and his multi-platinum record.

∘ ∘ ∘

I was brought up on Billie Holiday, Lena Horne, Peggy Lee, and Nat King Cole. My dad was in the navy in Malta, and the family used to listen to the American Armed Forces Radio Network, and that was the music we heard.

When I got back to England, the music that was on the radio at the time was Otis Redding and rock 'n' roll. It just moved me. To me it was like rebel music. So I struck up some correspondence with a record store in New York, and they would send me all the Stax, Motown, and Atlantic single releases. It got to the point where I would try to get the latest single by the Four Tops. We'd get it, learn it, and then play it with my band, which was the Mandrakes at that time.

I would do the arranging and work out the chords. I'd listen to the high-hat and imagine what that cat was like. And then years later I'd meet the guy, and he was exactly like that sound he made. The cats behind Aretha Franklin were the men I walked in on when I made my first album. I kept saying to myself, "Don't think about it, don't think about it. They've been playing together for years. Just get into it." They weren't even paying attention to me. About eight bars into the first tune one of them asked me what my name was.

I wasn't part of the mainstream in England during the sixties. Groups like the Beatles, Stones, the Who, Led Zeppelin seemed rather cut and dry. There was no digging into something and trying to take it out and put it all back. Their influences seemed very obvious, and I was never that crazy about their interpretations. I had listened to a lot of Marvin Gaye songs that the Stones had been doing for years, so it didn't seem particularly interesting. The bands I had evolved with, like DaDa, were at least into experimenting and introducing arrangements into the rhythm section. Later on I developed to the point where I could control what was happening with the rhythm section. At least, it was a means of expression rather than a bandwagon to jump on. I never wanted to be like this or that. I wanted to be however it turned out.

Of course, the others were getting successful doing what they were doing, and I was not. But it wasn't frustrating at all. I loved it. I must have loved it because it was hell doing tours in those days. For instance, the first tour we did in America, the British half of the company was supposed to deliver half the money, and America was giving the other half. When the British side didn't come through with their half, we did the whole of America living off breadsticks. We were asking for money up front from gigs in Nyack, New York. I remember saying, "If we can put up with this, just imagine how wonderful it will be, like, to have an outrageous audience and have the money going better."

I guess I always treated this as a hobby. And it still is a hobby. If I find a new high-hat act, or a new way for the groove to sit by doing something totally unorthodox, it just makes my week. Writing is the hardest thing. Someone once said that Frank Sinatra cut 1,300 tunes, none of which did he write. I've written about 80 in my time and every one of them has been real work.

Speaking of Frank Sinatra, the first inkling I had of how singers looked was from seeing Frank Sinatra dressed in a suit on a record sleeve. My mother tells me how really fussy I was about my school uniform. Because I was brought up around naval people, particularly the Italian wave, I was very meticulous. I've always felt more comfortable dressing conservatively. I just don't like to call attention to myself.

John Cougar Mellencamp

○ ○ ○

A leader in the blue-collar rock world, John was interviewed in his
Bloomington, Indiana, home, where he gave us a look inside a
dynamic career and the methodology of keeping ahead of the rock-
lyric game.

○ ○ ○

When I started, I thought all I needed to do was just write songs for people
in bars. I was playing in bars. I behaved like people in bars. So those were
the kind of songs I wrote.

There's this basketball coach in my hometown in Indiana, and his rap
has always been, "I've always been honest. I've never kissed ass." I've tried
to live that way.

I've never claimed to be a musician. I'm the same guitar player now
that I was when I was fifteen. I learned a bunch of chords and how to sing
melodies over them, and that's all I ever wanted to do. I think it's good that
I'm the same player now that I was then. I like keeping a "garage" sound
on my records. I've never been one for slick productions. When I pick up
a guitar, everybody goes, "Oh, God, there he goes. Is he gonna be in time
or not?"

My performing goes back to me being mad and angry all the time.
When you first start out, audiences aren't particularly hospitable to you,
particularly when your manager has gone ahead and booked you in Germany,
opening for Blue Oyster Cult. I come on with my acoustic guitar, and I say
to myself, "What am I doing here? They're not going to understand this."

But I could write songs like "Hurt So Good," which guys in bars liked.
I said, "Hey, they like it. Better stick with it." Then one day it dawned on
me that there were a lot of guys writing the same things, only better. The
Stones always wrote "Brown Sugar" better than I could ever write it.

So at thirty-five, I realize I need to be writing for my own age group.
Like this song of mine, "Check It Out." It's about having a house in escrow,
and the anxiety of buying your first house, and the anxiety of looking at your
kids and asking yourself, "Am I being responsible?"

I went to Washington in the early seventies to protest against the war.
Afterwards, I went home to my mom and dad's house and back to college.
How committed was I, really? Did I go to Washington for the party? For
the drugs? I thought I was concerned about the war, and I probably was
concerned about it to an extent, but not concerned enough to be laying in
some rice field. My Vietnam experience is basically what I saw on television.

The farm crisis, on the other hand, is real for me. Drive around my
town and you see that it's closing down. Are all the grain stores in town
going to go out of business? Are all the farm implement companies going
to go out of business? Are the small Chevrolet dealers going to go out of

business? These corporate farms are taking over and buying up everything directly. It destroys the look of this country.

Do we want our produce and bread and corn and soybeans controlled by a couple of people who will dictate to us what's going to happen? Do I want my kids paying $355 for a loaf of bread, when a loaf of bread costs 16¢? It's just unfair, but then so is life.

I always feel like the record I'm making is my last record. Somehow I always think that the record company is going to drop me next week, that the next record is going to come out and sell five copies, and I'll be back pouring concrete.

I've quit making records a hundred times. "I've had it," I say. "It's not worth it."

So I approach every record as if it were my last. And then I think to myself, "Well, at least I got this far before it all went to hell."

Phil Ramone

○ ○ ○

A tasteful man who has been behind the mixing board for some of the best music, from Peter, Paul and Mary through Billy Joel, Phil is the prototypical New York record man with a great résumé.

○ ○ ○

I got my chops listening to all the people I was working with—Leiber and Stoller, Bacharach and David, Jeff Barry and Ellie Greenwich. You can't learn any better than that. Eventually you learn to experiment with what you have, and that's what makes you different from the next guy.

A lot of my learning experience had to do with the speed in which you did a date. Today it's not even discussed whether you can get a track in a day or two days, or a week, for that matter. Then, the big thing was to do three or four songs on a session. If you could do it in three hours, you were a king. You got to be known as a fast guy who could get the band in and out in a few hours. People used to come in prepared. There was an arranger. Very little was said by the artist. Whatever it was, they discussed it with the arranger—or the A & R man, who really was king. The engineer had to be superfast to be able to deal with it all.

I started in show business as a little boy, a childhood performer. I played fiddle, but I was really interested in jazz and humor. I went on the road for a while with "The Ted Mack Amateur Hour." I learned from almost every possible place I could. The kids I went to school with didn't understand. And then performance pieces started getting boring to me. Once you play Vegas, once you play clubs and rock 'n' roll theaters with the Four Aces, and you're touring with the Crew Cuts, you learn by accident. I learned the record business by accident. There I was with Dick Clark in Cleveland, playing all these record hops, curly hair and cute. You know—at least I did—that this was not going to last. I don't think anybody who has been around doesn't feel the same way. But in my case, my goal was not necessarily to perform. It was to get backstage. I just realized that the performing thing wouldn't go on forever.

The Beatles, of course, were a heavy influence on me. I studied George Martin and everything the guy did. In America, we still weren't into stacking voices. I mean, if you really want to look at the history, the guy who probably influenced all of us was Les Paul.

Eventually the songwriters became producers, and if you had some ingenuity and some idea of trying, and they gave you time, you could come up with something. You kept playing Beatles records for other people. They said, "Sure, that is good. But they're huge." Nobody ever gave the Beatles credit for this, but they used to do three songs a session, too. We all came out of that. The demand was, if you couldn't do three or four tunes at a time, you weren't good. Connie Francis would come in for two days. You're scared because you have a sixty-piece orchestra, and you're getting ready to do it live.

I remember the long-hair–hippie days. We used to laugh. It was so easy. If you said you were from Kranitz, U.S.A., and you said you had this group called the Slugs, forget it, you had a hit. They asked you, "What do you need?"

"We need a lot of equipment." That would be the first move. Then, "We don't like to record in your studios. We will pick the place." This was heavy duty for a lot of people.

But it always came back to the songs. Jeff Barry and Ellie Greenwich, Leiber and Stoller, Bacharach and David—these are people who never gave up on their songs. There was an extreme fussiness to make great songs happen. It goes back to the real basics of the recording business itself: When you turn around every five years and something emerges, it's usually because it has great songs.

Billy Joel is a perfect example of someone who came around with some great songs. In '76 I went up to the CBS convention in Toronto. Phoebe Snow was playing at the convention. Paul Simon was closing it. The opening act was Billy, and he just tore the place apart. I said, "Oh boy, how do you follow this guy?" You don't. I said, "I better take notice of this guy. This guy is going to be around."

I knew "Piano Man," and I knew a couple of his records. I think *Turnstiles* had just come out. I got a call from his wife at the time, Elizabeth, and she asked me to meet with Billy. Several producers were being considered. We had lunch. I went to his Carnegie Hall performance, and I said what I felt. I said, "I listened to all of your albums, and truthfully I think they are too glitzy, too shiny, and they don't represent what I saw when I saw you perform in Toronto and what I saw at Carnegie Hall." Obviously,

I said the right thing. We started working together, and the next year Billy broke wide open.

Billy Joel

○ ○ ○

Billy is simply a great survivor and a consummate artist. He overcame more than anyone's share of tough times at the start to establish a strong personality and a fine reputation as a writer and performer.

○ ○ ○

Everybody, deep down, who is an artist has got to wonder, "What if they find out?" I mean, you think you're good at certain things, but the fact that people listen to you time and time again makes you wonder. Once in a while I try to intellectualize, which is a dumb thing to do if you're onstage.

I'll say something like, "What the hell are they all doing out there?" Of course, if people sense that you don't know what you're doing up there, they'll eat you up. I think an audience expects to be sort of led, or swept away. They have to believe you. It's not a matter of selling them, but you have to have such a strong belief in what you're doing at that moment. That is part of what show business is, what being an entertainer is all about. Entertaining is believing you are doing so much that you can cast a spell, for lack of a better word. With me, it gets to the point that when I get off the stage, sometimes I go, "Who the hell was that? What was that that just went on? What happened?" It's almost like a trance. People tell me that I've done things on stage that I don't even remember.

Part of the armor is confidence. I think of myself as a real sensitive and vulnerable person, like a bad review could destroy me. But onstage, that's my job, my gig. This is what I'm going to do, and I better do it right because if I stink, they are going to remember. I don't get nervous. I get psyched. It's an adrenaline flow. The mouth gets a little dry, and you go, "OK, here you go." I grab onto the piano because it's my shield, my crutch, and I do it.

When I was nineteen or twenty, I said, "I don't want to be a rock 'n' roll star anymore." I had been in bands for years, and to get up onstage to want to be a star, you have to have a tremendous self-centered thing. You have to shut out a lot of things in your life. You have to give up a lot of your social life. You have to concentrate on your art. Music has to be your mistress. So I said at nineteen or twenty, "I have had it with trying to be a rock 'n' roll star. I just want to be a songwriter."

So I wrote a lot of songs and people in the music business said, "Well, OK, if you want people to hear your songs, maybe you should record them."

OK, I got a record deal in the era of the singer-songwriter, on Michael Lang's label. Then I got switched to Artie Ripp's label, like a baseball trade, and I ended up on Family Records. All right, I made the record and then they told me, "Now you have to go out on the road and promote it."

I'm on the road six months and I'm thinking, "This is a kind of weird way to be a songwriter." It ended up that I became Billy Joel, rock star, which was not what I intended. Don't get me wrong, it's great. But I didn't realize what I'd signed away. The guy who was managing me at the time was in cahoots with the company that signed me, so he became a part of the company. For six months I didn't get any money, nobody in the band got any money. We didn't have any food, and the company would say, "Get some white bread and peanut butter and just eat peanut butter and jelly sandwiches."

I said, "Something isn't right here. I got to get out of these bad contracts, these deals." That is when I went out to Los Angeles and sort of disappeared. Got a job working in a piano bar. Because of the song "Piano Man," people think I was working in that bar for years, but I only did it for six months. It was a way to pay the rent. It was a way for me to be anonymous in L.A.

Then I got a music business lawyer, I got a guy who was a manager, and fortunately Clive Davis at Columbia had seen me at some music festival, and so Columbia initiated a signing. The old company still gets a piece of me, but I came to grips with it. I used to get mad, but I honored an agreement, however dishonorable it was. I lived with it and I got on with my life. It was either negotiate a compromise or don't do anything. See, somebody wins if you stay bitter. If it eats you up, if you stay angry, if you change and become hateful, they win. I made more money than I ever expected to make. And besides, all those deals are just about over. The next record I make I am free and clear.

I think I've dreamed all the songs I've written. I don't dream regular dreams. I dream stories. When people tell me they had a strange dream last night, they were riding down a street, and blah, blah, blah, I don't relate to that. I dream in abstractions, in colors. I dream music and shapes and paintings and sculptures. I have awakened at four-thirty in the morning with a whole symphony in my head. I say to myself, "This is so good I don't even have to get up now. I'll remember it when I wake up later." And then later when I wake up, it's gone. And then weeks, maybe months, maybe years later it reoccurs to me that the song I have just written is from some old dream.

I was in the middle of a meeting with someone, and "Just the Way You Are" popped out of my head. I said, "I gotta go home right now and write this song." I just stopped the meeting. That's how all my songs get written. It's another dimension. I hate to speak in cosmic ways. Other people say they have to get in the mood, do their yoga, and maybe that works for them. I am unable to do that. I can never go to the song computer. When I'm dry, I'm dry. I understand Stevie Wonder writes a song a day. This guy keeps in shape, like it's a musical workout. I tried that once. It was very,

very frustrating. Writing for me is like going through a pregnancy and labor and a painful birth. Here comes this kid. And like with kids, some songs I like the way they age, and with other songs I don't.

More than anything, I like when other people do my songs. That was my original intention, to be a songwriter. I've gotten criticism over the years for not being enough of a stylist. I change my voice a lot. Like sometimes I sing like Ray Charles. In my early days I was trying to sing like the Beatles. The criticism about that never bothered me because, as a songwriter, I am always trying to fit my vocal limitations into what the song should be. I don't think of myself as a song stylist. Sometimes I try to sing like a black man.

I don't think I'm much of a singer. I always wanted to sing like Ray Charles or Sam Cooke or Wilson Pickett. I am a white kid from Levittown, but I always wanted to do that. There are some white guys who have had great careers singing like black men. Steve Winwood, Joe Cocker. When I sing like that, I feel good but it's not my real voice. Maybe it's becoming my real voice because I used to sing in a pure kind of Irish tenor like Paul McCartney.

But I know who I am, I know where I came from, and I know what I look like when I get up in the morning. It's ironic. When my name is mentioned and people yell and scream, I know I gotta give my all. I don't hold anything back. I just don't think of myself as a rock star. When I'm walking down the street, it's just me. People say, "Look, there's Billy Joel," I am snapped back to, "Oh, yeah, rock star." It's funny to me, but I don't make light of it. I don't want to hurt anyone's feelings, 'cause if I saw Paul McCartney walking down the street and I went up to him and he made light of it, I would be heartbroken.

Phil Collins

○ ○ ○

Dynamic drummer and exciting vocalist, Phil's an artist who combines the roles of solo star and group leader. His work with Genesis and his Grammy-winning records on his own have put him way up in the lineup of eighties leaders.

○ ○ ○

Everybody wanted to get into a serious band in the early seventies. Everybody was trying to be a bit complicated, trying to turn out things that made them scratch their heads.

My background is different. Two or three years previous to joining Genesis I had been acting on the West End stage. I had a precocious side to me. I was usually the most humorous one in the group. Funny, but a lot of the humor on our early albums went over a lot of people's heads. They were taking us far too seriously. A lot of the songs like "Musical Box" and "Return of the Giant Hogweed" had a lot of humor in them, but people tended to think that we were deadly serious. We were serious about trying to do well, but there was an awful lot of dry humor in the lyrics.

I enjoyed the live work, I enjoyed my drumming and the playing of more complicated things and showing everybody that I could play, but we were all frustrated with the fact that, in America especially, people couldn't see past what Peter Gabriel was wearing as opposed to what we were playing. So that was very frustrating. I know now that a lot of people never saw Genesis with Peter in it, but back then we had to accept—Mike Rutherford, Steve Hackett, Tony Banks, and myself—that Peter, by nature of the fact that the rest of us were all seated and he was standing up singing, would be the one that everybody would watch.

The real frustration was when record people and fans came backstage after a show and they would say, "Great show, man," as they walked straight by us to him. Everybody was responsible for the music, not just Peter. Either all of us would write a song, or three of us, or two of us. The real music fans could watch Tony Banks play keyboards all night. And I guess some people came to see me. But your average fan related to Genesis because of what Peter did and the costumes he wore.

We were doing *The Lamb Lies Down on Broadway* in '74, and halfway through, Peter left to work on something with William Friedkin. We said, "Peter, either do this or do that. If you want to do that, fine, leave." He said he wanted to do that, and he left. When Friedkin heard about it, he didn't like the idea that he had been involved in splitting up the band. He had an idea to see if something could work with Peter, a collaboration.

So Peter came back, a little bit with his tail between his legs, and saying, "Well, let's start again." But the rest of us knew at that point that there were real problems. His wife was having a difficult time with the arrival of their first baby. Lots of things were going on that the rest of us didn't understand at that time. Finally, two-thirds of the way through *The Lamb Lies Down on Broadway* tour, he said he was going to leave, that he wanted to spend more time at home with his wife and new baby. Peter was the first of all of us to even have children, so at the time none of us could relate to his experience.

The good news was, after he left reviewers stopped thinking that he had written all the music. To come out from under that underdog situation was very satisfying.

For the rest of us, the first thing that happens when you have solo success is that everybody expects you to leave the group. As the years have gone by, I think we've all made space for each other, and we are quite adult about it. Tony, Mike, and myself all write too much music to just be confined into one group. We also need to do things on our own. Some groups, you can see it in the past, even with us, bands that go up the charts, they say, "If you want to put out your own record, it's either that or us. If that's more important to you, you better leave." People would have their backs up against the wall, and they had to leave.

We say, "Great, do an album, fine. Maybe I'll have a go at one, too." And then we come back together in a year and a half and do a band album. We've always tried to give one another space without even talking about it.

I've been very lucky. I've had success with Genesis and success on my own. My gut reaction is that I haven't changed a bit. The difference is, I go into a supermarket today and people say hello. They recognize me. That's the only difference. Having more success doesn't mean to say it makes anything easier. The easiest thing for me to do is stop and say, "Now that I'm ahead, I'm calling it a day." It's just as much pressure for me to do an album now as it was before *No Jackets Required*, as it was before *Hello, I Must Be Going*. I put the pressure on myself. Me saying, "Can you top that?"

I'm just trying to do as many normal things as possible. My wife and I go shopping, I push the trolley, and she puts the stuff in. Like everybody else does. I buy toilet paper, and people look at me like, "God, he uses toilet paper like everybody else." Well, yes, I do.

Sting

○ ○ ○

Somewhat enigmatic, very handsome, and extremely talented, Sting was at the heart of the Police and then moved into film and solo records. His future has no limit.

○ ○ ○

I am from a place called Newcastle, and there has always been a thriving jazz community in Newcastle. It was hip in the fifties to play Dixieland in Newcastle. I ended up at the age of fifteen, sixteen, playing with guys, beatniks, who had been playing since the fifties. I played standards with guys in their late forties and fifties. I was known as "the kid." I would do anything to play, and rather than learn Led Zeppelin riffs, as people my age were doing on guitar, I was learning how to play jazz standards. I was in a dance band, a mainstream jazz band. It was modern jazz, cabaret.

Led Zeppelin was the megaband then, and it was the kind of music I didn't really like. Being brought up on jazz, I was locked out when I started going around to record companies. I went to every major record company with my songs, and they all said it wasn't commercial enough. That is what really made me feel a rapport with the punk movement. Although the music was a little shallow, the anger and the sense of wanting to revolutionize the music industry was something I felt strongly about. So the Police flew that banner for a while. We were energetic, loud, and noisy, and as the punk bands fell by the wayside, for various reasons we stayed and survived. We came through the door and we put our own flag up. Then we became the establishment.

In the beginning with the Police it was all a fantasy. We fantasized having a Number 1 hit, and everything happened with us step by step. I did not imagine we would become as mega as we did, but it did happen step by step. I am not sure we had a formula, but we knew what we wouldn't do and what we would do. We knew we did not want to support anybody. We felt if we had to go out and play in front of four people, it was better than supporting Foreigner and have the audience throw rocks at us. We played places like Poughkeepsie at the Last Chance Saloon for three people, and one of them was a DJ.

We traveled by station wagon with the gear in the back. We took turns driving. We shared a motel room. Came back after eight weeks on the road with ten dollars in my fist, which I gave to my wife. It was bloody-mindedness, and it was discouraging at the start when people said, "You shouldn't do this. It is madness." The record company would say, "What are you doing this for? No one does this." To us, that was a good reason to do it. We never asked our record company, A&M, for an advance, so we never had that kind of feudal relationship with them. They never felt as if they owned us, and the partnership continues today.

"Roxanne" was an import that broke out of Austin, Texas. We played a little club in Austin, and the stations started playing the record. When success hit, we were in our mid-twenties, with pretty strong personalities. We were egotistical and the whole rocket ship of success amplified everything. In a way it was very positive and it made us a very angry little group. The music was very tight and feisty and that kind of pressure and negativity worked for a while. Then it became debilitating. After about four albums it became something you would rather avoid. At first it was good, it gave us personality. After a while it became debilitating, and that is why I stopped it.

On my own it's been very interesting. Jazz is still important to me. Not as something that is a religion, but I like it. It is not what I do now, even though I play with jazz musicians. I hope the music we make can't be labeled. My whole point about music is that labeling is limiting. It prejudices people. As soon as you introduce a name, a type of music, you introduce a preconception. My whole crusade at the moment is confounding stereo-types. I have records on the charts that shouldn't be there. They aren't formula, they aren't programmable. I have a single called "Englishman in New York," which has a jazz section in it, and then a hip-hop section. The contemporary hit radio format—they don't like jazz, they don't like hip-hop. It is against their formula. But because it is my record they have to take it seriously. They can reject it or play it, but they have to decide. They can't just throw it away, and I find that interesting.

I actually sang with Gil Evans, at one of his last concerts in Italy. He arranged some of my songs at this big Italian festival, and he became for me a kind of father figure in a way. He was present during my last record, pointing and helping me out, giving me advice. His loss is a big one. He was the youngest seventy-six-year-old man I ever met. I went to see his band one night, and I plucked up enough courage to go backstage and introduce myself. I said, "I am a rock singer called Sting."

And he said, "Yeah, I've heard of you." I couldn't believe it. He said that he liked the song, "Walking on the Moon," and the bass line. I was totally blown away. I admired this guy since I was fifteen, and he knew one of my pieces.

I said, "I want you to help me make an album."

He said, "Sure, make me an offer." It didn't happen for another two years, but having made the connection, I then sang with him at Sweet Basil in New York. It was an impromptu thing one night, but we had a relationship.

That's what I mean about not limiting oneself. I have to be myself, and if being in rock music forces me to pretend I am an idiot, or that I have to wear tight trousers, or a wig, then I have to get another job. At the moment I can actually be myself and people will accept it. It is not nerve at all. It just feels very natural. As soon as it feels unnatural, I will get the hell out and do something else.

George Michael
∘ ∘ ∘

We talked just before he smashed through with his own record. There was some insecurity about image, but the worldwide acceptance for this young man has removed all doubts.

∘ ∘ ∘

I wanted with a passion to be a star. It sounds very easy to say in hindsight, but I've always had a very strange sense of my own future. As a child, even though I had no idea that I could write and sing, I was convinced I was going to be a pop star. I mean, now that I'm here, I don't feel special for being here, but I had this feeling that I was going to do something special.

The image of Wham! was not so much contrived. I find it hard to accept the word "contrived," because contrived suggests some element of deception, and there never was any deception.

Probably our first image was a little contrived. We looked kind of cocksure, like street kids, which we weren't. I mean, Andrew Ridgely and I were street kids in a sense that we both thought we'd be out of work. We came from working-class backgrounds initially, but we moved into middle-class areas. Even though we didn't have any money in our pockets, our parents did. So we always had a security blanket, as it were.

So that was kind of contrived because it was streetish, but at the same time the lyrics were always tongue-in-cheek, so we didn't feel that we were deceiving because we were parodying all the things the songs were about. "The Wham! Rap" was about unemployment. "Young Guns" was about the perils of marriage at an early age. And "Bad Boys" was about teenage rebellion, child versus parent. They were all very tongue-in-cheek. We weren't taking any of those subjects seriously because they really didn't affect us. Neither of us was really rebellious. We were both doing things our parents didn't want us to do, like following careers our parents didn't want us to follow, but other than that, we weren't rebels. Neither of us had any plans of getting married at that age. Even though we were unemployed a lot of the time, it was no great hardship. So, that was contrived in a very tongue-in-cheek way.

Our first American image, two grinning guys in front of a camera, wasn't contrived because we were both extremely up that year. It was our first taste of real success. I think whatever we radiated was fairly genuine confidence. Obviously, we were marketed. That wasn't really me as a person. That wasn't really Andrew either. Our goals were, let's say, more adult than that.

At one point, image was vital to the success of the records. I never really understood it, but in England we had gone from being kind of street looking to being kind of pop-starrish looking, almost like we had suddenly struck it lucky, and people were fascinated with that. With records like "Wake Me Up Before You Go-Go" and "Freedom," we took a whole sixties image and put it to records in the eighties, which did two things. One, it brought people into the record shops and made them buy that confidence we were exuding.

Secondly, it turned around people who couldn't stomach us. Andrew and I simply did not accept the cynicism that had been taken for granted in England. You were supposed to adopt it if you had an intelligent attitude towards music. As far as I was concerned, I was far more musical than the people I was reading about in *New Musical Express*. I would pick up *New Musical Express* and read about this ridiculous cynicism which had actually begun seeping into kids' attitudes. It wasn't just the journalists thinking that way anymore. It was the kids, too, and the pair of us just didn't accept that.

Society is very cynical. That doesn't mean there's no place for pure entertainment. That doesn't mean that pure entertainment cannot be done in a very intelligent manner. I consider myself to be an intelligent person, I consider myself to be a very musical person, and the two combined is the main reason for the success of our records. I don't think I have anything to be ashamed of in the trivia of a record like "Go-Go."

When I was twelve years old—and this is true for Andrew, as well— we both bought "Good-bye Yellow Brick Road." I was a huge Elton John fan from the time I was nine. I'm kind of surprised his influence hasn't shown up more in my writing. His melodies were always so strong. My natural leanings are R & B, which is a music you either appreciate or you don't. You either have it in you, or you don't. I have it in me. But I wasn't exposed to much black music as a child, simply because I listened to white radio. I came from a very white suburban area. Until the "Saturday Night Fever" boom, there wasn't much black music on the radio. As a very small child, I had three records that I would play over and over. Literally, I had one of those windup things out in my garage, and my parents had thrown out three records—"Delilah," by Tom Jones, which is a strange one to start off with, and "Stop in the Name of Love" and "Baby Love," by the Supremes. Those were the records I grew up listening to.

Bono

○ ○ ○

Bono and his U2 mates exploded in 1987. They won awards, they sold millions of records, and while their style and attitude have come to be appreciated by every level of the rock world, these are people who steadfastly continue to march on to their own dreams.

○ ○ ○

Success for us was a bit of blind faith and ignorance. We wrote songs because we couldn't play other people's songs. We could hardly play our own instruments. This was a band that could not form an E chord. To walk onstage with instruments strapped on our backs is not easy. We always struggle to play right and give a good show. We are not "musician" musicians. When we were on the Amnesty tour, we asked ourselves, "How are we going to do this and go out there and play when all you see are these great musicians like Peter Gabriel and Sting?" We're not like that. We're a garage band.

We had no real role models. You have to understand, this was a time of real arrogance amongst the youth culture we came out of. We were a punk band that did up our hair. We were more punk than the Monkees. We had the attitude that with three chords and the truth you could do anything you wanted to do.

This might be a cliché, but I didn't know I was Irish until I came to America. You don't look at what's under your feet. You always look at what's around you. But recently, we started looking at what was under our feet, and we developed an interest in Irish folk music and then realized its relationship with American folk music. It's quite interesting, actually, if you studied it in some depth, going right back to the slave days. You would think that the Irish, having come out from under the boot, would not be bigots. They were the worst bigots. They worked on the farms, and they were just one rung above the blacks. And as a result, a lot of Irish songs got picked up on the plantations—black gospel songs, Scottish melodies, Irish melodies. There's a real link between Irish folk music and American folk music.

Our interest in American music has become fascinating. Some people would say we're obsessed with America. To me, it's something I'm wrestling with because I really love it in America, yet I hate some aspects of what America is becoming. I have confused feelings, but at the moment my love for America is much more overpowering than any other feeling.

The Irish will always feel that America is the promised land for them. Also, the Irish will always side with a nation like Nicaragua because we remember what it's like to be a small nation facing a big bully.

U2 is a group. We go up and down. We work hard as a band, and we decided very early that if we had to survive and play every second night, we needed to write songs. So we wrote a pile of songs. It was sort of a gangland mentality. Somebody once said that we'll be stars as long as we don't become celebrities. No matter what happens, we can always go running back to Ireland because the Irish look down on success. Say nobody likes our next record and it sells 1 million copies instead of 15 million. So what? That's more money than we need anyway. We're just going to make music. I object to the idea of getting bigger. I think it kills things. We didn't necessarily want to be the biggest. But we did want to be the best.

In the last few years I think there's been a blurring of what I would call the "awesome" band. It's hard for me to talk about this without slagging off other bands. You'll notice I don't do that, but when I was growing up and I was sixteen, I was into this kind of music, whether it was Patti Smith or the Rolling Stones, but as much as I was into this music, I was not into that music. There was us and there was them. You always pick up on a few pop songs here and there, but you wouldn't admit to liking them or buying the record. So that's what it was then, us and them.

But over the last five years I've noticed that it's blurring. There are famous stars of my generation being called "rock" singers. Half of these people are "pop" singers. I want to unblur that. I want to separate pop from rock. The truth of the way I feel right now is that anger is about what is going on. People say our songs make social statements. Anyone who's not blind or dumb could write the songs we write. The question is, why don't they write them, and why are we the odd ones?

I never set myself up as any kind of political guru. I probably know less than most people about what is going on in the world. People have a way of describing you, or tagging you in thirty seconds. For example, U2, the band with great rock music that makes social statements with their songs. As a band, we are very selfish with our goals. And, yes, it is true that we feel strongly about issues and human rights and what's going on in America and in the land. But we refuse to say yes to anything that we don't feel is right.

David Lee Roth

o o o

Flamboyant would be an understatement. David began with Van Halen and is currently a rock idol and sex symbol in between his mountain climbing and jungle exploring.

o o o

History is rife with bands with groups of people who didn't get along with one another. It's the same with rock bands as it is with governments. The audience loves pain. They love to see pain up there. But the audience doesn't know where it's coming from. They have no idea that between the band members it can be miserable.

Most bands don't think of the future. Most musicians can't even spell future. Lunch is how far we think ahead. If you're not getting along with people in that frame of reference, it gets very difficult.

Our producer, Ted Templeman, and I clicked right away. We could sit around and drink beer and toss out tunes until the sun came up. "Hey, remember that Sam Cooke tune? How did it go. Oh, that Beatles one? Who did 'Fever'?" And on and on.

When we were in the studio welding songs together, we would go, "OK, let's steal this little part from the Ohio Players. Now we'll do this little drum feel from that Dave Clark 5 song."

The Van Halen brothers came from what was essentially a classical music background. They learned to play piano and some theory in orchestration in the same classes I did at Pasadena City College. But beyond that, their frame of reference in popular music was very limited. For them, it was either a twenty-minute Cream jam or Deep Purple or Black Sabbath. But it never extended beyond Led Zeppelin, which is the end of the alphabet, so go figure?

Whenever we were in the studio, there was always friction between the brothers and Teddy. The brothers had a very specific sound in mind, a very different direction from Teddy. The brothers always approached the studio as if it were a half-blank easel.

I don't buy anything. The pants I'm wearing right now I bought in 1979. I'm not into material things, like the jet ski or the motorbike. Before I got in the band there was a Mercedes parked in my front yard. It didn't belong to me, but I saw it there. When I got some bucks, running out and buying a Mercedes was not the first thing I thought of doing.

People think I'm outrageous. I don't think I'm so outrageous. A lot of people get into music because they're inarticulate vocally. "Let's use the guitar, let's emote through the drum, let's dance." Feel everything, but don't talk. I'm a talker, and the combination of rock 'n' roll and speaking openly with a sense of humor is taken as outrageousness.

Musicians by and large take their music very seriously. They're the ones with the Day-Glo cheekbones and that studio pallor that goes back to the days of the Left Banke. I may repeat stories from bar to bar, but I don't take myself very seriously. I suspect there are a lot of musicians out there who have the same kind of sense of humor, but they'll never let on because it'd fuck up their image.

If I were concerned about my image, I never would have done "Just a Gigolo." I never would have left Van Halen.

Things are different for me since I left the band. People like Jerry Lewis are taking my phone calls. Even though they're not rock fans, people have become titillated with me. It's like I give them a chuckle. But at least they're not laughing at "that dummy."

I now have more energy, more stamina. Nothing is more typical than the musician who walks offstage in the middle of his tour and goes, "Yeah. Nothing like the road for getting in shape." Bullshit. As I get older, I find that I can stay awake longer and think more coherently than I ever used to be able to do.

The dentist asked me the other day, "Why do you get up so early?" I get up at six in the morning. He said, "What gets you up so early? Where do you get your energy from?"

I told him, "Fear and revenge."

Joe Smith

○ ○ ○

Well, that's it. We tried to get all the heavy hitters. I used all my connections, and in a lot of cases I was still turned down. The Springsteen people, in particular Jon Landau, treated this like it was the SALT talks. "Maybe we will. Let us think about it further. Maybe yes, maybe no. Bruce doesn't have time."

We weren't talking about changing the direction of mankind here. It was just about spending thirty minutes to an hour with someone discussing music. But I understand the protective nature of people. Frank Sinatra was a big disappointment to me. Here was a guy I had been involved with in business for a number of years. My efforts in helping him develop his record company made him a lot richer. He claimed he'd never been interviewed for a book. He said, "Go ahead, take all the things I've ever said in print and put them together." Sinatra isn't exactly overly quoted in print, so there wasn't much to take.

Col. Tom Parker was hilarious. I wanted something definitive on Elvis Presley, who is unable to speak for himself, so I went to Parker. He asked me for $25,000 for a ten-story interview, $2,500 per anecdote. I could do without that, and besides, there are a lot of Elvis books out there already.

Before James Brown finally said yes, he wanted a condition on the interview that I sign two or three acts he was working with. Wilson Pickett declined to do the interview, but told me I could write anything I wanted. I tried to explain it wasn't that kind of book, but he didn't want to hear it. Chuck Berry was concerned that anything he said in my book would interfere with a future book of his.

And then halfway through the project I took on the CEO position of Capitol/EMI in the United States. It was an enormous job. I was not exactly stepping into the catbird seat in the music business; it was a company with great values that had been suffering over the last few years and required some major reorganization and restructuring to get it back to where it was. It was not the kind of job where I came riding in on a white horse and everything would be wonderful. It's a big company—a couple of thousand employees, four record labels, huge distribution problems. Certainly not a part-time job. Now I had to fit the interviews and all other aspects of the book into the job at Capitol. I can't tell you what it took.

Johnnie Ray made a 4:30 appointment with me at his house in the hills, not far from the Capitol Records building. I cleared all my business from 4:15 to 5:45, I go up to Johnnie's house and Johnnie's not home. Here I am, president of Capitol Records, sitting in a Mercedes outside a home in the Hollywood Hills. Dogs were barking at my car, neighbors were staring at me—they probably figured a drug deal was going down.

Entertainers are used to having people cater to their schedules. They had no idea what havoc it wreaked when they would call and say, "I know we're supposed to do the interview at two o'clock on Thursday. But how about noon on Monday?" I tried to explain that I had a flight to catch, and they'd say, "Well, I'd like to be with my kids today. Why not another time?"

I remember going to see Sting at a San Francisco hotel. It was the start of an Easter weekend. I had my return flight and there were no seats on any other plane. I called his room at 11, as planned, and they say it's set for 12. I say, "I have a flight to catch. How about eleven thirty?"

They say, "How about eleven forty-five?" I was negotiating with them over 15 minutes.

Joe Cocker lives in the mountains above Santa Barbara. I asked him the directions to his house and he says, "You get off the main road, and you proceed up a dirt road until you see a blue truck. Take the side road at the blue truck."

I ask him, "What happens if someone moves the blue truck?"

He says, "They usually don't."

Some of these meetings were set up like a CIA drop. Van Morrison, who has always been a mystery, wanted to meet me in a London hotel lobby under an assumed name. I entered the lobby, saw him, and said, "Hello, Mr. Johnson." Not a person in the lobby recognized him. We walked into a private room and he said, "Hi, Joe," and I said, "Hi, Van." I have no idea why he wanted to be Mr. Johnson.

Richard Branson, the head of Virgin Records, has an office on a houseboat on the Thames. The day we did the interview it was so windy I was getting seasick. I would rather have done it on the sidewalk in the rain.

Roger Waters of Pink Floyd lives in suburban London. I took a cab. It was pitch-black outside. Even the cabdriver couldn't find the place. He wanted to take off, so he dropped me off on a country road with my tape recorder and piece of paper, and I'm asking myself, "What am I doing?"

Cliff Richard was starring in a show in London. We had it set up that I would interview him backstage before the show. It's pouring out and I'm schlepping this heavy Haliburton case with professional recording equipment and I can't get a cab. Forget trying to get a cab when it's raining in London. It's impossible. I start walking a mile and a half and I'm saying to myself, "Why am I doing this? Is Cliff Richard going to make or break this book?"

Well, no, but he's here along with a couple hundred others who made a difference in popular music. That's the thing. To sit with all these people and talk about music and their lives was extraordinary. If this book doesn't sell a copy, it will have been an amazing journey for me through fifty years of popular music.

I'd like to think that by the time we're ready to do Volume II that the SALT talks will have progressed to a point that maybe we could get Bruce and some of the others we missed on tape. In the meantime, I'm very proud of how the book turned out. The entire process has been an incredible source of satisfaction.